Tolley's
Taxation in the
Republic of Ireland
1995–96

by
Glyn Saunders MA
from an original text by
Eric L Harvey FCA AITI

Consultants
Deloitte & Touche
Dublin

Tolley Publishing Company Limited
un A United News & Media publication

H.J -9. OCT. 1995

Published by
Tolley Publishing Company Ltd
Tolley House
2 Addiscombe Road
Croydon CR9 5AF
Surrey, England
0181-686 9141

Typeset by Phoenix Photosetting, Chatham, Kent

Printed and Bound by
BPC Wheatons Ltd, Exeter

ISBN 1 86012 019-9

About This Book

This book contains all the important legislative provisions relating to income tax, capital gains tax, corporation tax, capital acquisitions tax and value-added tax, and to advance corporation tax and residential property tax. There is also coverage of double taxation relief agreements with the United Kingdom. It includes the provisions of the Finance Act 1995 and there is a separate summary of that Act towards the end of the book.

As usual, the contents are divided into chapters arranged in alphabetical order for ease of reference. Legislative references are given throughout so that the provisions may quickly be found in the various Acts. There is a detailed index at the end of the book.

The Finance Act 1995, as long and complex as has become customary, is particularly notable for the large number of areas in which changes of more or less significance are made. Amongst these are the familiar new batch of special reliefs for building works, this time in certain traditional seaside resorts, as well as an extension to the similar urban renewal reliefs. A number of small general personal reliefs are introduced, and the reliefs under capital gains tax, capital acquisitions tax and residential property tax are generally improved. There is a raft of new anti-avoidance and anti-evasion provisions, and some amelioration of the more draconian aspects of the self-assessment system. As always, value-added tax receives a substantial measure of attention. It is notable that, despite the extent and complexity of the new provisions generally, the legislation continues to be relatively clearly expressed, in stark contrast to the tortuous nature of current UK tax legislation.

As for previous editions, Messrs Deloitte & Touche of Dublin have, as consultants, provided their distinctive practical knowledge and experience, and thanks are due to Brian McDonald for his invaluable contribution.

TOLLEY PUBLISHING CO. LTD.

Contents

The following subjects are in the same alphabetical order in the book.

Contents

Abbreviations and References

References throughout the book are to legislation of the Republic of Ireland and numbered sections and schedules are from the Income Tax Act 1967 unless otherwise stated.

ABBREVIATIONS

ACT	=	Advance Corporation Tax.
Art	=	Article.
CAT, CATA	=	Capital Acquisitions Tax (Act 1976).
CGT, CGTA	=	Capital Gains Tax (Act 1975).
CGT(A)A	=	Capital Gains Tax (Amendment) Act 1978.
CT, CTA	=	Corporation Tax (Act 1976).
DTR	=	Double taxation relief.
EC	=	European Communities.
EEC	=	European Economic Community.
FA	=	Finance Act.
F(MP)A 1968	=	Finance (Miscellaneous Provisions) Act 1968.
F(Mines)A 1974	=	Finance (Taxation of Profits of Certain Mines) Act 1974.
FY	=	Financial year.
H/C	=	High Court.
IT	=	Income tax.
ITA	=	Income Tax Act 1967.
KB(I)	=	King's Bench Division of the High Court of Justice in Southern Ireland.
NI	=	Northern Ireland.
PRSI	=	Pay-Related Social Insurance
q.v.	=	quod vide (= which see).
RI	=	Republic of Ireland.
RPT	=	Residential Property Tax.
s	=	section.
S/C	=	Supreme Court.
Sch	=	Schedule [*4 Sch 10* = 4th Schedule, paragraph 10].
Sec	=	Section of the Income Tax Act 1967.
UK	=	United Kingdom (including Northern Ireland).
VAT, VATA	=	Value-Added Tax (Act 1972).
VAT(A)A	=	Value-Added Tax (Amendment) Act 1978.

LAW REPORTS

All E R	=	All England Law Reports (Butterworth & Co (Publishers) Ltd, Bell Yard, London WC2A 2LG).
ATC	=	Annotated Tax Cases (Gee & Co (Publishers) Ltd, 7, Swallow Place, London W1R 8AB).
ILRM	=	Irish Law Reports Monthly (Irish Academic Press, Kill Lane, Blackrock, Co. Dublin).
IR	=	Irish Reports (Law Reporting Council, Law Library, Four Courts, Dublin).
ITC	=	Irish Tax Cases (Government Publications, 1 and 3, G.P.O. Arcade, Dublin 1).
TC	=	Official Reports of UK Tax Cases (HMSO, PO Box 276, London SW8 5DT).
TL	=	Tax Case Leaflets (as for ITC above).

1 Administration and General

1.1 The Republic adopted UK tax law (with a few modifications) up to, and including, the *FA 1922* and so the two tax codes are broadly similar but with substantial divergences arising in subsequent Finance Acts. The *Income Tax Act 1967* consolidated the legislation relating to income tax and sur-tax. Sur-tax was abolished from 6 April 1974 onwards [*FA 1974, s 10*] and replaced by higher rates of tax in a new unified tax system, see 2.2 ALLOWANCES AND RATES. Companies are charged to corporation tax under the *Corporation Tax Act 1976*; before that Act companies were charged to income tax and corporation profits tax. Value-added tax was enacted in 1972, wealth tax and capital gains tax in 1975, and capital acquisitions tax in 1976. Wealth tax was suspended from 5 April 1978 onwards. Youth employment and income levies were introduced from 1982/83 and 1983/84 respectively, the latter ceasing after 1985/86. Advance corporation tax applies to most distributions after 8 February 1983, and residential property tax was first imposed in respect of property value on 5 April 1983. Farm Tax was introduced by the *Farm Tax Act 1985* with effect from 6 October 1986, and its proposed repeal was announced in the 1987 Budget Statement, making the tax applicable for one year only. All legislation, regulations, etc. can be obtained from Government Publications, Sun Alliance House, Molesworth Street, Dublin 2.

1.2 UK High Court decisions before 1923/24 are part of the law adopted by the Republic but subsequent UK cases are not binding on RI Courts although regard is had to them in matters of interpretation where the law is similar.

1.3 As from 1969/70 the former Schedules A and B were abolished [*FA 1969, s 65 and 5 Sch*] and assessments to income tax are now made under three Schedules, C, D and E. [*Secs 47, 52, 109*]. Schedule D is dealt with under five Cases, I, II, III, IV and V (V replacing Schedule A). [*Sec 53*]. A new Schedule F was added from 6 April 1976. [*CTA s 83*].

1.4 The administration of the Income Tax Acts is in the charge of the Revenue Commissioners [*Sec 155*] who are appointed by the Government and form a branch of the Department of Finance. Their address is The Revenue Commissioners, Dublin Castle, Dublin 2. Appeal Commissioners are appointed by the Minister for Finance to hear appeals [*Sec 156; F(MP)A 1968, s 1*] and Inspectors of Taxes, appointed by the Revenue Commissioners, are responsible for making assessments (with a few exceptions) [*Secs 161, 181, 526; F(MP)A 1968, s 2; CTA s 144, 2 Sch 5; FA 1986, s 116*] and may grant allowances etc. [*Sec 182*]. Collection of tax is by the Collector-General and his nominated officers. [*Sec 162; FA 1987, s 52*].

1.5 Notes on Revenue practice are not generally published, but if the following Principal Inspectors of Taxes are contacted, information may be obtained as to whether or not a practice exists in any given situation.

	Telephone no.	Tax districts
Mr A. O'Connor	Dublin 6718295	Personnel and Management Services, Training School.
Mr P. C. O'Laoghaire	Dublin 6716779	Customer Services Policy, Dublin IT and CT, Directors and Retirement Benefits.
Mr E. P. O'Coindealbhain	Dublin 6716813	Castlebar, Letterkenny, Sligo, Dundalk, Galway and Computer Branch.

	Telephone no.	Tax districts
Mr S. Breathnach	Dublin 6718675	Waterford, Athlone, Thurles, Wexford and Kilkenny.
Mr T. M. Tiuit	Dublin 6716424	Arrears Project and Compliance Policy, Dublin Compliance.
Mr P. MacGiolla Mhaith	Dublin 6718097	Technical Services (incl. CT, CGT, VAT and Anti-Avoidance).
Mr J. A. Browne	Dublin 6716168	Technical Services (IT and PAYE/PRSI).
Mr A. K. Hanrahan	Dublin 6716612	DAD 1–10.
Mr P. S. O'Donghaile	Dublin 6718560	I.B., S.E.B.
Mr P. O'Morain	Dublin 6718726	Audit Policy.
Ms M. Hughes	Dublin 6718975	Cork, Limerick and Tralee.
Mr L. O'Laocha	Dublin 6718304	Dublin PAYE, TCRO, CRIO.

1.5A   For general guidance on enquiries, see the Revenue Commissioners' publication 'Guidelines for Practitioners on making enquiries to Revenue Offices', which does, however, note that the enquiry system is not 'a vehicle for debate on arguable issues, advance rulings or assistance in relation to tax planning'.

1.6   The Exchequer financial year (and local authorities' financial year) was changed to the calendar year by *The Exchequer and Local Financial Years Act 1974*. There was a transitional period from 1 April 1974 to 31 December 1974 and 1975 was the first full calendar year for Budget purposes. For tax purposes the year of assessment continues to be from 6 April to 5 April.

1.7   The Revenue Commissioners may disclose information to authorised persons (as specified) for the purpose of establishing the entitlement of a claimant to relief under the *Rates on Agricultural Land (Relief) Acts 1939–1978* and any subsequent enactment. [*FA 1978, s 47; FA 1980, s 89*]. Power to disclose information in matters concerning pay-related social welfare benefits is conferred by the *Social Welfare (Pay-related Benefit) Act 1973, s 12*. Information may also be disclosed to the Ombudsman for the purposes of any investigation under the *Ombudsman Act 1980*. [*FA 1981, s 52*]. The Revenue Commissioners are also required to compile an annual list or lists of tax defaulters, for inclusion in their Annual Report and, at their discretion, publication in *Iris Oifigiúil*. The lists include all persons upon whom a fine, etc. was imposed by a court during the year for a tax offence, or with whom a negotiated settlement in respect of tax, interest and penalties forgone was reached in the year in lieu of initiation of proceedings for such a fine, etc. Settlements following complete voluntary disclosure, or for a sum not exceeding £10,000, are excluded. [*FA 1983, s 23; FA 1992, s 240*].

1.8   Any records which a person is obliged to keep, to issue or to produce for inspection for any tax purposes may be dealt with by any electronic, etc. process approved by the Revenue Commissioners, and the requirements in evidence are appropriately adjusted. The Revenue is similarly empowered to carry out its functions by electronic, etc. means. [*FA 1986, s 113; FA 1993, s 99*]. There are appropriate inspection powers relating to computer documents and records. [*FA 1992, s 237*].

1.9   The *Finance Act 1992* introduced considerably increased powers of entry and inspection for the Revenue Commissioners in relation to the full range of tax liabilities, with increased penalties for non-compliance (see *FA 1992, ss 231–236*).

1.10   See *FA 1995, s 175* for Revenue Commissioners' powers to obtain information regarding payments by or on behalf of Ministers.

1.11   **Relevant offences.** A 'relevant person' in relation to a company who, having regard to information obtained in the course of assisting or advising the company in relation to its accounts or tax returns, etc., becomes aware that the company has committed or is committing one or more material 'relevant offences', is obliged without undue delay to notify the company in writing of particulars of the offence(s) and to request the company, within six months, either to rectify the matter or to notify the appropriate officer (as designated by the Revenue Commissioners, see below) of the offence(s). Unless satisfied that such action has been taken by the company, the 'relevant person' must cease to assist or advise the company (except in relation to legal proceedings extant or pending at a time six months after the original notification to the company), and must not do so again until three years after the original notification (or, if earlier, when satisfied that the required action has been taken by the company).

An auditor ceasing to act by virtue of the above is required to give the company written notification of his or her resignation and to send a copy of that notification to the appropriate officer (as above).

A 'relevant person' is liable to a penalty of up to £5,000 and two years' imprisonment for failure to comply with the above, or for knowingly or wilfully making an incorrect notification of a 'relevant offence'. Proceedings in relation to such failures may be commenced at any time within six years from the date the original notification to the company was (or should have been) given. It is, however, a good defence against failure to comply to show that awareness that a 'relevant offence' had been committed arose from assisting or advising the company in preparing for litigation in the ordinary course of professional engagement.

The taking of any action required by these provisions cannot be regarded as a contravention of any duty or give rise to any liability or action in any Court.

The name of the officer of the Revenue Commissioners to whom copies of notices should be sent is published in *Iris Oifigiúil.*

A *'relevant person'* is an auditor (as defined), or a person who assists or advises the company for reward in the preparation or delivery of any document which he or she knows is, or is likely, to be used for tax purposes (but excluding PAYE employees of the company). *'Relevant offence'* is defined to include a wide range of knowing or wilful failures in relation to taxes, duties, levies or charges under the care and management of the Revenue Commissioners, including the making of incorrect returns, failure to make returns, false relief claims and falsification of documents.

These provisions apply to tax assessable for 1995/96 and subsequent years of assessment and for company accounting periods beginning after 30 June 1995, to tax payable after, or for taxable periods beginning after, that date, to tax chargeable on gifts or inheritances taken on or after that date and to tax on chargeable instruments executed on or after that date.

[*FA 1995, s 172*].

1.12   **Tax clearance certificates.** With effect from **1 July 1995**, application may be made to the Collector-General for a tax clearance certificate (valid for a specified period) stating that the holder is in compliance with all obligations imposed under the *Tax Acts*, the *Capital Gains Tax Acts* and the *Value-Added Tax Act 1972* in relation to payment of tax, interest or penalties and the delivery of returns. Such a certificate is required as a condition for the award of certain public sector contracts. The conditions for issue of a certificate are contained in *FA 1995, s 177(3)(4)*. [*FA 1995, s 177*].

1.13   For amnesties relating to arrears of tax, see 25.5 PAYMENT OF TAX.

2 Allowances and Rates—for Income Tax

Headings in this section are:

2.1 In the following pages of this section, all rates and allowances for 1989/90 onwards are shown, and where a rate in force for 1989/90 commenced in an earlier year that earlier year is shown also. Changes are shown for and from the year in which they commenced with the current rates etc. in bold type. A separate **six-year summary** appears inside the front cover.

The year of assessment (or 'tax year') runs from 6 April to 5 April. [*Sec 5*].

Total Income is the income from all sources as estimated in accordance with the Income Tax Act. [*Sec 1 inserted by FA 1974, s 1*]. It consists of earned and unearned income less charges, losses, etc., and less certain maintenance payments (see 23.4 MARRIED PERSONS) and other specified deductions (see e.g. 12.17 CORPORATION TAX and 21.7 INVESTMENT IN CORPORATE TRADES AND RESEARCH AND DEVELOPMENT).

Taxable Income is Total Income less personal allowances and items treated as such (see 2.6 to 2.20 and 2.22 to 2.25 below). [*Sec 137*].

2.2 THE UNIFIED TAX SYSTEM FOR 1974/75 ONWARDS

On 6 April 1974 a unified system of income tax on individuals replaced the previous dual structure of income tax and sur-tax (now abolished). A single graduated tax comprising reduced, standard and higher rates became applicable to all income, whether earned or unearned.

2.3 RATES OF TAX FOR 1995/96 [*FA 1995, s 2*].

For 1995/96 two separate graduated scales of tax apply as follows.

(*a*) For a husband whose wife's income (if any) is, by election (see 23.1 MARRIED PERSONS), treated as his own:

4

Taxable Incomes £	On Taxable Income £	Rate	Equal to tax of £
Standard Rate			
First 17,800	0–17,800	27%	4,806
Higher Rate			
Above 17,800	17,801 upwards	48%	

(*b*)   In any other case:

Taxable Incomes £	On Taxable Income £	Rate	Equal to tax of £
Standard Rate			
First 8,900	0–8,900	27%	2,403
Higher Rate			
Above 8,900	8,901 upwards	48%	

These rates apply to any individual charged to income tax unless he is acting in a fiduciary or representative capacity. Standard rate applies to annual payments etc., see 13 DEDUCTION OF TAX AT SOURCE.

For the purpose of ascertaining the total amount of income which is to be charged at the rates shown above, any income which has suffered (or is deemed to have suffered) tax at source is included at the gross amount. A credit is then given for the tax suffered in order to determine the net amount of tax payable. Such taxed income shall be regarded as income chargeable under Schedule D, Case IV. [*FA 1974, s 4; CTA 2 Sch 41, 3 Sch*].

2.4   **RATES OF TAX FOR 1989/90 TO 1994/95** [*FA 1980, s 8; FA 1990, s 2; FA 1991, s 2; FA 1992, s 2; FA 1993, s 2; FA 1994, s 2*].

For 1994/95 two separate graduated scales of tax apply as follows.

(*a*)   For a husband whose wife's income (if any) is, by election (see 23.1 MARRIED PERSONS), treated as his own:

Taxable Incomes £	On Taxable Income £	Rate	Equal to tax of £
Standard Rate			
First 16,400	0–16,400	27%	4,428
Higher Rate			
Above 16,400	16,401 upwards	48%	

(*b*)   In any other case:

Taxable Incomes £	On Taxable Income £	Rate	Equal to tax of £
Standard Rate			
First 8,200	0–8,200	27%	2,214
Higher Rate			
Above 8,200	8,201 upwards	48%	

For 1993/94 two separate graduated scales of tax apply as follows.

(*a*)   For a husband whose wife's income (if any) is, by election (see 23.1 MARRIED PERSONS), treated as his own:

2.4 Allowances and Rates—for Income Tax

Taxable Incomes £	On Taxable Income £	Rate	Equal to tax of £
Standard Rate			
First 15,350	0–15,350	27%	4,144.50
Higher Rate			
Above 15,350	15,351 upwards	48%	

(*b*)   In any other case:

Taxable Incomes £	On Taxable Income £	Rate	Equal to tax of £
Standard Rate			
First 7,675	0–7,675	27%	2,072.25
Higher Rate			
Above 7,675	7,676 upwards	48%	

For 1992/93 two separate graduated scales of tax apply as follows.

(*a*)   For a husband whose wife's income (if any) is, by election (see 23.1 MARRIED PERSONS), treated as his own:

Taxable Incomes £	On Taxable Income £	Rate	Equal to tax of £
Standard Rate			
First 14,950	0–14,950	27%	4,036.50
Higher Rate			
Above 14,950	14,951 upwards	48%	

(*b*)   In any other case:

Taxable Incomes £	On Taxable Income £	Rate	Equal to tax of £
Standard Rate			
First 7,475	0–7,475	27%	2,018.25
Higher Rate			
Above 7,475	7,476 upwards	48%	

For 1991/92 two separate graduated scales of tax apply as follows.

(*a*)   For a husband whose wife's income (if any) is, by election (see 23.1 MARRIED PERSONS), treated as his own:

Taxable Incomes £	On Taxable Income £	Rate	Equal to tax of £
Standard Rate			
First 13,400	0–13,400	29%	3,886
Higher Rates			
Next 6,200	13,401–19,600	48%	2,976
Above 19,600	19,601 upwards	52%	

6

(*b*)   In any other case:

Taxable Incomes £	On Taxable Income £	Rate	Equal to tax of £
Standard Rate			
First 6,700	0–6,700	29%	1,943
Higher Rates			
Next 3,100	6,701–9,800	48%	1,488
Above 9,800	9,801 upwards	52%	

For 1990/91 two separate graduated scales of tax apply as follows.

(*a*)   For a husband whose wife's income (if any) is, by election (see 23.1 MARRIED PERSONS), treated as his own:

Taxable Incomes £	On Taxable Income £	Rate	Equal to tax of £
Standard Rate			
First 13,000	0–13,000	30%	3,900
Higher Rates			
Next 6,200	13,001–19,200	48%	2,976
Above 19,200	19,201 upwards	53%	

(*b*)   In any other case:

Taxable Incomes £	On Taxable Income £	Rate	Equal to tax of £
Standard Rate			
First 6,500	0–6,500	30%	1,950
Higher Rates			
Next 3,100	6,501–9,600	48%	1,488
Above 9,600	9,601 upwards	53%	

For 1989/90 two separate graduated scales of tax apply as follows.

(*a*)   For a husband whose wife's income (if any) is, by election (see 23.1 MARRIED PERSONS), treated as his own:

Taxable Incomes £	On Taxable Income £	Rate	Equal to tax of £
Standard Rate			
First 12,200	0–12,200	32%	3,904
Higher Rates			
Next 6,200	12,201–18,400	48%	2,976
Above 18,400	18,401 upwards	56%	

(*b*)   In any other case:

Taxable Incomes £	On Taxable Income £	Rate	Equal to tax of £
Standard Rate			
First 6,100	0–6,100	32%	1,952
Higher Rates			
Next 3,100	6,101–9,200	48%	1,488
Above 9,200	9,201 upwards	56%	

2.5 Allowances and Rates—for Income Tax

2.5 **STANDARD RATE** [*FA 1984, s 2; FA 1989, s 2; FA 1990, s 2; FA 1991, s 2; FA 1992, s 2; FA 1993, s 2; FA 1994, s 2; FA 1995, s 2*].

For	1989/90	32%
For	1990/91	30%
For	1991/92	29%
From	**1992/93**	**27%**

Tax credit. For tax credit purposes, the standard rate was deemed to be 28% for 1989/90 and 1990/91, and 25% for 1991/92 onwards. [*FA 1978, s 28; FA 1983, s 28; FA 1988, s 31, 2 Sch; FA 1990, s 36, 1 Sch*].

2.6 **AGE ALLOWANCE** [*FA 1974, s 8 and 2 Sch; FA 1982, s 2 and 1 Sch; FA 1986, s 3 and 1 Sch*].

The allowance may be claimed in addition to the personal allowances under 2.9 to 2.11 below if a person (or his wife whose income is, by election, treated as his, and she is living with him) is aged 65 or over at any time in year of assessment. A person may also be entitled to the age exemption under 2.7 below.

		Single £	Married £
From	**1986/87**	**200**	**400**

2.7 **AGE EXEMPTION** [*FA 1980, s 2; FA 1989, s 1; FA 1990, s 1; FA 1991, s 1; FA 1992, s 1; FA 1993, s 1; FA 1994, s 1; FA 1995, s 1*].

A person receiving the age allowance (see above) may claim exemption from income tax if his total income does not exceed a *specified amount*, as follows.

		Single £	Married £
For	1989/90	3,400	6,800
For	1990/91	3,750	7,500
For	1991/92	3,900	7,800
For	1992/93	4,000	8,000
From	1993/94	4,100	8,200
For	**1995/96**	**4,300**	**8,600**

Where the person or his spouse is aged 75 or over at any time in the year of assessment, increased exemption limits apply as follows.

		Single £	Married £
For	1989/90	4,000	8,000
For	1990/91	4,350	8,700
For	1991/92	4,500	9,000
For	1992/93	4,600	9,200
From	1993/94	4,700	9,400
For	**1995/96**	**4,900**	**9,800**

From **1994/95** onwards, the specified amounts are increased by £450 in respect of the first 'qualifying child' (see 2.16 below) living at any time in the year of assessment, by £450 in respect of the second such child, and by £650 in respect of each of the third and subsequent such children. For 1993/94, the increases are £350, £350 and £550 respectively. For 1991/92 and 1992/93, they are £300, £300 and £500 respectively. For 1989/90 and 1990/91, they are increased by a fixed amount in respect of each such child, of £300 for 1990/91 and of £200 for 1989/90. Only one increase is allowed in respect of a child, and, where appropriate, the increase is apportioned by reference to expenditure on maintenance.

Marginal relief applies to limit tax in appropriate cases. The limit is **40%** (48% for 1993/94 and 1992/93, 52% for 1991/92, 53% for 1990/91, 60% for 1989/90 and earlier years) of the excess over the appropriate exemption limit, up to a total income of twice that exemption limit. If the claimant was subject to the restriction of personal allowances relating to farming (see 18.3 FARMING), the exemption limits were reduced in the same way as if they had constituted the claimant's personal reliefs.

'Total income' includes that arising outside RI and not chargeable to tax.

2.8 **LOW INCOME EXEMPTION** [*FA 1980, s 1; FA 1989, s 1; FA 1990, s 1; FA 1991, s 1; FA 1992, s 1; FA 1993, s 1; FA 1994, s 1; FA 1995, s 1*].

Complete exemption from income tax is granted to individuals whose total income (including that arising outside RI and not chargeable to tax) does not exceed a *specified amount*, which depends on whether the individual is entitled to the married allowance or not. The specified amounts are as follows.

		Single	Married
		£	£
For	1989/90	3,000	6,000
For	1990/91	3,250	6,500
For	1991/92	3,400	6,800
For	1992/93	3,500	7,000
From	1993/94	3,600	7,200
For	**1995/96**	**3,700**	**7,400**

From 1994/95 onwards, the specified amounts are increased by £450 in respect of the first 'qualifying child' (see 2.16 below) living at any time in the year of assessment, by £450 in respect of the second such child, and by £650 in respect of each of the third and subsequent such children. For 1993/94, the increases are £350, £350 and £550 respectively. For 1991/92 and 1992/93, they are £300, £300 and £500 respectively. For 1989/90 and 1990/91, they are increased by a fixed amount in respect of each such child, of £300 for 1990/91 and of £200 for 1989/90. Only one increase is allowed in respect of a child, and, where appropriate, the increase is apportioned by reference to expenditure on maintenance.

Marginal relief applies to limit tax to **40%** (48% for 1993/94 and 1992/93, 52% for 1991/92, 53% for 1990/91, 60% for 1989/90 and earlier years) of the excess of income over the specified amount, up to a total income of twice the specified amount. The exemption or deduction is treated as a personal relief for all income tax purposes. [*FA 1980, s 25*].

2.9 **SINGLE ALLOWANCE** [*Sec 138(1); FA 1980, s 3; FA 1988, s 3 and 1 Sch; FA 1991, s 3 and 1 Sch; FA 1993, s 3 and 1 Sch; FA 1994, s 3 and 1 Sch; FA 1995, s 3 and 1 Sch*].

(Unmarried, separated or divorced person, or each of husband and wife electing to be treated as a single person)

From	1988/89	£2,050
From	1991/92	£2,100
For	1993/94	£2,175
For	1994/95	£2,350
For	**1995/96**	**£2,500**

2.10 Allowances and Rates—for Income Tax

2.10 WIDOW(ER) ALLOWANCE *[Sec 138(2); FA 1980, s 3; FA 1988, s 3 and 1 Sch; FA 1991, s 3 and 1 Sch; FA 1993, s 3 and 1 Sch; FA 1994, s 3 and 1 Sch; FA 1995, s 3 and 1 Sch]*.

From	1988/89	£2,550
From	1991/92	£2,600
For	1993/94	£2,675
For	1994/95	£2,850
For	**1995/96**	**£3,000**

For a widow, or widower not entitled to the married allowance (see 2.11 below), whose spouse dies in the year of assessment, the allowance is £5,000 (£4,700 for 1994/95, £4,350 for 1993/94, £4,200 for 1991/92 and 1992/93, £4,100 for 1988/89 to 1990/91 inclusive).

See also 2.16 below as regards certain child allowances due to widow(er)s.

2.11 MARRIED ALLOWANCE *[Sec 138(1); FA 1980, s 3; FA 1988, s 3 and 1 Sch; FA 1991, s 3 and 1 Sch; FA 1993, s 3 and 1 Sch; FA 1994, s 3 and 1 Sch; FA 1995, s 3 and 1 Sch]*.

(Married man whose wife is living with him or wholly or mainly maintained by him or, from 1994/95, *vice versa*.)

From	1988/89	£4,100
From	1991/92	£4,200
For	1993/94	£4,350
For	1994/95	£4,700
For	**1995/96**	**£5,000**

A husband and wife may, if either spouse so wishes, be treated as two single people for income tax purposes, each then qualifying for the single allowance (see 2.9 above). No married allowance will then be due. *[Sec 193 as amended by FA 1980, s 18]*. See also 23.1 MARRIED PERSONS as regards the year of marriage.

2.12 EMPLOYEE ALLOWANCE *[Sec 138B; FA 1980, s 3; FA 1988, s 3 and 1 Sch; FA 1991, s 7; FA 1994, s 4]*.

A special deduction may be given to any individual whose total income includes emoluments subject to the PAYE system (i.e. *ITA Pt V Chap IV*). Emoluments paid by an individual to spouse or child, by a partnership to partner's spouse or child, or by body corporate etc. to a 'proprietary director' (beneficial owner or controller of over 15% of ordinary share capital) or spouse or child of such director, are not eligible for the deduction, *except that* for 1994/95 and subsequent years, this does not apply to exclude emoluments paid to a child (unless a proprietary director in his/her own right) provided that

(a) the emoluments paid in the year exceed £3,600,

(b) the child is required to, and does, devote substantially the whole of his/her time throughout the year to the duties of the employment, and

(c) either the child is entitled to the PRSI allowance (see 2.13 below) or the PAYE regulations, in so far as they apply, have been complied with in the year in relation to the emoluments.

		Amount of deduction
From	**1988/89**	**£800**

The relief is available only against emoluments as defined above.

In any case where both a husband's and his wife's income are to be treated as the husband's for income tax purposes, a deduction up to the full amount may be allowed against each spouse's emoluments.

For **1991/92** onwards, the allowance is also available in respect of emoluments of an individual's overseas office or employment, where the emoluments are chargeable in the country in which they arise under a system similar to the PAYE system and are also chargeable in full to tax under Schedule D in RI, and where they would, if the office etc. was held in RI by an RI resident, qualify for the allowance as above.

2.13   **PRSI ALLOWANCE** [*FA 1982, s 6; FA 1987, s 1; FA 1988, s 4; FA 1989, s 3; FA 1990, s 3; FA 1991, s 9; FA 1992, s 3; FA 1993, s 4; FA 1994, s 5; FA 1995, s 4*].

A special deduction may be made from emoluments of employees who pay the higher rates of pay-related social insurance.

From	1983/84	£286
For	1995/96	£140

In the case of a married man whose wife's income is, by election, treated as his, this deduction may be made from each of the husband's and the wife's emoluments meeting the required conditions.

2.14   **EMPLOYED PERSON TAKING CARE OF INCAPACITATED INDIVIDUAL** [*FA 1969, s 3; FA 1984, s 8; FA 1985, s 3 and 1 Sch; FA 1990, s 4*].

Claimable if taxpayer (or his wife whose income is, by election, treated as his) is totally incapacitated throughout the year of assessment and employs a person to take care of himself or his wife.

From	1985/86	£2,500 maximum
From	1990/91	£5,000 maximum

The allowance is limited to the cost in the year of employing the employed person.

2.15   **CHILD ALLOWANCE** [*Sec 141; FA 1986, s 4; FA 1991, s 126*].

For 1986/87 and subsequent years, the allowance is available only in respect of incapacitated children. (For additional allowance for a single parent, see 2.16 below.)

		Incapacitated child £	Income limit £
From	1986/87	600	720
From	1991/92	600	2,100

The allowance is available in respect of any child permanently incapacitated by mental or physical infirmity from maintaining himself (or, if under age 16, whose infirmity is such that he would be so incapacitated if over 16) who became so incapacitated before age 21 or while in full-time education or training (e.g. apprentice or articled clerk). The allowance is reduced by every £1 of the child's income (excluding scholarships, bursaries, etc.) over the income limit, and, if the child is over 16 at the beginning of the year of assessment, is limited to the amount expended by the claimant on maintaining the child. The taxpayer may claim for each child of his own or for any child of which he has the custody and which he maintains at his own expense (subject to restrictions to prevent double allowance). Where two or more individuals are entitled to the allowance in respect of a child, the allowance is apportioned according to the amount expended by each on maintenance (and see 23.4 MARRIED PERSONS).

See 2.16 below as regards the meaning of 'child'.

2.16 **SINGLE PARENT ALLOWANCES** [*Sec 138A; FA 1985, s 4; FA 1988, s 3 and 1 Sch; FA 1991, ss 3, 4 and 1 Sch; FA 1993, s 3 and 1 Sch; FA 1994, s 3 and 1 Sch; FA 1995, s 3 and 1 Sch*].

Applies to a widow(er) or other person not entitled to the married allowance, or to the allowance to a widow in the year of bereavement, who during the year has a 'qualifying child' resident with him/her.

		Widow(er)	Other person
From	1988/89	£1,550	£2,050
From	1991/92	£1,600	£2,100
For	1993/94	£1,675	£2,175
For	1994/95	£1,850	£2,350
For	**1995/96**	**£2,000**	**£2,500**

A '*qualifying child*' is a child under 16 at the beginning of (or born in) the year of assessment, or over 16 at that time but either in full-time education or permanently incapacitated by reason of physical or mental infirmity from maintaining himself (having been so incapacitated before age 21 or while still in full-time education). The child must be the child of the claimant, or in the custody of the claimant and maintained at the claimant's expense for at least part of the year of assessment.

'Child' includes a stepchild and a child adopted under the *Adoption Acts* or equivalent foreign law. Before 6 April 1987, it also included an illegitimate child whose parents subsequently married. For 1987/88 and subsequent years, and for accounting periods ending after 13 January 1988, the *Status of Children Act 1987, s 3* applies in that

(*a*) relationships between persons are to be determined without regard to whether the parents of any person are or have been married to each other, unless the contrary intention appears, and

(*b*) an adopted person shall, for the purposes of (*a*) above, be deemed from the date of adoption to be the child of the adopter or adopters, and not the child of any other person(s).

This applies for the purposes of the *Tax Acts* generally. See also 7.4 CAPITAL ACQUISITIONS TAX, 9.4 CAPITAL GAINS TAX, and 23.1 MARRIED PERSONS. [*FA 1977, s 36; FA 1988, s 74; FA 1992, s 16*].

Only one deduction is available per claimant. The relief is not available to either spouse where the wife is living with the husband, and it is not available in the case of a man and woman living together as man and wife. The relief is reduced by any amount by which the child's own income (excluding scholarships, bursaries, etc.) exceeds £720.

Special allowance for widowed parent following death of spouse. For **1991/92** and subsequent years of assessment, an individual whose spouse died in any of the three preceding years of assessment, and who has not remarried before the commencement of the year of assessment and has a 'qualifying child' (see above) resident with him/her for the whole or part of that year, is entitled to an allowance as follows.

First year after year of bereavement	**£1,500**
Second year after year of bereavement	**£1,000**
Third year after year of bereavement	**£500**

The allowance is not, however, available in the case of a man and woman living together as man and wife. Only one allowance is available per claimant.

2.17 **DEPENDENT RELATIVE ALLOWANCE** [*Sec 142; FA 1979, s 1; FA 1982, s 2 and 1 Sch*].

Granted for

(*a*)   each relative incapacitated by old age or infirmity, or widowed mother or mother-in-law, if maintained by claimant, and

(*b*)   a son or daughter resident with and maintained by claimant, whose services the claimant is compelled to depend on because of his own old age or infirmity.

Where income of relative exceeds the limit below, the allowance is reduced by £1 for each £1 of excess. The income limit is the sum of the maximum contributory old age pension plus living alone allowance payable to a single person over 80.

The allowance is denied where child allowance (see 2.15 above) is claimed in respect of the same person. [*Sec 141(1); FA 1986, s 4*].

		Allowance	Income limit
For	1989/90	£110	£3,417
For	1990/91	£110	£3,566
For	1991/92	£110	£3,725
For	1992/93	£110	£3,877
For	1993/94	£110	£4,023
For	1994/95	£110	£4,149
For	**1995/96**	**£110**	**£4,270**

2.18 **BLIND PERSON ALLOWANCE** [*FA 1971, s 11; FA 1980, ss 4, 5 and 1 Sch; FA 1985, s 3 and 1 Sch*].

Claimable if taxpayer (or his wife) is blind (as defined) for any part of year of assessment. If both husband and wife are blind, then the total allowance claimable is as shown.

		Blind person	Both spouses blind
From	1985/86	**£600**	**£1,400**

2.19 **HEALTH EXPENSES**

(*a*)   **Insurance.** [*Sec 145; FA 1994, s 7*]. Relief is given for payments in preceding year for insurance covering medical, surgical, nursing, hospital etc. fees re sickness or accident to self, spouse or dependants. For 1996/97 and subsequent years relief is restricted to the standard rate of income tax, and only 50% of the premiums relievable in 1995/96 may attract relief at the higher rate.

(*b*)   **Costs.** [*FA 1967, s 12; FA 1969, s 7; FA 1972, s 9; FA 1986, s 5; FA 1994, s 8*]. An allowance is given (by tax repayment) for the cost (not recoverable by insurance or compensation etc.) of certain medical, hospital etc. fees, drugs etc. in respect of self, spouse, dependants, housekeeper, so far as they exceed £100 per individual or £200 per family in any year (£50 and £100 respectively for 1993/94 and earlier years) without maximum.

(*c*)   **Permanent health benefit schemes.** [*FA 1979, s 8; FA 1986, s 7; FA 1992, s 7*]. An individual who makes a claim is entitled to a deduction for any premiums etc. paid by him to a *bona fide* permanent health benefit scheme approved by the Revenue Commissioners (or in a standard form approved by them), up to a **maximum of 10% of his total income for the tax year**. Relief is also given where the premiums etc. are paid by the employer so as to be a taxable benefit in kind.

Benefits paid to an individual under such a permanent health benefit scheme are chargeable under SCHEDULE E (34.1).

2.20   **LIFE INSURANCE RELIEF (1991/92 AND EARLIER YEARS)** [*Secs 143, 151, 152; FA 1973, s 23, 1 Sch; FA 1974, s 9; FA 1975, s 2; FA 1978, s 2; FA 1980, s 6; FA 1982, s 7; FA 1985, s 60; FA 1989, s 8; FA 1991, s 119; FA 1992, s 4*].

Premiums paid under an insurance policy (or contract for a deferred annuity) taken out after 22 June 1916 by a claimant on life of self or spouse were allowed as a deduction from total income for income tax (not sur-tax) at a rate of *one-half of the amount paid* (two-thirds in certain cases, see below) subject to the limits below. The policy or contract had to be made with an insurance company established in RI, UK or the British Commonwealth or carrying on business in RI, or with a registered friendly society, or (for a deferred annuity) with the National Debt Commissioners. The relief also applied to persons liable under statute or under terms of employment for deductions or payments to secure a deferred annuity for widow or provision for children after death. Relief was given, conditionally, on premiums to non-RI etc. companies by persons becoming resident after ten years continuous non-residence, on policies effected before becoming resident.

Relief was denied where:

(*a*)   the policy did not secure a capital sum on death; or

(*b*)   a premium was payable during a period of deferment of a policy of deferred assurance; or

(*c*)   the policy proceeds attracted relief from inheritance tax (see 7.5(*n*)(*q*) CAPITAL ACQUISITIONS TAX).

[*Sec 143; FA 1985, s 60; FA 1991, s 119(6)*].

For policies and contracts made after 21 May 1953 and before 2 February 1978 with an insurance company or friendly society registered, managed and controlled in RI, relief was given at *two-thirds of the amount paid*. For policies and contracts made before 2 February 1978 by a higher rate taxpayer entitled only to relief at the half rate, the tax payable was reduced to the aggregate of (*a*) the tax which would have been payable if two-thirds of the premium had been deductible and (*b*) tax at the standard rate on one-sixth of the premium paid. [*Sec 143(3); FA 1978, s 2*].

Relief was limited to

(i)   one-sixth of total income or £1,000 (£2,000 where a husband and wife had elected for both their incomes to be treated as the husband's), whichever was the lesser (but premiums in excess of £1,000 (or £2,000 as appropriate) already being paid on contracts made on or before that date continued to qualify for relief),

(ii)   seven per cent of capital sum assured (excluding bonuses etc.) as regards each policy, but this restriction was modified where health of insured causes unfavourable terms of policy, and

(iii)   £100 in total of premiums for benefits other than securing a capital sum at death.

Where the premiums paid under an insurance policy (or deferred annuity contract) containing special terms relating to the health of the insured person exceeded those which would have been payable but for the special terms, relief was given in respect of the excess notwithstanding the above limitations, and the excess was ignored in considering those limitations in regard to other premiums.

Relief was further restricted, for 1989/90 onwards, to 25% (50% for 1990/91, 80% for 1989/90) of that which would otherwise have been available as above.

[*Sec 152; FA 1982, s 7; FA 1989, s 8; FA 1990, s 6; FA 1991, s 5*].

Endowment policies issued (or varied) to persons under 56 years of age only qualified for relief if (*a*)   term was at least ten years,

(*b*)   premiums were payable annually or at shorter intervals throughout term, or until death,

(*c*)   premiums payable in any twelve months did not exceed twice amount payable in any other twelve months nor one-eighth total of premiums payable throughout term,

(*d*)   amount payable on death was guaranteed at least 75% of total premiums payable throughout term, and

(*e*)   there was no provision, other than on surrender, for any capital benefit other than by way of bonuses or on disability.

[*FA 1973, s 23, 1 Sch*].

Relief for life assurance premiums is abolished after 5 April 1992. [*FA 1992, s 4*].

2.21   **RETIREMENT ANNUITIES** [*Secs 235, 236, 238, 5 Sch; FA 1974, ss 65/67; FA 1978, s 4; FA 1979, s 28*].

An individual may deduct from his 'net relevant earnings' (see below) chargeable to tax in a year of assessment any qualifying premium paid by him under an annuity contract (approved by the Revenue Commissioners) with a person carrying on a life annuity business in RI and which precludes

(*a*)   any payment during the life of the individual other than an annuity commencing not earlier than age 60 nor later than age 70, and

(*b*)   any payment after his death other than an annuity (not greater than the original annuity) to the surviving spouse or, if no annuity becomes payable either to the individual or spouse, the return of premiums paid, with reasonable interest or bonuses out of profits.

The Revenue Commissioners may conditionally approve a contract with other specified provisions, including a right for the individual, at the commencement of the annuity, to commute up to one-fourth of its value. [*Sec 235(1)–(5); FA 1974, s 65*]. An annuity contract which allows transfer by the assured of his accrued rights under the contract to be applied under a new contract with a different assurer (an 'open market option') may be approved by the Commissioners, and the annuity paid under the substituted contract will be earned income in the same way as under the original contract. [*FA 1979, s 28*].

Contracts for dependants or for life assurance. The Commissioners may approve a contract under which

(i)   the main benefit is an annuity for a spouse or one or more dependants of an individual, or

(ii)   the sole benefit is a lump sum, on death before age 70, payable to the personal representatives.

Conditions are laid down, which must be met by contracts falling within (ii) above, but the Commissioners may approve a contract under (i) above even if it does not meet the conditions. [*Sec 235A inserted by FA 1974, s 66*].

Contributions to approved trust schemes providing similar benefits as above are treated as qualifying premiums. [*Secs 235(4) and 235A(5)*].

Total premiums deductible are limited to 15% of net relevant earnings. Within the limits, qualifying premiums under *Sec 235A* (see above) are restricted to 5% and are deducted before any other premiums. [*Sec 236(1)–(1B); FA 1978, s 4*].

For individuals born before 1918 and not in receipt of a pension under a sponsored super-annuation scheme as defined in *Sec 235(9)* in respect of a former employment or entitled to such a pension at a future time, the limits are increased to:

Born	1916 or 1917	16%
	1914 or 1915	17%
	1912 or 1913	18%
	1910 or 1911	19%
	1909 or earlier	20%

[*5 Sch; FA 1978, s 4, 1 Sch Pt 1*].

If qualifying premiums up to the maximum limit cannot be fully allowed because of an insufficiency of net relevant earnings, the disallowed part may be carried forward until it can be allowed within the limits for a later year. [*Sec 236(2); FA 1974, s 67(1)*].

For 1990/91 and later years, where a qualifying premium is paid after the end of a year of assessment, but before 31 January in the year of assessment next following, an election may be made, before that 31 January, to treat the premium as if it had been paid in the earlier year of assessment. Previously, where the assessment for a year of assessment became final after 5 October in the year and a qualifying premium was paid after the end of the year but within six months after the assessment became final, an election could be made within that six months for the premium to be treated as paid in that year. [*Sec 235(11); FA 1974, s 67(2); FA 1990, s 27(1)*].

Relevant Earnings comprise income

(i)   from non-pensionable employments etc.,

(ii)   from property attached to such employment forming part of the emoluments,

(iii)   chargeable under Schedule D as immediately derived from a trade, profession etc. carried on personally or as an active partner, or

(iv)   from patent rights treated as earned income,

but not including remuneration from any investment company to a person controlling more than 15% of its ordinary share capital, nor the relevant earnings of the individual's wife. [*Sec 235(6)–(9)*].

Net Relevant Earnings are relevant earnings, as above, less deductions for tax purposes

(*a*)   in respect of payments, or

(*b*)   in respect of losses or of capital allowances relating to activities, profits from which would be 'relevant earnings'.

Where such deductions may be treated as made out of either 'relevant earnings' or other income, then so far as possible, deductions under (*b*) are treated as made from 'relevant earnings' but if treated in any year as made from income other than 'relevant earnings' the net relevant earnings for the next year are treated as reduced to that extent with any balance being carried forward to the third year, and so on. [*Sec 236(3)–(7)*].

2.22   ALLOWANCE TO OWNER-OCCUPIERS—URBAN RENEWAL ETC.

Expenditure incurred in the period 1 August 1994 to 31 July 1997 inclusive. Relief against total income may be claimed by an individual in respect of 'qualifying expenditure' attributable to work carried out in the period 1 August 1994 to 31 July 1997 inclusive (the '*qualifying period*'). The relief is available for the year of assessment in which the 'qualifying premises' were first in use as a dwelling after the incurring of the expenditure, and for any of the following nine years of assessment in which the 'qualifying premises' in respect of

16

which the expenditure was incurred is the only or main residence of the individual. The amount of the relief is:

(*a*)   where the 'qualifying expenditure' was on construction of the 'qualifying premises', 5% of that expenditure;

(*b*)   where the 'qualifying expenditure' was on 'refurbishment' of the 'qualifying premises', 10% of that expenditure.

'*Qualifying expenditure*' is expenditure incurred by an individual on the construction or 'refurbishment' of a 'qualifying premises' which is first used, after the incurring of that expenditure, as the individual's only or main residence, net of any grants etc. from the State or any statutory board or public or local authority. It includes expenditure on the development of the land (including gardens, access, etc.), in particular demolition, groundworks, landscaping, walls, mains supplies and outhouses, etc. for use by the occupants of the house. Expenditure borne by two or more persons is apportioned between or amongst them in the proportion in which they actually bore the expenditure.

'*Refurbishment*' of a building means either or both of

(i)   the carrying out of any works of construction, reconstruction, repair or renewal, and

(ii)   the provision or improvement of water, sewerage or heating facilities,

certified by the Minister for the Environment, in a certificate of reasonable cost relating to any house contained in the building, as necessary to ensure the suitability as a dwelling of any house in the building, regardless of whether or not the number of houses in the building, or the shape or size of any such house, is altered in the course of the refurbishment.

'*Qualifying premises*' means a house (which includes any building or part of a building suitable for use as a dwelling, and land or outbuildings appurtenant thereto or usually enjoyed therewith) used solely as a dwelling:

(*a*)   the site of which is wholly within a designated area, or which fronts onto a designated street, so designated for the purpose by the Minister for Finance, which designation may specify a shorter period within the qualifying period referred to above;

(*b*)   of floor area not less than 30 sq. metres or more than 125 sq. metres (90 sq. metres for expenditure incurred before 12 April 1995, except in the case of refurbishment expenditure) in the case of a self-contained flat or maisonette in a building of two or more storeys, or of not less than 35 sq. metres or more than 125 sq. metres in any other case;

(*c*)   in respect of which, if it is not a new house (within *Housing (Miscellaneous Provisions) Act 1979, s 4*), there is in force a 'certificate of reasonable cost', granted by the Minister for the Environment, in which the construction or refurbishment cost specified is not less than that actually incurred;

(*d*)   complying with such conditions as to construction or improvement standards and service provision as the Minister may lay down under *Housing (Miscellaneous Provisions) Act 1979, s 4* or *s 5*;

(*e*)   open to inspection by persons authorised in writing by the Minister at all reasonable times; and

(*f*)   which (or the development of which it is part) must comply with guidelines issued by the Minister for the Environment concerning:

(i)   design, construction and refurbishment of the houses;

(ii)   total floor area and dimensions of rooms;

(iii)   provisions of ancillary facilities; and

(iv)   the 'balance' between the houses, the development and the location.

Where the qualifying premises front onto a designated street, relief under these provisions is available only in respect of refurbishment expenditure.

A house occupied by a person connected (within *F(MP)A 1968, s 16*) with the person claiming the deduction is excluded unless the lease is on arm's length terms.

An appeal lies to the Appeal Commissioners on any question arising under these provisions as it would in relation to an assessment to tax.

[*FA 1994, ss 38, 39, 46, 47; FA 1995, s 35(1)(a)(b)(i)(2)*].

See below as regards continuing reliefs for urban renewal expenditure in the Temple Bar or Custom House Docks Areas of Dublin, and earlier reliefs for such expenditure in certain other areas. Where those earlier reliefs apply to certain expenditure incurred on or after 1 August 1994 as if it had been incurred before that date, the above provisions do not apply to such expenditure. [*FA 1986, s 44(1)(g); FA 1994, s 35(1)(c)(iv)*]. See also 8.10 CAPITAL ALLOWANCES, 30.22 SCHEDULE D, CASES I AND II and 33.11 SCHEDULE D, CASE V.

Expenditure incurred (or treated as incurred) before 1 August 1994 or in the Temple Bar or Custom House Docks Areas of Dublin. Relief against total income of a year may be claimed by an individual in respect of 'qualifying expenditure' on an owner-occupied dwelling the site of which is wholly in the Custom House Docks Area, the Temple Bar Area, or in certain other areas of Dublin, Athlone, Castlebar, Cork, Dundalk, Kilkenny, Letterkenny, Limerick, Waterford, Galway, Sligo, Tralee, Tullamore and Wexford, as designated by *FA 1986, 4 Sch Pts III–VII* and see *SIs 1988, Nos 92, 287, 314.* The relief given to the person incurring the expenditure is 5% (10% in the case of refurbishment expenditure in the Temple Bar Area and, after 26 January 1994, in the Custom House Docks Area) of the amount of the 'qualifying expenditure' in the year of assessment in which the expenditure is incurred and in any or all of the following nine consecutive years of assessment in which the dwelling continues to be that person's only or main residence.

'*Qualifying expenditure*' is the net amount of expenditure incurred by the individual (after deducting any grants, etc.), in the period commencing on 23 October 1985 (6 April 1988 in relation to expenditure in the Custom House Docks Area, 6 April 1991 in the Temple Bar Area) and ending on **31 July 1994** (and where at least 15% of the total construction expenditure on qualifying premises was certified before 24 February 1994 by the relevant local authority (under the relevant guidelines) to have been incurred before 26 January 1994, further such expenditure incurred between 1 August and 31 December 1994 inclusive is treated as having been incurred in the qualifying period), **5 April 1998** in the Temple Bar Area and **24 January 1999** in the Custom House Docks Area), on the 'construction or refurbishment' of 'qualifying premises' which are first used, after the expenditure is incurred, by the individual as his only or main residence. Expenditure on the refurbishment of buildings existing on 1 January 1991 in the Temple Bar Area is deemed to include the lesser of the cost of acquisition of the building (excluding land) and the value of the building at 1 January 1991, provided that the actual expenditure incurred is at least equal to that lesser amount.

Expenditure in the Temple Bar Area qualifies for relief only if the building is approved by Temple Bar Renewal Ltd.

'*Qualifying premises*' means residential premises which would qualify for relief as described under 33.4 or 33.5 SCHEDULE D, CASE V if the conditions as to letting were satisfied, and expenditure is within the meaning of 'construction or refurbishment' if it would be so for those purposes. For expenditure incurred after 25 January 1994 on the refurbishment of flats and maisonettes in the Custom House Docks and Temple Bar Areas, the maximum permissible floor area is increased from 90 to 125 square metres, and from 12 April 1995 this applies also in relation to construction expenditure.

For the purposes of granting the relief, expenditure is treated as incurred on the earliest date on which the premises were in use as a dwelling after it was actually incurred. Expenditure incurred by more than one person is apportioned on a just and reasonable basis by the inspector, subject to revision on appeal by the Appeal Commissioners or Circuit Court. Appeals are generally to the Appeal Commissioners and are dealt with in the same way as appeals against assessments (see 4 APPEALS).

[*FA 1986, ss 41, 44, 4 Sch; FA 1987, s 27; FA 1988, ss 25, 26; FA 1990, s 30(1); FA 1991, ss 54, 55, 2 Sch; FA 1992, ss 29(a)(c), 30; FA 1993, s 30(1)(b); FA 1994, ss 35(1)(c), 36, 37(1)(a)(i)(ii); FA 1995, ss 32, 33, 34(1)(a)(b)(2)*].

See also 33.4, 33.5 SCHEDULE D, CASE V.

Relief may also be claimed in prescribed form by an individual against his total income in respect of 'relevant expenditure' on an owner-occupied dwelling in a designated area (as above) which is determined (on application) by the Commissioners of Public Works in Ireland to be a building of significant scientific, historical, architectural or aesthetic interest.

For the year of assessment in which the 'relevant expenditure' is incurred, a deduction of 25% is allowed, with a further 5% in each of the following five years of assessment, provided that no other relief may be claimed in respect of the expenditure.

'*Relevant expenditure*' is expenditure incurred by the individual, in the period commencing on 24 May 1989 and ending on **31 July 1994**, in respect of any work of repair or restoration, or of maintenance of a similar nature, consistent with the original character or fabric of the building, after deducting any grants, insurance receipts etc. The building must be used at the time of the expenditure, or first used thereafter, as the individual's only or main residence. Expenditure incurred by two or more individuals is apportioned on a just and reasonable basis by the inspector (or, on appeal, by the Appeal Commissioners or Circuit Court).

The determination may be revoked, and relief withdrawn, where a building is altered, and there are powers of entry for the purpose of inspecting a building at any reasonable time. [*FA 1989, s 4; FA 1990, s 30(2); FA 1992, s 31; FA 1993, s 31*].

2.23   **RENT ALLOWANCE** [*Sec 142A; FA 1982, s 5; FA 1985, s 7; FA 1991, s 8; FA 1995, s 5*].

An individual who is aged 55 or over at any time in the year of assessment may claim a deduction from his total income for rent paid in respect of premises which were his only or main residence. See further below for relief for individuals aged under 55. Any deduction given is in *substitution* for any other deduction to which the claimant might be entitled in respect of the payments.

The deduction is the aggregate of all payments of rent in the year of assessment (but see below) meeting the requisite conditions (see below) paid by the claimant or, if he is a married man whose wife's income is, by election, treated as his, by his wife, subject to a **maximum deduction of £2,000** for a married man whose wife's income is, by election, treated as his, or of **£1,500** for a widowed person, or of **£1,000** in any other case. (Before 1991/92, the figures were £1,500, £750 and £750 respectively.)

For 1994/95 and earlier years, relief was given for rent paid in the year to 31 December ending in the previous year of assessment, and for 1995/96 only relief will continue to be so given where relief would not otherwise be available.

The rent, including certain periodical payments in the nature of rent, must be for the bare right to use, occupy and enjoy a building (or part) and grounds, and must not be reimbursed to, or the subject of a subsidy enjoyed by, the person paying it. It must be payable under a tenancy (including a contract, licence or agreement), which must not be for a freehold estate or interest or for a definite period of 50 years or more (ignoring any statutory extension), and under which

(i)   the rent must not be payable to certain public authorities, and

(ii)   no part of the rent may be treated as (part) consideration for a greater interest in the premises (or in any other property).

There are provisions for apportionment of composite payments by the inspector (subject to the usual appeal rights), and for time apportionment of rent for periods falling in more than one year of assessment. The Revenue Commissioners may make regulations as required to bring the scheme of allowance into effect (see *Income Tax (Rent Relief) Regulations 1982* (*SI 1982 No 318*)).

For 1995/96 onwards, relief is extended to individuals who would qualify for relief as above but for their being aged under 55 at the end of the year of assessment. For such individuals, relief is given by a reduction of liability to income tax for the year of assessment (except insofar as required to cover charges, see 13.1 DEDUCTION OF TAX AT SOURCE) by the lesser of

(*a*)   an amount equal to standard rate tax (see 2.5 above) on the rent paid in the year of assessment (but limited to standard rate tax on £1,000 for a married man whose wife's income is, by election, treated as his, or on £750 for a widowed person, or on £500 in any other case), and

(*b*)   the amount required to reduce that income tax liability to nil.

Claims must be accompanied by details (in a form prescribed by the Revenue Commissioners) of the claimant, the person(s) entitled to the rent (including, for 1995/96 and subsequent years, their tax reference number), the premises concerned, and the tenancy agreement, and by a receipt or acknowledgement in respect of the rent for which relief is claimed. On a request by the claimant, such a receipt, etc. must be provided within seven days by the person(s) entitled to the rent. For 1994/95 and earlier years, following such a request, a receipt, etc. had to be supplied within seven days of all subsequent payments of rent. The receipt, etc. must be in writing and contain the names and addresses of the claimant and of the person(s) entitled to the rent (and, for 1995/96 and subsequent years, the tax reference number of the latter) and details of the amount and period of the rent paid.

The inspector may, however, waive the requirement for details of the person(s) entitled to the rent if he is satisfied that the claimant is unable to supply them. He may also waive the requirement for a receipt, etc. if satisfactory proof is produced of the rent paid and of the name and address of the payee. Any decision by the inspector is subject to the usual appeal rights as if the claim were an appeal against an assessment.

2.24   **GIFTS FOR EDUCATION IN THE ARTS** [*FA 1984, s 32*] **AND TO COSPÓIR** [*FA 1986, s 8*].

Relief against total income of a year may be claimed in respect of gifts, to certain approved educational bodies, totalling £100 or more in the year, to the extent that they do not total more than £10,000 in the year, gifts in all cases being taken as net of any consideration received as a result of making the gift. The gift(s) must not be deductible in computing profits or gains, nor income dispositions within *Sec 439*, and must be for the purpose of assisting the recipient body to promote the advancement in RI of an 'approved subject' and applied by the body for that purpose.

Where the donor is a wife whose income is, by election, treated as that of her husband, the deduction is made from her own income, her husband's total income being adjusted accordingly.

The Minister for Finance may give, and withdraw, his approval for this purpose to or from any RI body or institution which

(a)   provides in RI any course with an entry requirement related to the results of the Leaving Certificate Examination, a matriculation examination of a recognised RI university or an equivalent non-RI examination, or

(b)   is permanently established solely for the advancement wholly or mainly in RI of one or more 'approved subjects', contributes to such advancement nationally or regionally, and is barred from distributing its assets or profits to its members.

'*Approved subject*' means the practice of architecture, art and design, music and musical composition, theatre or film arts, or any other subject approved for the purpose by the Minister for Finance.

Identical relief is available for 1986/87 onwards for gifts to the Minister for Education for the benefit of Cospóir, the National Sports Council.

See 12.9 CORPORATION TAX for the associated relief for companies.

2.25   **GIFTS TO THE PRESIDENT'S AWARD SCHEME** [*FA 1985, s 16; FA 1986, s 47*].

For 1985/86 and 1986/87, relief against total income of the year may be claimed in respect of gifts to the trustees of the President's Award Scheme exceeding £100 in the year, to the extent that they do not total more than £10,000 in the year. The gifts must not be deductible in computing profits or gains, nor income dispositions within *Sec 439*. Where the donor is a wife whose income is, by election, treated as that of her husband, the deduction is made from her own income, her husband's total income being adjusted accordingly.

See 12.9 CORPORATION TAX for the associated relief for companies.

2.26   **RELIEF FOR FEES PAID TO PRIVATE COLLEGES** [*FA 1985, s 6*].

For 1996/97 onwards, an individual may claim relief for 'qualifying fees' proved to have been paid in respect of an 'approved course' for the academic year commencing after 31 July in the year of assessment. Relief is given by a reduction of liability to income tax for the year of assessment (except insofar as required to cover charges, see 13.1 DEDUCTION OF TAX AT SOURCE) by the lesser of

(a)   an amount equal to standard rate tax (see 2.5 above) on the fees so paid, and

(b)   the amount required to reduce that liability to nil.

The fees may be paid on the taxpayer's own behalf or on behalf of a spouse or child of the taxpayer or a person whose legal guardian the taxpayer is.

'*Qualifying fees*' are tuition fees approved by the Minister for Education for this purpose for the course and for the academic year in question, and an '*approved course*' is a full time undergraduate course of study, lasting at least two academic years, which is approved for this purpose by the Minister for Education, and in an RI college so approved. The Minister for Education is required, before 1 July in each year of assessment, to furnish the Revenue Commissioners with full details of approved colleges, courses and fees. Approval of a course or college may be withdrawn by notice to the college, with effect from the following year of assessment (such notice also to be published in the *Iris Oifigiúil*).

Claims to relief will only be admitted where a return in prescribed form of total income for the year of assessment is made, and relief is denied to the extent that a sum is received in respect of, or by reference to, the fees by way of grant, scholarship or otherwise.

2.27   **ALLOWANCE FOR SERVICE CHARGES** [*FA 1995, s 7*].

For 1996/97 onwards, an individual may claim relief for local authority or similar service charges for which he or she was liable for the financial year to 31 December immediately prior to the year of assessment, provided that they were paid on time and in full. Relief is given by a reduction of liability to income tax for the year of assessment (except insofar as required to cover charges, see 13.1 DEDUCTION OF TAX AT SOURCE) by the lesser of

(*a*)   an amount equal to standard rate tax (see 2.5 above) on the charges so paid (but limited to standard rate tax on £150), and

(*b*)   the amount required to reduce that liability to nil.

Any relief under these provisions is in substitution for, and not in addition to, any other deduction to which the individual might be entitled in respect of the payment.

Where the taxpayer is a married man whose wife's income is, by election, treated as his, he may claim relief for payments made by his wife. Where the service charges are paid on behalf of the claimant by an individual residing on a full-time basis in the premises to which they relate, the claimant may disclaim the relief in favour of that individual.

The service charges for which relief may be claimed are charges under certain *Acts* for the provision by or on behalf of a local authority (i.e. a council of a county or urban district, or a corporation of a county or other borough), of domestic water supply, domestic refuse collection or disposal or domestic sewage disposal facilities.

An individual wishing to claim relief under these provisions must furnish to the local authority to which charges are paid his Revenue and Social Insurance ('RSI') Number. If the conditions (as above) have been met in relation to the financial year in which he has so furnished his RSI number (and any arrears for earlier years have been paid in accordance with guidelines issued by the Department of the Environment), the local authority will then include the claimant in the return it is required to provide to the Revenue Commissioners for these purposes. Where, exceptionally, a valid claimant is not included in the return, the local authority must supply the claimant with a certificate, which must accompany the claim.

There are provisions for relief similarly to be available in respect of payments by members of group water supply schemes within *SI 1983 No 330.*

In the case of refuse collection or disposal services provided and charged for by a person or body of persons, other than the local authority, which has provided the local authority with specified information, and has given the claimant the appropriate certificate, a claim (accompanied by the certificate) may be made as if a payment of £50 had been made for the service. Similarly where such services, whether provided by the local authority or by some other such person or body, are charged for other than by way of a specified annual charge, relief may be claimed as if a payment of £50 had been made for the services. Where a service charge applies in respect of services other than domestic refuse collection and disposal, these £50 reliefs are available only where the claimant qualifies for relief in respect of such service charge.

3   Anti-Avoidance Legislation

Cross-references.   See 30.24 SCHEDULE D, CASES I AND II for certain 'Bond Washing' and 'Dividend Stripping' transactions; 8.2 CAPITAL ALLOWANCES; 9.8 CAPITAL GAINS TAX; 38.90 TAX CASES; and generally under 12 CORPORATION TAX.

3.1   TRANSACTIONS TO AVOID LIABILITY TO TAX [*FA 1989, s 86*].

A general anti-avoidance provision is introduced as respects any 'tax avoidance transaction' any part of which is undertaken or arranged after 24 January 1989, and which (apart from this provision) gives rise to a reduction, avoidance or deferral of tax arising by virtue of any other transaction carried out wholly on or after a date which could not fall before 25 January 1989, or a refund, repayment or increased repayment of tax which would otherwise first become payable on a date which could not fall earlier than that date. The provision applies to any tax, levy or charge under the care and management of the Revenue Commissioners, and any interest, penalty etc. thereon.

A transaction (as widely defined) is a '*tax avoidance transaction*' if, having regard to the results of the transaction, its use in achieving those results, and any other means by which the results (or part) could have been achieved, the Revenue Commissioners form the opinion that (apart from these provisions) it gives rise to a 'tax advantage' and was not undertaken or arranged primarily for any other purpose. Excluded is any case in which the Revenue Commissioners are satisfied that either

(*a*)   although some other transaction giving rise to greater tax liability could have achieved the same purpose(s), the transaction was undertaken or arranged by a person with a view to realising profits in his business activities, and not primarily to give rise to a tax advantage, or

(*b*)   it was undertaken or arranged for the purpose of obtaining a relief, allowance or abatement under any provision *of the Acts* and would not result in a misuse or abuse of the provision having regard to its purpose.

A '*tax advantage*' is a reduction, avoidance or deferral of any charge or assessment to tax, or a refund or repayment of tax, or increase therein, whether current, potential or prospective, arising out of a transaction, including a transaction where another transaction would not have been undertaken or arranged to achieve the intended results.

The Revenue Commissioners are to take into account the form and substance of the transaction and of any other related or connected transactions, and the final outcome and result of all such transactions.

Having formed the opinion that a transaction is a tax avoidance transaction, the Revenue Commissioners are required to calculate the tax advantage from the transaction and the tax consequences, to withdraw or deny that advantage, that would flow from the decision that the transaction fell within these provisions (and any adjustment they consider necessary to afford relief from double taxation), and to notify those details to any person whose tax advantage it is proposed to cancel, or to whom relief from double taxation would be given. Appeal may be made (within 30 days) to the Appeal Commissioners, but only on the grounds that the transaction is not an avoidance transaction, or that the tax advantage (or relief) is incorrectly calculated, or that the tax consequences would not be just or reasonable. The appeal proceeds in like manner to an appeal against an income tax assessment (other than the restriction as to grounds), and appeals against the same opinion may (at the request of the appellants) be heard together. The Appeal Commissioners may accept, reject or amend a notice where the appeal is on the ground that the transaction is not a tax avoidance transaction, and they may confirm or adjust the tax advantage or tax consequences or relief in the notice if the appeal is on those grounds. The Revenue Commissioners may amend, add to or withdraw a notice by further notice, which is treated as a new notice under these provisions, but not so as to set aside or alter any matter which has become final and conclusive on appeal made with regard to that matter.

Requirements as to confidentiality are waived in relation to the giving of notice under these provisions, or in relation to appeals against such notices. Any Revenue officer may be nominated to carry out the functions of the Revenue Commissioners under this provision.

Where the Revenue Commissioners' opinion (subject to any amendments) becomes final and conclusive (i.e. if there is no timeous appeal or if the appeal is determined without the notice being cancelled), all such adjustments may be made as are just and reasonable, and are specified in the notice, to withdraw or deny the tax advantage. These include the allowance or disallowance of deductions etc., the allocation or denial of deductions, losses, reliefs, exemptions etc., and the recharacterisation of the nature of payments etc., and the granting of relief from any resulting double taxation. There is no further right of appeal against such adjustments.

3.2   **SCHEMES TO AVOID LIABILITY UNDER SCHEDULE F** [*FA 1989, s 88*].

An anti-avoidance provision applies where a shareholder disposes of shares in a close company (see 12.7 CORPORATION TAX) after 24 January 1989 and, following the disposal or the carrying out of a scheme or arrangement of which it is a part, the interest of the shareholder in any trade or business (the '*specified business*') carried on by the company at the time of the disposal is not significantly reduced, whether or not the company continues to carry it on.

The question of whether an interest is 'not significantly reduced' is determined by reference to beneficial ownership of, or entitlement to, ordinary share capital, or profits or assets available for distribution to equity holders, at any time after the disposal as compared with any time before the disposal.

A disposal of shares for this purpose includes a part disposal and a deemed disposal for CGT purposes, and certain arrangements which result in shares in another close company being issued to shareholders in respect of or in proportion to their holdings in the close company, but with those shares being either retained or cancelled, are nonetheless treated as a disposal (or part disposal) of those shares in exchange for the new shares.

Unless it is shown to the satisfaction of the inspector (or, on appeal, the Appeal Commissioners or Circuit Court judge) that the disposal was made for *bona fide* commercial reasons and not as part of a scheme or arrangement a purpose of which was the avoidance of tax, the proceeds of the disposal in money or money's worth or, if less, the excess of those proceeds over any new consideration given for the issue of the shares (and not previously taken into account under this provision), is treated as a distribution (see 12.10 CORPORATION TAX) made at the time of the disposal. The amount so treated at any time may not exceed the aggregate of 'capital receipts' (i.e. amounts received in money or money's worth (other than the company's shares) and not, apart from this provision, chargeable to income tax) received by the shareholder in respect of the disposal or as part of a scheme or arrangement of which the disposal is part. Capital receipts received after the time of the disposal continue to result in deemed distributions at the time of the disposal. Interest on unpaid tax (see 25.4 PAYMENT OF TAX) runs in respect of the distribution as if it were due and payable from the day on which the shareholder received the capital receipt. A tax credit is available in respect of the distribution only to the extent that ACT (see 12.25 CORPORATION TAX) has been accounted for (or would have been but for being set off against distributions received).

3.3.   **LOAN TRANSACTIONS** [*FA 1974, s 41; CTA 2 Sch 45*].

Where, with reference to lending money or giving credit (or varying the terms of a loan or credit):

(*a*)   a transaction provides for the payment of any annuity, or other annual payment, the payment is treated for all tax purposes (including CT) as if it were interest;

(*b*)   a transaction provides for the subsequent repurchase or reacquisition by the former owner of any securities or other income-producing property transferred, the former owner is assessable under Schedule D, Case IV on any income arising from the property before repayment of the loan etc.;

(*c*)   a transaction provides for a person to assign, surrender, waive or forgo income on property (without a sale or transfer), he is assessable under Schedule D, Case IV on the amount of that income (without prejudice to the liability of any other person);

(*d*)   credit is given for the purchase price of property and, during the subsistence of the debt, the purchaser's rights to income from the property are suspended or restricted, he is treated as if he had surrendered that income under (*c*) above.

3.4   **TAX-RELIEVED DIVIDENDS AS EMOLUMENTS** [*FA 1974, s 54; CTA 2 Sch 46, 3 Sch; FA 1977, s 8*].

Employees etc., and directors, of a tax-relieved company (i.e. a company qualifying for exported goods relief or 'Shannon' relief) or persons connected therewith (as defined) who receive distributions on shares in that company and, in the opinion of the Revenue Commissioners, receive inadequate remuneration, will be assessed under SCHEDULE E (34) on such part of those distributions as the Revenue Commissioners consider represents emoluments. These provisions also include dividends paid to a company in which the employee etc. is a 'participator' (as defined at 12.7 CORPORATION TAX) or to a settlement in which he or any person connected with him is a beneficiary. There is a right of appeal.

3.5   **CERTIFICATES OF DEPOSIT ETC.** [*FA 1974, s 55; CTA 2 Sch 21*].

Gains, not otherwise chargeable to tax, arising from the disposal of certificates of deposit and assignable deposits (as defined) are chargeable to tax under Schedule D, Case IV on so much of the gain as is time-apportionable to the period from 3 April 1974 to disposal date. There is a right to set off losses against other Case IV income, including interest on the certificate.

3.6   **BOND WASHING** [*FA 1984, s 29; FA 1991, s 27; FA 1993, s 21; FA 1994, s 26*].

This provision applies (subject to certain exceptions) on the sale or transfer after 25 January 1984 of 'securities' other than company shares, including Government and other securities exempt from capital gains tax (see 9.7 (*e*) CAPITAL GAINS TAX) and any stocks, bonds and obligations of any Government, municipal corporation, company or other body corporate, whether or not creating or evidencing a charge on assets.

For such sales, etc. before 18 May 1991, if interest becomes payable in respect of the securities other than to the vendor, then the interest which would have accrued to the date of contract for the sale, etc. (or to the date of payment of the consideration if later) if it had accrued on a day-to-day basis from the date of the last interest payment to the vendor (or from his date of acquisition if he has not previously received any interest in respect of the security) is chargeable on the vendor under Schedule D, Case IV.

For such sales, etc. of securities after 17 May 1991, if interest in respect of a security is receivable otherwise than by the owner, interest is deemed to have accrued on a day-to-day basis during his whole period of ownership, and he is chargeable under Schedule D, Case

IV on interest so accrued up to the date of contract for the sale, etc. (or the date of payment of consideration for the sale, etc. if later), less any interest in respect of which he is otherwise chargeable to tax. If there are arrangements under which the owner agrees to buy back or reacquire the security (or to buy or acquire similar securities), or acquires an option (subsequently exercised) to do so, the charge under these provisions is on the interest deemed to accrue up to the next interest payment date after the sale, etc. On any subsequent resale, etc., the charge does not apply to interest treated as accruing before that payment date.

The exceptions are:

(*a*) where the security has been held by the vendor for a continuous period of at least two years up to the date of contract for the sale, etc. (or the date of payment of the consideration if later);

(*b*) where the sale proceeds are taken into account under Schedule D, Case I in the vendor's trade of dealing in securities;

(*c*) where the sale or transfer is between spouses at a time when the wife is treated as living with her husband (see 23.1 MARRIED PERSONS);

(*d*) where interest on the security is treated as a distribution (see 12.10 CORPORATION TAX); and

(*e*) where the owner in an 'undertaking for collective investment' (see 12.21 CORPORATION TAX), and any gain or loss on the sale or transfer is a chargeable gain or an allowable loss.

For the purposes of (*a*) above,

(i) the personal representatives of a deceased person, during administration of the estate, and the deceased are treated as the same person, and

(ii) a husband and wife to whom (*c*) above applies are treated as the same person.

As regards (*b*) above, for accounting periods beginning before 1 January 1993, the exception does not apply if the trade consists wholly or partly of exempt life business (as defined in *CTA s 50(2)*, see 12.15 CORPORATION TAX).

Identification. Securities disposed of are identified with securities of the same class (i.e. where they entitle the owner to the same rights against the same person as to capital and interest, and the same remedies for enforcement of those rights) acquired later before those acquired earlier.

Information. The inspector has wide powers to require such particulars as he considers necessary for the purposes of these provisions from the issuer of a security (or his agent) and from the owner of a security.

See also 30.24 SCHEDULE D, CASES I AND II for earlier provisions relating to share dealers, etc.

3.7 **SHARES ISSUED IN LIEU OF CASH DIVIDENDS** [*FA 1974, s 56; CTA 3 Sch Pt II; FA 1993, s 36*].

Where shares are received as an alternative to cash dividends, the cash amount will be taxable under Schedule D, Case IV if received from a company in RI, or Case III if from a foreign company. From 1 June 1993 this does not apply to distributions by companies whose shares are quoted on a stock exchange or dealt in on the smaller companies, unlisted securities or exploration securities markets of the Irish Stock Exchange or similar markets on other stock exchanges.

3.8   **TRANSFER OF ASSETS ABROAD** [*FA 1974, ss 57–61; FA 1977, s 3*].

Where an individual ordinarily resident in the RI has the power to enjoy (as widely defined), either forthwith or in the future, any income of a non-resident or non-domiciled person which arises as a result of a transfer of assets (or of any associated operation) *at any time*, then the income shall be deemed to be income of the resident individual for all tax purposes, unless he shows that the transfer (together with any associated operations) was made for genuine business reasons and not for tax-avoidance purposes.

The tax chargeable will be under Schedule D, Case IV for the year in which the benefit is received with the same deductions and reliefs as if the income had actually been received. There are provisions against a double charge on the same income or benefit. Certain provisions which exempt from tax the income of non-residents (e.g. on government securities payable to non-residents) will not apply. The Revenue have power to obtain information. See 38.158, 38.159 TAX CASES.

3.9   **TRANSACTIONS IN LAND**

(i)   **Extension of charge under Schedule D, Case I** [*F(MP)A 1968, ss 17, 18; FA 1981, ss 28, 29*].

Profits from dealing in or developing land otherwise not within Schedule D are charged to tax under Case I if they would be so charged if all disposals were of a full interest in land acquired in the course of business by the disponer. The computation of such profits varies from normal Case I rules in several respects.

(*a*)   Any consideration other than rent (or premiums treated as rent—see 33.6 SCHEDULE D, CASE V) for the disposal of an interest in land is treated as a trading receipt.

(*b*)   Any consideration for the granting of development rights in land (other than easement rights chargeable under SCHEDULE D, CASE V (33)) is treated as a trading receipt.

(*c*)   Any interest in land held as trading stock remains so until the trade ceases.

(*d*)   Any interest in land acquired other than for money or money's worth, or otherwise than as trading stock, is treated as acquired at market value at the time of becoming trading stock.

(*e*)   No deduction is allowed in respect of any payment for the surrender of a right to an annuity or other annual payment, subject to the exception of certain annuities, etc. arising under a will or liability incurred for consideration, or the payment for which is chargeable to income or corporation tax on the payee.

(*f*)   A trader's expenditure in acquiring an interest in land subject to an annuity, etc. is adjusted where a sum (not chargeable to income or corporation tax on the payee) is payable for the forfeiture or surrender of the right to the annuity, etc. by some other person (other than in the course of a land dealing or development trade carried on by that other person). The expenditure is reduced to that payable if the right had not been forfeited or surrendered, the balance of the trader's expenditure being treated as payable by him for the forfeiture, etc. of the right. All necessary apportionments and valuations are made by the inspector, or, on appeal, the Appeal Commissioners.

(*g*)   Any provision applied by *F(MP)A 1968, s 18* as originally enacted, but not applied following amendment by *FA 1981, s 29* is disregarded in valuing trading stock at the commencement of periods ending after 5 April 1981.

(ii)   **Charge under Schedule D, Case IV** [*F(MP)A 1968, ss 20–22; FA 1981, ss 28, 29*].

27

3.9 Anti-Avoidance Legislation

Where

(*a*)   land (or any property deriving its value from land) is acquired with the sole or main object of realising a gain from disposing of it, or

(*b*)   land is held as trading stock, or

(*c*)   land is developed with the sole or main object of realising a gain from disposing of it when developed,

any capital gain from disposal of the land or any part of it (i.e. any amount not otherwise includible in any computation of income for tax purposes) which is realised (for himself or for any other person) by the person acquiring, holding or developing it (or by any connected person, as defined by *F(MP)A 1968, s 16*, or a person party to, or concerned in, any arrangement or scheme to realise the gain indirectly or by a series of transactions) is, subject as below, treated for all tax purposes as income of the person realising the gain (or the person who transmitted to him, directly or indirectly, the opportunity of making that gain) assessable, under Schedule D, Case IV, for the chargeable period in which the gain is realised.

These provisions apply to a person, whether RI-resident or not, if all or any part of the land in question is in RI.

'*Land*' includes buildings, and any estate or interest in land or buildings.

'*Property deriving its value from land*' includes any shareholding in a company, partnership interest, or interest in settled property, deriving its value, directly or indirectly, from land, and any option, consent or embargo affecting the disposition of land. But see 'Exemptions' below.

Land is '*disposed of*' for the above purpose if, by any one or more transactions or by any arrangement or scheme (whether concerning the land or any property deriving its value therefrom), the property in, or control over, the land is effectively disposed of. Any number of transactions may be treated as a single arrangement or scheme if they have, or there is evidence of, a common purpose. See also under 'General' below.

Exemptions

(i)   An individual's gain made from the *sale, etc., of his residence* exempted from capital gains tax under *CGTA 1975, s 25* or which would be so exempt but for *CGTA 1975, s 25(10)* (acquired for purpose of making a gain).

(ii)   A gain on the sale of *shares in a company holding land as trading stock* (or a company owning, directly or indirectly, 90% of the ordinary share capital of such a company) *provided that* the company disposes of the land by normal trade and makes all possible profit from it, and the share sale is not part of an arrangement or scheme to realise a land gain indirectly.

(iii)   (If the liability arises solely under (ii) (*c*) above). Any part of the gain fairly attributable to a *period before the intention was made* to develop the land.

Gains are to be computed 'as is just and reasonable in the circumstances', allowance being given only for expenses attributable to the land disposed of, and the following may be taken into account.

(A)   If a leasehold interest is disposed of out of an interest in land, the Schedule D, Case I treatment in such a case of a person dealing in land.

(B)   Any adjustments under *Secs 84(2), 85(4)* for tax on lease premiums.

Where the computation of a gain in respect of the development of land (as under (*c*) above) is made on the footing that the land or property was appropriated as trading stock that land, etc., is also to be treated for purposes of capital gains tax (under *CGTA 1975, 1 Sch 15*) as having been transferred to stock.

Where, under these provisions, tax is assessed on, and paid by, a person other than the one who actually realised the gain, the person paying the tax may recover it from the other party (for which purpose the Revenue will, on request, supply a certificate of income in respect of which tax has been paid).

General. See *F(MP)A 1968, s 20(7)(8)* as substituted by *FA 1981, s 29* for provisions to prevent avoidance by the use of indirect means to transfer any property or right, or enhance or diminish its value, e.g., by sales at less, or more, than full consideration, assigning share capital or rights in a company or partnership or an interest in settled property, disposal on the winding-up of any company, partnership or trust etc. For ascertaining whether, and to what extent, the value of any property or right is derived from any other property or right, value may be traced through any number of companies, partnerships or trusts to its shareholders, etc., 'in such manner as is appropriate to the circumstances'. For the above purposes the inspector may require, under penalty, any person to supply him with any particulars thought necessary, including particulars of

(I)   transactions, etc., in which he acts, or acted, on behalf of others, and

(II)   transactions, etc. which in the opinion of the inspector should be investigated, and

(III)   what part, if any, he has taken, or is taking, in specified transactions, etc.. (Under this heading a *solicitor* who has merely acted as professional adviser is not compelled to do more than state that he acted and give his client's name and address.)

(iii)   Miscellaneous

(*a*)   There are provisions for adjustment of sale price to market value in the case of certain transfers other than at market value between connected persons (as defined by *F(MP)A 1968, s 16*). [*F(MP)A 1968, s 19*].

(*b*)   The tax payable under these provisions may be postponed in certain circumstances. [*F(MP)A 1968, s 23*].

3.10   ANNUAL PAYMENTS FOR NON-TAXABLE CONSIDERATION [*FA 1989, s 89*].

This provision applies to a payment made after 8 May 1989 which is an annuity or other annual payment chargeable under Schedule D, Case III, not being interest, an annuity granted in the ordinary course of a business of granting annuities, or a payment to an individual for surrender, assignment or release of an interest in settled property in favour of a person with a subsequent interest. Where such a payment is made under a liability incurred for a consideration in money or money's worth, which is not wholly brought into account for income or corporation tax purposes in computing the income of the payer, then the payment is not made under deduction of tax (see 13.1 DEDUCTION OF TAX AT SOURCE), is not allowed as a deduction in computing the income of the payer, and is not a charge on income for corporation tax purposes (see 12.9 CORPORATION TAX).

3.11   ARRANGEMENTS FOR REDUCING VALUE OF COMPANY SHARES [*FA 1989, s 90; FA 1993, ss 126, 127*].

See generally 7 CAPITAL ACQUISITIONS TAX.

The following anti-avoidance arrangements have effect as respects a gift or inheritance taken as a result of arrangements made after 24 January 1989.

(*a*)   Where a person has an absolute interest in possession in shares in a private company (within *CATA 1976, s 16(2)*), and as a result of any arrangement the market value of those shares, or of any property representing them, is reduced, then for CAT

29

purposes a 'specified amount' is treated as a benefit taken, immediately after the making of the arrangement, from that person, as disponer, by the beneficial owners of the shares whose market value is increased as a result of the arrangement or, if the shares are held in trust without any ascertainable beneficial owners, by the disponer in relation to that trust as if he were the beneficial owner. The 'specified amount' is apportioned according to the increase in value of the shares held.

The '*specified amount*' is the difference between the market value of the shares immediately before the arrangement was made (calculated under *CATA 1976, s 16* (or, before 24 February 1993, *s 17*) as if each share were in a company controlled by a donee or successor) and that of the shares (or property) immediately after the arrangement was made (calculated under *CATA 1976, s 15*), and is situate where the company is incorporated. For these purposes, where the arrangement is made after 5 May 1993, *CATA 1976, s 16* has effect as if

(i) references to the donee or successor were references to the disponer of the specified amount,

(ii) the relevant time in relation to control of a company were the time immediately before the arrangement came into effect, and

(iii) the shares were, immediately before the arrangement came into effect, the absolute property of the disponer of the specified amount.

(*b*) Where an interest in property is limited by the disposition creating it to cease on an event (including a death and the expiry of a specified period), and immediately before the making of an arrangement the property includes shares in a private company, and the arrangement reduces the value of those shares (or of property representing them), then:

(i) where the interest is an interest in possession, the property under the disposition is treated as including a 'specified amount' (as in (*a*) above);

(ii) where the interest is not an interest in possession, (i) above applies as if it were; and

(iii) the event on which the interest was to cease is, to the extent of the specified amount, treated as having happened immediately before the arrangement was made.

(*c*) Where shares in a private company are subject to a discretionary trust, under or in consequence of a disposition, immediately before the making of an arrangement which reduces the value of the shares (or of property representing them), then for CAT purposes the specified amount is treated as a benefit taken, immediately after the making of the arrangement, by the beneficial owners of the shares whose market value is increased as a result of the arrangement or, if the shares are held in trust without any ascertainable beneficial owners, by the disponer in relation to that trust as if he were the beneficial owner. The specified amount is apportioned according to the increase in value of the shares held.

(*a*), (*b*) and (*c*) above do not prejudice any charge in respect of any gift or inheritance under any disposition on or after the making of the arrangement in question comprising shares in a company (or property representing such shares). Where shares held in trust under a disposition by any disponer are shares whose value is increased as a result of such arrangements as are referred to in (*a*), (*b*) or (*c*) above, any gift or inheritance taken under the disposition on or after the making of the arrangement and comprising those shares (or property representing them) is deemed to be taken from that disponer.

Where under (*a*) or (*c*) above the specified amount is treated as a benefit taken by the disponer in relation to a trust, the trustee of that trust shall, and the disponer shall not, be a person primarily accountable for the payment of tax in respect thereof. The tax, interest and expenses may be raised by the person accountable for the tax in respect of a specified amount by the sale or mortgage of, or of a terminable charge on, the shares whose value is increased as a result of the arrangement, whether or not those shares are vested in him. The tax remains a charge on the shares whose value is increased as a result of the arrangement.

Where shares in a company have been redeemed immediately after, and as a result of, an arrangement made after 5 May 1993, the redeemed shares are, for the purposes of (*a*), (*b*) or (*c*) above, and unless they are actually represented by property, deemed thereon to be represented by property with a market value of nil.

For the purposes of the special tax on discretionary trusts (see 7.13 CAPITAL ACQUISITIONS TAX), the increase in value of shares subject to such a trust immediately after the arrangement is made (as above) is treated as property.

4 Appeals

[Secs 415–432; FA 1968, ss 15, 16; FA 1974, s 69; FA 1976, s 30; FA 1980, s 54; FA 1983, s 9; FA 1984, s 6; FA 1992, s 5].

Cross-references. See 7.12 CAPITAL ACQUISITIONS TAX, 26.13 RESIDENTIAL PROPERTY TAX for appeals relating to those taxes, 28.12 RETURNS regarding the self-assessment provisions and 38.2–38.17 TAX CASES for relevant case law.

4.1 Appeals on all tax matters are made to the Appeal Commissioners (subject, on application within ten days of their determination, to a complete rehearing, fact and law, by a Circuit Judge) and thence to the High Court (law only) by transmission of a Stated Case (fee £20 for assessments made after 8 June 1983, previously £1). Cases may be continued to the Supreme Court. *[Secs 416, 428, 432; FA 1983, s 9].* One Commissioner may hear and determine an appeal *[Sec 416(5)]* and issue a precept. *[Sec 422(3)].* A barrister, solicitor, accountant or member of the Institute of Taxation, or any other person at the Commissioners' discretion, may represent taxpayer before Commissioners or Circuit Judge. *[Sec 421(2); FA 1980, s 54; FA 1990, s 28; FA 1995, s 173(d)(ii)].* Appeals to the Circuit Court are held in camera. *[Secs 416(10), 420].* See 38.3–38.17 TAX CASES regarding admission of appeals and procedures generally.

4.2 Appeals against assessments and most other appeals must be made within 30 days with grounds of appeal specified. The inspector must then notify the appellant of the time and place of the hearing of the appeal unless an agreement has been reached with the appellant or the appellant has withdrawn the appeal (see 4.3 below). The inspector may also refrain from giving such notice, or withdraw a notice already given, if the inspector considers that the appeal may be settled by agreement. Failure to attend hearing of an appeal against an assessment results in assessment being treated as if no appeal made. Such appeals will be dismissed (subject to appeal to the High Court on a point of law) if no adjournment application is made to the Appeal Commissioners, or any such application is refused, and the required return or evidence in support of the appeal has not been made. The Appeal Commissioners may not refuse an adjournment application within nine months of the earlier of the date of the making of the assessment and the end of the year of assessment to which the assessment relates. They may determine the appeal if they are satisfied that sufficient information has been provided to enable them to do so. *[Sec 416; FA 1976, s 30(7); FA 1983, s 9; FA 1984, s 6].* See further below, and also, as regards payment of tax pending appeal, 4.5 below. A late appeal may be accepted by the inspector if there is reasonable cause for the delay, but if the application is made 12 months or more after the date of the notice of assessment, it may only be accepted if at the time of the appeal the necessary returns, etc. have been submitted to enable the appeal to be settled by agreement *and* the tax charged by the assessment, together with any interest due thereon, paid. A refusal to accept a late appeal application may be referred to the Appeal Commissioners within 15 days of notification of the refusal and their consideration is subject to similar conditions. No interest (see 4.5 below) will be added to any tax repaid following settlement of an appeal made 12 months or more after the date of the notice of assessment. A late appeal application will not be entertained as long as certain recovery proceedings are incomplete. *[Sec 416(7); FA 1983, s 9].*

For appeals against assessments made **after 1 June 1995**, an inspector who considers that an appellant was not entitled to make an appeal may, by written notice to the appellant, refuse to accept the appeal. The appellant may appeal against such refusal within 15 days of the notice, and the Appeal Commissioners may then allow or refuse to allow the appeal to proceed, or arrange a hearing to determine the matter. Also in relation to such assessments, the appellant's agreement must be sought to the withdrawal of an appeal which has been listed for hearing, and the appellant also has the right to apply to the Appeal Commissioners (in writing) for a direction to the inspector to list an appeal for hearing, which they must give if satisfied that the appeal is likely to be determined at the first hearing. Also, the grounds on which the Appeal Commissioners may dismiss an appeal are expanded to cover cases of failure by the appellant to supply information required by the Appeal Commissioners. [*Sec 416(1), (2)(b)(ii)(c), (6)(c)(ii)(B) as inserted and amended by FA 1995, s 173(1)(a)*].

See also 28.12 RETURNS regarding self-assessment.

4.3   The taxpayer and the inspector may reach an agreement to settle the appeal, but inspector cannot oppose withdrawal of appeal by taxpayer, and the assessment then has effect as if no appeal had been made. [*Sec 416(3); FA 1974, s 69(b)*].

4.4   Appeals on question of domicile, residence etc. are to Appeal Commissioners with time limit of two months in certain cases. [*Secs 50, 76, 462, 6 Sch 3(2)*]. See *Sec 549(5)* re unremittable income. See also 38.55 TAX CASES as regards jurisdiction.

4.5   **Payment of tax pending appeal.** An appeal against an assessment must specify (*a*) the grounds of the appeal and (*b*) the amount of tax in the assessment (or in each instalment of tax payable) which, in the taxpayer's opinion, is likely to become payable after determination of the appeal. The amount of tax so specified is then payable (see 25 PAYMENT OF TAX) as if no appeal was pending. If no tax is specified under (*b*), or if the amount specified is greater than the amount assessed, the amount assessed is payable. On the determination of the appeal, any difference in the tax paid will be charged or repaid. Tax repaid will carry interest (unless under £1) at 0.6% per month (1.0% before 1 August 1990, 1.25% before 27 May 1986) free of tax. Where the specified tax is paid within two months of its due date and is not less than the lesser of (i) the tax assessed and (ii) 90% of the tax chargeable on determination of the appeal (80% in the case of assessment other than to income tax, corporation tax or capital gains tax), no interest will be charged on the balance of tax if that balance is paid within two months of the determination of the appeal.

Where the assessment as finally determined includes income chargeable (or annual payments deductible) on an actual year basis and the appeal is made before the end of the year of assessment, the taxpayer may elect (at the time of determination of the appeal) for the amounts of such items arising in the preceding year to be used in the assessment under appeal. [*FA 1976, s 30; FA 1984, s 30; FA 1986, ss 49, 114; SI 1990 No 176*]. See 38.17A TAX CASES as regards entitlement to interest on overpaid tax.

These provisions do not apply in relation to certain self-assessing procedures, see 28.12 RETURNS.

5   Assessment Bases

The taxes dealt with in this book and their bases of assessment are as follows but see the further details in the other sections of the book under the headings shown in the first column below.

Assessed Under	Source Chargeable	Basis on which Assessed
Income Tax		
Schedule C	Government stocks etc. taxed at source.	Actual interest etc. paid in tax year.
Schedule D, Case I Schedule D, Case II	Trades, etc. } Professions. }	Profits on usual annual account ending in tax year.
Schedule D, Case III	Interest, discounts, annuities, annual payments, income from foreign securities (except charged under Schedule C) and foreign possessions.	Amount arising in tax year.
Schedule D, Case IV	Sundry income not included in any other Case or Schedule.	Usually on actual income of tax year.
Schedule D, Case V	Rents or easements.	Amount arising in tax year.
Schedule E	Office, employment or pension.	Actual income of tax year.
Schedule F	Dividends and distributions, plus tax credits, from companies resident in RI.	Actual dividends etc. payable in tax year.
Advance Corporation Tax	Distributions.	Tax credit attached.
Capital Acquisitions Tax	Gifts and inheritances.	Value received.
Capital Gains Tax	Chargeable gains.	Gains on disposals in tax year.
Corporation Tax	Profits of company.	Profits of actual accounting period.
Farm Tax	Taxable farm.	Adjusted acreage.
Residential Property Tax	Residential property.	Relevant residential property on 5 April.
Value-Added Tax	Import of certain goods; supply of certain goods and services.	Value of imports; consideration received for goods and services.

6   Assessments to Income Tax

For assessments to other taxes, see under relevant sections of this book. See 28.12 RETURNS as regards assessments under self-assessing procedures.

6.1   Assessments are made by inspectors (with minor exceptions) and notices of assessment must state the time limit for making appeals. [*Sec 181; F(MP)A 1968, s 2; CTA 2 Sch 5*]. Estimated assessments may be made in absence of satisfactory information. [*Sec 184; CTA 2 Sch 7*]. See 38.2, 38.2A TAX CASES as regards additional assessments.

Where income is assessable and payable on the actual year basis (e.g. RI dividends, ground rents etc.) the inspector shall estimate such income and any deductible charges (e.g. mortgage interest), for assessment purposes, and in computing the tax payable shall estimate any tax to be credited. Adjustments of these estimates are made automatically, without notice of appeal being given, provided the taxpayer notifies the inspector of the correct figures within one year after the end of the year of assessment. [*Sec 528; FA 1974, 1 Sch Pt III (xiii)*].

6.2   The time limit for making assessments (except in cases of fraud or neglect) is ten years after year of assessment [*Sec 186; F(MP)A 1968, s 4*] except assessments on personal representatives for which the time limit is two years after end of year in which grant of representation or additional affidavit is lodged for estate duty or CAT, unless grant etc. was made or lodged in year of death, when time limit is three years. [*Sec 211; FA 1973, s 6; FA 1978, s 11*].

6.3   Income, profits etc. are assessed to income tax under four Schedules, C, D, E and F [*Secs 47, 52, 109; CTA s 83; FA 1980, s 55*] with Schedule D divided into five Cases [*Sec 53*]. Schedules A and B (ownership and occupation of property) do not apply after 5 April 1969. [*FA 1969, s 65 and 5 Sch*].

7 Capital Acquisitions Tax

See also 3.11 ANTI-AVOIDANCE LEGISLATION.

7.1 The *Capital Acquisitions Tax Act 1976 (CATA)* became law on 31 March 1976. It introduced two new and complementary taxes, a gift tax on gifts taken on or after 28 February 1974 and an inheritance tax on inheritances on a death taken on or after 1 April 1975. Certain transactions occurring on or after 28 February 1969 are relevant in determining the rate of tax on a gift or inheritance. The person chiefly accountable for payment of the tax is the recipient of the gift/inheritance (donee/successor). The provisions of the Act are summarised below.

7.2 GIFT TAX

A gift will be deemed to be taken (by a donee) where, under or in consequence of any disposition, he becomes beneficially entitled in possession, otherwise than on a death, to any benefit otherwise than for full consideration in money or money's worth paid by him. Where the benefit is in a property which consists wholly or partly of private company shares (see 7.8 below), the 'full consideration' exclusion does not apply after 23 February 1993 where the consideration, being in relation to a disposition, could not reasonably be regarded as representing full consideration to the disponer for making the disposition, taking into account the disponer's position prior to the disposition. A gift completed on or after 26 March 1984 bears tax on its taxable value (see 7.9 below) at a rate determined by aggregating that taxable value with the taxable value of all taxable gifts and inheritances taken previously on or after 2 June 1982. For gifts taken after 1 June 1982 and before 26 March 1984, earlier gifts and inheritances were aggregated only where the same Table (see 7.4 below) applied. The rate applicable to a gift completed after 27 February 1974 and before 2 June 1982 was determined by aggregating the taxable gift with the value of all relevant gifts from the same disponer since 28 February 1969 and of all taxable inheritances taken after 31 March 1975. [*CATA ss 4, 5(1), 9, 2 Sch 4; FA 1982, s 102; FA 1984, s 111; FA 1993, s 121; FA 1994, s 147*]. The rate of gift tax is 75% of that for inheritance tax. [*CATA 2 Sch 6*].

Where the disponer died before 1 April 1975, gift tax was not payable. [*CATA s 6(3)*]. Where the disponer dies within two years of a gift made after 31 March 1975, inheritance tax is payable. [*CATA s 3*].

'The date of the gift' is the date on which the donee becomes beneficially entitled in possession [*CATA s 2*] but see *CATA s 5(6)* as amended by *FA 1982, s 99* as regards certain gifts under contract or agreement. See also 38.153 TAX CASES.

7.3 INHERITANCE TAX

An inheritance will be deemed to be taken (by a successor) where, under or in consequence of any disposition, he becomes beneficially entitled in possession on a death to any benefit otherwise than for full consideration in money or money's worth paid by him. Where the benefit is in a property which consists wholly or partly of private company shares (see 7.8 below), the 'full consideration' exclusion does not apply after 23 February 1993 where the consideration, being in relation to a disposition, could not reasonably be regarded as representing full consideration to the disponer for making the disposition, taking into account the disponer's position prior to the disposition. [*CATA s 11(1); FA 1993, s 123; FA 1994, s 148*].

'On a death' means

(*a*)   (i)   on a person's death or at a time ascertainable only by reference to a death;

    (ii)   under a will or intestacy, or under the *Succession Act 1965, Part IX* or *s 56*; or

    (iii)   in consequence of the failure by a person to exercise a right or power where that person was immediately before his death capable of exercising such right or power;

    (when 'the date of the inheritance' is the date of the death); or

(*b*)   under a gift made on or after 1 April 1975 where the disponer dies within two years of the gift (when 'the date of the inheritance' is the date of the gift); or

(*c*)   on any further change in the interests under a trust after the cesser of an intervening life interest (when 'the date of the inheritance' is the date of the change).

[*CATA ss 2(1), 3*].

See, however, *CATA s 5(6)* as amended by *FA 1982, s 99* as regards the date of certain inheritances under contract or agreement.

Where the date of an inheritance is 1 April 1975 or later it will be subject to tax on its taxable value (see 7.9 below) at a rate calculated from Tables in the Act (see 7.4 below), and for this purpose a taxable inheritance (see 7.6 below) taken on or after 2 June 1982 is aggregated with all previous taxable gifts and inheritances taken on or after 2 June 1982 (excluding gifts or inheritances to which the same Table (see 7.4 below) did not apply for gifts taken before 26 March 1984). A taxable inheritance taken before 2 June 1982 was aggregated with all previous taxable inheritances from the same disponer and with all relevant gifts (see 7.2 above) since 28 February 1969 from the same disponer. [*CATA s 10, 2 Sch 4; FA 1982, s 102; FA 1984, s 111*].

Surviving joint tenant(s) will take an inheritance of the share of a deceased joint tenant which accrues on his death. [*CATA s 14*].

Disclaimer of an inheritance is not itself a gift; nor is waiver or abandonment of a claim to an inheritance. Liability to tax on the inheritance or claim will disappear unless any consideration in money or money's worth is received for the disclaimer, waiver or abandonment (in which case tax is payable on that consideration as though it was the inheritance from the disponer). [*CATA s 13*].

7.4   RATES OF TAX

For gifts and inheritances taken after 25 March 1984, a single table applies to all gifts and inheritances, but with different thresholds according to the relationship between disponer and donee/successor. The taxable gift or inheritance is added as the top slice to the aggregate of earlier relevant gifts or inheritances (see 7.2, 7.3 above) and the tax chargeable is the excess of the tax on the aggregate over that on the earlier relevant gifts, etc. (but limited to the amount of the tax on the aggregate attributable to the taxable value of the taxable gift, etc.). For inheritances, the taxable value is charged at the rate so determined, for gifts at 75% of that rate. The table is as follows.

Portion of Value (£)	Rate of Tax (%)	Portion of Value (£)	Rate of Tax (%)
The threshold amount	Nil	The next £30,000	30
The next £10,000	20	The balance	40

For gifts etc. taken before 11 April 1994 but after 29 January 1991, the 30% band was £40,000 and there was an additional £50,000 band taxable at 35%. For gifts etc. taken before 30 January 1991, there were additional £50,000 bands taxable at 40% and 45%, the balance being taxable at 55%.

7.4 Capital Acquisitions Tax

The 'threshold amount' is the greatest of the 'revised class thresholds' that apply in relation to all of the taxable gifts and inheritances included in the aggregate figure. A 'revised class threshold' is the lesser of the 'class threshold' applying to a gift or inheritance and the total of the taxable values of all taxable gifts and inheritances included in the aggregate and to which that 'class threshold' applies, with a minimum of the smallest of the 'class thresholds' that apply in relation to all of the taxable gifts and inheritances included in the aggregate. The 'class thresholds' are, for gifts and inheritances taken after 31 December 1989, indexed by reference to the consumer price index for the immediately preceding year. The base figures (which apply to gifts and inheritances taken before 1 January 1990) are

£150,000   where the donee or successor is the spouse (but see 7.5 below re exemption), child, or minor child of a deceased child, of the disponer, or in relation to an inheritance taken on the date of death, the parent of the disponer where the interest taken is not a limited interest.

£20,000   where the donee or successor is a lineal ancestor or descendant (other than a child, or minor child of a deceased child), brother or sister, or child of a brother or sister, of the disponer.

£10,000   where the donee or successor does not stand to the disponer in any of those relationships.

The figures applicable for subsequent years are accordingly:

1990	£156,000	£20,800	£10,400
1991	£161,400	£21,520	£10,760
1992	£166,350	£22,180	£11,090
1993	£171,750	£22,900	£11,450
1994	£174,000	£23,200	£11,600
1995	£178,200	£23,760	£11,880

For gifts and inheritances taken before 26 March 1984, different tables apply according to the relationship between disponer and donee/successor. The taxable gift or inheritance is added as the 'top slice' to the aggregate of earlier relevant gifts or inheritances (see 7.2, 7.3 above), and, if an inheritance, taxed at the rate in the appropriate table, if a **gift, at 75%** of such rate. The tables are as follows.

TABLE 1

Where the donee or successor is the spouse, child, or minor child of a deceased child, of the disponer.

Value (£)	Rate of Tax (%)
0–150,000	Nil
150,000–200,000	25
200,000–250,000	30
250,000–300,000	35
300,000–350,000	40
350,000–400,000	45
400,000 and over	50

TABLE II

Where the donee or successor is a lineal ancestor or a lineal descendant (other than a child) of the disponer.

Value taken after 31 March 1978 (£)	Rate of Tax (%)	*Value taken before 1 April 1978* (£)
0– 30,000	Nil	0– 15,000
30,000– 33,000	5	15,000– 18,000

33,000– 38,000	7	18,000– 23,000
38,000– 48,000	10	23,000– 33,000
48,000– 58,000	13	33,000– 43,000
58,000– 68,000	16	43,000– 53,000
68,000– 78,000	19	53,000– 63,000
78,000– 88,000	22	63,000– 73,000
88,000–103,000	25	73,000– 88,000
103,000–118,000	28	88,000–103,000
118,000–133,000	31	103,000–118,000
133,000–148,000	34	118,000–133,000
148,000–163,000	37	133,000–148,000
163,000–178,000	40	148,000–163,000
178,000–193,000	43	163,000–178,000
193,000–208,000	46	178,000–193,000
208,000–223,000	49	193,000–208,000
223,000 and over	50	208,000 and over

TABLE III

Where the donee or successor is a brother or a sister, or a child of a brother, or of a sister, of the disponer.

Value taken after 31 March 1978 (£)	Rate of Tax (%)	*Value taken before 1 April 1978* (£)
0– 20,000	Nil	0– 10,000
20,000– 23,000	10	10,000– 13,000
23,000– 28,000	12	13,000– 18,000
28,000– 38,000	15	18,000– 28,000
38,000– 48,000	19	28,000– 38,000
48,000– 58,000	23	38,000– 48,000
58,000– 68,000	27	48,000– 58,000
68,000– 78,000	31	58,000– 68,000
78,000– 93,000	35	68,000– 83,000
93,000–108,000	40	83,000– 98,000
108,000–123,000	45	98,000–113,000
123,000 and over	50	113,000 and over

TABLE IV

Where the relationship between donee/successor and disponer is not one referred to in Table I, II or III.

Value taken after 31 March 1978 (£)	Rate of Tax (%)	*Value taken before 1 April 1978* (£)
0–10,000	Nil	0– 5,000
10,000–13,000	20	5,000– 8,000
13,000–18,000	22	8,000–13,000
18,000–28,000	25	13,000–23,000
28,000–38,000	30	23,000–33,000
38,000–48,000	35	33,000–43,000
48,000–58,000	40	43,000–53,000
58,000–68,000	45	53,000–63,000
68,000–83,000	50	63,000–78,000
83,000–98,000	55	78,000–93,000
98,000 and over	60	93,000 and over

7.5 Capital Acquisitions Tax

[*CATA 2 Sch; FA 1978, s 41, 3 Sch; FA 1984, s 111; FA 1990, s 128; FA 1991, ss 115, 116; FA 1994, ss 142, 145*].

Notes:

(i) A widow(er) whose relationship to the disponer is not as close as that of his/her deceased spouse is attributed with the deceased spouse's relationship to the disponer.

(ii) A nephew or niece of the disponer is treated as a child of his in relation to tax on gifts or inheritances taken (other than under a discretionary trust) after 30 April 1989 provided that the property comprised in the gift etc. is either

(*a*) business assets used in connection with the trade, business or profession of the disponer, or

(*b*) shares in a private trading company (see 7.8 below) controlled by the disponer (being also a director) throughout the 'relevant period',

and, throughout the 'relevant period', the nephew or niece has worked substantially on a full-time basis for the disponer in his trade etc. (where (*a*) applies) or for the company in its trade etc. (where (*b*) applies). For this purpose 'full-time' means more than 24 hours per week worked at a place where the trade etc. is carried on (15 hours if it is carried on only by the disponer and spouse and the nephew or niece). '*Relevant period*' means the five years (excluding, in relation to work, reasonable periods of annual or sick leave) ending on the date of the disposition, or on the subsequent coming to an end of certain interests in possession of the disponer in the property comprised in the disposition. For gifts or inheritances taken before 1 May 1989, a similar simplified provision applies but without reference to the coming to an end of an interest in possession of the disponer. See 38.18 TAX CASES.

(iii) Where a person receives a gift or inheritance from a grandparent, following the cesser of his parent's limited interest in possession, under a disposition made before 1 April 1975 in consideration of his parents' marriage, he is treated as the grandparent's child in computing the tax payable on the gift or inheritance. This provision was introduced by *FA 1981* with retrospective effect. Any consequential repayment of tax will not carry interest, notwithstanding *CATA s 46* (see 7.11 below).

(iv) 'Child' includes step child and adopted child. For gifts made and inheritances taken after 13 January 1988, the *Status of Children Act 1987, s 3* applies in that

(*a*) relationships between persons are to be determined without regard to whether the parents of any person are or have been married to each other, unless the contrary intention appears, and

(*b*) an adopted person shall, for the purposes of (*a*), be deemed from the date of the adoption to be the child of the adopter or adopters, and not the child of any other person or persons.

[*CATA s 2, 1, 2 Schs; FA 1978, s 41, 3 Sch; FA 1981, s 46; FA 1988, s 74; FA 1989, s 83; FA 1992, s 223; FA 1993, s 130*].

7.5 EXEMPTIONS

(*a*) Small gifts. The first £500 of taxable value taken from any one disponer during any year to 31 December is exempt. Additionally, the first £250 of aggregable value was, before 26 March 1984, ignored in computing tax. [*CATA s 53; FA 1978, s 44; FA 1984, s 110(2)*].

(*b*) Gifts or inheritances received by charities and applied for public or charitable purposes (which, for gifts, etc. before 9 July 1987, had to be in RI or NI) are exempt, as are gifts so applied by such charities. [*CATA s 54; FA 1984, s 110(3); FA 1987, s 50*].

(c) House or garden in RI of national, scientific, historic or artistic interest, provided reasonable viewing facilities have been allowed to the public since that date, or for three years immediately preceding the date of the gift/inheritance, and continue to be allowed. The property must not be held for trading purposes and the exemption is lost on a sale or breach of conditions as under (*d*) below. [*CATA s 55; FA 1978, s 39; FA 1984, s 110(4); FA 1995, s 160*]. See also (*t*) below.

(d) Objects of national, scientific, historic or artistic interest, not held for trading, provided they remain in RI and there are reasonable viewing facilities, and provided they are not sold (other than to a museum, university, etc. in the State) within six years after the valuation date, and before the death of the donee or successor (for gifts or inheritances taken before 12 April 1995, before they form part of the property comprised in a subsequent gift or inheritance). The exemption also ceases if the conditions are breached after the valuation date and before either the sale of the object or its forming part of a subsequent gift or inheritance (in respect of which an absolute interest is taken by a person other than the spouse of the donee or successor) or the death of the donee or successor (for gifts or inheritances taken before 12 April 1995, before it again forms part of the property comprised in a gift or inheritance). [*CATA s 55; FA 1995, s 160*]. See also (*t*) below.

(e) Payments by employer to employee by way of retirement gratuity, redundancy payment or pension (this may not apply if the employer is a relative of or a company controlled by the employee). But benefits under a superannuation scheme taken by persons other than the employee himself will be deemed to be taken from the employee, as disponer. [*CATA s 56*].

(f) Securities (and units of a unit trust scheme holding only such securities) received by donee/successor neither domiciled nor ordinarily resident in RI, the income from which is exempt from tax when owned by such a person, if

    (i) the disponer was either domiciled or ordinarily resident in RI at the date of the disposition (as defined, i.e. date of death or of act of disposition by disponer) and at the date of the gift/inheritance; and

    (ii) the disponer was beneficial owner from 14 April 1978 to the date of the gift/inheritance, or for three years prior to the gift/inheritance; and

    (iii) the securities were comprised in the gift/inheritance at both the date thereof and the valuation date.

    [*CATA s 57; FA 1978, s 40; FA 1984, s 110(5); FA 1991, s 121*].

(g) *Bona fide* betting receipts or prizes. [*CATA s 58(1)*].

(h) Compensation or damages received by a person for a wrong or injury suffered by him or in respect of a fatal accident. [*CATA s 58(1)*].

(j) Certain payments in a bankruptcy situation. [*CATA s 58(1)*].

(k) Reasonable payments during the donor's lifetime for the support, maintenance or education of a spouse or child. [*CATA s 58(2)*].

(l) Gifts or inheritances taken by a disponer under his own disposition, and gifts between associated companies (as defined). [*CATA s 59*].

(m) An inheritance taken by the spouse of the disponer after 29 January 1985, and a gift taken by the spouse of the disponer after 30 January 1990. [*FA 1985, s 59; FA 1990, s 127*]. It is understood that the inheritance tax exemption extends to an appointment made after that date under a discretionary trust to the surviving spouse of the disponer.

7.5   Capital Acquisitions Tax

(*n*)   With effect from 30 May 1985, an inheritance consisting of an interest in an insurance policy

    (i)   which is in a form approved by the Commissioners,

    (ii)   annual premiums on which are paid by the insured during his life, and

    (iii)   which is expressly effected under *FA 1985, s 60* for the purpose of paying 'relevant tax',

to the extent that the proceeds are applied in paying the 'relevant tax'. Any part of the proceeds not so applied is deemed to be taken on the day immediately after the later of the date of death of the insured and the latest date (if any) on which an inheritance is taken in respect of which 'relevant tax' is payable.

'*Relevant tax*' means inheritance tax payable in respect of an inheritance (excluding interests in qualifying insurance policies) taken on (or not later than one year after) the death of the insured under a disposition made by the insured. From 30 May 1990, it also includes inheritance tax payable in respect of an inheritance taken under a disposition made by the spouse of the insured, taken on the date of death of the insured or only in the event of the insured not surviving the spouse by a period of up to 31 days, where the proceeds of the policy are payable either on the death of the survivor of the spouses (or on their simultaneous death), or on the contingency of the insured surviving the spouse. From 29 May 1991, it also includes inheritance tax payable in respect of an inheritance taken under a disposition made by the spouse of the insured where the inheritance is taken on the date of death of the insured.

With effect from 24 May 1989, relief is extended to policies effected by spouses, the proceeds of which are payable on the death of the survivor of the spouses, or on their simultaneous death.

An insurance policy within (*q*) below is within these provisions where the proceeds become payable on the death of the insured, provided that it would have been within these provisions if expressed to be so.

See 2.20 ALLOWANCES AND RATES as regards withdrawal of income tax relief for premiums under such policies.

[*FA 1985, s 60; FA 1989, s 84; FA 1990, s 130; FA 1991, s 118*].

See Statement of Practice SP-CAT/2/91, issued by the Revenue Commissioners in June 1991, for examples of this relief and for the Revenue requirements for approval of policies.

(*o*)   With effect from 24 May 1989, units in certain collective investment undertakings (see 12.21 CORPORATION TAX) comprised in a gift or inheritance at the date of the gift etc. and at the valuation date (see 7.7 below), where, at the date of the disposition, either the disponer is neither domiciled nor ordinarily resident in RI or the proper law of the disposition is not that of RI, and, at the date of the gift etc., the donee or successor is neither domiciled nor ordinarily resident in RI. [*FA 1989, s 85*].

(*p*)   Where an inheritance taken after 29 January 1991 consists, at the date of the inheritance and at the valuation date, of a dwelling-house (or part), and is taken by a person who, at the date of the inheritance, is a brother or sister of the disponer who is at least 55 and who has resided with the disponer for at least five years up to the date of the inheritance, and who is not beneficially entitled in possession to any other dwelling-house (or part), the estimated market value of the house (or part) is reduced by the lesser of £60,000 and 60% (for inheritances taken before 11 April 1994, £50,000 and 50%). This does not apply if the house is agricultural property and the successor is a farmer (see 7.9 below). [*FA 1991, s 117; FA 1994, s 144*].

(q)   With effect from 29 May 1991, the proceeds of an insurance policy

   (i)   which is in a form approved by the Commissioners,

   (ii)   in respect of which annual premiums are paid by the insured,

   (iii)   the proceeds of which are payable on the 'appointed date', and

   (iv)   which is expressly effected for the purpose of paying 'relevant tax',

are, to the extent used to pay 'relevant tax', exempt from tax and not taken into account in computing tax. Subject to (b) and (m) above, an *inter vivos* disposition of the proceeds (or part) of such an insurance policy (other than in paying 'relevant tax') is not exempt from tax.

'*Relevant tax*' means gift or inheritance tax payable in connection with an *inter vivos* disposition made by the insured within one year after the 'appointed date', excluding such tax payable on an appointment out of an *inter vivos* discretionary trust set up by the insured.

The *'appointed date'* is a date occurring not earlier than eight years after the date on which the insurance policy is effected, or an earlier date on which the proceeds of a policy become payable either on the critical illness or on the death of the insured.

The 'insured' for these purposes may comprise an individual and spouse, together or separately, in the case of a joint insurance.

An insurance policy within (n) above is within these provisions where the proceeds are used to pay relevant tax (as above) arising under an *inter vivos* disposition made by the insured within one year after the appointed date.

See 2.20 ALLOWANCES AND RATES as regards withdrawal of income tax relief for premiums under such policies.

[*FA 1991, s 119*].

See Statement of Practice SP-CAT/2/91, issued by the Revenue Commissioners in June 1991, for Revenue requirements for approval of such policies.

(r)   Policies issued after 30 November 1992 to non-residents by life assurance companies operating in the International Financial Services Centre in Dublin are exempt from gift and inheritance tax provided that the donee or successor is neither domiciled nor ordinarily resident in RI at the date of the gift or inheritance, and that, at the date of the disposition, either the disponer is neither resident nor ordinarily resident in RI or the proper law of the disposition is not that of RI. [*FA 1993, s 133*].

(s)   With effect from 12 April 1995, an inheritance taken by a parent from a child on the death of the child if the child had, within the preceding five years, taken a non-exempt gift or inheritance from a parent or parents. [*FA 1995, s 165*].

(t)   A gift or inheritance taken after 11 April 1995 consisting in whole or part of shares in a private company (within *CATA s 16*) which (after the taking of the gift or inheritance) is, on the date of the gift or inheritance, controlled (within *CATA s 16*) by the donee or successor, to the extent that the value of the shares at the valuation date is attributable to 'relevant heritage property'. That property must have been in the beneficial ownership of the company (or a subsidiary within *Companies Act 1963, s 155*) on 12 April 1995.

'*Relevant heritage property*' is property to which *CATA s 55* applies (see (c)(d) above).

There are provisions for dealing with shares which are also relevant business property (see 7.9 above), and for the withdrawal of the exemption where either the shares or the relevant heritage property are sold (other than to a museum, university, etc. within the State) within six years after the valuation date and before the death of the donee or successor, or the conditions referred to in (*d*) above are breached such that the exemption in (*c*) or (*d*) above would cease to apply.

[*FA 1995, s 166*].

7.6 MEANING OF 'GIFT' AND 'INHERITANCE'

A gift or inheritance is deemed to consist of the whole or a proportionate part of the property in which the benefit is taken or on which it is or can be charged or secured. A gift or inheritance of a periodic payment which cannot be charged or secured is deemed to consist of a sum which would if invested on the date of the gift/inheritance in specified RI Government securities give an annual yield equal to the periodic payment. [*CATA ss 5(2)(5), 11(2)*].

Taxable gift and taxable inheritance mean the whole property wherever situate, or the whole sum where

(*a*)   the disponer is, or was until his death, domiciled in RI, or

(*b*)   (in the case of gifts or inheritances taken before 17 June 1993) the proper law of the disposition (or, for a gift taken under a discretionary trust, of the discretionary trust) was RI law;

otherwise (but not in the case of a periodic payment above) all the property situate in RI at the date of the gift/inheritance. [*CATA ss 6, 12; FA 1993, ss 122, 124*].

7.7 VALUATION DATE

(*a*)   For a **taxable gift**, the valuation date will be the date of the gift.

(*b*)   For a **taxable inheritance**, the valuation date will be

(i)   where the inheritance is taken as a *donatio mortis causa* or by reason of failure to exercise a power of revocation, the date of death;

(ii)   where a gift becomes an inheritance because disponer dies within two years, the date of the gift;

(iii)   for other inheritances, the earliest date of the following: earliest date on which the personal representative or any other person is entitled to retain the subject matter of the inheritance for the benefit of the successor; the date on which it is so retained; or the date of delivery, payment or other satisfaction of the subject matter to the successor.

[*CATA s 21*].

Where an inheritance is received in parts, each part will be treated as a separate inheritance. The Commissioners may determine valuation dates, subject to appeal. [*CATA s 21(5)(6)(8)(9)*].

7.8 MARKET VALUE

Market value of any property will be the price, in the Commissioners' opinion, it would fetch if sold in the open market on the date it is to be valued, in circumstances which would obtain the best price for the vendor. The Commissioners may have property valued at their expense. In valuing unquoted shares it shall be assumed that all the relevant information which might be required by a prudent purchaser is available to him. [*CATA s 15*].

For gifts or inheritances taken after 23 February 1993, the market value of shares in a private company (as defined) which is controlled by the donee or successor shall be ascertained as if it formed an apportioned part of the market value of a 'group of shares', the apportionment, as between shares of the same class, being by reference to nominal amount, and as between shares of different classes, having due regard to the attached rights. The *'group of shares'* to be considered is the aggregate of those of the donee or successor, of relatives, nominees and nominees of relatives of the donee or successor, and of trustees of settlements whose objects include the donee or successor or such relatives. There are further detailed rules relating to certain private company holdings of shares.

Previously, private trading companies and private non-trading companies (as defined) controlled by the donee or successor were dealt with differently. The market value of shares in the former was ascertained as if each was part of a holding giving control, that of shares in the latter as if the company had been voluntarily wound up and all the assets realised and payment made on each share.

[*CATA ss 16, 17; FA 1993, ss 125, 134*].

7.9 TAXABLE VALUE

The market value will be reduced by any debts or other liabilities to which the gift or inheritance is subject. The balance is the *incumbrance-free value* from which is deducted any *bona fide* consideration in money or money's worth by the donee or successor to give the taxable value. No deduction is allowed for specified items, including contingent liabilities (unless subsequently paid, when a claim may be made for adjustment of the tax), reimbursable amounts (unless reimbursement not obtained), liabilities created by the donee or successor, tax etc. chargeable on the gift or inheritance, and any liability on exempt property. Foreign debts will be deducted primarily from foreign property. [*CATA s 18*]. Where the disponer and donee/successor are related, the grant to the disponer of an annuity for life is not consideration for the gift or inheritance. [*CATA ss 5(4), 11(2)*]. Where a gift or inheritance is taken free of tax, the taxable value includes the tax chargeable on the gift etc., but, for a gift etc. taken after 17 July 1982, not tax chargeable on such tax. [*FA 1982, s 98*].

For events happening after 29 January 1985 which give rise to both gift or inheritance tax and capital gains tax, the capital gains tax is *not* deducted in arriving at taxable value. See 7.16 below for relief against the gift/inheritance tax liability. [*FA 1985, s 63*].

For a limited interest in property the incumbrance-free value will be reduced according to the age and sex of the donee or successor or the period of time for which the interest is to last. Rules and tables for calculating the reduction are set out in *CATA 1 Sch*. Any consideration will be deducted from the reduced value. [*CATA s 18(4)*].

For agricultural property (i.e. agricultural land, woodlands, farmhouses, buildings and, after 10 April 1994, farm machinery, livestock and bloodstock) in RI *taken by a farmer* (as defined) as donee or successor, the market value is reduced to give the 'agricultural value', from which debts, liabilities and any consideration will be deducted in the proportion the agricultural value bears to the market value. The net result will be the taxable value. For farm machinery, livestock and bloodstock, the reduction is 50% for gifts or inheritances taken after 7 February 1995, 25% for those taken after 10 April 1994 and before 8 February 1995. For gifts of other agricultural property, the reduction is 50% plus the lesser of 30% and £90,000 (i.e. 80% up to £300,000 plus 50% on the excess) for gifts taken after 7 February 1995, 30% plus the lesser of 50% and £150,000 (i.e. 80% up to £300,000 plus 30% on the excess) for those taken after 10 April 1994 and before 8 February 1995. For inheritances of other agricultural property, the reduction is 50% plus the lesser of 15% and £45,000 (i.e. 65% up to £300,000 plus 50% on the excess) for inheritances taken after 7 February 1995, 30% plus the lesser of 35% and £105,000 (i.e. 65% up to £300,000 plus

30% on the excess) for those taken after 10 April 1994 and before 8 February 1995. The limit of £90,000 (£150,000) or £45,000 (£105,000) applies to the aggregate of all taxable gifts taken after 27 February 1969 and all taxable inheritances taken after 31 March 1975 which consist in whole or part of agricultural property (other than farm machinery, live-stock and bloodstock) and which are taken by the same person from the same disponer. For earlier gifts and inheritances, the market value of all agricultural property (other than farm machinery, livestock and bloodstock) is reduced by a specified percentage subject to a spec-ified limit, the amount of the specified limit again applying to the aggregate of taxable gifts and inheritances as above. For gifts, the specified percentage and limit are 75% and £250,000 respectively from 17 June 1993 to 10 April 1994. Otherwise, for gifts and inheri-tances the specified percentage is 55% from 30 January 1991 to 10 April 1994, previously 50%, and the limit is £200,000 from 1 April 1982 to 10 April 1994, £150,000 from 1 April 1980 to 31 March 1982, previously £100,000.

These special reliefs will not apply if the property (for gifts etc. taken after 10 April 1994, excluding crops, trees or underwood, but including replacement agricultural property) is sold by the donee/successor, or compulsorily acquired, in his lifetime and within six years of the date of the gift/inheritance, without being replaced by further agricultural property. For gifts or inheritances taken on or after 2 June 1995, they do not apply if the donee or successor is non-RI resident for any of the three years of assessment immediately following that in which the valuation date of the property concerned falls. [*CATA s 19; FA 1980, s 83; FA 1982, s 100; FA 1991, s 114; FA 1993, s 128; FA 1994, s 141; FA 1995, s 158*].

For '**relevant business property**', the taxable value of gifts and inheritances taken after 7 February 1995 is reduced by 50%. For gifts or inheritances taken after 10 April 1994 and before 8 February 1995, the reduction is 50% in respect of the first £250,000 acquired by a donee or successor and 25% in respect of the balance. The £250,000 limit applies to the aggregate of all such property taken after 10 April 1994 and before 8 February 1995 by the same donee or successor. The reduction does not apply in relation to discretionary trust tax or probate tax (see 7.13, 7.17 below respectively). [*FA 1994, ss 125, 126; FA 1995, s 161*].

Subject as below, '*relevant business property*' means any of the following.

(*a*)   Property consisting of a business, or an interest in a business, carried on for gain.

(*b*)   'Unquoted' shares or securities (i.e. shares or securities not quoted on a recognised stock exchange) in or of a company incorporated in RI (and not within (*c*) below) which on the valuation date (alone or with others in the beneficial ownership of the donee or successor) give control of more than 25% of the votes on all matters affect-ing the company as a whole.

(*c*)   Unquoted shares or securities in or of a company incorporated in RI which on the valuation date (alone or with others in the beneficial ownership of the donee or suc-cessor) represent 10% or more of the nominal value of the company's share capital and securities, *provided that*, after the gift or inheritance is taken, the company is on that date controlled by the donee or successor within *CATA 1976, s 16* (i.e. control by the donee or successor together with certain relatives, trustees etc.).

(*d*)   Unquoted shares or securities in or of a company incorporated in RI which do not fall within (*b*) or (*c*) above and which on the valuation date (alone or with others in the beneficial ownership of the donee or successor) represent 10% or more of the nominal value of the company's share capital and securities, *provided that* the donee or successor has devoted substantially the whole of his time to the service, in a man-agerial or technical capacity, of the company (or of a fellow group company or com-panies) throughout the five years prior to the date of the gift or inheritance.

(*e*)   Any land, building, machinery or plant situated in RI which, immediately before the gift or inheritance, was used wholly or mainly for business purposes by a company of which the disponer then had voting control or by a partnership of which the disponer was then a partner.

(*f*)   Quoted shares in or securities of a company which would be within (*b*), (*c*) or (*d*) above if they were unquoted, *provided that* they, or other shares or securities represented by them, were in the beneficial ownership of the disponer immediately before the disposition and were unquoted at the date of commencement of that beneficial ownership or (if later) at 23 May 1994.

A business or interest in a business or shares in or securities of a company are *not* relevant business property if, on the date of the gift or inheritance, the business (or the business carried on by the company) was carried on wholly or mainly outside RI (in the case of a holding company, considering for this purpose the businesses carried on by the holding company and its subsidiaries as a whole). There is a similar exclusion where the business carried on consists wholly or mainly of dealing in currencies, securities, stocks or shares, land or buildings, or making or holding investments (but not so as to exclude holding companies of one or more companies whose business is not in any of those categories). As regards (*e*) above, there is a similar exclusion unless the disponer's interest in the business is, or the shares etc. in the company are, relevant business property in relation to the gift or inheritance or a simultaneous gift or inheritance taken by the same donee or successor from the same disponer. [*FA 1994, s 127*].

Property is not relevant business property unless it was in the beneficial ownership of the disponer or spouse for a period of two years (in the case of an inheritance taken on the death of the disponer) or five years (in any other case) immediately prior to the date of the gift or inheritance. [*FA 1994, s 128*]. Where property is replaced by other property, these requirements are satisfied by ownership for two out of the three, or five out of the six, years immediately prior to the date of the gift or inheritance, but not so as to increase the amount of the relief above what it would have been without such replacement(s). [*FA 1994, s 129*]. Property acquired on a death is deemed to have been beneficially owned by the successor from the date of death. [*FA 1994, s 130*]. There are provisions dealing with successive benefits within the two-year period. [*FA 1994, s 131*].

Valuation. The value of a business or of an interest in a business is the market value of the net business assets (including goodwill), disregarding (in the case of an interest in a business) any assets or liabilities other than those by reference to which the value of the entire business would be ascertained. Company shares or securities are valued excluding any group company whose business consists of dealing in currencies, etc. (see above) (unless that business consists in holding land or buildings for fellow group companies not carrying on such business), and there is a similar exclusion for the value of companies in a group whose shares or securities are quoted, except in certain cases where they were previously unquoted. [*FA 1994, ss 132, 133*].

Excepted assets. The part of the taxable value of a gift or inheritance attributable to relevant business property excludes that attributable to agricultural property (see above), 'excepted assets' and 'excluded property'. For gifts or inheritances taken after 11 April 1995, agricultural property in the beneficial ownership of a company, and not an 'excepted asset' or 'excluded property', is not excluded. An '*excepted asset*' is broadly an asset which was not used wholly or mainly for the purposes of the business (disregarding use for a business consisting of dealing in currencies, etc. (see above) or, where the business is not carried on by a company, for farming) throughout the two years prior to the date of the gift or inheritance (or for the period of ownership if shorter). Special rules apply in relation to use of land, buildings, machinery or plant within (*e*) above. Parts of land and buildings may be considered separately for these purposes. '*Excluded property*' is broadly a business (or interest in a business) owned by a company whose shares are relevant business property (or by a fellow group member of such a holding company), unless that business (or interest) would itself qualify as relevant business property if included in the gift or inheritance and owned by the disponer at all times when it was in the ownership of the company (or a fellow group member). [*FA 1994, s 134; FA 1995, s 162*].

Withdrawal of relief. There are provisions for the clawback of relief broadly where, within a period of six years from the valuation date (or, for gifts or inheritances taken before 12 April 1995, in the period until it is the subject of a subsequent gift or inheritance, if less), the property would not be relevant business property on a gift of such property at any time within that period, and where relevant business property is sold, redeemed or compulsorily acquired within that period without being replaced by qualifying property (in each case with a saving where the situation is restored within one year). Land, buildings, machinery or plant within (*e*) above (and replacements thereof) continue to be relevant business property for these purposes for so long as they are used for the business concerned. For gifts or inheritances taken after 11 April 1995, relief is not withdrawn where the donee or successor dies before the event which would otherwise cause the withdrawal. [*FA 1994, s 135; FA 1995, s 163*].

7.10   RETURNS AND ASSESSMENTS

The person primarily accountable for tax is the donee or successor. The following are also accountable: (*a*) the disponer (if a gift, or an inheritance taken after 30 April 1989 but before the disponer's death) and (*b*) every trustee, guardian, committee, agent (if agent previously notified in writing) or other person with care of any of the property or income, other than a person who is or derives title from a *bona fide* purchaser or mortgagee for full consideration in money or money's worth. The persons in (*b*) are only accountable for an amount of tax equal to the value of the property or income actually held by them. [*CATA s 35; FA 1980, s 84; FA 1989, s 81*].

From 1 September 1989, any person primarily liable for the tax must, within four months of the valuation date (or, if later, 1 September 1989) (see 7.7 above), or of the date of the notice requiring a return:

(*a*)   render a return of every taxable gift or inheritance, with its estimated market value on the valuation date and particulars relevant to assessment of the tax thereon;

(*b*)   assess the tax (and interest) which ought to be charged at that date; and

(*c*)   pay the tax, with the return, to the Accountant-General of the Commissioners.

Instalment payment and payment by certain Government securities (see 7.11 below) continue to be available. The above procedure applies to the charge under *FA 1984, s 106* (see 7.13 below), and to any other gift or inheritance where the aggregate taxable value exceeds 80% of the relevant threshold (see 7.4 above), or where a return is required by notice. Any of the persons accountable for the tax by virtue of *CATA s 35* (see above) may be required, within not less than 30 days of being given notice, to make the return as above.

The Commissioners have powers to call for such particulars and evidence as they consider may be relevant to assessment of the tax, and may authorise a person to inspect any property comprised in the gift or inheritance and any relevant books, records etc. They may also require an additional return if they consider that a return is materially defective, and any accountable person becoming aware of a defect in a return he has delivered must, within three months, deliver an additional return.

Where a return substantially underestimates the value of any property comprised in a gift or inheritance, the tax attributable to that property is subject to a surcharge as follows, the surcharge (subject to the usual appeal provisions) being treated as tax for the purposes of interest and collection.

Estimated value as % of ascertained value	Surcharge
Under 40%	30%
At least 40% but under 50%	20%
At least 50% but under 67%	10%

[*CATA s 36 as inserted by FA 1989, s 74; FA 1989, s 79*].

Previously, the return required did not include the assessment details or payment of the tax. [*CATA s 36* as originally enacted and amended by *FA 1978, s 42; FA 1982, s 101; FA 1984, s 110(1)*].

A return for these purposes must be made on a form provided by the Commissioners or in a form approved by them, and may be delivered by approved electronic etc. means. [*CATA s 37; FA 1989, s 82*].

The information required for the Revenue affidavit for probate is extended to cover details of the property subject to inheritances and of the successors thereunder. [*CATA s 38*].

Assessments may still be made by the Commissioners according to the return submitted or, if the returns are inadequate, to the best of their knowledge, information and belief. [*CATA s 39; FA 1989, s 75*].

7.11 PAYMENT AND INTEREST

Tax will be due on the valuation date from accountable persons, as defined. Interest will be chargeable at 1.25% per month or part month unless payment is made within three months of valuation date. If payment is made within 30 days after an assessment, no interest accrues for that period. Where the tax is self-assessed (see 7.10 above), interest is not payable on tax paid within four months of the valuation date, and any conditional or incorrect amount of tax paid is treated as a payment on account. [*CATA s 41; FA 1978, s 43; FA 1989, s 76*].

Except to the extent that the property of which a taxable gift or inheritance consists is personal property in which the donee or successor takes an absolute interest, payment may be made by five equal annual instalments (with interest as above on unpaid balances) commencing twelve months after the valuation date. All unpaid instalments become due on the sale or compulsory acquisition of the property of which the gift or inheritance consists (unless the interest of the donee or successor is a limited interest), but no instalments will be payable which, were the tax payable by instalments, would have been due after the death of a donee or successor with a life interest. In relation to gifts and inheritances taken after 7 February 1995 (but not an inheritance taken by a 'relevant trust' (see 7.17 below) or a discretionary trust (see 7.13 below)), to the extent that the tax is attributable to agricultural property (see 7.9 above) or 'relevant business property', the exclusion of tax in respect of personal property in which the donee or successor takes an absolute interest does not apply, and the interest rate on the unpaid balance is 0.75% per month (variable by regulations) rather than 1.25% per month (as above) (although the higher rate continues to apply on overdue instalments). '*Relevant business property*' is as in 7.9 above, but excluding quoted shares in or securities of a company and disregarding the minimum period of ownership requirements and certain exclusions in relation to 'excepted assets'. [*CATA s 43; FA 1995, s 164*].

Payment may be made by transfer of certain Government securities. [*CATA s 45*].

Interest up to 30 April 1991 (and any penalties incurred, see 7.16 below) are waived where gift or inheritance tax in respect of a gift, etc. taken before 31 January 1991 is due and payable by a donee or successor before 1 October 1991, and between 30 January 1991 and 30 September 1991 inclusive, a return is delivered and the tax assessed under *CATA s 36* (self-assessment, see 7.10 above) or *FA 1986, s 104* (discretionary trusts, see 7.13 below), and the tax is paid before 1 October 1991. Instalment payments and payments on account otherwise applicable against interest liability are applied towards discharge of the tax (but without repayment of any excess). The waiver does not apply where any other gift or inheritance tax is outstanding after 30 September 1991, or where any capital gains tax liability (including any interest and penalties) in respect of the disposal of the property comprised in the gift, etc. remains unpaid at the time the gift or inheritance tax is paid. Interest on additional tax following the revaluation of property included in a self-assessed return delivered after 29 January 1991 is not waived. Fines, penalties and interest imposed by a court may not be waived. [*FA 1991, s 120*].

Tax overpaid will be refunded with tax-free interest at 0.6% per month (1% before 1 August 1990, 1.25% before 27 May 1986). The Commissioners may postpone or remit tax. Tax on a gift which becomes an inheritance by death of disponer within two years will be set off against the inheritance tax. [*CATA ss 42, 44, 46; FA 1986, s 109; SI 1990 No 176*].

Tax will be a charge on the property (not money or negotiable instruments) comprised in the gift or inheritance in priority to any charge or interest created by the donee/successor (except as against a *bona fide* purchaser or mortgagee for full consideration in money or money's worth without notice), but the charge will not preclude sale or exchange of settled property (in which case the charge will apply to the proceeds of sale or substituted property). [*CATA s 47*].

From 23 May 1994, applications for the registration of title to land based on possession will not be granted without the production of a clearance certificate from the Revenue Commissioners confirming that, in the 'relevant period', any liabilities to gift or inheritance tax (including probate tax) charged on the land (and not charged prior to the date ownership was last registered) have been or will (within a reasonable time) be discharged. The *'relevant period'* is generally the period from 28 February 1974 to the date as of which the registration was made, but a certificate ending at an earlier date is deemed to satisfy these conditions if the Registrar has no reason to believe that a death relevant to the application occurred in the intervening period. Where the owner of the property (if any) at the date of the application was registered as such after 28 February 1974, the relevant period begins on the date of that registration. [*FA 1994, s 146*].

7.12 APPEALS

Appeals in relation to value of real property will be made to the Land Values Reference Committee under provisions of *F(1909–10)A 1910, s 33*. Appeals in other cases must be made within 30 days after date of assessment, and the provisions relating to income tax appeals generally apply (see 4 APPEALS). [*CATA ss 51, 52; FA 1995, s 159*].

Appeals may be made against any assessment or written decision of the Commissioners relevant to tax. Certain other decisions of the Commissioners are specifically appealable. [*CATA ss 21(9), 52, 56(3)*].

7.13 SPECIAL CHARGE ON DISCRETIONARY TRUSTS

Initial charge. New and existing discretionary trusts on or after 25 January 1984 are to be treated as becoming beneficially entitled in possession to property subject to the trust on the latest of

(*a*)   the date the property became subject to the trust,

(*b*)   the date of death of the disponer, and

(*c*)   the date on which there ceases to be a 'principal object' (if any) of the trust under 21 (25 in relation to property becoming subject to the trust before 31 January 1993), and as taking an inheritance on that latest date accordingly as if the trust and its trustees were a person. A 'principal object' of the trust is a spouse or child of the disponer (and, if such a child predeceases the disponer, any children of such a child) for whose benefit trust income or capital (or part) may be applied.

As regards (c) above, all property subject to a discretionary trust on 31 January 1993 is treated as becoming subject to the trust on that date.

Where property would be charged to tax more than once under the same disposition, tax is charged only on the earliest occasion it became so chargeable. [*FA 1984, s 106; FA 1985, s 64; FA 1992, s 224*].

An interest in expectancy or in a life assurance policy is not property for this purpose until respectively it ceases to be in expectancy or matures. [*FA 1984, ss 105, 106*].

The tax payable on a charge under these provisions is 6% (for inheritances taken before 11 April 1994, 3%) of the taxable value (see 7.9 above) of the inheritance. [*FA 1984, s 109; FA 1994, s 143*]. However, the increase in the charge (from 3% to 6%) is refunded (without interest) if, within five years of the death of the disponer or, in the case of trusts with principal objects, within five years of the youngest reaching 21 years of age, all property within the relevant trusts has been transferred absolutely to the beneficiaries. See in particular 7.10 above as regards returns and payment of the tax.

Discretionary trusts created for the following purposes are, however, exempt from the above charge:

(i)   public or charitable purposes in RI or in Northern Ireland;

(ii)   the purposes of any retirement benefits scheme established under any enactment, or of certain other such schemes but excluding, after 4 April 1990, certain schemes relating to matters other than service in particular offices or employments;

(iii)   the purposes of a registered unit trust scheme;

(iv)   for the benefit of one or more named individuals incapable of managing their affairs through age, improvidence, or physical, mental or legal incapacity; or

(v)   for the upkeep of heritage property within 7.5(c) above,

as are also such a trust in respect of property subject to the trust which, on termination, is gifted or bequeathed to the State, and an inheritance consisting of free use of property, etc. which would otherwise be chargeable by virtue of *CATA s 31* (see 7.14 below). [*FA 1984, s 108; FA 1985, s 65; FA 1990, s 129*].

Appropriate modifications are applied to *CATA 1976* for the purposes of the above charge. [*FA 1984, s 107; FA 1989, s 78; FA 1993, s 131*].

Annual charge.   Subject to the same exceptions and exemptions [*FA 1986, ss 103, 105*], a charge is levied on 5 April (the '*chargeable date*') in every calendar year commencing with 1986 in which property is on that date subject to a discretionary trust in relation to which the disponer is dead and none of the principal objects, if any, is under 21 (25 in relation to 5 April 1993 and earlier chargeable dates), as if the trust and trustees were a person taking an inheritance on that date. Property previously subject to the discretionary trust which is not subject to the trust on the chargeable date only because of the existence of an interest in possession which is revocable, or which is limited to cease other than on the death of the person entitled to the interest in possession or the expiry of a period certain of five years or more from the date of appointment of the interest, is treated as being subject to the trust. The charge does not arise where an initial charge as above arises on the same property, or on property representing it, on, or within one year prior to, the chargeable date. [*FA 1986, ss 102, 103; FA 1992, s 225*].

The tax payable on a charge under these provisions is 1% of the taxable value (see 7.9 above) of the inheritance. [*FA 1986, s 106*]. The valuation date is the chargeable date, except that for the first charge under these provisions following an initial charge as above, the valuation date is the same as that for the initial charge. A trustee at or after the date of the inheritance is required to make appropriate returns within three months after the valuation date, and to assess and pay the due tax to the Accountant-General of the Commissioners. A penalty of the lesser of £1,000 and twice the tax payable may be imposed for failure to comply. [*FA 1986, ss 104, 108; FA 1993, s 132*].

There are provisions enabling the market value of real property and unquoted shares agreed for one chargeable date to apply, subject to limitations, to the following two chargeable dates. [*FA 1986, s 107*].

7.14   OTHER PROVISIONS

Distributions from discretionary trusts will be taxed, as and when made, as an inheritance if the creation of the trust related to a death, and as a gift otherwise. [*CATA s 22*].

Joint tenants are treated for tax purposes as tenants in common in equal shares. [*CATA ss 7, 14(2)*].

Powers of appointment.   Where the disposition is an exercise of, or failure to exercise, a general power of appointment the disponer is the holder of the power. In the case of a special power of appointment the disposition is the disposition creating the power and the disponer the creator of the power. [*CATA s 27*]. A general power of appointment is deemed to exist in certain situations (e.g. in a tenant in tail in possession). [*CATA s 2(2)*].

Enlargement of a limited interest into an absolute interest (e.g. by receiving a reversion) is taxed on the taxable value of the absolute interest minus the value [*CATA 1 Sch*] of the unexpired balance of the limited interest unless both interests are taken under the same disposition. [*CATA s 26*].

Free use of property, free loans etc. will be taxed annually as a gift or inheritance of the value of the free facility for the year. [*CATA s 31*].

Gift terminable on contingency is treated as an absolute interest unless and until the contingency occurs (when it is reassessed as a limited interest for a term certain) [*CATA s 20*], but a **gift subject to a power of revocation by the disponer** is deemed not to render the donee beneficially entitled until the power ceases to be exercisable. [*CATA s 30*]. See also 38.153 TAX CASES.

Gift-splitting will be ineffective because where a disposition enlarges the value of property already held by the donee/successor (but acquired by him since 28 February 1969) and derived from the same disponer, the difference between (*a*) the value of the original property and the newly received property taken as a unit and (*b*) the sum of their values taken separately is a deemed gift or inheritance. [*CATA s 29*].

Life assurance policy is deemed an interest in possession only when the policy matures or is surrendered or to the extent of any payment in whole or partial discharge. [*CATA s 32*].

Double aggregation and double charge: trust property.   Property in respect of which tax is chargeable more than once on the same event, in relation to a gift or inheritance taken after 1 June 1982, is not to be included more than once in relation to that event in any aggregate referred to at 7.4 above, or in relation to the apportionment of tax due in respect of gifts or inheritances taken on the same day. No interest is added to tax repaid under this provision. [*FA 1985, s 61*].

With effect from the introduction of capital acquisitions tax, where tax is charged more than once in respect of the same property on the same event, the net tax which is earlier in priority is deducted against the tax later in priority. Again, no repayment interest supplement is payable. [*FA 1985, s 62*].

Other provisions include: dealings with or settlement of future interests [*CATA ss 23, 25, 64*], release of limited interest [*CATA s 24*], cesser of liabilities [*CATA s 28*], connected successive dispositions [*CATA s 8*] and where *Succession Act 1965, s 98* applies. [*CATA s 33*].

7.15   COMPANIES

Dispositions by or to a private company are treated as if the beneficial owners of shares and of certain entitlements in the company are the disponers, donees or successors, in proportion to the value of their interests in the company. [*CATA s 34; FA 1993, s 129*].

A company resolution affecting company shares which benefits the estate of shareholder A at the expense of that of shareholder B is a deemed disposition by B if he could have prevented the resolution. [*CATA s 2(3)*].

7.16   MISCELLANEOUS

Joint accounts (not current accounts) containing more than £5,000 are frozen if one of the holders dies, and no payments out are allowed without the Commissioners' consent. [*CATA s 61*]. This does not apply where one of the holders dies after 29 January 1985 and was then the spouse of the other. [*FA 1986, s 110*].

Capital gains tax.   Where an event after 29 January 1985 gives rise to both gift or inheritance tax liability and capital gains tax liability, the capital gains tax paid is credited against the gift or inheritance tax liability in respect of that event. The credit given is to be confined to the lesser amount of these two taxes attributable to each asset, or to a part of each asset, which is property charged with both taxes on the same event. Any necessary apportionment of reliefs or expenditure is made on a just and reasonable basis by the Commissioners (or, on appeal, by the Appeal Commissioners). [*FA 1985, s 63; FA 1988, s 66*].

Double tax relief. Foreign tax on a gift/inheritance taken under a disposition on the happening of an event is allowed as a credit against gift tax/inheritance tax on the same event. If the date of the gift/inheritance was before 1 June 1977 the amount of foreign tax may be deducted from the taxable value. There is power to make double tax agreements. [*CATA ss 66, 67(2)(4); FA 1977, s 54(3), 2 Sch*]. See 14 DOUBLE TAX RELIEF—CAPITAL TAXES for the agreement with the United Kingdom.

Regulations may be made by the Commissioners as they think necessary. [*CATA s 71*].

Penalties apply for failure to comply with *CATA s 36* (see 7.10 above) and for the delivery of incorrect returns or statements etc.. [*CATA s 63; FA 1989, s 77*]. See 7.11 above for the waiver of certain penalties.

7.17   PROBATE TAX

Where, under or in consequence of any disposition, property becomes subject to a 'relevant trust' on a death after 17 June 1993, the trust is deemed on the date of death to become beneficially entitled in possession to an absolute interest in that property and to take an inheritance accordingly as if the trust and the trustees were together a person for *CATA 1976* purposes (the date of death being the date of the inheritance). This is without prejudice to any charge to tax in respect of any inheritance, affecting the same property (or part) taken under the same disposition, by an object of the relevant trust or by a discretionary trust by virtue of *FA 1984, s 106(1)* (see 7.13 above) (any such inheritance being deemed to be taken after the deemed inheritance (except for the purposes of the exemptions under *CATA 1976, s 55(3)(4)*, see 7.5(*d*) above)). A '*relevant trust*' is any trust under which, by virtue of *Succession Act 1965, s 10(3)*, the executors hold the estate of the deceased as trustees for the persons by law entitled thereto. It also includes certain trusts deemed to be created where a deceased estate vests in the President of the High Court under *section 13* of that *Act*. *Sections 10* and *13* are both deemed to apply irrespective of the domicile of the deceased or the locality of the estate. [*FA 1993, ss 109, 110; FA 1994, s 137*].

Effectively, the tax applies to the property in an estate passing on the death of a person under his will or intestacy. It does not apply to e.g. joint property passing on a death by survivorship. If the deceased was domiciled in RI, all his assets, no matter where situate, come within the charge unless specifically exempted; otherwise, only RI assets come within the charge.

The provisions of *CATA 1976* apply appropriately adapted in relation to the above charge. In particular, the market value of agricultural property is reduced by 30%, and the penalties under *CATA 1976, s 63* (see 7.16 above) are reduced by 80%. [*FA 1993, s 111; FA 1994, s 138*]. In relation to the exemption at 7.5(*r*) above, the requirement that the successor is not domiciled or ordinarily resident in RI does not apply. [*FA 1993, s 119*].

Exemptions. The following property attracts exemption from probate tax:

(*a*)   certain rights to receive benefits under superannuation and other retirement schemes;

(*b*)   property willed for public or charitable purposes which is, or will be, applied for such purposes;

(*c*)   the dwelling-house (including grounds up to one acre and normal furniture and household effects) where (subject to various conditions and limits) it is occupied by a dependent child or relative by whom it is taken under the will etc. (For deaths before 24 May 1994, the dwelling-house was also exempt where the deceased was survived by a spouse, but see now below as regards general surviving spouse reliefs.)

[*FA 1993, s 112; FA 1994, s 139*].

Rate of tax. Tax is charged at the rate of **2%** on the taxable value of the taxable inheritance under these provisions. No tax is payable where the taxable value does not exceed £10,000 multiplied, in years after 1993, by the figure obtained (to three decimal places) by dividing the consumer price index for the year preceding the year of death by 108.2. Where the taxable value exceeds £10,000 (as indexed), the tax is limited to the excess. [*FA 1993, s 113*].

Quick succession relief applies where the spouse of the deceased dies within one year, or within five years if the surviving spouse is survived by a dependent child. [*FA 1993, s 114*].

Incidence of tax. Property representing any share in the deceased's estate (so far as not exempt or not chargeable) bears its due proportion of the tax. Disputes may be determined, on application by any interested person, in the High Court or, if the amount in dispute is less than £15,000, the Circuit Court. [*FA 1993, s 115*].

Surviving spouse. Tax on property which, at the date of death of the deceased, represents the absolute share of the surviving spouse of the deceased in the estate is abated to nil. Except in the case of certain limited interests (see below), where property represents the shares of both the spouse and other person(s) in the estate, the tax borne by the property is abated in the proportion that the value of the spouse's interest (disregarding any interest in expectancy) bears to the total value of the property. Where a limited interest passes to the surviving spouse, the tax is not abated but does not become due and payable until the limited interest comes to an end. Certain other persons and trustees with an interest in the property on the cessation of the limited interest, or in whose care that property (or income therefrom) is placed at that time, are then accountable for the tax, which is a charge on the property.

Any tax borne by the dwelling-house where the spouse survives the deceased (i.e. where it is not, or not fully, comprised in the spouse's share in the estate and not within the exemption at (*c*) above) does not become due and payable until the date of death of the spouse. Certain other persons and trustees in whom property comprised in the original will etc. is vested at or after the date of the spouse's death, and persons who took an inheritance thereunder including the dwelling-house (or part) or property representing it, are then accountable for the tax.

[*FA 1993, s 115A; FA 1994, s 140*].

Payment and postponement of tax. The person applying for probate or letters of administration of the estate is required to make an assessment in prescribed form of the tax arising on the death, including any interest payable (as below), and to deliver it, with the Inland Revenue Affidavit, to the Commissioners, accompanied by payment of that tax (and interest). Where there are insufficient liquid assets in the estate to meet the tax, payment may be postponed as the Commissioners think fit. [*FA 1993, ss 116, 118*].

Interest on tax. The tax is due and payable on the valuation date (see 7.7 above), in effect the date of death, and simple interest runs from nine months after that date until payment at the rate of 1.25% per month (or part). The interest may not, however, exceed the amount of the tax. Where a payment on foot of the tax is made before the end of that nine-month period, it is discounted at 1.25% per month (or part) of the nine-month period remaining. Any repayment under *CATA 1976, s 46* (see 7.11 above) is made without regard to such discount. [*FA 1993, s 117*].

8 Capital Allowances

Cross-references. See also 18.5 FARMING; 22.4 LOSSES for allowances on significant buildings; 24.2 and 24.6 MINES for capital allowances applicable to mining; 30 SCHEDULE D, CASES I AND II at 30.19 for patents, 30.22 for scientific research and 30.25 for staff recruitment.

Note: The *Corporation Tax Act 1976* replaced or amended much of the existing legislation in order to adapt it for both corporation tax and income tax. See also 12.9 CORPORATION TAX.

8.1   Capital allowances include the allowances mentioned in this section and in the cross-references above. [*FA 1975, s 33*]. They are generally a deduction from the profits of trades etc. (for corporation tax purposes, they are treated as trading expenses) and must be claimed. Where profits are insufficient, excess allowances are carried forward [*Sec 241; CTA 1 Sch 47*] or may create or augment a loss (see 22 LOSSES) [*Secs 318, 319*]. Apportionment of consideration (including exchanges etc.) is made where a lump sum is paid for various assets. [*Sec 298*]. There is a right of appeal. [*Sec 301; CTA s 14, 1 Sch 6*].

8.2   Anti-avoidance provisions apply to sales of assets

(*a*)   between persons under common control or where one party controls the other, or

(*b*)   where sole or main benefit was obtaining capital allowances.

Generally, market value will apply and, for machinery and plant, no initial allowance is claimable by buyer unless sale is in ordinary course of seller's business. However, if only (*a*) applies, the parties may elect (provided no allowance or charge accrues to a non-resident) to substitute for market value the written down value, if lower, and any subsequent balancing charge will be made on the buyer as if he had always been the owner. [*Sec 299; CTA 1 Sch 46*].

8.3   **BASIS PERIODS**

Initial and investment allowances and balancing charges are made in the year of assessment related to the basis period in which the expenditure or sale etc. occurred and wear and tear and writing-down allowances are given on assets in use at the end of that period.

The basis periods for capital allowances follow the appropriate rules of assessment i.e. under Schedule D, normally the current (or, before 1990/91, preceding) year with provisions for commencement and cessation; under Schedule E, the year of assessment; and for corporation tax, the accounting period.

There are transitional provisions which apply for 1990/91 in connection with the changeover to the current year basis of assessment. Where there is an interval between the basis periods for 1989/90 and 1990/91 (the 'intervening period'), and relevant capital expenditure is incurred in that intervening period, an election may be made for either

(i)   the expenditure of the intervening period, or

(ii)   that of the basis period for 1990/91

to qualify for the increased capital allowances described at 8.5, 8.6 below. [*FA 1990, s 21*].

Where

(*a*)   basis periods overlap, the period common to both falls into the first period,

(*b*)   there is an interval between basis periods, it forms part of second period, *unless* the business is discontinued in second period, in which case the interval is part of the first period. [*Sec 297; CTA 1 Sch 6, 45; FA 1990, s 22*].

8.4   DREDGING [*Sec 294; CTA 1 Sch 43*].

Rates from 1960/61 onwards on capital expenditure incurred after 29 September 1956 are

(*a*)   **Initial Allowance**—10%.

(*b*)   **Writing-down Allowance**—2% p.a. for 50 years subject to restriction on total of initial and writing-down allowances to amount of capital expenditure.

8.5   INDUSTRIAL BUILDINGS [*Secs 254–270; FA 1969, ss 31, 64; FA 1970, s 19; FA 1973, s 40; CTA 1 Sch 17–27, 72; FA 1984, ss 35, 36, 38; FA 1985, s 20; FA 1988, ss 44, 45, 48–51; FA 1991, ss 22–24; FA 1993, ss 33, 34; FA 1994, ss 22, 23; FA 1995, ss 26, 27*].

Allowances are on capital outlay after 29 September 1956 on construction of building for use in a trade

(i)   carried on in a mill, factory etc., or dock etc. (including expenditure after 24 January 1984 on a laboratory mainly concerned with mineral analysis in connection with mineral, including oil and gas, exploration and extraction);

(ii)   of hotel keeping (including from 1960/61 use as a holiday camp and from 1969/70 as holiday cottages);

(iii)   from 1966/67, of market gardening (writing-down allowances available for constructions after 5 April 1971);

(iv)   from 1974/75, of intensive production of livestock or eggs, other than in the course of farming as defined by *FA 1974, s 13* (writing-down allowances available for constructions after 5 April 1971); or

(v)   (for expenditure incurred after 23 April 1992) consisting of the operation or management of an airport, where the building, etc. is an airport runway or apron used solely or mainly by aircraft carrying passengers or cargo for hire or reward,

including expenditure on recreational facilities for employees and on site preparation, but excluding expenditure on dwellings, retail shops, offices, etc., land acquisition, plant or machinery (although site preparation costs for installation are allowable), and certain other expenditure attracting other allowances. [*Secs 255–258; FA 1975, s 34; CTA 1 Sch 18, 19, 72; FA 1984, s 36*].

Allowances for expenditure incurred after 23 April 1992 on holiday cottages may only be set against income from the lettings (or from the trade for which the cottages are used), unless the expenditure was incurred before 6 April 1993 and either the construction work was contracted for, or a contract for the lease or purchase of the land entered into and planning permission applied for. [*FA 1992, s 25*].

Buildings, etc. bought *unused* (or, after 5 April 1991, and provided that no allowances have previously been claimed, within one year after first use) attract allowances on the cost of construction or the purchase price, whichever is the lesser. If bought from a person who constructed the building as part of his trading activities, the allowance is on the purchase price. After 5 April 1990, expenditure on the land and certain other items which do not attract industrial buildings allowances are excluded from the cost of construction and, proportionately, from the purchase price. [*FA 1970, s 19; FA 1990, s 75; FA 1991, s 23*].

Part of a building may qualify for allowance where the conditions are met in respect of that part. Where not more than one-tenth of the expenditure on a building relates to parts which do not qualify, the whole of the expenditure qualifies for allowance. [*Sec 255(5)(6)*]. See also 38.24, 38.25 TAX CASES.

8.5 Capital Allowances

Provision is made for the apportionment of construction expenditure where an industrial building or structure forms part of a building, or part or the whole of a building which is part of a single development consisting of a number of buildings. [*Secs 254(3A), 256(2); FA 1990, s 74(c); FA 1994, s 22(1)(a)(b)*].

A building in temporary disuse after use as an industrial building continues to be treated as an industrial building. Where the trade for which it was in use, or the relevant interest, comes to an end during such disuse, allowances are made by way of discharge or repayment of tax and charges are made under Schedule D, Case IV (or, where appropriate, allowances and charges are made in charging income under Schedule D, Case V). [*Sec 270*].

Where any such building is let for use in a trade (or, for expenditure incurred after 28 January 1981, to the Industrial Development Authority, the Shannon Free Airport Development Company Ltd, or Údarás na Gaeltachta, and then under a sub-lease for use in a trade), allowances are similarly available. [*Sec 254; FA 1981, s 27*].

Allowances are also available on expenditure incurred before 1 April 1991 on the construction of car parks of three or more storeys for general public use. [*FA 1981, s 25; FA 1984, s 38*].

Persons holding interests under certain '*property investment schemes*', which provide facilities for the public to share in the profits arising from industrial buildings, etc., are entitled to set their industrial buildings allowances in respect of those interests only against income arising from the interests, and not (where excess allowances arise) against their general income. [*FA 1991, s 24*].

(*a*)   **Initial Allowances** may be claimed in the chargeable period, or its basis period, in which expenditure (net of grants etc.) is incurred or, where let, in the chargeable period, or its basis period, in which the tenancy begins. [*Sec 254; FA 1975, s 34; CTA 1 Sch 17, 72; FA 1993, s 34(1)(a)*].

Basic Allowance	**— 10%**

The **increased allowances** are as follows

Mill, factory etc. or dock etc. From 14 December 1961	— 20%
From 16 January 1975 to 31 March 1996 (but see below)	— 50%*
Multi-storey car parks From 29 January 1981 to 31 March 1991 (and see 8.10 below)	— 50%
Market gardening From 6 April 1974 to 31 March 1992	— 20%
Livestock production From 6 April 1974 to 31 March 1992	— 20%

[*Sec 254(2)(2A); CTA 1 Sch 17, 72; FA 1975, s 34; FA 1977, s 37; FA 1979, s 26; FA 1981, s 25; FA 1984, s 35; FA 1985, s 20; FA 1986, s 51; FA 1988, ss 49, 50; FA 1991, s 22*].

Initial allowances are generally abolished after 31 March 1992. [*Sec 254(2B); FA 1990, s 74(b)*].

*50% initial allowances continue to be available from 1 April 1992 to 31 December 1995 (or 31 December 1996) for expenditure to which 100% increased wear and tear allowances continue to be available after 31 March 1988 (see 8.5(*b*) below).

They also continue to be available for expenditure incurred:

(i)   up to 31 December 1997 (31 December 2002 where the company was included on a list of those entitled to 'Section 84A loans', see 12.10(ii) CORPORATION TAX) for a project approved after 31 December 1988 and before 1 January 1991 for grant assistance by the Industrial Development Authority, the Shannon Free Airport Development Co Ltd or Údarás na Gaeltachta; or

(ii)   up to 31 December 1995 on certain tourist accommodation registered within six months of completion with Bord Fáilte Éireann, provided that a binding contract for the building was entered into before 31 December 1990.

[*FA 1988, s 51(4); FA 1990, ss 80, 81; FA 1995, ss 26, 27*].

(*b*)   **Writing-down allowances**

These are available to the person entitled to the 'relevant interest' in an industrial building or structure on which allowable capital expenditure has been incurred after 29 September 1956. An allowance may be claimed annually while the building or structure remains in use as specified. See below for the percentages applicable to the expenditure (net of any grants, etc.) and periods when available. The total allowances claimed must not exceed 100% of the expenditure. [*Secs 264, 266, 303(3); FA 1975, s 34; CTA 1 Sch 23, 25; FA 1977, s 37; FA 1978, s 25; FA 1979, ss 25, 26; FA 1981, s 25; FA 1984, ss 35–36, 38; FA 1985, s 20; FA 1986, ss 51, 52(2); FA 1988, ss 48–50; FA 1990, s 76; FA 1991, ss 22, 26; FA 1993, s 34(1)(b); FA 1994, s 22(1)(c); FA 1995, ss 26, 27*]. No allowance is available for expenditure incurred after 31 March 1989 for a chargeable period for which an initial allowance (see (*a*) above) is made. [*FA 1989, s 14*].

Basic allowance   —   2% p.a. for 50 years

It is increased to **4% p.a. for 25 years** for expenditure from 16 January 1975 to **31 March 1996**. Other **increased allowances** are as follows.

Mill, factory etc. or dock etc.
Constructions from 2 February 1978
to 31 March 1988   —   up to 100% p.a.*
„   from 1 April 1988
to 31 March 1989   —   up to 75% p.a.*
„   from 1 April 1989
to 31 March 1991   —   up to 50% p.a.*
„   from 1 April 1991
to 31 March 1992   —   up to 25% p.a.*

Hotels etc.
Constructions after 31 December 1959   —   **10% p.a. for 10 years**
Constructions
(not holiday
cottages)   **from 27 January 1994**   —   **15% p.a. for 7 years**
Constructions from 2 February 1978
to 31 March 1988   —   up to 100% p.a.*
„   from 1 April 1988
to 31 March 1989   —   up to 75% p.a.*

59

8.5 Capital Allowances

| | from 1 April 1989 to 31 March 1991 | — | up to 50% p.a.* |
| | from 1 April 1991 to 31 March 1992 | — | up to 25% p.a.* |

Market gardening—constructions after 5 April 1964

From 6 April 1966   —   **10% p.a. for 10 years**

Livestock production—constructions after 5 April 1971

From 6 April 1974   —   **10% p.a. for 10 years**

*Only available where the person incurring the expenditure actually occupies the building. There is an additional requirement in the case of hotels that the premises must be registered with Bord Fáilte Éireann (Irish Tourist Board). The 100% increased allowance continues to be available after 31 March 1988 on expenditure:

(i)   relating to certain activities in Shannon Airport or the Custom House Docks Area (see 12.17 CORPORATION TAX);

(ii)   relating to certain other qualifying premises (see 8.10 below);

(iii)   incurred before 31 December 1995 for a project approved by an industrial development agency before 1 January 1986;

(iv)   incurred before 31 December 1996 for a project approved by an industrial development agency after 31 December 1985 but before 1 January 1989; or

(v)   incurred before 31 December 1995 under a binding contract entered into before 28 January 1988.

For other expenditure incurred after 31 March 1988, increased allowances are not available where an initial allowance has been made (see (*a*) above). [*FA 1978, s 25; FA 1988, ss 44, 48, 51; FA 1990, ss 76, 80; FA 1993, s 33; FA 1995, s 26*].

50% allowances continue to be available after 31 March 1991 for expenditure incurred:

(i)   up to 31 December 1997 (or 31 December 2002 where the company was included on a list of those entitled to 'Section 84A loans' – see 12.10(ii) CORPORATION TAX) for a project approved after 31 December 1988 and before 1 January 1991 for grant assistance by the Industrial Development Authority, the Shannon Free Airport Development Co Ltd or Údarás na Gaeltachta; or

(ii)   up to 31 December 1995 on certain tourist accommodation registered within six months of completion with Bord Fáilte Éireann, provided that a binding contract for the provision of the building was entered into before 31 December 1990.

[*FA 1978, s 25; FA 1990, s 81; FA 1995, s 27*].

No initial allowance is available for expenditure incurred after 5 April 1989 for a chargeable period for which accelerated writing-down allowances are claimed or for any subsequent chargeable period. [*FA 1989, s 16*].

In the case of an industrial building outside the scope of *Sec 264* above which is used by the owner for business purposes, five-twelfths of the rateable valuation may be deducted from profits for 1969/70. [*FA 1969, s 31*]. For previous years see *Secs 65, 67*.

(*c*)   **Balancing allowances or charges** may apply on sale, etc. after 15 April 1959 of buildings constructed after 29 September 1956 which are industrial buildings at the time of sale, etc. After 5 April 1988, any consideration, other than rent or a premium to be treated as rent, in respect of an interest subject to the relevant interest, gives rise to a balancing charge (except where the expenditure qualifies for continuation of the 100% allowance (see above)). After 5 April 1990, balancing adjustments apply to all buildings which have at any time attracted industrial buildings allowances. Balancing adjustments do not apply on sale etc. more than 25 years (ten years for holiday cottages and market gardening buildings, ten years for hotel expenditure prior to 27 January 1994 (seven years for hotel expenditure after 26 January 1994), and fifty years in certain other cases) after the first use of the building (or the incurring of certain refurbishment expenditure attracting allowances). [Sec 265, CTA 1 Sch 24; FA 1977, s 37; FA 1979, s 26; FA 1980, s 58; FA 1988, ss 45, 50, 51(5); FA 1990, s 78; FA 1991, ss 22, 26; FA 1994, s 22(1)(d); FA 1995, s 24]. See FA 1973, s 40 for restriction of balancing allowances on sales after 2 July 1973 between connected persons.

It is understood that, by concession, balancing charges arising after cessation of a trade may be offset by unused trading losses and capital allowances in that trade.

8.6   MACHINERY AND PLANT (INCLUDING SHIPS)

For the meaning of 'plant', see 38.20–38.23 TAX CASES. With effect from 23 May 1994, where a right to use or deal with computer software is acquired for trade purposes, then for capital allowance purposes the right and the software are regarded as machinery or plant provided for trade purposes and belonging to the person entitled to the right. Similarly computer software acquired for trade purposes which would not otherwise constitute machinery or plant is treated as such. [Sec 241A; FA 1994, s 24(a)].

(a)   **Initial Allowances** may be claimed in the chargeable period or its basis period in which the capital expenditure was incurred on new machinery etc. (not cars, lorries etc. but including used and secondhand ships) after 5 April 1956 for trades, professions and market gardens. [Secs 251–253; CTA 1 Sch 15, 16]. Initial allowances and 'free depreciation' allowances (see (b) below) cannot be claimed on the same expenditure.

Basic allowance   —   20%

This applies to expenditure between 6 April 1956 and 13 December 1961. The **increased allowances** are as follows

From 14 December 1961	—	40%
From 1 April 1967	—	50%
From 1 April 1968	—	60%
From 1 April 1971 to 31 March 1988	—	100%
From 1 April 1988 to 31 March 1989	—	75%
From 1 April 1989 to 31 March 1991	—	50%
From **1 April 1991 to 31 March 1992**	—	25%

Initial allowances are generally abolished after 31 March 1992.

The 100% increased allowance continues to be available after 31 March 1988 on expenditure:

(i)   relating to certain activities in Shannon Airport or the Custom House Docks Area (see 12.17 CORPORATION TAX);

(ii)   relating to certain other qualifying premises (see 8.10 below);

(iii)   incurred before 31 December 1995 for a project approved by an industrial development agency before 1 January 1986;

(iv)   incurred before 31 December 1996 for a project approved by an industrial development agency after 31 December 1985 but before 1 January 1989;

(v)   incurred before 31 December 1995 under a binding contract entered into before 28 January 1988; or

(vi)   in a hotel-keeping trade where a binding contract for the provision of the building was entered into after 27 January 1988 and before 1 June 1988.

For other expenditure incurred after 31 March 1988, increased allowances are not available where an initial allowance has been made (see (*a*) above).

[*FA 1978, s 25; FA 1988, ss 44, 48, 51; FA 1990, ss 76, 80; FA 1993, s 33; FA 1995, s 26*].

50% increased allowances continue to be available after 31 March 1991 on expenditure:

(1)   incurred up to 31 December 1997 (31 December 2002 where the company was included on a list of those entitled to 'Section 84A loans' (see 12.10(ii) CORPORATION TAX)) for a project approved after 31 December 1988 and before 1 January 1991 for grant assistance by the Industrial Development Authority, the Shannon Free Airport Development Co Ltd or Údarás na Gaeltachta; or

(2)   incurred up to 31 December 1995 on certain tourist accommodation registered within six months of completion with Bord Fáilte Éireann, provided that a binding contract for the provision of the building was entered into before 31 December 1990.

[*FA 1978, s 25; FA 1990, s 81; FA 1995, s 27*].

(*b*)   **Wear and Tear Allowances**

Before 1 April 1992

New machinery etc. (other than cars, lorries and ships)   —   10%, 12½% and 25% p.a. on a reducing balance basis according to the nature of the asset.

Used and older assets   —   Various rates as for earlier periods.

No allowance may be claimed for expenditure incurred after 31 March 1989 for a chargeable period for which an initial allowance (see (*a*) above) is made unless the expenditure qualifies for the continuation of 100% increased allowances (see below and (*a*) above).

After 31 March 1992

Machinery and plant (new or used) provided for use after 31 March 1992 (other than cars or lorries, see below) attracts a 15% annual wear and tear allowance on a straight line basis for any chargeable period at the end of which the machinery, etc. is in use for trade purposes, provided that it has not been used other than for trade purposes. The allowance is proportionately reduced for chargeable or basis periods of less than twelve months. No allowance may be claimed for a chargeable period for which an initial allowance is made, except where the expenditure qualifies for the continuation of the 100% increased allowances (see below). No allowance may be claimed for expenditure incurred after 23 April 1992 on the construction of an industrial building or structure (or deemed industrial building or structure) (see 8.5 above).

[*Sec 241; FA 1968, s 4; FA 1970, s 14; CTA 1 Sch 6, 54, 56; FA 1989, s 13; FA 1990, s 70; FA 1992, s 26*].

Free depreciation

This applies to new machinery etc. (other than cars and lorries but including ships) provided for use as follows

From 1 April 1971 to 31 March 1988	—	up to 100%*
From 1 April 1988 to 31 March 1989	—	up to 75%
From 1 April 1989 to 31 March 1991	—	up to 50%
From 1 April 1991 to 31 March 1992	—	**up to 25%**

These accelerated allowances are generally abolished after 31 March 1992 (but see below).

[*FA 1971, s 26; CTA 1 Sch 60; FA 1977, s 37; FA 1978, s 22; FA 1988, s 47; FA 1990, ss 72, 80*].

*The 100% or 50% allowance will continue to be available for expenditure for which a 100% or 50% initial allowance would have continued to be available (see (*a*) above). [*FA 1988, s 51(3); FA 1990, s 81; FA 1995, ss 26, 27*].

Free depreciation is also claimable, where available, on

(i)   new machinery (other than cars, lorries etc.) purchased after 31 March 1967 for use in 'designated area' (as defined) [*FA 1967, s 11; CTA 1 Sch 53; FA 1988, s 46; FA 1990, ss 71, 80, 81*], and

(ii)   new machinery etc. purchased before 6 April 1971 for purposes of decimalisation changeover [*FA 1969, s 4; CTA 1 Sch 55*].

Free depreciation and initial allowances (see (*a*) above) may not be claimed on the same expenditure, except where the expenditure qualifies for the continuation of 100% increased allowances (see above). [*FA 1988, s 43*].

Cars and lorries are traditionally rated at 20% p.a.. Allowances for expenditure incurred after 8 February 1995 on cars costing over £14,000 are restricted as if the actual cost was £14,000. The limit was £13,000 from 27 January 1994 to 8 February 1995, £10,000 from 30 January 1992 to 26 January 1994, £7,000 from 26 January 1989 to 29 January 1992, £6,000 from 28 January 1988 to 25 January 1989, £4,000 from 6 April 1986 to 27 January 1988, previously £3,500. The increases from £13,000 to £14,000 and from £10,000 to £13,000 apply only to new cars registered on or after 9 February 1995 and 27 January 1994 respectively, and do not apply in relation to expenditure incurred in the twelve months following each of those dates under a contract entered into before that date, the latter restriction having applied also on the earlier increases in the limit. Similar restrictions apply for renewal allowances, hire purchase and hiring charges. [*Sec 241(1); FA 1973, ss 25–30; FA 1976, s 31; CTA 1 Sch 62; FA 1986, s 50(1); FA 1988, s 24(1); FA 1989, s 12(1); FA 1992, s 21(1); FA 1994, s 21(1); FA 1995, s 23(1)*].

Taxis and hire-cars. For chargeable periods ending after 5 April 1987, the wear and tear allowance is increased from 20% to 40% p.a. for taxis and for cars let on short-term hire, i.e. on self-drive hire under agreements of eight weeks or less (with provisions to prevent consecutive lets to the same or connected persons). The conditions as to use must be satisfied for at least 75% of the time for which the vehicle is in use or available for use (although the qualifying usage may drop to 50% or more for a chargeable period provided that the 75% level was satisfied in either the immediately preceding or in the immediately succeeding chargeable period). [*FA 1987, s 24*].

As regards both (*a*) and (*b*), expenditure incurred after 28 January 1986 is for allowance purposes taken as net of any grants, etc. received, unless the terms of the agreement for the grant, etc. were finally approved on or before 29 January 1986 or were under negotiation on that date and are finally approved before 1 January 1987. Allowances for actual expenditure by a company carrying on a food processing trade on food processing machinery or plant for use in that trade are, however, given without taking account of any grant, etc. received. [*FA 1986, s 52; FA 1987, s 25; FA 1993, s 34(3)*].

8.7   Capital Allowances

(c)   **Investment Allowances** were also available (and not deductible in calculating initial or wear and tear allowances or free depreciation) on *new* machinery etc. (not cars and lorries) for use in a 'designated area' (as defined in the *Industrial Development Act 1969*). The allowance was calculated on the cost less any grant, etc. received, and was withdrawn if the asset was sold without being used for the trade, etc. or within two years of first being so used.

From 1 April 1971 to 31 December 1980 — 20%

[FA 1971, ss 22–26; CTA 1 Sch 57–60; FA 1977, s 37; FA 1979, s 24].

New ships purchased from 6 April 1957 to 23 July 1973–10%. This was withdrawn if the ship was not used in trade or sold within five years of commencement of use. *[Secs 246–250; FA 1973, s 8; FA 1975, s 8; CTA 1 Sch 11–14; FA 1977, s 38; FA 1978, s 23].*

See also 38.23 TAX CASES.

(d)   Balancing allowances or charges arise on sale or cessation of use, etc.. *[Secs 271–278; CTA 1 Sch 28–31; FA 1990, s 79; FA 1994, s 24(b); FA 1995, s 25].*

An election may be made to deduct a balancing charge on old machinery from the cost of new machinery replacing it. *[Sec 273].*

If any grant, etc. is received in respect of wear and tear, for the purpose of determining a balancing allowance or charge a wear and tear allowance is treated as having been made in the chargeable period of the disposal, etc. to the extent that the grant has not already been deducted from the expenditure. *[Sec 280].* It is, however, understood that in practice the Revenue will not apply this so as to reduce a written-down value on disposal, etc. below zero.

Where the proceeds, etc. consist of payments under the EC scheme for decommissioning fishing vessels, any balancing charge is spread equally over three successive years commencing with the year of disposal. *[FA 1995, s 25].*

8.7   LEASING OF MACHINERY OR PLANT

Separate trade of leasing. Where machinery or plant or a film is, after 24 January 1984, provided for a trade of leasing, relief for capital allowances thereon (see 8.6 above) is restricted as below, unless the expenditure on its provision (or the cost of making the film) is either:

(i)   met wholly or partly, directly or indirectly, by the Industrial Development Authority, the Irish Film Board, the Shannon Free Airport Development Company Limited or Údarás na Gaeltachta; or

(ii)   incurred under an obligation entered into before 25 January 1984; or

(iii)   incurred under an obligation entered into before 1 March 1984, pursuant to negotiations in progress before 26 January 1984.

The exclusion at (i) ceases to apply to expenditure on machinery or plant, other than a film, provided for leasing after 12 May 1986, unless it is under an obligation entered into either before 13 May 1986, or before 1 September 1986 pursuant to negotiations in progress before 13 May 1986. However, for expenditure incurred on the provision of machinery or plant (other than a film) for leasing after 12 May 1986 (and not under an obligation entered into before 13 May 1986, or before 1 September 1986 pursuant to negotiations in progress before 13 May 1986), a further exclusion applies where the terms of the lease (provided that it is not between connected persons, as specially defined) include an undertaking that, during a period of at least three years following first use of the machinery or plant by the lessee, it will be used only for the purposes of a 'specified trade' carried on in RI by the lessee or his successor. A *'specified trade'* means a trade at least 75% of whose turnover during the period of restriction under the undertaking derives from a trade consisting of the manufacture of goods (see 12.17 CORPORATION TAX) or exempted trading operations in the customs-free airport (see 16.2 EXEMPT INCOME). There are provisions to correct the situation where it appears to the inspector (or, on appeal, to the Appeal Commissioners) that the undertaking has not been fulfilled.

Where a trade ceases to be a specified trade by virtue of the exclusions from manufacturing companies' relief in *FA 1990, s 41(1)* or *FA 1994, s 48(1)* (see 12.17 CORPORATION TAX), it is treated as continuing to be a specified trade in relation to expenditure incurred before 20 April 1990 or 11 April 1994 respectively under an obligation entered into before that date.

For accounting periods ending **after 30 December 1993**, the exclusion is extended to expenditure on machinery or plant provided for leasing by a lessor in the course of 'relevant trading operations' within *FA 1980, s 39A* or *s 39B* (i.e. certain operations within Shannon Airport or the Custom House Docks Area attracting manufacturing companies' relief, see 12.17 CORPORATION TAX), *provided that* no initial or accelerated capital allowances (see 8.6(*a*)(*b*) above) have been or will be made in respect of the expenditure.

For these purposes, 'leasing' includes letting on hire any item of machinery or plant and letting on charter a ship or aircraft (other than ship charters as part of trade activities of ship-operating companies), and the leasing part of a mixed trade is treated as a separate trade, with any appropriate apportionment.

Any excess of such 'restricted' allowances over income from leasing may not be set against other income. Where a trade (including a deemed separate trade, see above) of leasing is carried on, losses attributable to 'restricted' allowances may only reduce profits or gains of the same trade, and may not be relieved in any other way.

For income tax purposes, 'restricted' allowances, rather than other capital allowances, are set against any balancing charges, with only the balance being included in the loss claim. Where the loss claim exceeds the individual's income, he may specify the manner in which the loss relieved is to be attributed as between trading losses, 'restricted' allowances and other capital allowances.

For corporation tax purposes, a loss is similarly treated as attributable to 'restricted' allowances only insofar as it cannot be attributed to any other source. Equivalent restrictions apply to non-trading lessors.

[*FA 1984, s 40; FA 1986, s 53; FA 1987, s 26; FA 1990, s 41(5); FA 1994, ss 48(3), 61*].

Further restrictions—'relevant leases'. Where, in the course of a trade, a person provides machinery or plant under a 'relevant lease', the letting is treated as a separate leasing trade (the *'specified leasing trade'*) distinct from all other activities. The restrictions on relief for allowances described above in relation to the separate trade of leasing under *FA 1984, s 40* then apply to allowances in the specified leasing trade. This applies with effect **on and from 23 December 1993**, except that a lease is not a 'relevant lease' if a binding written contract for the letting was concluded before that day, or if the leasing was in the course of 'relevant trading operations' within *FA 1980, s 39A* or *s 39B* (see 12.17 CORPORATION TAX), or in certain other cases where the value of the asset(s) concerned does not exceed £50,000. The detailed definition of a *'relevant lease'* is contained in *FA 1994, s 30(1)*, but broadly it is any lease where there is an uneven spread of taxable lease payments involving a deferral of payments. Provided that lease payments are broadly on an even basis throughout the period during which 90% (in certain cases, 95%) of the original value of the leased machinery or plant is recovered, the lease is not a *'relevant lease'*. Seasonal factors in the case of leased agricultural machinery or plant are discounted, and there are special arrangements where expenditure is incurred on leased machinery or plant provided for certain new projects and attracting grant aid, and for which accelerated 50% allowances are available under *FA 1990, s 81* (see 8.6(*a*) above).

Anti-avoidance. Where, after 11 April 1994, either the terms of a machinery or plant lease entered into before that date are altered, or a machinery or plant lease is terminated and a further agreement for a lease of the machinery or plant entered into by the same or connected persons, and as a result lease payments after any given time are greater than they would otherwise have been, then unless the termination or change can be shown to have been effected for *bona fide* commercial reasons, the lease (including the terminated lease) is a relevant lease. There are arrangements for the withdrawal of any relief given which would not have been given if the lease was a relevant lease. Similarly, where a person who owned machinery or plant before 11 April 1994 disposes of it on or after that date to another person, and at or about that time the machinery or plant is leased back by that person to the original owner (or by or to connected persons), then unless the machinery or plant is new and unused, or the lease meets certain other conditions, the lease is a relevant lease.

[*FA 1994, s 30*].

8.8   **RESIDENTIAL BUILDINGS** [*FA 1981, s 23; FA 1985, s 21; FA 1986, s 43*].

See 33.4, 33.5 SCHEDULE D, CASE V for relief on expenditure on certain such premises.

8.9   **ROADS, BRIDGES, ETC.** [*FA 1981, s 26; FA 1984, s 39; FA 1989, s 17*].

Where, under an agreement with a road authority, capital expenditure (including interest where agreement was entered into after 5 April 1987) is incurred after 28 January 1981 and before 1 April 1992 (1 April 1989 where agreement was entered into before 6 April 1987) on the construction of toll roads, bridges, etc., 50% of the expenditure may be set against income arising under such agreements in the same chargeable (or basis) period. Any balance of the allowable expenditure unrelieved may be carried forward without time limit against such income. In relation to expenditure incurred under agreements entered into after 5 April 1987, relief is available only against income arising under the agreement by virtue of which the expenditure was incurred, but all prior expenditure is treated as incurred in the chargeable period in which such income first arises, and further relief is available at the rate of 10% of the expenditure in each of the next five chargeable periods in which such income arises.

The expenditure must not be the subject of any other tax relief or allowance.

8.10   **URBAN RENEWAL RELIEFS**

Expenditure incurred in the period 1 August 1994 to 31 July 1997 inclusive. Enhanced industrial buildings allowances (see 8.5 above) are available for capital expenditure attributable to work carried out in the period 1 August 1994 to 31 July 1997 inclusive (the '*qualifying period*') on the construction or 'refurbishment' of a building or structure used for the purposes of a trade carried on in a mill, factory or other similar premises, where the site of the building, etc. is wholly within a designated area, or the building, etc. fronts onto a designated street etc. (or part). Such areas and streets, etc. are designated by the Minister for Finance, which designation may specify a shorter period within that referred to above. For such expenditure, an initial allowance of **25%** or (in the case of expenditure by the occupier of the building, etc.) annual writing-down allowances of up to **50%** may be claimed. In the case of a building, etc. fronting on a designated street, the enhanced allowances apply only to capital expenditure on the 'refurbishment' of buildings, etc. existing on 1 August 1994, and are restricted to relief of expenditure up to the amount (if any) of expenditure on the existing building, etc. which attracts relief under *FA 1994, s 44* or *s 45* or (as refurbishment expenditure) under *FA 1994, s 46* (reliefs for certain expenditure on residential accommodation, see 33.11 SCHEDULE D, CASE V, 2.22

ALLOWANCES AND RATES). The balance of the expenditure may continue to attract the normal 4% annual allowance.

With effect from 12 April 1995, no balancing charge will be made in relation to a building, etc. attracting allowances as above, where the event which would otherwise give rise to a charge occurs more than 13 years after first use (or, where relevant, after the incurring of the refurbishment expenditure).

'*Refurbishment*' means any construction, reconstruction, repair, renewal or maintenance work in the course of repair or restoration.

Industrial buildings allowances are also available in respect of capital expenditure attributable to work carried out in the qualifying period on the construction or refurbishment of '*qualifying premises*', i.e. premises within designated areas or fronting on designated streets, etc., which are not industrial buildings or structures, but which are used for trade or professional purposes or let on *bona fide* arm's length commercial terms. Any part of such premises in use as, or as part of, a dwelling-house is excluded, as is any part of premises, any part of the site of which is within the county boroughs of Dublin, Cork, Limerick, Galway or Waterford, in use as, or as part of, an office (except that use as an office is disregarded where the construction or refurbishment expenditure in the qualifying period on the part so used amounts to one-tenth or less of the total such expenditure on the premises). The allowances otherwise available (and any related balancing charges) are reduced by **one-half** in all cases, the total allowances being limited to 50% of the qualifying expenditure. The allowances which may be claimed, after such reduction, are an initial **25%** and annual allowances of **2%** or (in the case of expenditure by the occupier of the building, etc.) accelerated annual allowances of up to **50%**. The restrictions applicable to expenditure on industrial buildings or structures fronting on designated streets (see above) apply equally to expenditure on qualifying premises, but to the extent that refurbishment expenditure on the commercial element of the building exceeds the expenditure on the residential element, the capital allowances will be denied. No balancing charge (see 8.5(*c*) above) will be made in respect of qualifying premises by reason of any event occurring more than 13 years after the premises were first used or, in the case of refurbishment expenditure, after that expenditure was incurred.

[*FA 1994, ss 38–41; FA 1995, s 35(1)(a)–(d)*].

See below as regards continuing allowances for urban renewal expenditure in the Temple Bar or Custom House Docks Areas of Dublin, and earlier allowances for urban renewal expenditure in certain other areas. Where those earlier allowances apply to certain expenditure incurred on or after 1 August 1994 as if it had been incurred before that date, the above provisions do not apply to such expenditure. [*FA 1986, s 42(9); FA 1994, s 35(1)(a)(ii)*]. See also 2.22 ALLOWANCES AND RATES, 30.22 SCHEDULE D, CASES I AND II and 33.11 SCHEDULE D, CASE V.

Enterprise areas. Industrial buildings allowances (see 8.5 above) are available on the special basis described below for all capital expenditure incurred in the qualifying period 1 August 1994 to **31 July 1997** inclusive on the construction or refurbishment of a 'qualifying building' as if it were an industrial building or structure. A '*qualifying building*' is a building or structure the site of which is wholly within an 'enterprise area' and in use for 'qualifying trading operations' carried on by a 'qualifying company', but excluding any part in use as, or as part of, a dwelling-house. Enterprise areas are specified by the Minister for Finance, which specification may be for a shorter period within that referred to above. '*Qualifying trading operations*' means the manufacture of goods within *FA 1980, Pt I, Ch VI* (see 12.17 CORPORATION TAX) or the rendering of internationally traded services in the course of a service industry within *Industrial Development Act 1986*. A '*qualifying company*' is a company approved for financial assistance under a scheme administered by Forfás, Forbairt or the Industrial Development Agency (Ireland) and to which a certificate for these purposes has been given by the Minister for Enterprise and Employment. Such a certificate may be conditional, may not be given unless the Minister is satisfied that the carrying on of the qualifying trading operations in the enterprise area will contribute to the balanced development of the area, and may be revoked (in particular if the company fails to comply with a notice requiring it to desist from activities having an adverse effect on the use or development of the area or otherwise inimical to its balanced development).

The allowances available are an initial allowance of **25%** or (where the person incurring the expenditure also occupies the building) free depreciation of up to **50%**, together with annual allowances of **4%** to a total of 100%. Only expenditure attributable to work actually carried out during the qualifying period (as above) is treated as having been incurred in that period. No balancing charge will be made by reason of any event in relation to a qualifying building occurring more than 13 years after first use (or, where relevant, after the incurring of refurbishment expenditure).

[*FA 1994, s 41A; FA 1995, s 35(1)(e)(2)*].

Multi-storey car parks. Expenditure incurred in the period from 1 July 1995 to **30 June 1998** inclusive (the 'qualifying period') on the construction or refurbishment of a public multi-storey car park certified by the local authority to be developed in accordance with criteria laid down by the Minister for the Environment attracts industrial buildings allowances (see 8.5 above) at enhanced rates. In the case of refurbishment, the expenditure incurred in the qualifying period must amount to at least 20% of the car park's market value immediately before the incurring of the expenditure. Expenditure is treated as incurred in the qualifying period only if it is properly attributable to work actually carried out in that period.

The allowances available are either an initial allowance of **25%** and **2%** annual allowances or (only in the case of owner-occupied buildings) free depreciation annual allowances, in either case to a maximum total allowance of **50%**. No balancing charge will be made by reason of any event in relation to a qualifying car park occurring more than 13 years after first use (or, where relevant, after the incurring of refurbishment expenditure).

[*FA 1994, s 41B; FA 1995, s 35(1)(f)(2)*].

Expenditure incurred (or treated as incurred) before 1 August 1994 or in the Temple Bar or Custom House Docks Areas of Dublin. Industrial buildings allowances and charges are given or made in respect of capital expenditure incurred in the 'qualifying period' on construction of 'qualifying premises' as if the premises were an 'industrial building or structure' in use for a trade carried on in a mill, factory, etc. (see 8.5 above), whether or not any such trading activity is carried on in the premises.

Relief is similarly available for expenditure on the refurbishment of buildings existing on 1 January 1991 within the Temple Bar Area (see (iii) below), and for this purpose expenditure is deemed to include the lesser of the cost of acquisition of the building (excluding land) and the value of the building at 1 January 1991, provided that the actual expenditure incurred is at least equal to the lesser of those amounts.

'*Qualifying premises*' means a building or structure the site of which is wholly within a 'designated area', which is not otherwise an 'industrial building or structure', and which is either in use for the purposes of a trade or profession or, whether or not so used, is let on bona fide arm's length commercial terms. Any building or structure in use as, or as part of, a dwelling house is excluded (but see 33.4 SCHEDULE D, CASE V). Buildings in the Temple Bar Area (see (iii) below) may fall within this definition whether or not they are otherwise 'industrial buildings or structures'.

A '*designated area*' is either

(i)   the Custom House Docks Area of Dublin (as specified in *FA 1986, 4 Sch Pt II* or as extended by order of the Minister for Finance under *FA 1987, s 27*),

(ii)   certain areas of Dublin, Athlone, Castlebar, Cork, Dundalk, Kilkenny, Letterkenny, Limerick, Tralee, Tullamore, Sligo, Wexford, Waterford or Galway (as specified in *FA 1986, 4 Sch Pts III–VII*), or

(iii)   the Temple Bar Area (as specified in *FA 1991, 2 Sch*).

See also *SIs 1988 Nos 92, 287, 314.*

Expenditure in the Temple Bar Area qualifies for relief only if approved by Temple Bar Renewal Ltd.

In relation to premises in a designated area within (i) above, the '*qualifying period*' is the period of eleven years ending on **24 January 1999**. For designated areas within (ii) above, it is the period commencing on 23 October 1985 and ending on **31 July 1994** (and where at least 15% of the total construction expenditure on qualifying premises was certified before 24 February 1994 by the relevant local authority (under the relevant guidelines) to have been incurred before 26 January 1994, further such expenditure incurred between 1 August and 31 December 1994 inclusive is treated as having been incurred in the qualifying period), and for the area within (iii) above, it is the period commencing on 6 April 1991 and ending on **5 April 1998**.

The normal rules for industrial buildings allowances apply (see 8.5 above) subject to the following amendments.

(*a*)   The allowances and charges apply for expenditure incurred up to the end of the qualifying period (see above).

(*b*)   The allowances and charges are reduced by one-half where the designated area is an area of Dublin not falling within (i) or (iii) above (and the allowances and charges are for this purpose computed as if this provision does not apply before the reduced allowance is given or charge made, but not so as to result in a balancing charge in excess of the allowances given).

(*c*)   Where the premises are in a designated area within (i) above, and the expenditure is incurred after 24 January 1998, the maximum enhanced annual allowance which may be claimed is 54%, and no initial allowance is available for a period for which an enhanced annual allowance is claimed.

(*d*)   Allowances for capital expenditure on multi-storey car parks which would otherwise be given under *FA 1981, s 25* (see 8.5 above) are instead given under the current provisions, unless the allowances would thereby be reduced under (*b*) above.

(*e*)   The prohibition on the granting of a writing-down allowance for a chargeable period for which an initial allowance is made does not apply.

(*f*)   From 6 May 1993, the period after first use (or after refurbishment) after the end of which no balancing charge may arise is reduced to 13 years (instead of 25 years) (see 8.5(*c*) above).

The inspector determines the amount of expenditure on qualifying premises which is properly attributable to work on construction of the premises actually carried out during the qualifying period, subject to revision on appeal by the Appeal Commissioners or by the Circuit Court.

[*FA 1986, ss 41, 42, 4 Sch; FA 1987, s 27; FA 1988, ss 26, 51; SI 1988 No 314; FA 1990, ss 30(1), 31, 80; FA 1991, ss 22(2), 54, 55, 2 Sch; FA 1992, ss 29(a)(b), 30; FA 1993, s 30(1)(a); FA 1994, ss 35(1)(a), 36, 37(1)(a)(i)(ii); FA 1995, ss 32(1)(a)(b), 33, 34(1)(a)(b)*].

See also 2.22 ALLOWANCES AND RATES, 30.22 SCHEDULE D, CASES I and II and 33.4, 33.5 SCHEDULE D, CASE V.

8.10A   Capital Allowances

8.10A QUALIFYING RESORT AREA RELIEFS

Special allowances are available for capital expenditure incurred in the period **1 July 1995 to 30 June 1998** inclusive on the construction or 'refurbishment' of certain buildings or structures wholly within a '*qualifying resort area*' i.e. a part of Achill, Arklow, Ballybunion, Bettystown, Bundoran, Clogherhead, Clonakilty, Courtown, Enniscrone, Kilkee, Lahinch, Laytown, Mosney, Salthill, Tramore, Westport or Youghal described in *FA 1995, 3 Sch*. The allowances are given as industrial buildings allowances consisting of an initial allowance of 50% and annual allowances of 5%, with free depreciation annual allowances of up to 75% where no initial allowance is claimed (up to a total of 100% allowances). They are, however, dependent, in the case of 'refurbishment' expenditure, on the total amount of such expenditure incurred in the qualifying period being not less than 20% of the market value of the building or structure (excluding land) immediately before the expenditure is incurred. Expenditure is treated as incurred in the qualifying period only if it is properly attributable to work actually carried out in that period.

'*Refurbishment*' for these purposes means any work of construction, reconstruction, repair or renewal, including the provision or improvement of water, sewerage or heating facilities, carried out in the course of repair or restoration, or maintenance in the nature of repair or restoration.

The allowances are given for:

(*a*)   industrial buildings or structures consisting of hotels, holiday camps or registered holiday cottages within 8.5(ii) above (displacing the allowances otherwise available); and

(*b*)   buildings or structures which are not industrial buildings or structures within 8.5 above, and which are in use for the purposes of the operation of one or more 'qualifying tourism facilities', but excluding any part of a building, etc. in use as, or as part of, a dwelling-house unless it is itself registered or listed as a 'qualifying tourism facility'.

'*Qualifying tourism facilities*' are tourist accommodation facilities registered by Bord Fáilte Éireann under *Tourist Traffic Act 1939, Pt III* or listed under *Tourist Traffic Act 1957, s 9*, and other facilities approved for the purpose by the Minister for Tourism and Trade.

As regards buildings, etc. within (*b*) above which are registered or listed tourism accommodation facilities, their ceasing to be so registered or listed is treated as an event giving rise to a balancing charge, with sale, etc. moneys equal to the aggregate of the residue of expenditure incurred on the construction or refurbishment immediately before that event and the allowances given (as above) in relation to that expenditure (so that all the allowances are in effect clawed back). However, no such balancing charge, nor such a charge by reason of any other event, will be made by reason of any event occurring more than eleven years after first use of the building, etc. (or, where relevant, after the incurring of the refurbishment expenditure).

[*FA 1995, ss 46, 47, 48*].

See also 30.22 SCHEDULE D, CASES I AND II and 33.12 SCHEDULE D, CASE V.

8.11   MISCELLANEOUS MATTERS

The total of annual wear and tear allowances and initial allowances claimed after 2 July 1973 must not exceed the cost of the asset, and disposals after that date will attract balancing charges where capital allowances exceed cost. Previous balancing allowances or charges will be taken into account. [*FA 1973, s 9; CTA 1 Sch 61*].

Expenditure on effluent treatment. Capital expenditure by a taxpayer for the purposes of treatment of trade effluent can qualify for capital allowances if it meets the normal conditions for such allowances. An equivalent relief is available for contributions to capital expenditure by a local authority on an effluent control scheme. If the contribution is for the purposes of his trade and the local authority expenditure is for provision of an asset for an approved scheme for treating trade effluent, then the taxpayer is entitled to capital allowances as though his contribution was expenditure by himself on such an asset. [*FA 1978, s 26*].

Film production, etc. expenditure. It is understood that film production expenses can qualify for capital allowances, provided that the master negative is retained by the production company and has an anticipated life of at least two years. Similar considerations apply to e.g. master copies of records and tapes.

Obsolescence allowance may be claimed as an expense in replacing any machinery etc. provided before 15 April 1959 for trade, profession, employment or office. [*Sec 243; CTA 1 Sch 8*].

Value-added tax claimable as a refund or deduction under *VATA ss 12, 20(3)* (see 39.12, 39.18 VALUE-ADDED TAX) is disregarded in any claim to capital allowances or where chargeable on any disposal proceeds. [*FA 1975, s 29*].

9   Capital Gains Tax

9.1   The *Capital Gains Tax Act 1975 (CGTA)* was enacted on 5 August 1975 and it introduced capital gains tax (CGT) for years of assessment commencing on or after 6 April 1974. As originally enacted, Irish CGT bore a close resemblance to UK capital gains tax, but substantial differences were introduced by the *Capital Gains Tax (Amendment) Act 1978 (CGT(A)A)* for years of assessment commencing on or after 6 April 1978. Under these modifications the amount of the gain is no longer computed by reference to historical cost; instead allowable expenditure is increased by reference to the increase in the consumer price index since the expenditure was incurred (see 9.9 below). In addition, except for companies, assets disposed of before 26 March 1982 which were held for more than 21 years were exempt and those held for a lesser period were subject to a tapering charge.

9.2   BASIS OF CHARGE

CGT is charged for 1974/75 and subsequent years of assessment (i.e. year commencing 6 April) in respect of chargeable gains accruing to a person on any disposal of assets. [*CGTA s 3*].

Persons chargeable are those resident or ordinarily resident in RI during the tax year, and anyone else who disposes of land or minerals or mineral rights in RI, or exploration or exploitation rights over the RI continental shelf, or unquoted shares or securities deriving their value from any of the assets mentioned above, or assets in RI used in a trade carried on by him in RI. Persons resident or ordinarily resident in RI but not RI domiciled are chargeable, as respects assets outside RI and UK, on remittances to RI. (Losses on such overseas disposals are not allowed.) [*CGTA s 4*].

Amount chargeable is the total of taxpayer's chargeable gains in the *actual year of assessment* after deduction of allowable losses for that year and, so far as not already deducted, in any previous year from 6 April 1974. [*CGTA s 5*].

9.3   RATES

From 6 April 1992 onwards, the rate of capital gains tax on all disposals is **40%**, except that for 1994/95 and subsequent years, for chargeable gains accruing to an individual on the disposal (not being a 'relevant disposal', see 9.16 below) of 'qualifying shares' in a 'qualifying company' held by the individual for a minimum 'period of ownership' (see below) of five years, the rate is 27%. For this purpose *'qualifying shares'* are fully paid-up ordinary shares carrying no present or future preferential rights to dividends or assets or to be redeemed, and a company is a *'qualifying company'* if, at the date of acquisition of the shares,

(*a*)   it is resident in RI and not elsewhere,

(*b*)   none of its shares etc. is listed on a stock exchange or dealt in on an unlisted securities market, and

(*c*)   the market value of its issued share capital does not exceed £25 million;

and provided that, throughout the five years preceding the disposal, it is resident in RI and not elsewhere and either

(i)   it exists (as regards at least 75% of its market value) for the purposes of the carrying on of one or more 'qualifying trades', or

(ii)   its business consists in the holding of shares in one or more 'connected companies', with or without the carrying on of one or more 'qualifying trades', and at least 75%

of its market value derives from the carrying on of 'qualifying trades' by those 'connected companies' (or by 'connected companies' of such companies where they are themselves holding companies) or by the company itself.

Where a new holding of qualifying shares is acquired by an individual on a reorganisation, etc. of share capital within *CGTA 1975, 2 Sch 2* (see 9.15 below), and the original shares were also qualifying shares, then provided that the individual is not treated under *CGTA 1975, 2 Sch 2(3)* as giving or becoming liable to give any consideration (other than the original shares) for the new holding, these provisions are adapted to take account of the period during which the original shares were held (see *FA 1994, s 66(7)(8)*). For disposals in 1995/96 only, the lower rate also applies to disposals of shares obtained following a reorganisation, etc. before 6 April 1994, where the original shares would have qualified and the new holding consists of non-qualifying shares or qualifying shares in a non-qualifying company, provided that the original shares had been held for at least five years before the reorganisation, etc..

A *'qualifying trade'* is a trade or profession which, throughout the five years preceding the disposal, consists of trading etc. operations other than dealing in shares, securities, land, currencies, futures or traded options (any such operations in that period being treated as a separate trade for these purposes). A company is *'connected'* with the company whose business consists of the holding of its shares (the 'holding company') where

(A) at the date of the acquisition of its shares by the holding company, its shares etc. were not listed on a stock exchange or dealt in on an unlisted securities market,

(B) it is resident in RI and not elsewhere, and

(C) at least 20% of the voting rights in the company are exercisable by the holding company.

[*CGTA s 3; FA 1992, s 60; FA 1994, s 66; FA 1995, s 75*].

Before 6 April 1992, the generally applicable rate was 30%, with higher rates for assets held for six years or less. The 30% rate applied to all disposals (other than certain disposals of development land, see 9.16 below) on the Smaller Companies Market of the Irish Stock Exchange of shares dealt in only on that Market. The higher rates were 50% where the 'period of ownership' of the asset did not exceed three years and 35% where it exceeded three years but did not exceed six years. For disposals before 6 April 1990, a 60% rate applied where the 'period of ownership' did not exceed one year. A *'period of ownership'* had to be continuous, and in the same capacity, up to the date of disposal, and, where property passed to a surviving spouse, included the period of ownership by the deceased spouse. [*CGTA s 3; FA 1986, ss 60, 61; FA 1989, s 30; FA 1990, s 82*]. See also 9.16 below as regards special rates applicable to certain disposals of development land.

9.4 ADMINISTRATION, RETURNS AND ASSESSMENT

The income tax provisions relating to administration, assessment, returns, collection of tax and appeals apply in general for CGT. [*CGTA 4 Sch; CGT(A)A s 15; FA 1983, s 55*]. For the self-assessment provisions applicable for 1990/91 and subsequent years of assessment, see 28.12 RETURNS. Proper books and records must be kept to enable true returns to be made, subject to a penalty up to £1,200. [*FA 1992, s 231*].

Returns may additionally be required from issuing houses etc.; stockbrokers; auctioneers or persons dealing with tangible movable property; nominee shareholders; parties to a settlement; and persons involved with a non-resident company or trust. [*CGTA 4 Sch 3–7; FA 1992, s 246; FA 1994, s 63; FA 1995, s 70*].

Assessment of married persons. Gains of a wife living with her husband are assessed on the husband, and rules on returns and collection apply accordingly, unless either spouse claims separate assessment. Such a claim remains in force until withdrawn by notice. Allowable losses (see 9.10 below) not exhausted against gains of one spouse may be transferred to the other, unless there is separate assessment. [*CGTA s 13, 4 Sch 10*].

Children. As regards disposals made after 13 January 1988, the *Status of Children Act 1987, s 3* applies in that

(*a*)   relationships between persons are to be determined without regard to whether the parents of any person are or have been married to each other, unless the contrary intention appears, and

(*b*)   an adopted person shall, for the purposes of (*a*), be deemed from the date of the adoption to be the child of the adopter or adopters, and not the child of any other person or persons. [*FA 1988, s 74*].

Assessment, where tax unpaid, on donees, beneficiaries or shareholders. Where CGT payable on a gift is not paid by the donor, the donee may be assessed for the same amount of tax. He may recover the tax from the donor or, if the donor is dead, from his personal representatives, as a debt. A beneficiary absolutely entitled against the settlement trustees (or so entitled but for age or disability etc.) who receives from the trustees an asset, or the proceeds of sale of an asset, on the previous disposal of which CGT has become due from the trustees but has been unpaid for six months or more, may be assessed in the name of the trustees. A person connected with an RI resident company who receives a capital distribution (other than a reduction of capital) in respect of shares in the company may be assessed in the company's name for CGT due but unpaid for six months or more in respect of a chargeable gain to which the distribution relates. He may recover the tax from the company. In all the above cases the assessment must be made *within two years* of the date on which the tax originally became payable. [*CGTA s 14(9), 4 Sch 17, 18*].

Assessment on liquidators, receivers, etc. Disposals by a company liquidator or by a person entitled to an asset by way of security, or to the benefit of a charge or encumbrance on an asset, or by a person appointed to enforce or give effect to the security, etc. (an '*accountable person*') are generally treated as being disposals by the debtor or company owning the asset subject to the charge, etc. [*CGTA ss 8(5), 41; CTA s 13(5)*]. See 38.28A TAX CASES. Any 'referable CGT' or 'referable corporation tax' (see below) attributable to the disposal is assessable on and recoverable from the accountable person out of the disposal proceeds, and is treated as a necessary disbursement out of those proceeds. The CGT or corporation tax liability of the owner of the asset is correspondingly reduced for the year of assessment or accounting period of the disposal, but the owner's chargeable gains are otherwise unaffected.

The assessment is made under Schedule D, Case IV for the year of assessment of the disposal on an amount such that income tax at the standard rate thereon equals the referable CGT or corporation tax to be brought into charge (see below).

'*Referable CGT*' generally means the amount of CGT assessable on the debtor (apart from these provisions) in respect of disposals such as are referred to above ('*referable gains*') reliefs and deductions being apportioned rateably. In cases where there are other gains in the year of assessment, the usual order of allowance of reliefs and deductions applies where tax would be chargeable at more than one rate or would be chargeable on both 'relevant disposals' (i.e. disposals of development land—see 9.16 below) and other disposals. Otherwise a proportion A/B of the liability on all gains in the year (apart from these provisions) is attributed to the referable gains, where

A is the CGT liability which would arise (apart from these provisions) if the referable gains were the debtor's only chargeable gains for the year, ignoring any deductions or reliefs, and

B is the CGT liability which would arise (apart from these provisions) on all the owner's chargeable gains for the year, ignoring any deductions or reliefs.

'*Referable corporation tax*' is similarly broadly the CGT which would be assessable on the company (apart from these provisions) in respect of the referable gains if companies were chargeable to CGT under the normal CGT provisions, except that the corporation tax chargeable on referable gains (apart from these provisions) is generally substituted if less. There are similarly provisions determining the tax attributable to referable gains where there are gains other than referable gains and 'relevant disposals' (see above). [*FA 1983, s 56*].

9.5   PAYMENT OF TAX

See also 28.12 RETURNS as regards self-assessment.

CGT is normally payable three months after the end of the year of assessment in which the gain accrued or, if later, two months after the date of assessment. Where consideration for a chargeable disposal is paid in instalments over a period beginning on or after the date of the disposal and exceeding 18 months, CGT may be allowed to be paid in instalments in cases of hardship. [*CGTA ss 5(2), 44*]. The chargeable gain on a disposal by a person neither resident nor ordinarily resident in RI at the time of disposal may, however, be assessed and charged before the end of the year of assessment of the disposal, and the tax is then payable within three months of the date of disposal or, if later, two months after the date of the assessment. [*FA 1982, s 33*].

Unremittable gains. Chargeable gains, included in an assessment, accruing on a disposal of assets outside RI may be disregarded by the Revenue Commissioners if they are satisfied that legislation or executive action of the foreign State prevents the gains being remitted to RI. [*CGTA s 43*].

Deduction of tax on certain disposals. A person by or through whom consideration exceeding £100,000 (£50,000 before 24 May 1989) is payable on the disposal of land, minerals or mineral rights in RI, or of exploration or exploitation rights over the RI continental shelf, or of unquoted shares deriving their value from any of the foregoing (or, on or after 2 June 1995, of unquoted shares exchanged for such shares), or of goodwill of an RI trade, must deduct and account for an amount of CGT equal to *15% of the consideration* unless the vendor produces to him a *clearance certificate*. On application by a vendor, an inspector of taxes must issue a clearance certificate, with a copy to the purchaser, if satisfied that the vendor is resident in RI (before 2 June 1995, ordinarily resident) or that CGT is not payable or has already been paid. [*CGTA 4 Sch 11; FA 1982, s 34; FA 1989, s 29; FA 1995, s 76(a)(b)*]. See 38.28, 38.28A TAX CASES. Where no clearance certificate is produced but the consideration is of a kind preventing the deduction being made, the purchaser must, for disposals on or after 2 June 1995, within seven days of the disposal, notify particulars to the Revenue Commissioners and pay to the Collector-General an amount of capital gains tax equal to 15% of the market value of the consideration, estimated to the best of the purchaser's knowledge and belief. This does not apply where the provisions of *CGTA 4 Sch 18*, enabling tax chargeable on a disposal by way of gift to be assessed and charged on the donee (see 9.4 above), apply. An assessment is not required, but may be made if the tax is not paid within seven days of the disposal. The purchaser may recover an amount equal to tax so paid from the vendor as a simple contract debt in any competent court (unless a certificate is subsequently produced, in which case the tax will be repaid). These provisions apply *mutatis mutandis* to joint purchasers. For disposals before 2 June 1995, the purchaser (or joint purchaser) was, in such circumstances, obliged, within three months of the disposal, to notify particulars to the Revenue Commissioners, failing which he could become liable for capital gains tax up to the amount of any tax remaining unpaid in respect of the disposal twelve months after it fell due. [*CGTA 4 Sch 11(7); FA 1995, s 76(c)*]. A disposal on or after 2 June 1995 by virtue of a capital sum being derived from assets (see 9.6(*c*) below) is for the above purposes treated as the acquisition of the assets for that sum (whether in money or in money's worth) by the person paying the capital sum. [*CGTA 4 Sch 11(10A); FA 1995, s 76(d)*].

See 25.3 PAYMENT OF TAX, 4.5 APPEALS as regards interest on unpaid and overpaid tax.

9.6 DISPOSAL OF ASSETS

Assets comprise all forms of property, whether or not in RI, including options, debts, and other incorporeal property, and property created by its owner or otherwise arising without being acquired. Certain assets are exempt, see 9.7 below. [*CGTA s 7*].

'**Disposal**' is not defined but it is regarded as meaning any transfer of ownership rights. The following are specifically stated to be disposals:

(*a*)   a gift made after 20 December 1974 [*CGTA s 9(2)(a)*];

(*b*)   satisfaction of a debt (including a debt on any security, other than an exempt security, see 9.7 below), although only a gain on disposal of a *debt on a non-exempt security* is chargeable, or grant (and in certain cases abandonment) of an option (including an option for a lease) (and see 9.15 below) [*CGTA ss 46, 47; FA 1992, s 63*];

(*c*)   receipt by the owner of an asset of a capital sum by way of compensation (including insurance moneys) for damage, loss or depreciation of the asset or by way of payment for use or for waiver of rights (see also 9.7 (*m*)) [*CGTA s 8(2)*] (and see 38.26A TAX CASES);

(*d*)   receipt of or entitlement to a capital distribution on shares (deemed to be a part disposal of the shares), also receipt of any sum, except new shares, on a reorganisation of capital, conversion of securities, etc. [*CGTA 2 Sch*].

Part disposal occurs where any rights over the asset remain undisposed of, including where an interest is created by disposal (e.g. grant of a lease by the freeholder). [*CGTA s 8(1)*].

The time of disposal if there is a contract is the date when the contract is made, or, if conditional, when the condition is satisfied. A hire-purchase or similar transaction is a disposal at the time when the use and enjoyment of the assets begin (with adjustment of tax if ownership never passes). Where land is compulsorily acquired, disposal occurs on the date when the compensation is initially determined or, if earlier, the date of the authority's entry onto the land. [*CGTA s 10*].

Death of owner is not a disposal, nor is any deed of family arrangement made within two years of death (or longer if Revenue Commissioners allow). [*CGTA s 14*].

Conveyance or transfer of an asset by way of security is not a disposal. Subsequent disposal under enforcement powers by mortgagee or receiver is deemed to be a disposal by the owner/mortgagor. [*CGTA s 8(4)(5)*]. See also 9.4 above.

9.7 EXEMPTIONS AND RELIEFS

(*a*)   **Gains not exceeding £1,000 for an individual** (£2,000 for 1991/92 and earlier years) in a year of assessment are exempt (gains are net after deduction of losses including losses brought forward from earlier years). If total gains exceed the exempt limit only the excess is chargeable. As regards married couples, each spouse is entitled to the full exemption, and any unused balance of either spouse may be transferred to increase the other's exemption limit. Strictly, a spouse's exemption is available only if that spouse makes a disposal in the year, but it is understood that, in practice, the double exemption is available where only one spouse is chargeable to CGT in the year. The exemption does not apply in cases of retirement relief (see (*q*) below). Where in a tax year an individual is chargeable to CGT at more than one rate (see 9.3 above), relief is allowed first against gains charged at the highest rate. [*CGTA ss 13(4), 16; CGT(A)A 1 Sch 8; FA 1980, s 61; FA 1982, s 32; FA 1992, s 59*].

(*b*) **Any disposal of tangible movable property for £2,000 or less** by an individual is exempt, with marginal relief limiting tax on disposals over £2,000 to one-half of the excess. Any loss arising is restricted by the consideration being deemed to be £2,000 if in fact it is less. The exemption does not apply to commodities sold by a dealer on a terminal market, to disposals of any kind of currency or to wasting assets. Splitting a set of assets is ineffective if the disposals are to the same person, or persons connected. [*CGTA s 17*].

(*c*) **Death** is not a disposal of property of which the deceased was competent to dispose. Personal representatives and legatees or persons succeeding on intestacy are deemed to have acquired such property at market value on the date of death. Deeds of family arrangement made within two years of death (or longer if the Revenue Commissioners allow) also do not constitute disposals. [*CGTA s 14; CGT(A)A s 6*].

(*d*) **Transfers between husband and wife** who are living together are treated as disposals on a no gain/no loss basis, but on a subsequent disposal by the donee spouse the gain is computed on the basis of the acquisition by the donor spouse. [*CGTA s 13*].

(*e*) **Exempt assets:** Irish currency [*CGTA s 7(1); FA 1980, s 62*]; Government and other securities, as specified, and savings certificates, and unconditional futures contracts relating to such securities etc. which require delivery (unless closed out). [*CGTA s 19; FA 1982, s 41; FA 1983, s 54; FA 1984, s 66; FA 1988, s 70; FA 1989, ss 31, 32, 95, 98; FA 1994, s 161*].

(*f*) **Life assurance policies and deferred annuity contracts** are exempt for the original beneficial owner and any subsequent owner who did not give consideration in money or money's worth (excluding certain policies, contracts or reinsurance contracts with foreign insurers issued or made after 19 May 1993). Also excluded from the exemption are certain policies or contracts entered into or acquired without consideration for investment purposes by companies after 10 April 1994, for which special charging provisions apply (see 9.12 below). [*CGTA ss 20, 20A; FA 1993, s 24; FA 1994, s 58; FA 1995, s 68*]. See also 28.4 RETURNS.

(*g*) **Private residence** (including additional grounds up to one acre) of an individual which has been the only or main residence throughout the period of ownership, except part or all of the last twelve months of ownership. Absences for periods of employment abroad do not break continuity of occupation, nor do absences not exceeding four years in all due to requirements of employer. Apportionment of gain applies where the owner was only resident for part of the time. A married couple can have only one main residence, but occupation as only or main residence by a separated spouse prior to transfer of the property to that spouse as part of the financial settlement will, by concession, count as occupation by the transferor up to the date of disposal. The exemption applies equally to disposal by a trustee of settled property occupied by a beneficiary, and, in practice, to disposals by personal representatives where the residence is occupied as only or main residence before and after the death of the deceased by beneficiaries entitled to the proceeds of disposal under the will or intestacy. It does not apply to disposals wholly or mainly with the object of gain. [*CGTA s 25*]. An additional similar relief is available for a gain on a dwelling-house and grounds which had been provided by the taxpayer rent-free and without consideration as the sole residence for his widowed mother or mother-in-law or other relative incapacitated by old age or infirmity (only one such house is eligible). [*FA 1979, s 35 as amended by FA 1980, s 61*].

Such relief will not in practice be denied where the dependent relative makes payments in respect of the property, provided that no net income is receivable by the individual entitled to the relief.

Where a property otherwise qualifying for private residence exemption would, apart from that exemption, give rise to a development land gain (see 9.16 below), then the exemption is restricted as below, the part of the gain not exempt being subject to the development land gains charge.

The part of the gain continuing to attract exemption is the excess of current use value (see 9.16 below) on disposal over

(i)   if the property was held on 6 April 1974, the current use value on that date, or

(ii)   if the property was not held on 6 April 1974, the lesser of current use value on the date of acquisition and the cost of acquisition, plus the incidental costs of acquisition reduced, if appropriate, to the proportion that current use value represents of cost of acquisition at the date of acquisition,

in either case after inflation indexing (see 9.9 below), less the proportion of incidental costs of disposal corresponding to the ratio of current use value on disposal to disposal consideration.

The restriction does not, however, apply where the total consideration in the year of assessment for disposals which would otherwise be subject to the restriction does not exceed £15,000. [*FA 1984, s 67*].

(*h*)   **Tangible movable wasting assets** (see 9.12 below) are exempt, except to the extent that capital allowances were or could have been claimed because of use in a trade or profession. The exemption does not apply to commodities sold by a dealer on a terminal market. [*CGTA s 18*].

(*j*)   **Exempt bodies**: local authorities; trade unions and friendly societies exempt from income tax; Central Bank of Ireland; National Treasury Management Agency; health boards; vocational education committees; committees of agriculture; Bord Fáilte Éireann and certain regional tourism organisations; Eolas; Forbairt; Forfás; Industrial Development Agency (Ireland); Industrial Development Authority; Shannon Free Airport Development Co Ltd; Údarás na Gaeltachta. [*CGTA s 23; FA 1989, s 33; FA 1991, ss 20(2), 44; FA 1994, s 32(5)*]. See 17.8 EXEMPT ORGANISATIONS as regards European Economic Interest Groupings.

(*k*)   **Charities** are exempt on gains applied for charitable purposes. [*CGTA s 22(1)*].

(*l*)   **Superannuation and similar funds** approved for income tax purposes are exempt. [*CGTA s 21; FA 1988, s 30; FA 1991, s 38*]. There is no charge to CGT on a disposal by a person of his rights to any payments from such a fund. [*CGTA s 24(3)(a)*].

(*m*)   **Exempt gains**: instalment savings scheme bonuses; prize bond winnings; betting, lottery or sweepstake winnings; gains on a disposal of any debt other than a debt on a non-exempt security. [*CGTA ss 24, 46, 2 Sch 3; FA 1980, s 62*].

(*n*)   **Compensation, or damages, for personal injury or professional injury** is exempt. [*CGTA s 24(1)*]. Capital sums received as compensation or insurance money on damage or destruction of an asset (not a wasting asset) are not chargeable if applied in restoring or replacing it (but the gain otherwise chargeable is, on a later disposal, deducted in the former case from allowable expenditure, before application of the inflation multiplier, and in the latter from the cost of acquiring the replacement). [*CGTA s 29; CGT(A)A 1 Sch 1*].

(*o*)   **Settlements, trusts etc.** Disposals of any interest under a settlement (including a life interest or annuity) are exempt for the original beneficial owner and any other person not giving consideration in money or money's worth or whose consideration was another such interest (but see 9.13 below for deemed disposals under settlements). Disposals of any annuity not granted by an insurance company or of annual payments under an unsecured covenant are exempt. [*CGTA s 24(3)(4)*].

(*p*)   **Disposals to the State, charities or certain national or public bodies** by way of gift or not by arm's length bargain are treated as made on a no gain/no loss basis. [*CGTA s 39; CGT(A)A s 10*].

(*q*)   **Retirement relief:** (i) *General.* There is relief for total consideration received up to £250,000 (£200,000 from 6 April 1991 to 5 April 1995 inclusive, £50,000 before 6 April 1991) on disposals by an individual aged 55 years or over of chargeable business assets (including goodwill, excluding shares etc. held as investments) used for his business or farm, or of rights over such assets of his 'family company' and shares or securities of his 'family company' or, after 5 April 1990, of a company which is a member of a trading group of which the holding company is his 'family company'. The relief for disposals of shares in family companies (and holding companies) is in the proportion which the value of its chargeable business assets (or those of the trading group) bears to that of its total chargeable assets (before 6 April 1995, to that of its total assets). Marginal relief applies to limit CGT to one-half of any excess consideration over £250,000 (£200,000/£50,000). Except for tangible movable property, the chargeable business assets must have been owned for at least the ten years prior to the disposal, and shares in the family or subsidiary company only qualify if the individual has been a working director for ten years, and a full-time working director for five years. (For disposals before 6 April 1991, the individual had to have been a full-time working director throughout the period of ten years prior to the disposal.) Separate disposals by an individual are aggregated. [*CGTA s 26; FA 1990, s 84; FA 1991, s 42; FA 1995, s 71*].

(ii) *Disposals within the family.* Similar relief is available without limit where the whole or part of the individual's qualifying assets are disposed of to his children (including nephews and nieces who have helped full-time in the business for the previous five years). If the child etc. later disposes of any of the assets within six years (ten years for disposals before 6 April 1995), he is taxable on the retiring person's gain as well as on any gain he himself makes. [*CGTA s 27; CGT(A)A s 8; FA 1990, s 85; FA 1995, s 72*]. The relief also applies to such a disposal by a mother to her illegitimate child. [*FA 1979, s 36*].

(iii) *Premiums for retiring farmers* paid under *European Communities (Retirement of Farmers) Regulations 1974* are not counted as part of the consideration for any retirement disposal. This relief is independent of (i) and (ii) above. [*CGTA s 30*].

(*r*)   **Replacement of business assets—'rollover' relief.** Gains arising on disposals, of assets used solely for a trade etc., from which the consideration is entirely spent on acquiring new assets solely for use in the trade etc. will (on a claim by the taxpayer) be treated as not accruing until the new assets (or subsequent new assets similarly acquired) cease to be used in the trade etc. This deferment also applies, but only to a proportion of the gain, where all of the consideration, save a part not exceeding the gain, is spent on replacement. It is understood that, in practice, relief will generally be available where the expenditure to which the proceeds of disposal of the existing asset is applied is to enhance the value of, or to acquire a further interest in, assets already in use for trade purposes, and may also be available where the new asset is not immediately used for trade purposes. Assets qualifying are plant and machinery, goodwill, and (except where the receipt would be a trade profit) land and buildings. The new assets must be acquired within twelve months before or three years after the disposal of the old assets. The relief is also available to public authorities, trade associations, non-profit-making bodies, bodies promoting sports etc., professional persons and employees, farmers and persons managing woodlands. [*CGTA s 28; CGT(A)A s 9*].

(s) **Replacement of land etc. compulsorily acquired.** There is similar relief where land (with certain related assets) is disposed of to the State, local authority etc., under the exercise of compulsory purchase powers or following formal notice of intention to exercise such powers, and where the whole of the compensation or consideration received is applied in acquiring other assets of the same kind. The replacement assets are identified with the original assets and no disposal is regarded as having occurred. The two kinds of assets are

(i) land and buildings, excluding trade assets in (ii) and houses entitled to relief under (*g*) above as principal private residences;

(ii) trade assets consisting of land and buildings used and occupied solely for the purposes of the trade, plant and machinery, and goodwill (a trade of dealing in or developing land or of providing landlord's services etc. is excluded if a profit on sale would be a trading profit).

The replacement assets must be acquired within twelve months before or three years after the disposal. If part of the compensation is not applied in acquiring the replacement assets there is a part disposal of the original assets; if money additional to the compensation is spent on acquiring the replacement assets, there is an acquisition of a proportionate part of those assets. [*CGT(A)A s 5*].

(t) **Reinvestment relief.** If an individual (the '*reinvestor*') makes a 'material disposal' **after 5 May 1993** of shares or securities in a company and, within three years, applies the consideration for the disposal in making a 'qualifying investment', he may claim to be treated for capital gains tax purposes as if the chargeable gain on the disposal did not accrue until he disposes of the qualifying investment. If the disposal of the qualifying investment itself attracts relief under these provisions, the gain on the original disposal may be further deferred until a disposal occurs which is not within these provisions. Any necessary apportionment of overall consideration for these purposes is made on a just and reasonable basis.

If only part of the disposal consideration is reinvested as above, and the part not so reinvested is less than the gain accruing on the disposal, the reinvestor may claim a reduction in the gain on the material disposal to the amount of the consideration not so reinvested, the balance of the gain being deferred until disposal of the qualifying investment.

When the deferred gain is brought into charge, inflation indexing (see 9.9 below) is on the basis of the actual date of the material disposal.

Relief is denied unless the acquisition of the qualifying investment was made for *bona fide* commercial reasons and not wholly or partly for the purposes of realising a gain from its disposal.

A claim may be made after the relevant disposal and acquisition where all the conditions have been or will be satisfied, but relief is withdrawn where in the event the claimant is not entitled to the relief. A return of the relevant information in relation to such withdrawal is required with the return under *FA 1988, s 10* (see 28.12 RETURNS).

Relief is withdrawn for the year of assessment relating to the event giving rise to the failure to meet the requisite conditions, by the bringing into charge of the deferred chargeable gain, adjusted in respect of unused losses and annual exemption of the year of the material disposal and notional interest during the period of deferral.

A disposal of shares in or securities of a company is a '*material disposal*' if throughout the three years preceding the disposal (or throughout the period from commencement of trading by the company to the disposal, if shorter):

(i)   the company has been a '*trading company*' or a '*holding company*' (i.e. its business has consisted wholly or mainly of the carrying on of trade(s) or, for disposals after 5 April 1995, professions, or of the holding of shares in or securities of 51% trading, etc. subsidiaries); and

(ii)   the reinvestor has been a full- or part-time employee or director (within *FA 1978, s 8*, see 20.3(*c*)(ii) INTEREST PAYABLE) of the company or of companies which are members of the same group of trading companies.

For disposals before 6 April 1995, (ii) above is replaced by a requirement for the reinvestor to have devoted substantially the whole of his time to the service of the company or companies as officer or employee in a managerial or technical capacity and to have been entitled to exercise at least 15% of the total voting rights in the company, and for none of the company's shares to have been listed on a stock exchange or dealt in on an unlisted securities market.

An individual acquires a '*qualifying investment*' if he acquires '*eligible shares*' (i.e. new ordinary shares which, for five years after issue, carry no present or future preferential rights to dividends, or to assets on a winding up, or to be redeemed) in a 'qualifying company' and:

(A)   he holds at least 5% of the ordinary share capital at any time in the period from acquisition of the shares to the date one year after the material disposal (or, where the material disposal was made after 5 May 1993 and before 6 April 1994, to 5 April 1995) (the 'initial period');

(B)   he holds at least 15% of the ordinary share capital at any time in the initial period and the following two years (the 'specified period');

(C)   the company is not the company whose shares were the subject of the material disposal, nor a member of the same trading group as that company;

(D)   the individual becomes a full-time employee or director of the company (for disposals before 6 April 1995, a full-time working officer or employee of the company) at any time in the initial period, and continues as such until the end of the specified period (or until the company commences to be wound up, or to be dissolved without being wound up); and

(E)   for disposals after 5 April 1995, the company uses the money raised through the share issue within the specified period to enable it, or enlarge its capacity, to undertake 'qualifying trading operations'.

A company incorporated in RI is a '*qualifying company*' if

(I)   throughout the specified period, it is resident only in RI, is not quoted on a stock exchange or dealt in on an unlisted securities market, and exists wholly for the purpose of carrying on one or more 'qualifying trades' wholly or mainly in RI, and

(II)   it is not, at any time in the specified period, under the control of another company (together with any connected persons within *CTA s 157*), or a 51% subsidiary (within *CTA s 156*) of another company.

With effect from 6 April 1994, a '*qualifying trade*' is a trade (or, for disposals after 5 April 1995, a profession) which, throughout the specified period, is conducted on a commercial basis and with a view to the realisation of profits, and which consists (as regards at least 75% of its trading, etc. receipts in the specified period) of '*qualifying trading operations*', i.e. operations other than dealing in shares, securities, land, currencies, futures or traded options. Before 6 April 1994, the definition of '*qualifying trade*' for the purposes of the business expansion scheme (see 21.6 INVESTMENT IN CORPORATE TRADES AND RESEARCH AND DEVELOPMENT) applied also for these purposes.

It ceases to be a qualifying company if, at any time in the specified period, a resolution is passed, or an order made, for the winding up of the company, or the company is dissolved without being wound up, unless the winding up or dissolution is for *bona fide* commercial reasons and is not part of a tax avoidance scheme and any net assets are distributed to members within three years from the commencement of the winding up or dissolution.

[*FA 1993, s 27; FA 1994, s 65; FA 1995, s 74*].

(*u*)   **Works of art loaned for public display.** A disposal after 17 April 1991 of any picture, print, book, manuscript, sculpture, piece of jewellery or work of art, after it has been loaned to an approved RI gallery or museum and placed on public display for at least six years, is treated as made at no gain or loss for CGT purposes, provided that its market value was £25,000 or more (in the opinion of the Revenue Commissioners) at the time it was loaned. [*FA 1991, s 43*]. See, however, 34.3 SCHEDULE E—EMOLUMENTS as regards certain art objects loaned by companies to directors or employees.

9.8   **COMPUTATION OF GAINS AND LOSSES** [*CGTA s 11, 1 Sch*]

The gain or loss on disposal is the consideration for the disposal *less*

(*a*)   consideration for its acquisition or, if asset created etc., expenditure in producing it;

(*b*)   incidental costs of acquisition (i.e. advertising, valuation costs, legal fees and expenses including stamp duty, etc.);

(*c*)   expenditure on enhancing value of asset and costs incurred in establishing or defending title;

(*d*)   incidental costs of disposal (as for (*b*) above).

[*CGTA 1 Sch 3*].

More detailed rules on allowable deductions are given below. Deductions under (*a*)–(*c*) are inflation indexed, see 9.9 below.

Consideration on disposal is not defined but it is regarded as meaning any benefit in money or money's worth, excluding any amount chargeable or otherwise taken into account for income tax (except balancing charges and capitalised value of income payments such as rent). [*CGTA 1 Sch 2*]. The consideration is deemed to be the *market value* of the asset where part of the consideration cannot be valued or where disposal is not by way of arm's length bargain (including gifts). [*CGTA ss 9(2), 49*].

Consideration for acquisition is not defined but it is regarded as meaning money and/or money's worth given, again excluding amounts taken into account for income tax. The exclusion does not apply to outlay on assets subject to capital or renewals allowance, or on construction or refurbishment expenditure allowed as a deduction from rental income (see 33.4, 33.5 SCHEDULE D, CASE V), unless a capital loss would arise, in which case such expenditure is excluded to the extent that a net allowance has been given in respect of it. [*CGTA 1 Sch 4, 5; FA 1981, s 23(10)*]. The consideration is deemed to be the *market value* of the asset where part of the consideration cannot be valued (including assets given for loss of office, diminution of emoluments, or services past or future), where acquisition is not by way of arm's length bargain (including gifts), and where a company distributes assets in respect of its shares (but this does not apply in relation to disposals after 6 May 1992 where there is no corresponding disposal of the asset and either there is no consideration in money or money's worth or the consideration is less than the market value of the asset). [*CGTA ss 9(1), 49; FA 1992, s 62*]. Where, however, after 23 June 1982, a company allots shares, in a bargain not at arm's length, to a connected person (as defined by *CGTA s 33*), the consideration given by that person for those shares is deemed to be the lesser of the actual consideration and the excess of the market value of his shares in the company immediately after the allotment over that (if any) immediately before the allotment. For this purpose shares includes stock, debentures, and any other interests in the company, and options in relation to such shares. [*FA 1982, s 62*]. Interest is not an allowable deduction unless it is charged to capital by a company and is in respect of money borrowed to finance expenditure, allowable for capital gains tax purposes, on construction work. [*CGTA 1 Sch 3*].

Where personal representatives, legatees etc. dispose of an asset devolving on death, the acquisition consideration is deemed to be the asset's market value on the date of death. [*CGTA s 14; CGT(A)A s 6*].

Appropriations to and from trading stock. Assets appropriated to trading stock on which, if they had then been sold at market value, a chargeable gain or allowable loss would have accrued, are treated as having been disposed of at market value on appropriation. If the trade profits are chargeable under Schedule D, Case I, an election may be made for the deemed disposal provision not to apply, and instead for the market value at the time of appropriation to be reduced, in computing trade profits for income tax purposes, by the amount of the chargeable gain (or increased by the amount of the allowable loss) which would otherwise have arisen. For appropriations on or after 30 May 1990, no election is available where an allowable loss would have accrued on the appropriated asset. [*CGTA 1 Sch 15(1)(3); FA 1990, s 86*].

On an asset ceasing to be trading stock (whether by appropriation for another purpose or by retention following cessation), it is treated as having been acquired at that time for a consideration equal to the value brought into the trade accounts in respect of it for income tax purposes. [*CGTA 1 Sch 15(2)*].

Acquisition deemed to be that of former owner. Where a married person has received an asset from spouse on a no gain/no loss basis (see 9.7 (*d*) above) and later disposes of it, he/she is deemed to have acquired it in the circumstances in which the spouse acquired it. [*CGTA s 13(7)*].

Part disposals. Except for any sums wholly attributable to the part disposed of, allowable deductions under (*a*)–(*c*) above are apportioned in the proportion the consideration received bears to that consideration plus the market value of the parts or rights undisposed of. [*CGTA 1 Sch 6*].

9.9 INFLATION INDEXING OF ALLOWABLE DEDUCTIONS

Any item of deductible expenditure (including acquisition costs, if appropriate, but excluding incidental disposal costs) incurred more than twelve months before the date of disposal is multiplied by a figure reflecting the rate of inflation (but see 9.11 below as regards assets held on 6 April 1974). The gain due to each item of enhancement expenditure is apportioned and treated as a gain on a separate asset for this purpose (with special provision for an unduly low acquisition consideration). This increase is not available to create or increase a loss (or gain) and if it would turn a gain into a loss (or vice versa) the disposal is deemed to have been on a no gain/no loss basis (see also 9.11 below for example of operation of these provisions). [*CGT(A)A s 3 and 1 Sch 2*]. The appropriate multiplier by reference to year of disposal and year expenditure incurred is shown in the table below. [*CGT(A)A s 3(4) and annual Capital Gains Tax (Multipliers) Regulations*].

CAPITAL GAINS TAX MULTIPLIERS											
Year in which expenditure incurred	Multipliers for disposals in the year ended										
	5.4.85	5.4.86	5.4.87	5.4.88	5.4.89	5.4.90	5.4.91	5.4.92	5.4.93	5.4.94	5.4.95	5.4.96
1974/75	4.140	4.397	4.598	4.756	4.848	5.009	5.221	5.355	5.552	5.656	5.754	5.899
1975/76	3.344	3.551	3.714	3.842	3.916	4.046	4.217	4.326	4.484	4.568	4.647	4.764
1976/77	2.881	3.059	3.200	3.309	3.373	3.485	3.633	3.726	3.863	3.935	4.003	4.104
1977/78	2.470	2.623	2.743	2.837	2.892	2.988	3.114	3.194	3.312	3.373	3.432	3.518
1978/79	2.282	2.423	2.534	2.621	2.672	2.760	2.877	2.951	3.059	3.117	3.171	3.250
1979/80	2.059	2.186	2.286	2.365	2.410	2.490	2.596	2.663	2.760	2.812	2.861	2.933
1980/81	1.782	1.893	1.979	2.047	2.087	2.156	2.247	2.305	2.390	2.434	2.477	2.539
1981/82	1.473	1.564	1.636	1.692	1.725	1.782	1.857	1.905	1.975	2.012	2.047	2.099
1982/83	1.239	1.316	1.376	1.424	1.451	1.499	1.563	1.603	1.662	1.693	1.722	1.765
1983/84	1.102*	1.170	1.224	1.266	1.290	1.333	1.390	1.425	1.478	1.505	1.531	1.570
1984/85		1.062*	1.111	1.149	1.171	1.210	1.261	1.294	1.341	1.366	1.390	1.425
1985/86			1.046*	1.082	1.103	1.140	1.188	1.218	1.263	1.287	1.309	1.342
1986/87				1.035*	1.055	1.090	1.136	1.165	1.208	1.230	1.252	1.283
1987/88					1.020*	1.054	1.098	1.126	1.168	1.190	1.210	1.241
1988/89						1.034*	1.077	1.105	1.146	1.167	1.187	1.217
1989/90							1.043*	1.070	1.109	1.130	1.149	1.178
1990/91								1.026*	1.064	1.084	1.102	1.130
1991/92									1.037*	1.056	1.075	1.102
1992/93										1.019*	1.037	1.063
1993/94											1.018*	1.043
1994/95												1.026*

*Does not apply to expenditure within twelve months of disposal

9.10   LOSSES

Losses are computed in the same way as gains, and if a gain on the disposal would not have been chargeable then a loss is not allowable. Allowable losses are set-off against gains in the same year and any amount remaining is carried forward to gains in later years. Losses brought forward from earlier years must be applied first against current year gains, and before applying the annual exemption. Losses arising in the year of assessment of tax-payer's death which are not deducted in that year may be carried back successively against gains of the three preceding years. [*CGTA ss 5(1), 12, 14(2)*].

Where in a tax year a person is chargeable (on capital gains) at more than one rate (see 9.3 above), losses are allowed first against gains chargeable at the highest rate [*CGT(A)A 1 Sch 7*], subject to the special rules relating to certain disposals of development land (see 9.16 below).

The entire loss or extinction of an asset is, with exceptions, deemed to be a disposal, so as to allow the loss to be claimed; as is the occasion of an asset's value becoming negligible (if the inspector is satisfied). Where a building is destroyed the loss is reduced by any increase in value of the adjacent land. [*CGTA s 12(3)–(5)*].

9.11   ASSETS HELD ON 6 APRIL 1974

For disposals on or after 6 April 1978, the acquisition cost is market value on 6 April 1974 and this market value is increased by the appropriate inflation index multiplier for 1974/75 as described in 9.9 above. If the indexed amount produces a higher gain or loss than the actual monetary gain or loss (without time apportionment) then the actual gain or loss is taken. If the indexed amount turns an actual monetary gain into a loss (or vice versa), the disposal is deemed to produce neither a gain nor a loss.

Thus, the inflation indexing is not available to create or increase an allowable loss (nor to create or increase a chargeable gain). [*CGT(A)A s 3(2)(3)*]. The following examples illustrate this.

Example 1—Indexed 1974 value greater than cost

		£
Cost 1970		5,000
Market value at 6.4.74	£6,000	
Indexed at sale in 1994/95		
6,000 × 5.754		34,524

(*a*)	Sale proceeds in 1994/95	35,000
	Actual gain (35,000–5,000)	30,000
	Indexed gain (35,000–34,524)	476
	The lower (indexed) gain of £476 is taken.	

(*b*)	Sale proceeds in 1994/95	10,000
	Actual gain (10,000–5,000)	5,000
	Indexed loss (10,000–34,524)	(24,524)
	Actual gain as compared with an indexed loss, so no gain/no loss results.	

(*c*)	Sale proceeds in 1994/95	4,000
	Actual loss (4,000–5,000)	(1,000)
	Indexed loss (4,000–34,524)	(30,524)
	The lower (actual) loss of £1,000 is taken.	

Example 2—Indexed 1974 value lower than cost

		£
Cost 1972		19,000
Market value at 6.4.74	£3,000	
Indexed at sale in 1994/95		
3,000 × 5.754		17,262

(*a*)	Sale proceeds in 1994/95	20,000
	Actual gain (20,000–19,000)	1,000
	Indexed gain (20,000–17,262)	2,738
	The lower (actual) gain of £1,000 is taken.	

(*b*)	Sale proceeds in 1994/95	18,800
	Actual loss (18,800–19,000)	(200)
	Indexed gain (18,800–17,262)	1,538
	Actual loss as compared with an indexed gain, so no gain/no loss results.	

(*c*)	Sale proceeds in 1994/95	10,000
	Actual loss (10,000–19,000)	(9,000)
	Indexed loss (10,000–17,262)	(7,262)
	The lower (indexed) loss of £7,262 is taken.	

9.12 SPECIAL RULES FOR ASSETS

Shares and securities. A 'first in/first out' rule applies to shares and securities of the same class. For disposals before 6 April 1978, shares and securities of the same class were pooled (except those held on 6 April 1974, to which 'first in/first out' applied in any case). Calls on shares or debentures, more than twelve months after their allotment, and expenditure on rights issues are deemed incurred when the consideration is given for the purposes of inflation and tapering relief. *[CGT(A)A 1 Sch 3, 5]*. *Shares and securities held on 6 April 1978*, from which disposals were made prior to that date, are identified by assuming that holdings originally acquired on different dates formed distinct parts of the pool and that each part, and the deductible expenditure attributable to it, is reduced proportionately by the pre-6 April 1978 disposals. Shares disposed of within four weeks after acquisition of shares of the same class are partly or wholly identified with the newly acquired shares. Where shares are acquired within four weeks after disposal of shares of the same class at a loss, the loss is only allowable against subsequent gains on the shares newly acquired. *[CGTA 1 Sch 13, 14; CGT(A)A 1 Sch 4]*.

Commodity futures and other assets not individually identifiable are subject to the same provisions as shares and securities. *[CGTA 1 Sch 13(6); CGT(A)A 1 Sch 4(4)]*.

Wasting assets are assets, excluding freehold land, which have a predictable life (for tangible movables, useful life for its original purpose) not exceeding 50 years. *Plant and machinery* are deemed to have a life of less than 50 years. A life interest in settled property is a wasting asset when the actuarial life expectancy of the life tenant is 50 years or less. Deductible expenditure on a wasting asset, except any expenditure qualifying for capital allowances, is written off at a uniform rate over the remaining life of the asset (except as regards any residual or scrap value). *[CGTA 1 Sch 8–10]*.

Leases of land are only wasting assets where the duration remaining is 50 years or less, but allowable expenditure is written off, not uniformly as above, but at a progressive rate laid down. Special provisions apply to premiums and sub-leases. *[CGTA ss 11, 51, 3 Sch]*.

Life assurance policies etc.: investment by companies. Special provisions apply for the computation of the chargeable gain on the disposal (see *CGTA 1975, s 20(3)(4)*) by a company of, or of an interest in, a policy of life assurance, or a deferred annuity contract on the life of any person, entered into, or acquired without consideration, after 10 April 1994 (not being a foreign policy etc. within *CGTA 1975, s 20A*). Policies entered into or acquired on or before that date are treated as entered into or acquired after that date where there are certain variations after that date.

Transitional provisions treat as having been made before 11 April 1994, and hence as excluded from these provisions, any contract entered into before 23 April 1994, where a broker's receipt was issued before 11 April 1994, and any policy taken out before 30 June 1994 as part of an endowment package in respect of a property which the company had contracted to acquire before 11 April 1994.

Unless the disposal results directly from the death, disablement or disease of a person (or one of a class of persons) specified in the policy, the exemption under 9.7(*f*) above does not apply, and the gain is treated as the net amount of a gain from the gross amount of which corporation tax has been deducted at the standard rate of income tax. The gross amount of the gain is brought into charge for the accounting period of the disposal, the corporation tax treated as deducted being set off against corporation tax for the period, any excess being repaid to the company. These provisions do not apply to the computation of allowable losses on such policies, etc. *[CGTA 1975, s 20B; FA 1994, s 58]*.

9.13   SETTLEMENTS AND TRUSTS

See also 36.4 SETTLEMENTS as regards foreign trusts.

'Settled property' means any property held in trust, but not property held in trust for a person absolutely entitled to it as against the trustees (or who would be absolutely entitled but for being an infant or under a disability). *[CGTA s 2]*.

Disposals by the trustees of assets constituting settled property attract CGT payable by the trustees out of trust moneys. Where the beneficiary is absolutely entitled (or would be but for infancy etc.) to assets, disposals of those assets by the trustees are regarded as disposals by the beneficiary, who is assessed accordingly. Any allowable loss on that part of settled property which has not already been deducted can then be claimed by the beneficiary. The ending of the trust by transferring the assets to a beneficiary absolutely entitled is not a chargeable disposal. [*CGTA ss 8(3), 15*].

Deemed disposals. [*CGTA ss 15, 22; CGT(A)A s 7*].

(*a*)   A gift in settlement (revocable or irrevocable) is deemed to be a disposal by the donor, even where the donor is a beneficiary and/or a trustee. (If the trust is for charitable purposes only the gift will be regarded as made on a no gain/no loss basis, see 9.7 (*p*) above.)

(*b*)   Termination (by death) of a life interest or annuity, without the relevant property ceasing to be settled property, is deemed to be a disposal of that property by the trustees (with reacquisition by them at market value).

(*c*)   The occasion of a person becoming absolutely entitled to settled property (or absolutely entitled but for infancy etc.) is deemed to be a disposal, by the trustees, of that property (which ceases to be settled property) with reacquisition at market value. Where the absolute entitlement arises by the termination of a life interest (not an annuity) by death, the gain is *exempt* and the reacquisition is at market value at the date of death.

(*d*)   Property held on charitable trusts which ceases to be held on those trusts is deemed to be disposed of by the trustees with reacquisition by them at market value, with a corresponding charge, and gains made up to ten years previously are brought into charge.

9.14   UNIT TRUSTS

Unit trusts which are collective investment undertakings are subject to a special tax regime (see 12.21 CORPORATION TAX). Otherwise, they are chargeable to CGT (in certain cases at half rate, see below) unless all the units are held by exempt persons (e.g. charities) or, for units disposed of before 1 September 1993, the assets held by the trust are exempt assets (this exemption being extended to 5 April 1994 in the case of government securities, and generally continuing for disposals of such securities after that date to the extent that any gain accrued up to that date). Receipt of a capital distribution by a unit holder is treated as a part disposal by him of the holding in consideration of the distribution and is charged to CGT accordingly. [*CGTA s 31; FA 1979, s 37; FA 1994, s 64*]. There is exemption for gains from disposals of units of an assurance linked unit trust by the assurance company which administers the trust, so long as the units do not at any stage become the property of the policy owner. [*CGTA s 31(5A); FA 1977, s 34*].

Charge at half rate. Before the introduction of the special regime for collective investment undertakings (see 12.21 CORPORATION TAX), CGT was charged at half the normal rate or half the appropriate reduced rate (for which qualifying unit trusts were eligible) on disposals by 'qualifying unit trusts' and on disposals of units held by persons in such a trust. For a unit trust to qualify for the half rate it had to be registered under *Unit Trusts Act 1972, s 3*; its trustees had to be resident and ordinarily resident in RI; all units had to be of equal value and carry equal rights; unit prices had to be published regularly; and certain other conditions had to be met (broadly, large public participation and substantially the greatest part of its investments in quoted securities). [*CGTA ss 3(3), 32; FA 1977, ss 33, 35; CGT(A)A s 4(6), 1 Sch 9*]. This provision was abolished as such trusts are collective investment undertakings. [*FA 1989, s 18(7)*].

9.15 SPECIAL PROVISIONS

Transactions in company shares or securities. Receipt of a capital (i.e. not income) distribution by a person in respect of shares held by him is a part disposal of the shares unless the following sentence applies. Subject to certain conditions, a new holding of shares and securities issued to a person in place of other shares or securities held by him will be treated as the same asset as the original holding, with no disposal regarded as having occurred, on a reorganisation of share capital or reduction of share capital (not paying off redeemable shares) or a conversion of securities. After 5 April 1990, this applies also to certain unit trust reorganisations or reductions. Similar rules apply on an amalgamation by exchange of shares or a scheme of reconstruction or amalgamation provided that it can be shown that the exchange, etc. was for *bona fide* commercial reasons and not part of any scheme or arrangement a main purpose of which was the avoidance of tax. On a transfer by an individual of an entire business as a going concern to a company, in return for shares, the net chargeable gains on the business assets are deferred by being apportioned among the shares and, on subsequent disposal of shares, this amount is deducted from the costs of acquisition of the shares, provided, in relation to transfers after 23 April 1992, that they are for *bona fide* commercial reasons and not part of any scheme or arrangement a main purpose of which was the avoidance of tax. [*CGTA 2 Sch; CGT(A)A 1 Sch 5; FA 1982, s 63; FA 1990, s 87; FA 1992, s 61*].

There is an anti-avoidance provision which ensures that an individual resident or ordinarily resident in RI who holds shares in a close company will be charged, on an increase in value in the company's assets being reflected in a capital gain by him on the sale of his shares, at the reduced rate (see 9.3 above) which related to the period for which the company held the assets and not to the period (if longer) for which the individual held the shares. [*CGT(A)A 1 Sch 6*].

Options. The grant of an option is a disposal of an asset (the option) but if the option is exercised then the grant of the option is treated as part of the larger transactions, so that the consideration for (or cost of) the option is aggregated with the consideration for (or cost of) its exercise in selling (or buying) the substantive asset. A *forfeited deposit* of purchase money is treated in the same way as a payment for an option which is not exercised. Most options are wasting assets, ceasing to exist when the rights to exercise them end. However, in the case of quoted or traded options, and options to acquire assets for use in a trade, abandonment of the option is a disposal thereof, and on the transfer or abandonment of the option the wasting asset provisions do not apply. After 6 May 1992, the abandonment of an option is similarly treated as a disposal in any other case, but not so as to give rise to an allowable loss. [*CGTA s 47; FA 1992, s 63*]. See also 38.26A TAX CASES.

Anti-avoidance provisions deal with transactions between connected persons, disposals in a series of transactions, and transfers at undervalue by a close company. [*CGTA ss 33–35; CTA 2 Sch Pt 11; FA 1989, s 87*].

Partnerships. It is understood that the UK Revenue Statement of Practice of 17 January 1975 'Partnerships' is acknowledged by the Revenue Commissioners to be a guide to the treatment of capital gains tax on partnerships. However, its application to any individual case may be considered on its merits. For an outline of the UK practice, see Tolley's Capital Gains Tax under Partnerships.

9.16 DEVELOPMENT LAND GAINS [*FA 1982, ss 36–40; FA 1990, s 83; FA 1992, ss 60, 68; FA 1995, s 73*].

Disposals of '*development land*' are called '*relevant disposals*' and are subject to special rules.

Development land is land in RI the consideration for the disposal of which, or the market value of which at the time of disposal, exceeds the '*current use value*' of the land at the time of disposal. It also includes unquoted shares deriving their value (or the greater part thereof) directly or indirectly from such land.

Current use value of land is the market value on the assumption that it can never be developed (excluding certain minor development by a local authority or statutory undertaker).

For disposals **before 6 April 1992**, the rate of capital gains tax on chargeable gains on relevant disposals was **50%**, except that on a compulsory disposal following a 'period of ownership' (see 9.3 above) exceeding three years the rate was **40%**. For disposals before 6 April 1990, a 60% rate applied where the period of ownership did not exceed one year.

Inflation indexing of allowable expenditure in computing the chargeable gain on a relevant disposal (see 9.9 above) applies only to an amount limited to the '*current use value*' (see above) of the land at the date of acquisition and to the proportion of incidental acquisition costs referable to that value; or, if the land was held at 6 April 1974, to the current use value at that date.

'Rollover relief' (see 9.7(*r*)(*s*) above) is not available in respect of consideration for a relevant disposal, except that:

(i)   such relief is available in respect of certain disposals by sports clubs;

(ii)   for disposals after 5 April 1995, relief under 9.7(*r*) above is not denied where the relevant local authority certifies, on the basis of guidelines issued by the Minister for the Environment, that the land disposed of is subject to a use which is inconsistent with the protection and improvement of the amenities of the general area within which the land is situated or is otherwise damaging to the local environment; and

(iii)   for disposals after 5 April 1995, relief under 9.7(*s*) is not denied where the land involved is farmland acquired by the authority for the purposes of road building or widening.

Losses from disposals *other than* relevant disposals may not be set against chargeable gains on relevant disposals. Losses on relevant disposals may be set against such gains, and are then not available for relief as allowable losses for the purposes of corporation tax on chargeable gains.

For individuals, these provisions apply only where the total consideration for relevant disposals in the year of assessment exceeds **£15,000**.

Companies are liable to capital gains tax on chargeable gains on relevant disposals under these provisions, and not to corporation tax on the chargeable gains, so that trading or other losses may not be set against such gains. Corporation tax provisions relating to groups of companies are applied to capital gains tax for this purpose, with appropriate modifications. See also 12.13 CORPORATION TAX as regards restrictions on certain distributions out of gains on such disposals, and 12.24 CORPORATION TAX as regards changes following implementation of EEC Directive 90/434/EEC.

9.17   **OVERSEAS MATTERS**

Non-resident companies and trusts. A person resident or ordinarily resident in RI (and, if an individual, RI domiciled) who holds shares in a non-resident close company is chargeable on a proportion of the gains accruing to the company. This does not apply to gains made on trading assets, gains distributed within two years, or gains chargeable in the State of the company's residence. The RI tax thus charged is deductible from gains on a disposal of the shares. An RI resident or ordinarily resident beneficiary (also, if an individual, RI domiciled) is chargeable on a proportion of the gains accruing to a non-resident trust, if the settlor was RI domiciled and resident or ordinarily resident in RI, either at the time of the settlement or when the gains arose. [*CGTA ss 36, 37; CTA 2 Sch Pt II*].

See also 36.4 SETTLEMENTS.

Double tax relief. The same power to make arrangements exists as for income tax. [*CGTA s 38*]. See 15 DOUBLE TAX RELIEF—INCOME TAXES.

10   Claims

10.1   Time limit for a claim to repayment of tax is generally ten years after end of year of assessment to which it relates, but claims regarding lost rent or shortfall in husbandry profits have a limit of one year. [*Secs 29, 35, 498; F(MP)A 1968, s 4(5)*].

10.2   Claims by a contingent beneficiary in respect of income accumulated, up to 5 April 1973 only, under a trust must be made within six years after end of tax year in which contingency happens [*Sec 154; FA 1973, s 5*] and claims for credit in respect of foreign tax are also limited to six years. [*10 Sch 13*].

10.3   Relief for **double assessment** of the same amount is claimable under *Sec 190*.

10.4   Relief for **'error or mistake'** in returns etc. may be claimed in respect of Schedule D and E (and, from 1995/96, Schedule F) assessments within six years after end of year of assessment to which it relates. [*Sec 191; FA 1995, s 15*].

11   Companies

11.1   Under the *Corporation Tax Act 1976*, companies are liable to CORPORATION TAX (12) on their profits. Previously companies were liable on their profits to both income tax (at the standard rate) and corporation profits tax.

11.2   **Dividends.** Dividends and certain other distribution payments are grossed-up by a tax credit (see 35 SCHEDULE F). The amount received by the shareholder plus the related tax is treated as his gross income and credit given for the tax suffered. The company must account for ACT (see 12.25 CORPORATION TAX).

12   Corporation Tax

Headings in this section are:

12.1   COMMENCEMENT OF CORPORATION TAX

Corporation Profits Tax (CPT) ceased to apply when a company came within the charge to corporation tax and does not apply to any income after 5 April 1976.

CPT was payable, in addition to income tax, on the profits of RI companies and on foreign companies trading in RI to the extent of profits made there [*FA 1940, s 52(2)*] but UK companies not trading in RI through a permanent establishment were exempt. [*FA 1949, 5 Sch*].

Corporation tax was introduced by the *Corporation Tax Act 1976 (CTA)*. The rules for corporation tax apply generally from 1 April 1974 but exclude any income which was used as the basis of an income tax assessment for 1975/76 or any earlier year.

A company came within the charge to CT at different times according to the source of income involved. A company came within the charge to CT

(*a*)   from the end of any 1975/76 income tax basis period ending before 6 April 1976, or the end of a 1974/75 basis period (if later); or

(*b*)   on 6 April 1976, if not charged to income tax for 1975/76 or if the 1975/76 income tax assessment was based on actual profits for that year.

[*CTA s 173*].

If not liable as above, an RI company came within the scope of CT (for purposes of accounting periods, see 12.3 below) on 6 April 1976 or, if not then operative, when it commenced business or first made a chargeable gain or an allowable loss. [*CTA s 9(4)(6)*].

'Company' means any body corporate (including, from 1 April 1993, a trustee savings bank) but excluding health boards, European Economic Interest Groupings, vocational education committees, agriculture committees and local authorities. [*CTA s 1(5)(a); FA 1990, s 29(4); FA 1993, s 42*].

Income tax (except on any income received by a company in a fiduciary or representative capacity), corporation profits tax and capital gains tax ceased to be chargeable when CT became chargeable. [*CTA ss 1, 174*]. Many provisions of the *Income Tax Acts* and the *Capital Gains Tax Acts* relating to the computation of income and chargeable gains are adopted for CT purposes. [*CTA s 140, 2 Sch*].

12.2   SCHEME AND RATES OF TAX

A company is chargeable to CT on its profits wherever arising (other than profits accruing to it in fiduciary or representative capacity) for each financial year, i.e. year ending 31 December (and see 12.3 below). [CTA ss 1, 6]. See 12.25 below as regards set-off of advance corporation tax.

Profits of a company comprise its **income** (computed by normal IT principles under each Schedule and then aggregated) and its **chargeable gains** (computed under CGT rules and then specifically reduced, see below). [CTA ss 1, 11, 13].

The rates of tax are (by reference to financial year = FY)

	FY 1989	FY 1990	FY 1991	FY 1992 to 1994	FY 1995	FY 1996
Full rate [CTA s 1; FA 1988, s 33(1); FA 1990, s 37(1); FA 1995, s 54].	47%/43%*	43%	43%/40%*	40%	40%/38%*	38%
Manufacturing companies rate (see 12.17 below) [FA 1980, s 41; FA 1982, s 26(2), 2 Sch; FA 1988, s 33(3), 3 Sch; FA 1990, 2 Sch Pt II; FA 1995, 4 Sch Pt II].	10%**	10%	10%	10%	10%	10%
Small companies rate (see 12.20 below) [CTA s 28; FA 1988, s 33(2), 3 Sch].	40%/—***	—	—	—	—	—
Special reduced rate (see below) [CTA s 79; FA 1988, s 33(2), 3 Sch].	35%/—***	—	—	—	—	—
On certain home loan interest (see (c) below)	45%/—***	—	—	—	—	—

* for periods to 31 March and from 1 April respectively.
** where full rate otherwise payable.
*** cease to apply after 31 March 1989.

Full rate applies to company's total profits. [CTA s 1].

Corporation tax on chargeable gains is calculated on an amount of chargeable gains so as to result in CT payable equalling the capital gains tax which would be payable on the same chargeable gains if capital gains tax applied to companies. The allowable losses which may be set against gains are those accruing in the accounting period and unallowed losses of earlier accounting periods while the company was within the charge to CT. Where parts of an accounting period ending after 31 March 1988 fall in two successive FYs (or deemed FYs, see below) for which different rates of CT apply, a time-weighted average rate of CT is used in determining the appropriate amount of chargeable gains to be taken into account. For this purpose, the following periods are treated as if each were a financial year.

1 January 1987 to 31 March 1988
1 April 1988 to 31 March 1989
1 April 1989 to 31 December 1990

and, in relation to accounting periods ending after 31 March 1991,

1 January 1990 to 31 March 1991
1 April 1991 to 31 December 1992

and, in relation to accounting periods ending after 31 March 1995,

1 January 1994 to 31 March 1995
1 April 1995 to 31 December 1996

For earlier accounting periods during which the rate of CT changed, the capital gains tax calculated as above was apportioned between the parts of the accounting period falling before and after the change in determining the imputed chargeable gains in each part. Chargeable gains on certain disposals of development land are excluded, companies being directly liable for capital gains tax on such gains (see 9.16 CAPITAL GAINS TAX). [*CTA s 13; FA 1982, s 31; FA 1988, 3 Sch; FA 1990, 2 Sch 1; FA 1995, 4 Sch 1*].

Special reduced rate of corporation tax (see above) applies to

(*a*)   any income of a trade or business carried on by a public utility company (i.e. tramway, dock or canal undertaking) in respect of which it is subject to statutory regulation of its prices and dividends,

(*b*)   income derived from a public utility company by a company controlling it,

(*c*)   approved rate interest on housing loans received by an approved bank on or after 1 July 1975 (the 45% rate being applicable on loans granted after 21 May 1987),

(*d*)   income of the Agricultural Credit Corporation Limited,

(*e*)   income of a railway company,

(*f*)   income of a building society (see 12.21 below),

(*g*)   income of an association registered under *Companies Act 1963, s 24* without addition of the word 'limited' to its name,

(*h*)   income of a company established solely for the advancement of religion or education and prohibited by its memorandum or articles of association from distributing its profits to its members,

(*j*)   income of a company formed before 4 August 1920 whose sole assets are public authority securities formerly held by the persons who formed the company,

(*k*)   income of a company precluded by its constitution from distributing its profits to its members,

(*l*)   any income of an investment trust company derived from a company whose profits have borne UK corporation tax.

Income has the same meaning as for small companies relief (see 12.20 below), i.e. profits before deductions which can be taken from profits of more than one description, less the part attributable to capital gains.

The special reduced rate **ceases to apply after 31 March 1989**, and for this purpose an accounting period straddling that date is treated as consisting of two separate accounting periods, one ending on that date, the other commencing on the following day.

[*CTA ss 31(9), 79; FA 1976, s 28; FA 1977, s 18; FA 1978, s 28(2)(d), (5); FA 1987, s 33; FA 1988, s 33(2), 3 Sch*].

12.3 ACCOUNTING PERIODS

While CT is charged on profits in a financial year (i.e. ending 31 December), assessments are made by reference to accounting periods. When an accounting period does not coincide with the financial year the profits for that accounting period are apportioned between financial years on a time basis. [*CTA s 6(3)*]. As respects accounting periods ending after 1 April 1988, the following periods are specially treated as if each was a financial year for this purpose (following the changes of corporation tax rate after 31 March in the actual financial years 1988, 1989, 1991 and 1995).

1 January 1987 to 31 March 1988
1 April 1988 to 31 March 1989
1 April 1989 to 31 December 1990

and, in relation to accounting periods ending after 31 March 1991,

1 January 1990 to 31 March 1991
1 April 1991 to 31 December 1992

and, in relation to accounting periods ending after 31 March 1995,

1 January 1994 to 31 March 1995
1 April 1995 to 31 December 1996

[*FA 1988, 3 Sch; FA 1990, 2 Sch 1; FA 1995, 4 Sch 1*].

An accounting period **begins** when the company first comes within the charge to CT, or when an accounting period ends and the company is still within the charge to CT. An accounting period lasts twelve months or otherwise **ends** on:

(i) the date to which a company makes up its accounts (so that for any company which makes up its accounts annually, subsequent accounting periods will coincide with its year of account);

(ii) the company beginning or ceasing a trade within the charge to CT;

(iii) the company beginning or ceasing to be resident in RI;

(iv) the company ceasing to be within the charge to CT.

[*CTA s 9(2)(3)*].

'Within the charge to CT' has an extended meaning so that every company resident in RI, whether or not assessable to CT, falls within the provisions relating to accounting periods on 6 April 1976 or (if later) the date when it starts to carry on business. [*CTA s 9(4)*].

Where a company carries on several trades and makes up separate accounts for each using different accounting dates, the Commissioners may determine to which of those accounting dates (i) above applies. [*CTA s 9(5)*]. If the beginning or end of any accounting period is uncertain an inspector may make an assessment for such period not exceeding twelve months as appears to him appropriate. [*CTA s 9(8)*].

12.4 ADMINISTRATION

CT is administered by the Revenue Commissioners and the same administrative provisions in general apply as under the Income Tax Acts. See 1 ADMINISTRATION AND GENERAL. [*CTA ss 6(5)–(7), 145, 147*].

An election made by a company under IT rules will continue in effect under CT, if appropriate. [*CTA s 172*].

12.5   RETURNS AND ASSESSMENT

Self-assessing procedures. See 28.12 RETURNS as regards new procedures for returns, payment of preliminary tax and assessment, which apply to accounting periods ending after 30 September 1989.

Returns of profits and of distributions received from Irish-resident companies and of surplus ACT (see 12.25 below), of certain payments from which income tax is to be deducted (see 12.19 below), and of the amounts of certain tax credits recoverable from the company must be made when required by notice from an inspector or officer of the Commissioners, and there are powers to demand information and production of books, accounts, documents, etc. where a company fails to deliver a required return, or the inspector is not satisfied with a return. [*CTA s 143 as amended by FA 1981, s 16; FA 1983, ss 36, 39; FA 1990, s 54; FA 1992, s 247*]. See 12.25 below as regards advance corporation tax returns.

Every company which starts trading or carrying on a profession or business (in RI in the case of non-resident companies) must deliver particulars within 30 days and a company chargeable to CT which has not made a return of its profits must give notice to the inspector within one year of the end of the accounting period. Special provisions apply to RI incorporated but non-resident companies. Penalties apply for non-compliance. [*CTA ss 141, 142, 149; FA 1995, s 58*].

Assessments are made by an inspector, and if the company is not resident in RI may be made on any agent, manager or representative of the company. Estimated assessments may be made in the absence of satisfactory information. In the absence of fraud or neglect no assessment may be made more than ten years after the accounting period to which it relates. [*CTA ss 7, 144, 153*].

Assessment—special rules for capital gains. A person connected with a company resident in RI may be assessed to unpaid CT in respect of a chargeable gain accruing to the company on a disposal of assets (see 9.6, 9.8 CAPITAL GAINS TAX) to the extent to which the gain was passed on to the connected person by a capital distribution (not being a reduction of capital) which also constituted a disposal of assets. Any person so assessed may reclaim the amount from the company. [*CTA s 126*].

On a transfer of the whole or part of a business for no consideration (other than the assumption of liabilities of the business) from one RI company to another in the course of a company reconstruction or amalgamation, the transferor company is treated as having made neither gain nor loss and the transferee is treated as having acquired the assets in the way in which the transferor company originally acquired them. [*CTA s 127; CGT(A)A s 13*]. Interest on a loan for construction work which enhances the value of an asset (see 9.8 CAPITAL GAINS TAX) is allowable if charged to capital. [*CTA s 128*].

12.6   APPEALS AND PAYMENT OF TAX

Appeals are governed by *Secs 415–431* in the same way as those sections apply for IT (see 4 APPEALS). [*CTA s 146; FA 1980, s 51; FA 1983, s 37*].

Payment of CT. See 28.12 RETURNS as regards payments of preliminary tax.

For accounting periods ended after 5 April 1990, CT is payable in a single instalment, six months (seven months for accounting periods ending before 1 May 1993) from the end of the accounting period or, if later, one month after the making of the assessment, but in either case, for accounting periods ending after 30 April 1993, by the 28th day of the month where it would otherwise be payable by a later day in the month. Previously, it was payable six months from the end of the accounting period or, if later, two months after the making of the assessment (the day following the making of the assessment where the self-assessment procedures apply, see 28.12 RETURNS).

There are transitional provisions for certain accounting periods ending before 28 February 1987. [*CTA s 6(4); FA 1990, s 24(c); FA 1993, s 39*].

Interest on unpaid tax is chargeable generally as for income tax (see 25.3 PAYMENT OF TAX) [*CTA s 145(3)–(5); FA 1982, s 27(4)*]. See 25.5 PAYMENT OF TAX as regards waiver of certain interest and penalties. See 4.5 APPEALS as regards interest on overpaid tax.

See 12.25 below as regards advance corporation tax.

Profits from land dealing or development. Payment may be postponed in respect of profits attributable to a right to obtain a lease-back of the property sold. [*CTA s 150*].

12.7   CLOSE COMPANIES

A close company is a company

(*a*)   which is under the control of

   (i)   five or fewer participators, or

   (ii)   participators who are directors, or

(*b*)   more than half of whose distributable income would, on a full distribution, be paid directly or indirectly to five or fewer participators or to participators who are directors.

[*CTA s 94*].

The following are not close companies:

  (i)   a company not resident in RI,

  (ii)   a registered industrial and provident society, or building society,

 (iii)   a company controlled by the State,

 (iv)   a company controlled by one or more non-close companies, where one of the five or fewer participators necessary to its being treated as close is also a non-close company (non-resident companies being treated as close for this purpose if they would be so if RI resident),

  (v)   a company in relation to which

   (A)   shares (not carrying a fixed rate of dividend) representing 35% or more of the voting power are unconditionally and beneficially held by the public (as defined), and some of those shares have been quoted and dealt with on a recognised stock exchange within the preceding twelve months, and

   (B)   the total voting power held by the principal members does not exceed 85% (a principal member being a person whose shareholding exceeds 5% in voting power and is one of the top five in voting power),

 (vi)   a company which cannot be a close company except by including, as having control, persons with rights to distribution of assets on a winding up or in other circumstances and which would not be a close company if the rights of such persons excluded those of loan creditors who are non-close companies.

[*CTA ss 94, 95*].

Control means control (whether direct or indirect) of the company's affairs, or possession of the greater part of the share capital or voting power or entitlement to the greater part of the company's whole income or (on a winding up, etc.) assets. [*CTA s 102*]. *Participator* means a person with a share or interest in the company's income or capital, and includes a shareholder, loan creditor, and a person entitled to secure that income or assets will be applied to his own benefit. *Director* includes both a manager and a beneficial owner of 20% of the company's ordinary share capital. [*CTA s 103*].

Surcharge on undistributed income. There is an additional charge to CT for each accounting period in which the excess of a close company's 'distributable investment income' plus its 'distributable estate income' over its distributions for a twelve-month accounting period is greater than £500 (with marginal relief for amounts slightly over £500). The £500 is reduced for lesser periods and where there are associated companies.

The rate of surcharge is 20% of the excess. For accounting periods ending after 31 March 1990, the surcharge is treated as corporation tax chargeable for the earliest accounting period which ends at least twelve months after the end of the accounting period in respect of which the surcharge is made. If there is no such accounting period so ending, it is chargeable for the accounting period in respect of which the surcharge is made. Previously, the surcharge was charged for the accounting period in respect of which it was made, and was payable within two months of the making of the assessment. [*CTA s 101; FA 1990, s 47*]. A company entitled to export sales relief (see 16.4 EXEMPT INCOME AND SPECIAL SAVINGS SCHEMES) is, it is understood, in practice allowed the same measure of relief from surcharge.

It is understood that, by concession, liability to surcharge may be waived where a company, 90% or more of whose ordinary share capital is beneficially owned by non-residents, wishes to retain its surplus funds in RI.

Distributable income is the sum of

(a)   the company's income for the period (excluding franked investment income), after all deductions except those applicable by carry-forward or carry-back from other periods, and after deduction of CT thereon (ignoring, for accounting periods ending after 5 April 1989, manufacturing companies relief), and

(b)   the company's franked investment income for the period minus the tax credits thereon;

except that it is understood that, in practice, only a part of a dividend out of profits the subject of export sales relief (see 16.4 EXEMPT INCOME AND SPECIAL SAVINGS SCHEMES) is included, corresponding to the amount of the dividend to which a tax credit equal to that (if any) attached to the dividend received would correspond if there were no export sales relief (i.e. 65/35ths of the reduced tax credit). Dividends paid by the company are to be correspondingly restricted.

Distributable investment income is the amount of distributable income attributable to income (other than 'estate income') which would not rank as earned income in the hands of an individual. *Estate income* means rent from land and buildings chargeable under Schedule D, Case III, IV or V, and *distributable estate income* is that amount of distributable income which is attributable to estate income. [*CTA s 100; FA 1989, s 27*]. There is no additional tax credit in respect of the surcharge if income surcharged is later distributed. The distribution carries the normal tax credit only. [*CTA s 101(4)*].

Trading company relief. Any close company which exists wholly or mainly for the purposes of carrying on a trade or whose income does not consist wholly of investment or estate income, or both, is a 'trading company' and its distributable investment income (computed as above) is reduced by 5% and its distributable estate income by 7.5% before they are added together and the distributions subtracted therefrom. [*CTA s 100(4)(5)*].

Service companies. A similar 20% surcharge applies to the excess of distributable income over distributions of close companies formed for the purpose of carrying on a profession, where the income if distributed would be charged to higher rate IT in the hands of the recipients, except that only 50% (80% for accounting periods ending before 1 April 1995) of such income other than investment or estate income is taken into account for this purpose. Accounting periods straddling 1 April 1995 are for this purpose divided into two separate accounting periods, ending immediately before and starting on that date. [*CTA s 162; FA 1990, s 48; FA 1995, s 55*]. See 38.33 TAX CASES.

Distribution is given an extended meaning for close companies. It includes expenses (valued in the same way as benefits in kind) incurred by the company in providing participators or their associates with accommodation, entertainment, facilities, etc. where such provision is *not* a taxable benefit in kind (see 34.3 SCHEDULE E). [*CTA s 96*]. Loan interest, exceeding a prescribed amount, paid to a director with a 'material interest' (broadly, more than 5% of the ordinary share capital), or to such a director's associate, is also a distribution. [*CTA s 97*].

Loans to participators. A close company whose business does not include the making of loans is charged to IT on any loan or advance to a participator or associate of a participator who is an individual or which is a company acting in a fiduciary or representative capacity or a company not resident in RI. The tax payable is an amount equal to IT at the standard rate on the grossed-up equivalent of the loan. *Loan* includes any debt (except normal credit for normal supply of business goods or services), but a loan of £15,000 or less to a borrower who works full-time for the company and does not have a material interest (see above) is exempt. All tax paid will be repaid on repayment of the loan. [*CTA s 98*]. Any interest charged due to late payment of the tax is not, however, repaid. [*FA 1981, s 22*]. On the release or writing off of such a loan the amount of the loan received by the debtor is treated as income from which standard rate IT has already been deducted but the tax credit attributed is not repayable. [*CTA s 99*]. For loans, etc. made after 22 May 1983, the exclusion at (ii) above of industrial and provident societies from being close companies does not apply for this purpose. [*FA 1983, s 35*].

12.8   COMPUTATION OF PROFITS

Total profits. The figures for income and capital gains (as reduced) are added to give a company's total profits. From this figure may be deducted

(i)   losses (see 12.16 below),

(ii)   charges on income (see 12.9 below),

(iii)   management expenses (see 12.9 below),

(iv)   group relief (see 12.14 below).

Income. In general, a company's income is computed for CT purposes in the same way as under income tax law, as though accounting periods were years of assessment. Thus, income from each source still falls to be computed under the Schedule and Case appropriate to that particular source, except that (*a*) income of any particular period is computed by reference to that period and no other (except for apportionment between accounting periods), and (*b*) income of a trade under Schedule D, Case III is computed according to Schedule D, Case I rules. [*CTA ss 11, 12(5)*]. However, the following provisions of *ITA 1967* do not apply: *Part XXV* (see 16.2, 16.4 EXEMPT INCOME AND SPECIAL SAVINGS SCHEMES); *Sec 76* (see 31.2 SCHEDULE D, CASE III); and, in computing the income of a trade, *Sec 64(1)*. [*CTA ss 11(6)(7), 12(8)*].

Capital allowances and balancing charges (see 12.9 below) are applicable only in computing *income*.

Distributions received by a company (see 12.7 above and 12.10 below) are not taken into account in computing income. [*CTA s 2*]. See 12.12 below as regards exemption of certain dividends from foreign subsidiaries.

Special rules for income [*CTA ss 11, 12*].

(i)   Beginning or ceasing to be within the charge to CT in respect of a trade is treated as the commencement or cessation of the trade (except where the trade is not regarded under tax law as permanently discontinued).

(ii) Income from letting rights to work minerals in RI — deduction is allowed, subject to restrictions, for management expenses, etc.

(iii) Foreign tax paid on income from foreign property is normally deductible against that income.

Chargeable gains and allowable losses are computed in the same way as under the *CGTA*, as though accounting periods were years of assessment, before being reduced (see 12.2 above). Provisions relating to CGT which can only apply to individuals do not apply under CT, in particular the reduced rates for periods of ownership exceeding three years and *1 Sch 4(1)* (exclusion of expenditure chargeable or allowable for IT) (see 9.3, 9.8 CAPITAL GAINS TAX). [*CTA s 13*]. For the charge on gains on certain life policies, etc., see 9.12 CAPITAL GAINS TAX.

Foreign currency considerations. *Exchange gains and losses.* For accounting periods beginning after 31 December 1994, the amount of any gain or loss, realised or unrealised, attributable to money held or payable for trade purposes, or to a related currency hedging contract, which results from an exchange rate change and which is properly credited or debited to the profit and loss account, is brought into account in computing trading income. Exchange gains and losses on 'relevant contracts' and on money held for trade purposes are correspondingly not chargeable gains or allowable losses (except in the case of certain companies carrying on exempt life assurance business). The 'profit and loss account' is the account of the company (or of the branch or agency business of a non-resident company) certified by the auditor as presenting a true and fair view of the profit or loss of the company (or business) in question. [*CTA s 12A; FA 1994, s 56(a)*].

Capital allowances. For accounting periods beginning after 31 December 1993, allowances to be made in taxing a trade for expenditure becoming payable after that date are computed in the 'functional currency' of the company, and given effect as a trading expense or receipt in computing the trading income or loss in that currency. Where there is a change in functional currency, any earlier expenditure (after 31 December 1993), and allowances in respect of that expenditure, are converted into the new functional currency by reference to the exchange rate on the day the expenditure was incurred. The *'functional currency'* is the currency of the primary economic environment in which the company operates, or, in the case of a non-resident company, in which the company carries on trading activities in RI, *except that* where the profit and loss account (as above) for a period of account has been prepared in IR£, that is the functional currency for that period. The currency of the primary economic environment is determined with reference to the currency in which revenues and expenses are primarily generated and the company primarily borrows and lends (in relation to the RI trading activities in the case of a non-resident company). [*CTA s 14A(1)(2); FA 1994, s 56(b)*].

Trading losses. For loss set-offs in accounting periods beginning after 31 December 1993, trading losses incurred in accounting periods ending after that date are computed in the 'functional currency' (as above) of the company, and are converted to IR£ by reference to the rate of exchange used to convert the trading income for the accounting period in which the loss is to be set off (or which would be used if there were such income). Where there is a change in functional currency, any loss incurred in an accounting period ending after 31 December 1993, and any set off referable to such a loss, which was previously computed by reference to the earlier functional currency is converted into the new functional currency by reference to the average exchange rate for the accounting period in which the loss was incurred. [*CTA s 14A(1)(3); FA 1994, s 56(b)*].

12.9 DEDUCTIONS

Capital allowances and balancing charges apply to companies, with suitable modifications, as under the corresponding income tax provisions in force for the year of assessment in which the accounting period ends and arise by reference to actual accounting periods instead of to basis periods. For the income tax provisions see 8 CAPITAL ALLOWANCES and the cross-references therein. The legislation now refers to 'chargeable periods' which are the accounting periods of companies (and years of assessment for individuals, etc.). Where chargeable periods are less than twelve months the allowances are reduced proportionately. [*CTA s 21, 1 Sch*].

Allowances and charges relating to a trade are treated respectively as trading expenses and receipts. Initial allowances may be disclaimed by notice in writing within two years of end of accounting period. Allowances available primarily against a specified class of income are deducted as far as possible from income of that class. Where there is an insufficiency of income for that accounting period the balance may, on a claim, be dealt with as a loss as in 12.16 below (but a claim for an accounting period ending after 31 March 1992 is restricted to one-half of the maximum claim where the return for the period is late, see 28.12 RETURNS). [*CTA s 14*].

Where a company takes over the business of another company which ceases to trade and at least a three-fourths interest in the trade remains in the same hands, there is no cessation or commencement of trading for the purposes of capital allowances. [*CTA s 20*].

Charges on income. Certain annual payments may be deductible from overall profits. These 'charges on income' include annuities and other annual payments, royalties and long lease rents but not distributions by the company nor any sum deductible in computing overall profits.

Interest payments within *FA 1974, ss 33, 35* (see 20.3(*c*) INTEREST PAYABLE) are charges on income. [*CTA s 10(6)–(8); FA 1982, s 23*].

Payments must be charged to income not capital, and (unless short-term transactions within *Sec 439(1)(ii), (iia)*) must be under a liability incurred for valuable and sufficient consideration and, if the payer is non-resident, incurred wholly and exclusively for the purposes of a trade it carried on in RI through a branch or agency. [*CTA s 10(5)*].

Payments made in accounting periods ending after 5 April 1990 to non-residents must be made under deduction of standard rate income tax (unless the Revenue Commissioners authorise the company to do otherwise) which the company accounts for, unless the payment is made out of income from securities and possessions outside RI brought into charge to tax under SCHEDULE D, CASE III (31). Previously, the paying company had in addition to be RI resident, and no provision was made for the Revenue Commissioners to waive the requirement to deduct tax. [*CTA s 10(4); FA 1990, s 43*].

See 12.17 below for restrictions on relief of charges for the purposes of activities within the manufacturing companies relief.

Management expenses of an RI *investment company* (excluding sums deductible from income under Schedule D, Case V) are deductible from total profits in so far as they exceed the amount of any income (excluding franked investment income) derived from sources not charged to tax. For these purposes, allowances under *FA 1968, s 37* or *FA 1972, s 16* (see 16.12 EXEMPT INCOME AND SPECIAL SAVINGS SCHEMES, 30.21 SCHEDULE D, CASES I and II, 17.15 EXEMPT ORGANISATIONS) are included as management expenses but see 30.10 SCHEDULE D, CASES I and II as regards business entertainment. 'Investment company' includes a savings bank. [*CTA s 15(1)(3)(6)*]. See also 38.168 TAX CASES regarding the definition of 'investment company'.

Where the management expenses, plus any *charges on income paid wholly and exclusively for the purposes of the company's business*, exceed the amount of profits from which they are deductible, the excess may be

(*a*)   carried forward to the succeeding accounting period and applied as though it had arisen in that succeeding accounting period, or (*b*)   on a written claim within two years, set off against any franked investment income in the accounting period, enabling the company to claim repayment of the tax credit (but this relief is not available for any amount carried forward from a previous year under (*a*) above).

[*CTA s 15(2)(4)(5)*].

Research and development activities. A special relief relating to certain expenditure on such activities may be claimed by a '*qualified company*', i.e. a company which:

(*a*)   carries on a trade consisting wholly or mainly of the manufacture of goods in RI by virtue of *FA 1980, s 39* (see 12.17 below) (and not by virtue of any other provision);

(*b*)   holds a certificate from Forbairt as to the potential of the activities to achieve the purposes of acquiring new knowledge with specific commercial application or creating new or improved materials, products, devices, processes or services;

(*c*)   notifies the inspector beforehand of its intention to carry out such activities (or have them carried out on its behalf);

(*d*)   maintains a record in accordance with a Forbairt-approved system of its expenditure on such activities; and

(*e*)   does not raise any money through the issue of eligible BES shares (see 21.2 INVESTMENT IN CORPORATE TRADES, ETC.) in the period from 10 May 1995 to the end of the three year period during which this special relief is available (see below).

'*Research and development activities*' means activities involving innovation or technical risk, carried on wholly or mainly in RI (i.e. at least 75% of the total amount expended in the course of such activities is expended in RI), being systematic investigative or experimental activities for the purpose of acquiring new knowledge with specific commercial application or creating new or improved materials, products, devices, processes or services, and other directly related activities. Excluded are activities carried on by way of market research, testing or development; sales promotion or consumer surveys; quality control; making cosmetic or stylistic changes to products, processes or production methods; management studies or efficiency surveys; and research in social sciences, arts or humanities.

A qualified company may claim a deduction in computing its trading income of **treble** its qualifying 'expenditure on research and development' (in addition to any deduction to which it would otherwise be entitled in respect of the expenditure). Where the additional deduction exceeds the amount of the company's income from the sale of goods (see 12.17 below) of the manufacturing trade for the period, the excess is treated as a loss incurred in the trade from the sale of goods. Relief is available for the year ending 31 May 1996 and for each of the two following twelve-month periods (the '*relevant periods*'), and is apportioned between accounting periods falling wholly or partly within such periods as necessary.

'*Expenditure on research and development*' is non-capital expenditure certified by the auditors as having been incurred by the company, being either a sum paid to a non-connected person (see *CTA s 157*) for carrying out research and development activities related to the company's trade, or an amount equal to 115% of the aggregate of

(i)   emoluments of employees engaged in such activities and laid out for the purposes of such activities, and

(ii)   expenditure on goods or materials used solely in carrying out such activities.

Expenditure is excluded where any research and development expenditure in the relevant periods or in the immediately preceding twelve months is met by the State or by any other person (and in the case of a qualified company which is a member of a group of companies (see below), this applies where any group member's expenditure on research and development in such periods is met by the State or by a person who is not a member of the group).

The expenditure on research and development qualifying for relief is the excess of such expenditure in a relevant period over that incurred in the year ended 31 May 1995 (or, in relation to the second and third relevant periods, over that incurred in an earlier relevant period, if greater), but disregarding the first £25,000 of that excess. The aggregate relief may not exceed the expenditure certificated by Forbairt.

A company claiming relief under these provisions may not be a qualifying company for BES purposes (see 21.4 INVESTMENT IN CORPORATE TRADES, ETC.) in respect of any amount raised at any time during the period from 10 May 1995 to the end of the three year period during which the relief is available.

Groups of companies. Where a qualified company (as above) is a member of a group of companies (consisting of a company and all those companies with which it is associated within *CTA s 102*), the limitation on relief is applied by reference to group qualifying expenditure as a whole (the initial base period for comparison being the twelve months preceding the first relevant period, see below), and the qualified company obtains relief for a proportion of such group qualifying expenditure corresponding to the proportion of group expenditure on research and development which is incurred by the qualified company. Expenditure on research personnel and goods or materials incurred on behalf of another group company is treated as incurred by the other company. The relevant periods for which relief is available are the twelve months to the end of the first accounting period commencing after 31 May 1995, provided that one or more group companies carried on a trade throughout that twelve months, and the two twelve month periods following that period. If group accounting periods do not coincide, there is provision for nomination of the first period, provided that it meets those conditions.

[*FA 1995, s 59*].

Approved profit sharing schemes. See 34.7 SCHEDULE E as regards deduction of scheme contributions.

Gifts for education in the arts and to Cospóir. The relief for individuals making such gifts (see 2.24 ALLOWANCES AND RATES) applies to gifts made by companies to educational bodies and to Cospóir (the National Sports Council), subject to the same conditions. Relief is given by treating the net gifts made in an accounting period as a loss incurred in a separate trade carried on in that accounting period. The monetary limits apply by reference to accounting periods of the company instead of years of assessment. [*FA 1984, s 32; FA 1986, s 8*].

Gifts to the President's Award Scheme. The relief for individuals making such gifts (see 2.25 ALLOWANCES AND RATES) applies to gifts made by companies after 5 April 1985 and before 6 April 1987, subject to the same conditions. Relief is given by treating the gift(s) made in an accounting period as a loss incurred in a separate trade carried on in that accounting period. [*FA 1985, s 16; FA 1986, s 47*].

Gifts to The Trust for Community Initiatives. A gift made by a company to the Trust after 19 April 1990 and before 31 March 1992 and applied solely for the purposes of the Trust, and which is neither (apart from this provision) deductible for trade purposes nor income within Sec 439 (see 36.2 SETTLEMENTS), may, on a claim, be allowed as a trading deduction or as a management expense (see above) as appropriate. Any direct or indirect consideration received by the company as a result of making the gift is deducted from the amount of the gift to be allowed. [*FA 1990, s 45; FA 1991, s 39*].

Gifts to The Enterprise Trust Limited. A gift made by a company to the Trust after 31 March 1992 and before 31 December 1996 and applied solely for the objects set out in its memorandum of association, and which is neither (apart from this provision) deductible for trade purposes nor income within *Sec 439* (see 36.2 SETTLEMENTS), may, on a claim, be allowed as a trading deduction or as a management expense (see above) as appropriate. Any direct or indirect consideration received by the company as a result of making the gift is deducted from the amount of the gift to be allowed. [*FA 1992, s 56; FA 1994, s 51*].

Gifts to First Step. A gift made by a company to First Step Ltd after 31 May 1993 and before 1 June 1997 and applied solely for the objects for which First Step was incorporated, and which is neither a trade or professional deduction for corporation tax purposes nor income within *Sec 439* (see 36.2 SETTLEMENTS), may, on a claim, be treated as a loss incurred in a separate trade carried on in the accounting period in which the gift was made. Any direct or indirect consideration received by the company as a result of making the gift is deducted from the amount of the gift for this purpose. Relief is limited to total gifts by the company to First Step Ltd of £100,000 in any accounting period, and is dependent upon a minimum contribution in excess of £500 in an accounting period (each amount being proportionately reduced for accounting periods of less than twelve months). There is also a limit on total gifts received by First Step Ltd which may obtain relief (£1,500,000 in each of the years to 31 May 1994, 31 May 1995, 31 May 1996 and 31 May 1997), and First Step must notify the company within 30 days of the making of the gift if relief is thereby denied. [*FA 1993, s 51; FA 1995, s 67*].

12.10 DISTRIBUTIONS

See 12.25 below as regards liability to advance corporation tax in respect of distributions.

In general, CT is not chargeable on dividends or other distributions by a company resident in RI, nor are they taken into account in computing CT. [*CTA s 2*]. Every distribution (as defined, see below) by a company resident in RI to a person resident in RI or to another company, subject to the exceptions below, carries a tax credit to the value of

$$\text{Value of distribution} \quad \times \quad \frac{\text{*Standard rate of income tax}}{100 - \text{*Standard rate of income tax}}$$

*For distributions made after 5 April 1978 and before 6 April 1983, standard rate is deemed to be 30% for tax credit purposes; for those made in 1988/89, 32%; for those made in 1989/90 or 1990/91, 28%; for those made in 1991/92 to 1994/95 inclusive, 25%; for those made after 5 April 1995, 23%.

From 6 April 1992, the liability of a person who is neither resident nor ordinarily resident to income tax in respect of a distribution is reduced by the amount by which that liability exceeds the available tax credit (if any), so that no net liability arises, and the income is not available to cover charges.

[*CTA ss 83, 88; FA 1978, s 28; FA 1983, s 28; FA 1988, s 31, 2 Sch; FA 1990, s 36, 1 Sch; FA 1992, s 38; FA 1994, s 27; FA 1995, ss 39, 45, 2 Sch*].

Distribution does not include distributions made in respect of share capital in winding up, but does include

(*a*)   any dividend, including a capital dividend,

(*b*)   any distribution out of assets in respect of shares in the company except a repayment of capital (see below) or an amount equal to any 'new consideration' (see below),

(*c*)   any amount met out of assets, otherwise than for new consideration, in respect of the redemption of any security issued by the company,

(*d*)   any interest or other distribution out of assets in respect of securities either

      (i)   issued other than for new consideration in respect of shares in or securities of the company; or

     (ii)   convertible into shares in, or carrying the right to receive shares in or securities of, the company, being neither quoted securities nor issued on comparable terms; or

(iii)   the interest on which

   (I)   varies with the issuing company's results, or

   (II)   (and to the extent that it) is at more than a reasonable commercial rate; or

(iv)   held by a non RI-resident company of which the issuing company is a 75% subsidiary, or where both are 75% subsidiaries of another company which, if RI-resident, owns less than 90% of the issuing company's share capital; or

(v)   'connected with' shares of the issuing company (i.e. it is necessary or advantageous for the holder of the securities to hold a proportionate number of those shares),

(*e*)   a transfer of assets or liabilities by a company to its members, or to a company (except dealings with subsidiaries) by its members, to the extent that it exceeds the value of any new consideration,

(*f*)   an issue of bonus shares following a repayment of share capital (as defined) on or after 27 November 1975, except where the share capital repaid consisted of certain fully paid-up preference shares.

[*CTA ss 84, 85*].

Repayment of share capital for the purposes of (*b*) and (*f*) above has a restricted meaning where share capital has been issued (after 26 November 1975) as paid up otherwise than for new consideration, and any amount so paid up is not a distribution. Subsequent distributions in respect of that share capital are only repayments of share capital to the extent that their total value exceeds that amount. [*CTA s 86*].

Non-close companies are excluded from (*f*) above and from *CTA s 86* (see preceding paragraph) where

(I)   the issue and repayment are separated by ten years or more, and

(II)   the issue (under (*f*)) or repayment (under *CTA s 86*) relate to non-redeemable share capital.

[*CTA ss 85(4), 86(6)*].

New consideration means consideration not provided directly or indirectly out of the assets of the company, and must in addition consist of money or value received or certain other things as specified. [*CTA s 87; FA 1991, s 29*].

'*Section 84A loans*'. Interest, etc. on a security within (*d*)(ii), (iii)(I) or (v) above (a '*relevant security*') paid after 11 April 1989 by the borrower to another company within the charge to corporation tax is, however, not treated as a distribution unless either

(A)   the lender's ordinary trading activities include lending on relevant securities, and the borrower uses the loan in a 'specified trade' carried on in RI, of which the interest would, were it not a distribution, be treated as a trading expense, or

(B)   it exceeds a reasonable commercial return for the use of the principal, in which case only the excess is to be treated as a distribution.

A '*specified trade*' is a trade consisting as to at least 75% (by reference to turnover) of the manufacture of goods or of activities which would, on a claim, be treated as such for the manufacturing companies relief (but not by virtue of a certificate under *FA 1980, s 39A*) (see 12.17 below) or, in the case of a 75% subsidiary of an agricultural or fishery society, either or both of the manufacture of goods and the wholesale sale of agricultural products or fish respectively. The use referred to in (A) above must be in the activities which qualify the trade as a specified trade.

Where a trade ceases to be a specified trade by virtue of the exclusions from manufacturing companies' relief in *FA 1990, s 41(1)* or *FA 1994, s 48(1)* (see 12.17 below), it is treated as continuing to be a specified trade in relation to interest on any principal advanced before 20 April 1990 or 11 April 1994 respectively.

(A) above does not apply to allow interest to be treated as a distribution to the extent that loans by the lender to the borrower on relevant securities held directly or indirectly by the lender exceed 110% of such loans (if any) on 12 April 1989.

After 30 January 1990, there is a ceiling on new loans interest on which may be treated as a distribution by virtue of (A) above. Broadly, the limit will be 75% (reduced to 40% after 30 December 1991) of such loans outstanding on 12 April 1989 (which may be reduced if the loans outstanding fall below this limit), although there is a limited provision for further loans in certain specified exceptional cases. Otherwise, the only new loans which will qualify for this treatment, subject to a global limit, are those relating to certain new manufacturing projects.

In all cases, distribution treatment under these provisions is restricted to a seven year period after the date on which the principal was advanced (or, in the case of principal advanced before 11 April 1994, to the period ending 11 April 2001).

Where the loan is denominated in a foreign currency, interest for a period beginning after 29 January 1991 which is computed on the basis of a rate in excess of 80% of three month DIBOR is not treated as a distribution in the hands of the recipient company. This does not apply where the principal was advanced:

(i)   before 30 January 1991 under an agreement made before that date, and the rate exceeded the 80% limit on that date (but subject to further restriction after 19 December 1991 if the currency in which the loan was denominated on 30 January 1991 is changed); or

(ii)   after 29 January 1991 for the purposes of certain trades specified in lists prepared by the Industrial Development Authority (broadly certain new manufacturing projects) (but subject to further restriction after 19 December 1991 where the rate exceeds that approved by the Minister for Finance in relation to such loans, or where the currency in which the loan was denominated when it was advanced is changed); or

(iii) after 17 April 1991, and the 80% limit was exceeded only because the loan was denominated in sterling; or

(iv)   to a non-manufacturing company carrying on trading operations within *Sec 39A* (see 12.17 below) in the Customs-free airport.

For these purposes the extension (after 5 May 1993) of a repayment period is treated as a repayment and further advance of the principal in question on the date on which it would otherwise have fallen to be repaid.

[*CTA s 84A as inserted by FA 1989, s 21; FA 1990, ss 41(4), 46; FA 1991, s 28; FA 1992, s 40; FA 1993, s 45; FA 1994, ss 48(3), 50*].

Similar earlier provisions, which applied to interest etc. paid after 24 January 1984, continue to have effect for payments up to 31 December 1991 for periods before that date in respect of securities issued before 12 April 1989, or (without time limit) where the principal secured by the relevant security has been advanced out of money subscribed for foreign-owned share capital of the lender. Under the earlier provisions, interest etc. on a relevant security is not treated as a distribution unless either:

(i)   the lender's ordinary trading activities include moneylending, and the interest, if not treated as a distribution, would be treated as a trading expense of a trade carried on in RI in the accounting period of payment consisting of at least 75% (by reference to turnover) of

(*a*)   the manufacture of goods (including trades defined as such under 12.17 below), or

(*b*)   'Customs-free airport' operations (see 16.2 EXEMPT INCOME AND SPECIAL SAVINGS SCHEMES), or

(*c*)   a service undertaking in respect of which an employment grant was made by the Industrial Development Authority under the *Industrial Development (No 2) Act 1981, s 2* (but see below),

or, in the case of a 75% subsidiary of an agricultural or fishery society, either or both of the manufacture of goods and wholesale sales of agricultural products or fish respectively; or

(ii)   it is payable under a binding written contract entered into before 25 January 1984 and is payable on or before 24 January 1989 or, if earlier, the last day of the period within which the loan, etc. (interest and principal) was due to be repaid under the contract as at 24 January 1984 (or the date of the making of the loan, etc. if later); or

(iii)   it is payable under a binding written contract entered into after 24 January 1984 and before 1 March 1984, pursuant to negotiations in the course of which preliminary commitments or agreements had been entered into before 26 January 1984, and is payable on or before 28 February 1989, or, if earlier, the last day of the period within which the loan, etc. (interest and capital) was due to be repaid under the contract as at the date of the contract (or the date of the making of the loan, etc. if later); or

(iv)   it exceeds a reasonable commercial return for the use of the principal, in which case only the excess is to be treated as a distribution.

For the purposes of (ii) and (iii) above, any extension of the repayment period coming into force after 24 January 1984 (or after 28 February 1984 pursuant to negotiations in the course of which preliminary commitments or agreements had been entered into before 26 January 1984) is ignored.

The exclusion at (i)(*c*) above does not apply unless the obligation to pay the interest, etc. arose under a binding written contract either entered into before 13 May 1986, or entered into before 1 September 1986 pursuant to negotiations in the course of which preliminary commitments or agreements had been entered into before 14 May 1986. [*CTA s 84A as originally inserted by FA 1984, s 41; FA 1986, s 54; FA 1992, s 41*].

The operation of (*d*)(iv) above may, on election, be excluded where a company providing certain financial services within a certificate issued by the Minister for Finance (see 12.17(viii) below) (or which could be so certified if carried on in the Custom House Docks Area rather than Shannon airport) would, but for that provision, be able to deduct the interest as a trading expense in computing income from operations covered by that certificate, and where the interest is payable to a company resident in the USA or in a territory with which arrangements under *Sec 361* (see 15.2 DOUBLE TAX RELIEF—INCOME AND CAPITAL GAINS) have been made. The election must be submitted with the company's return of profits for the accounting period for which the interest is payable. [*FA 1988, s 37; FA 1994, s 49*].

See 12.7 above for extended meaning of distribution for close companies and see also 12.25 as regards ACT on certain distributions within (*d*) above.

Foreign currency transactions. Where the lender in relation to a security within (*d*)(ii), (iii)(I) or (v) above denominated in a foreign currency is a company whose ordinary trading activities include money-lending, and the interest (treated as a distribution) is computed on the basis of a rate which at any time in an accounting period exceeds 80% of three-month DIBOR (or comparable rate), then any profit or loss arising to the borrower from any foreign exchange transaction in connection with the loan is treated as a trading profit or loss of the accounting period. See, however, 12.17(xvi) below as regards the rate of tax applicable to such exchange gains. [*FA 1993, s 47*].

Company purchasing own shares—trading or holding companies. *Part IX* of the *Companies Act 1990* permits a company to purchase its own shares, subject to various requirements. Following *FA 1991, ss 59–72*, when certain conditions are satisfied, the purchase, repayment or redemption by a company of its own shares is not to be treated as a distribution, and the vendor will be liable to capital gains tax rather than income tax on the payment received. This may also apply to certain purchases by subsidiary companies of shares of the parent company. The conditions to be satisfied are broadly as follows.

(i)   The company must be either a trading company or a holding company, the main business of which is to hold shares in one or more 51% subsidiaries in a 'trading group'. A *'trading group'* is a holding company plus one or more subsidiary companies whose business, taken together, consists wholly or mainly of the carrying on of a trade or trades. 'Trade' does not include dealing in shares, securities, land, futures or options.

(ii)   Neither the company's shares nor those of a company of which it is a 51% subsidiary may be quoted on a stock exchange list or dealt in on an unlisted securities market.

(iii) Either (*a*) or (*b*) as follows is satisfied.

    (*a*)   (I)   The purchase etc. must be made wholly or mainly for the benefit of the trade of the company or any of its 51% subsidiaries, and

            (II)   the purchase etc. must not form part of a scheme a main purpose of which is to enable the shareholder to participate in the profits of the company or any of its 51% subsidiaries without receiving a dividend, and

            (III)   the conditions relating to the shareholder detailed at (iv)–(xi) below must be satisfied where applicable.

    (*b*)   The person to whom the payment is made must apply the whole, or substantially the whole, of the payment (less any sum applied in discharging a liability to capital gains tax, if any, in respect of the purchase etc.) to discharging

            (I)   within four months of the valuation date (as defined in *CATA 1976, s 21*: see 7.7 CAPITAL ACQUISITIONS TAX) of a taxable inheritance of the company's shares, an inheritance tax liability in respect of that inheritance, or

            (II)   within one week of the purchase etc., a debt incurred by him for the purpose of discharging the inheritance tax liability in (I) above,

    and he could not have otherwise discharged that liability without undue hardship.

(iv)   The vendor of the shares must be resident and ordinarily resident (see 27.1 RESIDENTS AND NON-RESIDENTS) in RI for the chargeable period in which the purchase etc. is made. Where the shares are held through a nominee, the nominee must also be so resident and ordinarily resident. The residence etc. of a personal representative is for these purposes the same as the residence etc. of the deceased immediately before his death. The residence etc. of trustees is determined in accordance with *CGTA 1975, s 15*.

(v) The vendor must have owned the shares for at least the five years ending on the day of the purchase etc. If during that period the shares were transferred to the vendor by a person who was then his spouse living with him, any period during which the spouse owned the shares shall be treated as an ownership period of the vendor, provided that the transferor either is still the vendor's spouse living with him or is deceased at the time of purchase etc.

If the vendor acquired the shares under a will or intestacy, or as a personal representative, ownership by the deceased person (and, in the former case, by his personal representative) count as ownership by the vendor, and the qualifying period is reduced to three years.

Where identification of different holdings of shares of the same class is necessary, earlier acquisitions are taken into account before later ones, and previous disposals identified with later acquisitions before earlier ones, for this purpose. The time of acquisition of shares acquired through a reorganisation of share capital or securities etc. is that determined under *CGTA 1975, 2 Sch*, except where the vendor is treated under *CGTA 1975, 2 Sch 2(3)* as giving consideration, other than the old holding, for the acquisition of the shares.

(vi) The vendor's shareholding must be 'substantially reduced' by the purchase etc. A shareholding is '*substantially reduced*' if and only if the proportion of the company's issued share capital held by him immediately after the purchase does not exceed 75% of that immediately before the purchase. It is not regarded as so reduced if the share of the profits available for distribution to which the vendor would be entitled (beneficially, except in the case of trustees or personal representatives) immediately after the purchase etc. is greater than 75% of his entitlement immediately before the purchase etc.

(vii) If, immediately after the purchase etc., any shares in the company are owned by an 'associate' of the vendor, the combined interests of the vendor and his associate(s) must satisfy the 'substantial reduction' condition at (vi) above.

'*Associate*' includes spouse and minor children, and a broad range of relationships whereby an individual or company may be able to influence the actions of another.

(viii) If the company making the purchase etc. is, immediately before the purchase etc., a member of a 'group of companies', and, immediately after the purchase etc., either

  (*a*) the vendor owns shares in other group member(s), or

  (*b*) he still owns shares in the company making the purchase etc. *and* had immediately before the purchase etc., owned shares in other group member(s),

then the 'substantial reduction' condition at (vi) above must be satisfied in relation to his interest in the group as a whole, taken as the average of his proportionate holdings of the issued share capital of the company purchasing the shares and of all other group members in which he holds shares immediately before or after the purchase etc.

A '*group of companies*' for this purpose is a company which has one or more 51% subsidiaries, but is not itself a 51% subsidiary of any other company, together with those subsidiaries.

Where the whole or a significant part of the business carried on by an unquoted company (the 'successor company') was previously carried on by the company purchasing the shares (or a member of the same group), then, unless the successor company first carried on the business more than three years before the purchase etc., the successor company and any company of which it is a 51% subsidiary are treated as being members of the same group as the company purchasing etc. the shares.

(ix) Where an associate (see (vii) above) of the vendor owns shares in any company in the same group (see (viii) above) as the company purchasing the shares immediately before the purchase etc., the combined interests of vendor and associate(s) must satisfy the 'substantial reduction' condition at (vi) above.

(x) The vendor must not, immediately after the purchase etc., be 'connected with' the company purchasing the shares or any other company in the same group (see (viii) above).

The vendor is so *'connected with'* a company if, together with his associates (see (vii) above), he directly or indirectly possesses or is (or will be) entitled to acquire

(*a*) more than 30% of its issued ordinary share capital, or its loan capital (i.e. any debt incurred by the company for money borrowed or capital assets acquired) and issued share capital, or its voting power, or

(*b*) more than 30% of its assets available for distribution to the company's equity holders (to be determined in accordance with *CTA 1976, ss 109, 111*, modified as appropriate),

or if he has control of it.

(xi) The purchase etc. must not be part of a scheme or arrangement which is designed or likely to result in the vendor or any associate of his acquiring interests in the company such that, if he had those interests immediately after the purchase etc., any of the conditions in (vi) to (x) above could not have been satisfied. Any transaction occurring within one year of the purchase etc. is deemed to be part of a scheme of which the purchase etc. is also a part.

Where any of the conditions in (vi) to (x) above are not satisfied in relation to the vendor, they will nevertheless be treated as satisfied where the vendor proposed or agreed to the purchase etc. in order that the conditions in (vii) or (ix) above regarding the substantial reduction of the combined interests of a vendor and his associate(s) could be satisfied in respect of a purchase etc. of shares owned by such an associate, to the extent that that result is produced by virtue of the purchase etc.

[*FA 1991, ss 59–66, 71, 72*].

When a company makes a payment which it treats as being not a distribution by virtue of these provisions, it must make a return in prescribed form to the inspector within nine months from the end of the accounting period in which it makes the payment. Alternatively, the inspector may by notice in writing require the company to make a return at an earlier time within the period (which is not to be less than 30 days) specified in the notice. [*FA 1991, s 67*].

If the inspector has reason to believe that a payment etc. treated by the company as being within the above provisions may form part of a scheme within (xi) above, he may require the company or any person connected with it (see (x) above) to furnish him, within not less than 60 days, with a written declaration as to whether, according to information reasonably obtainable, any such scheme or arrangement exists or has existed, and with such other information reasonably required by him as the company or person can reasonably obtain. Where a company makes a payment which it treats as being within the above provisions, any person connected with the company who knows of a scheme or arrangement within (xi) above which affects the payment shall within 60 days after he first knows of the payment and the scheme, give a notice to the inspector containing details of that scheme.

Any person receiving a payment etc. treated as falling within the above provisions, or on whose behalf such a payment etc. is received, may be required to notify the inspector as to whether he received the payment on his own or another's behalf and, in the latter case, to supply the other person's name and address.

The penalty provisions of *Secs 500–503* apply to returns required as above. [*FA 1991, s 68*].

Dealers in securities. Where a company purchases its own shares (or those of a company of which it is a subsidiary) from a dealer (i.e. a person on whom the price received would normally be included in Schedule D, Case I or II profits), then

(*a*)   the purchase price is brought into account on the dealer under Schedule D, Case I or II,

(*b*)   tax is not chargeable under Schedule F, and no tax credit is available, and

(*c*)   the normal corporation tax exemption for RI company distributions does not apply.

This does not, however, apply in relation to the redemption of fixed-rate preference shares (as defined), or certain other preference shares issued before 18 April 1991, which were issued to and continuously held by the person from whom they are redeemed. [*FA 1991, s 60*].

Advance corporation tax. For certain ACT purposes, purchases etc. by a company of its own (or its parent's) shares which are deemed to be distributions are treated in the same way as dividend payments. [*FA 1991, s 69*].

Treasury shares (within *Companies Act 1990, s 209*) are for tax purposes treated as cancelled when purchased by the issuing company. Cancellation gives rise to neither chargeable gain nor allowable loss for CGT purposes. [*FA 1991, s 70*].

Company purchasing own shares—non-distributing investment company. A 'relevant company' may claim to have every payment made by it for the redemption, repayment or purchase of its own shares treated as not being a distribution, so that no ACT is accounted for and no tax credit is available to the recipient. A claim must be made in writing to the inspector in prescribed form, and be accompanied by the company's return of profits for the accounting period in which it first makes such a payment. A *'relevant company'* is an investment company (within *Companies Act 1990, Pt XIII*) which is a qualified company within *FA 1980, s 39B* (see 12.17(viii) below) which makes only one payment in respect of any share or security issued by it, being a payment for its redemption, repayment or purchase. [*FA 1983, s 47A; FA 1995, s 37*].

Preference shares. Dividends on certain preference shares, paid after 24 January 1984 to another company within the charge to corporation tax, do not entitle the holder to a tax credit, and are chargeable to corporation tax under Schedule D, Case IV. The following preference shares are, however, excluded from such treatment:

(i)   those quoted on an RI stock exchange;

(ii)   those not so quoted but carrying rights comparable with those general for fixed dividend shares which are so quoted;

(iii) those issued before 25 January 1984, *but only* in respect of dividends payable before 25 January 1989;

(iv)   those issued after 24 January 1984 where the subscriber was obliged under a written contract entered into before 25 January 1984 to subscribe for the shares, *but only* in respect of dividends payable before 25 January 1989;

(v)   those issued after 24 January 1984 where the subscriber was obliged under a written contract entered into before 1 March 1984 to subscribe for the shares and where, before 26 January 1984, preliminary commitments or agreements had been entered into to that effect, *but only* in respect of dividends payable before 1 March 1989; and

(vi)   non-transferable shares issued after 5 April 1989 in the course of trading operations attracting the manufacturing companies relief (see 12.17 below) by virtue of

12.17(viii) below (being carried on within the International Financial Services Centre) or of the issue of a certificate in relation to operations carried on within Shannon airport, where the shares are issued to a company none of whose shares is beneficially owned, directly or indirectly, by an RI resident and which, apart from this exclusion, would not be chargeable to corporation tax on any profits other than dividends chargeable by virtue of these provisions.

[*FA 1984, s 42; FA 1989, s 26*].

Reciprocal arrangements between companies to make distributions to each other's members to avoid the above provisions will be ineffective. [*CTA s 87(3)*].

Shares with assured income or capital return. Special restrictions apply to distributions in respect of shares where an agreement, arrangement or understanding exists to eliminate the risk that the owner of the shares, or a connected person (within *CTA s 157*), might at a particular time be unable to realise a particular amount, or might not receive a particular level of distributions, in respect of the shares. Where any person receives a distribution in respect of such shares after 20 July 1989, and the distribution would otherwise come within the special provisions relating to Shannon relief (see 16.2 EXEMPT INCOME AND SPECIAL SAVINGS SCHEMES), export sales relief (see 16.4 EXEMPT INCOME AND SPECIAL SAVINGS SCHEMES), stallion fees and commercial woodlands (see 30.1 SCHEDULE D, CASES I and II) or patent royalties (see below), then those provisions do not apply to the distribution, no tax credit is available, and the distribution is taxable under SCHEDULE D, CASE IV (32). See also 21.5 INVESTMENT IN CORPORATE TRADES AND RESEARCH AND DEVELOPMENT for restriction of relief in respect of such shares.

These restrictions do not apply to such distributions received by non-residents, or by companies owned by non-residents which would otherwise only have been chargeable to corporation tax in respect of such distributions. This does not, however, affect the liability of any other RI resident. [*FA 1990, s 34*].

Bonus issue stripping. No distribution falling within (*c*), (*d*) or (*f*) above or disqualified from being a repayment of share capital by *CTA s 86* will

(i)   entitle the recipient to deduct or recover the tax credit, or

(ii)   rank as franked investment income (see below),

except insofar as it represents a normal return on the kind of investment held by the recipient. [*CTA s 89*].

Patent royalties which are exempt for all tax purposes (see 16.12 EXEMPT INCOME AND SPECIAL SAVINGS SCHEMES) are also, if distributed, exempt in the hands of recipients and carry no tax credit. As regards distributions received after 23 April 1992, this exemption is available to companies only where the distribution is in respect of '*eligible shares*', i.e. fully paid ordinary share capital carrying no present or future preferential rights to dividends or assets, or to be redeemed, and not subject to any different treatment from other shares of the same class. Similarly as regards distributions received by individuals, the exemption is phased out except (in relation to distributions in respect of eligible shares) to the extent that the distribution is made out of income referable to a qualifying patent of which the recipient was the deviser (or joint deviser). The exemption is phased out by being applied to only two-thirds of the total distributions received after 23 April 1992 and before 6 April 1993 which would otherwise be exempt, and to only one-third of such distributions for 1993/94. It is abolished after 1993/94. [*CTA s 170; FA 1992, s 19(2)*]. See, however, above as regards certain shares carrying an assured return.

Distributions out of exempt or relieved profits. Certain distributions out of income bearing a reduced rate of corporation tax under the manufacturing companies relief (see 12.17 below) carry a correspondingly reduced rate of tax credit, and similarly reduced or nil tax credits apply to distributions out of certain exempt income (Shannon airport relief, export sales relief, patent royalties, commercial woodlands and stallion fees, see 16.2, 16.4, 16.12 EXEMPT INCOME AND SPECIAL SAVINGS SCHEMES, 30.1 SCHEDULE D, CASES I AND II). There are provisions allowing the company to specify the accounting period(s) in which such distributions are to be treated as having been made, which for distributions made before 1 June 1994 apply only to the manufacturing companies relief (and see in particular 12.17 CORPORATION TAX). [*CTA ss 64, 76, 93, 170; FA 1980, s 45; FA 1988, s 32; FA 1989, ss 24, 25; FA 1994, s 59; FA 1995, s 45, 2 Sch*].

12.11   DOUBLE TAXATION RELIEF

The present rules and agreements under IT are adopted for CT, and for that purpose are extended to cover capital gains subject to CT. [*CTA, ss 22, 23, 166, 4 Sch*]. See also 15.2 to 15.14 DOUBLE TAX RELIEF—INCOME AND CAPITAL GAINS.

The amount of corporation tax against which foreign tax on income or gains may be credited is limited to corporation tax on the income or gains computed, broadly, by reference to the amount of the income or gains as measured for the purposes of RI tax, with all necessary apportionments being made, and taking account of effective reduced rates of corporation tax (e.g. manufacturing companies relief, see 12.17 below) where relevant. No corporation tax is attributable to certain income or gains taken out of charge by the allocation of deductions. [*CTA s 23; FA 1995, s 60*].

Distribution by non-resident company to RI-resident parent. Where, after 31 December 1991, an RI-resident company receives from a non-resident 'subsidiary' a distribution (other than in a winding-up) chargeable to RI corporation tax, credit is allowed against that corporation tax (so far as not otherwise allowed) for withholding taxes charged on the distribution by other EEC Member States, and for so much of other Member State taxes, not chargeable in respect of the distribution but borne by the subsidiary and attributable to profits represented by the distribution, as exceeds any tax credit in respect of the distribution repayable to the parent. The normal foreign dividend payment arrangements under *Secs 459–462* do not apply to such distributions. The provisions of *10 Sch* apply as if the relief were under a double taxation agreement. The above relief is without prejudice to any provision of a double tax agreement.

'*Subsidiary*' generally means a company at least 25% of whose share capital is owned by the parent, but a double taxation agreement may apply the test by reference to voting rights, and may impose a condition that the 25% relationship exist for an uninterrupted two–year period.

These provisions are in implementation of *Council Directive No 90/435/EEC* of 23 July 1990. [*FA 1991, s 36*].

12.12   EXEMPTIONS AND RELIEFS

With the exceptions of *Secs 373–414* all existing income tax exemptions and reliefs apply to CT as they apply to IT. [*CTA s 11(6)*]. Consequently, such provisions noted elsewhere in this book also apply to CT, the exceptions being Exported Goods relief and Shannon Airport relief which are re-enacted with slight modifications (see 16.2, 16.4 EXEMPT INCOME AND SPECIAL SAVINGS SCHEMES). [*CTA Parts IV, V, VI*].

National Co-operative Farm Relief Services Ltd. Grants to, and transfers of monies to members by, National Co-operative Farm Relief Services Ltd after 31 March 1993, under the agreement with the Minister for Agriculture, Food and Forestry dated 4 July 1991 for support of farm relief services, or after 11 December 1994 under the agreement dated 16 May 1995 for support of agricultural services development, are disregarded for corporation tax purposes. [*FA 1994, s 52; FA 1995, s 57*].

Foreign branch profits. Profits or gains or losses from the carrying on of 'qualified foreign trading activities' are disregarded for corporation tax purposes, and gains on disposal of assets (other than land and minerals in RI and related assets) used wholly and exclusively for the trade consisting of those activities are not chargeable gains. Charges, management expenses, etc. incurred for the purposes of that trade may not be relieved against any other profits.

'*Qualified foreign trading activities*' are trading activities carried on by a 'qualified company' through a branch or agency outside RI in a territory specified in the certificate given by the Minister for Finance certifying that the company is a 'qualified company', and a '*qualified company*' is an RI-resident company to which the Minister has given such a certificate which has not been revoked. The conditions for the issue of such a certificate are broadly that the Minister must be satisfied that an investment plan submitted by the company will, before a date specified in the plan and agreed by the Minister, result in the company or an associated company (as defined for this purpose) making a substantial permanent capital investment in RI to create substantial new employment in trading operations in RI, the maintenance of which will depend on the carrying on of qualified foreign trading activities. There are provisions for the drawing up of guidelines relating to these requirements, and for the granting and revocation of certification.

Where the qualified foreign trading activities are carried on as part of a trade, those activities are treated as constituting a separate trade. There are provisions for the necessary attributions and apportionments on an arm's length basis for this purpose.

[*FA 1995, s 29*].

Dividends from foreign subsidiaries. Certain dividends received **after 5 April 1988** by an RI resident company from a 51% subsidiary resident in the USA or in another territory with which arrangements under *Sec 361* (see 15.2 DOUBLE TAX RELIEF—INCOME AND CAPITAL GAINS) are in force are exempted from corporation tax. The dividends must be applied (after 5 April 1988) within the period from one year before to two years after receipt in RI, although after 31 December 1990 this period may be extended at the Revenue Commissioners' discretion. They must be applied for the purposes of a plan certified by the Minister for Finance as being directed towards the creation or maintenance of employment in trading operations carried on or to be carried on in RI, and must be specified in that certificate as qualifying for relief. Details of plans and of the dividends concerned must be submitted to the Minister, and relief may be withdrawn or denied where dividends are not applied within the time limits referred to above. After 31 December 1990, plans may be submitted up to one year after implementation if there is reasonable cause for their being submitted after implementation. Claims for relief where a certificate has been given are to be submitted with the company's return of profits for the period in which the dividends are received in RI. [*FA 1988, s 41; FA 1991, s 40*].

For reliefs generally, see paras 12.2, 12.11, 12.14, 12.15, 12.21 and Chapters 16 and 17 below.

12.13   FRANKED INVESTMENT INCOME

Franked investment income means the tax-credited distributions received by a company resident in RI, and consists of the distributions plus the total tax credit thereon. Similarly, *franked payment* means the amount of a distribution made by a company resident in RI plus the tax credit thereon. [*CTA s 24*].

See 12.25 below as regards use of such payments to frank distributions otherwise giving rise to liability to ACT.

Where the total profits of a company for an accounting period are insufficient to exhaust all or any of its

(i)   trading losses,

(ii)   charges on income,

(iii)   capital allowances deductible against total profits (i.e. exceeding the income of the specified class, see 12.9 above),

for that period, the company may claim to have the remaining balance of those deductions set off against all or part of its franked investment income for the period and claim repayment of the tax credit (but see 12.25 below as regards restrictions on repayment of tax credit). Such a claim must be made within two years. [*CTA s 25; FA 1983, ss 43, 48*]. An investment company can additionally claim repayment of the tax credit by setting off its excess management expenses (see 12.9 above) against its franked investment income. [*CTA s 15(4)*].

See 38.37A TAX CASES as regards date of receipt of dividend for these purposes.

A company may subsequently claim to carry forward a deduction which has already been set off against franked investment income and instead have it set off against profits of a later accounting period. In such a case the company will be charged under Schedule D, Case IV for an amount of IT equal to the amount of repaid tax credit. For accounting periods ending after 31 March 1992, the liability is, for the purposes of charge, assessment, collection and recovery, treated as a corporation tax liability. [*CTA s 25(5); FA 1986, s 55; FA 1992, s 49(1)*].

Losses carried forward and terminal losses carried back (see 12.16 below) of certain financial concerns may similarly be set off against franked investment income for an accounting period which would be trading income but for having been taxed under other provisions, insofar as such losses exceed the profits available for set-off in that period. [*CTA s 26; FA 1986, s 55; FA 1992, s 49(2)*].

To the extent that any distribution received by a company from a fellow group member (see 12.14 below) is made out of gains accruing on **certain disposals of development land** (see 9.16 CAPITAL GAINS TAX), the distribution is treated, in the hands of the recipient, as being a gain accruing from a disposal of development land (see 12.2 above), and the distribution plus related tax credit is not treated as franked investment income for the purposes of set-off of trading losses as above. [*FA 1982, s 40(3)*].

12.14 GROUPS

Definition of subsidiary. Whether a company is a 51% or 75% or 90% subsidiary is determined by reference to beneficial ownership, direct or indirect, of the company's ordinary share capital. Indirect ownership through a chain of companies is traced as follows:

Where A Company holds ordinary shares in B Company which holds ordinary shares in C Company which in turn holds ordinary shares in X Company, the interest of A Company in X Company equals

$$\frac{\text{Holding of A Co. in B Co.}}{\substack{\text{Total ordinary share} \\ \text{capital of B Co.}}} \times \frac{\text{Holding of B Co. in C Co.}}{\substack{\text{Total ordinary share} \\ \text{capital of C Co.}}} \times \frac{\text{Holding of C Co. in X Co.}}{\substack{\text{Total ordinary share} \\ \text{capital of X Co.}}}$$

For a 75% or 90% subsidiary the shareholding of the parent must be at least 75% or 90%; for a 51% subsidiary the shareholding must exceed 50%. [*CTA s 156*].

Group relief. Any relief for losses etc. available to a company (the surrendering company) may be transferred by a 'payment for group relief' to another company (the claimant company) where

(*a*)   both companies are resident in RI, and

(*b*)   both are members of the same group of companies (i.e. one is a 75% subsidiary of the other or both are 75% subsidiaries of a third), or, *where the surrendering company is not a member of such a group*, the surrendering company is

(i)   a trading company which is owned by a consortium, or which is a 90% subsidiary of a holding company which is owned by a consortium, or

(ii)   a holding company which is owned by a consortium,

and the claimant company is a member of that consortium. [*CTA s 107*].

Holding company means a company whose sole or main business is the holding of shares or securities of trading companies which are its 90% subsidiaries. A company is *owned by a consortium* if all its ordinary share capital is owned *directly* and beneficially by five or fewer companies.

Any shareholding in a company resident outside RI is ignored, as is any shareholding a profit on sale of which would fall to be treated as a trading receipt. [*CTA s 107(5)(7)*].

To qualify as a 75% or 90% subsidiary under group relief the following conditions must be fulfilled in addition to the general definition above. The parent company must be entitled to 75%/90% of the profits of the subsidiary available for distribution to equity holders and to 75%/90% of the assets which would be available for distribution to equity holders if the subsidiary were at that moment wound up. [*CTA ss 108–115*].

(i)   Any trading loss of a surrendering company, or

(ii)   any excess of its capital allowances, or charges on income, or (if an investment company) management expenses, over its profits (computed without deduction of any such allowances etc.) in an accounting period,

may be deducted from the total profits of the claimant company (ignoring any subsequent reliefs carried back) in its corresponding accounting period. Where the claimant company is a member of a consortium, it is only entitled to such fraction of the relief as reflects the proportion of its holding in the surrendering company. [*CTA ss 116–118; FA 1990, s 44*]. Where companies join or leave a group or consortium, relief is restricted by reference to the period during which both claimant and surrendering companies were members. [*CTA s 119*].

The payment for group relief is not taken into account in computing the profits or losses of either company, nor does it rank as a distribution or a charge on income. [*CTA s 107(4)*].

Claims must be made within two years of the end of the accounting period of the surrendering company, and be with the written consent of the surrendering company and (if appropriate) of the other members of the consortium. [*CTA s 125*]. Two or more companies may claim in respect of the same relief of a surrendering company but the total relief cannot exceed what would have been available to a single claimant company. [*CTA ss 197(3), 124*]. A claim for an accounting period ending after 31 March 1992 is restricted to one-half of the maximum claim where either the claimant company or the surrendering company has failed to submit its return for the period to which the claim relates by the required date (see 28.12 RETURNS).

Anti-avoidance provisions deal with limited or diminishing entitlement of equity holders [*CTA ss 112, 113*], and with transfer of a surrendering company between groups [*CTA s 120*], capital allowances in respect of machinery and plant [*CTA s 121*], and shares of a company in a partnership. [*CTA s 122*]. An inspector has power to require information in respect of these three latter situations. [*CTA s 123*].

See also 12.25 below as regards surrender of advance corporation tax.

Interaction with manufacturing companies relief. For accounting periods falling within the period from 1 January 1989 to 31 December 2010, group or consortium relief for losses or charges on income attributable to the sale of goods by a company within the scheme of the manufacturing companies relief (see 12.17 below) is restricted to set-off against similar income of other group or consortium members, as reduced by certain losses and charges on income under *CTA ss 16A, 10A*. For this purpose an accounting period straddling 31 December 1988 is deemed to consist of two separate accounting periods, one ending on that date and the other commencing on the following day, and similar provision is made in relation to 31 December 2010. Where relief for such losses etc. is allowed, it acts to reduce income before terminal loss relief but after relief for other trading losses.

The restriction on relief does not apply to losses etc. in a trade

(i)   in an accounting period (or part) falling before 6 April 1990 where export sales relief was claimed in the latest preceding accounting period in which there was income from the trade which gave rise to a corporation tax liability, or

(ii)   where the loss was referable to capital allowances for certain commercial buildings in use by financial services companies operating in the Custom House Docks Area (see 12.17(viii) below).

Where relief is surrendered under the above provision, it is set against the income from the sale of goods, which would otherwise give rise to manufacturing companies relief in the hands of the claimant company. The amount surrendered may not exceed the claimant company's income from the sale of goods. [*CTA s 116A; FA 1988, s 34; FA 1992, s 46(2)*].

Payments without deducting tax. Certain payments (chiefly charges on income) made between two RI resident companies must be made without deduction of tax where

(*a*)   one is a 51% subsidiary of the other or both are 51% subsidiaries of a third resident company, or

(*b*)   the payer company is a trading or holding company owned by a consortium of which the payee company is a member.

Holding company has the same meaning as above, and the same rules apply for disregarding shares held in non-resident companies or held for the purposes of a trade; but here a company is *owned by a consortium* if three-fourths or more of its ordinary share capital is beneficially owned by five or fewer resident companies none of which owns less than one-twentieth of the share capital.

Before 28 May 1992, these provisions applied only where the companies concerned jointly elected for them to do so. The relief ceased if either company ceased to be entitled to make the election or immediately on either revoking the election. [*CTA ss 105, 106; FA 1992, s 50*].

See also 12.25 below as regards dividends payable without accounting for advance corporation tax.

Deferment of tax on capital gains. A transfer of assets between companies in a group will be treated as being for a consideration such that no loss or gain accrues to the transferor company. This relief will not apply where the disposal consists of satisfying a debt or redeeming shares, or is a disposal of an interest in shares on a capital distribution. [*CTA s 130*]. The relief only applies to companies resident in RI, and a *group* is defined as consisting of a principal company and its 75% subsidiaries (see above), and the 75% subsidiaries of those subsidiaries, and so on. The relief is carried over where the principal company itself becomes a 75% subsidiary thus enlarging the group. [*CTA s 129*].

Further provisions clarify the situation as regards appropriations to and from stock in trade in the course of such transfers, provide for aggregation of capital allowances for the purpose of restricting an ultimate loss, and treat as one for the purposes of 'roll-over' relief all businesses carried on by the group. [*CTA ss 131, 132(1), 133; CGT(A)A s 14*]. Ownership of an asset by another group member prior to an intra-group transfer is treated as ownership by the transferee company in determining period of ownership for inflation indexing (see 9.9 CAPITAL GAINS TAX) and the rate applicable to transactions generally before 6 April 1992 (see 9.3 CAPITAL GAINS TAX) but not to such transfers of development land (see 9.16 CAPITAL GAINS TAX). [*CTA s 132(2); CGT(A)A s 3; FA 1982, ss 31(1), 36(7)*].

There is a retrospective charge to CT where the company in possession of an asset leaves the group within ten years of acquiring the asset under a relieved transaction. A 'deemed disposal and re-acquisition' provision renders the difference between (*a*) the no loss/no gain consideration under the relief, and (*b*) the market value of the asset on the date the company acquired it, a chargeable gain by the company for the accounting period in which it acquired the asset. This retrospective charge does not apply where the company left the group as part of a genuine commercial merger. [*CTA ss 135, 136*]. Further anti-avoidance provisions deal with sales of shares of subsidiaries, losses manufactured by intra-group transfers at an undervalue or by share dealing or share cancellation, and losses caused by dividend stripping. [*CTA ss 137–139*].

12.15   LIFE ASSURANCE COMPANIES

CTA ss 33–50 (as amended) contain detailed provisions for the taxation of assurance companies (within *Insurance Act 1936, s 3*), including relief for management expenses similar to that in 12.9 above. For these purposes, life assurance business is split between pension business, general annuity business, (from 1 January 1993) special investment business, and other life assurance business. Major changes are introduced from 1 January 1993 (for which see generally *FA 1993, ss 11, 12*), involving a reduction in the rate of tax generally applicable to 27% and a widening of the tax base, including taxation of certain unrealised gains (subject to spreading, generally over seven years, but to be phased in by the year 2000). 'Special investment business' (relating to business connected with 'special investment policies') is taxable at a special rate of 10% (although the normal rules applicable from 1 January 1993 are for this purpose further broadened in that the spreading of certain chargeable gains on deemed disposals does not apply to such business, and Irish government securities are included in such deemed disposals). Such business is 'ring-fenced' in relation to management expenses and asset transfers into and out of the fund. There are restrictions on the investment of funds representing liabilities on special investment business (in particular a minimum requirement as to Irish equity and smaller Irish company investment) and on the amount to which an individual may be entitled under such a policy (broadly £50,000, but see 16.22 EXEMPT INCOME AND SPECIAL SAVINGS SCHEMES as regards further limitations on investment). See 16.21 *et seq.* EXEMPT INCOME AND SPECIAL SAVINGS SCHEMES generally as regards this and other special savings schemes.

12.16   LOSSES

Relief for a loss (computed generally in the same way as income) incurred during an accounting period may be claimed

(*a*)   by **set-off** against profits of any kind in that accounting period [*CTA s 16(2)*];

(*b*)   except for trades within Schedule D, Case III, by **carry-back** against profits of any kind in a previous accounting period ending within a period immediately preceding, and of the same length as, the accounting period of the loss (with time apportionment of income etc. of accounting periods partly within that period) [*CTA s 16(2)*];

(*c*)   by **carry-forward** against trading income from the same trade in succeeding accounting periods (charges on income, relating wholly and exclusively to a trade, which exceed the *total profits* for the accounting period may create or augment a loss for this purpose) [*CTA s 16(1)*];

(*d*)   if a **terminal loss,** i.e. any loss in a trade incurred in an accounting period wholly or partly falling within the twelve months prior to cessation of that trade, by carry-back against trading income of any accounting period falling wholly or partly (and if partly, by apportionment) in the three years preceding the twelve months [*CTA s 18*];

(*e*)   by **carry-forward against income of the same trade in a successor company** where the successor company takes over the business of the predecessor company which ceases to trade and at least a three-fourths interest in the trade remains in the same hands [*CTA s 20*];

(*f*)   if a **Schedule D, Case IV** transaction, by carry-forward against later income of such transactions [*CTA s 19(1)*];

(*g*)   if a **Schedule D, Case V** transaction, by carry-back against the income of such transactions in the preceding accounting period, and carry-forward of any remaining balance against subsequent such transactions [*CTA s 19(2)*];

(*h*)   by set-off against **surplus franked investment income,** see 12.13 above;

(*j*)   by way of **group relief,** see 12.14 above.

Claims under (*a*), (*b*), (*d*) and (*g*) must be made within two years. A claim under (*a*), (*b*) or (*g*) for an accounting period ending after 31 March 1992 is restricted to one-half of the maximum claim where the return for the period is late (see 28.12 RETURNS). Relief under (*d*) is precluded in a situation to which (*e*) applies. [*CTA ss 16(10), 18(1)*].

Farming losses are subject to the same conditions as for income tax under *FA 1974, s 27,* see 18.6(*d*) FARMING. [*CTA s 17*].

Financial concerns operating in RI through a branch or agency are subject to restriction of loss relief arising from holdings of exempt government securities issued under *Sec 464* (see 19.2 GOVERNMENT AND OTHER PUBLIC LOANS) and certain other exempt securities issued under the authority of the Minister for Finance. [*FA 1992, s 42(2)–(4)*].

'Loss buying' — if there is a change in the ownership of a company and either (i) a major change in the nature or conduct of a trade occurs or has occurred within three years or (ii) at the time of the change of ownership the company's scale of activities is small, carry-forward relief under (*c*) for losses incurred before the change of ownership will be disallowed. [*CTA s 27*]. See 38.42 TAX CASES.

Expenditure on 'significant buildings' may attract relief as if it were a trading loss. See 22.4 LOSSES.

Limited partnership losses. See 22.5 LOSSES.

Manufacturing companies relief. See 12.17 below for restrictions on relief for losses from activities within the relief.

12.17   MANUFACTURING COMPANIES RELIEF

For all accounting periods (or parts) falling within the period **1 January 1981 to 31 December 2010** (31 December 2000 in relation to the special category listed at (vii) below), any company engaging in a trade which includes the manufacture and sale of 'goods' (as defined below) may claim relief from part of its CT liability.

'Goods' means goods manufactured (see 38.38–38.39D TAX CASES) by the claimant company within RI. The provision within RI of services to another person consisting of the subjection of commodities or materials belonging to that person to a process of manufacturing is treated as being the manufacture of 'goods'. (The inspector may require information in support of such a claim.) Where goods are manufactured within RI by one company and sold by another, and either one company is a 90% subsidiary of the other or both are 90% subsidiaries of a third, the goods sold by the selling company are deemed to have been manufactured by it. Goods sold, directly or ultimately, to any intervention agency under EC regulations are excluded from this definition of 'goods', as are goods sold by retail by the claimant company. As respects accounting periods ending after 31 March 1992, the 90% subsidiary test must also be satisfied in relation to distributions of profits and of assets in a winding-up (see *CTA ss 108–113*). [*FA 1980, s 39; FA 1990, s 41(6); FA 1991, s 35; FA 1992, s 47(a)*].

The following are also classed as the manufacture of goods for the purposes of this relief:

(i)   the production of fish on a fish farm within RI [*FA 1981, s 17*];

(ii) (for accounting periods beginning before 1 June 1994) the cultivation of mushrooms within RI [*FA 1981, s 17; FA 1994, s 48*];

(iii) the repairing of ships within RI [*FA 1981, s 17*];

(iv) the rendering within RI of design and planning services in connection with engineering works executed outside the EC [*FA 1981, s 17*];

(v)   (from 13 April 1984) the rendering of data processing or software development services (and, from 6 April 1989, related technical or consultancy services) (which is treated as being within RI) where the work was carried out in RI in a service undertaking in respect of which an employment grant was made under *Industrial Development Act 1986, s 25* (previously *Industrial Development (No 2) Act 1981, s 2*) or, after 31 December 1987, in respect of which certain grants or financial assistance were made available by the Shannon Free Airport Development Co Ltd or Údarás na Gaeltachta [*FA 1984, s 45; FA 1989, s 22; FA 1990, ss 40, 41(1)(a)*];

(vi) (from 1 January 1987) the carrying on of 'qualifying shipping activities' in the course of a 'qualifying shipping trade' [*FA 1987, s 28; FA 1988, s 40*];

(vii) (from a date to be appointed by the Minister for Finance) the wholesale sale of export goods by a 'Special Trading House', i.e. a company whose trade consists solely of the carrying out of such sales [*FA 1987, s 29*];

(viii) (from a date to be specified in the relevant certificate) the provision by a company (the 'qualified company') of certain financial services in the Custom House Docks Area (as described in *FA 1986, 4 Sch Pt II*) in respect of which the Minister for Finance has given (and not revoked) a certificate for this purpose which remains in force until 31 December 2005. The circumstances in which the Minister may give (or revoke) such a certificate are laid down in detail, but are broadly designed to contribute to the development of the Custom House Docks Area as an International Financial Services Centre. A certificate may be granted where operations are temporarily carried on outside the Area for reasons beyond the control of the company concerned. A limit of 10% is also placed on the rate of tax applying to income or chargeable gains from investments held abroad relating to certain foreign life assurance or unit trust business covered by such a certificate. [*FA 1980, s 39B; FA 1987, s 30; FA 1988, s 36; FA 1991, s 34; FA 1992, s 53; FA 1994, s 53; FA 1995, s 65*];

(ix) (from 9 July 1987) cultivating plants in RI by the process of micro-propagation or plant cloning [*FA 1987, s 31*];

(x)   (for accounting periods beginning after 31 March 1990) repair or maintenance of aircraft within RI (other than in Shannon Airport, see below) [*FA 1990, s 41(1)(b)*];

(xi) (for accounting periods beginning after 31 March 1990) film production on a commercial basis primarily for public exhibition or for training or documentary purposes, on which at least 75% of production work is carried out in RI [*FA 1990, s 41(1)(b)*];

(xii)   (for accounting periods beginning after 31 March 1990) meat processing within RI (in an establishment approved and inspected under *SI 1987 No 284*) and fish processing within RI [*FA 1990, s 41(1)(b)*], but without prejudice to the exclusion of goods sold into intervention (see above) [*FA 1991, s 32*], although this does *not* exclude the provision of processing services in relation to meat owned by the Intervention Agency [*FA 1993, s 44(1)(a)*];

(xiii) (for accounting periods beginning after 31 March 1990) the manufacture or repair of computer equipment or of sub-assemblies by the company which manufactured them (or by a connected company within *CTA s 157*) [*FA 1990, s 41(1)(b)*];

(xiv)   (for accounting periods ending after 31 March 1992) the sale by wholesale by certain agricultural and fishery societies of goods purchased from their members, which are themselves entitled to the manufacturing companies relief in respect of those goods (or would be but for the prohibition of sales into intervention) [*FA 1992, s 47(c)*];

(xv)   (for accounting periods ending after 31 March 1992) the sale by certain agricultural societies of milk purchased from their members and sold to certain milk product manufacturing companies certified for the purpose by the Minister for Agriculture. [*FA 1992, s 47(c); FA 1993, s 44(1)(a)*];

(xvi)   exchange gains in respect of certain loans, which are deemed to be trading profits or gains (see 12.10 above) [*FA 1993, s 47*]);

(xvii) (for accounting periods ending after 31 March 1992) newspaper production (including the provision of related advertising services) [*FA 1993, s 44(1)(c)*] (and see now 38.39E TAX CASES).

As regards (viii) above, see also 12.10 above, 16.6 EXEMPT INCOME AND SPECIAL SAVINGS SCHEMES as regards certain interest exemptions and 20.1(vi) INTEREST PAYABLE as regards deduction of tax from interest payments.

It is understood that the activities at (x) and (xii) above have always been regarded as qualifying for relief, despite the enacted commencement dates referred to.

The inspector may require information in support of a claim under (iii)–(viii), (x), (xi) or (xiii)–(xvii) above.

The following are, for accounting periods beginning after 31 March 1990, specifically excluded from being treated as the manufacture of goods for the purposes of relief:

(A)   processes applied to any produce, product or material acquired in bulk to prepare it for sale or distribution;

(B)   application of methods of preservation, pasteurisation or maturation etc. to foodstuffs;

(C)   preparation of food or drink for human consumption shortly after preparation;

(D)   improvements or alterations to articles or materials which do not change their character;

(E)   repair, refurbishment, restoration etc. of any articles or materials,

and relief is similarly denied, for accounting periods ending after 31 March 1992, in respect of advertising receipts of companies producing newspapers, magazines etc.

Relief is also denied where the manufacturing process is not carried out by the company claiming relief (subject to the exception referred to above in the case of 90% subsidiaries). [*FA 1980, s 39(5); FA 1990, s 41(1)(c); FA 1992, s 47(b)(d)*].

A '*qualifying shipping trade*' consists of the carrying on of '*qualifying shipping activities*', i.e. the carriage of passengers or cargo for reward (and provision of certain ancillary services) in a 'qualifying ship', the letting out on charter of such a ship for such purposes where the operation of the ship remains under the company's direction and control, (after 5 April 1988) the subjection of fish to a manufacturing process aboard such a ship, or (after 5 April 1990) the transport of supplies or personnel or provision of services to offshore installations. A '*qualifying ship*' is an Irish registered, self-propelled, sea-going vessel of not less than 100 tons gross tonnage at least 51% owned by RI ordinary residents, but excluding fishing vessels (other than factory ships, as indicated above), tugs (other than certain deepsea tugs), platforms, service vessels (but only before 6 April 1990) and other vessels not normally used for qualifying shipping activities.

Where qualifying shipping activities are carried on as part of a trade, they are treated as constituting a separate trade (except for the purposes of the commencement and cessation provisions and the carry-forward of trading losses). Capital allowances for a qualifying ship are available only in the separate trade, unless the ship is let on charter other than as described in (vi) above, in which case they are available against income from such letting. (Such letting is, however, brought within the restriction on allowances for leased plant and machinery under *FA 1984, s 40* (see 8.7 CAPITAL ALLOWANCES) notwithstanding the general exclusion of ship-operating companies.) Similarly, losses in the separate trade may only be set against other profits or surrendered as group relief (see 12.14 above) to the extent that the income against which they are set is from qualifying shipping activities. The separate trade is not excluded from the operation of the capital allowance leasing restrictions in *FA 1984, s 40* (see 8.7 CAPITAL ALLOWANCES) or the '*Section 84* loans' restrictions in *CTA s 84A* (see 12.10 above) despite its being brought within the manufacturing companies relief. [*FA 1987, s 28; FA 1988, s 40; FA 1990, s 42; FA 1994, s 62*].

It is understood that, in practice, the Revenue accept that magnetic tapes and discs etc. representing software or data processing input are 'goods' for these purposes.

In addition, the Minister for Finance may issue a certificate with the effect that certain trading operations carried on within Shannon airport are similarly treated as the manufacture of goods. Such operations must consist of the repair or maintenance of aircraft or operations contributing (in the opinion of the Minister) to the use or development of the airport, or be ancillary to such operations or to the manufacture of goods as defined apart from this specific provision.

Specifically excluded are operations consisting of

(*a*)   the rendering of services to passengers or in connection with the movement of aircraft or cargo,

(*b*)   the operation of a scheduled air transport service

(*c*)   retail selling, or

(*d*)   the sale of fuel or other aircraft stores.

Such a certificate may be conditional, and may be revoked where any conditions are not met or where the trade ceases to be carried on within Shannon airport or by agreement. It is otherwise valid until 31 December 2005.

The inspector may again require information in support of a claim under this provision. [*FA 1980, ss 39, 39A as amended and introduced by FA 1981, s 17; FA 1988, s 35; FA 1989, s 23; FA 1991, s 33; FA 1992, s 52*]. See also 16.6 EXEMPT INCOME AND SPECIAL SAVINGS SCHEMES for exemption of certain interest paid in the course of such operations, and 20.1(vi) INTEREST PAYABLE as regards deduction of tax from interest payments.

It is understood that, for new projects, the Revenue Commissioners are prepared, on receipt of satisfactory detail, to give an opinion on whether the process described is likely to qualify for relief.

Apportionment on a time basis applies where an accounting period falls only partly within the date limits for relief. [*FA 1980, s 40*].

Basis of relief is a reduction of that part of the liability to CT (ignoring certain reliefs and surcharges and amounts treated as CT) referable to income from the sale of 'goods'. The reduction is 4/5ths for profits attributable or apportioned to periods falling before 1 April 1988, 37/47ths for those attributable or apportioned to the period 1 April 1988 to 31 March 1989 inclusive, 33/43rds for those attributable or apportioned to periods falling between 1 April 1989 and 31 March 1991 inclusive, 3/4rs for those attributable or apportioned to periods falling between 1 April 1991 and 31 March 1995 inclusive, and 28/38ths for those attributable or apportioned to periods falling after 31 March 1995. (See 12.3 above for apportionment of profits to actual or deemed financial years.) The effective rate is thus 10% except where a reduced rate (see 12.3 above) applies before 1 April 1989. The CT thus relieved is that attributable to the company's income for the relevant period (i.e. profits chargeable to CT less that part attributable to chargeable gains without deduction of any amounts which may be set against profits or gains of more than one description) reduced in the proportion that the income from the sale of 'goods' bears to total income. The income from the sale of 'goods' as a proportion of the income from the sale of both 'goods' and other merchandise is determined by the amounts receivable (excluding any duty or VAT) in respect of each category. If the trade has income other than from the sale of 'goods' and merchandise, the proportion of total income attributable to such sales is such as appears just and reasonable to the inspector (or the Commissioners on appeal). [*FA 1980, s 41(1)–(5); CTA s 16A(5); FA 1982, 2 Sch Pt II; FA 1988, 3 Sch; FA 1989, s 27; FA 1990, s 52, 2 Sch Pt II; FA 1992, ss 46(1)(c), 54; FA 1995, ss 54, 61, 4 Sch Pt II*].

There are provisions by which a smaller reduction in the rate of corporation tax may be applied in any particular case where a company qualifying for the relief is wholly or partly owned by a non-RI resident company or companies (or is itself non-resident and trades in RI through a branch or agency) and its operations contribute, or will do so, to the development of an International Financial Services Centre or Customs-free Airport (within *FA 1980, ss 39A, 39B* respectively, see above). [*F(No 2)A 1992, s 1*]. This is intended to deal with the situation where, due to anti-avoidance legislation in a foreign jurisdiction (e.g. Germany) a higher overall tax rate would otherwise apply.

Before 6 April 1989, relief could be restricted in the case of a company which, at the end of an accounting period, employed 50 or more people full-time on operations the subject of a certificate entitling them to relief under *FA 1980, s 39A* (see above under 'Goods'). The total of all reliefs given under that section up to the end of the accounting period could not exceed an amount determined in accordance with EC principles on State aid. Such assessments and adjustments as are required were authorised, as was the making of the necessary regulations. [*FA 1980, s 39A(8)(9) as introduced by FA 1981, s 17 and repealed by FA 1989, s 23*].

Credit for foreign tax. Where the Irish treaty system does not provide for double taxation relief, a measure of unilateral credit is available against foreign taxes paid on profits arising in accounting periods ending **after 30 April 1994** and derived from sales of computer software or services or from Shannon Airport activities qualifying for manufacturing companies relief. The *'relevant foreign tax'* is foreign tax (which, for accounting periods ending after 31 December 1994, must correspond to income or corporation tax) deducted from the amount receivable and not repaid to the company.

The corporation tax attributable to an amount receivable is, for accounting periods ending after 31 December 1994, 10% of the company's income attributable to that amount (correspondingly increased where reduced manufacturing relief applies). Previously, it was the amount which would not be payable if the amount were disregarded. Income from the sale of goods is reduced for this purpose in the proportion which the amount in question bears to the total amount receivable from the sale of goods in the period, the total income from the sale of goods being determined as in relation to the basis of relief (see above). [*FA 1980, s 39C; FA 1994, s 54; FA 1995, s 63*].

Certain companies carrying on 'stand alone' non-banking financial trades which qualify as 'relevant trading operations' within *FA 1980, ss 39A, 39B* (see above) may elect, for accounting periods ending after 31 December 1994, to receive enhanced relief for foreign withholding tax deducted under double taxation agreements from interest payments from 'related' companies. In the case of *section 39A*, the operations must be such as could be certified for the purposes of *section 39B* if they were carried out in the Custom House Docks Area (i.e. broadly the provision of international financial services). Companies which are, or are '25% subsidiaries' of, 'credit institutions' are excluded. Broadly, where an election is made for an accounting period (before the 'specified return date' for the period, see 28.12 RETURNS), such foreign tax may be deducted from corporation tax attributable to income other than that which suffered the foreign tax, subject to a maximum additional credit in aggregate of 35% of the corporation tax which would otherwise be payable on income attributable to interest received (whether or not from 'related companies') subject to double taxation agreements. [*FA 1980, s 39D; FA 1995, s 62*].

Restrictions on relief for charges on income and losses. For accounting periods falling within the period 1 April 1992 to 31 December 2010, relief for charges paid for the purposes of the sale of goods within the manufacturing companies relief, and for losses arising from such sales, is restricted. An accounting period straddling 1 April 1992 or 31 December 2010 is for these purposes split into two accounting periods, so that the restrictions apply to the deemed accounting period starting on 1 April 1992 or ending on 31 December 2010.

Charges on income (see 12.9 above) are allowed as a deduction from total profits only to the extent that they do not exceed income (net of losses carried back) from the sale of goods within the relief in the period.

Losses (see 12.16 above) are only allowed against other income of the accounting period to the extent that that income arises from the sale of goods within the relief, and relief against income of earlier accounting periods (see 12.6(*b*) above) is similarly restricted. These restrictions do not, however, apply to the extent that a loss is attributable to plant and machinery or industrial buildings allowances in respect of expenditure incurred before 31 March 1995 on a project approved by the Industrial Development Authority in the two years to 31 December 1988 (see 8.5, 8.6 CAPITAL ALLOWANCES), provided that one-half of the expenditure was incurred or contracted for before 1 April 1992, or to certain urban renewal relief capital allowances (see 8.10 CAPITAL ALLOWANCES). See *CTA s 16A(5)* for the effect of loss reliefs on the income taken into account in the computation of the manufacturing companies relief. [*CTA ss 10A, 16A; FA 1992, s 46(1); FA 1993, s 50*].

Where 'Shannon' relief (see 16.2 EXEMPT INCOME AND SPECIAL SAVINGS SCHEMES) is claimed in respect of any part of the company's trading operations, amounts receivable from such exempt trading operations are disregarded for the purpose of the manufacturing companies relief, as are amounts receivable on exempted transactions by an agricultural society or fishery society (see 12.21 below). [*FA 1980, s 41(6)–(7)*].

Claims to relief must be made before the assessment for the period of claim becomes final and conclusive. [*FA 1980, s 41(8)*].

Exported goods relief is not available for any accounting period following one for which a claim to the new manufacturing companies relief is made. [*FA 1980, s 42*].

Mining and construction operations income is excluded from relief. Also, where part or all of the minerals etc. obtained are not sold but used in a combined trade which includes the manufacture of 'goods', such part of the income as appears just and reasonable to the inspector (or to the Commissioners on appeal) is treated as income from mining operations and excluded from relief. Similarly, where part of the amount receivable from the sale of 'goods' is consideration for carrying out construction operations, a 'just and reasonable' part of the income is excluded from relief. [*FA 1980, s 50*].

Associated persons. An anti-avoidance section prevents tax avoidance by transactions between associated persons at artificial prices, the test of association being by reference to 'control' within the meaning of *CTA s 158*. An inspector may require information for this purpose. [*FA 1980, s 44*].

Distributions. There are complex provisions relating to the tax credit attached to distributions where manufacturing companies relief has been claimed. For distributions made before 6 April 1989 (except where the election referred to below applies), distributions are first treated as paid out of a 'primary fund' of profits which have benefited from manufacturing companies relief, and distributions treated as so paid have a correspondingly reduced tax credit attached to them of 1/18th of the distribution. For distributions made **on or after 6 April 1989** (or, on written election by the company, on or after a specified day after 5 April 1988) distributions are attributed to profits attracting manufacturing companies relief in the ratio that such profits bear to total profits, and profits so attributed have a correspondingly reduced tax credit attached to them of 1/18th of the distribution.

For this latter purpose, distributions are treated as having been made for a specified period which is generally that ending most recently before the date of the distribution (but with special rules for interim dividends or distributions within 12.10(*d*)(ii), (iii)(I), or (v) above, for distributions on certain preference shares, on commencement or cessation, and in certain other cases where distributions exceed distributable income). A company may, however, specify, within six months after the accounting period in which a distribution is made, in which accounting period(s) it is to be treated as having been made. The amount so attributed to any accounting period may not exceed the undistributed income of the period, and the attribution may not be to accounting period(s) ending more than nine years before the date of the distribution unless the distribution exceeds the undistributed income of accounting periods ending before, but not more than nine years before, that date. A company may not generally specify that a distribution is to be treated as paid in the accounting period in which it was paid, but again subject to special rules for the categories of distribution referred to above.

The provisions are modified in cases where a lesser reduction in the rate of corporation tax applies by virtue of *F(No 2)A 1992, s 1* (see above).

In all cases, any balance of distributions not attributed to profits benefiting from manufacturing companies relief attract the normal tax credit (see 12.23 below). The company must identify such distributions in its returns, and if it appears to the inspector (who has powers to call for information) or the Commissioners on appeal that any excess tax credit has been vouched to the recipient of a distribution, a corresponding adjustment is made to the relief given or, in relation to distributions made after 5 April 1989, by assessment under Schedule D, Case IV on the company, unless there is 'good and sufficient reason' why it is just and reasonable that such an adjustment should not be made. [*FA 1980, ss 45, 46; CTA s 10A(3); FA 1988, s 32, 2 Sch; FA 1989, ss 24, 25; FA 1990, s 38; FA 1991, s 37; FA 1992, ss 37, 46(1)(a); F(No 2)A 1992, s 2*]. See also *FA 1993, s 46* as regards certain distributions by companies carrying on 'specified trades' within *CTA s 84A* (see 12.10 above).

An individual resident in, and only in, RI who is beneficially entitled to any such dividends paid after 5 April 1986 and **before 29 January 1992** by a company resident in RI is entitled to a deduction from total income of one half of the amount of the dividends plus attached tax credits (maximum deduction in any year of assessment £7,000), but is allowed the full amount of the tax credits. From 1987/88

(i)   relief is only granted in respect of qualifying dividends paid on *bona fide* ordinary share capital, and

(ii) the maximum deduction is increased to £9,000 where such dividends are received directly from a company at least 75% of whose sales are of goods within the manufacturing companies relief, and which has an approved profit sharing scheme for its employees (see 34.6 SCHEDULE E). The relief remains at £7,000 for dividends from other companies, with an overriding relief limit per individual of £9,000 from both sources.

This deduction is **abolished** in relation to dividends paid after 28 January 1992. [*FA 1986, s 14; FA 1987, s 5; FA 1992, s 13*].

Where a company is obliged to make distributions expressed at a gross rate or of a gross amount, and the obligation is, by *CTA s 178*, satisfied by a payment equivalent to the gross amount less tax at the deemed standard rate (see 12.10 above) on that amount, and the distribution carries a reduced tax credit as above, the company is required to make a supplementary distribution of an amount equal to the excess of the amount of the tax credit which would have applied if the reduced rate of tax credit above had not been applicable over that reduced tax credit. No tax credit is attached to the supplementary distribution, which must again be identified in the company's returns. [*FA 1980, s 49; FA 1988, s 32, 2 Sch*].

Group relief. See 12.14 above for the restriction on group relief of losses arising to companies within the manufacturing companies relief scheme.

12.18 NON-RESIDENTS

A **non-resident company** which carries on a trade in RI through a branch or agency is chargeable to CT on

(*a*) its trading income arising directly, or indirectly through the branch or agency (excluding distributions received from resident companies), and

(*b*) such capital gains as would be chargeable in the hands of non-residents under the *CGTA* on the disposal of any assets used, held or acquired for the purposes of the branch or agency.

[*CTA s 8*].

Non-resident companies remain liable to IT or CGT on income or chargeable gains arising in RI which is not or are not chargeable to CT. Where a non-resident company is chargeable to CT for one source of income and to IT for another, the capital allowances and balancing charges relating to particular income shall have effect in respect of the particular tax. [*CTA s 21(4)*].

Non-resident banks, insurance companies and investment companies carrying on business in RI are charged to CT on foreign interest and dividends received by them in respect of their RI business. (Such sums are normally exempt, see 29.2 SCHEDULE C; see also 12.11 above.) Certain reliefs are restricted. [*CTA ss 50, 51*].

Distributions. From 6 April 1992, a non-resident company is entitled to a tax credit in respect of any distribution received, and its liability to income tax in respect of the distribution is reduced by the amount by which that liability exceeds the available tax credit. Previously, no tax credit was available to non-resident companies (unless provided for in a double taxation agreement). [*CTA s 88; FA 1992, s 38; FA 1994, s 27; FA 1995, s 39*].

12.19 PAYMENTS–DEDUCTIONS OF TAX

All annual payments made by a resident company after 5 April 1976 are deemed not to have been made out of profits brought into charge to tax and accordingly the company is obliged under *Sec 434* to deduct standard rate IT from the payment (even if made to another resident company) and account separately to the Revenue for the tax. [*CTA s 3*]. Where such a payment is received by a company the tax so deducted will be set against the company's liability to CT, and may be reclaimed if there is no CT liability. [*CTA ss 3(2),4*]. The IT deducted may also be set off against the company's liability to IT deducted from payments it has itself made. [*CTA s 151(7)*].

For accounting periods ending after 31 March 1990, a return of every payment from which a company has been obliged to deduct income tax, including any deemed payment in respect of a loan by a close company to a participator (see 12.7 above), must be made within nine months of the end of the accounting period in which the payment was made, and the tax becomes due and payable without assessment at the same time as any preliminary tax for the period (see 28.12 RETURNS). The (net) income tax payable is treated for the purposes of charge, assessment, collection and recovery (and interest and penalties) as corporation tax payable for the accounting period, but without prejudice to the right to repayment as if it were income tax where appropriate. Returns of payments not made in an accounting period are required within six months after the date of the payment, and the income tax is due at the time by which the return must be made. Any assessment is treated as an income tax assessment for the year of assessment in which the payment was made. For accounting periods ending before 1 April 1990, returns and payments were in all cases required within six months of the end of the accounting period or, where the payment was not made in an accounting period, of the date of payment. [*CTA s 151; FA 1990, s 49*]. For accounting periods ending before 1 April 1990, and for income tax assessments in relation to later periods, the normal income tax provisions relating to assessments, appeals, payment and interest apply. [*CTA s 152; FA 1990, s 50*].

For accounting periods ending after 31 March 1990, a non-resident company within the charge to corporation tax must make a return of payments made in an accounting period from which it is required to deduct income tax under *Sec 434*. The income tax required to be deducted is treated as corporation tax chargeable for the accounting period for the purposes of charge, assessment, collection and recovery from the company, and of interest and penalties. [*FA 1990, s 51*].

Charges on income. An annual payment may be deductible for CT purposes as a charge on income, see 12.9 above.

12.19A PETROLEUM TAXATION

There are special provisions, contained in *FA 1992, ss 75–88 as amended*, for the taxation of petroleum activities of exploration, exploitation, or the acquisition, enjoyment or exploitation of petroleum rights. Broadly, such activities are ring-fenced, and a special reduced rate of corporation tax applies. There are also provisions dealing specifically with reliefs for development, exploration and abandonment expenditure and for petroleum valuations.

12.20 SMALL COMPANIES RELIEF (TO 31 MARCH 1989)

This reduced rate (see 12.2 above) applies to the *income* of an RI resident company whose *profits* for a twelve month accounting period do not exceed £25,000 (or proportionately for a shorter period). *Income* is profits charged to CT less the part attributable to chargeable gains (before any deduction for charges on income, expenses of management or other amounts which could otherwise be deducted from profits of more than one description). *Profits* are those charged to CT (including chargeable gains) plus any franked investment income (see 12.13 above) from companies not in the same group.

Taper relief applies where profits are between £25,000 and £35,000. The full rate is applied but the amount of the tax payable is (subject to below) reduced by

$$25\% \text{ of } (£35,000 - \text{profits}) \quad \times \quad \frac{\text{Income}}{\text{Profits}}$$

If a small company has one or more associated companies, the figures of £25,000 and £35,000 above are divided by one plus the number of associated companies in the accounting period (but an associated company which has not carried on any trade or business during that accounting period is disregarded). A company is an 'associated company' of another company if one of the two has control of the other or both are under common control of the same person or persons (see 12.7 above for 'control'). [*CTA s 28; FA 1977, s 17; FA 1978, s 21*]. See 38.41 TAX CASES as regards non-resident associated companies.

The reduced rate **ceases to apply after 31 March 1989,** and for this purpose an accounting period straddling that date is treated as consisting of two separate accounting periods, one ending on that date, the other commencing on the following day. For accounting periods ending after 31 March 1988, the figure of 25% in the tapering relief formula referred to above is changed to 17.5%, and for this purpose an accounting period straddling that date is similarly treated as two separate accounting periods, one ending on and one beginning immediately after that date. [*FA 1988, s 33(2), 3 Sch*].

12.21 SPECIAL BODIES

Industrial and provident societies. Any share or loan interest paid by a society registered under the *Industrial and Provident Societies Acts 1893–1971* is not subject to deduction of tax if paid to an RI resident (chargeable instead under Schedule D, Case III) and is not a distribution. [*CTA s 30(2) as inserted by FA 1978, s 19*].

Any discount, rebate, dividend or bonus granted by a society to members or others in respect of transactions with the society is deductible as an expense so long as the discount etc. was based on the magnitude of the transaction and not on any share or interest in the capital of the society. Share or loan interest ranks as a deductible expense if wholly and exclusively for the purposes of a trade. [*Sec 219; CTA s 30(5); FA 1978, s 19*].

Every society must make a return on or before 1 May each year showing the name and address of every person to whom it has paid share or loan interest of £70 or more in the previous year of assessment and showing the amount actually paid. If such a return is not duly made, the society is precluded from relief under *Sec 85(1)(e)* (short leases, see 33.6 SCHEDULE D, CASE V) or *Sec 219* (see above) or *CTA s 10* (charges on income) for that year of assessment. [*CTA s 30(4); FA 1978, s 19*].

In computing shareholdings for the purpose of group relief for trading losses, etc., or for group capital gains (see 12.14 above), any share capital of a registered industrial and provident society is treated as ordinary share capital. [*CTA ss 107(6), 129(1)(d)*].

Agricultural and fishery co-operatives. Up to 31 March 1992, any trading income or loss of industrial and provident societies which are agricultural societies or fishery societies (see below) from 'exempted transactions' is disregarded for all tax purposes. The exemption applies to a society if throughout the accounting period it has 50 members or more (20 for a fishery society), the majority of whom are mainly engaged in and derive their income principally from husbandry/fishing, or if it is certified for exemption by the Minister for Finance. Certificates granted for the earlier exemption under *Sec 220* have effect for this purpose. [*FA 1978, s 18(1)–(3), 4 Sch*].

Exempted transactions covers wholesale sales, except to an EC intervention agency, of goods and the provision of services, listed in *FA 1978, 2 Sch* (as amended by *FA 1983, s 34* and

FA 1984, s 43). Income from a sale of goods which is an exempted transaction is not eligible for exported goods relief. [*FA 1978, s 18(1)(6)*].

Trading income for exemption purposes is income after deduction of capital allowances etc. but before loss relief. Where part of a society's income is exempt there is proportionate reduction in its charges on income and allowable losses. Unclaimed allowances under *FA 1976, s 33(4)* may not be carried forward to the period beginning on 1 April 1978. [*FA 1978, s 18(4)–(9); FA 1979, s 21(4)*].

Where the exemption is claimed, an inspector may request to see appropriate books and records. [*FA 1978, s 18(10)*].

This exemption is abolished (subject to transitional provisions, see below) for transactions after 31 March 1992. Losses incurred prior to abolition are available after that date as if the previous exemption had not applied. Income attributable to transactions which would have attracted exemption but for its abolition, and which does not attract manufacturing companies relief (see 12.17 above), is relieved as to two-thirds where it arises before 1 January 1993 and as to one-third where it arises in 1993. For these purposes accounting periods are treated as split into separate accounting periods up to and from appropriate dates, and income is attributed to transactions in proportion to amounts receivable in respect of such transactions. [*FA 1992, s 48*].

Transfers to members of shares held in co-operatives. Transfers after 5 April 1993 by agricultural and fishery co-operatives of shares in subsidiary companies are granted certain tax exemptions, provided that the shares are distributed in proportion to the members' shares held in the co-operative before the transfer, that a corresponding proportion of each member's shares in the co-operative is cancelled following the transfer, that there is no other consideration for the transfer or cancellation, and that the transfer is effected for *bona fide* commercial reasons and does not form part of a scheme or arrangement a main purpose of which is the avoidance of corporation tax or capital gains tax. Where these conditions are met:

(*a*)   the transfer is not treated as a distribution (see 12.10 above);

(*b*)   the transfer is treated as being at no gain/no loss to the society for chargeable gains purposes;

(*c*)   the cancellation of each member's shares in the co-operative is not treated as a disposal for capital gains tax purposes; and

(*d*)   the shares transferred to a member are treated for capital gains tax purposes as acquired at the same time and for the same consideration as the member's cancelled shares in the co-operative. [*FA 1993, s 35*].

See 12.12 above as regards exemption of certain grants.

Bank levy. There are special provisions for a bank or banking group which is liable to pay the bank levy under *FA 1992, s 200* to set off a part of the levy against its corporation tax liability. [*FA 1992, s 45; FA 1995, s 56*].

Building societies: change of status. Where a building society converts into a company under *Building Societies Act 1989, Pt XI*, the following special provisions apply.

Capital allowances. The conversion does not give rise to any balancing adjustments, and the successor company stands in the shoes of the society as regards subsequent allowances and charges.

Financial assets. Financial assets constituting trading stock are valued at cost on the conversion for the purposes of *Sec 62* (trading stock of discontinued trade, see 30.27 SCHEDULE D, CASES I AND II). The vesting in the successor company of financial assets, profits on whose disposal would be chargeable under Schedule D, Case I, does not constitute a disposal, and the profit on disposal of those assets by the successor company is calculated by reference to the cost to the society.

Capital gains: assets vested in successor company. The conversion does not constitute a disposal for capital gains purposes, and all actions by the society in relation to such assets are treated as actions of the company for all subsequent capital gains matters.

Capital gains tax: shares etc. in successor company. Any right to acquire shares in the successor company on favourable terms conferred on a member of the society is treated as an option acquired for no consideration and having, at the time of grant, no value (see 9.15 CAPITAL GAINS TAX).

Shares issued to members are treated as acquired for the new consideration (if any) given and as having a value equal to that acquisition cost at the time of acquisition. Where the shares are issued to trustees as settled property on terms providing for their transfer to members for no consideration, they are treated as acquired by the trustees for no consideration, the member's interest in the shares is treated as acquired for no consideration and as having no value, and when the member becomes absolutely entitled to the shares (or would do so but for a legal disability), the shares are treated as disposed of and reacquired by the trustees at no gain/no loss.

Groups of companies. In relation to groups of companies (see 12.14 above), 'company' includes a building society incorporated under the *Building Societies Act 1989*, or deemed to be incorporated under *section 124(2)* of that *Act*.

[*FA 1990, ss 57, 58, 3 Sch*].

Collective investment undertakings. From 6 April 1994 (25 May 1993 if business was not commenced before that date, **6 April 1998** in the case of 'designated' and 'guaranteed undertakings for collective investment'), a new taxation regime applies to '*undertakings for collective investment*', i.e. those set up and authorised under the *European Communities (Undertakings for Collective Investment in Transferable Securities) Regulations 1989 (SI 1989 No 78)*, schemes which are, or are deemed to be, authorised unit trust schemes within the meaning of the *Unit Trusts Act 1990* (other than unit trusts within *CGTA 1975, s 31*, see 9.14 CAPITAL GAINS TAX, and special investment schemes within *FA 1993, s 13*, see 16.23 EXEMPT INCOME AND SPECIAL SAVINGS SCHEMES), and any authorised investment company, within the meaning of *Companies Act 1990, Pt XIII*, which has been designated in that authorisation as being able to raise capital by promoting the sale of its shares to the public, but excluding any 'offshore fund' (see 32.8 SCHEDULE D, CASE IV) and 'specified collective investment undertakings' (see below). For those categories of collective investment undertaking excluded from these provisions (as above), the earlier provisions described below continue to apply.

Broadly, the income and gains of such undertakings are taxable at a rate equivalent to the standard rate of income tax. *Non-company unitholders* are not entitled to any credit for or repayment of tax paid by the undertaking, but have no further liability as regards any payments received from the undertaking in respect of the units, and no capital gains tax liability on the disposal of units acquired after 5 April 1994 (or 5 April 1988 where applicable). As regards any units held on 5 April 1994 (or 5 April 1998), a chargeable gain or allowable loss arises on disposal by a non-company unitholder by reference to the market value of the units on that date (with inflation indexing and exemption under *CGTA 1975, s 31(5)* (see 9.14 CAPITAL GAINS TAX) as if disposed of on that date), unless

(*a*)   a smaller gain or a smaller loss accrued by reference to the actual disposal, in which case the normal rules apply by reference to the actual disposal, or

(*b*)   (in the case of a gain) a loss accrued by reference to the actual disposal or (in the case of a loss) a gain accrued by reference to the actual disposal, in which case the disposal is treated as giving rise to neither gain nor loss.

For *company unitholders*, any payment received from the undertaking in respect of units is treated as the net amount of an annual payment, chargeable under Schedule D, Case IV, from which income tax has been deducted at the standard rate. Any chargeable gain accruing on the disposal of units after 5 April 1994 (or 5 April 1998 where applicable) is similarly treated as the net amount of a gain from the gross amount of which capital gains tax has been deducted at the standard rate of income tax. The gross amount of the gain is brought into charge for the accounting period of the disposal, the capital gains tax treated as deducted being set off against corporation tax for the period, any excess being repaid to the company. As regards any units held on 5 April 1994 (or 5 April 1998), the above provisions apply only to that part of the chargeable gain which would have accrued had the units been disposed of at market value on 5 April 1994 (or 5 April 1998). These provisions do not apply to the computation of allowable losses. Special provisions apply in relation to financial traders such as banks and insurance companies.

For all unitholders, where the units were acquired in a no gain/no loss transaction, ownership is treated as having included that of the previous owner(s) prior to such transactions. The capital gains tax provisions relating to units held on 5 April 1994 (or 5 April 1998) do not apply in the case of units in undertakings which commenced business after 25 May 1993.

As regards the determination of the profits of an undertaking for collective investment which are liable to standard rate tax as above, the following specific provisions apply:

(i)   distributions (including the attached tax credit) received by the undertaking are taxable, the tax credit being available against its taxation liabilities, any excess being repayable;

(ii) the capital gains tax exemption of government securities (see 9.7(*e*) CAPITAL GAINS TAX) does not apply;

(iii) assets (other than government securities) are treated as disposed of and reacquired at market value at the end of each chargeable period, the resultant net gain or loss being spread over that period and subsequent chargeable periods, at the rate of one-seventh per twelve months chargeable period (the whole remaining balance being chargeable if the undertaking ceases business before the whole gain or loss has been charged or allowed);

(iv) if the undertaking was carrying on business on 25 May 1993, it is treated as having acquired its assets at market value on 5 April 1994 (or 5 April 1998 where applicable);

(v)   inflation indexing (see 9.9 CAPITAL GAINS TAX) does not apply to disposals; and

(vi) net allowable losses for a chargeable period are set against income arising in that period, any excess being carried forward.

A '*designated undertaking for collective investment*' is a collective investment undertaking 80% of whose assets (in terms of consideration given), on 25 May 1993, were land or unquoted securities. A '*guaranteed undertaking for collective investment*' is such an undertaking all of the issued units of which, on 25 May 1993, carried a right to a single payment of a fixed amount plus an amount (which may be nil) related to a stock exchange index or indices. The references to 5 April 1988 in relation to designated and guaranteed undertakings may be amended to an earlier 5 April (1994 or later) where, in the case of a designated undertaking, the 80% limit ceases to be exceeded in the preceding year, and in the case of a guaranteed undertaking, a payment is made to unitholders in the preceding year other than in cancellation of the units.

CGTA 1975, s 32 (see 9.14 CAPITAL GAINS TAX) has no effect in relation to undertakings for collective investment, and the provisions in *FA 1976, s 13* and *CTA s 101* (see 36.1 SETTLE-

MENTS and 12.7 above respectively) for surcharges on undistributed income do not apply. 'Relevant payments' out of 'relevant profits' (as defined under the earlier legislation, see below), and payments for the cancellation, redemption or repurchase of units are similarly not treated as distributions (see 12.10 above).

[*FA 1989, s 18(7)–(9); FA 1993, ss 17, 18; FA 1994, s 57*].

Before 6 April 1994 (or **25 May 1993** or **6 April 1998** as appropriate, see above), a separate tax regime is applicable to collective investment undertakings (defined broadly as above, see *FA 1989, s 18(1) as amended by FA 1991, s 19(1)(a); FA 1994, s 25(1)(a); FA 1995, s 38*), from 24 May 1989 in the case of a '*specified collective investment undertaking*' (i.e. broadly one most of whose RI business is carried on in the Custom House Docks Area (see *FA 1986, 4 Sch Pt II*) or in the customs-free airport, and all the holders of units in which are resident outside RI), and from 6 April 1990 (or such earlier day in the preceding year as may be agreed) in any other case. This regime continues to apply after 5 April 1994 in the case of those collective investment undertakings excluded from the provisions generally applicable after that date (see above), and may also from a specified date apply to certain property investment limited partnerships of non-RI residents (subject to their authorisation by the Central Bank).

Where this applies, the '*relevant profits*' (i.e. 'relevant income' and 'relevant gains') are not chargeable to tax on the undertaking, but are chargeable in the hands of any unit holder to whom a '*relevant payment*' is made (i.e. a payment by virtue of rights as a unit holder, other than in respect of the cancellation, redemption or repurchase of a unit) out of those profits, and who would have been taxable in RI on those profits if they had been received direct. Income is treated as arising at the time of the payment and is chargeable under Schedule D, Case IV, and gains are treated as capital distributions made by a unit trust (see 9.14 CAPITAL GAINS TAX).

As originally enacted, the unit trust schemes within these provisions were registered schemes within the meaning of the *Unit Trusts Act 1972*, but after 25 December 1990 this was amended to refer to schemes which are, or are deemed to be, authorised schemes (whose authorisation has not been revoked) within the meaning of the *Unit Trusts Act 1990*. Also within the provisions, after 31 January 1991, is any authorised investment company (whose authorisation has not been revoked), within the meaning of *Companies Act 1990, Pt XIII*, which has been (and continues to be) designated in that authorisation as being able to raise capital by promoting the sale of its shares to the public.

With effect after 5 April 1990, certain unit trust schemes which require, or have required, any or all participators to effect a policy of assurance upon human life (but without the units in respect of which the requirement applied becoming the property of the owner of the policy) are not collective investment undertakings for these purposes. Such schemes are, however, treated as collective investment undertakings with effect from 1 April 1992 where, not later than 1 November 1992, the trustees pay one-half of the capital gains tax which would have been chargeable if they had disposed of all scheme assets at market value on 31 March 1992, and notified the Revenue Commissioners accordingly. Unit holders are treated for capital gains tax purposes as having acquired their units on 31 March 1992.

After 31 March 1991, certain limited companies wholly owned by specified collective investment undertakings (as above), or by the trustees thereof, to enable them to invest in certain financial instruments, are themselves specified collective investment undertakings.

In relation to collective investment undertakings, *CGTA 1975, s 32* (see 9.14 CAPITAL GAINS TAX) has no effect, and the provisions in *FA 1976, s 13* and *CTA s 101* (see 36.1 SETTLEMENTS and 12.7 above respectively) for surcharges on undistributed income do not apply. Relevant payments out of relevant profits, and payments for cancellation, redemption or repurchase of units, are similarly not treated as distributions (see 12.10 above).

Double tax arrangements under *Sec 361* (see 15.2 DOUBLE TAX RELIEF) may not apply to collective investment undertakings, but *Sec 200* is not to apply to treat a non-resident as taxable in the name of an agent in RI in respect of a relevant payment out of relevant profits.

'*Relevant income*' is income, profits or gains which in the hands of an RI resident individual would be taxable as income, and '*relevant gains*' are gains which would similarly constitute chargeable gains in the hands of an RI resident.

Undertakings other than specified collective investment undertakings (see above) are required to deduct and to account to the Revenue for (as to which see *FA 1989, 1 Sch*) the 'appropriate tax' in respect of any relevant payment made out of profits to an RI-resident unit holder, and of any undistributed income at the end of an accounting period from which tax has not previously been deducted. The '*appropriate tax*' is tax at the standard rate of income tax at the time of the payment or at the end of the accounting period, as appropriate, less an allowance for any tax previously deducted from undistributed income out of which a relevant payment is made, and for tax deducted under any other provision of the Taxes Acts from profits out of which a relevant payment is made or from undistributed income. The unit holder receiving a relevant payment from which appropriate tax has been deducted (or out of relevant profits from which such tax has been deducted) is liable (as above) on the sum of the actual payment and the appropriate tax deducted therefrom, and is entitled to a credit for the appropriate tax and to repayment where the credit exceeds his liability to tax in respect of the relevant payment (e.g. where he is in fact not RI resident at the time of the payment). Any necessary apportionment of the appropriate tax is made on a just and reasonable basis by the inspector (or, on appeal, by the Appeal Commissioners).

[*FA 1989, s 18, 1 Sch; FA 1990, s 35; FA 1991, s 19; FA 1992, s 36; FA 1994, s 25*].

General. There are information requirements relating to RI resident holders of units in collective investment undertakings, which must be satisfied by any intermediary for an undertaking which markets its units in RI but is situated in another member state. [*FA 1989, s 19; FA 1992, ss 226, 228, 229*]. See also Statement of Practice SP–IT/1/92 and 28.14 RETURNS.

Company carrying on a mutual business or not carrying on business. The provisions relating to tax credit, etc. will not apply to any distribution by such a company unless it is made out of profits charged to CT or out of franked investment income. [*CTA s 29*].

Partnerships involving companies. As under IT, partners are assessed individually (see 30.6 SCHEDULE D, CASES I AND II). There are provisions for apportionment of accounting periods and the relevant amount of any capital allowance or balancing charge which would be applicable under IT rules is transformed into a trading expense or receipt, respectively, for CT purposes. [*CTA s 32*].

Securitisation of assets. A company carrying on only a business of managing mortgage loans, acquired at arm's length from companies whose trade consists of or includes the making of such loans, is treated as carrying on a trade within Case I of Schedule D, with appropriate deductions in respect of bad and doubtful debts. [*FA 1991, s 31*].

Trustee savings banks: amalgamations. Where any assets or liabilities of a trustee savings bank are transferred (or deemed to be transferred) to another under *Trustee Savings Banks Act 1989, Pt VI*, those banks are treated for tax purposes as the same person. [*FA 1990, s 59*].

Trustee savings banks: corporation tax. Trustee savings banks are brought within the charge to corporation tax from 1 April 1993. [*FA 1993, s 42*]. From that date, the exemptions under *Sec 337* (see 17.16 EXEMPT ORGANISATIONS) are withdrawn. However, trading income of a trustee savings bank is for corporation tax purposes reduced by 75% for the year ending 31 March 1994, by 50% for the year ending 31 March 1995, and by 25% for the year ending 31 March 1996, accounting periods being deemed to end on 31 March and commence on 1 April for this purpose. [*FA 1993, s 43*].

Trustee savings banks: reorganisation into companies. Special provisions apply on the reorganisation of one or more trustee savings banks into a company (whether controlled by the Minister for Finance or not), or of a company within *subparagraph (i)* of the *Trustee Savings Banks Act 1989, s 57(3)(c)* (company controlled by the Minister) into a company within *subparagraph (ii)* of that *subsection* (company not so controlled).

Capital allowances. The transfer does not give rise to any balancing adjustment, and the successor stands in the shoes of the trustee savings bank as regards subsequent allowances and charges, except that no carry-forward is permitted of allowances unused by the trustee savings bank.

Trading losses incurred by a company controlled by the Minister may not be carried forward for set off against profits of a company not so controlled.

Financial assets. Financial assets constituting trading stock are valued at cost on the reorganisation for the purposes of *Sec 62* (trading stock of discontinued trade, see 30.27 SCHEDULE D, CASES I AND II). The acquisition by the successor company of any assets, profits on whose disposal would be chargeable under Schedule D, Case I, does not constitute a disposal, and the profit on disposal of those assets by the successor company is calculated by reference to the original cost to the bank.

Capital gains. The disposal of an asset by the bank to the successor company in the course of the reorganisation is treated as being at no gain/no loss, and on any subsequent disposal the successor is treated as if the original acquisition were the successor's acquisition. Unused allowable losses may be transferred to the successor. For rollover relief purposes (see 9.7(*r*) CAPITAL GAINS TAX) the bank and the successor are treated as if they were the same person, and in relation to any debt transferred to the successor, for capital gains tax purposes (see 9.7(*m*) CAPITAL GAINS TAX) the successor is treated as the original creditor.

[*FA 1990, ss 60, 61, 4 Sch*].

12.22 INVESTMENT IN FILMS

An 'allowable investor company' which makes a 'relevant investment' in a 'qualifying company' during the 'qualifying period' commencing on 9 July 1987 and ending on 31 March 1996 may claim an investment not exceeding £350,000 in a 12 month period ending on 8 July (£200,000 in relation to investments before 6 May 1993, £100,000 for each of the two periods ending on 8 July 1988 and 8 July 1989) as a deduction against profits. The relief is extended to 'qualifying individual' investors during a 'qualifying period' commencing on 6 May 1993 and ending on 5 April 1996, but with a limit of £25,000 in each year of assessment (and a minimum of £200).

The 'qualifying company' must be engaged solely in the production and distribution of 'qualifying films' on a commercial basis. This means cinema and television films, and excludes commercial and advertising films (and see below).

An *'allowable investor company'* is a company which is not connected with the 'qualifying company' in which the investment is made.

A *'relevant investment'* means a sum of money which is

(a)   paid in a qualifying period to a 'qualifying company' whether in respect of shares in that qualifying company, or otherwise, by an allowable investor company (or, after 5 May 1993, a 'qualifying individual') on its (or his) own behalf; and (*b*)   paid by such an allowable investor company (or qualifying individual) for the purpose of enabling the 'qualifying company' to produce a 'qualifying film'; and

(*c*)   used by the 'qualifying company', within two years of the receipt of that sum, for that purpose.

As regards (*a*) above, investments made before 14 January 1994 otherwise than in respect of shares could also qualify as relevant investments (and this also applies to investments made before 2 August 1994 where the Revenue Commissioners had before 14 January 1994 expressed an opinion that a particular such investment would be a relevant investment in a qualifying company).

A relevant investment does not include a sum of money paid to the 'qualifying company' on terms that it will be repaid.

A '*qualifying company*' is a company which

(i)   is incorporated in the State; and

(ii)   is resident in the State; and

(iii)   exists solely for the purposes of the production and distribution of a 'qualifying film' or 'qualifying films'.

A '*qualifying individual*' is an individual not connected with the qualifying company.

For relevant investments made after 22 May 1994, a '*qualifying film*' is a film in respect of which the Minister for Arts, Culture and the Gaeltacht has given a certificate under *FA 1987, s 35(1A)* (inserted by *FA 1994, s 20(1)(b)*). The Minister may give such a certificate in accordance with guidelines issued by the Minister for Finance, and the general conditions for the issue of such a certificate are broadly unchanged from those previously applicable, although the Minister may impose such other conditions as he thinks proper. The definition applicable for investments before 23 May 1994, which (as stated above) continues generally to apply, is that a qualifying film in respect of which not less than 75% of the work on the production of the film is carried out in the State, and not more than 60% of the cost of production of the film is met by relevant investments. In relation to investments after 5 May 1993, where at least 10% but less than 75% of production work is carried out in the State, the Minister for Arts, Culture and the Gaeltacht may give a certificate that the film is to be treated as a qualifying film. In such cases, however, the percentage of production costs which may be met by relevant investments is the lesser of the percentage of production work carried out in the State and 60%.

Grant of relief. Relief is given to an allowable investor company as a deduction from total profits in the accounting period in which the investment is made, and, subject to the overall annual maximum (as above), any excess of investment made over profits may be carried forward to the succeeding accounting period. Relief is given to a qualifying individual as a deduction from total income for the year of assessment in which the investment is made as if it were a personal allowance, and, subject to the overall annual limits (as above), any unused relief due to an insufficiency of total income or to investment in excess of the annual limit may be carried forward and treated as a relevant investment of the next year of assessment, or (if still unused) to a later year. For this purpose, relief is treated as referable first to brought forward investments (earliest first) and then to current year investments. No relief may be carried forward beyond 1995/96.

Where a company, together with companies connected with it, makes an investment or investments exceeding the annual maximum (see above) in a 12-month period ending on 8 July, no relief is given for the excess and the available relief, where necessary, is apportioned by the inspector of taxes (or, on appeal, the Appeal Commissioners) when more than one investment has been made or connected companies are involved.

In relation to investments after 8 July 1989, where the total investment in a qualifying company by the investor company (and any companies connected with it) in a twelve-month period ending on 8 July exceeds £350,000 (£200,000 in relation to investments before 6 May 1993), and is made for the purpose of enabling one, and only one, qualifying film to be made, the investor company (and any companies connected with it) may elect for relief for that year to be given in respect of £1,050,000 (£600,000 in relation to investments before 6 May 1993), reduced by any other relevant investments made by the investor company (and companies connected with it) in the two immediately preceding years (but disregarding investments made before 9 July 1989). No further relief is then available to the investor company or any connected company in that year or the following two years.

In relation to investments after 22 May 1994, a claim must be accompanied by a certificate stating that the conditions for relief in relation to the company and the qualifying film are or will be satisfied, issued by the company with the authority of an authorised officer of the Revenue Commissioners (to whom the company must make a statement to similar effect and, after 12 April 1995, furnish a copy of the qualifying film certificate issued by the Minister (as above)). A penalty of up to £500 (£1,000 in cases of fraud) may be imposed on a company making such a certificate or statement fraudulently or negligently, or issuing a certificate without due authority.

Relief may not also be claimed concurrently under any other section of the *Income Tax, Corporation Tax* or *Capital Gains Tax Acts*.

Withdrawal of relief. Relief may be withdrawn if conditions are not satisfied, and the relevant investment must be

(A)   made for *bona fide* commercial purposes and not as part of a tax avoidance scheme; and

(B)   used by the qualifying company within two years of receipt for the production of a qualifying film; and

(C)   made at the risk of the investor company or individual on the basis of an arm's length commercial arrangement.

Assessment of withdrawn relief, without time limit, may be made under Schedule D, Case IV for the accounting period or year of assessment in which the relief was originally given.

Disposal of shares. When the allowable investor company or qualifying individual retains new ordinary shares in the qualifying company for more than three years, and the shares are subsequently sold, the original cost of purchase is not reduced for capital gains tax purposes by the tax relief granted unless the relief exceeds the sale consideration. When this occurs the cost is reduced by the lesser of the excess of tax relief over consideration and the relief itself. These provisions do not, however, apply on a transfer between spouses.

In relation to investments after 8 July 1989, where the shares are disposed of not less than twelve months after acquisition, and the consideration used within twelve months to make a further relevant investment in a qualifying company's shares (the sum being used to produce a different qualifying film), then the capital gains tax relief (as above) applies in respect of that consideration as if the shares had been held for three years. If the qualifying investment exceeds £350,000 (or £200,000, as appropriate) and an election is made for relief of a larger sum up to £1,050,000 (or £600,000, as appropriate) (see above), this treatment applies without the requirement for reinvestment of the consideration, to the whole of the consideration for the qualifying shares if the qualifying investment (or the total of such investments relating to the qualifying film) is £1,050,000 (£600,000), otherwise to the proportion thereof corresponding to the proportion of the relevant investment(s) which exceeds £350,000 (£200,000). Where this does not apply, the requirement for reinvestment is similarly waived for disposals not less than twelve months after acquisition in relation to an investment in the period from 9 July 1994 to 8 July 1995 inclusive in a qualifying company existing solely for the purposes of the production and distribution of a film or films the cost of production of which (or of each of which) does not exceed £1,050,000, and which (or each of which) is certified for the purpose by the Minister for Arts, Culture and the Gaeltacht (such certification being separate from that required for a film to be a 'qualifying film').

[*FA 1987, s 35; FA 1989, s 28; FA 1992, s 58; FA 1993, s 48; FA 1994, s 20; FA 1995, s 36*].

12.23 TAX CREDIT

In general, any person receiving a distribution is treated as receiving it net of standard rate income tax (but see below) and credited with having paid that amount of tax. An individual whose liability to income tax is less than his total tax credits may claim repayment of the balance while an individual liable to higher rate income tax on the distribution (plus the tax credit) will have to make an additional payment. [*CTA s 88(4)*]. A company receives tax-credited distributions in the form of 'franked investment income'. See above, 12.10 and 12.11.

From 6 April 1992, a person who is neither resident nor ordinarily resident is entitled to a tax credit in respect of any distribution received, to be set against the liability to income tax for the year of receipt, and its liability to income tax in respect of the distribution is reduced by the amount by which that liability exceeds the available tax credit. In certain cases of individual non-residents claiming proportionate personal allowances under *Sec 153(2)*, any excess tax credit may be repaid. Previously, no tax credit was available to non-residents (unless provided for in a double taxation agreement or in relation to *Sec 153(2)* claims, see above). [*CTA s 88; FA 1992, s 38; FA 1994, s 27; FA 1995, s 39*].

A reduced amount is credited in respect of certain distributions out of income bearing a reduced rate of CT as a result of a claim to manufacturing companies' relief (see 12.17 above). [*FA 1980, s 45; FA 1988, s 32; FA 1989, ss 24, 25*]. See also 12.10 above.

The amount of the credit represents tax at the standard rate (see 2.5 ALLOWANCES AND RATES — currently 35%) of income tax. For distributions made in 1988/89, the standard rate was assumed to be 32%; for those made in 1989/90 and 1990/91, 28%; for those made in 1991/92 to 1994/95 inclusive, 25%; for those made after 5 April 1995, 23%. [*FA 1988, s 31, 2 Sch; FA 1991, s 36, 1 Sch; FA 1995, s 45, 2 Sch*].

A company which issues a warrant, cheque or order in payment of a dividend or of interest which is a distribution must (under penalty) accompany it with a statement of details in writing, including the amount of the tax credit which would apply if the recipient was a person entitled to a tax credit. [*CTA s 5*]. In the case of any other kind of distribution the recipient may by notice in writing require the company to furnish him with such details. [*CTA s 83(5)*].

See 12.25 below as regards a company's liability to advance corporation tax in respect of distributions.

12.24 TRANSFERS OF ASSETS — EEC DIRECTIVE 90/434/EEC

FA 1992, ss 65–74 give effect to certain elements of the 'Mergers Directive' (90/434/EEC) which were not already covered by RI legislation. These relate in the main to transfers of assets where trades are transferred in exchange for shares. They apply generally to transfers after 31 December 1991.

Transfers of assets generally. Where a company transfers the whole or part of a trade carried on in RI to another company in return for securities of the transferee, then:

(i)   the transferee takes over the capital allowances position of the transferor, no balancing allowances or charges arising on the transfer;

(ii)   the transferee takes over the chargeable gains position of the transferor, the transfer giving rise to no disposal for this purpose; and

(iii)   if the transferee disposes of the assets acquired within six years, the allowable deductions on the disposal are reduced by the appropriate proportion of the net chargeable gains which would have been arisen on the transferor but for (ii) above.

(i)–(iii) above do not, however, apply if

(*a*)   immediately after the transfer, the assets are not used by the transferee in an RI trade, or the transferee would not be chargeable in respect of any gains were it to dispose of any of the assets, or any of the assets are exempt from RI tax on disposal under a double taxation agreement, or

(*b*)   the transferor and transferee jointly so elect (by the due date for the return for the transferor's accounting period of the transfer, see 28.12 RETURNS).

[*FA 1992, s 65*].

Transfer of asset to parent company. Where an asset in use for an RI trade is transferred to a company owning the whole of the transferor's capital, and the transfer would not otherwise fall within *CTA s 130* (transfers within a group, see 12.14 above), then *CTA ss 130–132* have effect as if the companies were RI-resident, provided that the asset is, immediately after the transfer, used in an RI trade, and that *FA 1992, s 65* (see above) does not apply. The exclusions from *section 65* described at (*a*) and (*b*) above apply also for these purposes. [*FA 1992, s 66*].

Transfer of development land. Where, after 23 April 1992, a company disposes of development land (see 9.16 CAPITAL GAINS TAX) to another company, *FA 1992, s 65* (see above) does not apply to the disposal, and *CTA s 127* (reconstructions and amalgamations, see 12.5 above) would apply had the disposal not been of development land, then the disposal is treated as being at no gain/no loss, the acquiring company taking over the chargeable gains position of the disposing company. [*FA 1992, s 67*].

The provisions of *CTA ss 130, 132, 135, 136* relating to transfers within a group are applied to disposals of development land [*FA 1992, s 68*], and an amendment made to *CTA s 132* (disposal or acquisition outside a group) where there have been multiple intra-group disposals of development land. [*FA 1992, s 73*].

Credit for tax. Where an RI-resident company transfers the whole or part of a trade carried on through a branch or agency in another Member State to a non-resident company, including all the assets used in the trade, and the consideration for the transfer consists wholly or partly of securities of the transferee company, then foreign tax which would have been payable on the transfer but for the Directive, or for domestic legislation deferring a charge to tax on gains in the case of such a transfer, is treated as tax payable for the purposes of double tax relief. [*FA 1992, s 69*].

Anti-avoidance. *FA 1992, ss 65–69* (see above) do not have effect as respects a transfer unless it can be shown that the transfer was effected for *bona fide* commercial reasons and not as part of a scheme or arrangement a main purpose of which was the avoidance of income tax, corporation tax or capital gains tax. [*FA 1992, s 70*].

Returns are required by the transferor company of transfers within *FA 1992, ss 65–69* (above), within nine months of the end of the accounting period of the transfer. [*FA 1992, s 71*].

There are also provisions for such further relief to be given as the Revenue Commissioners consider just and reasonable in implementation of the Directive [*FA 1992, s 72*], and for adjudication on any necessary apportionments. [*FA 1992, s 74*].

12.25   ADVANCE CORPORATION TAX

Following the making of any distribution (see 12.10 above), an RI-resident company becomes liable to make a payment of advance corporation tax (ACT). The amount of the payment is the amount of the tax credit (see 12.23 above) to which a person entitled to tax credit would be entitled in respect of the distribution. [*FA 1983, s 38*].

Company also receiving distribution(s). The ACT for which a company is liable in respect of an accounting period is reduced by the amount of the tax credit attached to distributions made by RI-resident companies and received by the company in the accounting period (see also 12.13 above). Any surplus of tax credits attached to such distributions received in a period (insofar as not repaid to the company) is carried forward and treated as a tax credit in respect of a distribution received by the company in the next accounting period (and so on for subsequent periods). This provision applies equally to the amount of a tax credit, attached to a distribution received, payment of which is obtained but which is subsequently recovered from the company by an assessment under SCHEDULE D, CASE IV (31) (e.g. because the company wishes to set losses against taxable profits and opts for such treatment). If the amount so carried forward to an accounting period is (or becomes) excessive, the inspector has powers to ensure that the ACT payable for the accounting period is as it would have been if the correct amount had been carried forward.

See below, however, as regards certain dividends which are not treated as distributions for these purposes. [*FA 1983, ss 41, 42*].

Repayment of tax credit in respect of distributions received in an accounting period is restricted to that part not used to reduce liability to ACT in respect of distributions made in the period. For this purpose, any surplus tax credit brought forward to the period is treated as reducing liability to ACT before tax credits in respect of distributions received in the accounting period. [*FA 1983, s 43*].

Returns and collection. A return must be made, within nine months (six months for accounting periods ending before 1 April 1990) of the end of an accounting period in which a distribution has been made, of the amounts of all distributions made or received in the period (specifying any not treated for ACT purposes as distributions — see below), of the related tax credits, of any tax credit brought forward in respect of distributions received in an earlier accounting period, and of the ACT payable. If a distribution is made on a date not falling in an accounting period, it is treated as if made on the last day of an accounting period. The ACT is payable without assessment within six months of the end of the accounting period, and may be assessed on the company. For accounting periods ending after 30 April 1993, it is payable by the 28th of the month if it would otherwise be payable by a later day in the month. The usual assessment provisions apply where the inspector is not satisfied with a return. The tax is then payable within one month of issue of the notice of assessment, and interest runs in respect of the tax assessed as if it was payable at the normal due date if a correct return had been made.

The inspector has powers to ensure that all liabilities (including interest) are correctly imposed where any item is included in a return in error.

The normal corporation tax provisions as regards returns, assessments, appeals and recovery apply with the necessary modifications to ACT, except that interest on unpaid tax is at the rate of 1.25% per month or part month whether or not an assessment has been made, with no period of grace, and no part of any tax assessed may be postponed pending appeal. [*FA 1983, s 50; FA 1990, s 55; FA 1993, s 41*].

Distributions to non-residents. The following distributions are not treated as such for ACT purposes, and no tax credit is available in respect of them if, with the recipient's consent, the payer so claims in the ACT return for the period during which the distribution was made.

139

(i)   Interest on company securities which is classed as a distribution under *CTA s 84(2)(d)(iv)* (see 12.10(*d*)(iv) above).

(ii) A dividend paid to a company resident in the US or in a territory with which a double taxation agreement is in force by virtue of *Sec 361* (see 15.2 DOUBLE TAX RELIEF — INCOME AND CAPITAL GAINS) and of which the issuing company is a 75% subsidiary.

[*FA 1983, s 47*].

Section 84 loans. Special provisions apply where an obligation was entered into before 9 February 1983 (or before 9 June 1983 pursuant to negotiations in progress on 9 February 1983) to pay interest on securities issued as under *CTA s 84(2)(d)(ii)(iii)(I)(v)* (see 12.10(*d*)(ii)(iii)(I)(v) above) to a company carrying on a money-lending business. Such interest (or the excess over a reasonable commercial rate) is not treated as a distribution for ACT purposes, and the tax credit attached to it may not be repaid. The exclusion and prohibition do not generally apply to interest paid in respect of any period by which the repayment period under the original agreement is extended after 8 February 1983. They do, however, apply to extensions of up to five years agreed before 9 June 1983 pursuant to negotiations in progress on 9 February 1983 (or to the first five years of a longer such extension). [*FA 1983, s 48*].

Set-off of ACT. ACT paid (and not repaid) by a company in respect of an accounting period may be set against the company's liability to corporation tax *on its income* (as defined for the purposes of small companies rate — see 12.20 above) for that period. Any surplus ACT may (on a claim made within two years of the end of the accounting period) be wholly or partly set against corporation tax liabilities on income of accounting periods ending in the twelve months before the start of the accounting period in which it arose (of more recent periods before earlier ones) (but a claim to carry back ACT of an accounting period ending after 31 March 1992 is restricted to one-half of the maximum claim where the return for the period is late, see 28.12 RETURNS). Otherwise, it is carried forward and treated as if paid in respect of distributions in the next accounting period, and so on for subsequent periods. The inspector may make any necessary assessments to secure that, if a set-off is wrongly made or has become excessive, the proper liabilities (including interest) are restored. [*FA 1983, ss 39, 40*].

Groups of companies. Dividends received by a company after 28 May 1992, including those received on behalf of, or in trust for, the company (but not those received by the company on behalf of or in trust for another person) are excluded from these provisions, both as regards the paying company and in the hands of the recipient company, where both are RI-resident and the paying company is

(i)   a 51% subsidiary of the recipient company, or of an RI-resident company of which the recipient company is a 51% subsidiary, or

(ii) a trading or holding company owned by a consortium the members of which include the recipient company,

unless a profit on the sale of the recipient company's investment in the paying company would be treated as a trading receipt. The provisions of *CTA s 105(5)(6)* apply in determining whether a company is a 51% subsidiary of another as they apply to certain other intra-group transactions (see 12.14 above). The inspector has powers to restore the correct liabilities (including interest) where a company pays a dividend without accounting for ACT, when ACT ought to have been paid. The powers include recovery from the recipient company.

Distributions on the redemption, repayment or purchase by a company of its own shares, or on the acquisition of those shares by a subsidiary (within *Companies Act 1963, s 155*), in an accounting period ending **after 30 December 1993** are treated as dividends for these purposes.

Tax credits in respect of such dividends may not be repaid to the recipient company.

A company paying dividends may, however, elect for ACT to apply in the normal way to any specified dividends. The election must be made in writing before the due date for payment of ACT for the accounting period in which the dividends are paid, and is valid only if the ACT in respect of the dividends concerned has been paid.

For dividends paid before 28 May 1992, the exclusion of dividends from the ACT provisions applied only if the paying and recipient companies jointly so elected.

[*FA 1983, s 44; FA 1992, s 51; FA 1994, s 55*].

Surrender of ACT. Where a company is throughout an accounting period treated as a member of a group for group relief purposes (see 12.14 above), the benefit of any ACT paid (and not repaid or offset) in respect of dividend(s) paid in the accounting period may (on a claim) be surrendered (in whole or part) to any company which was a member of the same group throughout the accounting period. Surrenders may be made to more than one such company in such proportion as the company may determine.

The surrendered amount is treated as ACT paid by the recipient company in respect of a distribution made on the date (or proportionately made on the dates) of the dividend(s) by the surrendering company in respect of which the ACT surrendered was paid.

The surrendered amount may not be set against the recipient company's corporation tax liability of an earlier accounting period than that in which the notional distribution is treated as having been made, but is set against the liability of that accounting period before any ACT in respect of distributions actually made by the recipient company in that period. The surrendered amount may not be offset in any accounting period of the recipient company unless both surrendering and recipient company are members of the same group throughout that period.

Any payment made by the recipient company to the surrendering company in consideration of the surrender is ignored for corporation tax purposes as regards both companies, provided that it does not exceed the surrendered amount.

A claim to surrender ACT requires the recipient company's consent, and must be made within two years of the end of the surrendering company's accounting period to which it relates. [*FA 1983, s 45*]. A claim to surrender ACT of an accounting period ending after 31 March 1992 is restricted to one-half of the maximum claim where the return for the period is late (see 28.12 RETURNS), and the claimant company's use of surrendered ACT is similarly restricted in any of its accounting periods for which the return is late.

Change of ownership in company. If a 'major change in the nature or conduct of a trade or business', which was not completed before 9 February 1983, takes place within three years of (or at the same time as) a change in ownership of the company (see *FA 1973, 5 Sch* with appropriate modifications) which occurred after 8 February 1983, a new accounting period is deemed to commence at the time of the change of ownership for the purposes of

(*a*)   set-off of ACT against corporation tax liability,

(*b*)   calculation of ACT where a company receives distributions, and

(*c*)   determining ACT return periods.

Furthermore, surplus ACT cannot be carried forward (see above) from the accounting period ending with the change of ownership (whether its termination is deemed or actual). Relief for the ACT may therefore be lost. ACT surrendered to a company as a member of a group is equally subject to these restrictions.

A *major change in the nature or conduct of a trade or business* includes

(i)   a major change in the type of property dealt in or services or facilities provided,

(ii)   a major change in customers, outlets or markets,

(iii) the company's ceasing to be a 'trading company' and becoming an 'investment company' (or vice versa), or

(iv)   where the company is an investment company, a major change in the nature of its investments.

The change may be the result of a gradual process which began outside the three-year period.

Trading company means a company the business of which consists wholly or mainly of the carrying on of trade(s).

Investment company means a company (other than a company the business of which consists wholly or mainly in the holding of securities or shares of companies which are its 90% subsidiaries and which are trading companies) the business of which consists wholly or mainly of making investments whence the principal part of its income is derived.

The same restrictions apply if there is a change in ownership of a company after the scale of activities in its trade or business has become small or negligible, and before any considerable revival of that trade or business has taken place. [*FA 1983, s 46*].

13   Deduction of Tax at Source

13.1   **Any annuity or other annual payment** (except annual interest, rents chargeable on the recipient under SCHEDULE D, CASE V (33), and certain maintenance payments, see 23.4 MARRIED PERSONS). In relation to such payments,

(*a*)   if payable wholly out of taxed income, no relief is given for the payment but the payer is entitled when making the payment to deduct and retain a sum representing standard rate tax from it [*Sec 433; FA 1989, s 89(1)*];

(*b*)   if not payable wholly out of taxed income, the payer *must* deduct standard rate tax and account to the Revenue for tax on so much of the payment as was made out of untaxed income [*Sec 434*].

Where a payment, due in a year in which it could have been paid wholly or partly out of taxed income, is paid in a later year otherwise than out of taxed income, it is understood that an allowance is, by concession, made, in fixing the amount payable under (*b*) above, for the tax the payer would have been entitled to deduct under (*a*) above if the payment had been made on the due date.

See, however, 3.10 ANTI-AVOIDANCE LEGISLATION.

All deductions will be made at the standard rate in force at the time of the payment. [*FA 1974, s 5; CTA 3 Sch*].

Annuities and annual payments by the National Treasury Management Agency are paid without deduction of tax. [*FA 1991, s 20(3)*].

13.2   **Annual interest.** All interest is paid without deducting tax except interest paid by a company (unless a bank etc.) or to a non-resident or on an instalment promissory note, in which cases deduction *must* be made and the *Sec 434* rules apply [*FA 1974, ss 31, 50*] and interest paid by certain deposit-takers (see 13.8 below). There are special provisions for interest on quoted Eurobonds. [*Sec 462A; FA 1994, s 15*]. See also 20.1 INTEREST PAYABLE and 38.175 TAX CASES.

13.3   **Patent royalties.** Payments for user of patent rights are governed by the provisions in 13.1 above. [*Secs 433(2), 434*].

13.4   **Tax under-deducted** because of a change in the standard rate may

(*a*)   in the case of interest, dividends etc. payable by an agent, be charged on the recipient under Schedule D, Case IV, or

(*b*)   in the case of annual payments, etc. by persons entitled to deduct at source, be deducted from the next payment or, if no next payment, recovered as a debt due.

The above does not apply to a distribution by a company. [*Sec 8; CTA 2 Sch 2*].

13.5   **Dividends.** Dividend etc. payments have a related tax credit (see 12.23 CORPORATION TAX). Dividends out of certain exempt and tax-relieved profits (e.g. certain patent royalties, profits of mines, exports etc.) have tax related only to the taxable proportion. [*Secs 396, 410; FA 1969, ss 18, 20; FA 1973, s 34; FA 1975, s 30; CTA ss 64–67, 3 Sch*]. See also 12.10 CORPORATION TAX as regards distributions out of such income and in respect of certain shares carrying assured returns. Dividend warrants, etc. must show the tax related to the payment. [*Secs 363, 458; CTA s 5, 2 Sch 25*].

Before 6 April 1976, tax was deducted from dividends, etc.. For *preference shares*, or other fixed rate distributions on stocks or shares, existing before that date companies may make a distribution on them of such an amount as, when the value of the tax credit for the year of assessment in which the dividend is paid is added to it, will equal the amount calculated at the fixed rate. [*CTA s 178; FA 1978, s 28(6); FA 1988, s 32, 2 Sch; FA 1990, s 36, 1 Sch; FA 1995, s 45, 2 Sch*].

13.6   **Purchased life annuities.** The capital element in such annuities (as defined) is not treated as income (except where, for other tax purposes, a lump sum payment has to be taken into account in computing profits or losses). [*Secs 239, 240; CTA 2 Sch 9*].

13.7   **Contractors in the construction industry** (or, from 6 October 1992, forestry or meat processing) must deduct tax at 35% from payments to sub-contractors, and account for the deductions monthly to the Revenue, unless the sub-contractor produces a certificate from the Revenue Commissioners enabling him to be exempted from such deduction. Before issuing an exemption certificate the Commissioners must be satisfied that the sub-contractor has permanent premises with proper equipment, stock and other facilities to carry out construction work (as defined) and has a satisfactory record of dealing with his tax affairs, etc. They may make regulations relating to administrative procedures. There is an appeal procedure where a certificate is refused. Penalties apply to cases of fraud or evasion. Interest on arrears of tax deducted and payable to the Revenue is at 1.25% per month or part month and is payable gross and *not* deductible. See 25.5 PAYMENT OF TAX as regards waiver of certain interest and penalties.

Regulations may require contractors and sub-contractors, before entering into a contract, to make a declaration in a specified form that, having regard to guidelines published by the Revenue Commissioners, they have satisfied themselves that in their opinion the contract they propose to enter into is not a contract of employment (without prejudice to whether it is in fact such a contract). They may also require sub-contractors to supply to contractors the necessary information and particulars, and that declarations be kept and made available for inspection.

Penalties of up to £1,000 may be imposed for a wide range of infringements of the requirements of the deduction scheme.

The tax deducted from the sub-contractor may be set against his liability to income tax, corporation tax, capital gains tax, VAT, PAYE, Social Welfare pay-related contributions; and any excess may be repaid.

[*FA 1970, s 17; FA 1971, s 21; FA 1975, ss 27, 28; FA 1976, s 21; FA 1978, s 46; FA 1981, s 7; FA 1990, s 131; FA 1991, s 128; FA 1992, s 28; FA 1995, s 18*].

The Revenue Commissioners have powers of entry and inspection similar to those which apply in relation to PAYE. [*FA 1992, s 235*].

See 38.32A TAX CASES.

13.8   **DEPOSIT INTEREST RETENTION TAX ('DIRT')**

Payments of interest by a 'relevant deposit taker' in respect of a 'relevant deposit' are made under deduction of basic rate tax (except in the case of 'special savings accounts', see below, where the deduction is at the rate of 15% (10% for 1994/95 and earlier years)). The provisions of *FA 1974, s 31* (see 20.1 INTEREST PAYABLE) regarding deduction of tax cease to apply to such payments. A 'relevant deposit taker' must treat every deposit as a 'relevant deposit' unless satisfied that it is not so, but once satisfied that a deposit is not a 'relevant deposit' it may continue so to treat it unless and until it comes into possession of information reasonably indicative that the deposit is, or may be, a 'relevant deposit'.

A '*relevant deposit taker*' is any of:

(*a*)   the holder of a licence under *Central Bank Act 1971, s 9* or EEC equivalent;

(*b*)   a building society under the *Building Societies Acts* or EEC equivalent;

(*c*)   a trustee savings bank under the *Trustee Savings Bank Acts*;

(*d*)   the Agricultural Credit Corporation plc, the Industrial Credit Corporation plc and (from 30 October 1992) ICC Investment Bank Ltd; and

(*e*)   the Post Office Savings Bank.

A '*relevant deposit*' is any deposit held by a relevant deposit taker other than a deposit:

(i)   made by a relevant deposit taker, the Central Bank of Ireland, the Insurance Corporation of Ireland plc (after 1 August 1990, Icarom plc), (after 2 December 1990) the National Treasury Management Agency (or the State acting through it), by whom the interest on the deposit is beneficially owned;

(ii)   which is a debt on a security issued by the relevant deposit taker and is listed on a stock exchange;

(iii)   which, where the relevant deposit taker is resident in RI, is held at a branch outside RI;

(iv)   which, where the relevant deposit taker is not resident in RI, is not held at a branch in RI;

(v)   denominated in a foreign currency (but this exclusion does not apply to deposits made by individuals after 31 May 1991, unless additional to deposits made on or before that date with the same deposit taker and denominated in the same currency, and ceases to apply to any deposit made after 31 December 1992);

(vi)   in respect of which no person beneficially entitled to the interest is resident (before 1995/96, ordinarily resident) in RI, provided that the appropriate declaration (see *FA 1986, s 37 as amended*) has been made to the relevant deposit taker;

(vii)   (from 1 January 1993) which is made by, and the interest on which is beneficially owned by, a company which is or will be within the charge to corporation tax in respect of the interest, or a 'pension scheme', which has made the declaration as under *FA 1986, s 37B* (as inserted by *FA 1992, s 22(c)* and amended by *F(No 2)A 1992, s 3(c)*) to the deposit taker; or

(viii)   the interest on which is exempt under *Sec 333(1)(b)* (charitable exemption), provided that the appropriate declaration (see *FA 1986, s 38*) has been made to the relevant deposit taker.

A '*pension scheme*' for the purposes of (vii) above is an exempt approved scheme under *FA 1972, s 17* (see 17.17 EXEMPT ORGANISATIONS) or a retirement annuity contract or trust scheme under *Secs 235, 235A* (see 2.21 ALLOWANCES AND RATES, 17.19 EXEMPT ORGANISATIONS).

'Interest' for these purposes includes any amount paid in consideration of the making of a deposit (including dividends or other distributions in respect of shares in a building society but excluding certain redemption bonuses on ACC Bonus Bonds), and any sum paid to a relevant deposit taker on terms under which it will be repaid on demand or at an agreed time or in agreed circumstances is a deposit. Interest credited is treated as paid.

[*FA 1986, ss 31, 32; FA 1991, s 11; FA 1992, s 22; F(No 2)A 1992, s 3(a); FA 1993, s 15(1)(a); FA 1995, ss 11(1), 167*].

The relevant deposit taker must, if requested, supply a statement to any person beneficially entitled to '*relevant interest*' (i.e. interest paid on a relevant deposit) of the interest paid and the tax deducted on any date. [*FA 1986, s 36*].

Penalty provisions apply for failure to comply with the above requirements. [*FA 1986, s 40*].

Special savings accounts are accounts not denominated in a foreign currency opened by an individual after 1 January 1993 in which a relevant deposit is made and which satisfies the conditions of *FA 1986, s 37A* (inserted by *FA 1992, s 22(c)*), including the making of a declaration as required under that *section* to the deposit taker. A deduction rate of 15% (10% before 6 April 1995) applies to interest on such accounts, and no further liability to income tax arises in respect of such interest. The conditions of *FA 1986, s 37A* are broadly as follows.

(*a*) The individual must be of full age and beneficially entitled to the interest.

(*b*) No withdrawals may be made within three months of opening the account.

(*c*) Withdrawals must be subject to 30 days notice.

(*d*) The balance in the account must not exceed £50,000.

(*e*) There must be no agreements or arrangements affecting the interest rate for periods in excess of 24 months.

(*f*) Except for married couples, joint accounts are excluded.

(*g*) Only one account may be owned by an individual, except that married couples may have two single or two joint accounts.

(*h*) The account must not be 'connected with' another account, i.e. neither account must have been opened or be operated in any respect by reference to the existence of the other.

(*i*) (from 6 April 1993) All moneys held in the account must be subject to the same terms.

(*j*) (from 9 July 1993) Interest must not directly or indirectly be linked to, or determined by, the performance of stocks, shares, debentures or securities.

[*FA 1986, ss 31(1), 37A; FA 1992, s 22; F(No 2)A 1992, s 3(b); FA 1993, s 15(1)(c); FA 1994, s 12(b); FA 1995, s 11(1)*].

See also 16.22 EXEMPT INCOME AND SPECIAL SAVINGS SCHEMES as regards restrictions on this and other investments.

Liability to account for tax retained. The relevant deposit taker must, within 15 days from the end of each year of assessment, make a return to the Collector-General of the relevant interest paid in the year and of the tax retained, and pay over the tax retained. An assessment is not required, but may be raised where the tax is not paid over by the due date.

The relevant deposit taker must also make a payment on account of the year-end liability by 20 October in each year of assessment, at least equal to the liability which would arise at the year end on the amount of relevant interest accrued (on a day-to-day basis) in the period from 6 April in the year to 5 October in the year inclusive. If the payment on account exceeds the full liability, the excess is carried forward against future liability under these provisions. Again an assessment is not required but may be raised where necessary.

Where the amount of retention tax paid for a year of assessment represents tax on less than a full year's accrued interest, the relevant deposit taker must make up the short-fall at the October payment date in the following year of assessment. In effect, a payment on that date will represent retention tax on a year's accrued interest less the payment made in the previous April. Credit will be given, where appropriate, against future payments.

There are provisions for the raising of assessments where no return is made or where the inspector is dissatisfied with a return, and for the adjustments necessary where an incorrect return is made. Interest at the rate of 1.25% per month will arise where tax is paid late.

The normal income tax rules generally apply in relation to assessments, appeals, collection and recovery. [*FA 1986, s 33; FA 1987, s 7*].

Taxation of relevant interest. Except as detailed below, tax retained out of relevant interest may not be repaid to any person who is not a company within the charge to corporation tax in respect of the payment. The gross amount is regarded as income chargeable under Schedule D, Case IV. For 1993/94 and subsequent years, credit is given for the tax deducted and retained out of the interest, the standard rate band of individual depositors is increased by the gross amount of the interest chargeable in the year, so that no further income tax liability arises, and (except for the purposes of repayment claims by the sick and elderly (see below)) the 'specified amount' for the age and low income exemptions (see 2.7, 2.8 ALLOWANCES AND TAX RATES) is similarly increased. (For 1994/95 onwards, marginal relief in relation to those exemptions is calculated by reference to the tax payable after credit for DIRT, and the marginal relief limit of twice the specified amount is increased by the amount of the deposit interest.) For 1992/93 and earlier years, no assessment to basic rate tax may be made, but higher rate tax and the surcharge on accumulation and discretionary trustees (see 36.1 SETTLEMENTS) may be assessed, with credit being given for the retained tax. Credit is similarly given against any corporation tax liability.

Where a deposit not previously within these provisions becomes a relevant deposit, it is treated for SCHEDULE D, CASE III (31) purposes as a separate source of income which ceases immediately before it comes within these provisions. Similarly where a deposit ceases to be a relevant deposit, it is treated for Schedule D, Case III purposes as a separate source of income commencing immediately thereafter.

The exemption for small amounts of interest from the Post Office Savings Bank and certain other banks (see 16.6 EXEMPT INCOME AND SPECIAL SAVINGS SCHEMES) does not apply to interest paid in respect of relevant deposits. [*FA 1986, s 35; FA 1993, s 15(1)(b); FA 1994, s 12(a)*].

Special rules apply to 'special savings accounts' (see above).

Repayments of retained tax may be made to a charity exempt under *Sec 333(1)* from income or corporation tax (where exemption may not have been agreed at the time of payment) and, on a claim not earlier than the end of the year to which the claim relates, to an individual who, or whose spouse, was aged 65 years or more at some time in the year, and to an individual who, or whose spouse, was, at the end of that year, permanently mentally or physically incapacitated from maintaining himself or herself. [*FA 1986, s 39*].

13.9   PAYMENTS FOR PROFESSIONAL SERVICES

After 5 June 1987, deduction of tax at the standard rate (see 2.3 ALLOWANCES AND RATES) must be made from payments in respect of 'professional services' made to individuals, partnerships and companies by 'accountable persons'. Deductions are made from amounts *net* of VAT.

Where, after 5 June 1988, the 'accountable person' is an authorised insurer (see (*y*) below), payments to a medical practitioner in discharge of an insurance claim in respect of certain medical expenses are brought within the scheme. For this purpose, provision is made for payment direct to the practitioner by the insurer in relation to amounts so claimed, and regulations may be made to give full effect to these provisions.

13.9   Deduction of Tax at Source

The procedure applies generally for fees and similar payments, but does not apply to payments already covered by PAYE or the construction industry scheme established by *FA 1970, s 17* (see 13.7 above). Payments to non-residents come within the scope of the scheme, but it is understood that recipients in countries with which Ireland has a double taxation agreement will be entitled to receive a full refund if the income is not chargeable to RI tax.

Fees represented by the payments still have to be taken into account in calculating the profits or gains of the recipient for tax purposes. The tax deducted at source is, however, available for set-off, and provision is made for interim refunds to alleviate hardship, where a substantial proportion of fees is paid out to meet the expenses of the business.

The list of '*accountable persons*', which can be extended by Regulation (but without retrospective effect), is as follows.

(*a*)   A Minister of the Government.

(*b*)   A local authority within the meaning of *section 2(2)* of the *Local Government Act 1941*, and includes a body established under the *Local Government Services (Corporate Bodies) Act 1971*.

(*c*)   A health board.

(*d*)   The General Medical Services (Payments) Board established under the *General Medical Services (Payments) Board (Establishment) Order 1972 (SI No 184 of 1972)*.

(*e*)   The Attorney General.

(*f*)   The Director of Public Prosecutions.

(*g*)   The Revenue Commissioners.

(*h*)   The Commissioners of Public Works in Ireland.

(*i*)   The Legal Aid Board.

(*j*)   A vocational education committee or a technical college.

(*k*)   (before 6 June 1992) An Chomhairle Oiliúna established under the *Industrial Training Act 1967*.

(*l*)   A harbour authority.

(*m*)   (after 5 April 1988) An Foras Áiseanna Saothair. (On and before that date, An Chomhairle Oiliúna Talmhaíochta.)

(*n*)   (before 6 June 1992) An Foras Talúntais.

(*o*)   Údarás na Gaeltachta.

(*p*)   The Industrial Development Authority (after 5 June 1994, The Industrial Development Agency (Ireland)).

(*q*)   (before 6 June 1992) Córas Tráchtála.

(*r*)   Shannon Free Airport Development Company Limited.

(*s*)   Bord Fáilte Éireann.

(*t*)   An institution of higher education within the meaning of the *Higher Education Authority Act 1971*.

The following are added to the list of '*accountable persons*' in respect of payments made after 5 June 1988.

(*u*)   CERT.

(v)   (before 6 June 1994) Eolas—The Irish Science and Technology Agency.

(w)   (before 6 June 1992) An Bord Fuirnimh Núicléigh.

(x)   Certain voluntary public or joint board hospitals.

(y)   An authorised insurer within *Sec 145*.

After 5 June 1992, the list is extended to include the commercial State bodies and a number of non-commercial State bodies, and further additions are made after 5 June 1994. The full list after that date is contained in *FA 1992, 2 Sch* as amended by *FA 1994, s 11*, but the Minister for Finance may further add to or delete from that list by Regulation.

'*Professional services*' include

(i)   services of a medical, dental, pharmaceutical, optical, aural or veterinary nature,

(ii)   services of an architectural, engineering, quantity surveying or surveying nature, and related services,

(iii)   services of accountancy, auditing or finance and services of financial, economic, marketing, advertising or other consultancies,

(iv)   services of a solicitor or barrister and other legal services,

(v)   geological services, and

(vi)   training services provided on behalf of An Foras Áiseanna Saothair (before 6 April 1988, An Chomhairle Oiliúna).

Information and deduction forms. Recipients of professional fees must supply to the relevant accountable person

(A)   in the case of a person resident in RI or a person having a permanent establishment or fixed base in RI,

   (i)   details of their income tax or corporation tax number, and

   (ii)   where relevant, their value-added tax registration number; or

(B)   in any other case, details of their country of residence and tax reference in that country.

Where that information has been supplied, the accountable person making a payment must give the recipient, in a form prescribed by the Revenue Commissioners, particulars of

(1)   name and address of recipient;

(2)   recipient's tax reference;

(3)   amount of gross payment;

(4)   amount of tax deducted; and

(5)   date of payment.

Accounting for tax deducted. Returns of all payments covered by the deduction scheme made in each income tax month, together with the tax deducted, must be submitted by the accountable person within ten days of the end of each income tax month. Nil returns are also required.

Credit for tax borne. Credit is given for tax deducted

(*a*)   in an accounting period of a company, for allowance against corporation tax for that period, or (*b*)   in the 'credit period' (before 1990/91, the basis period) for a year of assessment in the case of an individual or partnership, for allowance against income tax for that year of assessment.

The '*credit period*' for a year of assessment means the basis period for the year of assessment immediately preceding the year of assessment for which the claim is made. (For 1990/91 only, the credit period is the period which would have been the basis period for that year but for *FA 1990, ss 14, 15* (see 30.3 SCHEDULE D, CASES I AND II).) For the year of discontinuance, it is in any event the year of assessment itself.

Where there is an interval between credit or basis periods or basis periods overlap, the common period or interval is deemed to be part of the second period only. The tax deduction form supplied by the accountable person (see above) must be produced in order to claim credit, with any necessary apportionment being made where the form refers to more than one person. Tax suffered cannot be set off more than once, or allowed both as a tax credit and as the basis for an interim refund (see below). Any excess of tax deducted over the corporation or income tax liability for a period may be repaid.

Interim refunds of tax suffered by deduction under these provisions in an accounting or basis period may be claimed in certain cases.

Ongoing businesses. Conditions for interim refund are that

(i)   the accounts of the immediately preceding accounting or basis period must have been finalised, agreed and the tax thereon paid, and

(ii)   the claim must be supported by the appropriate tax deduction forms.

The amount of the interim refund will be the excess of the tax deducted and vouched as in (ii) above (less any previously refunded) over the tax liability referred to in (i) above, *less* any VAT, PAYE, or PRSI due but unpaid.

Commencing businesses. Where an interim refund is claimed for the first accounts period of a business, condition (ii) above applies as for ongoing businesses, but there are special provisions to determine the amount to be refunded. The inspector will, for that first period, determine tax at the standard rate on the figure resulting from the formula

$$E \times \frac{A}{B} \times \frac{C}{P}$$

where   A = estimated payments for professional services of the period from which tax has been deducted at source

B = estimated total income for the period

E = estimated allowable business expenditure during the period

P = estimated number of months and fractions of months in the period in respect of which the refund is made

C = estimated number of months and fractions of months in the period in respect of which the refund claim is made.

The resulting figure is compared with tax actually deducted (and not previously refunded) and the refund made is the lesser of the two figures.

Particular hardship. In cases of particular hardship, the Revenue Commissioners are enabled to waive any of the conditions and to authorise the inspector to make such refund as they consider to be just and reasonable.

[*FA 1987, ss 13–21; FA 1988, s 8; FA 1990, s 26(1); FA 1992, ss 10, 11, 2 Sch; FA 1994, s 11*].

14   Double Tax Relief—Capital Transfers

Cross-references. For double tax relief on income tax, capital gains tax and corporation tax, see 15 DOUBLE TAX RELIEF—INCOME AND CAPITAL GAINS.

14.1   A Convention between UK and RI to avoid double taxation over capital transfer tax (UK) and gift tax and inheritance tax (capital acquisitions tax—RI) was signed on 7 December 1977. It will also apply to any identical or substantially similar taxes imposed by either State in addition to or in place of these taxes. [*Art 2*]. Due to the differences between the provisions concerning the persons liable for CAT and CTT, the relief given under this Convention attaches not to the persons who pay tax but to the property subject to the charge. Note also that 'settlement' is defined by reference to the UK legislation (see 14.4 below) and that the 'grossing-up' on UK lifetime gifts is taken into account for DTR purposes.

Commencement. [*Art 14*]. The Convention entered into force on 2 October 1978 upon an Exchange of Notes and thereupon took effect retrospectively to the date of the introduction of each of the taxes. These dates are

RI   —   gift tax—28 February 1974
inheritance tax—1 April 1975

UK   —   capital transfer tax not on death—27 March 1974
capital transfer tax on a death—13 March 1975

14.2   SCHEME FOR ELIMINATING DOUBLE TAXATION

In general each State retains the right to levy tax according to its own laws. [*Art 5(1)*]. In cases where double taxation would occur, the rules provide for one State to allow as a credit against its own charge to tax any tax imposed by the other State. [*Art 8*]. This is worked out as follows.

(*a*)   Where one State taxes property which is situated in the other State, the State where the property is *not* situated must allow a credit for tax payable in the other State on the same event (i.e. death, gift, etc.).

(*b*)   Where both States impose tax on the same event and the property is situated in a third State, it is the State which has *subsidiary taxing rights* (see below) which must allow credit for the tax charged by the other State.

[*Art 8(1)(2)*].

Computation. The property on which tax is charged is to be treated as reduced by any deductions (e.g. for debts, charges) allowed by the tax law of the State imposing the tax. [*Art 7*]. The tax chargeable by a contracting State is to be reduced by any amount allowed as a credit in respect of tax levied on the same property by any non-contracting State. [*Art 8(4)(a)*].

The credit is only available in RI if the gift/inheritance bears its own tax. If the tax is payable out of the residue then the credit is available against tax in the UK on the residue. A lifetime gift liable to UK tax payable by the transferor is, for RI credit purposes, treated as reduced by the amount of the UK tax (i.e. the 'grossing-up' is taken into account). [*Art 8(3)*].

Claim for credit or repayment of tax must be made within six years of the event giving rise to the charge. [*Art 9*].

14.3 PLACE WHERE PROPERTY IS SITUATED

The place where property is situated is to be determined initially by each State under its own law. If this results in a disagreement then the question is to be determined solely according to the law of the State with *subsidiary taxing rights* (or, if there is no such State, by agreement). [*Art 6*].

14.4 SUBSIDIARY TAXING RIGHTS

The State with subsidiary taxing rights is the State which must allow a credit for tax charged by the other State, where the property is situated in a third State. (In effect, the other contracting State is regarded as having the 'primary' taxing rights.) Identifying the State with subsidiary taxing rights greatly depends on determining fiscal domicile.

Fiscal domicile. The domicile of a person (individual, company or body of persons) is initially determined according to the law of domicile or tax law of each contracting State. [*Art 4(1)*]. If this results in the person being domiciled in both States, the question is determined by reference, successively, to permanent home, personal and economic ties, habitual abode and nationality. In default, the question is to be settled by agreement between the RI and UK revenue authorities. [*Art 4(2)*].

Subsidiary taxing rights. Except for settlements, the State with subsidiary taxing rights will be the State where, under the rules in *Art 4(2)* above, the disponer or transferor is *not* domiciled. [*Art 5(2)(a)*]. In relation to property comprised in a settlement (as defined by UK law—*UK Finance Act 1975, 5 Sch 1(2)*) the State with subsidiary taxing rights is determined as follows. [*Art 5(2)(b)*].

Proper law of settlement when made	*Domicile of settlor at that time under Art 4(1)*	*State*
RI	UK	UK
Not RI*	UK*	RI
Not RI	Both—domicile falling to be determined by *Art 4(2)*	State of non-domicile under *Art 4(2)*

*Property becoming liable to RI tax due to a later change, in proper law or settlor's domicile, to the RI jurisdiction.

14.5 OTHER PROVISIONS

A contracting State may not discriminate by imposing more onerous tax on property owned by nationals of the other State, nor on the permanent establishment of an enterprise of the other State, nor on enterprises whose capital is controlled by residents of the other State. (This does not entitle the nationals of the other State to parity of personal allowances, reliefs and reductions.) [*Art 10*].

Complaints that the Convention is not being complied with may be made direct to the revenue authority of either State, and problems are to be resolved by agreement between the UK and RI revenue authorities. [*Art 11*]. Information to be exchanged between revenue authorities not only for DTR purposes but also for purposes of domestic tax, such information to be treated as confidential. [*Art 12*].

Diplomatic and consular officials. The Convention does not affect the international fiscal privileges of such persons. [*Art 13*].

14.6 TERMINATION

The Convention may be terminated from the beginning of any calendar year after 1980 by either State giving at least six months' prior notice. [*Art 15*].

15 Double Tax Relief—Income and Capital Gains

Cross references. See also 14 DOUBLE TAX RELIEF—CAPITAL TRANSFERS. See 31 SCHEDULE D, CASE III for foreign income etc. See Tolley's Income Tax, Tolley's Corporation Tax and Tolley's Capital Gains Tax for further details of taxation in UK.

15.1 Where the same income is liable to be taxed in both RI and another country, relief may be available

(*a*)   under the terms of a double tax agreement between RI and that other country — see generally 15.2 below and see 15.3 et seq. for agreements with the UK;

(*b*)   under the unilateral double tax relief provisions contained in RI tax legislation — see 15.14 below.

15.2   **DOUBLE TAX AGREEMENTS** [*Secs 358–362 and 10 Sch; FA 1987, s 23*].

The Republic of Ireland has agreements with the following countries (statutory instrument numbers in round brackets).

	In force*
Australia (406/1983)	1984
Austria (250/1967 and 29/1988)	1964 (protocol 1974/1976)
Belgium (66/1973)	1973
Canada (212/1967)	1968
Cyprus (79/1970)	1962
Denmark (286/1993)	1994
Finland (289/1993)	1990
France (162/1970)	1966
Germany, Federal Republic (212/1962)	1959
Italy (64/1973)	1976
Japan (259/1974)	1974
Korea (290/1991)	1992
Luxembourg (65/1973)	1968
Netherlands (22/1970)	1965
New Zealand (30/1988)	1989
Norway (80/1970)	1967
Pakistan (260/1974)	1968
Portugal (102/1994)	1995
Spain (308/1994)	1995
Sweden (19/1960, 348/1987 and 398/1993)	1960
Switzerland (240/1967 and 76/1984)	1965 (protocol 1974/1976)
United Kingdom (319/1976)	**
United States of America (381/1951 and 87/1956)	1951
Zambia (130/1973)	1967

Treaties with Hungary and Russia await ratification, and negotiations are in progress for revisions to the treaties with Austria, Belgium, Canada, France, Italy, Japan, the Netherlands, Norway and the USA. It is expected that they will commence shortly for revisions to the treaty with Australia. A treaty with Poland is expected shortly, and new treaties are also being negotiated with The Czech Republic, Greece, Israel and Mexico. A protocol to the UK treaty dealing with pensions will be ratified during 1995.

*The date of entry into force is 6 April in the year for income tax and capital gains tax; and 1 April for corporation or corporation profits tax (except agreements with Canada, Korea and Australia, 1 January).

15.3 Double Tax Relief—Income and Capital Gains

**Various dates for entry into force, see 15.3 below.

Note: Arrangements relating to corporation profits tax (abolished from 6 April 1976) are adopted and preserved for the purpose of corporation tax. [*CTA ss 22, 23, 166, 4 Sch Pt I*].

15.3 ARRANGEMENTS WITH UK

A revised double tax agreement between UK and RI came into effect on 23 December 1976. It consists of a Convention signed on 2 June 1976 and a Protocol signed on 28 October 1976. The agreement is broadly based on the 1963 OECD model treaty and applies in respect of RI income tax, corporation tax and capital gains tax, and in respect of UK income tax, corporation tax, petroleum revenue tax and capital gains tax. It will apply to subsequent taxes of a similar nature. [*Art 2*]. It took effect from the following dates:

(i) income tax — except on salaries, wages, remuneration and pensions — and capital gains tax: **for years of assessment beginning after 5 April 1976**;

(ii) income tax on such salaries, etc.: **for years of assessment beginning after 5 April 1977**;

(iii) corporation tax: **for the financial year 1976** and thereafter.

The previous arrangements ceased to have effect when the new agreement became law, except, as regards salaries, etc., for any year of assessment ending before 6 April 1977. [*Art 28(2)(3)*].

15.4 ARRANGEMENTS UNDER 1976 AGREEMENT

Special meaning of residence ('fiscal domicile'). For DTR purposes a person cannot be resident in both UK and RI. The residence of an *individual* is first determined under normal tax rules relating to abode, domicile, etc. If this results in him being technically resident in both States the question is decided by reference successively to permanent home, personal and economic ties, habitual abode, and nationality, and if necessary is decided by agreement between the States. A *company or body of persons* is deemed to be resident where its place of effective management is situated. [*Art 4*].

15.5 **Enterprises.** *Permanent establishment* of an enterprise carried on by a person resident in UK or RI means a fixed place of business where the business of the enterprise is wholly or partly carried on, including a place of management, an office, factory, etc. Certain fixed places of business are excluded (e.g. if used for advertising or storage). Carrying on business in State A through a broker or other agent of independent status will not cause a State B enterprise to have permanent establishment in State A. [*Arts 3(1), 5*].

Business profits of a State A enterprise are taxable only in State A, unless the enterprise has a permanent establishment in State B in which case the profits attributable to the permanent establishment may be taxed in State B. Rules are laid down for identifying the profits of a permanent establishment. These provisions do not affect specific legislation in either State relating to non-resident life assurance companies. [*Art 8*].

15.6 **Taxable in State of source.** Certain kinds of profits or gains are taxable in the State in which the source of the profits or gains is situated. If the taxpayer is resident in the State which is not the State of source (see above for residence), the tax paid in the State of source is allowed as a credit against the tax on the same profits or gains in the State of residence. [*Art 21*]. The kinds of profits or gains to which these arrangements apply are the following.

(*a*) Income from immovable property, including income from agriculture and forestry. 'Immovable property' is as defined by the law of the State where it is situated, and further includes livestock and equipment used for agriculture or forestry, and other rights and property. [*Art 7*].

(*b*)   Business profits of a UK or RI enterprise which has a permanent establishment in the State of source, to the extent that these profits are attributable to that permanent establishment. Rules apply for identifying the profits of a permanent establishment. [*Art 8*].

(*c*)   Dividends, interest and royalties connected with the business done by such a permanent establishment in the State of source. [*Arts 11(6), 12(3), 13(3)*].

(*d*)   Capital gains arising from sale of assets forming part of such a permanent establishment. [*Art 14(3)*].

(*e*)   Capital gains derived from immovable property or unquoted shares deriving their value from immovable property. [*Art 14(1)(2)*].

(*f*)   Salaries, wages and remuneration of employees, and director's fees, if

   (i)   the employee/director is present in the State of source (i.e. where the employment/directorship is exercised) for more than 183 days in the fiscal year, or

   (ii)   the employer/company is a resident of the State of source or has a permanent establishment there from which the remuneration is paid.

[*Art 15*].

If neither condition is fulfilled, see 15.8 (*c*) below.

(*g*)   Income of public entertainers and athletes. [*Art 16*].

(*h*)   Profits from operation of ships or aircraft as regards voyages confined solely to State of source. [*Art 6*].

15.7   Taxable only in the State of source. Remuneration and pensions paid by central or local government (see 38.42A TAX CASES) are taxable in the State of source and exempt in the State of residence (if different), *but only if*

(*a*)   the remuneration or pension relates to services which were not rendered in connection with a trade or business (i.e. relates to governmental duties); and

(*b*)   the recipient is a *national* of the State of source or a dual UK/RI national.

[*Art 18*].

If these conditions are not met the usual rules apply (see 15.6 (*f*) and 15.8 (*c*) for remuneration, and 15.8 (*d*) for pensions).

15.8   Taxable only in the State of residence. The following kinds of profits or gains are taxable only in the State of residence.

(*a*)   Interest and royalties, except where the rule in 15.6 (*c*) applies. [*Arts 12, 13*].

(*b*)   Capital gains not covered by the rules in 15.6 (*d*) or (*e*). [*Art 14*].

(*c*)   Salaries, wages and other remuneration and director's fees, if

   (i)   the employee/director is present in the State of source (i.e. where the employment/directorship is exercised) for 183 days or less in the fiscal year, and

   (ii)   the employer/company is not a resident of the State of source and does not have a permanent establishment there from which the salary etc. was paid.

[*Art 15*].

(*d*)   Pensions and annuities, other than government and local authority pensions falling within 15.7 above. [*Art 17*].

(*e*)   Profits and capital gains derived from operation of ships or aircraft except where the rules in 15.6 (*d*) or (*h*) above apply. [*Arts 9, 14(4)*].

(*f*)   Other income not expressly mentioned, except trust income (see 15.10 below). [*Art 20*].

15.9   **Dividends** [*Art 11*]. There are different rules depending on whether the dividend (meaning any distribution under RI or UK tax law, as appropriate) carries a tax credit. Where, as under current law in each State, the dividend would carry a tax credit if the recipient were resident in the same State as the company issuing the dividend (called 'the State of source' below), but in fact the recipient is resident in the other State, the following rules apply.

(*a*)   The dividend is taxable in the State of the recipient's residence.

(*b*)   The dividend is also taxable in the State of source. However, a tax credit is allowed to the recipient in the same way as if he were resident in the State of source, provided he is beneficially entitled to the dividend. This includes the right to obtain repayment of any excess of the tax credit.

(*c*)   If the recipient is a company which alone or together with any associated companies controls directly or indirectly 10% of the voting power in the distributing company, the dividend is exempt from tax in the State of source; however, no tax credit is allowed.

Article 11(1) provides for the situation where the dividend would not entitle a resident of the State of source to a tax credit. In these circumstances, there is 'withholding tax' in the State of source up to the following maximum:

(i)   generally, 15% of the gross amount of the dividend; or

(ii)   if the recipient is a company which controls directly or indirectly at least 10% of the voting power in the distributing company, 5% of the gross amount of the dividend.

The above rules do not apply:

(A)   where the dividend is connected with the business of a permanent establishment in the State of source (see 15.6 (*c*) above);

(B)   to a recipient who holds 10% or more of the class of shares to which the dividend attaches, as regards any dividend which can only have been paid out of profits earned in a period ending twelve months before the recipient's holding reached 10%. This disqualification will not apply if the recipient can show that he acquired the shares for *bona fide* commercial reasons;

(C)   to a recipient who is exempt from tax in one State in such circumstances that if he were resident in, and exempt in, the other State his exemption in the first State would be limited or removed. [*Art 11(5)(6)*].

Where a dividend suffers withholding tax in the State of source the tax thus paid will be allowed as a credit against the recipient's tax liability in his State of residence, to the extent that the overall rate of tax in the State of source does not exceed the overall rate in the State of residence. There is no credit for tax on the profits of the distributing company out of which the dividend is made except where the recipient is a company which controls directly or indirectly 10% of the voting power in the distributing company. [*Art 21*].

15.10   **Trust income.** The Convention does not specify how trust income is to be treated. It will continue to be dealt with by agreement between the Revenue authorities of UK and RI according to the nature of the income concerned.

15.11 **Charities, superannuation schemes, and pension businesses of insurance companies.** The above Convention rules do not apply and the following *reciprocal exemption* applies to such a body resident in one State in respect of

(*a*)   dividends received from a company resident in the other State;

(*b*)   income from immovable property in the other State; and

(*c*)   capital gains taxable in the other State.

Where the Revenue authorities of the first-mentioned State certify that such dividends, income or gains are not taxable in that State by virtue of an exemption for such a body, then there is a reciprocal exemption from tax in the other State on the dividends, income or gains. [*Art 11(3); Protocol Arts I and II*].

15.12 **Other provisions.** A resident of one State is entitled to the same personal allowances in the other State as a national of the other State not residing there. [*Art 22*]. Non-discrimination by one State against nationals of the other State. [*Art 23*]. Allegations that an assessment does not comply with the Convention are to be presented to the State of residence. Difficulties are to be resolved by agreement between the Revenue authorities. [*Art 24*]. Exchange of information between the Revenue authorities not only for purposes of DTR but also for purposes of domestic tax. [*Art 25*]. A number of anti-avoidance provisions apply. [*Arts 10, 11(5), 12(4)(5), 13(4)*].

15.13 **EXAMPLE OF RELIEF UNDER 1976 AGREEMENT**

For year of assessment 1995/96, an RI resident, who is married with two children under 11 and who spends 90 days of the year in the UK as director of a UK company, has the following income.

	RI Sources £	UK Sources £
Directorship of RI company	20,000	—
Directorship of UK company	—	3,000
Rents from RI property	2,000	—
Rents from UK property	—	1,800
Other RI income	1,000	—
Dividends from UK companies (including tax credit of £50)	—	200
	£23,000	£5,000

UK tax liability

The income from UK sources above is all liable to UK income tax as follows

Directorship (see 15.6 (*f*))	3,000	
Rents (see 15.6 (*a*))	1,800	
	4,800 at 20%/25%	1,040
Dividends (tax limited to 15%, see 15.9 above)		30
	Tax liability	£1,070

Effective rate of tax is $\dfrac{1,070}{5,000} \times 100 = 21.4\%$

Notes   (i)   The maximum tax on the dividends is 15% (£30) and the taxpayer is entitled to repayment by the UK revenue authorities of £20 out of the £50 tax credit.

157

15.14   Double Tax Relief—Income and Capital Gains

(ii)   In some circumstances, a claim may be made for personal allowances (see Tolley's Income Tax, under Overseas Matters) but such a claim is usually only advantageous where the RI effective rate is *lower* than the UK effective rate.

RI tax liability

The income from all sources is liable to RI income tax as follows

RI sources	23,000
UK sources	5,000
	28,000
Less allowances	5,000
Taxable Income	£23,000
Tax on £23,000 at 27% or 48%	7,302

Effective rate of tax is $\dfrac{7,302}{28,000} \times 100 = 26.07\%$

Double taxation relief at lower effective rate (i.e. 21.4%) is given against RI tax liability. Since the lower rate is the UK tax rate, the entire UK liability is deductible.

Deduct UK tax liability as above	1,070
	£6,232

15.14   PROVISIONS FOR UNILATERAL RELIEF

Ten years previous residence abroad. A person who (*a*) is domiciled, resident and ordinarily resident in RI in the relevant year of assessment, and (*b*) was previously resident for an aggregate of ten years in USA, Canada, Australia, New Zealand, South Africa or any 'British possession' within *Income Tax Act 1918, Schedule C*, may be given unilateral relief on doubly taxed income from that country. The relief is of such amount as the Revenue Commissioners think fit, with the following restrictions

(A)   not to exceed the lesser of (i) the foreign tax on the doubly-taxed income or (ii) half the RI tax on the doubly-taxed income (computed by reference to the overall RI tax rate on world income); and

(B)   not to reduce the aggregate of RI and foreign tax on the doubly-taxed income below what would be payable if the income had arisen in RI.

[*Sec 365*].

Overseas dividends etc. derived from tax relieved income. Dividends or interest arising from the investment of RI profits exempted under Exported Goods relief or Shannon Airport relief (see 16.2, 16.4 EXEMPT INCOME AND SPECIAL SAVINGS SCHEMES) in a territory with which there is no double tax agreement may be granted such relief as is just (with the same restrictions as in (A) and (B) above). [*CTA s 163*].

See also *Sec 366* for relief on non-UK income in case where person qualified for relief on UK income under *FA 1941, s 2*.

16   Exempt Income and Special Savings Schemes

Cross-references. See also 12.12 CORPORATION TAX; 18.4 FARMING; 19.3 GOVERNMENT AND OTHER PUBLIC LOANS; 29.2 SCHEDULE C; 34.9 SCHEDULE E.

16.1   **Children's allowances** under the *Social Welfare (Children's Allowances) Acts* are exempt from income tax. [*Sec 354*].

16.2   **Customs-free airport.** Profits of certain companies trading within the customs-free airport were exempt until 5 April 1990. [*Secs 302, 373–381; FA 1969, s 15; CTA ss 69–77, 1 Sch 48*].

From 1 January 1981, this exemption was available to a company only where

(i)   any trading operations of the company were already exempt on 31 December 1980, or

(ii)   any trading operations of the company, which would, before the *FA 1980* legislation, have attracted exemption, commenced after 31 December 1980, and, before 1 January 1981, an assurance in writing was given by the Minister for Finance or his agent that the trading operations would be exempt notwithstanding the provisions of *FA 1980, s 43(1)*. Such an assurance was given only where the Minister was satisfied that the trading operations would (or did) contribute significantly to regional or national development.

For a company whose trade consisted only of exempted trading operations, those operations ceased to be exempt for all periods beginning with one for which a claim to relief under the manufacturing companies relief provisions effective from 1 January 1981 was made. For companies part only of whose trade consisted of exempted trading operations, a claim to the new manufacturing companies relief did not include income from such operations (see 12.17 CORPORATION TAX). [*FA 1980, s 43*].

The certification of a company by the Minister as qualifying for this relief could be revoked if the company engaged in activities 'inimical to development' of the airport, from which it failed to desist after being served with a warning notice. [*FA 1986, s 56*].

See *FA 1968, s 36; CTA s 78* for extension of this 'Shannon' relief, or exported goods relief (see 16.4 below), to profits on sales between certain associated companies.

The income tax exemption for distributions out of relieved profits is phased out for distributions after 28 January 1992, being abolished after 5 April 1994. See *CTA s 76A* inserted by *FA 1992, s 35(b)*.

See 12.10 CORPORATION TAX as regards attribution of distributions out of exempt profits and as regards distributions in respect of certain shares carrying assured returns.

16.3   **Payments** made by the Minister for Labour under the **Employment Incentive Scheme**, the **Employment Maintenance Scheme**, the **Enterprise Allowance Scheme** or the **Enterprise Scheme**; or under the **Enterprise Scheme** or the **Employment Subsidy Scheme** of An Foras Áiseanna Saothair; or out of the **Employer's Temporary Subvention Fund**; or under the **Employers' Employment Contribution Scheme**; or under the **Market Development Fund** of An Bord Tráchtála; or by the **Industrial Development Authority** under *Industrial Development (No 2) Act 1981, s 2*, are disregarded for tax purposes. [*FA 1976, s 25; FA 1979, s 27; FA 1981, s 18; FA 1982, s 18; FA 1988, s 22; FA 1993, s 38*]. This applies also to certain **employment grants** under *Údarás na Gaeltachta Act 1979* or *Industrial Development Act 1986*. [*FA 1993, s 37; FA 1995, s 43*].

16.4 Exempt Income and Special Savings Schemes

16.4 **Exported goods relief.** Up to 1975/76 this relief was contained in *ITA Part XXV, Chap IV*. These provisions were repealed for 1976/77 onwards by *CTA 3 Sch*, but were effectively re-enacted by *CTA ss 53–68 except for the alternative relief noted below*.

Relief is given to **RI companies** which

(a) manufacture goods for export (including wholesalers) [*Secs 398, 399, 404; CTA ss 53, 54, 58*], or

(b) process in RI, and then send out of RI, goods owned by a non-resident [*Sec 406; CTA s 59*], or

(c) sell bacon/milk products to the Pigs and Bacon Commission (or Pigs and Bacon Commission Ltd)/Dairy Board (An Bord Bainne Co-operative Ltd) which the Commission/Board exports. [*Sec 401; FA 1974, s 68; CTA s 56; FA 1983, s 33*].

Temporary 100% relief from income tax/corporation tax on profits from *increased* exports for maximum period of 20 years, tapering after 15th year with reduction of the relief to 80%, 65%, 50%, 35% and 15% successively in the following years, but not later than 1989/90. [*Secs 402–404; FA 1969, s 26; CTA ss 57, 58; FA 1980, s 42*]. Certain amounts treated as corporation tax are excluded from relief (see *FA 1990, s 53*).

For computation of relief, see 38.34 TAX CASES. For meaning of 'exporter', see 38.35 TAX CASES. For scope of relief, see 38.36 TAX CASES.

For ship repairs see *Sec 400; CTA s 55* and for adjustment of relief on dutiable goods see *Sec 411; CTA s 6*.

For provisions against artificial prices, etc. between associated companies and other abuses, see *Secs 412, 413; CTA ss 62, 63*.

For tax credits relating to distributions made, see *CTA ss 64–67 as amended by FA 1978, s 28; FA 1980, s 42; FA 1983, s 28; FA 1988, s 31, 2 Sch; FA 1990, s 36, 1 Sch*. Income tax exemption is phased out for distributions after 28 January 1992, being abolished after 5 April 1994. See *CTA s 66A inserted by FA 1992, s 35(a)*.

See also 12.10 CORPORATION TAX as regards attribution of distributions out of exempt profits and as regards distributions in respect of certain shares carrying assured returns.

For extension to companies rendering 'engineering services' see *FA 1968, s 34; CTA s 60*.

From 1 January 1981, exported goods relief is available only to

(i) companies exporting goods in the course of trade before 1 January 1981, or companies succeeding to the trade, or part of the trade, of such companies after 31 December 1980.

(ii) a company which, before 1 January 1981, receives an assurance in writing in respect of a trade from the Minister for Finance or his agent that the relief will be available to the company notwithstanding the provisions of *FA 1980, s 42(1)*. Such an assurance will be given only where the Minister is satisfied that the trade will (or does) contribute significantly to regional or national development.

No claim to exported goods relief may be made for any accounting period after one for which a claim to the manufacturing companies relief available from 1 January 1981 is made. [*FA 1980, s 42*].

16.5 **Haemophilia HIV Trust.** Income consisting of payments made by the trustees of the Trust for a beneficiary are disregarded for all income tax purposes. [*FA 1990, s 7*].

16.6 **Interest** is exempt from income tax:

(i)   to the extent of the first £120 for each spouse from the Post Office Savings Bank or trustee savings banks, or to the extent of the first £50 from specified commercial banks, subject to an overall limit of £120. The £120 and £50 limits are doubled for an individual of the age 65 years or more at any time during the year of assessment. The specified commercial banks are the Bank of Ireland, the Allied Irish Banks Ltd, the Northern Bank Ltd, the Ulster Bank Ltd, Ansbacher & Co Ltd, Barclays Commercial Bank Ltd, Guinness & Mahon Ltd, Chase Bank (Ireland) Ltd and the Agricultural Credit Corporation Ltd. [*Sec 344; FA 1967, s 8; FA 1968, s 41(9); FA 1980, s 13; FA 1983, s 8; FA 1984, s 7; FA 1985, s 8*]. See, however, 13.8 DEDUCTION OF TAX AT SOURCE as regards payments of 'relevant interest' which are not exempted;

(ii) on securities used for payment of income tax. [*Sec 345*];

(iii) on bonus payable to an individual under an instalment savings scheme (as under *FA 1970, s 53*). [*FA 1970, s 18*];

(iv) where it is paid to persons not ordinarily resident in RI by a company in the course of 'relevant trading operations' within *FA 1980, ss 39A, 39B* (see 12.17 CORPORATION TAX). [*FA 1995, s 40*].

16.7   **Interest on 'housing loans'** received by approved banks is exempt. [*FA 1976, s 28*].

16.8   **Investment bonds etc.** (under *Central Fund Act 1965*). The premium on redemption is exempt from income tax and corporation tax except where it is part of trading profits. The relief does not apply to Agricultural Commodities Intervention Bills issued by the Minister for Agriculture, or to Exchequer Bills and (after 30 May 1990) other securities issued at a discount by the Minister for Finance. Any profit or gain on sale or redemption of such a security is, however, exempt from income and corporation taxes where the owner is non-RI ordinarily resident (except in the case of corporation tax chargeable on the income of an RI branch or agency of a non-resident company). [*Sec 465; F(No 2)A 1968, s 8; FA 1969, s 63; FA 1984, s 28; FA 1990, s 138*].

16.9   **Irish securities.** Interest from stocks, shares and securities beneficially owned by individuals resident only in RI in

(*a*)   certain non-manufacturing companies as certified by Minister for Finance, and

(*b*)   certain manufacturing companies as certified by Revenue Commissioners,

has a 20% exemption from income tax. [*Secs 329–332; FA 1970, s 16; CTA 2 Sch 10–12*]. This exemption ceases to apply to any payment made after 8 February 1983. [*FA 1983, s 7*].

Certain government and other securities may be issued exempt from RI taxation so long as the beneficial owner is not ordinarily resident in RI (although the exemption does not apply to certain holdings of financial concerns) [*Secs 464, 474; FA 1992, s 42(1)(a)*] and the interest on certain securities issued to and continuously held by foreign-controlled companies may be exempt from corporation tax. [*FA 1985, s 69*].

16.9A **Judges' expenses.** An annual allowance paid to a judge of the District Court, the Circuit Court, the High Court or the Supreme Court under *Courts of Justice Act 1953, s 5(2)(c)*, in full settlement of necessary expenses as a judge not otherwise reimbursed out of moneys provided by the Oireachtas, is disregarded for all income tax purposes (and accordingly no Schedule E deduction is allowed for such expenses). [*FA 1994, s 164*].

16.10 **Military pay, pensions, etc.** The following are exempt from tax: wound and disability pensions and related gratuities under *Army Pensions Acts 1923–62*, etc.; military gratuities

16.11   Exempt Income and Special Savings Schemes

and demobilisation pay to officers of National or Defence Forces; deferred pay and gratuities under *Defence Act 1954*; pensions under *MacSwiney (Pension) Act 1950*; gratuities for services with the Defence Forces; any yearly sum under the *Griffith Settlement Act 1923*; and certain pensions, etc. payable to veterans of the War of Independence (or their widows or dependants). [*Secs 340, 554(3); FA 1980, s 12; FA 1982, s 9; FA 1983, 4 Sch*].

16.11   **National lottery profits** are exempt from corporation tax in the hands of a company licensed by the Minister for Finance to hold the National lottery. [*FA 1987, s 34*].

16.12   **Patent royalties** arising to RI residents from patents devised etc. in RI, and certain other sums arising from such patents, are exempt from income tax and corporation tax. [*FA 1973, s 34; CTA 2 Sch 35; FA 1994, s 28*]. For individuals other than the deviser (or joint deviser) of the patent, relief is restricted to two-thirds of such payments arising after 23 April 1992 and before 6 April 1993, to one-third of payments arising in 1993/94, and is abolished thereafter. [*FA 1992, s 19(1)*]. See also 12.10 CORPORATION TAX as regards certain distributions of such royalties.

16.13   **Personal injuries.** For 1990/91 and subsequent years of assessment, income arising from the investment of damages paid, following institution of a civil action, in respect of personal injury is exempt. The injury must have given rise to mental or physical infirmity by reason of which the injured person is permanently and totally incapacitated from maintaining himself, and the income must be the sole or main income of the injured person. [*FA 1990, s 5*].

16.14   **Redundancy payments** under *Redundancy Payments Act 1967* are exempt from income tax under Schedule E. [*FA 1968, s 37(2)*].

16.15   **Scholarship** income and bursaries etc. are exempt. [*Sec 353*].

16.16   **Stallion fees.** See 30.1 SCHEDULE D, CASES I and II.

16.17   **Sweepstakes.** Profits of sweepstakes held under *Public Hospitals Act 1933*, as amended, and lotteries licensed under *Gaming and Lotteries Act 1956* are exempt from tax under Schedule D. [*Secs 346, 350*].

16.18   **Thalidomide children.** Payments received from the German foundation and from the Minister of Health are exempt, as is income derived from investing such payments. [*FA 1973, s 19; FA 1975, s 9; FA 1978, s 7*].

16.19   **Writers, composers, painters and sculptors** solely resident in RI may claim exemption from tax on all earnings from works of cultural or artistic merit. For claims made after 2 May 1994, the Revenue Commissioners may not determine that a work meets these criteria unless it complies with guidelines (which are available free of charge from the Revenue Commissioners) drawn up by the Arts Council and the Minister for Arts, Culture and the Gaeltacht with the consent of the Minister for Finance. See 38.177, 38.178 TAX CASES.

The exemption operates for the year of assessment in which the claim (if accepted) is first made and subsequent years of assessment. An appeal procedure is available where the Revenue Commissioners fail to make a determination in relation to a work or works within six months of the claim to relief being made in respect of that work or works. [*FA 1969, s 2; FA 1989, s 5; FA 1994, s 14; FA 1995, s 173(2)*].

16.20   **Miscellaneous concessions.** It is understood that the following are, by concession, not normally charged to tax.

(i)   Meal vouchers to the value of 15p per day supplied to employees.

(ii)   Payments to foster parents under *Health Act 1953, s 55*.

(iii)   Long service awards at a cost not exceeding £12 per year of service.

(iv)   Continuing sick benefit during a period of absence from work under a taxpayer's own insurance policy, unless the benefit has continued for at least twelve months prior to commencement of the year of assessment.

(v)   Suggestion schemes. Certain payments under formally constituted schemes are exempted.

(vi)   Training courses. Certain expenses paid or reimbursed by employers are exempted, and a deduction similarly allowed for expenditure by employees not so reimbursed.

The inspector concerned should be consulted for the detailed conditions for exemption.

16.21 **SPECIAL SAVINGS SCHEMES**

Following *FA 1993*, there are four savings schemes or investment products which in effect offer the investor a special tax rate of 10% or 15% on an investment up to a maximum of £50,000 (£75,000 in certain cases). (See 16.22 below as regards restrictions where more than one type of investment is acquired and the application of the £75,000 limit.) The four types of scheme are:

(*a*)   special savings accounts, introduced with effect from 1 January 1993 by *FA 1992, s 22*, under which interest is received under deduction of 15% tax (10% before 6 April 1995), no further liability arising on the depositor. See 13.8 DEDUCTION OF TAX AT SOURCE;

(*b*)   special investment policies with life assurance companies, introduced with effect from 1 January 1993 by *FA 1993, ss 11, 12*, underlying funds of which are subject to a special corporation tax rate of 10% (but with special rules for the determination of taxable profits). Restrictions on fund investments apply similar to those in relation to schemes within (*c*) below. See generally 12.15 CORPORATION TAX;

(*c*)   special investment schemes, introduced with effect from 1 February 1993 by *FA 1993, s 13*, under which special investment units may be purchased in authorised unit trusts, the income and gains arising to the scheme being taxable at a special rate of 10%. See 16.23 below;

(*d*)   special portfolio investment accounts, introduced with effect from 1 February 1993 by *FA 1993, s 14*, under which income and gains of investments held in such accounts with designated stockbrokers are taxable at 10%, to be accounted for by the stockbroker. See 16.24 below.

16.22 **Restrictions on investments under schemes within 16.21 above.** An individual may normally have only one of the four types of investment described at 16.21 above. However, provided he does not have a joint interest in any such investment, he may have both a special savings account within 16.21(*a*) and one of the three types of investment within 16.21(*b*), (*c*) or (*d*), but a limit of £25,000 (rather than £50,000) must be applied to one of those investments. Alternatively, if the individual has only one investment, whether joint or not, and it is within 16.21(*b*), (*c*) or (*d*) above, the limit is increased to £75,000. Married couples who have only joint investments may have two or three investments, including at least one within 16.21(*a*) above and at least one within 16.21(*b*), (*c*) or (*d*) above, or they may have four investments, two from each category, but limits of £25,000 (rather than £50,000) must then be applied to both of the accounts in one of those categories. Similar restrictions applied before 6 April 1994, except that the £25,000 limit applied to all accounts rather than just those in one category where multiple accounts were held, and married couples were allowed only two joint investments without the £25,000 restriction applying, and the increased limit of £75,000 did not apply.

Any other restriction on investments by reference to the £50,000 limit applies by reference to the £25,000 limit where applicable.

[*FA 1993, s 16; FA 1994, s 34*].

16.23 **Special investment schemes.** A '*special investment scheme*' is an authorised unit trust scheme meeting the following conditions:

(*a*)   the beneficial interests in the scheme assets must be divided into 'special investment units'; and

(*b*)   the proportion of the aggregate consideration (calculated as under *CGTA 1975, s 9* and *CGT(A)A 1978, 1 Sch 4*) given for scheme shares which must relate to 'qualifying shares' and to 'specified qualifying shares' is:

   (i)   at any time before 1 February 1994, 40% and 6% respectively;

   (ii)   at any time in the year ending 31 January 1995, 45% and 9% respectively;

   (iii) at any time in the year ending 31 January 1996, 50% and 10% respectively;

   (iv)   at any time after 31 January 1996, 55% and 10% respectively.

'*Qualifying shares*' are ordinary shares in RI-resident companies, or companies listed on the Irish Stock Exchange or dealt in on the smaller companies or unlisted securities markets of that Exchange, other than shares in investment companies or UCITS or whose value approximates to the market value of the company's assets. '*Specified qualifying shares*' are qualifying shares in companies with market capitalisation (at the time of the acquisition of the shares) of less than £100 million.

'*Special investment units*' are units so designated which are sold to an individual after 31 January 1993 by the management company or trustee of the scheme, and in respect of which the following conditions are met.

(A)   The aggregate investment by an individual in such units (jointly or otherwise) must not exceed £50,000, and the market value of his units must not exceed £50,000 at any time on or after the fifth anniversary of his first scheme investment. Disposals of units are identified with acquisitions on a last in, first out basis for these purposes.

(B)   Units must not be sold to or owned by an individual under full age.

(C)   Units must only be sold to individuals who are beneficially entitled to all amounts payable in respect of those units, and to whom all such amounts are to be paid.

(D)   Units may only be jointly owned by married couples to whom the units were sold as such.

(E)   Except in the case of married couples' jointly-owned units, units may not be held in more than one scheme, and married couples may only jointly hold units in a maximum of two schemes. Married couples with jointly-owned units may not also hold units on their own account.

(F)   A signed declaration must be made, in prescribed form and containing such information and undertakings as the Revenue Commissioners may reasonably require, to the management company or trustee in writing by the individual to whom units are sold, to the effect that the conditions in (B)–(E) are satisfied in relation to those units. The declaration must contain the full name and address of the person beneficially entitled to the units, and an undertaking to notify the management company or trustee if any of conditions (B)–(E) subsequently ceases to be satisfied. It must also contain such other information as the Revenue Commissioners may reasonably require.

As regards (A), (B), (D) and (E), ownership must be beneficial ownership. Declarations under (F) are to be retained and made available to the inspector as required.

A special investment scheme is not treated as a collective investment scheme (see 12.21 CORPORATION TAX) (except in relation to certain stamp duty and VAT requirements). Income and gains arising to the scheme and accruing for the benefit of unitholders give rise to no liability on the unitholders, and within the scheme are chargeable to income tax and capital gains tax at a special rate of 10% (before reduction by any other credit or relief). Distributions from RI-resident companies are generally chargeable, the tax credit being available for set off against the scheme's tax liabilities, any excess being repaid. This does not apply, however, to distributions in respect of eligible shares in qualifying companies under the business expansion scheme (see 21.2 INVESTMENT IN CORPORATE TRADES AND RESEARCH AND DEVELOPMENT), which are exempt from charge, any tax credit being ignored. Chargeable gains in respect of such eligible shares are also exempted (without prejudice to the relief of allowable losses). Otherwise, for the purposes of determining the scheme chargeable gains, assets are treated as disposed of and reacquired at market value on each 5 April. Indexation does not apply, nor does the exemption of government securities. (Special rules apply for shares disposed of within four weeks of acquisition.) Any net allowable capital losses in a year are treated as reducing chargeable income for that year, any excess being carried forward as a loss of the following year.

The 'DIRT' scheme (see 13.8 DEDUCTION OF TAX AT SOURCE) applies to deposits made by the scheme trustees or managers.

Payments made to holders of units by the managing company or trustees by reason of rights as unitholders are disregarded for income tax purposes, and no chargeable gain arises on the disposal of units.

[FA 1993, s 13, 16(3); FA 1994, s 34(g)].

16.24 **Special portfolio investment accounts.** A '*special portfolio investment account*' is an account, designated as such, opened after 31 January 1993 in which a 'relevant investment' is held and in respect of which the following conditions are met.

(*a*)   The account must not be opened by or held in the name of an individual under full age.

(*b*)   The account must be opened by and held in the name of the individual beneficially entitled to the income and gains in respect of the relevant investments therein.

(*c*)   The account may not be a joint account, except in the case of an account opened and held as such by a married couple.

(*d*)   Only one account may be held by an individual. Married couples may jointly hold two such accounts. Married couples with jointly-held accounts may not also hold accounts of their own.

(*e*)   A signed declaration must be made, in prescribed form and containing such information and undertakings as the Revenue Commissioners may reasonably require, to the 'designated broker' in writing by the individual to whom interest is payable in respect of the relevant investment(s), to the effect that the conditions in (*a*)–(*d*) are satisfied in relation to the account. The declaration must contain the full name and address of that individual, and an undertaking to notify the designated broker if any of the conditions in (*a*)–(*d*) subsequently ceases to be satisfied. It must also contain such other information as the Revenue Commissioners may reasonably require.

(*f*)   Each account and the related assets must be kept separately from all other accounts.

(*g*)   The aggregate investment in an account must not exceed £50,000, and the market value of the investments must not exceed £50,000 at any time on or after the fifth anniversary of the first investment.

(*h*)   The investment requirements described at 16.23(*b*) above apply also to such accounts.

For the purposes of (*g*) above, disposals are, where necessary, identified with later acquisitions before earlier.

A '*relevant investment*' is an investment in 'qualifying shares' and 'specified qualifying shares' (for the definitions of which see 16.23 above), in addition to which certain government and other securities may be held. A '*designated broker*' is a dealing member firm of the Irish Stock Exchange which has notified the Revenue Commissioners of its intention to accept deposits from individuals for the purpose of acquiring relevant investments.

The provisions relating to special savings accounts (see 13.8 DEDUCTION OF TAX AT SOURCE) apply equally to special portfolio investment accounts, with certain modifications, in particular with the retention of a 10% rate of tax deduction after 5 April 1995 (when the rate for special savings accounts was increased to 15%). The designated broker is deemed to have made a payment on 5 April in each year of assessment of the aggregate income and gains arising from the relevant investments held in the account, and is required to account for tax equivalent to 10% of that payment by 1 November following the end of the year of assessment. No other tax liability arises on the account holder. The calculation of the income and gains is on broadly the same basis as applies in relation to special investment schemes (see 16.23 above), including the exemption of business expansion scheme investments. Additionally, the small chargeable gains exemption does not apply. A net loss is carried forward to set against income and gains of the following and future years.

The period from 1 February 1993 to 5 April 1993 is treated as forming part of year of assessment 1993/94 for these purposes.

[*FA 1993, s 14; FA 1995, s 11(2)*].

17   Exempt Organisations

The following organisations etc., are specifically exempt from tax as indicated.

17.1   **Agricultural societies.** Profits of shows, etc., applied to purposes of society, exempt from income tax. [*Sec 348*]. See 38.165 TAX CASES.

17.2   **Athletic or amateur games or sports.** Exempt from income tax on income applied to promotion. [*Sec 349*]. The conditions for exemption were tightened by *FA 1984, s 9*, which enables the Revenue Commissioners (subject to the usual appeal rights) to deny exemption where they are satisfied that the body was not established, or no longer exists, solely for the promotion of athletic or amateur games or sports, or was, wholly or partly, established to secure a tax advantage. Bodies exempt before 6 April 1984 continue to qualify, but relief may be withdrawn after 5 April 1984 from any body failing to meet the above conditions. See also 38.167 TAX CASES.

17.3   **Bord Gáis Éireann** is exempt from corporation tax. [*FA 1983, s 32*].

17.4   **An Bord Pinsean** is exempt from corporation tax. [*FA 1991, s 41*].

17.5   **Charities** (including hospitals, public schools, almshouses, ecclesiastical bodies) are exempt on income and gains applied to charitable purposes. This includes any profits from a trade of farming, and profits of any other trade where the work is mainly carried on by the beneficiaries of the charity. Gifts for maintenance of graves, memorials etc. up to £60 p.a. or up to £1,000 lump sum are treated as gifts for charitable purposes. [*Secs 333, 334; Charities Act 1961, s 50; CGTA s 22(1); CTA 2 Sch 13; FA 1981, s 11*]. It is understood that, by concession, trading profits from occasional bazaars, jumble sales, gymkhanas, etc. organised to raise funds for charity are generally exempted from liability to tax.

See 38.30–38.32 TAX CASES.

Donations to Third World charities. Where a 'qualifying donation' is made to a 'designated charity', it is treated in the hands of the charity as an annual payment received under deduction of tax at the standard rate (see 2.5 ALLOWANCES AND RATES) for the year in which the donation was made. The charity may claim repayment of the notional tax deducted in the normal way (but restricted, where the donor has not paid all the tax referred to in the 'appropriate certificate' (see below), to the amount of that tax which has been paid).

A '*qualifying donation*' is a donation made after 30 June 1995 by an RI-resident individual who has given an 'appropriate certificate' to the charity in relation to the donation, and has paid the tax referred to in the certificate (and is not entitled to claim a repayment of any part of that tax). The donation must be a sum or sums of money totalling not less than £200 in the year of assessment of payment, and must neither be subject to a condition as to repayment nor give rise to a benefit for the donor or a connected person (within *F(MP)A 1968, s 16*). It must not be related to the acquisition of property by the charity from the donor (or a connected person) other than by way of gift.

There is an overall limit of £750 on qualifying donations by an individual in a year of assessment.

A '*designated charity*' is a charity designated for these purposes by the Minister for Foreign Affairs, who is required to maintain a list of designated bodies, to be published from time to time in the *Iris Oifigiúil*. The conditions for designation are set out in *FA 1995, s 8(2)*, broadly requiring the sole object of the charity to be relief and development in countries in

Part 1 of the OECD List of Aid Recipients. Notice of withdrawal of designation must be published in the *Iris Oifigiúil* within one month, and is effective from the start of the year of assessment in which such notice is given.

An '*appropriate certificate*' is a certificate in prescribed form containing the donor's Revenue and Social Insurance Number, and a statement by the donor to the effect that the donation satisfies the above requirements, and that the donor has paid or will pay income tax of an amount equal to tax at the standard rate on the grossed-up amount of the donation, being neither tax the donor may charge against any other person or deduct, satisfy or retain out of any payments the donor is liable to make to any other person, nor tax deducted under the DIRT scheme (see 13.8 DEDUCTION OF TAX AT SOURCE).

[*FA 1995, s 8*].

17.6 **Credit unions** registered under *Industrial and Provident Societies Acts* are exempt from income tax, corporation profits tax, and corporation tax. [*FA 1972, s 43*].

17.7 **Custom House Docks Development Authority** is exempt from corporation tax. [*FA 1988, s 42*].

17.8 **European Economic Interest Groupings (EEIGs)** within *EEC Directive No 2137/85* and *SI 1989 No 191* are not within the charge to income tax, corporation tax or capital gains tax. Any assessment required to be made in respect of profits or gains arising to the EEIG is made on (and losses allowed to) members of the EEIG. The income tax and capital gains tax provisions relating to partnerships apply generally, with appropriate modification, to the activities of an EEIG, as if members of the EEIG were partners therein. [*FA 1990, s 29*].

17.9 **Friendly societies.** Unregistered societies with income not exceeding £160 p.a. and registered societies not assuring to any person a gross sum in excess of £1,000 or £52 p.a. annuity are exempt under Schedules C, D and F. [*Sec 335; FA 1967, s 7; FA 1969, s 33; CTA 2 Sch 14*].

A registered society must also

(i)   be established solely for purposes under *Friendly Societies Act 1896, s 8(1)* and not for securing a tax advantage, and

(ii)   since establishment, have engaged solely in activities for those purposes and not in trading activities (other than insurance re members).

The society may appeal against a determination that it does not satisfy these conditions. [*FA 1973, s 44*].

17.10 **The Great Book of Ireland Trust.** Income arising to the trustees from sales of The Great Book of Ireland is disregarded for all tax purposes, as are payments made by the trustees to Clashganna Mills Trust Ltd or Poetry Ireland Ltd. [*FA 1991, s 13*].

17.11 **Harbour authorities** within RI are exempt under Schedule D on profits arising from maintaining normal port facilities. [*Sec 343*].

17.12 **The Housing Finance Agency** is exempt from corporation tax on trading income arising from the making of loans and advances under *Housing Finance Agency Act 1981, s 5* and, for accounting periods ending after 5 April 1990, on income otherwise chargeable under SCHEDULE D, CASE III (31). [*FA 1985, s 24; FA 1990, s 56*].

17.12A The **Irish Horseracing Authority, Irish Thoroughbred Marketing Ltd** and **Tote Ireland Ltd** are exempt from corporation tax on profits for accounting periods ending after 30 November 1994, and gains on disposals after that date are not chargeable gains. [*FA 1995, s 44*].

17.13 Local authorities, health boards, agriculture committees and vocational education committees in respect of income tax (other than the requirement to deduct basic rate tax from certain interest payments, see 13.8 DEDUCTION OF TAX AT SOURCE) [*FA 1990, s 13*] and capital gains tax (see 9.7(*j*) CAPITAL GAINS TAX). See also 12.1 CORPORATION TAX.

17.13A National Co-operative Farm Relief Services Ltd. See 12.12 CORPORATION TAX.

17.14 National Treasury Management Agency profits and gains are exempt from corporation tax. [*FA 1991, s 20*].

17.15 Nítrigin Éireann Teoranta is exempt from corporation tax on any income (otherwise chargeable under Schedule D, Case I) arising in any accounting period ending between 1 January 1987 and 31 December 1999 inclusive from the supply of gas (purchased from Bord Gáis Éireann) under contract to Irish Fertilizer Industries Ltd. [*FA 1988, s 39; FA 1992, s 57*].

17.15A   Non-commercial state-sponsored bodies (as listed in *FA 1994, 2 Sch*, which is subject to amendment by order by the Minister for Finance). Income of such bodies which would otherwise be chargeable under Schedule D, Case III, IV or V (i.e. *excluding* trade or professional income) is disregarded for all purposes of the *Tax Acts*, except the liability to deduct and account for tax on interest payments under the Deposit Interest Retention Tax scheme (see 13.8 DEDUCTION OF TAX AT SOURCE) (and such a body is not treated as a company within the corporation tax charge for the purposes of the exception from treatment of a deposit as a 'relevant deposit' detailed at 13.8(vii), nor as a person to whom the repayment provisions of *FA 1986, s 39* under the scheme apply). The exemption applies from the date of incorporation or establishment of the body, but no repayment may be made of income or corporation tax paid by such a body. [*FA 1994, s 32, 2 Sch*].

17.16 Savings banks have certain exemptions on income under Schedules C, D and F and on profits or gains on certain securities. [*Sec 337; CTA 2 Sch 16; FA 1990, s 61; FA 1993, s 43*]. See 12.21 CORPORATION TAX as regards trustee savings banks.

17.17 Superannuation funds and occupational pension schemes (see *FA 1972, ss 13–25, 1 Sch; FA 1974, s 64* for general provisions and *FA 1991, s 12* as regards medical practitioners' scheme) approved by the Revenue Commissioners are exempt from tax on investment income. After 5 April 1988, investment includes dealing in financial futures or traded options (including, after 31 March 1991, on a non-RI exchange). There is a charge to tax of 25% (10% before 29 January 1992 and in certain other cases) on refunds of employee contributions. [*FA 1972, s 16; CTA 3 Sch; FA 1988, s 30; FA 1991, s 38; FA 1992, s 6*].

17.18 Trade unions. Registered unions which are precluded by statute or rules from assuring to any person a gross sum exceeding £2,000 or annuity exceeding £750 p.a. are exempt under Schedules C, D and F on investment income applied solely to provident benefits. [*Sec 336; FA 1971, s 15; FA 1973, s 12; CTA 2 Sch 15; FA 1980, s 11*].

17.19 Trust schemes approved by the Revenue Commissioners for providing retirement annuities to individuals etc. in particular occupations are exempt from income tax on investment income. [*Secs 235(4) and 235A(5)–(6) inserted by FA 1974, s 66*].

17.20 United Nations Organisation or Council of Europe. Certain bodies having consultative status with these organisations may claim the same exemptions as charities [*FA 1973, s 20*], but with the additional benefit that deeds of covenant to them for three years or longer will be recognised for tax purposes. [*FA 1973, s 15*].

17.21 Voluntary Health Insurance Board is exempt from corporation tax in respect of income arising from the carrying out of schemes of voluntary health insurance. [*CTA s 80*].

18 Farming

[*FA 1974, ss 13–28 as amended*].

Cross-reference. See also 33.3 SCHEDULE D, CASE V — PROPERTY INCOME as regards leasing of farm land.

18.1 Profits from farming in RI are assessable under Schedule D, Case I as a single trade (whether carried on solely or in partnership). This does not, however, prevent the commencement and cessation basis (see 30.5 SCHEDULE D, CASES I AND II) applying where a partnership trade is set up or ceases. [*FA 1974, ss 14, 15; FA 1983, s 11*]. See 17.5 EXEMPT ORGANISATIONS as regards farming carried on by charities. See 38.166 TAX CASES as regards 'farming'.

The *Farm Tax Act 1985* became law on 25 July 1985, and imposed a charge based on adjusted farm acreage. It was effective for one year only and is to be repealed. See 18.9 below.

18.2 INDIVIDUALS—BASIS OF ASSESSMENT

Individuals are assessed under Schedule D, Case I. The normal accounts basis applies (see 30.3 SCHEDULE D, CASES I AND II), *except that* a 'full-time farmer' may elect (in writing, within 30 days of the date of the notice of assessment for the year) to be charged by reference to an average figure (see below), provided that he was charged to tax under Schedule D, Case I on the current year (for 1989/90 and earlier years, the preceding year) basis in respect of farming profits in each of the two preceding years of assessment. [*FA 1974, s 20B(1)*].

An individual carrying on 'farming' in a year of assessment is a '*full-time farmer*' unless he, or his spouse living with him, carried on at any time during the year of assessment, solely or in partnership, another trade or profession (but excluding provision of accommodation in farm buildings by wife as ancillary activity in farm trade), or was a director controlling, directly or indirectly, more than 25% of the ordinary share capital of a trading company. 'Farming' means farming land in RI, other than market garden land (see 30.1(ii) SCHEDULE D, CASES I AND II), 'occupied' wholly or mainly for the purposes of husbandry, and '*occupation*' of land means having the use thereof or the right to graze livestock thereon. [*FA 1974, ss 13, 16; FA 1975, ss 12, 14*].

The 'average figure' for a year of assessment is arrived at by taking a 'fair and just' average of the profits or losses of the three years ending on the normal accounting date in the year of assessment concerned (for 1989/90 and earlier years, in the year preceding the year of assessment concerned) or, if there is no normal accounting date, 5 April in that year. Any necessary aggregation of profits and losses in those three years is made. Where an overall loss results, one-third of that loss will be allowable in the normal way for the year of assessment concerned. Losses so aggregated may not be relieved in any other way.

An election, once made, continues in force for all subsequent years until withdrawn, except that it does not apply to years in which the individual is not a full-time farmer (see above). The election may be withdrawn for a year of assessment and subsequent years (by notice in writing with the return required under *FA 1988, s 10* (see 28.12 RETURNS) or, for 1989/90 and earlier years, within the six months before 6 July in that year of assessment) provided that in each of the three preceding years of assessment the averaging basis was applied. The election is in any event deemed to have been (validly) withdrawn for any year in which the individual is not a full-time farmer, and for subsequent years.

170

Following such a withdrawal election (whether actual or deemed), the assessment for each of the first two of the last three years assessed on the averaging basis is increased to the amount of the profits assessed for the last such year, if either or both of them would otherwise have been less than that figure.

Capital allowances and charges continue to be given or made as if the profits were assessed on the normal basis, and the cessation provisions under Schedule D, Case I (see 30.5 SCHEDULE D, CASES I AND II) will have effect, where appropriate, notwithstanding any election under these provisions.

The normal rules regarding computation of profits, delivery of returns, etc. apply where assessments are raised on the averaging basis. [*FA 1974, s 20B; FA 1981, s 10; FA 1990, s 20(2)*].

18.3 COMPANIES

Companies are liable to CORPORATION TAX (12) on all farming profits. Previously, they were assessable to income tax on such profits but without the benefit of the special rules for individuals (see 18.2 above).

18.4 COMPULSORY DISPOSAL

A special relief may be claimed where cattle forming part of trading stock of a farming business are all compulsorily disposed of after 5 April 1993 under any statute relating to the eradication or control of livestock diseases (including all cattle required to be disposed of under a brucellosis eradication scheme), and there is an excess of amounts received as a result of that disposal over the value of the stock at the beginning of the accounting period of the disposal. The farmer may elect (by the specified return date for the period of the disposal — see 28.12 RETURNS — or, if that date was before 2 June 1995, by 31 December 1995) to have the excess treated as arising in two equal instalments, either in the accounting period of the disposal and the following accounting period, or in the two accounting periods following that of the disposal.

Where, not later than the end of the second of the two accounting periods in which the excess is treated as arising (as above), expenditure of not less than the amount received as a result of the compulsory disposal is incurred on replacement of the cattle, stock relief (see 18.8 below) at a special rate of 100% may be claimed in respect of the excess brought in in each period. Where, however, such replacement expenditure is less than the amount so received, the relief in each of those two accounting periods is correspondingly reduced.

[*FA 1995, s 22*].

See also 18.8 below.

18.5 CAPITAL ALLOWANCES

A farm buildings allowance may be claimed for capital expenditure (net of grants etc.) incurred after 5 April 1971 on farm buildings (excluding buildings or parts of buildings used as dwellings), fences etc., allowing the expenditure to be written off over up to ten years. For expenditure incurred after 31 March 1989, this is extended to include roadways, holding yards, drains and land reclamation. For expenditure incurred before 6 April 1982, farmhouses and cottages also qualified, but allowances were restricted to one-third of the expenditure in the case of farmhouses. For expenditure incurred after 26 January 1994, the allowances are made during a writing-down period of seven years beginning with the chargeable period in which the expenditure is incurred, at the rate of 15% p.a. for the first six years and 10% p.a. for the last year. Previously, the normal annual allowance was 10%, but accelerated allowances could be claimed up to 31 March 1992. In respect of expenditure incurred after 31 March 1991 and before 1 April 1992, the maximum accelerated allowance was 25% (whether claimed in one or more than one chargeable periods). Between 1 April 1989 and 31 March 1991 inclusive, the maximum allowance was 50%, and between 6 April 1982 and 31 March 1989 inclusive, 30%. There was a special accelerated allowance of up to 50% (in one or more chargeable periods) for expenditure between 1 April 1991 and 31 March 1993 inclusive on farmyard pollution control works in respect of which grant-aid has been paid under the Farm Improvement Programme or the Scheme of Investment Aid for the Control of Farmyard Pollution. Where an individual was exempt from assessment or elected for notional assessment, any annual allowances which would otherwise have been claimable are deemed to have been made and not carried forward. Where property is transferred, any allowances remaining for subsequent years continue to be claimable by the transferee. [*FA 1974, s 22; CTA 1 Sch 70; FA 1980, s 27; FA 1982, s 16; FA 1983, s 15; FA 1988, s 52(1); FA 1989, s 15; FA 1990, s 77; FA 1991, s 25; FA 1993, s 34(2); FA 1994, s 23*].

An initial allowance of 20% was also claimable on such expenditure incurred between 6 April 1974 and 5 April 1980. [*FA 1974, s 22(2)(a); CTA 1 Sch 70; FA 1980, s 27*].

Free depreciation may be claimed for capital expenditure incurred after 5 April 1977 and before 1 April 1989 on constructing fences, roadways, holding yards, or drains, or in land reclamation. [*FA 1977, s 14; FA 1988, s 52(2)*].

Capital allowances on machinery and plant. In determining wear and tear allowances and balancing allowances and charges, the appropriate wear and tear allowances are deemed to have been made to the farmer for any years in which he did not farm, or was not taxable under Schedule D, Case I, or was charged on the notional basis, or during which the machinery or plant was not used for farming purposes. [*FA 1974, s 25; CTA 1 Sch 71; FA 1978, s 14*].

For a chargeable period beginning after 5 April 1980 and before 6 April 1989, initial allowances and free depreciation on machinery or plant (excluding fixed machinery or plant used only in a farm building) are restricted. No such allowances are available where either (*a*) the expenditure on such machinery or plant, or (*b*) the aggregate of all other capital allowances available, amounts to 30% or more of the profits or gains from farming in the period. In any other case, such allowances are to be limited so that the total of capital allowances for the period does not exceed 30% of the profits or gains. [*FA 1980, s 26; FA 1988, s 52(3)*].

See under 8.3 CAPITAL ALLOWANCES for basis periods in which expenditure is incurred, and generally.

18.6   LOSSES

Relief for losses (see 22.2 LOSSES) will **not** be given

(*a*)   by carry-forward to 1978/79 or subsequent years of a loss incurred in a year of assessment for which the farmer was not chargeable to tax in respect of his farming profits. [*FA 1978, s 15*].

(*b*)   by carry-forward of losses incurred prior to 1974/75. [*FA 1974, s 24*].

(*c*)   by set-off against other income in cases where farming profits would not be charge-able under Schedule D, Case I. [*FA 1974, s 26; FA 1983, s 14*].

(*d*)   by set-off against other income, or profits of another trade, unless it is shown that, for the year of loss, the trade was being carried on on a commercial basis and with a view to profit. Nor will relief be given if a loss was incurred in each of the three previous years of assessment unless the activities in the year are carried on so as to justify a reasonable expectation of profits in the future and the activities in the three previous years could not reasonably have been expected to become profitable until after the year under review.

These restrictions also apply to losses in market gardening but do not apply (i) where the trade is part of, and ancillary to, a larger undertaking, or (ii) where the trade commenced during the previous three years (ignoring changes where a person is carrying on the trade before and after the change). [*FA 1974, s 27*].

18.7   PAYMENT AND INTEREST

For 1983/84 onwards, full-time farmers pay the tax on their farming profits at the same time as others chargeable under Schedule D, Case I or II. See 25.1 PAYMENT OF TAX. See also 25.3 PAYMENT OF TAX as regards interest on unpaid tax.

18.8   STOCK RELIEF

The scheme of stock relief described below applied with some modifications to a wide range of trades for company accounting periods ending before 6 April 1983 and for individual and partnership years of assessment to and including 1983/84. For company accounting periods ending after 5 April 1983 and before 6 April 1997, and for years of assessment 1984/85 to 1996/97 inclusive, it applies only to persons carrying on the trade of **farming**.

There are now two kinds of relief for an increase in value of trading stock, and although basically similar and complementary there are some differences.

Relief B applies to eligible RI resident companies carrying on farming trades for CORPORATION TAX (12) for accounting periods ending before 6 April 1997. [*FA 1975, s 31A, 5 Sch, as inserted and amended*].

Relief C applies to eligible individuals and partnerships carrying on farming trades, resident in RI and not resident elsewhere, for years of assessment 1974/75 to 1996/97 inclusive (i.e. normally for the same accounting periods as for companies above, tax under Schedule D, Case I being usually charged on the 'current year' basis). [*FA 1976, s 12 as amended*].

Where relief has been given it may be 'clawed back' where a *decrease in stock value* occurs (see below). This ceases to apply for 1993/94 onwards, and for company accounting periods ending after 5 April 1993.

Persons eligible for the reliefs must be carrying on a farming trade, chargeable under Schedule D, Case I, which accounts for at least 75% of their gross sales receipts. No relief is given for an accounting period which ends because the person ceases to trade, or ceases to be resident, or ceases to be within Schedule D, Case I. [*FA 1975, ss 31, 31A, 3 Sch 4, 5 Sch 4; FA 1976, s 26(1); FA 1977, s 43, 1 Sch Pt V*].

The **amount of the relief** for 1993/94 to 1996/97 inclusive, and for company accounting periods ending after 5 April 1993 but before 6 April 1997, is generally 25% of the '*increase in stock value*' (i.e. value of opening stock *minus* value of closing stock), but restricted to the amount of the trading profits. It is, however, increased to 100% in certain cases in relation to 'qualifying farmers' (see below). The amount to be deducted is treated as a trading expense. Previously, the relief was 110% of the increase in stock value. [*FA 1975, ss 31(2), 31A(2)(4); FA 1982, s 13; FA 1983, s 13; FA 1984, s 33; FA 1985, s 17; FA 1986, s 15; FA 1987, s 22; FA 1988, s 23; FA 1989, s 11; FA 1991, s 18; FA 1993, s 28; FA 1995, s 21(1)(2)*]. In relation to Relief B, and for accounting periods ending before 6 April 1993, there are provisions to ensure that the increase in stock value is determined by reference to the 'highest stock value' over all accounting periods (see below).

A '*qualifying farmer*' is an individual

(A)   who, in the year 1993/94 or any subsequent year of assessment, first qualifies for grant aid under the Scheme of Installation Aid for Young Farmers operated by the Department of Agriculture, Food and Forestry, or

(B)   who first becomes chargeable under Schedule D, Case I in respect of farming profits in a year of assessment after 1992/93, who is aged under 35 at the commencement of that first year of assessment, and who, at any time in that first year of assessment, either:

  (i)   holds a qualification included in *FA 1994, 6 Sch* (or certified by Teagasc (The Agricultural and Food Development Authority) as corresponding to such a qualification) and also (in certain cases) a certificate issued by Teagasc of satisfactory attendance of more than 80 hours at a course of farm management training; or

  (ii)   has satisfactorily attended any full-time course of at least two years' duration at a third-level institution, and holds a certificate issued by Teagasc of satisfactory attendance of more than 180 hours at a course of agriculture and/or horticulture training; or

  (iii)   having been born before 1 January 1968, holds a certificate issued by Teagasc of satisfactory attendance of more than 180 hours at a course of agriculture and/or horticulture training.

The 100% relief (as above) is available for 1995/96 to 1998/99 inclusive to individuals who become qualifying farmers before 6 April 1996, and for 1996/97 to 1999/2000 for those who become qualifying farmers after 5 April 1996 and before 6 April 1997. [*FA 1995, s 21(3)(4)*].

Compulsory disposal. There is a special relief, for individuals and partnerships only, where trading stock includes livestock which is compulsorily disposed of under any statute relating to the eradication or control of diseases in livestock, resulting in a fall in the value of trading stock over the relevant accounting period. An election may be made (in writing within two years (one year as respects disposals before 6 April 1990) of the end of the accounting period) for the closing stock value of the accounting period and the opening stock value of the immediately following accounting period (and, for disposals after 5 April 1990, where appropriate, the opening stock value of the next period after that) to be computed as if the stock compulsorily disposed of had not been disposed of. For disposals after 5 April 1992, the election may alternatively apply to the opening stock values of each of the three accounting periods following that of disposal. No stock relief claim may be made for an accounting period to which such an election applies. This relief does not apply to affect the valuation of closing stock where a farmer ceases to carry on his trade, or to be chargeable in respect of it under Schedule D, Case I, or to be RI resident. [*FA 1980, s 28(3); FA 1990, s 9; FA 1991, s 18(3); FA 1992, s 20*]. See also 18.4 above.

'Accounting period' is a period of twelve months ending on the date to which the accounts are usually made up (or otherwise it is a period of twelve months as determined by the Revenue Commissioners). [*FA 1975, ss 31(1), 31A(1); FA 1976, ss 12(1), 26(1)*]. Where the beginning or end of an accounting period does not coincide with accounting dates, there will be no opening (or closing) stock to use in ascertaining any increase in value. In these cases a 'reference period' will extend back to the beginning, or forward to the end, of the period of account which bridges the beginning or end of the accounting period. In any other case the reference period will begin or end with the date of an accounting period. Where a reference period applies, the increase or decrease in stock values and the trading profits are apportioned (in months and fractions of months) to the accounting period. [*FA 1975, 3 Sch 1, 2, 5 Sch 1, 2; FA 1976, s 26(1); FA 1977, s 43, 1 Sch Pt V*].

'Trading stock' is as defined in *Sec 62* (see 30.27 SCHEDULE D, CASES I AND II but excludes any stock to the extent that any payments on account have been received (for which see 38.110 TAX CASES). [*FA 1975, ss 31(1), 31A(1); FA 1976, s 26(1)*]. A person commencing to trade at the beginning of an accounting period for which relief is claimed without opening stock taken over from a previous business will have an opening stock value attributed to it by the inspector who 'shall have regard to all the relevant circumstances of the case' particularly the movements in costs of stock items and changes in volume of trade during the period. There is a right to appeal against the inspector's decision. [*FA 1975, 3 Sch 5, 5 Sch 5; FA 1976, s 26(1)*]. The inspector may also (subject to appeal) treat opening or closing stock as having such value as appears 'reasonable and just' where stock is acquired or disposed of otherwise than in the normal conduct of the trade. Where the basis of calculation for opening and ending stock differs, the opening stock will be amended to conform. [*FA 1975, ss 31(7), 31A(6); FA 1976, s 26(1)*].

'**Trading income**' means (except as noted below) the profits or gains computed under Schedule D, Case I before deduction of any losses or capital allowances, or addition for balancing charges. [*FA 1975, ss 31(1), 31A(1); FA 1976, s 26(1)*]. For Relief B, the company's trading profit (which the total relief may not exceed) is that income *after* deduction of losses and capital allowances and additions for balancing charges. [*FA 1975, s 31A(4) (a) proviso; FA 1977, 1 Sch Pt V; FA 1979, s 23*]. For Relief C, there is a similar ban on carrying forward losses or capital allowances or carrying back losses. [*FA 1976, s 12(7) (7A); FA 1977, 1 Sch Pt V; FA 1979, s 23*].

Claims to relief for accounting periods ending after 5 April 1993 (Relief B) and for 1993/94 to 1996/97 (Relief C) must be made on or before the specified return date (see 28.12 RETURNS) for the chargeable period. For earlier years, they must be made before the assessment becomes final or (Relief B) by 31 December in year of assessment following that in which period ends and (Relief C) by 31 December in the year of assessment. [*FA 1975, ss 31(5), 31A(5); FA 1976, ss 12(4), 26(2); FA 1979, s 23; FA 1993, s 28*].

Highest stock value. For company accounting periods ending before 6 April 1993, a 'decrease in stock value' in an accounting period (i.e. the amount, if any, by which opening value exceeds closing value) is carried forward in certain circumstances to reduce (to nil, if appropriate) the amount of increase in stock value in successive subsequent accounting periods ending before 6 April 1993. Thus any decrease in an accounting period which is not deemed to be a trading receipt (see below) must be subtracted in the next accounting period in which an increase in stock value occurs, and any balance carried forward, but not to an accounting period ending after 5 April 1993.

[*FA 1975, s 31A(8); FA 1977, 1 Sch Pt V; FA 1993, s 28*].

Relief 'clawback'. As regards Relief B any decrease in stock value in an accounting period ending before 6 April 1992 is treated as a trading receipt for that period, but only up to the amount by which the aggregate of earlier such deemed receipts is less than the total relief which has been obtained by the company. Only reliefs and deemed receipts for accounting periods ending in the ten years before the start of the period in which the decrease in stock value took place are to be taken into account for this purpose. In relation to clawback of stock increases attracting relief in accounting periods ending after 5 April 1989, the ten-year clawback period is reduced to seven years. Any decrease not treated as a trading receipt is used to restrict future relief under the 'highest stock value' rules above. Where this does not result in all the relief obtained having been 'clawed back' in accounting periods ending before 6 April 1992 (subject to the ten-year or seven-year restriction as above), a decrease in stock value occurring in any accounting period ending on or after that date results in certain additional deemed receipts until the balance is achieved. [*FA 1975, s 31(A)(7)(9); FA 1977, 1 Sch Pt V; FA 1978, s 27; FA 1980, s 53; FA 1981, s 20; FA 1982, s 24; FA 1983, s 26; FA 1984, s 33; FA 1985, s 17; FA 1986, s 15; FA 1987, s 22; FA 1988, s 23; FA 1989, s 11; FA 1991, s 18; FA 1993, s 28*].

Individuals. Similar rules apply as regards Relief C so that a decrease in an accounting period is treated as a trading receipt, but not so as to exceed the aggregate relief obtained, and similarly subject to the ten-year or seven-year restriction on reliefs and deemed receipts to be taken into account. Additional receipts will also be deemed, where necessary, in accounting periods ending on or after 6 April 1992. [*FA 1976, s 12(5)(6); FA 1977, 1 Sch Pt V; FA 1978, s 27; FA 1979, s 23; FA 1980, s 53; FA 1981, s 20; FA 1982, s 24; FA 1983, s 26; FA 1984, s 33; FA 1985, s 17; FA 1986, s 15; FA 1987, s 22; FA 1988, s 23; FA 1989, s 11; FA 1991, s 18*].

Where there is a decrease in stock value in a period after one in which 110% relief (as above) was obtained, then, in determining the amount to be treated as a trading receipt of that later period, the decrease is deemed to be increased by 10% or, if less, by the net benefit for preceding periods from the 110% provisions (i.e. relief given in respect of *deemed* stock increases less clawback of *deemed* stock decreases).

Ceasing to be chargeable. For Reliefs B and C there is a deemed trading receipt where the person ceases to carry on a trade or to be chargeable under Schedule D, Case I or to reside in RI. In such a case the closing stock value of the final accounting period is deemed to be nil, creating a total decrease in stock value to which the above rules apply. [*FA 1975, s 31A(10); FA 1976, s 12(8); FA 1977, 1 Sch Pt V*].

None of these clawback provisions applies in respect of years of assessment 1993/94 onwards or accounting periods ending after 5 April 1993.

Companies in a group (i.e. where one company is wholly owned by the other or where both companies are wholly owned by another company). Where one company ('the transferor company') manufactures goods which it transfers to the transferee company whose business consists of selling those goods (and which is not otherwise entitled to stock increase relief) and both companies have the same accounting or reference period, then a claim for relief by the transferor company shall apply as if both companies are one and the aggregate of their stock values and trading profits are taken in computing the total relief, which is then apportioned between them in proportion to the closing stock value of each. [*FA 1975, 3 Sch 3, 5 Sch 3; FA 1976, s 26(1)*].

Successions. Special rules apply where a farming trade ceases to be carried on by a person (the 'predecessor'), whether on death or otherwise, and is immediately thereafter carried on by a person (the 'successor') resident in RI in the year he commences to carry on the trade (and not resident elsewhere) who is either

(i)   the personal representative of the predecessor, or

(ii)   the spouse or child (as defined in *CGTA 1975, s 27*, see 9.7(*q*) CAPITAL GAINS TAX) of the predecessor, who does not at the time of commencement possess any other trading stock of a trade of farming.

The special rules apply equally where a person within (ii) above succeeds to a trade carried on by a person within (i) above in respect of the same trade, and where two or more persons both within (i) or (ii) above (as appropriate) continue to carry on the trade in partnership.

Where that condition is met, and the trade in question and trading stock thereof pass in their entirety to the successor, the predecessor (or his personal representative) and successor jointly (or, if the successor is himself the personal representative of the predecessor, the successor alone) may elect (in writing within two years of the end of the year of assessment in which the successor commenced to carry on the trade) that:

(*a*)   *Sec 62* (valuation of stock on discontinuance — see 30.26 SCHEDULE D, CASES I AND II) is not to apply on the transfer; and

(*b*)   stock relief allowances and charges are to be given to or made on the successor as if the carrying on of the trade by the predecessor had been his carrying on of the trade.

[*FA 1984, s 33(5)*].

18.9 FARM TAX

Farm tax was introduced by the *Farm Tax Act 1985* with effect from 6 October 1986 and, in the 1987 Budget Statement, the Government made a commitment to abolish the tax, making farm tax applicable for one year only. Formal repeal of the tax has not yet taken place. However, in the case described at 38.43A TAX CASES, it was held that the *Act* was unenforceable for both future and past years.

For details of the farm tax, see 1989/90 or earlier editions of this book.

19   Government and Other Public Loans

[Secs 463–474]. See also 29 SCHEDULE C.

19.1   The Minister for Finance issues securities the interest on which is payable gross, but recipient is then assessable under Schedule D, Case III. *[Sec 466]*. Extended to debentures, etc., and other securities of the Agricultural Credit Corporation *[Sec 468]*, certain securities issued outside RI by local authorities, provided they are not held by persons domiciled or ordinarily resident in RI (or, for securities acquired after 15 May 1992, by or for a branch or agency through which a financial concern carries on business in RI) *[Sec 470; FA 1992, s 42(1)(b)]*, stock issued by Bord na Móna after July 1957 *[Sec 473]* and securities of certain European bodies *[FA 1973, s 92; FA 1989, s 98]*. Also stock, etc., of Electricity Supply Board, and C.I.E. *[Sec 471]*, stocks issued under *Local Government Act 1946, s 87 [Sec 472]*, debentures, etc., of Aer Lingus, Aer Rianta or Aerlínte Éireann *[Sec 467]*, of Bord Telecom Éireann and Irish Telecommunications Investments plc *[Sec 467A; FA 1988, s 70]*, of Radio Telefís Éireann and the Industrial Credit Corporation plc *[Sec 467B; FA 1989, s 95]*, of Bord Gáis Éireann *[Sec 467C; FA 1992, s 24]* and of the International Bank for Reconstruction and Development *[FA 1994, s 161]*, and Central Bank Reserve Bonds *[FA 1972, s 11]*. In these cases terms of issue may include complete exemption (capital and interest) of beneficial owners not domiciled nor ordinarily resident in RI, or income tax exemption of such owners domiciled but not ordinarily resident (except that, for securities acquired after 15 May 1992 and held by or for a branch or agency through which a financial concern carries on business in RI, neither exemption applies). *[Sec 474; FA 1992, s 42(1)(c)]*.

Further extended by *FA 1970, s 59* to securities guaranteed by a Minister of State (in these cases the paying company may deduct from Schedule D, Case I profits the amount of interest so paid gross).

See 16.8 EXEMPT INCOME AND SPECIAL SAVINGS SCHEMES as regards securities issued at a discount.

19.2   Government securities may also be issued exempt from RI taxation so long as in the beneficial ownership of persons not ordinarily resident there (although the exemption does not apply to securities acquired after 29 January 1992 and held by or for a branch or agency through which a financial concern carries on business in RI). *[Sec 464; FA 1992, s 42(a)]*.

19.3   Accumulated interest on RI National Savings Certificates is exempt *[Sec 463]*, but not interest on UK Government Stocks paid tax-free or on UK National Savings Certificates.

20   Interest Payable

20.1   DEDUCTION OF TAX

Interest is payable without deduction of tax, except where paid

(*a*)   by a company (otherwise than in a fiduciary or representative capacity), or

(*b*)   to a person whose usual place of abode is outside RI, or

(*c*)   on an instalment promissory note signed before 6 April 1974, or

(*d*)   by certain deposit-takers (see 13.8 DEDUCTION OF TAX AT SOURCE).

But (*a*), (*b*) and (*c*) do not apply and no tax is deductible from interest paid

(i)   to or by a bank carrying on business in RI,

(ii)   by a company authorised by the Revenue Commissioners to make payments gross,

(iii)   on certain government securities,

(iv)   by industrial and provident societies to RI residents,

(v)   by a close company which is a distribution under *CTA s 97* (excess interest to certain directors),

(vi)   to a person within (*b*) above by a company in the course of operations covered by a certificate relating to certain financial services or Shannon airport operations (see 12.17 CORPORATION TAX), or

(vii)   by the National Treasury Management Agency.

[*FA 1974, ss 31, 50; CTA 2 Sch 42; FA 1988, s 38; FA 1991, s 20(3)*].

There are special provisions for interest on quoted Eurobonds. [*Sec 462A; FA 1994, s 15*].

Any agreement providing for payment of interest less tax shall be construed as requiring payment of the gross amount. [*FA 1974, s 39*].

20.2   BUSINESS INTEREST

Where interest paid under deduction of tax is incurred for business purposes, it is deductible from profits assessable under Schedule D, Cases I and II and under Case V (rental income). [*FA 1974, ss 40, 42, 51*]. See also 20.3(*c*)(i) below. See 12.9 CORPORATION TAX as regards yearly interest paid by companies.

20.3   PERSONAL INTEREST RELIEF

(*a*)   Interest on '**qualifying loans**' from a bank, stockbroker or discount house carrying on business in RI, or being yearly interest charged to tax under Schedule D, attracts relief up to a limit, for 1989/90 onwards, of **80%** (increased to **90% for 1993/94** only, and previously, for 1987/88 and 1988/89, 90%) of the *lesser* of

    (A)   the amount of interest actually paid, and

    (B)   (i)   **£5,000** (£4,000 for 1992/93 and earlier years) for a married man whose wife's income is, by election, treated as his,

          (ii)   **£3,600** (£2,900 for 1992/93 and earlier years) for a widowed person, or

          (iii)   **£2,500** (£2,000 for 1992/93 and earlier years) for other individuals.

20.3 Interest Payable

For **1993/94** and subsequent years, the percentage restriction does not apply for the first five years of assessment (three years in relation to 1993/94 relief only) for which relief falls to be given to a taxpayer in respect of a qualifying loan or loans. (This applies equally where the taxpayer first claimed relief before 1993/94, so that e.g. a taxpayer whose first claim was in 1990/91 is entitled to 80% relief for 1993/94, 100% relief for 1994/95 and 80% relief thereafter.) Any resultant additional relief in the case of a married person is given equally to each spouse.

Also for **1993/94** and subsequent years, the amount of interest, calculated as above, for which relief may be obtained is reduced by **£100** (**£200** in the case of a married man within (B)(i) above) or, if it is less than that amount, is reduced to nil, *except that* for 1994/95 and subsequent years, there is no reduction for the first five years of assessment for which relief falls to be given to a taxpayer in respect of a qualifying loan or loans (any resultant additional relief in the case of a married person being given equally to each spouse).

All limits apply to the aggregate of interest allowed under these provisions and certain annual payments paid abroad and set against income from abroad.

Relief is given by means of a claim for repayment of tax. Before 1994/95, relief was at the claimant's marginal rate of tax, but for 1997/98 and subsequent years relief is restricted to the standard rate of income tax, and is given by a reduction in income tax liability. The proportion of the relievable interest for which relief is given by a reduction in total income is reduced to 75% for 1994/95, to 50% for 1995/96 and to 25% for 1996/97, the balance attracting standard rate relief by a reduction in income tax liability. Except for the purposes of the age and low income exemptions (see 2.7, 2.8 ALLOWANCES AND TAX RATES), no deduction is made from total income for that part of the relievable interest for which relief is given by a reduction in income tax liability. [*Sec 496 as amended by FA 1974, s 29; FA 1979, s 9; FA 1980, s 7; FA 1982, s 21; FA 1983, s 10; FA 1987, s 6(1); FA 1989, s 7; FA 1993, s 5; FA 1994, s 6*]. Interest on money borrowed to pay death duties also attracts relief under these provisions, but is not subject to the above mentioned limits. [*Sec 496(4); FA 1982, s 21(8); FA 1987, s 6(2)*].

A *qualifying loan* is a loan, or replacement for a loan, not being an overdraft, used by an individual solely for the purchase, repair, development or improvement of a building (or part) and grounds situated in RI, Northern Ireland or Great Britain, being the sole or main residence of the individual, his former or separated spouse, or a dependent relative other than a child (in the latter case, provided that the occupation is rent-free). It does not, however, include a loan used to defray payment to a spouse (unless separated) for the purchase of property, or (where the payment is excessive) any payment to a person connected with the borrower (as defined by *F(MP)A 1968, s 16(3)*), and a loan ceases to be a qualifying loan if the property purchased (or a superior interest in it) is disposed of after 25 March 1982. [*FA 1982, ss 21(1)(5)(10), 22(1)*]. It is understood that, for these purposes, temporary absences of up to one year are in practice ignored, as, generally, are periods of absence of up to four years during which a person is required to move home by reason of his employment (and successive such periods separated by a minimum of three months of occupation).

Personal representatives of a deceased person, and trustees of a settlement under a will, generally continue to receive relief for interest on a loan which was a qualifying loan at the time of the deceased's death, as long as the property continues to be occupied by his widow, former or separated spouse or dependent relative (other than a child). [*FA 1982, s 21(7)*].

Subsidies. A repayment as above in respect of interest paid may however be restricted for any year of assessment in which an individual has received any sum(s) from the Minister of the Environment under a first-time buyers special mortgage subsidy scheme. Any part of the repayment arising from loans in relation to which such a subsidy has been granted ('specified loans') is reduced by the amount (if any) by which (i) below exceeds (ii) below.

(i) is the aggregate of the tax repayment for the year otherwise arising from 'specified loans' and the subsidy or subsidies (as above) received in the year.

(ii) is the total of all payments of principal and interest made in the year on 'specified loans'.

A subsidy granted in respect of a period is treated as being made in the year of assessment in which the period falls, with time apportionment where the period falls in more than one year of assessment. [FA 1981, s 6].

Preferential loans. See 34.3 SCHEDULE E for the charge to tax of notional interest on certain loans.

Aggregation. Interest paid by connected persons is aggregated, but this does not apply to married persons who are treated for income tax purposes as if they were not married. There is also aggregation where a company is connected with an individual or another company. [FA 1974, s 38; CTA 2 Sch 44; FA 1979, s 9; FA 1980, s 7].

(b) **Bridging loans.** On a move from one 'only or main residence' to another, the previous 'only or main residence' continues to be treated as such for a period of twelve months from acquisition of the new residence, provided that all appropriate steps are taken to dispose of the previous residence. Also, where an only or main residence is sold and replaced by means of a loan used only for that purpose, the interest *for the first twelve months* on that loan (including any subsequent loan wholly or partly replacing it) is eligible for relief up to the limits in (a) above (apportioned on a time basis if the twelve months extends over two tax years) *in addition to any other interest* paid during that time. [FA 1974, s 32; FA 1982, s 21(6)].

(c) **Loan for purchasing ordinary shares in, or making a loan to, certain companies.** Two alternative forms of relief are available for interest payable on such a loan, or a loan to repay an eligible loan, where the company concerned is a trading or property company (or a company whose business is holding stocks, shares or securities of a trading or property company). The reliefs only apply if there has been no recovery of capital (as defined). If any capital has been recovered, including any connected consideration, without reducing the loan, the relief for interest is reduced proportionately. It is understood that, in practice, relief will continue to be available where shares in the company are exchanged for shares in another close company as a result of a company reorganisation, provided that relief would have been available for investment in that other company.

(i) There is unrestricted relief if (A) the investor (borrower) has a material interest in the company (more than 5% control) when the interest is paid, and (B) during the period of the loan, if the investor is a *company*, at least one of its directors is also a director of the company concerned or a connected company or, if an *individual*, his main work was the management or conduct of the company or a connected company. [FA 1974, ss 33–35; CTA 2 Sch 43].

(ii) An *individual* is entitled to unrestricted relief on such loans relating to a *private* company if, during the period of the loan, he was (A) if the company is a trading or property company, an employee (full-time or part-time) or director (full-time or part-time), or (B) if a holding company, a full-time employee or full-time director. He will not be eligible if the company or any person connected with it had made any loan or advance to him (or any connected person) except in the ordinary course of a business (as defined).

Public company. Similar relief applies, up to a maximum of £2,400, to eligible loans relating to a public company. The individual must be a full-time employee or full-time director and the relief only applies in relation to a public 'holding company' if it is resident in RI.

Full-time employee/director. An individual qualifies if he is required to devote substantially the whole of his time to the service, as employee or director, of the company concerned or a company which is a 90% subsidiary of the company concerned. [*FA 1974, s 34; FA 1978, s 8; FA 1979, s 9*].

Relief for individuals under (i) or (ii) above is phased out after 5 April 1992 where the company concerned is a '*quoted company*', i.e. a company whose shares are listed on a stock exchange or dealt in on certain other markets, on a 'specified date'. The '*specified date*' is the later of

(*a*)   6 April in the second year of assessment next after that in which the company became a quoted company, and

(*b*)   (i)   if the loan was applied before 6 April 1989, 6 April 1992,

     (ii)   if the loan was applied during 1989/90, 6 April 1993,

     (iii)   if the loan was applied after 5 April 1990, 6 April 1994.

Relief is restricted to 70% of that otherwise available for the year of assessment starting on the specified date, to 40% in the following year of assessment, and is abolished thereafter. However, no relief at all is given for interest on a loan applied after 28 January 1992 at a time when the company concerned is a quoted company. [*FA 1992, s 14(1)–(3)*].

For loans applied after 23 April 1992, relief to individuals under (i) and (ii) above is denied unless the loan in question is applied for *bona fide* commercial purposes and not as part of a scheme or arrangement a main purpose of which is the avoidance of tax. [*FA 1974, s 34(3); FA 1992, s 14(4)*].

Business expansion scheme and film investment shares. Relief is not available to individuals under the above provisions where a claim for relief under *FA 1984, Pt I, Ch III* (see 21.2–21.13 INVESTMENT IN CORPORATE TRADES AND RESEARCH AND DEVELOPMENT) is made in respect of the amount subscribed for the shares for whose purchase the loan was made and the shares were issued after 19 April 1990, or where a claim for relief is made under *FA 1987, s 35* (investment in films, see 12.22 CORPORATION TAX) in respect of the amount subscribed for the shares for whose purchase the loan was made and the shares were issued after 5 May 1993. (*Note.* This does not apply to relief for shares issued in research and development companies, see 21.14 *et seq.* INVESTMENT IN CORPORATE TRADES AND RESEARCH AND DEVELOPMENT.) [*FA 1990, s 11; FA 1993, s 6*].

(*d*)   **Loans for purchasing a share of, or making a loan to, a partnership** (or in replacing a prior eligible loan). Unrestricted relief is given to an individual on interest on such a loan provided that he personally acted in the conduct of the partnership trade between purchase or loan and payment of the interest and has recovered no part of the capital. If any capital has been recovered (including any connected consideration) the relief for interest will be reduced proportionately. [*FA 1974, s 36*]. The Revenue have indicated that their practical requirements are that:

    (i)   the borrowings must be introduced into the partnership by way either of loan or of contribution of capital;

(ii)   the money must be used wholly and exclusively for the purposes of the trade or profession; and

(iii)   any recovery of capital must be used to repay the loan, if relief is not to be restricted.

However, in respect of loans received before 1 December 1985, interest relief will continue to be available concessionally where the strict conditions are not met, provided that:

(*aa*)   no relief would otherwise be available;

(*bb*)   the borrowings were individually identified so as to show the lender, the principal outstanding and the terms of repayment;

(*cc*)   the purpose for which the moneys were borrowed was stated (not necessary where total borrowings did not exceed about £10,000);

(*dd*)   there was no departure from or variation of the terms of the original loan, so as to extend the borrowing indefinitely; and

(*ee*)   there is, in the Revenue's view, no abuse of the concessional relief.

It is understood that, in practice, relief will continue to be available where the partnership is incorporated into a close company, provided that relief would have been available under (*c*) above for investment in that company.

(*e*)   **Loans for replacement of business capital.** Interest on loans to replace business capital withdrawn within the five years preceding the date of the loan will not be regarded as business interest. [*FA 1974, s 37*].

21 Investment in Corporate Trades and Research and Development

Cross-reference. See also 12.9 CORPORATION TAX as regards certain alternative reliefs for research and development and 12.22 CORPORATION TAX as regards investment in film production companies, for which relief is (from 6 April 1993) available to both individual and corporate investors.

21.1 The relief for investment in corporate trades (frequently referred to as the Business Expansion Scheme) was introduced by *FA 1984, ss 11–27*, and these provisions are dealt with at 21.2–21.13 below. The relief was extended by *FA 1986, ss 17–30* to investment in research and development companies, and although the relief is broadly similar to that for investment in corporate trades, the various new definitions and differences in the research and development relief scheme are dealt with at 21.14–21.21 below. Following *FA 1993*, certain research and development activities are themselves treated as within the main relief.

21.2 BUSINESS EXPANSION SCHEME

Conditions for relief. A 'qualifying individual' who subscribes for 'eligible shares' in a 'qualifying company' which are issued after 5 April 1984 and **before 6 April 1996 (6 April 1998** in the case of a 'relevant investment', see 21.7 below) may claim income tax relief on his investment, provided that

(i) the purpose of the issue is to raise money for a 'qualifying trade' carried on by the company (or by certain subsidiaries of the company, see 21.11 below) or which it intends to carry on and in fact commences within two years of the issue (three years in relation to issues after 5 April 1985 if the company spends at least 80% of the money subscribed for the issue on research and development work connected with, and undertaken with a view to the carrying on of, the trade), and

(ii) the money was used, is being used or is intended to be used

    (*a*) with a view to creating or maintaining employment in the company or, in the case of advance factory building construction and leasing (see 21.6(*e*) below), in either or both a company contracted to construct the building and a company leasing it, and

    (*b*) for the purpose of enabling the company to undertake or enlarge 'qualifying trade' operations; to carry out research and development; to acquire technological information and data; to develop new or existing products or services, provide new products or services; to identify new markets and develop new and existing markets for its products and services; or to increase its turnover.

From 6 April 1987 to 29 January 1991, in the case of a qualifying shipping trade, relief for investment for the purpose of purchase of a ship is conditional on certification by the Minister for the Marine regarding eligibility for grant-aid and, for shares issued after 11 April 1989, benefit to the RI shipping fleet.

In the case of advance factory building construction and leasing (see 21.6(*e*) below):

(*a*) relief is dependent on certification by an appropriate industrial development agency as to the status and location of the building; and

(*b*) as regards (i) above, the trade is deemed to have commenced on commencement of construction of the building.

In the case of qualifying trading operations consisting of research and development within 21.6(*f*) below, relief is dependent on certification by an appropriate industrial development agency that operations have commenced and that the operations have the potential to lead to the commencement of trading operations within 21.6(i) (manufacturing), (ii) (certain services) or (*d*) (plant cultivation).

[*FA 1984, s 12(1),(4)(b),(11); FA 1985, s 13(b); FA 1986, s 13; FA 1987, s 8(a); FA 1989, s 9(a); FA 1990, s 10(b); FA 1991, ss 14, 15(1)(a); FA 1993, s 25(b)(i)(vi); FA 1995, s 17(1)(b)(vi)*].

Relief is allowed only when the company (or subsidiary) has carried on the trade for four months (or in the case of a 'relevant investment' (see 21.7 below), has commenced to carry on the relevant trading operations), and not before 1 January 1985. In the case of qualifying trading operations consisting of research and development within 21.6(*f*) below, the trade is deemed to have commenced on the date of issue of the appropriate certificate. If, before the trade has been carried on for four months, the company (or subsidiary) is dissolved or wound up for bona fide commercial reasons, and not as part of a scheme the main purpose (or one such purpose) of which was tax avoidance, relief will nevertheless be available. [*FA 1984, s 12(4)(a),(5)(8); FA 1993, s 25(b)(iii)(iv); FA 1995, s 17(1)(b)(iii)*].

Relief is also available where shares are subscribed for by a nominee for the individual claiming relief, including the managers of an investment fund designated by the Revenue Commissioners for this purpose. The Revenue Commissioners have wide powers to designate funds for this purpose, and to withdraw such designation (withdrawal being effective for subscriptions by the fund after the date of publication of the notice of withdrawal in Iris Oifigiúil). Specifically they must so designate a fund if, but only if, it is established under irrevocable trusts for the sole purpose of enabling 'qualifying individuals' to invest in 'eligible shares' of a 'qualifying company', and the terms of those trusts satisfy certain conditions as to the manner in which shares are purchased, dividends distributed, and moneys held, as to fund charges, and prohibiting connections between fund managers or trustees and the companies for whose shares the fund subscribes. The fund must close before the first investment is made, and annual audited accounts must be submitted to the Revenue Commissioners. Shares must be held by the fund for five years before they can be transferred into the name of a participant in the fund. [*FA 1984, s 27*].

21.3 A '*qualifying individual*' must subscribe for the shares on his own behalf, must not during the 'relevant period' receive from the issuing company a dividend within the 'customs-free airport' or 'exported goods relief' provisions (see 16.2, 16.4 EXEMPT INCOME), and must not, at any time in that period, be 'connected with' the issuing company (or a subsidiary of that company). He is so '*connected with*' any company:

(i)   of which he is a partner, director or employee, or of a partner of which he is a director or employee, *except that* as a director or employee he is only 'connected with' a company if he (or a partnership of which he is a member) receives (or is entitled to receive) from that company (or from a company which is a partner of that company), during the five years following the issue, a payment other than by way of

   (*a*)   payment or reimbursement of allowable expenditure under Schedule E,

   (*b*)   interest at a commercial rate on money lent,

   (*c*)   dividends, etc. representing a normal return on investment,

   (*d*)   payment for supply of goods at no more than market value, or

   (*e*)   any reasonable and necessary remuneration for services rendered which is chargeable under Schedule D, Case I or II (other than secretarial or managerial services, or those rendered by the company itself) or which is emoluments of the directorship or employment;

(ii) of which an associate (as defined by *CTA s 103(3)* but, after 5 April 1985, excluding a relative of the participator) meets any of the conditions at (i);

(iii)   if he directly or indirectly possesses or is entitled to acquire

    (*a*)   more than 30% of its voting power, its issued ordinary share capital, or its loan capital and issued share capital together (loan capital including any debt incurred by the company for money borrowed, for capital assets acquired, for any right to income created in its favour, or for insufficient consideration, but excluding a debt incurred by overdrawing a bank account in the ordinary course of the bank's business), or

    (*b*)   rights entitling him to more than 30% of its assets available for distribution to the company's equity holders (as defined in *CTA ss 109, 111*); or

(iv)   of which he has control (as defined in *CTA s 158*):

and in applying (iii) and (iv), rights and powers of his associates (as in (ii) above) are attributed to him. A person is treated as entitled to acquire anything he is entitled to acquire at a future date or will at a future date be entitled to acquire.

For shares issued after 16 June 1993, an individual is not connected with a company by reason only of (iii) or (iv) above

(A)   if, throughout the 'relevant period', the aggregate of all amounts subscribed for the issued share capital and loan capital of the company does not exceed £250,000 (£150,000 as respects eligible shares issued before 6 April 1994), or

(B)   in the case of a 'specified individual' (see 21.7 below), by virtue only of a 'relevant investment' in respect of which relief has been given for the period prior to issue of the shares (see 21.7 below).

Relief given as a result of (A) or (B) above is not withdrawn by reason only that the individual subsequently becomes connected with the company under (iii) or (iv) above.

Relief is also denied where a person is 'connected with' (as above) a subsidiary of the issuing company (see 21.11 below) if it is a subsidiary during the 'relevant period', whether or not it becomes a subsidiary before, during or after the year of assessment in respect of which the individual claims relief and whether or not it is a subsidiary during the time that the circumstances in (i) to (iv) above exist; or where a person has at any time in the 'relevant period' had control (see (iv) above) of a company which has since that time, and before the end of the 'relevant period', become a subsidiary of the issuing company; or where a person directly or indirectly possesses or is entitled to acquire (as above) any loan capital (see (iii)(*a*) above) of such a subsidiary.

'*Relevant period*' in this context means the period from the date of incorporation of the company (or, if later, two years before the shares were issued) to five years after the issue of the shares.

Relief is denied where reciprocal arrangements are made aimed at circumventing this provision.

[*FA 1984, ss 12(7)(a), 14, 2 Sch 2; FA 1985, s 13(a); FA 1993, s 25(e); FA 1994, s 16(1)(b)*].

21.4   A '*qualifying company*' must be incorporated in RI, resident only in RI, and none of its shares, etc. may be listed in the official list of a stock exchange or dealt in on an unlisted securities market. Its business must consist wholly of either

    (*a*)   carrying on one or more 'qualifying trades' wholly or mainly in RI, or

    (*b*)   holding shares or securities of, or making loans to, 'qualifying subsidiaries' (see 21.11 below), with or without the carrying on of one or more 'qualifying trades' wholly or mainly in RI. Although a winding-up or dissolution in the 'relevant period' generally prevents a company meeting these conditions, they are deemed met if the winding-up or dissolution is for bona fide commercial reasons and not part of a scheme the main purpose (or one such purpose) of which is tax avoidance, provided that any net assets are distributed to its members before the end of the 'relevant period' or (if later) the end of three years from commencement of winding-up.

As regards (b) above, for shares issued (except as below) after 11 March 1991, money raised for a subsidiary's qualifying trade must be used only to acquire eligible shares in the subsidiary. This applies after 31 August 1991 where the transitional provisions of *FA 1991, s 16* (see 21.8 below) apply, and after 29 June 1994 in certain cases where work preparatory to an issue was in hand before 12 March 1991. [*FA 1991, s 17(2)(3); FA 1994, s 17*].

For 1987/88 onwards, a company carrying on qualifying tourism activities (see 21.6 below) which is seeking qualification must satisfy the Revenue Commissioners that it has had approved by Bord Fáilte Éireann a three year development and marketing plan designed to attract foreign tourists. Similarly from 2 June 1995, a company carrying on a trade of the cultivation of horticultural produce must have had approved by the Minister for Agriculture, Food and Forestry a three-year development and marketing plan to increase exports or replace imports.

'*Relevant period*' in this context means the period from the date of issue of the shares to three years after that date, or, if later, three years after the 'qualifying trade' was commenced following issue of the shares.

The company must also not at any time in the relevant period either

(i)   have share capital which includes any issued shares not fully paid up;

(ii)   control another company (other than a 'qualifying subsidiary' (see 21.11 below)) or be controlled by another company (control in either case being as defined in *CTA s 102(2)–(6)*, and being considered with or without persons connected with the company as defined in *CTA s 157*);

(iii)   be a 51% subsidiary (see 12.14 CORPORATION TAX) of another company or itself have a 51% subsidiary (other than a 'qualifying subsidiary', see 21.11 below); or

(iv)   be capable of falling within (ii) and (iii) by virtue of any arrangements.

A company in which a 'relevant investment' is made by a 'specified individual' (being that individual's first such investment in that company) (for shares issued before 2 June 1995, a 'relevant company') (see 21.7 below) is not a qualifying company if any transactions in the relevant period with another company were not at arm's length, and that other company was the immediate former employer of the individual concerned (or controlled or was controlled by a company which was the immediate former employer).

There is an additional exclusion if an individual who, after 5 April 1984, has acquired a 'controlling interest' in the company's trade, or in the trade of any subsidiary of the company, also has or has had such an interest in another trade concerned with similar goods or services, or serving a similar market, at any time in the period from two years before to three years after the later of the date of issue of the shares and the date the company or subsidiary commenced the trade.

In the case of a trade carried on by a company, a person has a '*controlling interest*' if he controls (within the definition of *CTA s 102(2)–(6)*) the company; or if the company is close and he is a director of the company and the owner of or able to control more than 30% of its ordinary share capital; or if at least half the trade could be regarded as belonging to him under *CTA s 20(12)*. In any other case it is obtained by his being entitled to at least half of the assets used for, or income arising from, the trade. In either case, the rights and powers of any person's 'associates' are attributed to the person ('associate' being as defined in *CTA s 103(3)*).

21.5 Investment in Corporate Trades etc.

[FA 1984, ss 12(7)(b), 15; FA 1987, s 10; FA 1993, s 25(f); FA 1995, s 17(1)(e)].

A company claiming enhanced relief for certain research and development expenditure is excluded from being a qualifying company. See 12.9 CORPORATION TAX.

21.5 *'Eligible shares'* means new ordinary shares which, for five years after issue, carry no present or future preferential rights to dividends or assets (on a winding-up) or to be redeemed. *[FA 1984, s 12(2)]*. Certain shares carrying an assured return (see 12.10 CORPORATION TAX) are excluded from relief. *[FA 1990, s 34(4)]*.

21.6 A *'qualifying trade'* must be conducted on a commercial basis and with a view to the realisation of profits and must, throughout the 'relevant period' (as defined in 21.4 above) consist wholly or mainly of either or both of

(i) the manufacture of goods as defined for the purposes of the manufacturing companies' relief (see 12.17 CORPORATION TAX), or

(ii) the rendering of services (other than certain financial services, see 12.17(viii) CORPORATION TAX) in the course of a service industry in respect of which an employment grant has been made by Forbairt or the Industrial Development Agency (Ireland) under *Industrial Development Act 1993, s 12(2)* (previously by the Industrial Development Authority under *Industrial Development Act 1986, s 25*) or, for shares issued after 31 December 1993, shares in the company were purchased or taken by either of those bodies under *Industrial Development Act 1986, s 31*, or, for shares issued after 30 May 1990, in respect of which certain grants or financial assistance have been made available by the Shannon Free Airport Development Co Ltd or Údarás na Gaeltachta,

and, in the case of (i), the company must have claimed and be entitled to manufacturing companies' relief (or would have claimed and been entitled but for an insufficiency of profits). Where a trade ceases to be within (i) by virtue of the exclusions from manufacturing companies' relief in *FA 1990, s 41(1)* or *FA 1994, s 48(1)*, and the company concerned would otherwise be a qualifying company, the current provisions continue to apply to subscriptions for shares in the company which were issued before 20 April 1990 or 11 April 1994 respectively (and provisions to similar effect apply in relation to research and development relief, see 21.17 below).

Trades brought within the manufacturing companies' relief by any enactment after *FA 1984* other than *FA 1990, s 41* are excluded from (i) above (and for shares issued after 5 May 1993, film production (see 12.22 CORPORATION TAX) is in any event excluded). The scheme is, however, extended to include

(*a*) on and after 1 January 1987 and before 30 January 1991, shipping activities which qualify for the 10% rate of corporation tax under *FA 1987, s 28* other than fish processing aboard a factory ship, chartering where the crew and the operation of the ship remain under the direction and control of the company or the servicing of offshore installations (see 12.17 CORPORATION TAX);

(*b*) after 5 April 1987 (but with restrictions applicable after 29 January 1991), defined tourist traffic undertakings;

(*c*) from a date to be appointed by the Minister for Finance, the sale of export goods by Trading Houses which qualify for the 10% rate of corporation tax under *FA 1987, s 29* (see 12.17 CORPORATION TAX);

(*d*) after 5 April 1988, cultivating plants by the process of micro-propagation or plant cloning;

(*e*) after 30 May 1990, the construction or leasing of an *'advance factory building'*, i.e. a factory building within *Industrial Development Act 1986, s 2(1)* promoted by a local community group for local development and employment creation and undertaken without any prior leasing commitment;

(*f*)   after 16 June 1993, research and development or other similar activity preliminary to the carrying on of trading operations within (i), (ii) or (*d*) above;

(*g*)   after 10 April 1994, the cultivation of mushrooms within RI;

(*h*)   after 1 June 1995, the cultivation of horticultural produce; and

(*i*)   after 1 June 1995, certain commercial research and development activities.

The changes in (*a*) and (*b*) above after 29 January 1991 are subject to transitional provisions (in *FA 1991, s 16*) in respect of certain issues before 1 September 1991.

Financial services carried on in the Custom House Docks site and brought within the manufacturing companies relief by *FA 1987, s 30* (see 12.17 CORPORATION TAX) are also excluded from (ii) above.

For shares issued after 11 April 1989, leasing of machinery or plant (other than as part of a trade within (*a*) above) or of land or buildings (other than within (*e*) above), and financing and refinancing activities, are not qualifying trading operations, and the definition of 'qualifying tourist undertakings' in (*b*) above is amended to exclude self-catering accommodation in certain urban areas.

A trade of which only a part qualifies under this definition is treated as qualifying provided that at least 75% of its turnover in the relevant period is from the qualifying part.

Adventures in the nature of trade are excluded.

[*FA 1984, s 16; FA 1987, s 11; FA 1988, ss 7, 40(2); FA 1989, s 9(c); FA 1990, ss 10(c), 41(2)(3), 42(2); FA 1991, s 15(1)(e); FA 1993, s 25(g); FA 1994, ss 16(1)(c), 48(3); FA 1995, s 17(1)(f)*].

21.7   **Method of giving relief.** Relief is given on the amount subscribed (subject to certain limits, see 21.8 below) as a deduction, in the year of assessment of the share issue, from the total income of the individual subscribing for the shares, as if the relief were a personal allowance. After 5 April 1987, an investor in a 'designated fund' (see 21.2 above) may instead claim relief for the year of assessment of his investment in the fund, provided the eligible shares are issued in the following year of assessment. [*FA 1984, s 12(3)(9); FA 1987, s 8(b)*].

A 'specified individual' may, however, elect, in relation to a 'relevant investment' made by him after 16 June 1993, for relief to be given instead for any one of the five years of assessment immediately prior to the year of issue of the shares. Relief in respect of a second 'relevant investment' in the same company, made on or after 2 June 1995 and within either of the two years of assessment immediately following that in which the first such investment was made, may similarly, by election, be referred back to any of the five years preceding the first investment. In either case, relief unused in that year may be carried forward (see 21.8 below) so as to obtain relief in nominated subsequent years before that in which the shares were issued (and limited to two such years in the case of shares issued before 2 June 1995), any relief still unused being carried forward to the year of issue of the shares. The limits at 21.8 below apply, so that relief to a maximum of £125,000 (£75,000 in relation to shares issued before 2 June 1995) in respect of any one 'relevant investment' may be obtained immediately provided that the general conditions are met.

An election for relief to be referred back as above may be made by an individual in respect of a maximum of two 'relevant investments' in shares issued on or after 2 June 1995. Previously, only one 'relevant investment' could be the subject of such an election.

In relation to subscriptions for shares issued on or after 2 June 1995, a '*specified individual*' is a qualifying individual who:

21.7   Investment in Corporate Trades etc.

(i) in each of the three years of assessment preceding the year of assessment immediately before that in which the individual makes his first or only 'relevant investment', was not chargeable to tax otherwise than under Schedule E or (in respect of an employment outside RI) Schedule D, Case III in respect of income in excess of the lesser of his income chargeable under Schedule E or (as aforesaid) Schedule D, Case III and £15,000 (where the 'relevant investment' is in a company set up to trade as an exchange facility established in the Custom House Docks Area, this condition need not be satisfied);

(ii) throughout the period beginning with the date of issue of the shares and ending two years later (or, if later, ending two years after the date on which the company began to carry on 'relevant trading operations') possesses at least 15% of the issued share capital of the company in which the 'relevant investment' is made; and

(iii) at the date of subscription for the shares comprised in the relevant investment (the last subscription where there is more than one), and in the preceding twelve months, does not possess and has not possessed, directly or indirectly, and is not and was not entitled to acquire, more than 15% of the issued ordinary share capital, or the loan capital and issued share capital, or the voting power of any other company other than a company which, during the five years ending on the date of that subscription (or last subscription),

    (A) was not entitled to any assets other than cash on hands, or a sum on deposit not exceeding £100,

    (B) did not carry on a trade, profession, business or other activity including the making of investments, and

    (C) did not pay charges within *CTA s 10* (see 12.9 CORPORATION TAX).

As regards (ii) above, a failure by reason of the company's being wound up or dissolved before the end of the period concerned is disregarded provided that the winding up or dissolution is for *bona fide* commercial reasons and not part of a scheme or arrangement a main purpose of which was the avoidance of tax.

As regards (iii) above, there is an exception for an individual owning more than 15% of only one other company where the company is a trading company (other than in land or financial services) with an annual turnover not exceeding £100,000.

In relation to shares issued before 2 June 1995, a broadly similar definition applied, except that the limit in (i) was £10,000, and the exception for companies within (A), (B) and (C) of (iii) did not apply. There was also a requirement that the individual exercised a 'relevant employment', which for shares issued after 2 June 1995 is replaced by a withdrawal of relief where the individual fails to commence such employment within the year of assessment in which the shares are subscribed for or, if later, within six months of the date of the subscription (or last subscription).

For shares issued on or after 2 June 1995, a '*relevant investment*' is the amount (or aggregate amounts) subscribed in a year of assessment by the specified individual for eligible shares in a qualifying company carrying on (or intending to carry on) 'relevant trading operations'; '*relevant employment*' is employment by the company in which the relevant investment is made, as a full-time employee or director (within *FA 1978, s 8*, see 20.3(*c*)(ii) INTEREST PAYABLE), throughout the period of twelve months beginning with the date of issue of the shares (or, if later, with the date of commencement of the employment); and '*relevant trading operations*' are defined in *FA 1984, s 16A* (inserted by *FA 1995, s 17(1)(g)*) broadly as qualifying trading operations (see 21.6 above) (other than those within 21.6(*e*) above) certified by Bord Fáilte Éireann, An Bord Iascaigh Mhara or An Bord Tráchtála, or by an industrial development agency, or by the Minister for Agriculture, Food and

Forestry or the Minister for the Marine to be a new venture which, having regard to its potential for the creation of additional sustainable employment, and the desirability of minimising the displacement of existing employment, may be eligible for grant aid (or, in the case of certain trading operations, within guidelines agreed to by the Minister for Finance). For the latter purposes, the category of 'qualifying trade' described at 21.6(ii) above is extended to include the rendering of certain services for which either an appropriate grant or financial assistance would have been available from the appropriate authority but for its having been made by some other person, or certain feasibility study grants have been provided by an industrial development agency, and, notwithstanding the exclusion referred to at 21.6(ii), certain financial services operations on an exchange facility in the Custom House Docks Area.

For shares issued before 2 June 1995, a '*relevant investment*' is the amount subscribed by an individual for eligible shares in a 'relevant company' in the year of assessment in which the individual commences 'relevant employment'; a '*relevant company*' is a qualifying company incorporated after 16 June 1993 which intends to carry on 'relevant trading operations'; '*relevant employment*' is defined as above; and '*relevant trading operations*' are defined in *FA 1984, s 11(1)* as amended by *FA 1993, s 25(a)(ii)* and *FA 1994, s 16(1)(a)(ii)*, broadly as above.

[*FA 1984, ss 11(1), 12(3)(6A)(7)(c)(d), 14A, 16A; FA 1993, s 25(a)(b)(ii)(v); FA 1994, s 16(1)(a)(c)(2); FA 1995, s 17(1)(a)(b)(d)(f)(g)*].

21.8   **Limits on relief.** Except in the case of investments through 'designated funds' (see 21.2 above), relief is restricted to investments of not less than £200 by any one person in any one company in a year of assessment. In all cases there is an upper limit on investments by an individual in a year (whether in one or more companies) in respect of which relief may be given of £25,000. For 1987/88 onwards, where relief in any year of assessment is limited, either because of insufficiency of income or because of the £25,000 maximum, the unrelieved investment may be carried forward for relief in succeeding years up to and including 1995/96 (1997/98 in the case of 'relevant investments', see 21.7 above). Relief carried forward is given in priority to current relief, earlier years being relieved first. As regards shares issued after 29 January 1991 and before 24 February 1993, no relief was given to the extent to which the lifetime total relief in respect of amounts subscribed by an individual would thereby exceed £75,000. [*FA 1984, s 13; FA 1987, s 9; FA 1991, ss 14, 15(1)(b); FA 1993, s 25(c); FA 1995, s 17(1)(c)*].

See also 21.12 below as regards married persons.

In relation to shares issued after 11 April 1989, there is an additional restriction on the amount which may be raised by a company and attract relief. This limits relief to the amount by which sums raised by all previous issues of eligible shares by the qualifying company fell short of £1,000,000 (£500,000 in relation to shares issued after 29 January 1991 and before 6 May 1993, £2,500,000 in relation to shares issued before 30 January 1991), disregarding sums raised which did not attract relief under these provisions. The sums in respect of which relief is available are apportioned where there is more than one individual entitled to relief in respect of the issue in question. [*FA 1984, s 13A; FA 1989, s 9(b); FA 1991, s 15(1)(c); FA 1993, s 25(d)(i)*]. There are transitional provisions allowing relief up to £1,000,000 (rather than £500,000) in certain cases where shares were issued before 1 September 1991. [*FA 1991, s 16*].

With respect (except as below) to shares issued after 11 March 1991, there are provisions to prevent the circumvention of the £1,000,000 (or £500,000) limit by any agreement, arrangement or understanding whereby trading operations are or are to be carried on by more than one company. The limit is in effect restricted by reference to, and apportioned between, all the companies concerned. [*FA 1991, s 17(1); FA 1993, s 25(d)(ii)*]. These provisions apply after 31 August 1991 where the transitional provisions of *FA 1991, s 16* (see above) apply, and after 29 June 1994 in certain cases where work preparatory to an issue was in hand before 12 March 1991. [*FA 1991, s 17(3); FA 1994, s 17*].

21.9 **Claims for relief.** A claim for relief in respect of any shares issued by a company in a year of assessment must be made not earlier than the date on which relief becomes allowable (see 21.2 above), and must be made within two years of the end of that year of assessment (or, if later, within two years of the end of the initial four months' trading giving rise to eligibility for relief, see 21.2 above). It must be accompanied by a certificate issued by the company stating that the conditions for relief, in respect of the company and the trade, are satisfied in relation to those shares. Before issuing such a certificate, the company must supply to the inspector a statement that those conditions were fulfilled from the beginning of the 'relevant period' (as defined in 21.3 or 21.4 above as appropriate), and such statement must contain such information as the Revenue Commissioners may reasonably require, and be in such form as they may direct, and must contain a declaration that it is correct to the best of the company's knowledge and belief. A certificate may not be issued without the inspector's authority, nor where a notice under *FA 1984, s 24(2)* (see 21.13 below) has been given to the inspector. If such a certificate is issued or statement made fraudulently or negligently, or the certificate should not have been issued (see above), the company is liable to a fine of up to £500 (£1,000 in the case of fraud). The provisions are suitably modified where relief is claimed in respect of shares held by a 'designated fund' (see 21.2 above).

For the purpose of calculating interest on overdue tax (see 25.3 PAYMENT OF TAX), tax charged by an assessment is regarded as due and payable notwithstanding that relief is subsequently given on a claim under these provisions, but is regarded as paid on the date on which a claim is made which results in relief being granted, unless it was either in fact paid earlier or not due and payable until later. Interest is not refunded in consequence of any subsequent discharge or repayment of tax giving effect to relief under these provisions. [*FA 1984, ss 22, 27(5)(6)(7); FA 1993, s 25(h); FA 1995, s 17(1)(h)*].

21.10 **Restriction or withdrawal of relief.** Relief allowed in the 'relevant period' (as defined in 21.3 or 21.4 above as appropriate) may be withdrawn if on any subsequent event it appears that the claimant was not entitled to relief. [*FA 1984, s 12(6)*]. See 21.6 above as regards withdrawal of relief in respect of 'relevant investments' where 'relevant employment' is not commenced within a certain time.

Disposal of shares. Where an individual disposes of, or of interest in or right over, shares, on the purchase of which relief was obtained, before the end of the 'relevant period' (as in 21.3 above), then:

(*a*)   if the disposal is not at arm's length, all relief is withdrawn;

(*b*)   otherwise, relief is withdrawn to the extent of the amount or value of consideration received.

Sales out of a holding of ordinary shares of any class in a company on only part of which relief has been obtained are treated as being of shares on which relief has been obtained rather than others. Where a holding includes shares attracting relief but issued at different times, shares issued earlier are deemed disposed of before those issued later. For this purpose, shares are treated as being of the same class only if they would be so treated if dealt in on an RI stock exchange.

Where, on a capital reorganisation, new shares or debentures are allotted (without payment) in proportion to a holding of shares which have attracted relief, and are treated for capital gains tax as being the same asset (see 9.15 CAPITAL GAINS TAX), the disposal of the new shares or debentures is treated as a disposal of shares which have attracted relief. [*FA 1984, s 17*].

Relief in respect of shares issued after 11 April 1989 is lost where the individual otherwise entitled to relief directly or indirectly enters into an option arrangement or an agreement, within the relevant period, either binding the individual to dispose of the shares, or requiring another person to acquire them, other than at market value at the time of the disposal/acquisition. [*FA 1989, s 9(d)*].

See, however, 21.12 below as regards transactions between married persons.

Value received from company. Entitlement to relief in respect of shares issued by a company is reduced by the amount of any 'value received' from the company (including any company which, during the 'relevant period' (as in 21.3 above), is a subsidiary of that company, whether it becomes a subsidiary before or after the individual receives any value from it) during the relevant period.

An individual '*receives value*' from a company if it:

  (i) repays, redeems or repurchases any part of his holding of its share capital or securities, or makes any payment to him for the cancellation of rights; or

 (ii) repays any debt owed to him other than an 'ordinary trade debt' (i.e. one incurred for normal trade supply of goods on normal trade credit terms (not in any event exceeding six months)) incurred by the company, or any other debt incurred by the company on or after the earliest date on which he subscribed for the shares which are the subject of relief and otherwise than in consideration of the extinguishment of a debt incurred before that date; or

 (iii) pays him for the cancellation of any debt owed to him other than such a debt as is mentioned in the exceptions in (ii) above or a debt in respect of such a payment as is mentioned in 21.3 (i)(*d*) or (*e*) above; or

 (iv) releases or waives any liability of his to the company (which it is deemed to have done if payment of the liability is twelve months or more overdue) or discharges or undertakes to discharge any liability of his to a third person; or

  (v) makes a loan or advance to him (defined as including the incurring by him of any debt either to the company (other than an 'ordinary trade debt', see (ii) above) or to a third person but assigned to the company); or

 (vi) provides a benefit or facility for him; or

(vii) transfers an asset to him for no consideration or for consideration less than market value, or acquires an asset from him for consideration exceeding market value; or

(viii) makes any other payment to him except one either falling within 21.3(i)(*a*) to (*e*) above or in discharge of an 'ordinary trade debt' (see (ii) above); or

 (ix) is wound up or dissolved in circumstances such that the company does not thereby cease to be a 'qualifying company' (see 21.4 above), and he thereby receives any payment or asset in respect of ordinary shares held by him.

The amount of the value received by an individual is that paid to or receivable by him from the company; or the amount of his liability extinguished or discharged; or the difference between the market value of the asset and the consideration (if any) given for it; or the net cost to the company of providing the benefit. In the case of value received within (i), (ii) or (iii) above, the market value of the shares, securities or debt in question is substituted if greater than the amount receivable.

An individual also '*receives value*' from the company if any person 'connected with' the company (as defined in 21.3 above) purchases any shares or securities of the company from him, or pays him for giving up any right in relation to such shares or securities. The value received is the amount receivable, or, if greater, the market value of the shares, etc.

All payments or transfers, direct or indirect, to, or to the order of, or for the benefit of, an individual or an 'associate' (as defined in 21.3 (ii) above) of his are brought within these provisions, as are payments, etc. made by any person 'connected with' the company (as defined in *CTA s 157*).

Relief is, where appropriate, withdrawn or withheld in respect of shares issued earlier before shares issued later. [*FA 1984, s 18, 2 Sch 3(1)*].

Value received other than by claimant. Relief is also reduced where, in the 'relevant period' (as in 21.3 above), the issuing company (including a subsidiary at any time in the relevant period) repays, redeems or repurchases any of its share capital belonging to any member other than (i) the individual, or (ii) another individual whose relief is thereby reduced (see above), or pays such a member for cancellation of his rights to its share capital. The reduction is the amount receivable by the member or, if greater, the nominal value of the share capital in question (with relief being restricted in proportion to the relief otherwise available where two or more individuals are involved). This restriction of relief does not apply in relation to the redemption on a date fixed before 26 January 1984 of any share capital, nor in relation to the redemption, within twelve months of issue, of any shares issued after 5 April 1984 to comply with *Companies (Amendment) Act 1983, s 6* (public company not to do business unless certain requirements as to share capital complied with). Relief is reduced in respect of shares issued earlier rather than shares issued later where relevant.

Where, in the 'relevant period' (as in 21.3 above), a member of the issuing company receives, or is entitled to receive, any 'value' from the company, then in applying the percentage limits referred to at 21.3 (iii) (*a*) above, the following amounts are treated as reduced:

(i)   the amount of the company's issued ordinary share capital;

(ii)   the amount of that capital 'relevant' to the provisions in question; and

(iii)   the amount at (i) not included in (ii).

The reduction in (ii) and (iii) is in each case the same proportion of the total amount as the 'value' received by the member(s) entitled to the shares comprising the amount bears to the sum subscribed for those shares. The reduced amount at (i) is the sum of those at (ii) and (iii).

The capital '*relevant*' to a provision is those shares whose proportion of the total issued ordinary share capital is in each case compared with the appropriate percentage of that capital.

A member receives '*value*' from the company for this purpose where any payments, etc. are made to him which, if made to an individual, would fall within (iv) to (viii) inclusive above, excluding those within (viii) made for full consideration. The amount of value received is as defined above. [*FA 1984, s 20, 2 Sch 3(1)(2)*].

Replacement capital. An individual is not entitled to relief in respect of shares issued by a company where, at any time in the 'relevant period' (as in 21.3 above), the company (or a subsidiary) begins to carry on a business (or part) previously carried on at any such time otherwise than by the company or a subsidiary, or acquires the whole or greater part of the assets used for a business so carried on, and the individual is a person who, or one of the group of persons who together, either

(i)   owned more than a half share (ownership and, if appropriate, respective shares being determined as under *CTA s 20(11)(a)(b)(12)(13)*) at any such time in the business previously carried on, and also own or owned at any such time such a share in the business carried on by the company (or by a subsidiary), or

(ii)   control (as in *CTA s 102(2)–(6)*), or at any such time have controlled, the company, and also, at any such time, controlled another company which previously carried on the trade.

For these purposes, the interests, rights and powers of a person's 'associates' (as in *CTA s 103(3)*) are attributed to that person.

An individual is similarly not entitled to relief in respect of shares in a company which, at any time in the relevant period, comes to acquire all the issued share capital of another company, and where the individual is the person who, or one of the persons who together, control or have at any such time controlled the company and who also, at any such time, controlled the other company. [*FA 1984, s 19*].

Assessments for withdrawing relief are made under Schedule D, Case IV for the year of assessment for which relief was given, and, if the event giving rise to the withdrawal occurred after the date of claim, may be made at any time within ten years after the end of the year of assessment in which the event occurs, without prejudice to the extension of the time limits in cases of fraud or neglect (see 6.2 ASSESSMENTS TO INCOME TAX). No assessment may be made by reason of any event occurring after the death of the person to whom the shares were issued.

See also 21.12 below as regards assessments on married persons.

Where a person has made an arm's length disposal of all the ordinary shares issued to him by a company in respect of which relief has been given, no assessment may be made in respect of those shares by reason of any subsequent event unless he is at the time of that event 'connected with' the company (as defined in 21.3 above).

The date from which interest runs on overdue tax (see 25.3 PAYMENT OF TAX) under these provisions is the date on which the event took place which gave rise to the withdrawal of relief, except that, where relief is withdrawn under the anti-avoidance provisions (see 21.13 below), it is the date on which relief was granted unless the relief was given under PAYE, in which case it is 5 April in the year of assessment in which relief was so given. [*FA 1984, s 23; FA 1993, s 25(i); FA 1995, s 17(1)(i)*].

21.11 **Subsidiary companies.** The existence of certain subsidiaries does not prevent the parent being a 'qualifying company' (see 21.4 above), and a 'qualifying trade' (see 21.6 above) being carried on by the subsidiary may enable shares issued by the parent to attract relief under these provisions. The necessary modifications to the provisions apply where such a subsidiary exists. [*FA 1984, s 26*].

The conditions imposed on any such subsidiary are that, until the end of the 'relevant period' (as in 21.4 above):

(i)   the subsidiary is a 51% subsidiary (see 12.14 CORPORATION TAX) of the qualifying company;

(ii)   no other person has control (as defined in *CTA s 158*); and

(iii) no arrangements exist whereby (i) or (ii) could cease to be satisfied,

and that the company either:

(*a*)   itself satisfies all the conditions for being a qualifying company as regards residence and purpose, and is an unquoted company and not wholly or partly a holding company (see 21.4 above); or

(*b*)   exists solely for the purpose of carrying on a trade consisting solely of any or all of

(i)   purchasing goods or materials for use by the qualifying company or its subsidiaries,

    (ii)   sale of goods or materials produced by the qualifying company or its subsidiaries, or

    (iii)   rendering services to or on behalf of the qualifying company or its subsidiaries.

Notwithstanding the above, a qualifying company carrying on qualifying shipping activities (which ceased to attract relief after 29 January 1991, see 21.6(*a*) above) could have one or more subsidiaries which did not satisfy either (*a*) or (*b*) above, provided that each such subsidiary existed for the purpose of carrying on qualifying shipping activities.

The winding-up or dissolution, in the relevant period, of the subsidiary or of the qualifying company does not prevent the above conditions being met, provided that the winding-up, etc. meets the conditions applied in relation to qualifying companies (see 21.4 above). [*FA 1984, s 26, 2 Sch 1; FA 1985, s 13(d); FA 1987, s 12; FA 1991, s 15*].

21.12 **Married persons.** The relief available under these provisions for subscriptions by a wife whose income is, by election, treated as that of her husband is available only against her total income, i.e. no excess of relief over total income may be set against her husband's total income. [*FA 1984, s 12(3)*].

Limits on relief. The £500 and £25,000 limits for investments attracting relief in a year of assessment (see 21.8 above) apply to the aggregate of the investments by a husband and wife where the wife's income is, by election, treated as that of her husband. Where in such a case a husband and wife are separately assessed, the relief is allocated to each in the proportion in which they subscribed for shares giving rise to relief. [*FA 1984, s 13(1)(3)*].

Disposal of shares. For the purposes of *FA 1984, s 17* (see 21.10 above), a disposal of shares which have been the subject of relief under these provisions from one spouse to another is ignored where the wife is treated as living with her husband (see 23.1 MARRIED PERSONS) at the time of the disposal. Where, following such a transfer inter vivos, the shares are subsequently disposed of to a third person, the disposal is taken into account for the purposes of *FA 1984, s 17*, any consequent assessment being raised on the transferee spouse (by reference to the inter-spouse transaction) if the wife is, at the time of that subsequent disposal, no longer treated as living with her husband. [*FA 1984, s 17(2)*].

Assessments for withdrawing relief. Where relief was obtained in respect of shares subscribed for by a spouse at a time when the wife's income was, by election, treated as that of her husband, and a subsequent withdrawal of relief falls to be made on a disposal of those shares at a time when the wife's income is no longer so treated, the assessment withdrawing relief is raised on the person making the disposal by reference to the actual reduction of tax flowing from the relief, regardless of any allocation of that relief. [*FA 1984, s 23(2)*].

Capital gains tax. On a disposal between spouses of shares in respect of which relief has been obtained, the restriction of allowable expenditure by reference to the excess of cost of subscription over consideration on disposal (or the relief obtained if less) (see 21.13 below) does not apply, i.e. the transfer continues to be treated as giving rise to neither gain nor loss. [*FA 1984, ss 12(10), 25(1)*].

21.13 **Miscellaneous.** The following general provisions apply in relation to the business expansion scheme.

Anti-avoidance. Relief otherwise due to an individual is denied where shares are issued other than for bona fide commercial reasons or as part of a scheme the main purpose, or one such purpose, of which was tax avoidance. [*FA 1984, s 21*].

Capital gains tax considerations. On a disposal (other than between spouses, see 21.12 above) of shares in respect of which relief has been given and not withdrawn, the allowable expenditure for capital gains tax purposes is determined without regard to that relief, except that where the expenditure exceeds the consideration (i.e. a loss), the expenditure is reduced by the lesser of (*a*) the amount of the relief and (*b*) the excess.

Any question of whether or not a disposal is of shares in respect of which relief has been given and not withdrawn, and as to which of such shares issued at different times a disposal relates, is determined as at 21.10 above.

Where only part of a holding of ordinary shares in a company has attracted relief, and there has been a reorganisation of share capital within *CGTA 1975, 2 Sch 2(1)*, the new holding of shares is treated as two new holdings, one identified with shares attracting relief, the other with the remainder of the shares originally held. [*FA 1984, ss 12(10), 25*].

Information. Certain events leading to withdrawal of relief must be notified to the inspector within 60 days by either the individual who received the relief, the issuing company, or any person 'connected with' that company (as defined in *CTA, s 157*) having knowledge of the matter. The inspector may require such a notice, and other relevant information, where he has reason to believe notice should have been given.

The inspector also has wide powers to require information in other cases where relief may be withdrawn, restricted or not due. The requirements of secrecy do not prevent his obtaining such information as he requires. [*FA 1984, s 24, 2 Sch 4*].

21.14 INVESTMENT IN RESEARCH AND DEVELOPMENT

A 'qualifying individual' who subscribes for 'eligible shares' in a 'qualifying research and development company' which are issued after 5 April 1986 and **before 6 April 1991** may claim income tax relief on his investment, provided that the purpose of the issue is to raise money for a 'qualifying research and development project' carried out by the company or which it intends to carry out and in fact commences to carry out within two years of the issue. [*FA 1986, s 18(1), (4)(b), (11)*].

Relief is allowed only when the company has carried out the 'qualifying research and development project' for four months, or for the 'project period' if shorter, and not before 1 January 1987. If, before the project has been carried on for the requisite period, the company is dissolved or wound up for bona fide commercial reasons, and not as part of a scheme the main purpose (or one such purpose) of which was tax avoidance, relief will nevertheless be available. [*FA 1986, s 18(4)(a)(5)(8)*].

'*Eligible shares*' are as defined in 21.5 above. [*FA 1986, s 18(2)*].

The '*project period*' is the period from commencement of work in connection with the 'qualifying research and development project' to the date on which all work in connection with it has ceased and all amounts due in relation to the project have been received by the 'qualifying research and development company'. [*FA 1986, s 17(1)*].

21.15 A '*qualifying individual*' is as defined in 21.3 above (with appropriate modification where necessary) except that:

(i)   the company with which the individual must not be connected is the 'qualifying sponsoring company' (see 21.17 below) on behalf of which the company issuing the shares carries out the 'qualifying research and development project';

(ii)   the restriction on dividends within the 'customs-free airport' or 'exported goods relief' provisions does not apply;

(iii) all employees of the 'qualifying sponsoring company' or of a partner of that company are excluded;

   (iv)   the exclusion of directors' emoluments from consideration under 21.3(i)(*e*) above does not apply;

   (v)   there are no provisions regarding reciprocal arrangements; and

   (vi)   relatives of the participator are treated as 'associates'.

The '*relevant period*' in this context is the period from the date of incorporation of the 'qualifying sponsoring company' (or, if later, two years before the date of issue of the shares) to the earlier of

(*a*)   five years after the issue of the shares, and

(*b*)   the end of the project period (see 21.14 above).

[*FA 1986, ss 18(7)(a), 20*].

21.16 A '*qualifying research and development company*' is defined in the same way as a 'qualifying company' in 21.4 above, except that:

   (i)   the company must exist solely for the carrying out of a 'qualifying research and development project' (which condition is treated as met if it is, or may become, entitled to receive any amount by reason of having carried out the project);

   (ii)   the share capital must consist entirely of eligible shares (see 21.14 above), which may, however, be part-paid;

   (iii) the shares may be listed in the official list of a stock exchange or dealt in on an unlisted securities market;

   (iv)   the restrictions by reference to persons acquiring a 'controlling interest' in the company's trade do not apply;

   (v)   the requirement in 21.4(*b*) above that, for a winding-up or dissolution not to debar relief, the net assets must be distributed to members within a certain time does not apply; and

   (vi)   there is an additional requirement that any 'qualifying sponsoring company' (see 21.17 below) in respect of which the 'qualifying research and development project' is carried out may not, in the 'relevant period', directly or indirectly possess or be entitled to acquire more than 20% of the qualifying research and development company's issued ordinary share capital, or of its loan capital and issued share capital, or of its voting power.

The '*relevant period*' in this context is either the project period (see 21.14 above) or, if it ends earlier, the period of five years commencing on the date of issue of the shares. [*FA 1986, ss 18(7)(b), 21*].

21.17 A '*qualifying sponsoring company*' must be incorporated in RI, resident only in RI, and must exist wholly for the purpose of carrying on wholly or mainly in RI one or more 'qualifying trades', as defined in 21.6 above, but excluding the rendering of services described in 21.6(ii) and without the requirements concerning claims for manufacturing companies' relief. The company must satisfy the Revenue Commissioners that any benefits from the 'qualifying research and development project' concerned will be applied by the company wholly or mainly for the purposes of its qualifying trade(s).

Although a winding-up or dissolution in the 'relevant period' generally prevents a company meeting these conditions, they are deemed met if the winding-up or dissolution is for bona fide commercial reasons and not part of a scheme the main purpose (or one such purpose) of which is tax avoidance.

The '*relevant period*' in this context is the period from the date of issue of the shares to the end of the project period (see 21.14 above) or, if later, to three years after commencement of the project period. [*FA 1986, ss 17(1), 18(7)(c), 22*].

21.18   A '*qualifying research and development project*' is a project carried out wholly or mainly in RI having as its sole object the development of new or improved industrial processes, methods or products. A research and development company is regarded as carrying out such a project only if it is carried out on behalf of a qualifying sponsoring company (see 21.17 above), and if the benefits of the project accrue wholly or mainly to that company. The project must be carried out at the risk of the research and development company, and there are specific provisions preventing such risk being directly or indirectly borne by the qualifying sponsoring company. The Revenue Commissioners must be satisfied that all money raised from individuals qualifying for relief in respect of subscriptions for eligible shares (see 21.14 above) in the research and development company was, is, or is intended to be, used for a qualifying research and development project.

The project, or any work on it, may be contracted out to any other person, including the qualifying sponsoring company. [*FA 1986, ss 17(1), 23*].

21.19   *Disposal of shares.* The provisions regarding disposal of shares described at 21.10 above apply, by reference to the 'relevant period' as defined in 21.15 above. There is an additional provision that if the qualifying research and development company is wound up or dissolved, any individual subscriber's eligible shares are treated as disposed of at arm's length for a price equal to the amount to which the individual is entitled on the winding-up or dissolution in respect of money subscribed for the eligible shares, insofar as the money has not been used for a qualifying research and development project. [*FA 1986, ss 18(7)(a), 25*].

21.20   The provisions described at 21.7, 21.8, 21.9, 21.12 and 21.13 above apply to research and development relief with appropriate modification, as do the provisions regarding withdrawal of relief in 21.10 above. [*FA 1986, ss 18(3)(6)(9)(10), 19, 26, 27, 28, 29, 30*]. The provisions regarding value received and replacement capital in 21.10 above, and those regarding subsidiaries in 21.11 above, do not apply for these purposes.

21.21   *Taxation of a qualifying research and development company.* The carrying out of a qualifying research and development project by such a company is deemed to be the carrying on of a separate trade consisting wholly of the manufacture of goods as defined for the purposes of the manufacturing companies' relief (see 12.17 CORPORATION TAX) for all purposes other than those of 21.17 above. Expenses in the course of carrying out the project, and receipts by reason of, or in connection with, carrying it out are treated as trade expenses or receipts if they would not otherwise be relieved or charged. The deemed trade ceases when the company is no longer entitled to any such receipts as are mentioned above. [*FA 1986, s 24*].

22 Losses

[*Secs 307–316*].

Cross-reference. See 12.16 CORPORATION TAX for losses by companies.

22.1 Losses are computed as for profits [*Sec 307(3)*] and may be created or augmented by capital allowances, so far as they exceed balancing charges. [*Secs 318, 319; FA 1979, ss 19, 20*]. Assessments under *Sec 434* (interest, annual payments etc. not payable out of taxed profits) are treated, conditionally, as losses, but not interest paid re patent rights; nor interest from which tax was deducted by virtue of *FA 1974, ss 30, 31* or *50* (see 20.1 INTEREST PAYABLE); nor retirement or other benefits assessed on directors or employees. [*Sec 316; FA 1976, s 5*].

22.2 **Relief** for losses may be claimed

(*a*) by **set-off** against other income in same year of assessment, first against income of the same kind (i.e. earned or unearned) as that to which the loss relates, then against the individual's other income, then spouse's earned/unearned income, and finally spouse's other income, except that a spouse's losses may only be set against the other spouse's income if, by election, the wife's income is treated as the husband's for income tax purposes. See 38.163 TAX CASES as regards 'income'. For 1989/90 and earlier years, a loss not fully set off against other income of the year in which it arose could be carried forward and set off against income of the following year (provided the same trade, profession or employment was still carried on), in priority to actual losses of that year. Claim for relief had to be made within two years of the year of assessment. [*Sec 307; FA 1979, s 17; FA 1990, s 27(2)*].

(*b*) by **carry-forward** (if not relieved under (*a*) above) against subsequent profits of the same trade without time limit. [*Sec 309*].

(*c*) by carry-back of a **terminal loss** arising on discontinuance (either permanent or notional) under *Sec 59* (changes of proprietorship). Any loss (as computed) incurred in the twelve months preceding date of cessation can be set against profits (as computed) assessed for the three years preceding year of cessation, using latest years first. Computed loss involves splitting of accounts and of relevant capital allowances (excluding those brought forward). Computed profit is reduced by capital allowances as above, any payments or losses deductible for tax purposes by an individual, any dividends paid by a company. (But if such payments are deducted from profits, a corresponding amount is deducted from the terminal loss applicable against earlier years, except where payments made wholly for purposes of the trade.) On notional succession, continuing partner has no claim for his share of losses. [*Secs 311–314*].

The above reliefs do not apply to any loss incurred in the occupation of commercial woodlands or from the sale of stallion services (for both of which the income is exempt, see 30.1 SCHEDULE D, CASES I AND II). [*Sec 307; FA 1979, s 17*]. There are restrictions for certain farming and market gardening losses, see 18.6 FARMING.

22.3 **Losses under Schedule D, Case IV or V** may be set off against profits of that Case of the same year or carried forward indefinitely against subsequent profits assessed under that Case. [*Secs 89, 310*]. See 32.3 SCHEDULE D, CASE IV and 33.7 SCHEDULE D, CASE V.

22.4 **Expenditure on approved buildings** in RI, or on ornamental gardens or grounds occupied or enjoyed with such buildings, incurred by the owner or occupier in respect of their repair, maintenance or restoration, may be treated as if it were a loss, sustained in the year of assessment (accounting period in the case of a company) in which it was incurred, in a separate trade carried on by that person. It may thus be relieved as under 22.2(*a*) above, or, in the case of a company, as under 12.16 CORPORATION TAX. Expenditure is reduced for this purpose by any payment received related to the work done, and by any part attracting relief under any other taxing provision. From 6 April 1993, the relief is extended to expenditure on the maintenance or restoration of approved gardens.

Approved buildings are those determined, on application by the owner or occupier,

(i)   by the Commissioners of Public Works in Ireland to be intrinsically of scientific, historical, architectural or aesthetic interest, and

(ii) by the Revenue Commissioners to afford *reasonable access* to the public or, from 2 June 1995, to be in use as a 'tourist accommodation facility' for at least six months in any calendar year (including at least four between 1 May and 30 September).

A '*tourist accommodation facility*' must be either in the register of guest houses kept by Bord Fáilte Éireann or in the list published by the Bord under *Tourist Traffic Act 1957, s 9*.

For chargeable periods beginning on or after 23 May 1994, relief may not apply for any chargeable period before that in which such application is made.

Approved gardens are similarly defined, with an additional qualifying category of horticultural interest.

Reasonable access requires

(*a*) access to the whole or a substantial part of the building at the same time,

(*b*) access at reasonable times for at least four hours on at least 60 days in any year, including at least 40 days in the period 1 May to 30 September (for chargeable periods beginning before 1 January 1995 where the Revenue Commissioners' determination was made before 23 May 1994, on at least 30 days in the year), subject to temporary closure for repairs, etc., and

(*c*) access at reasonable cost (if any).

For chargeable periods beginning on or after 23 May 1994, evidence has to be produced that details of opening dates and times, or of periods of use as a tourist accommodation facility, have been supplied for publication to Bord Fáilte Éireann by 1 January both in the chargeable period and in previous chargeable periods (up to a maximum of five) beginning with the chargeable period beginning on or after 23 May 1994 or (if later) with that in which the building was first approved for relief. Similarly for such periods, evidence that a tourist accommodation facility was included in the appropriate register or list (as above) must be provided.

There is provision for withdrawal of approval, with consequential adjustments, and for powers of inspection by representatives of the approving authority. A change from satisfying the 'reasonable access' requirement to being in use as a 'tourist accommodation facility', or *vice versa*, does not give rise to a withdrawal of approval, the revised approval being in effect treated as given at the time of the original approval.

Claims are made to the Revenue Commissioners in such form as they may prescribe.

[*FA 1982, s 19; FA 1993, s 29; FA 1994, s 18; FA 1995, s 20*].

See 34.3 SCHEDULE E—EMOLUMENTS as regards exemption from treatment as a benefit of certain loans of art objects on display in approved buildings or gardens.

22.5   LIMITED PARTNERSHIPS

Where an **individual** 'limited partner' sustains a loss or incurs capital expenditure in the partnership trade, or pays interest by reason of his participation therein, relief may be restricted. The restriction applies to a loss, etc. sustained in, or an allowance for expenditure made for, 1985/86 or a later year of assessment. An allowance for capital expenditure which creates or augments a trading loss under *Sec 318* (see 22.1 above) is for this purpose treated as made for the year of loss and not for the year of assessment for which the year of loss is the basis year.

A '*limited partner*' is a partner carrying on a trade

(*a*) as a limited partner in a limited partnership registered under the *Limited Partnerships Act 1907*, or

(*b*) as a general partner in a partnership, but who is not entitled to take part in the management of the trade, and who is entitled to have his liability for debts or obligations incurred for trade purposes discharged or reimbursed by some other person, in whole or beyond a certain limit, or

(*c*) who, under the law of any territory outside RI, is not entitled to take part in the management of the trade, and is not liable beyond a certain limit for debts or obligations incurred for trade purposes.

In relation to contributions made after 10 April 1994, a general partner is treated as within (*b*) above where, in connection with a contribution to the partnership trade, either:

(1) there exists any agreement, arrangement, scheme or understanding under which the partner is required to cease to be a partner before he is entitled to receive back from the partnership the full amount of his contribution; or

(2) by virtue of any such agreement, etc., a creditor's entitlement to recover any debt of the partner or partnership from the partner is in any way limited or restricted.

As respects a contribution made after 23 April 1992, any loss, etc. sustained by, or allowance for expenditure made to, a limited partner in respect of a trade as above for a year of assessment may be relieved under the '*relevant provisions*' only against profits of the same trade, and no relief is available for the excess of the loss etc. over his 'contribution' to the trade at the end of the year of assessment (or at the time he ceased to carry on the trade if he did so during that year of assessment). For earlier contributions, relief was available in full against profits of the same trade, but relief was not available against other income for the excess of the loss etc. over his contribution (as above). In relation to trades of managing and letting holiday cottages, where construction work was contracted for and commenced before 24 April 1992 and is completed before 6 April 1993, these changes apply from 1 September 1992 instead of 24 April 1992.

If relief has been allowed under any of the 'relevant provisions' (see below) for an earlier year of assessment (ignoring years before 1985/86) at any time during which the individual carried on the trade as a limited partner, the loss, etc. or allowance for the year of assessment is restricted by the excess of the sum of the loss, etc. or allowance for that year and the earlier amounts relieved over the 'contribution'.

The '*relevant provisions*' are

(i) *Sec 296* (relief of certain excess capital allowances against general income),

(ii) *Sec 307* (relief of losses against general income, see 22.2(*a*) above), and

(iii) *FA 1974, Ch III, Part I* (relief for certain interest payments, see 20.3(*a*) INTEREST PAYABLE).

The partner's '*contribution*' to the trade at any time is the aggregate of

(A) capital contributed and not subsequently, directly or indirectly, withdrawn or received back from the partnership or from a person connected (within *F(MP)A*

1968, s 16) with the partnership (other than anything, in relation to expenditure for the trade, which the partner is or may be entitled to withdraw or receive at any time he carries on the trade as a limited partner, or which he is or may be entitled to require another person to reimburse to him), and

(B)   any profits or gains of the trade to which he is entitled but which he has not received in money or money's worth.

In determining whether or not relief is obtained under a relevant provision as respects a contribution made after 23 April 1992, any relief which would not have been obtained but for a contribution made after that date is treated as obtained as respects such a contribution.

A partner is treated as receiving back an amount contributed to the partnership if he received that amount or value for the sale of his interest (or part) in the partnership; if the partnership (or a person connected with it within *F(MP)A 1968, s 16*) repays that amount of a loan or advance from him; or if he receives that amount of value for assigning any debt due to him from the partnership (or from a person connected with it, as above).

Similar provisions apply where a company which is a limited partner sustains a loss or incurs capital expenditure in the partnership trade, or where it or any other company pays a charge by reason of its participation in the trade, in an accounting period ending after 21 May 1985. The 'relevant provisions' under which relief is restricted are

(*aa*)   *CTA s 10* (relief for charges on income, see 12.9 CORPORATION TAX),

(*bb*)   *CTA s 14(6)* (relief for certain capital allowances against profits generally, see 12.9 CORPORATION TAX),

(*cc*)   *CTA s 16(2)* (relief for trading losses against profits generally, see 12.16 CORPORATION TAX), and

(*dd*)   *CTA s 116(1)(2)(6)* (group relief, see 12.14 CORPORATION TAX).

[*FA 1986, s 46; FA 1992, s 23; FA 1994, s 29*].

See also 38.90 TAX CASES.

23   Married Persons

Cross-references. See ALLOWANCES AND RATES at 2.9 for the single allowance applicable to married persons on election and at 2.11 for the married allowance plus the additional allowance for the year of marriage.

23.1   Where a wife is 'living with her husband' (see below), income tax is assessed, charged and recovered on the income of each as if they were not married. [*Sec 193 as amended by FA 1980, s 18*]. A husband and wife may, however, jointly elect for both incomes to be deemed to be the husband's for income tax purposes, and assessable on him (unless separate assessment has been claimed — see 23.2 below). [*Sec 194 as amended by FA 1980, s 18*]. He will then be entitled to married allowance. Such an election may be made at any time during the year of assessment for which election is made, and will continue to have effect until withdrawn by either spouse. An election will in any case be deemed to have been made for any year unless one spouse has, during the year or previously, given notice that he or she wishes to be assessed as a single person. [*Sec 195 as amended by FA 1980, s 18*]. Any overdue tax which is attributable to the wife's income may be collected direct from her, and a husband may disclaim liability for unpaid tax attributable to his deceased wife's income (so that it becomes payable out of her estate). [*Sec 196 as amended by FA 1980, s 18*].

For the year of marriage husband and wife are taxed as if unmarried throughout the year. However, where the tax paid and payable by both for that year exceeds that which would have been paid and payable had they been married throughout the year, they may jointly claim (in writing) a repayment of one-twelfth of that excess for each income tax month or part month in the year during which they were married. The repayment is allocated in proportion to the tax paid and payable in the year by each spouse. [*Sec 195A as inserted by FA 1983, s 6*].

A married woman is treated as '*living with her husband*' unless they are (*a*) separated under a Court Order or separation deed, or (*b*) in fact separated in circumstances where permanent separation is likely. [*Sec 192 as amended by FA 1980, s 18*].

For 1987/88 and subsequent years the *Status of Children Act 1987, s 3* applies in that

(*a*)   relationships between persons are to be determined without regard to whether the parents of any person are or have been married to each other, unless the contrary intention appears, and

(*b*)   an adopted person shall, for the purposes of (*a*), be deemed from the date of the adoption to be the child of the adopter or adopters, and not the child of any other person or persons. [*FA 1988, s 74*].

Assessment on either spouse. For **1994/95** and subsequent years, where an election under *Sec 195* (see above) has been (or is deemed to have been) made, the husband and wife may jointly elect for the wife, rather than the husband, to be assessed under *Sec 194* in respect of both their incomes. This will also apply without election in certain cases where the year of marriage is after 1992/93, the election under *Sec 195* is deemed to have been made but has not in fact been made, and the inspector considers that the wife's income exceeds that of the husband. In either case, the income of both husband and wife is deemed to be that of the wife, and the wife is assessed and charged in respect of both incomes. All other relevant provisions of the *Taxes Acts* specified to apply to the husband then apply to the wife (including entitlement to the married allowance, see 2.11 ALLOWANCES AND TAX RATES). A joint election by the spouses under these provisions must be made before 6 July in the first year of assessment to which it is to apply, and continues to apply for subsequent years until withdrawn by joint notice given before 6 July in the first year for which it is withdrawn. [*Sec 195B(1)–(3)(5)(6); FA 1993, s 10*].

Where this provision applies other than as a result of an election by the spouses, it continues to apply, whether or not the wife's income exceeds that of the husband, unless and until the spouses either elect under *Sec 195* for *Sec 194* to apply in relation to the husband, or apply for separate assessment (see 23.2 below). Where a notice under *Sec 195(4)(a)* or an application under *Sec 197* for separate assessment is withdrawn, and but for the original notice or election the wife would have been assessed and charged on both spouses' incomes for the year of withdrawal, then unless an election has actually been made under *Sec 195(1)* for joint assessment on the husband, the wife will, for the year of withdrawal and subsequent years, be assessed and charged on the joint income. [*Sec 195B(4); FA 1993, s 10*].

Where either husband or wife is assessed on their joint income and separate assessment under *Sec 197* (see 23.2 below) does not apply, any repayment of tax is allocated to husband and wife in proportion to the tax deducted or paid on their respective total incomes (subject to a *de minimis* limit of £20 in respect of a repayment to the spouse who is not assessed and charged under *Sec 194*). The inspector may, however, allocate a repayment on a just and reasonable basis where he is satisfied that it arises (or arises in greater part) by reason of an allowance or relief attributable to one spouse only. [*Sec 195C; FA 1993, s 10*].

23.2   **Separate assessment** to income tax may be claimed by either spouse within the six months before 6 July in the year of assessment (or the following 6 July if the year of assessment is the year of marriage), and will be effective for that year and subsequent years until withdrawn (in writing before 6 July). The total tax liability is unaffected. [*Sec 197 as amended by FA 1980, s 18*].

If separate assessment is claimed, certain basic allowances are divided between the spouses half and half. These are the married allowance, child allowance for own or adopted children, age allowance and blind person's allowance. Other allowances are, in general, divided in proportion to the amount of payments, etc. The special deduction for PAYE taxpayers is divided in proportion to the respective emoluments giving rise to the deduction. The amount of taxable income in the standard and higher rate bands is that applicable where both incomes are deemed to be those of the husband, and is divided equally. Any amount of unused allowance, or of unused tax rate band, is carried over to the other spouse.

Any reduction of income tax due to marginal age exemption or marginal low income exemption (see 2.7, 2.8 ALLOWANCES AND RATES) is apportioned between spouses in proportion to the income tax payable by each but for such exemption.

[*Sec 198 as amended by FA 1980, s 18; FA 1981, s 5; FA 1982, s 5; FA 1984, s 13; FA 1986, ss 14, 19, 44; FA 1989, s 4; FA 1992, s 2(2); FA 1993, s 48; FA 1994, s 46(6); FA 1995, ss 6(7), 7(9)(a)*].

23.3   **Following the Supreme Court ruling** on the unconstitutionality of aggregation of husband's or wife's incomes (see 38.52 TAX CASES), all assessments for years prior to 1980/81 are now required to be made on the basis of non-aggregation. Provision is accordingly made to prevent any advantage being gained by taxpayers in this respect for 1979/80 and earlier years.

(i)   For any such year, no repayment will be made or credit given in respect of any overpayment of tax (by deduction or otherwise) suffered through such aggregation unless, before the start of that year, the claimant had instituted legal proceedings to assert the unconstitutionality of the Income Tax Acts purporting to authorise such aggregation. This is in line with the Supreme Court ruling on entitlement to repayment. [*FA 1980, s 20*].

(ii)   Where an assessment for any such year requires to be made on an individual treated as living with his or her spouse in that year, and the tax payable thereon would be less than the 'relevant tax' — that which would have been payable had the assessment been raised on 6 October in that year — the assessment is to be raised on the basis of non-aggregation, but without personal reliefs and at the highest rate of tax for that year (including sur-tax). Relief will then be given to reduce the aggregate tax payable to the 'relevant tax'. [*FA 1980, s 21*]. See, however, 38.53 TAX CASES where it was held that this provision is unconstitutional and invalid.

23.4   **Maintenance payments** as specified below, which are made by one party to a marriage for the benefit of the other, are payable without deduction of tax, but are deductible in computing total income of the payer (see 2.1 ALLOWANCES AND RATES) and are chargeable under SCHEDULE D, CASE IV (32) on the other party. Payments for the maintenance of a child are also made without deduction of tax, but are not deductible from the payer's total income and are not treated as the child's income. For child allowance purposes (see 2.15 ALLOWANCES AND RATES), the payment is treated as spent by the payer (and only by the payer) on maintaining the child, regardless of whether it was in fact paid to the other party to the marriage.

For any year of assessment in which such a maintenance payment has been made, and in which the parties to the marriage are separated (but the marriage is neither dissolved nor annulled) but both RI-resident, they may jointly elect for the wife's income to be treated as that of her husband as under *Sec 194* (see 23.1 above). The maintenance payments are then ignored in calculating total income, and separate assessment (see 23.2 above) applied to determine respective liabilities.

For these purposes a *maintenance payment* is a legally enforceable periodical payment (or part) made under or pursuant to a maintenance arrangement (i.e. a court order, etc. giving rise to a legally enforceable obligation and made or done in consideration or consequence of the dissolution or annulment of a marriage or the legal separation of the partners) at a time when the wife is not living with the husband. It must be made for the benefit of the other party to the marriage or of the payer's child (including any child in respect of which he had previously been entitled to child allowance (see 2.15 ALLOWANCES AND RATES)).

Maintenance arrangements made before 8 June 1983 are excluded until either the arrangement is varied or replaced, or both parties to the marriage jointly elect (in writing) for their inclusion, whereupon any future such payments are included.

[*FA 1983, ss 3, 4*].

24   Mines

See generally the *Finance (Taxation of Profits of Certain Mines) Act 1974*, as amended in particular by *FA 1990, s 39*.

24.1   COAL MINES

Marginal Coal Mine Allowance. The Minister for Finance, after consultation with the Minister for Industry and Commerce, may direct that the tax chargeable on the profits of a marginal coal mine for any particular year of assessment or accounting period is to be reduced to an amount (including nil) as specified by him. [*FA 1974, s 74; CTA 2 Sch 48*].

24.2   MINE DEVELOPMENT ALLOWANCE

An annual allowance is given for capital expenditure incurred in searching for, discovering, testing or winning access (by underground or surface working) to minerals, including works likely to have little value when operation ceases, but not the cost of acquiring the site or the minerals.

The allowance is calculated to spread the difference between the cost and the residual value over the estimated life of the deposits (up to 20 years). The allowance must be claimed within 24 months of the end of the year of assessment. Balancing allowances and charges are made on cessation or sale. [*Sec 245; CTA 1 Sch 10; FA 1980, s 17*].

24.3   'NON-BEDDED' MINERAL MINES

Any company carrying on mining operations for 'non-bedded' minerals (as specified in *13 Sch*) is chargeable to corporation tax (previously to income tax under Schedule D, Case I, and to corporation profits tax).

[*CTA 1 Sch 64, 65*].

24.4   Marginal mine allowance is applicable as in 24.1 above. [*F(Mines)A 1974, s 10*].

24.5   Groups of companies.

Exploration expenditure by one member of a group of companies may, by election, be deemed the expenditure of another member (whether or not in existence at the time of the expenditure). [*F(Mines)A 1974, s 4; CTA 1 Sch 66*].

24.6   Capital allowances apply for income tax and corporation profits tax as follows

(a)   *Exploration investment allowance* of 20% on expenditure incurred after 5 April 1974.

(b)   *Plant and machinery* (other than cars, lorries etc.)

    (i)   investment allowance of 20% on new assets purchased after 5 April 1974.

    (ii)   free depreciation on purchases after 5 April 1974.

    (iii)   any earlier expenditure still unallowed may be fully claimed for 1974/75.

(c)   *Mineral depletion allowance* is given under *Sec 245* (see 24.2 above) on capital expenditure in *acquiring*, after 31 March 1974, any entitlement to work deposits of minerals (provided they are actually worked).

[*F(Mines)A 1974, ss 6–8; CTA 1 Sch 68, 69*].

24.7   Sale of a scheduled mining asset (including a licence to work) for a capital sum is taxable (less any original purchase price) under Schedule D, Case IV for the year of assessment (or accounting period of a company) in which received. Tax is deductible from a payment to a non-resident. An individual may elect, within 24 months after end of the year of assessment in which the sum is received, for it to be treated as six annual receipts. [*F(Mines)A 1974, s 11; CTA 2 Sch 39; FA 1981, s 9*].

25 Payment of Tax

Cross-references. See also 7.11 CAPITAL ACQUISITIONS TAX; 9.5 CAPITAL GAINS TAX; 12.6 COR-PORATION TAX; 13.8 DEDUCTION OF TAX AT SOURCE; 26.11 RESIDENTIAL PROPERTY TAX; and 39.10 VALUE-ADDED TAX. See 4.5 APPEALS for payment of tax pending appeal.

25.1 INCOME TAX

For individuals and partnerships income tax is payable

(a) On profits or gains of any trade or profession assessed under Schedule D (except, before 1983/84, full-time farming, see below), and on any other income except as (b) below, as follows:

for 1980/81 onwards: on 1 November in the year of assessment (1 October for 1989/90 and earlier years) or within one month following the date of assessment, if later.

[*Sec 477(1)(2); FA 1980, s 14; FA 1990, s 24(a)*].

See 28.12 RETURNS as regards certain payments of preliminary tax under self-assess-ment procedures.

(b) On income charged under Schedule E:

(i) where deduction at source is applied — by deduction from emoluments as and when paid. [*Secs 126, 127*]. See 34.7 SCHEDULE E for the PAYE system.

(ii) where the income is assessed — as in (a) above. [*Sec 477(2); FA 1980, s 14*].

Farming. Tax attributable to full-time farming is payable on the following dates, or within one month following the date of assessment, if later:

for 1983/84 onwards, on 1 November in the relevant year of assessment (1 October for 1989/90 and earlier years).

for 1982/83, by two equal instalments on 1 October 1982 and 1 January 1983.

for 1981/82, by two equal instalments on 1 October 1981 and 1 January 1982.

for 1980/81, by two equal instalments on 1 October 1980 and 1 January 1981.

[*FA 1980, s 14; FA 1981, s 12; FA 1982, s 14; FA 1990, s 24(a)*].

Companies pay income tax (when liable to it) on 1 January falling within the tax-year, or the day after the date on which the assessment is made, whichever is the later. [*Sec 477(1)*].

25.2 COLLECTION

Tax is collected by the Collector-General and his officers with rights of distraint and court proceedings. For procedure see *Secs 478–480, 482, 484–494; FA 1972, ss 7, 8; FA 1974, s 70; FA 1979, s 12; FA 1980, s 35; FA 1988, s 71; FA 1994, s 162*. For priority in bank-ruptcy and liquidation see *Companies Act 1963, ss 98, 285* and *Sec 132; FA 1968, s 11; CGTA 4 Sch 15; CTA s 145(5); FA 1976, s 14; FA 1989, s 10*. Tax deducted from sub-contractors in the construction industry may be set against tax liabilities, see 13.7 DEDUC-TION OF TAX AT SOURCE.

PAYE and VAT payments in default may be collected from the holder of a fixed charge (created after 27 May 1986) over the book debts of the defaulting company, up to the amount received by the holder of the charge from the company, in payment of debts due to the holder, after notification by the Revenue Commissioners of the liability of the holder under this provision. The amount for which the holder of the charge may be liable is further restricted where the existence or creation of the charge has been notified to the Revenue Commissioners. [*FA 1986, s 115; FA 1995, s 174*].

Attachment of third-party debts to tax defaulters, other than wages and salaries and amounts in dispute, may be made after 30 September 1988. This extends to VAT and other Government levies. For procedure see *FA 1988, s 73* as amended by *FA 1992, s 241*.

For the meeting of tax liabilities by the donation to certain national institutions of cultural items whose export would diminish the accumulated cultural heritage of Ireland, see *FA 1995, s 176*.

25.3   INTEREST ON UNPAID TAXES

Interest, without deduction of tax, is payable from the due date for payment of any income tax, sur-tax, corporation profits tax or corporation tax. (Before 1990/91, and for accounting periods ending before 6 April 1990, a period of grace was allowed for payment before interest was charged from the due date.) From 5 July 1978, the rate is 1.25% per month or part month. From 6 April 1975 the rate was 1.5%, from 28 July 1971 it was 0.75%, and before that it was 0.5%. [*Sec 550; FA 1971, ss 17, 47–49; FA 1975, s 28; FA 1978, s 46; FA 1988, s 18; FA 1990, s 24(b)*]. Recoverable under same powers as income tax, etc. [*Secs 550, 551; FA 1985, s 12*]. See *Sec 183* re composite charge and *FA 1971, ss 17(2), 19* re interest on assessments under appeal. Interest on tax undercharged because of fraud or neglect runs from the date when the tax would have been payable but for that fraud or neglect, and from 1 November 1982 is charged at a higher rate of 2% per month or part month. [*FA 1971, ss 20, 50; FA 1976, s 6; FA 1977, s 4; FA 1978, s 16; FA 1980, s 14; FA 1982, s 59*]. Interest on PAYE not paid over by an employer is at 1.25% per month from 5 July 1978 (previously 1.5% and prior to 6 April 1975 1%) with a minimum amount of £5. [*Sec 129; FA 1973, s 1; FA 1975, s 28; FA 1978, s 46*]. For interest on tax deducted from sub-contractors in the construction industry and not paid over, see 13.7 DEDUCTION OF TAX AT SOURCE.

Interest on unpaid wealth tax or capital acquisitions tax is not deductible for IT or CPT. [*FA 1976, s 29*].

For interest on overpaid tax, see 4.5 APPEALS.

25.4   SURCHARGE FOR LATE SUBMISSION OF RETURNS

For 1986/87 and subsequent years of assessment, and in relation to accounting periods ending after 5 April 1986, delivery of certain returns of income after a 'specified date' will result in a surcharge being added to any income, corporation or capital gains tax due for the year of assessment or accounting period in respect of income, profits or chargeable gains which are, or would be, contained in the return and on, or by reference to, which the tax would have been chargeable. The surcharge need not be separately assessed, and if the related assessment does not include the surcharge, all the provisions regarding collection and recovery of tax and interest on unpaid tax, etc. apply as if the assessment were increased by the amount of the surcharge. Any tax deducted and not repaid (other than PAYE deductions relating to a director or spouse), or tax credit or set-off available, is taken into account before the surcharge is calculated.

For 1995/96 and subsequent years of assessment, and for company accounting periods ending after 5 April 1995, the surcharge is 5% (maximum **£10,000**) where the return is delivered within two months of the 'specified date', otherwise **10%** (maximum **£50,000**). Previously it was **10%** in all cases.

Returns to which the surcharge applies are those which the person is required by the inspector to deliver under

(*a*)   *Sec 70* (sources and amounts of partnership income), (*b*)   *Sec 94(a)* (details of terms and provisions of leases and payments made),

(*c*)   *Sec 94(d)* (return by agent of payments arising from premises),

(*d*)   *Sec 169* (profits or gains),

(*e*)   *Sec 170* (returns for incapacitated persons and non-residents),

(*f*)   *Sec 172* (sources of income),

(*g*)   *Sec 197* (total incomes of husband and wife),

(*h*)   *FA 1976, s 11* (married women),

(*j*)   *CTA s 143* (return of company profits),

(*k*)   *FA 1988, s 10* and *FA 1990, s 23(4)* (self-assessment returns, see 28.12 RETURNS), and

(*l*)   *FA 1992, s 230(6)* (foreign bank accounts, see 28.4 RETURNS),

and include the extension of any of those provisions to capital gains tax. A return for a year of assessment is a return requiring details of income of that year of assessment (before 1990/91, details of income of the year ended on 5 April in the immediately preceding year of assessment).

The '*specified date*' is: 31 December 1987 in relation to year of assessment 1986/87 and accounting periods ending after 5 April 1986 and before 6 April 1987; 31 December in the year of assessment in relation to 1987/88 to 1989/90 inclusive; 31 January in the year following the year of assessment in relation to 1990/91 and later years of assessment; and the last day of the nine-month period commencing on the day after the end of the accounting period in relation to accounting periods ending after 5 April 1987. In all cases the last day of the six-month period commencing on the day after the person concerned was required by notice to deliver the return is substituted if later. For 1995/96 onwards, for the first year of assessment of a new business, it is instead the specified date which applies for the second year of assessment, provided that neither the taxpayer nor (unless the spouse is assessed as a single person under *Sec 193*) the spouse of the taxpayer was at any time in that first year carrying on a trade, etc. commenced in an earlier year.

Incorrect returns delivered on or before the specified date are deemed to have been delivered after that date unless the error is remedied on or before that date (or unless, where neither fraud nor negligence is involved, the error is corrected without unreasonable delay). If the inspector serves notice requiring the production of accounts, books, etc. under *Sec 174* by reason of his dissatisfaction with any statement of profits or gains from a trade or profession contained in a return delivered on or before the specified date, the return is treated as delivered after that date unless the inspector's requirements are met within the time specified in the notice. [*FA 1986, s 48; FA 1988, s 16; FA 1990, s 25; FA 1992, s 245; FA 1995, s 30*].

Late returns—Statement of Practice. Returns received within seven days of the filing date will normally be accepted as being made on time (although this will not apply to taxpayers or practitioners who abuse the procedure and regularly make returns within the seven-day period of grace). Similarly occasional late filing by a taxpayer up to four weeks after the filing date will be accepted without penalty provided that the correct amount (if any) of preliminary tax was paid on time and that there are reasonable grounds to believe that the default represents an uncharacteristic slip by an otherwise complying taxpayer. In the latter case, a note should be attached to the late return outlining why it is considered that the relief should apply. (Statement of Practice SP–GEN/1/93, April 1993).

25.5   AMNESTIES

The *Waiver of Certain Tax, Interest and Penalties Act 1993* introduced two amnesties relating to periods ending on or before 5 April 1991. Some amendments were made by *FA 1994, s 163*.

A general amnesty waived interest and penalties in relation to arrears of all taxes and levies, subject to certain requirements, including the payment of all arrears of tax by 14 January 1994. It applied to all categories of taxpayer, e.g. individuals, companies and trustees.

The 'incentive' amnesty applied only to individuals and only to income tax, capital gains tax and the income, health and youth employment levies, and to interest and penalties thereon. It enabled liabilities for such periods to be settled by a payment of 15% of the amount of the undisclosed income and gains, provided that a full declaration of those amounts was made by 21 December 1993, the 15% paid by 14 January 1994 and the 1992/93 tax return filed by 31 January 1994 (in certain cases, 28 February 1994). It did not apply where an audit of the taxpayer's affairs had commenced before 25 May 1993.

The publication of the names of tax defaulters (see 1.7 ADMINISTRATION AND GENERAL) does not apply in the case of settlements under the amnesties.

An earlier amnesty under the *Finance Act 1988* provided for the waiver of certain interest and penalties where arrears were reported between 27 January 1988 and 30 September 1988.

---

26 Residential Property Tax

26.1 **Residential property tax** (RPT) was introduced by *FA 1983, ss 95–116* with effect on and from 5 April 1983. It is an annual tax on individuals owning and occupying residential property. The tax is administered by the Capital Taxes Branch of the Revenue Commissioners. The provisions are summarised below.

For the constitutionality of RPT, see 38.59 TAX CASES.

26.2 **COMMENCEMENT AND BASIS OF ASSESSMENT**

RPT is charged annually on the net market value (see 26.6 below) of relevant residential property (see 26.5 below) of every assessable person (see 26.4 below) on 5 April in each year, commencing on 5 April 1983. It is subject to relief for resident children (see 26.9 below), to an income exemption limit and relief (see 26.8 below), and to a market value exemption limit (see 26.7 below). [*FA 1983, s 96*].

26.3 **RATE**

For valuation dates 5 April 1995 and after and 5 April 1993 and earlier, the rate of RPT is 1.5% of net market value (see 26.6 below). For valuation date 5 April 1994 only, the rate on property with net market value in excess of £25,000 is 1% on the first £25,000 of net market value, 1.5% on the next £50,000 and 2% on the remainder. The £25,000 and £50,000 band limits are reduced to the proportion of those amounts that the market value exemption limit bears to the general exemption limit. Where the net market value (multiplied by the proportion that the general exemption limit bears to the market value exemption limit) does not exceed £25,000, tax is computed in accordance with the following bands.

Net market value	*Tax due*
Up to £5,000	£25
Over £5,000 but does not exceed £10,000	£75
Over £10,000 but does not exceed £15,000	£125
Over £15,000 but does not exceed £20,000	£175
Over £20,000 but does not exceed £25,000	£225

Each of the figures in the table above is reduced, where appropriate, to the proportion that the market value exemption limit bears to the general exemption limit. [*FA 1983, s 96; FA 1994, s 116, 7 Sch; FA 1995, ss 151, 152, 155*].

26.4 **ASSESSABLE PERSONS**

Any individual the net market value (see 26.6 below) of whose relevant residential property (see 26.5 below) on 5 April in any year exceeds the market value exemption limit (see 26.7 below) is assessable to RPT. For an individual **not domiciled** in RI (see 27.3 RESIDENTS AND NON-RESIDENTS) on the valuation date, only relevant residential property situate in RI is taken into account on 5 April in that year. Otherwise, all such property, wherever situate, is included. [*FA 1983, ss 95, 97*].

26.5 **RELEVANT RESIDENTIAL PROPERTY**

Relevant residential property of an individual means any 'residential property' he owns and has the use of as a dwelling. He is treated as having the use of a dwelling on 5 April in any year, even if he does not have such use on that date, if he had such use for the greater part of the year ending on that date and of the following year.

Residential property includes garden (excluding certain gardens of historic, etc. interest, see 7.5(*c*) CAPITAL ACQUISITIONS TAX) or grounds of an ornamental nature occupied and enjoyed with a building (or part) used (or suitable for use) as a dwelling, but excludes certain approved buildings to which the public has reasonable access (see 22.4 LOSSES). *Ownership* of residential property is widely defined, including the holding of property under mortgage, or under a lease, etc. exceeding 50 years, or at no rent or at a rent less than 80% of an arm's length rent. This last category, however, does not include the provision of property in respect of which the occupier is chargeable to tax as a benefit in kind (see 34.3 SCHEDULE E) or as a close company distribution (see 12.7 CORPORATION TAX), or the holding of property as a caretaker under an arm's length agreement, or of property which is relevant residential property of the lessor, etc. [*FA 1983, s 95*].

26.6   NET MARKET VALUE

The net market value of a person's relevant residential property is the excess of the aggregate market values of each property comprised therein over the market value exemption limit (see 26.7 below). [*FA 1983, s 95*].

Market value is the price which the unencumbered fee simple would fetch if sold in the open market for residential use in circumstances calculated to obtain the best price for the vendor. That price is estimated by the person in whose relevant residential property the property is included (without taking into account possible liability to RPT), but the Revenue Commissioners may substitute a higher estimate if they consider it necessary to do so. For this purpose, the Revenue Commissioners may authorise an inspection of the property by any person (who must be allowed access at reasonable times), and any costs so incurred are borne by the Revenue Commissioners. For valuation date 5 April 1994 and subsequently, the estimate may be reduced by the value attributable to any alterations or improvements necessary to accommodate or facilitate a permanently incapacitated person who normally resided in the property in the year to the valuation date from maintaining himself. [*FA 1983, s 98; FA 1994, s 117*].

Apportionment of market value of property comprised in the relevant residential property of two or more persons is on the basis of equal division amongst all such persons. [*FA 1983, s 99*].

26.7   MARKET VALUE EXEMPTION LIMIT

The general market value exemption limit is:

	£
at 5 April 1983	65,000
at 5 April 1984	65,622
at 5 April 1985	66,491
at 5 April 1986	68,728
at 5 April 1987	69,971
at 5 April 1988	74,321
at 5 April 1989	82,772
at 5 April 1990	91,000
at 5 April 1991	96,000
at 5 April 1992	90,000
at 5 April 1993	91,000
at 5 April 1994	75,000
at 5 April 1995	**94,000**

For subsequent years, it will be increased in line with the Trends in Private New House Price Index Number compiled by the Department of the Environment. For the 5 April 1989 and earlier valuation dates, the increase was by reference to the index number for the three months to the 31 March preceding the appropriate valuation date. For the 5 April

1990, 5 April 1991 and 5 April 1993 and for 5 April 1996 and subsequent valuation dates, the increase is by reference to the index number for the three months to the 31 December preceding the appropriate valuation date, and the resulting figure is rounded up to the next £1,000. The 5 April 1992 figure was set by *FA 1992*, that for 5 April 1994 by *FA 1994*, that for 5 April 1995 by *FA 1995*.

The market value exemption limit applicable to any person at 5 April in any year is the aggregate of the 'unit exemption limits' attributed to each item in that person's relevant residential property at that date, but subject to an overall limit of the general market value exemption limit at that date.

The *'unit exemption limit'* attributed to a property is the fraction of the general market value exemption limit corresponding to the proportion of the aggregate of the market values of all the properties included in the person's relevant residential property represented by the property in question. For this purpose, the *whole* of the market value of any property comprised in the relevant residential property of two or more persons is included in any market value computation, but the unit exemption limit attributed to that property is apportioned in the same way as its market value is generally apportioned (see 26.6 above). [*FA 1983, s 100; FA 1990, ss 121, 123; FA 1992, ss 218, 219; FA 1994, s 118; FA 1995, ss 151, 153*].

26.8   INCOME EXEMPTION LIMIT

Exemption from RPT in respect of net market value at 5 April in a year may be claimed by an assessable person if the total of his 'income' and that of any 'relevant person' for the year ended on that date does not exceed the income exemption limit applying on that date. For valuation date 5 April 1994 and subsequently, the income of a relevant person who is not an assessable person is disregarded if, in relation to the valuation date, either

(*a*)   the owner or any of joint owners occupying the property is aged 65 or over, or

(*b*)   the owner or any of joint owners occupying the property is permanently incapacitated from maintaining himself, and the relevant person resides in the property as a consequence of that incapacity, or

(*c*)   the assessable person is a widowed person and the relevant person resides in the property as a consequence of the assessable person having a 'qualifying child' (see 26.9 below).

The income exemption limit is:

	£
year ended 5 April 1983	20,000
year ended 5 April 1984	22,030
year ended 5 April 1985	23,395
year ended 5 April 1986	24,468
year ended 5 April 1987	25,307
year ended 5 April 1988	25,795
year ended 5 April 1989	26,654
year ended 5 April 1990	27,800
year ended 5 April 1991	28,500
year ended 5 April 1992	27,500
year ended 5 April 1993	28,100
year ended 5 April 1994	25,000
year ended 5 April 1995	**29,500**

This is increased in line with increases in the All Items Consumer Price Index Number compiled by the Central Statistics Office, by reference to index numbers in mid-February preceding the appropriate valuation date (base November 1989 = 100). For the year ended 5 April 1990 and subsequent years, the limit is rounded up to the next £100. The figure for the year ended 5 April 1992 was set by *FA 1992*, that for the year ended 5 April 1994 by *FA 1994*, that for the year ended 5 April 1995 by *FA 1995*.

Income for this purpose is total income from all sources as estimated for tax purposes (ignoring the married persons taxation provisions, see 23 MARRIED PERSONS), but after adding back reliefs in respect of trading, etc. or property letting losses, retirement annuity premiums, retirement benefit contributions, and personal interest, and initial allowances in respect of machinery and plant, industrial buildings or residential premises construction, and various free depreciation and investment allowances. Income from savings bonds under *FA 1970, s 54* is excluded. Income not chargeable to tax is included, but this does not apply to interest on savings certificates and bonus or interest payable under instalment savings schemes, certain children's allowances, military pensions, etc., redundancy payments, scholarship income or payments for Thalidomide children (see 16.1, 16.6, 16.10, 16.12, 16.14, 16.15 EXEMPT INCOME AND SPECIAL SAVINGS SCHEMES and 19.3 GOVERNMENT AND OTHER PUBLIC LOANS).

A relevant person in relation to calculation of an individual's income for a year ending on 5 April means any person who, in that year, normally resided at any relevant residential property of the individual, and who (or whose spouse) paid no rent, etc. in respect of such residence, or paid rent representing less than 80% of an arm's length rent. It does not, however, include an employee of the individual whose employment was wholly or mainly concerned with the property nor, in relation to the year ended 5 April 1994 and subsequent years, any person who is not an assessable person and who is either aged 65 or over or permanently incapacitated from maintaining himself.

Marginal relief is available, on a claim within two years of the valuation date, where the income exemption limit is exceeded by £10,000 (£5,000 for valuation date 5 April 1993 and earlier) or less. The RPT payable will be reduced to a proportion of that otherwise payable corresponding to that excess divided by 10,000 (5,000). For valuation date 5 April 1994 and subsequently, the £10,000 limit is increased to £15,000 where the owner or any of joint owners occupying the property is aged 65 or over, and the aggregate relevant income is rounded down to the next multiple of £1,000. [*FA 1983, ss 101, 102; FA 1990, ss 121, 124; FA 1992, ss 218, 220; FA 1994, ss 115, 119, 120; FA 1995, ss 151, 154*].

26.9 **RELIEF FOR RESIDENT CHILDREN**

Where for a year of assessment ending on a valuation date 5 April 1990 or later an individual has one or more 'qualifying children' normally resident with him at a relevant residential property (see 26.5 above), any RPT otherwise payable by him in respect of his relevant residential property at 5 April in that year is reduced by one-tenth for each such child (maximum ten) on a claim being made within two years of the valuation date.

A *'qualifying child'* is a child under 16 at the beginning of (or born in) the year of assessment, or over 16 at that time but either in full-time education or training or permanently incapacitated by reason of physical or mental infirmity from maintaining himself (having been so incapacitated before age 21 or while still in full-time education or training). Excluded are children whose income in their own right for the year of assessment exceeds £720 (£1,320 in the case of permanently incapacitated children aged over 16). 'Child' includes a stepchild and an adopted child, and a person in the custody, and maintained at the expense, of the assessable person and/or spouse.

For earlier years of assessment, similar relief was available by reference to entitlement to child allowance (see 2.15 ALLOWANCES AND RATES), and was thus (after 1985/86) restricted to incapacitated children.

[*FA 1983, s 102(2)–(4); FA 1990, ss 121, 125; FA 1992, s 221*].

26.10   RETURNS AND ASSESSMENT

A **return** is required by **1 October** following 5 April in each year (commencing 1 October 1983) by every assessable person (see 26.4 above) of all that person's relevant residential property at that 5 April. The return (on a form (RPI) provided) must state the market value at that date of all property included therein, and must include a signed declaration (on oath if required) as to its correctness and completeness.

Any person required by written notice from the Revenue Commissioners to do so must make a similar return.

Further evidence, statements or documents may be required by the Revenue Commissioners by written notice. [*FA 1983, s 103*].

RPT payable is due without assessment, but may be assessed at any time on the assessable person (or person the Revenue Commissioners believe to be such) or the personal representative of such a person. The usual assessment provisions apply where the Revenue Commissioners are not satisfied with a return, or in the absence of a return, which assessment may be amended following a review by the Revenue Commissioners, or withdrawn and substituted by an assessment based on a satisfactory return made within 30 days after the date of the assessment. Any tax due under an assessment or amended assessment is payable on the day next after the date of the assessment, etc. [*FA 1983, s 104; FA 1991, s 112*].

26.11   PAYMENT AND INTEREST

RPT is due and payable to the Collector without assessment on **1 October** following the 5 April by reference to net market value on which it is calculated. See 26.10 above as regards RPT the subject of assessment. For valuation date 5 April 1994 and subsequently, the liability to RPT may alternatively be discharged, at the taxpayer's option and subject to regulations, by an initial payment on 1 October immediately following the valuation date of 25% of the tax due and by ten equal instalments on the immediately following 15 November and monthly thereafter of the balance of the liability plus 5% (i.e. ten instalments of 7.875% of the tax due). The normal recovery provisions apply on any default in relation to payments due following exercise of such an option. The option is not available in respect of tax or additional tax due under an assessment or amended assessment made by the Revenue Commissioners. Where the Commissioners are satisfied that the tax cannot be paid, either in one sum or by instalments as above, without excessive hardship, they may allow postponement for such period, to such extent and on such terms as they think fit. They may also, where, in their opinion, the complication of circumstances in any case justify them in doing so, compound the tax payable upon such terms as they think fit. [*FA 1983, ss 104, 106; FA 1994, s 121*].

Interest runs from 1 October (as above) until the date of payment at 1.25% per month or part month, subject to a de minimis limit of £5. It is recoverable as if it were part of the tax. [*FA 1983, s 105(1)*]. Interest does not run where the liability is satisfied by instalment payments (as above). Interest is not due in respect of tax due on an assessment made by the Revenue Commissioners as a result of their dissatisfaction with a return (see 26.10 above) provided that

(*a*)   the return was made in time, and any tax payable on the basis of the return paid by the due date, and

(*b*)   the tax assessed is paid within one month of the date of the assessment (or the latest determination of any appeal(s) against it), and

(*c*)   the tax assessed does not exceed £100 or, if the assessment was for an additional amount of tax, 10% of the total tax due.

Payments on account may be made at any time after the due date, and are applied against interest due in priority to tax due. Interest ceases to run on tax covered by such a payment from the date of the payment. [*FA 1983, s 105; FA 1994, s 122*].

26.12 OVERPAYMENTS

RPT (and interest) overpaid may be repaid, or (at the Revenue Commissioners' option) set against any RPT or interest due at the time the repayment falls to be made. A non-taxable repayment supplement of 0.6% (1% before 1 August 1990, 1.25% before 27 May 1986) per month or part month is added from the date of the excess payment to the date of repayment or retention. [*FA 1983, s 107; FA 1986, s 114; SI 1990 No 176*].

26.13 APPEALS

Procedures generally similar to those for income tax appeals (see 4 APPEALS) apply to appeals against assessments to RPT, except that 75% of the tax assessed must be paid before an appeal may be proceeded with before the Appeal Commissioners unless the appeal is on the ground that the appellant is exempt under the income exemption limit provisions (see 26.8 above) or is not an assessable person (see 26.4 above). [*FA 1983, s 109*]. Appeals in relation to the Commissioners' decision as to the market value of any relevant residential property (see 26.6 above) are, however, made to the Land Values Reference Committee under the provisions of *F(1909–1910)A 1910, s 33* (suitably modified). [*FA 1983, s 108*].

26.14 DOUBLE TAXATION RELIEF

The Government may by order make arrangements for relief from double taxation in respect of RPT or similar taxes imposed in any other country. In the absence of such an agreement, the Commissioners may grant unilateral relief for such foreign taxes on property outside RI. [*FA 1983, s 113*].

26.15 CLEARANCE ON SALE—LIABILITY OF PURCHASER

Special provisions for the recovery of unpaid RPT apply in relation to sales of residential property under contracts made after 31 July 1993. Where the consideration exceeds the market value exemption limit (see 26.7 above) on the immediately preceding 5 April (or on the date of the contract if it is 5 April), the person by or through whom the consideration is paid (the 'purchaser') must deduct a 'specified amount' from the consideration unless the vendor has obtained a clearance certificate from the Revenue Commissioners (see below). The purchaser must forthwith deliver a return on the appropriate form to the Revenue Commissioners, accompanied by payment of the amount deducted (subject to a penalty of up to £1,000 for failure to comply). On proof of such payment the purchaser is treated as having discharged his liability to pay the 'specified amount' to the vendor. Any amount deducted which is not accounted for is recoverable from the purchaser in the same way as RPT. There are provisions for an estimated amount to be recovered from the purchaser where, in the opinion of the Revenue Commissioners (and subject to appeal), the purchaser has failed to meet his obligation in full.

The '*specified amount*' is one and one-half per cent of the difference between the purchase consideration and the relevant market value exemption limit (as above) multiplied by the number of 5 Aprils (after 4 April 1983) on which the property has been in the ownership of the vendor, up to a maximum of five.

The vendor may, before the date of the contract for sale, apply (on the appropriate form) to the Revenue Commissioners for a certificate that there is no outstanding RPT on the property in question, and if such a certificate is issued, no deduction is required to be made by the purchaser.

There are provisions dealing with sales involving more than one vendor and for cases in which a vendor holds the property as trustee. Also, where a property is transferred between spouses (after 16 June 1993), any outstanding RPT liability of the transferor remains as a first charge on the property for a period of twelve years, unless the property is subsequently transferred for full consideration which does not exceed the market value exemption limit on the 5 April immediately preceding that later transfer.

[*FA 1983, s 110A; FA 1993, ss 107, 108*].

26.16 MISCELLANEOUS

Penalties. Failure to comply with the requirements as to returns (see 26.10 above) renders the person so failing liable to a penalty of up to £1,200, and to a continuing penalty of £50 per day after judgment has been given by the court. A penalty of up to £1,200 also applies where a person authorised by the Revenue Commissioners to inspect a property is prevented from doing so. The furnishing by or with the consent of an assessable person of incorrect returns, statements, evidence or valuations which would result in a reduction below the true RPT liability renders him liable to a penalty of up to £2,500 plus the amount (in case of fraud, twice the amount) of that reduction, unless the error was innocent and was remedied without unreasonable delay after coming to his notice. A penalty of up to £1,200 is also imposed on any person assisting in or inducing an incorrect return, etc. Otherwise, the normal penalty provisions apply with appropriate modifications, and criminal proceedings may be instituted notwithstanding any specific penalty provision. [*FA 1983, s 112; FA 1992, s 248*].

Regulations may be made by the Revenue Commissioners (subject to Dáil approval) as required. [*FA 1983, s 115; FA 1994, s 123*].

27   Residents and Non-Residents

Cross-reference. For non-resident companies, see 12.18 CORPORATION TAX.

27.1   RESIDENTIAL STATUS

A person resident in RI for a year of assessment is normally chargeable to RI tax on all his income whether arising inside or outside RI, subject to any double tax agreements which may apply. Subject to any double tax agreement which provides for a single 'fiscal domicile' (see 27.2 below), a person will be treated as resident in RI in accordance with the following.

New provisions for 1994/95 onwards. For 1994/95 and subsequent tax years (subject to certain transitional provisions), *FA 1994, ss 149–158* apply to determine whether an individual is resident and/or ordinarily resident in RI, to grant a new relief in relation to certain employment income earned outside RI, and to deal with certain other residence-related matters.

Residence. An individual is treated as resident in RI for a year of assessment only if either:

(*a*)   more than 183 days are spent in RI during that year; or

(*b*)   more than 280 days are spent in RI in that and the preceding year of assessment.

A day at the end of which the individual is present in RI is counted as a day spent in RI for this purpose. A year during which not more than 30 days are spent in RI will, notwithstanding (*b*) above, not be a year of residence.

An individual may elect to be treated as resident for a year, provided that the Revenue Commissioners are satisfied that he or she is in RI with the intention, and in such circumstances, that he or she will be resident for the following year of assessment.

These provisions do not apply for 1994/95, but commence for 1995/96, where the individual

(i)   was RI-resident in 1991/92 but not in 1992/93 or 1993/94, or

(ii)   was RI-resident in 1992/93 but not in 1993/94, or

(iii)   was RI-resident in 1993/94 but, apart from the above provisions, would not be so for 1994/95, or

(iv)   left RI in 1992/93 or 1993/94 for the purpose of commencing a period of ordinary residence outside RI, and did not recommence RI ordinary residence before 6 April 1994.

[*FA 1994, ss 150, 158*].

Split year residence. For the purposes of a charge to tax on employment income, where, during a year of assessment (the '*relevant year*') an individual who has not been resident in RI for the preceding year of assessment satisfies the Revenue Commissioners that he or she is in RI with the intention, and in such circumstances, that he or she will be resident for the following year of assessment, and the individual would otherwise be resident for the relevant year, he or she is resident in that year only from the date of arrival in RI. Similarly where a resident individual leaving RI other than for a temporary purpose satisfies the Revenue Commissioners that he or she will not be resident in the following year of assessment, residence will cease in the relevant year from the day after the date of departure from RI. The relevant year in either case is in effect split into separate years of assessment of residence and non-residence for these purposes. [*FA 1994, s 153*].

Individuals non-resident but ordinarily resident in RI are treated as resident for the purposes of taxation under Schedule C or Schedule D (other than in respect of employment income from employment the duties of which are performed wholly outside RI (disregarding incidental RI duties) and income from a trade or profession carried on wholly outside RI). With effect from 23 May 1994, other income not exceeding £3,000 in any year of assessment is also excluded. [*FA 1994, s 152; FA 1995, s 169*].

Ordinary residence. An individual is ordinarily resident in RI for a year of assessment where he or she has been resident in RI for each of the three preceding years. Ordinary residence only ceases after three consecutive years of non-residence in RI. [*FA 1994, s 151*].

Deduction for income earned outside RI. A special relief may be claimed by RI-residents in relation to emoluments from

(*A*)   an office of director of a company carrying on a trade or profession which is within the charge to corporation tax (or would be if it were RI-resident), and

(*B*)   an employment which is not with any statutory body and the emoluments from which are paid otherwise than out of State revenue.

The relief does not apply to offices or employments the emoluments from which are UK employment income, or income from employments exercised in the UK, or where the emoluments are taxed on the remittance basis, or where the split year residence basis described above applies.

Provided that the duties of the office or employment are performed wholly or partly outside RI, and that in any year of assessment the number of 'qualifying days' in that year (or in a 'relevant period' in relation to that year) is at least 90, then a deduction is allowed from the assessable emoluments. A '*qualifying day*' is a day of absence from RI for the purpose of performing the duties of an office or employment, which is one of at least 14 consecutive such days which are substantially devoted to the performance of such duties. The individual must be absent from RI at the end of the day for it to qualify, and a day may only be counted once. A '*relevant period*' is a continuous period of twelve months part of which coincides with the year of assessment in question, and no part of which is comprised in any other relevant period.

The deduction is the proportion of all income, profits or gains from an office, employment or pension (including income, etc. from offices or employments the duties of which are performed in RI) represented by the fraction

$$\frac{D}{365}$$

where D is the number of 'qualifying days' in the year of assessment concerned. Before 23 May 1994, D was for this purpose reduced by N, where N is 15 reduced, where relief is by reference to a relevant period, to the proportion of the qualifying days in the relevant period which fall in the year of assessment.

[*FA 1994, s 154; FA 1995, s 170*].

Personal allowances of citizens, subjects or nationals of EU Member States. Non-RI resident citizens, etc. of Member States are entitled to personal allowances proportionate to the amount of their income which is subject to RI tax. If such a non-resident is a resident of another Member State, the entitlement will be increased to 100% where at least 75% of total income is subject to RI tax. [*Sec 153(2)(c)(3); FA 1994, s 155*].

Appeals on any question where an individual is required to satisfy the Revenue Commissioners under the above provisions must be made within two months of the date on which notice of the adverse decision is given, and lies to the Appeal Commissioners in the same way as an appeal against an assessment. [*FA 1994, s 156*].

Repeals. Secs 76(4) (foreign employment income — discretionary relief, see 31.2 SCHEDULE D, CASE III), *199* (temporary residence outside RI, see below) and *206* (temporary RI residence, see below) and *FA 1987, s 4* (residence of persons working abroad, see 31.3 SCHEDULE D, CASE III) are repealed, except that in relation to the repeal of *Sec 76(4)* the Revenue Commissioners may grant such relief as they consider just for 1994/95. [*FA 1994, s 157*].

For 1993/94 and earlier years (subject to certain transitional provisions as above) a person is treated as resident in RI if he falls within one of the following cases. See 38.6, 38.54–38.58 TAX CASES as regards judicial clarification of requirements.

(a) '*Ordinarily resident in RI*'. This denotes greater permanence than residence and means habitual residence. It need not be the person's principal residence, a person can be ordinarily resident in more than one State at a time. An ordinary resident remains chargeable to RI tax on leaving RI if he leaves only for the purpose of 'occasional residence outside the State'. It is understood that, in practice, the Revenue will treat an individual as ordinarily resident from the date of arrival to take up permanent residence, and as ceasing to be ordinarily resident from the date of departure provided he does not become resident for a further three years. [*Sec 199*].

(b) *Presence in RI for six months.* A temporary visitor who is in RI for six months or more in any year of assessment is regarded as resident. To escape chargeability the visitor must prove that he spent less than six months in RI, for a temporary purpose only and not with a view to establishing residence. [*Sec 206*].

(c) *Accommodation available in RI.* If the person maintains a place of abode in RI which is available for his personal use and if he makes one visit to RI (however short), he is regarded as resident for that year of assessment.

For 1987/88 onwards, this does not apply to an individual domiciled in RI who is engaged full-time in a trade, profession, office or employment carried on wholly outside RI (apart from any RI duties of an office or employment which are merely incidental to the duties performed outside RI). [*FA 1987, s 4*]. See 31.2 OVERSEAS INCOME.

(d) *Habitual lengthy visits.* A person who visits RI for a substantial period year after year is regarded as resident. (The Revenue Commissioners give as a rough example visits of three months annually for four consecutive years.)

It is understood that, by concession, an individual is regarded as not resident and not ordinarily resident in RI in the tax year of his arrival up to the date of his arrival, and similarly as ceasing to be so resident and ordinarily resident in the year of his departure from the date of his departure. Entitlement to full personal allowances and reliefs for the year concerned is not affected. Similarly, for capital gains tax purposes, disposals by individuals and other persons before the date of arrival or after the date of departure are not charged to tax on the basis of residence or ordinary residence unless, in the case of arrival in RI, the person concerned had been so resident or ordinarily resident at any time in the previous 36 months or, in the case of departure, the person continues to be treated as so resident or ordinarily resident after departure.

A company is regarded for tax purposes as resident in the country in which its affairs are controlled (usually the country in which its directors' meetings are held). RI resident companies pay CORPORATION TAX (12) on their profits and gains wherever arising.

27.2 EXEMPTIONS

'Fiscal domicile' under double tax agreement. A double tax agreement may provide that although a person is resident in RI under the rules above he is to be regarded as resident only in the other State and not in RI (e.g. conventions based on the OECD model — see 14 DOUBLE TAX RELIEF–CAPITAL TRANSFERS and 15 DOUBLE TAX RELIEF–INCOME AND CAPITAL GAINS for agreements with the UK). It is understood that, in practice, an individual transferring his permanent residence from the UK will normally be given full personal allowances for the year of transfer, and any earnings from non-Irish employments ceasing before the date of transfer will be ignored in computing Irish tax liability for that year.

Individuals who give property to the State on leaving RI after 31 August 1974, and who become resident in another State for tax purposes, are not regarded as ordinarily resident thereafter, nor will return visits to RI to advise on administration of the property render the person resident or ordinarily resident, provided the visits total 182 days or less in the year of assessment. This applies to income tax, capital acquisitions tax, capital gains tax, and wealth tax. [*FA 1977, s 53*].

27.3 DOMICILE AND NATIONALITY

Domicile is quite distinct from residence or nationality. An individual can only have one domicile and, broadly speaking, it is the *legal system* in which he has, or is presumed to have, his permanent home (i.e. a person cannot be domiciled in the United Kingdom, he must be domiciled in England and Wales, or Scotland or Northern Ireland, etc.). A child acquires a 'domicile of origin' from his parents (usually father) and retains this domicile unless as an adult he acquires a 'domicile of choice'. Domicile is a very technical legal matter but occasionally arises in tax law, see e.g. 31.2(i) SCHEDULE D, CASE III and 38.56–38.58 TAX CASES.

Nationality denotes the sovereign State to which the person belongs. Citizenship of Ireland is governed by the *Irish Nationality and Citizenship Act 1956* and occasionally arises in tax law, see e.g. 27.4(*b*) below.

27.4 NON-RESIDENTS

Subject to any double tax agreement which may apply, non-residents are taxable on income derived from RI, under the normal Schedules (but see 19.1, 19.2 GOVERNMENT AND OTHER PUBLIC LOANS for certain exemptions). It is, however, understood that, by concession, such liability will not be pursued, except by set-off in a relief claim, where a non-resident who is not assessable in the name of an agent receives interest without deduction of tax, unless the interest is under the management and control of a branch in RI.

In addition, non-residents

(*a*)   are not eligible for the initial and reduced rates of income tax which applied for 1983/84 and earlier years [*Sec 153(1); FA 1977, 1 Sch Pt II*], although it is understood that, where appropriate, they will be taxed at the married persons' rates without taking into account income not chargeable to RI tax.

(*b*)   are not eligible for personal allowances (see 2.6–2.25 ALLOWANCES AND RATES), with the following exceptions.

    (i)   a citizen of Ireland;

    (ii)   a person previously resident in RI but compelled to live elsewhere on account of his health or the health of a member of his family;

    (iii)   a national etc., of a State in respect of which an exemption order under *Aliens Act 1935, s 10* applies (includes UK subjects) or of an EU Member State;

(iv)   a person who was before 6 April 1935 entitled to relief under *FA 1920, s 24* (under which certain non-UK residents were entitled to tax allowances, e.g. through being British subjects, residents of Channel Islands or Isle of Man, or in Crown service overseas).

In these cases, the non-resident is entitled to a proportion of the personal allowances to which he would be entitled (if resident) equal to the proportion the amount of his income taxable in Ireland bears to his total income from all sources. [*Sec 153(2)*]. See also 27.1 above.

(*c*)   may be assessed in the name of a trustee, agent, etc., as though resident in RI and in actual receipt of the income. Exception for transactions through brokers, etc. There is a deemed agency if a resident appears to be making less than a normal profit in his business dealings with a non-resident. In certain circumstances, assessment may be made on a percentage of the turnover of the agent etc. There is special provision for a non-resident manufacturer assessed on the sale through an RI agent of goods manufactured by him. [*Secs 200–205*].

28 Returns

Cross-references. For capital gains, see 9.4 CAPITAL GAINS TAX. For companies, see 12.5 CORPO-RATION TAX. See 10.4 CLAIMS regarding error or mistake in return. For penalties for late returns, see 25.4 PAYMENT OF TAX. See also 13.8 DEDUCTION OF TAX AT SOURCE.

28.1 Subject to the self-assessment provisions detailed at 28.12 below, returns must be made when required by a notice given to the taxpayer by an inspector. [*Sec 169*]. Service of notice by post is sufficient. [*Sec 542; FA 1975, s 25*]. Requirements for individuals as in *Sec 172* and for employers regarding employees as in *Sec 178; FA 1979, s 10(3)*. Any person who does not receive a notice but who is chargeable to tax must inform the inspector within one year after the end of the year of assessment. [*F(MP)A 1968, s 5*]. If a taxpayer informs the inspector, within 21 days of receiving his own return, that his wife is in receipt of an income, or if the inspector otherwise decides, the inspector may require the wife to render a separate return of her income. [*FA 1976, s 11*].

If the inspector is not satisfied with a person's return of income or gains, he may require that person (and his spouse if she is living with him) to deliver a statement of his assets and liabilities at the date of the notice. Further supporting evidence and statements may be required.

The statement must include:

(i)   in the case of an individual, unless the return was made in a representative capacity or as trustee, all the assets to which he is beneficially entitled and all the liabilities for which he is liable;

(ii) in the case of a person making a return in a representative capacity, all the assets to which the owner of the income or gains concerned is beneficially entitled, and in relation to which that person acts in a representative capacity, and all the liabilities for which the owner of the income or gains concerned is liable;

(iii) in the case of a trustee returning trust income or gains, all the assets and liabilities comprised in the trust.

In relation to (i), assets of an unmarried child under 21 are included where either they were previously disposed of by the individual or the consideration for their acquisition by the child was directly or indirectly provided by the individual.

The return must include full details of each asset or interest, including its location and date of acquisition and all expenditure incurred in respect of it, with further information in the case of a non-arm's length acquisition. The usual declaration as to completeness and cor-rectness may be required under oath. [*FA 1983, s 20; FA 1992, s 239*].

If the inspector is not satisfied with a return or statement of profits or gains by any person, or no such return or statement has been made when required by the inspector, and he, or an authorised Revenue officer, considers that that person has maintained an undisclosed account with a financial institution (or that such an institution's books may contain infor-mation indicative of material irregularities in his return or statement), an authorised officer may apply to a High Court judge for an order for the production of full details of all such accounts maintained in the preceding ten years and of all such information as is specified in the order. The order may also prohibit any dealings or transfers on such accounts. All pro-ceedings before the judge are held in camera. [*FA 1983, s 18*]. See 38.172 TAX CASES for an unsuccessful application under this provision.

28.2 Penalties may be exacted for failure to make returns or for making incorrect returns (including accounts) fraudulently or negligently etc. or assisting in making incorrect returns etc. Increased penalties may be imposed on bodies of persons and personally on the secretary of such bodies. [*Secs 499–521; FA 1973, s 46; FA 1978, s 11; FA 1979, s 29; FA 1980, ss 57, 59; FA 1982, s 59; FA 1992, s 248*]. Serious tax offences in relation to returns may be punishable on conviction on indictment by a fine of up to £10,000 and/or five years' imprisonment. [*FA 1983, s 94; FA 1992, s 243*]. See also 1.7 ADMINISTRATION AND GENERAL as regards publication of names of tax defaulters and 38.169–38.171 TAX CASES.

28.3   **Accounts, books etc.** An inspector may demand accounts and inspection of books and records if no return is made or he is not satisfied by return. [*Sec 174; FA 1976, s 3*]. See 30.8 SCHEDULE D, CASES I AND II for obligation of taxpayer to keep books and records. See 38.172A TAX CASES.

28.4   **Banks** (including Post Office Savings Banks) **and financial institutions** may be required to give particulars of interest paid exceeding £50 in any year ending after 8 February 1983 (previously £70 p.a.) received or retained in RI (and such returns may be required without notice, see 28.14 below). Such payments may be excluded from return if the recipient serves notice on the payer that the person beneficially entitled to the interest is not resident (before 1995/96, not ordinarily resident) in RI. As respects interest paid or credited after 8 June 1983, if the payer is not satisfied that the recipient was resident (or ordinarily resident) outside RI at the date of payment, the recipient must provide an affidavit stating his name and address and country of residence (or ordinary residence), and, if appropriate, those of the person beneficially entitled to the interest. If the payer is so satisfied, but the person beneficially entitled to the interest is not the recipient and is resident (or ordinarily resident) in RI, the recipient must state, in a notice to the payer, the name and address of the beneficial owner. The payer must retain the notice and accompanying affidavit(s) for six years. If so requested by the Revenue Commissioners, the payer must confirm whether or not such a notice has been served by a named person from a specified address, and furnish the Revenue Commissioners with the relevant notice and affidavit(s). [*Sec 175; FA 1968, s 13; FA 1970, s 12; FA 1983, s 17; FA 1995, s 168*]. These provisions do not apply to payments of interest after 5 April 1986 on 'relevant deposits', see 13.8 DEDUCTION OF TAX AT SOURCE.

Foreign deposit accounts. Any person carrying on an RI business in the course of which he acts as an intermediary in connection with the opening of foreign deposit accounts by or on behalf of RI residents is required to make a return giving full details (which he must take reasonable care to confirm) in relation to all RI residents for whom he has so acted in a chargeable period (year of assessment or accounting period as appropriate), and the account holders are obliged to supply such details to him. The return must be made by 31 January following the year of assessment, or nine months after the end of the accounting period, as appropriate, the first returns being required for 1992/93 and for accounting periods ending after 31 May 1992. Penalties of up to £2,000 apply to both the intermediary and the account holder in relation to failures to comply with the above requirements. Also, an RI resident opening a foreign deposit account is required to provide the inspector with full details within three months. The return provisions of *FA 1988, s 10* (see 28.12 RETURNS) apply, and any failure falls within the surcharge provisions of *FA 1986, s 48* (see 25.4 PAYMENT OF TAX). [*FA 1992, s 230*]. See also Statement of Practice SP – IT/1/92 and 28.14 below. *FA 1992, s 230* is applied *mutatis mutandis* in relation to certain life assurance policies and deferred annuity contracts with foreign insurers by *FA 1993, s 24* (see 9.7(*f*) CAPITAL GAINS TAX) and, for 1995/96 onwards, in relation to material interests in offshore funds (see 32.8 SCHEDULE D, CASE IV), other than certain undertakings for collective investment (for which see 12.21 CORPORATION TAX), by *FA 1995, s 41*.

28.5 Returns

28.5 Customers, business contacts etc. Persons carrying on business and companies may by written notice be required (under penalty) to give details of business transactions with a taxpayer and to furnish any documents (including books, accounts and records) relevant to his tax liability, where the inspector is dissatisfied with the taxpayer's returns relating to his company's business (not banking), or where the taxpayer has failed to deliver such a return, and the inspector notifies the taxpayer that he intends to require such information. There is a saving for confidential information or advice given by a professional person to a client. [*FA 1979, s 31; FA 1992, s 238*].

28.6 Lodgers etc. Lists of lodgers and inmates resident in his dwelling house must be given by any person if required by inspector. [*Sec 177*].

28.7 Nominee holders. Any registered holder of securities (as widely defined) may be required to furnish the inspector with the name and address of the beneficial owner of any such securities which he does not himself beneficially own, and with details of the holding concerned and of the date of registration. [*FA 1983, s 21; FA 1992, s 228*]. Such returns may be required without notice (see 28.14 below).

28.8 Partnerships. The senior partner is responsible, when required by notice, for making a return of all partnership income and any other statements required, and for producing accounts, books etc. [*Sec 70; FA 1979, s 30*]. See also 28.12 below.

28.9 Payments exceeding £500 p.a. to any RI resident. Returns may by specific notice be required from any trader (including a body of persons carrying on a non-trading activity) of such payments made either to non-employees for services rendered or in respect of copyright (but not for any tax-year more than three years before date of notice). [*Sec 173; FA 1992, ss 227(b), 228*]. Such returns may be required without notice (see 28.14 below).

28.10 Rating authorities must provide information concerning rates and rateable valuations when required by notice from an inspector. [*FA 1974, s 73; FA 1983, s 104(9)*].

28.11 Representatives of incapacitated persons and non-residents are held responsible for returns. [*Secs 170, 208, 209*]. So also are personal representatives of deceased persons [*Sec 211(3)*] and other persons in receipt of income of others in excess of £500. [*Sec 176; FA 1992, ss 227(c), 228*]. A return under *Sec 176* may be required without notice (see 28.14 below).

28.12 SELF-ASSESSMENT [*FA 1988, ss 9–21; SI 1989 No 178; FA 1990, ss 23, 24, 27(2); FA 1991, ss 45–53; FA 1992, ss 32, 33, 55, 244; FA 1993, s 40; FA 1994, s 13; FA 1995, ss 31, 66*].

With effect for 1988/89 and subsequent years of assessment for income tax, for company accounting periods ending on or after 1 October 1989 for corporation tax, and for 1990/91 and subsequent years of assessment for capital gains tax, *FA 1988, ss 9–21* require certain 'chargeable persons' to make returns, without notice, and payment of 'preliminary tax', as part of the move towards a self-assessment tax system.

The '*chargeable persons*' concerned are all persons chargeable to income or corporation or capital gains tax for the chargeable period, other, as respects income tax, than those all of whose income is dealt with under PAYE (or by restriction of PAYE allowances), or who are exempted by an inspector by notice, or who are chargeable only by reason of being required to account for tax deducted from annual payments. A return under *Sec 197(4)* by one spouse satisfies the obligations of both spouses in this respect. Returns may be made by an agent, and will be accepted as duly authorised unless the contrary is proved.

For 1992/93 and subsequent years, the exclusion of those whose income is dealt with under PAYE does not apply to directors (or their spouses) of companies which, during the year of assessment and the two preceding years, were not entitled to any assets other than cash not exceeding £100, did not carry on any trade, business or other activity (including investment), and did not pay any charges. See also Statement of Practice SP – IT/1/93, April 1993 as regards the exclusion in practice of certain non-proprietary directors.

The return is required to be made by 31 January in the year following the year of assessment (for 1989/90 and earlier years, by 31 December in the year of assessment), or by the last day of the period of nine months following the end of an accounting period (or the day three months after the commencement of winding-up in certain cases), and to contain broadly the information required by a notice under *Secs 169* or *172* or *CTA s 143* as appropriate. The precedent partner in a partnership is required to make the appropriate return which would be required by a notice under *Sec 70*. The normal provisions relating to incorrect returns apply as if the return had been made under notice, and the late submission surcharge (see 25.4 PAYMENT OF TAX) applies.

Under *FA 1992, s 55; FA 1995, s 66*, various claims by companies to loss reliefs (including group relief), capital allowances, ACT set-off and ACT surrender (see 12.9, 12.14, 12.16, 12.25 CORPORATION TAX) are restricted where a return for an accounting period ending after 31 March 1992 is not made, or is treated as not made, by the required date. For accounting periods ending after 5 April 1995, where the return is made within two months after that date, loss relief and capital allowance claims are restricted to 75% of the maximum claim (maximum restriction £25,000 in relation to each such claim), and ACT surrender claims and claims for ACT set-off are restricted to 75% of the maximum claim (maximum restriction £10,000). Otherwise, loss relief and capital allowance claims are restricted to 50% of the maximum claim (maximum restriction £125,000 in relation to each such claim), and claims for ACT set-off and ACT surrender claims are restricted to 50% of the maximum claim (maximum restriction £50,000). For earlier accounting periods, the restriction was to 50% of the maximum claim (with no maximum restriction) in all cases.

A special return (the '1990 Income Tax Return') may be required for 1990/91, giving information which would have been required in the return for that year if the provisions of *FA 1990, Ch II*, for changes consequential on the changes in assessment bases, had not been enacted.

The '*preliminary tax*' for a chargeable period is the amount which, in the opinion of the chargeable person, is likely to be assessable for that period, and it is payable on or before 1 November in the year of assessment for income tax, or within six months of the end of the accounting period for corporation tax (but by the 28th day of the month where it would otherwise be payable later in the month), or on or before 1 November next following the year of assessment for capital gains tax. Preliminary income tax before 1990/91 was payable by 1 October in the year of assessment, and preliminary corporation tax for accounting periods ending after 5 April 1990 and before 1 May 1993 was payable within seven months of the end of the accounting period (previously six months). Preliminary tax is treated as a payment on account of the liability assessed for the period. No preliminary tax is payable where an assessment has been received for the chargeable period on or before the due date for payment.

Preliminary tax for 1995/96 and subsequent years of assessment for income tax may be paid by direct debit where appropriate arrangements are made with the Collector-General. The tax due will generally be collected in equal monthly instalments on the ninth day of each month in the calendar year in which the due date falls, and is treated as having been paid by the due date.

For income and corporation taxes, where there is default in the payment of preliminary tax, or where, at any time prior to the due date for payment, the inspector considers it appropriate, he may issue a notice of the amount of preliminary tax he considers ought to be paid for the period (except that no such notice may be issued after the chargeable person has delivered a return (as above) for the period). That amount is then payable by the due date unless, on or before the date by which the return for the period is due, the chargeable person either makes a payment of preliminary tax in the normal way or notifies the Collector that he considers no liability will arise for the period. However, where the return for the period is not made by the due date, and the amount of preliminary tax notified by the inspector (increased by any surcharge for late submission, see 25.4 PAYMENT OF TAX) exceeds any preliminary tax paid (again including any surcharge), the excess continues to be payable. The inspector may at any time he considers it appropriate reduce (including to nil) the amount specified in a notice. A notice ceases to have effect on and from the date on which an assessment is made for the period unless enforcement action has at that time been taken for recovery of the tax notified. Preliminary tax so notified is collectible as if it were assessed tax in respect of which no appeal was outstanding.

Preliminary tax in excess of liability for a period is repaid, and carries interest as if the tax were paid under assessment (see 4.5 APPEALS), subject to a £10 *de minimis* limit, unless it arises from a relief under *CTA s 98(4)* (see 12.7 CORPORATION TAX).

Assessments. Where the inspector is satisfied that the preliminary tax paid meets the assessable liability for the period, he may elect not to make an assessment for the period, and must notify his decision to the chargeable person, who may, provided that he has made a return for the period, nonetheless require the making of an assessment. The giving of such notice by the inspector does not, however, prevent the inspector subsequently making an assessment for the period concerned. An assessment may not be made before the date by which a return is required for the period unless the return has already been made. Otherwise, provisions broadly similar in effect to the general assessment provisions apply to the making of an assessment under these provisions, and the inspector has the necessary powers (subject to appeal) to make enquiries and amend assessments. There is a time limit on the making or amending of assessments of six years from the end of the chargeable period in which a return is delivered provided that the return makes full and true disclosure of all material facts. Subject to appeal, this does not, however, prevent the making of an assessment to give effect to determination of an appeal, to take account of events occurring after delivery of the return, to correct a computational error or an error of fact, or where income is assessed on a current year basis. Provided that points subject to genuine doubt as to the application of law are drawn to the inspector's attention in the return, they do not prevent a full and true disclosure.

Nothing in the above prevents an inspector making an assessment under *CGTA 1975, ss 5(3)* (non-residents), *4 Sch 11(3)(4)* (disposals over £100,000 of land, minerals, goodwill etc.) or *4 Sch 17(2), 18(1)(2)* (assessments on third parties), and the tax under such an assessment is due and payable under the appropriate *CGTA 1975* provision, notwithstanding the self-assessment arrangements.

Appeals. There is no appeal against a notice of preliminary tax, or against items in an assessment based on accepted particulars either contained in the return for the period or agreed with the chargeable person. Appeal, on specified grounds, may be made against assessments raised in cases of failure to deliver, or unsatisfactory, returns only when the return is delivered and an amount of tax has been paid on foot of the assessment at least equal to the liability if the assessment were based on that return. Similar rights of appeal apply in respect of amended assessments.

Payment. See above as regards preliminary tax. Where an assessment is made before the date for payment of preliminary tax, it is due on or before that date. Where an assessment is made on or after that date and the requirements for preliminary tax have been satisfied, the balance payable is due:

(i)   for income tax for 1995/96 onwards, by 30 April in the next but one year of assessment;

(ii)   for income tax for earlier years of assessment and for any year of assessment for capital gains tax, by the *specified return date* for the year of assessment (i.e. 31 January following that year) or, if later, within one month of the date of the assessment;

(iii) for an accounting period of a company, within one month of the date of assessment.

Where, however, either

(*a*) the chargeable person has defaulted in payment of preliminary tax for the period, or

(*b*) the preliminary tax paid was less than, or less than the lower of, as the case may be:

    (i)   90% of the tax payable for the period;

    (ii)   in the case of income tax liabilities, 100% of the tax payable for the immediately preceding chargeable period (subject to certain adjustments for additional tax payable for that period, for reliefs for INVESTMENT IN CORPORATE TRADES AND RESEARCH AND DEVELOPMENT (21) and for investment in films (see 12.22 CORPORATION TAX), and for income levy, see 41.2 YOUTH EMPLOYMENT ETC. AND INCOME LEVIES); and

    (iii) in the case of income tax liabilities for a year of assessment 1995/96 or later in relation to which arrangements have been made to pay the preliminary tax by direct debit (see above), 105% of the income tax payable for the preceding year of assessment but one (subject to the same adjustments as in (ii) above), unless the income tax payable, or taken as payable (see below), for that year was nil, or

(*c*) the preliminary tax was not paid by (for 1989/90 and earlier years, within one month of) the date of its becoming due and payable,

the tax charged by the assessment is treated as having become due and payable on the due date for payment of the preliminary tax for the period. The alternative '100% test' in (b)(ii) above applies only for 1990/91 and later years. Additional tax due following amendment of an assessment is treated as due and payable as if it were charged under the original assessment, unless the assessment was made after a full and accurate return had been delivered or the assessment had previously been amended following such delivery, in which case the additional tax is treated as having become due and payable not later than one month from the making of the amendment (for 1989/90 and earlier years, on the day after the making of the amendment). On determination of an appeal, any excess of the tax found to be payable over the amount paid on foot of the assessment is treated as due and payable as if charged by the original assessment unless

(I)   that excess does not exceed 10% of the tax payable, and

(II)   the payment date under the original assessment was not determined under (*a*), (*b*) or (*c*) above,

in which case the excess is treated as due and payable within one month from the date of determination of the appeal (before 1990/91, on that date).

As regards (*b*)(ii) and (iii) above, for a year in which the person concerned was not a chargeable person, the income tax payable is taken as nil. For 1995/96 onwards, however, there are special provisions preventing married couples exploiting their ability to alternate periods of chargeability, in effect requiring their joint liability to be taken into account for these purposes.

The capital gains tax postponement provisions of *CGTA 1975, s 37(4)* (beneficiary of non-resident trust) and instalment provisions of *CGTA 1975, s 44* (hardship) are not affected by the above self-assessment provisions as regards due dates for payment.

28.13 Returns

Commencements and cessations. The Revenue Commissioners' Statement of Practice SP-IT/2/91 sets out the practice to be adopted in paying preliminary tax and filing returns in cases of commencement and cessation. It replaces the Statement of Practice issued in September 1988, which is inapplicable for 1990/91 and subsequent years following the introduction of the current year basis of assessment.

For the year of assessment in which a taxpayer commences to be a chargeable person, the tax payable for the preceding year is taken to be nil, so that no interest charge can arise by virtue of preliminary tax not being paid for the first year of assessment. The full liability for that year will, however, have to be paid within one month of the assessment for the year being received, otherwise an interest charge will arise. Preliminary tax for the second and subsequent years of assessment must be accounted for in the usual way. The Revenue Commissioners consider that taxpayers should, in their own best interests, pay their best estimate of the preliminary tax for the first year of assessment, to avoid cash flow problems arising from having to pay preliminary tax for the second and third years of assessment, the full liability for the first year of assessment and the balance of liability for the second year of assessment within the period from 1 November in the second year of assessment to 1 November in the third year of assessment.

A taxpayer already a chargeable person but commencing a new source of income must account for preliminary tax in the usual way.

As regards returns for the year of assessment in which a Schedule D, Case I or II source commences, if the first year's accounts are not completed by the filing date (see above), the return should show 'Source commenced on (date). Estimated profit (£   )'. The accounts should, at the latest, be submitted with the return for the second year of assessment. Estimated figures are not acceptable for other sources of income commencing in the year of assessment.

For the year of assessment in which a taxpayer ceases to be a chargeable person, preliminary tax must be accounted for in the usual way.

Returns for the final year must show the actual figures to the date of cessation. Any penultimate year revision under Schedule D, Case I or II should not be overlooked.

See 7.10 CAPITAL ACQUISITIONS TAX as regards self-assessment of that tax.

28.13 **A Statement of Practice** was issued by the Revenue Commissioners in September 1988 specifying the documents required to be enclosed with the various types of return. These are as follows, although specific circumstances may of course require further documentation.

Type of income	*Documentation*
Trade/profession	Accounts and computations (including losses, capital allowances and balancing charges).
Investment income	Schedules by category as per return of income received and tax credits. Dividend counterfoils etc. to be submitted only at inspector's request.
Rental income	Statement of gross receipts and expenses for each let premises, with computation of assessable profit (or allowable loss).
Salary, wages, fees etc.	P60.
Allowances, deductions	Details of interest, VHI, retirement contributions etc. paid (certificates only on request). RICT forms and F45s should be attached (unless already submitted).

Capital gains   Computation of chargeable gains/allowable losses.

Other matters   Details of expressions of doubt, special features etc. where relevant.

Accounts should not be sent to inspectors in advance of returns (on e.g. form CT1) as they will not be dealt with until the return is received.

28.14 RETURNS REQUIRED WITHOUT NOTICE

In addition to those required under the self-assessment system (see 28.12 above), returns of certain information etc. may, under *FA 1992, s 226*, be required to be made without notice. These are the returns under:

(a)   *Sec 94(d)(e)* (by managing and collecting agents of premises and bodies paying rent subsidies, etc., see 33.10 SCHEDULE D, CASE V);

(b)   *Sec 173* (fees, commissions etc., see 28.9 above);

(c)   *Sec 175* (interest paid or credited without deduction of tax, see 28.4 above);

(d)   *Sec 176* (income received on behalf of others, see 28.11 above);

(e)   *FA 1983, s 21* (by nominee holders of securities, see 28.7 above);

(f)   *FA 1989, s 19* (by certain intermediaries in relation to collective investment undertakings, see 12.21 CORPORATION TAX).

Any person having information or making, crediting or receiving payments within any of those provisions must make such a return as would be required if a notice were issued under the provision. The return must be made by 31 January following the year of assessment where the chargeable period to which the payment etc. relates is a year of assessment, or nine months after the end of the accounting period where it is an accounting period of a company. The first periods for which a return is required without notice are 1992/93 and accounting periods ending after 5 April 1993.

Returns without notice under a particular provision are not required from any person who would be excluded from making a return under the provision. The inspector may give written notice excluding any person from the requirement to make returns without notice, or limiting the information to be included therein.

The validity of a notice under any of the provisions at (a)–(f) above is not affected by the requirement to make a return without notice, and the issue of such a notice does not remove the obligation to make a return without notice.

The penalty provisions of *Secs 500, 503* (see 28.2 above) apply in cases of failure to deliver a return without notice as required under these provisions.

[*FA 1992, ss 226, 228*].

See also 1.11 ADMINISTRATION AND GENERAL as regards certain reportable offences and 28.4 above as regards returns relating to foreign deposit accounts.

Statement of Practice. The Revenue Commissioners have issued a Statement of Practice (SP – IT/1/92) clarifying the extent to which information has to be reported automatically, and deferring the application of the above provisions so as not to apply to any period before 1 January 1993. The Statement also sets out the matters to be included in returns in each category, and the person(s) on whom the obligation to make the return falls, and deals with various procedural matters.

29   Schedule C—Paying Agents

[*Secs 47–51, 1 Sch*].

Cross-reference. See also 19 GOVERNMENT AND OTHER PUBLIC LOANS.

29.1   Schedule C applies to paying agents (bankers and others) who are entrusted with the payment in RI of interest, annuities, dividends etc., out of public revenue. They must deduct tax at the standard rate (which is then charged on them under Schedule C) and pay the net amount to the persons entitled to the interest etc. [*Secs 47, 48, 51, 1 Sch*].

29.2   Dividends on securities of foreign territories beneficially owned by non-residents are exempt. [*Sec 50*].

29.3   The collection or realisation of coupons is charged under this Schedule [*Secs 47*] and see *Sec 449* (as amended by *CTA 2 Sch 22*) where the right to interest from securities is sold but not the securities themselves and see *Sec 475* (which is applied also to corporation tax by *CTA 2 Sch 26*) where funding bonds are issued in respect of interest.

30   Schedule D, Cases I and II—Profits of Trades, Professions etc.

30.1   Tax is charged under **Schedule D, Case I** on the profits or gains of trades of all kinds carried on in RI or by RI residents elsewhere [*Sec 53*] including

  (i)   mines, quarries, gravel pits, sand pits, ironworks, gasworks, canals, railways and the rights of markets, fairs and tolls etc. [*Secs 53, 56*].

  (ii)   market gardens (i.e. nurseries and gardens in RI used for the sale of produce other than hops). [*Sec 54*].

  (iii) cattle dealers and milk sellers occupying farmland insufficient for the keeping of cattle on it. [*FA 1969, s 19*]. The word 'cattle' in this context refers only to bovine animals, and does not include sheep or pigs (see 38.119 TAX CASES).

  (iv) exploration or exploitation activities on the continental shelf. [*FA 1973, s 33*].

Profits from the occupation of commercial woodlands and stallion fees are exempt from tax except where assessable under Schedule D, Case V. Profits from farming in RI were similarly exempt up to 1973/74 (see under 18 FARMING for position thereafter). [*FA 1969, ss 18, 22; FA 1974, s 14*]. From 1985/86 onwards and for company accounting periods ending after 5 April 1985 (but not so as to apply to profits or gains arising before 6 April 1985), the exemption of stallion fees is generally restricted to stallions and services within RI, except that it is extended to part-owners of stallions kept outside RI who acquired and hold their part-ownership for the purposes of servicing mares owned or part-owned by them in the course of an RI bloodstock breeding trade. [*FA 1985, s 14*]. Certain restrictions may apply to distributions out of such exempt profits, see 12.10 CORPORATION TAX.

Trades carried on abroad are charged under SCHEDULE D, CASE III (31).

30.2   Tax is charged under **Schedule D, Case II** in respect of any profession not contained in any other Schedule. [*Sec 53*].

30.3   **BASIS OF ASSESSMENT**

With effect for 1990/91 and later years, except in the case of new or discontinued businesses (as to which see below), the assessment is on the full amount of the profits (as adjusted) of the accounts for the year of assessment [*Sec 58; FA 1990, s 14(1)(a)*] (but see 18.2 FARMING for an alternative basis for full-time farmers). For 1989/90 and earlier years, the assessment is on the adjusted profits of the accounts for the year preceding the year of assessment.

Transitional provisions apply for 1990/91 for trades which commenced on or before 5 April 1989. Under the new rules, the accounts period ending in 1990/91 will form the basis period for that year. The assessment for 1990/91 will be reduced to the average of the adjusted profits of that basis period and those of the twelve months immediately preceding that period (the 'corresponding period'), except that it will not thereby be reduced to less than 125% of the profits of the corresponding period. In the case of farmers assessed on the 'averaging' basis (see 18.2 FARMING), the average of 'corresponding periods' is similarly considered. This transitional relief will not apply if the amount of the assessment for 1990/91 is determined under *Sec 58(5)(a)(ii)* on the permanent cessation of the trade during 1991/92 (see 30.5 below). [*FA 1990, s 16*].

For 1990/91 and later years, where

(*a*)   the only account made up to a date in a year of assessment is not for a period of one year, or

(*b*)   accounts are made up to more than one such date,

the assessment is based on the profits or gains of the twelve months to the date of the accounts in (*a*) or to the last of the dates in (*b*) or, in cases not within (*a*) or (*b*), on the actual profits for the year. If the profits of the corresponding period of twelve months before the basis period for the year of assessment exceed the amount assessed in the year preceding the year of assessment, the assessment for that preceding year is to be based on the profits of the corresponding period. Similar provisions apply before 1990/91 by reference to accounts made up for periods ending in the year preceding the year of assessment. [*Sec 60; FA 1990, s 15*].

Apportionments etc. are to be made by reference to months and fractions of months. [*Sec 107*].

See also under 8 CAPITAL ALLOWANCES and 22 LOSSES.

30.4   NEW BUSINESSES

First tax year. On actual profits (as adjusted for tax purposes) from date of commencement to the following 5 April. [*Sec 58(2)*].

Second tax year. On profits of one year from commencement. For 1989/90 and earlier years, if a claim was made within 24 months of the end of the year of assessment, adjustment to actual profits of the tax year could be made. [*Sec 58(3); FA 1980, s 17; FA 1990, s 14(1)(b)*].

Third tax year. On profits of accounts for the third year, with right to claim reduction of assessment by any amount by which the profits of the first twelve months trading exceeds the actual profits for the second tax year. Claim must be made with the return required under *FA 1988, s 10* (see 28.12 RETURNS). If, after reducing the assessment for the third year to nil, a balance of that excess remains, the balance may be carried forward as a trade loss and utilised in subsequent years of assessment. For 1989/90 and earlier years, assessment was normally on profits of the preceding year, but if a claim was made within 24 months of the end of the year of assessment, the assessment could be reduced by any amount by which the aggregate of the assessments for the second and third years exceeded the aggregate profits of those two years. [*Sec 58(4); FA 1980, s 17; FA 1990, s 14(1)(b)*].

Short-lived businesses. A special relief is available for businesses permanently discontinued within their third year of assessment of operation, and in the case of which the aggregate profits which would otherwise be assessed exceed the aggregate profits arising over the whole period of operation. Any person chargeable to tax on those profits may give notice by 31 January following the year of assessment of cessation (i.e. the normal return date, see 28.12 RETURNS) requiring the assessment for the penultimate year of assessment to be reduced to the actual profits arising in that year. [*Sec 58A; FA 1995, s 19*].

30.5   BUSINESSES PERMANENTLY DISCONTINUED

See 30.4 above as regards short-lived businesses.

The assessment for the final year is on the actual profits from 6 April to the date of discontinuance. The Revenue have the right to increase the assessment for the previous year to the actual profits for that year. If the trade was discontinued before 6 April 1991, the Revenue have the right to increase the assessments for the two preceding years to the actual profits for those years. [*Sec 58(5); FA 1971, s 3; FA 1990, s 14(2)*].

Discontinuance applies on the death of an owner, although it is understood that, in practice, where a wife succeeds to the trade of her deceased husband, the cessation provisions are not normally applied. [*Secs 58(6), 211*]. Also a change in ownership, including a transfer to or from a partnership (but see 30.6 below), is cessation of old business and commencement of new. [*Sec 59*]. See also 38.118 TAX CASES.

Post-cessation receipts are usually assessable (but under Case IV). See *FA 1970, ss 20–26* for provisions, including debts written off and subsequently realised, and a change from the 'conventional basis' to the 'earnings basis' in computing earnings on cessation.

30.6 PARTNERSHIPS

Each partner is individually assessed on his share of adjusted profits, including partnership salary, interest on capital etc. Assessments will be adjusted in opening and final years as in 30.4 and 30.5 above for the partner joining or leaving partnership but assessments on other partners will be unaffected. Partnership business as a whole is not treated as having ceased unless business actually terminated, or all partners retire except one so that it becomes a sole proprietorship, or completely different partners take over from all retiring partners.

The senior partner must make a return showing apportionments between partners and capital allowances claimed by him for division in the same ratio as profit sharing, including allowances brought forward from earlier years, even though partners are different. Similarly with balancing allowances and charges. If all partners agree hardship is caused by this treatment, they may request re-apportionment. A partner's share of accumulated losses is lost when he leaves partnership. [*Secs 69–74*].

Limited partnerships. See 22.5 LOSSES as regards restriction of relief.

ASSESSABLE PROFITS, ALLOWABLE DEDUCTIONS ETC.

See also 8 CAPITAL ALLOWANCES, 22 LOSSES and 38.60–38.119 TAX CASES. Headings below after 30.7 are in alphabetical order.

30.7 GENERAL

Provisions as to assessable and non-assessable income, allowable and non-allowable deductions are generally similar to those for purposes of UK income tax. Unless otherwise provided in the Tax Acts no sum is deductible in computing profits or gains unless expended wholly and exclusively for the purposes of the trade or profession. Prohibitions include capital expenditure or withdrawals, sums recoverable under contracts of insurance or indemnity, annuity or other annual payments and patent royalties. [*Sec 61; FA 1974, s 42*]. For relevant case law, see 38.60–38.119 TAX CASES.

Professional accounts. The Revenue Commissioners have issued a Statement of Practice (SP–IT/2/92) setting out the basis on which professional accounts may be drawn up for tax purposes. Except in the case of barristers (for whom special arrangements apply), the 'earnings basis' (see *FA 1970, s 20(5)*) is considered to be the strict legal basis, but certain 'conventional' bases, including a cash basis and anything between a full earnings basis and a simple cash basis, may be acceptable (except in the first three years following commencement). The basic requirements that must be demonstrated for a conventional basis to be acceptable are that

(*a*)   profits will not, taking one year with another, differ materially from those determined on the earnings basis,

(*b*)   bills are issued at regular and frequent intervals, and

(*c*)   precise details of the basis used appear as a note to the accounts.

Debtors and creditors must normally be included, but work-in-progress need be included only where its exclusion would materially affect the annual taxable profits. Specific debt provisions are acceptable, including a proportion of long-standing small debts justifiable by reference to previous experience.

As a transitional measure, where accounts have previously been prepared on an unacceptable basis, earlier years will not be reopened where an acceptable basis is adopted for the accounts forming the basis for 1992/93 (1993/94 where the 1992/93 accounts were finalised before the issue of the Statement of Practice), and any uplift in the opening balances taxable under *FA 1970, s 26* may be spread up to 1997/98 (subject to a cessation intervening).

30.8   BOOKS AND RECORDS

Every person carrying on, on his own or another's behalf, any trade, profession, etc., assessable under Schedule D must maintain proper books and records as specified relating to that trade, etc., and retain them for six years subject to a penalty up to £1,200. [*FA 1968, s 6; FA 1992, s 231*]. Authorised officers of the Revenue have power of entry to inspect such books etc., except of a banking business, subject to a penalty up to £1,000, but this power does not extend to documents relating to clients of professional persons. [*FA 1976, s 34; FA 1992, s 232*].

Any individual carrying on a business (the precedent partner in the case of a partnership) must ensure that any invoice, credit note, debit note, receipt, account, statement of account, voucher or estimate relating to an amount of £5 or more issued in the course of the business bears one of his 'tax reference numbers', i.e. his RSI number, or any reference number issued by the inspector, or his VAT registration number. If he has no tax reference number, he must state his full name and address. [*FA 1983, s 22*].

See also 1.8 ADMINISTRATION AND GENERAL as regards electronic data processing and 28 RETURNS.

30.9   CAR RUNNING EXPENSES

Car running expenses incurred for business purposes (including any deduction claimed from emoluments, see 34.3 SCHEDULE E, or as an expense of management under *CTA s 15*) in respect of a car costing more than £14,000 (£13,000 for expenses incurred before 9 February 1995, £10,000 before 27 January 1994, £7,000 before 30 January 1992, £6,000 before 25 January 1989, £4,000 before 28 January 1988 and £3,500 before 6 April 1986), will be reduced (i) by one-third of the amount by which the cost of the car exceeds £14,000 (£13,000/£10,000/£7,000/£6,000/£4,000/£3,500), or (ii) where the taxpayer elects, by the proportion which the excess of the cost of the car over £14,000 (£13,000/£10,000/

£7,000/£6,000/£4,000/£3,500) bears to the cost of the car. There is proportionate reduction for periods of less than one year. [*FA 1976, s 32; FA 1986, s 50(2); FA 1988, s 24(2); FA 1989, s 12(2); FA 1992, s 21(2); FA 1994, s 21(2); FA 1995, s 23(2)*].

The allowable cost of leasing a car of retail price over £14,000 (£13,000/£10,000/£7,000/£6,000/£4,000/£3,500) is also restricted to the proportion of that cost that £14,000 (£13,000/£10,000/£7,000/£6,000/£4,000/£3,500) bears to the retail price. The increase from £13,000 to £14,000 applies only to new cars registered on or after 9 February 1995, and does not apply in relation to expenditure incurred in the twelve months following that date under a contract entered into before that date, the latter restriction having applied also on the earlier increases in the limit. Running costs of such cars are restricted as above. [*FA 1973, s 27; FA 1986, s 50(1); FA 1988, s 24(1); FA 1989, s 12(1); FA 1992, s 21(1); FA 1994, s 21(1); FA 1995, s 23(1)*].

30.10 ENTERTAINMENT EXPENSES

Such expenses (including the provision of accommodation, food, drink or any other form of hospitality, and the provision of gifts) are not deductible in computing profits or gains, or as management expenses. Similarly, no allowance is available in respect of assets used for business entertainment. Entertainment of *bona fide* staff members is excluded from the prohibition unless only incidental to its provision for others. The cost of any business entertainment may be determined by the inspector, subject to the usual right of appeal. [*FA 1982, s 20*]. It is understood that, by concession, expenditure on certain small gifts to charities of a local nature, and subscriptions to local trade associations, made for trade purposes are not regarded as within the exclusion under *FA 1982, s 20*.

These provisions apply equally to the reimbursement to an employee of entertainment expenses incurred on the employer's behalf by the employee.

30.11 EXPORTS

For tax relief on exports by RI companies, see 16.4 EXEMPT INCOME.

30.12 FARMING

Profits from farming in RI were exempt up to 1973/74 but thereafter are chargeable, with (before 1983/84) certain exemptions, under Schedule D, Case I. See under 18 FARMING.

30.13 GIFTS OF MONEY

Gifts of money accepted by the Minister for Finance for public purposes are allowable as a deduction from profits (or as a deduction from total income if made by an individual, or as a loss in a separate trade if made by a company). [*Sec 547; CTA 2 Sch 27*]. See also 2.24, 2.25 ALLOWANCES AND TAX RATES and 12.9 CORPORATION TAX as regards gifts for education in the Arts.

30.14 ILLEGAL TRADING

See under 32.4 SCHEDULE D, CASE IV and also 38.104–38.106 TAX CASES.

30.15 INDUSTRIAL AND PROVIDENT SOCIETIES [*Secs 218–220*].

See under 12.21 CORPORATION TAX.

30.16 'KNOW-HOW'

Expenditure on acquiring know-how for use in a trade (but not the cost of know-how purchased together with the trade) is an allowable deduction under Case I. [*FA 1968, s 2*].

30.17 LAND TRANSACTIONS

See under 3.9 ANTI-AVOIDANCE.

30.18 MINING ACTIVITIES

See under 24 MINES.

30.19 PATENTS

Capital expenditure incurred by a trader or individual deriving income therefrom on purchase of patent rights allowed by equal annual instalments over 17 years, the remainder of first 17 years of life of patent, or the period for which rights acquired, whichever is less. Balancing allowances or charges are made when patent lapses or is sold with suitable adjustment for part sale. Capital sum received is assessable under Schedule D, Case IV (after deducting capital cost where purchased) but spread equally over year of receipt and five succeeding years (or charged for year of receipt if taxpayer so elects within one year thereafter or, within same period, taxpayer may apply to be charged for some other period). [*Secs 284–293; CTA 1 Sch 35–42*].

30.20 PENSION SCHEMES

The costs of setting up, or amending, and contributions to, approved schemes are allowed. [*Sec 63; FA 1972, s 16; CTA 2 Sch 31*].

30.21 REDUNDANCY PAYMENTS

Lump sum payments made under *Redundancy Payments Act 1967* are deductible and corresponding rebates are assessable. [*FA 1968, s 37; CTA 2 Sch 30*].

30.22 RENT—DOUBLE ALLOWANCE FOR CERTAIN PREMISES

Urban renewal: lease granted in the period 1 August 1994 to 31 July 1997 inclusive. Where a deduction is allowed for rent under a 'qualifying lease' in respect of 'qualifying premises' occupied for trade or professional purposes, a further deduction is allowed, for the first ten years for which rent is payable in relation to any qualifying lease of those premises, equal in amount to the deduction in respect of the rent. The relief is restricted where such a deduction is claimed in relation to a 'qualifying lease' of 'qualifying premises' created out of an interest held by a person, and that person or a connected person (within *F(MP)A 1968, s 16(3)*) takes a qualifying lease in respect of other qualifying premises, which he occupies for the purposes of his trade or profession, and which would otherwise attract a further deduction as above. A further deduction will then only be available in respect of the other premises if that person can show that the lease was not undertaken for the sole or main benefit of obtaining such a reduction.

A '*qualifying lease*' is a lease of 'qualifying premises' granted in the period 1 August 1994 to 31 July 1997 inclusive (in the case of a qualifying multi-storey car park (see below), the period 1 July 1995 to 30 June 1998 inclusive) (the '*qualifying period*') on *bona fide* commercial terms by a lessor to a person not connected (within *F(MP)A 1968, s 16(3)*) with the lessor or with any other person entitled to a rent in respect of the premises. A 'finance lease' as defined in *FA 1990, s 33* (broadly a lease at the inception of which the aggregate of the present discounted value of the minimum payments under the lease and any initial payment amounts in value to 90% or more of the arm's length net value of the premises, or a lease which in all the circumstances provides for the lessee all the risks and benefits of ownership of the premises other than legal title thereto) is not a qualifying lease for these purposes.

'*Qualifying premises*' means premises in a 'enterprise area', or a qualifying multi-storey car park, for which capital allowances are available by virtue of *FA 1994, ss 41A, 41B* (see 8.10 CAPITAL ALLOWANCES), or premises in an area designated for this purpose by the Minister for Finance (which designation may specify a shorter qualifying period within that referred to above) consisting of either

(i)   an industrial building or structure for construction or refurbishment expenditure on which, in the qualifying period, capital allowances are available by virtue of *FA 1994, s 40 or s 41* (see 8.10 CAPITAL ALLOWANCES), or

(ii)   an hotel on which all entitlement to industrial buildings initial or annual allowances has been irrevocably disclaimed (see *FA 1994, s 42(5)(6)*) in relation to construction or refurbishment expenditure in the qualifying period

and which is let on *bona fide* arm's length commercial terms. In the case of refurbishment expenditure, there is a further condition that the expenditure is at least 10% of the market value of the premises (excluding land) immediately before the expenditure was incurred.

[*FA 1994, ss 38, 39, 42; FA 1995, s 35(1)(a)(b)(g)(2)*].

See below as regards leases on premises in the Temple Bar or Custom House Docks Areas of Dublin, and as regards earlier leases in certain other areas. Where further deductions continue to apply in relation to rent under such earlier leases, the above provisions do not apply. [*FA 1986, s 45(6); FA 1994, s 35(1)(d)(iii)*]. See also 2.22 ALLOWANCES AND RATES, 8.10 CAPITAL ALLOWANCES and 33.11 SCHEDULE D, CASE V.

Lease granted before 1 August 1994 or in relation to premises in the Temple Bar or Custom House Docks Areas of Dublin. Where a deduction is allowed for rent under a 'qualifying lease' in respect of 'qualifying premises' occupied for trade or professional purposes, payable in the ten-year period commencing on the day on which rent is first payable in respect of those premises under any 'qualifying lease', a further deduction is allowed equal in amount to the deduction in respect of rent. This relief is restricted where such a deduction is claimed in relation to 'qualifying premises' in which a person holds an interest, and that person takes a 'qualifying lease' in respect of other 'qualifying premises', which he occupies for the purposes of his trade or profession, and which would otherwise attract a further reduction as above. Relief will then only be available in respect of the other premises if that person can show that the lease was not undertaken for the sole or main benefit of obtaining a further reduction under these provisions. The restriction is extended, as regards rent payable under leases entered into after 5 May 1993, to refer to both the claimant and persons connected with him within *F(MP)A 1968, s 16*.

As respects 'qualifying leases' entered into after 17 April 1991, the double allowance is by reference to rent paid *for* a rental period rather than that paid *in* a rental period, and where in a period or periods preceding the commencement of a 'qualifying lease' rent was payable by the same person (or a person connected with him within *F(MP)A 1968, s 16*) in relation to the same premises under a 'qualifying lease', double allowances are due only for the first ten years of the aggregate of such periods. As respects qualifying leases entered into after 10 April 1994, this applies to confine double allowances in respect of any one qualifying premises to a maximum of ten years, regardless of whether or not the claimants (if more than one) are connected.

The aggregate reduction in tax liability of an individual from the original reduction in respect of the rent and from the further reduction under these provisions may not exceed the amount of the rent giving rise to the allowances.

'*Qualifying premises*' means an 'industrial building or structure' (see 8.5 CAPITAL ALLOWANCES), or premises treated as such under *FA 1986, s 42* (see 8.10 CAPITAL ALLOWANCES), which is on a site wholly within certain designated areas of Dublin, Athlone, Castlebar,

Cork, Dundalk, Kilkenny, Letterkenny, Limerick, Sligo, Tralee, Tullamore, Wexford, Waterford or Galway (see *FA 1986, 4 Sch Pts II-VII* and *SIs 1988, Nos 92, 287, 314*) and which is let on *bona fide* arm's length commercial terms. It also includes such a building in the Temple Bar Area (see *FA 1991, 2 Sch*), whether or not it is an industrial building or structure, provided that it was in existence on 1 January 1991 or constructed in the period 6 April 1991 to 5 April 1998 and is approved by Temple Bar Renewal Ltd.

After 23 April 1992, only industrial buildings or structures in respect of which capital expenditure incurred in the 'qualifying period' attracts industrial buildings allowances satisfy the conditions for industrial buildings or structures to be qualifying premises. As regards rent payable under a lease entered into after 5 May 1993, where the capital expenditure is incurred on refurbishment of the premises, there is a further requirement that the refurbishment expenditure is at least 10% of the market value of the premises (excluding land) immediately before the expenditure was incurred.

A '*qualifying lease*' is a lease of such premises granted in, or within two years of the end of, the 'qualifying period' on *bona fide* commercial terms by a lessor to a person not connected (as defined for the purposes of *F(MP)A 1968, s 16*) with the lessor or with any other person entitled to a rent in respect of the premises. A 'finance lease' as defined in *FA 1990, s 33* (broadly a lease at the inception of which the aggregate of the discounted present value of the minimum payments under the lease and any initial payment amounts in value to 90% or more of the arm's length net value of the premises, or a lease which in all the circumstances provides for the lessee all the risks and benefits of ownership of the premises other than legal title thereto) is not a qualifying lease for these purposes.

The '*qualifying period*' is:

(i)   in relation to premises in the Custom House Docks Area of Dublin, the period of eleven years ending on **24 January 1999**;

(ii) in relation to premises in the Temple Bar Area, the period commencing on 6 April 1991 and ending on **5 April 1998**; or

(iii) in relation to premises in other designated areas, the period commencing on 23 October 1985 and ending on **31 July 1994**.

[*FA 1986, ss 41, 45, 4 Sch; FA 1987, s 27; FA 1988, s 26; SI 1988 No 314; FA 1990, ss 30(1), 31, 32, 33; FA 1991, ss 21, 54, 55; FA 1992, ss 29(a)(d), 30; FA 1993, s 30(c); FA 1994, ss 35(1)(d), 36, 37(1)(a)(i)(ii); FA 1995, ss 32(1)(a), 33, 34(1)(a)(b)*].

See also 2.22 ALLOWANCES AND RATES, 8.10 CAPITAL ALLOWANCES and 33.4, 33.5 SCHEDULE D, CASE V.

Qualifying resort areas. Where a deduction is allowed for rent under a 'qualifying lease' in respect of 'qualifying premises' occupied for trade or professional purposes, a further deduction may be claimed, for the first ten years for which rent is payable in relation to any qualifying lease of those premises, equal in amount to the deduction in respect of the rent. The relief is restricted where such a deduction is claimed in relation to a 'qualifying lease' of 'qualifying premises' created out of an interest held by a person, and that person or a connected person (within *F(MP)A 1968, s 16(3)*) takes a 'qualifying lease' in respect of other 'qualifying premises', which he occupies for the purposes of his trade or profession, and which would otherwise attract a further deduction as above. A further deduction will then only be available in respect of the other premises if that person can show that the lease was not undertaken for the sole or main benefit of obtaining such a reduction.

A '*qualifying lease*' is a lease of 'qualifying premises' granted in the period **1 July 1995 to 30 June 1998** inclusive (the '*qualifying period*') on *bona fide* commercial terms by a lessor to a person not connected (within *F(MP)A 1968, s 16(3)*) with the lessor or with any other person entitled to a rent in respect of the premises. A 'finance lease' as defined in *FA 1990,* *s 33* (broadly a lease at the inception of which the aggregate of the present discounted value of the minimum payments under the lease and any initial payment amounts in value to 90% or more of the arm's length net value of the premises, or a lease which in all the circumstances provides for the lessee all the risks and benefits of ownership of the premises other than legal title thereto) is not a qualifying lease for these purposes.

'*Qualifying premises*' means a building or structure the site of which is wholly within a '*qualifying resort area*' i.e. a part of Achill, Arklow, Ballybunion, Bettystown, Bundoran, Clogherhead, Clonakilty, Courtown, Enniscrone, Kilkee, Lahinch, Laytown, Mosney, Salthill, Tramore, Westport or Youghal described in *FA 1995, 3 Sch*, let on *bona fide* arm's length commercial terms, in respect of capital expenditure on the construction or refurbishment of which capital allowances fall or will fall to be made under *FA 1995, s 47* or *s 48* (see 8.10A CAPITAL ALLOWANCES), begin either

(*a*)   an industrial building or structure consisting of a hotel, holiday camp or registered holiday cottage (see 8.5(ii) CAPITAL ALLOWANCES), or

(*b*)   a building or structure which is not an industrial building or structure, and which is in use for the purposes of the operation of one or more 'qualifying tourism facilities'.

[*FA 1995, ss 46, 49*].

See also 8.10A CAPITAL ALLOWANCES, 33.12 SCHEDULE D, CASE V.

30.23 SCIENTIFIC RESEARCH EXPENDITURE

Expenditure on scientific research (as defined) is allowed as an expense if non–capital and incurred after 5 April 1946. Capital outlay from 6 April 1946 to 5 April 1965 was written off equally over five years, including year of outlay. After 5 April 1965 it is written off wholly in first year. Balancing allowances and charges arise on cessation of use. Allowance must be claimed within 24 months of end of year of assessment. [*Sec 244; CTA 1 Sch 9; FA 1980, s 17; FA 1992, s 39*]. See also 30.29 below and 38.109 TAX CASES.

30.24 SHARES, SECURITIES ETC.

(*a*)   '**Bond Washing**' transactions where income is received from securities bought and sold within six months or from securities held for over one month and either the purchase or the sale was not at current market price or an agreement regarding the sale was made at, or before, the purchase. [*Sec 367; CTA 2 Sch 17*]. If the transaction is by a share dealer (other than bona fide discount house in RI or a recognised dealer member of a stock exchange in RI) then purchase price used for computing profit or loss for tax purposes is reduced by 'appropriate amount' of the income. [*Sec 368*]. For traders other than share dealers, the 'appropriate amount', and tax thereon, is ignored in any loss repayment claim. [*Sec 370; CTA 2 Sch 19*]. Any exemption entitlement to a person shall not extend to the 'appropriate amount' of the income unless the exemption arises from residence in the UK. [*Sec 369; CTA 2 Sch 18*]. The 'appropriate amount' is the pre–acquisition portion of the dividend, interest etc. calculated from the last 'ex–div' day. It is the net dividend etc. after deduction of tax for purposes of *Sec 368* and gross dividend etc. for *Secs 369* and *370*. [*11 Sch*].

(*b*)   '**Dividend Stripping**' transactions. Where a person carrying on a trade of dealing in shares etc. holds 10% or more of the issued shares of one class (other than fixed rate preference shares) acquired within ten years (six years for dividends received before 26 March 1982) of receiving a dividend or distribution on them which is wholly or partly paid out of pre–acquisition profits, then such part of the net dividend etc. paid out of pre–acquisition profits is treated as a trading receipt which had not borne tax. [*Sec 371(1); CTA 2 Sch 20, 3 Sch; FA 1982, s 61*]. An exemption entitlement to a person shall not extend to such receipts out of pre-acquisition profits [*Sec 371(2)*] and a person not dealing in shares etc. may not claim repayment for loss relief against the gross amount of such dividends. [*Sec 372; CTA 2 Sch 21*]. Provisions include persons acting in concert etc. and see *12 Schedule (as amended by CTA 2 Sch 28; FA 1979, s 34)* for determination of pre-acquisition profits.

See also 3.6 ANTI-AVOIDANCE LEGISLATION.

30.25 STAFF RECRUITMENT AND COVENANTS

The cost (net of grants etc.) of recruiting and training staff (all or majority of whom are Irish citizens) prior to setting up manufacturing business is allowed equally over first three years of assessment in the same way as CAPITAL ALLOWANCES (8). [*Sec 305; CTA 1 Sch 51; FA 1993, s 34(1)(c)*].

See 34.11 SCHEDULE E as regards allowance of certain payments, etc. for restrictive covenants by employees.

30.26 TRADE MARKS

Costs of registration or renewal are allowed. [*FA 1971, s 5*].

30.27 TRADING STOCK

Trading stock is defined as property of any description, whether real or personal, which is either

(*a*)   property such as is sold in the ordinary course of trade or would be so sold if it were mature, or if its manufacture, preparation or construction were complete, or

(*b*)   materials used in the manufacture etc. of property in (a) above.

Trading stock on hand when business is discontinued is valued at amount realised on sale (or value of consideration) if transferred to a person carrying on (or intending to carry on) a trade in RI and who can deduct the cost as an expense for tax purposes, otherwise value is open market value at date of discontinuance (but not discontinuance due to death of a single individual who carried on the trade). [*Sec 62*]. See also 38.115 TAX CASES.

30.28 TRADING STOCK—RELIEF FOR OPENING STOCK VALUE

The greatly simplified scheme of stock relief described below was introduced by *FA 1984* for company accounting periods ending after 5 April 1983 and before 6 April 1985, and for individuals and partnerships for 1984/85 and 1985/86. For the earlier scheme of relief (which continues to apply to trades of farming), under which charges may arise for periods covered by the new scheme of relief and later, see 18.8 FARMING. [*FA 1984, ss 49(3), 51(1), 57; FA 1985, s 18*].

Eligible persons. Relief is available to persons resident in RI (except individuals also resident elsewhere) who, in an 'accounting period', carry on a 'qualifying trade' within the Schedule D, Case I charge. A '*qualifying trade*' is a trade carried on in RI consisting as to at least 75% (by reference to turnover in the accounting period) in:

(i)   the manufacture of goods;

(ii)   construction operations (see *FA 1970, s 17*); or

(iii)   selling machinery or plant (excluding passenger vehicles) or goods to persons for use in trades within (i) or (ii) or in trades of farming.

No relief is given, and any relief given is withdrawn, for an accounting period in which the trader ceases to trade, or to be within the Schedule D, Case I charge in respect of the trade, or to be RI-resident. [*FA 1984, ss 48, 49(1), 50, 51(2)*].

'*Accounting period*' is a company's accounting period (see 12.3 CORPORATION TAX), and for other traders the twelve-month period to the usual accounting date (or, if there is no such twelve-month period, such period not over twelve months as the Revenue Commissioners may determine). [*FA 1984, s 48*].

Amount of relief is 3% of opening trading stock of the accounting period, reduced proportionately for accounting periods of less than twelve months, and limited to the trading profits, computed under Schedule D, Case I rules and, in the case of a company, after deduction of losses and capital allowances and addition of any balancing charges. Relief is deductible as a trading expense. [*FA 1984, ss 49(1)(2), 51(1)(2)(3)*].

For income tax purposes, where stock relief is claimed for an accounting period, no unutilised losses may be carried forward to later periods, nor may a terminal loss be carried back to earlier periods, and utilisation of excess capital allowances is similarly restricted. [*FA 1984, s 51(4)*].

'*Trading stock*' is as defined in *Sec 62* (see 30.27 above), but excluding any stock to the extent that any payment on account has been received in respect of it (for which see 38.110 TAX CASES). [*FA 1984, s 48*].

Valuation of trading stock at intermediate dates (i.e. where a period for which accounts are made up does not coincide with an accounting period), where valuation has not been carried out on such a date, is on a 'reasonable and just' basis by the inspector (or, on appeal, by the Appeal Commissioners). He (or they) must in particular have regard to opening and closing stock values of the period of accounts including the date in question, and to stock cost and trade volume changes in that period. [*FA 1984, s 53*].

Anti-avoidance. The inspector's (or Appeal Commissioners') 'reasonable and just' valuation may be substituted for opening stock valuation where, before or after the beginning of the period of accounts, trading stock has been acquired or disposed of otherwise than in the normal conduct of the trade. [*FA 1984, s 55*].

Claims to relief must be made before the later of:

(i)   the date the assessment for the period becomes final and conclusive; and

(ii)   31 December in

(*a*)   (for income tax) the year of assessment,

(*b*)   (for corporation tax) the year of assessment following that in which the accounting period ends. [*FA 1984, ss 49(4), 51(5)*].

New businesses. Opening stock of a new business is valued on 'reasonable and just' basis by the inspector (or, on appeal, by the Appeal Commissioners), having regard in particular to stock cost and trade volume changes in the opening period, *unless* the trade was previously carried on by another person from whom the opening stock (as valued) was acquired. [*FA 1984, s 54*].

'Clawback' of relief. Subject to the 'succession' provisions (see below), for any accounting period during which a person ceases to carry on a trade, or to be within the Schedule D, Case I charge in respect of it, or to be RI-resident,

(i)   no stock relief is available, and

(ii)   any stock relief given under these provisions in respect of the trade for accounting periods ending in the five years before the beginning of the accounting period in which that event occurs is treated as a trading receipt.

[*FA 1984, ss 50, 52*].

Successions. The above 'clawback' provisions do not apply on a 'relevant disposal' of a trade, if predecessor and successor so elect (in writing within two years of the relevant disposal), and the successor is then treated for this purpose as having carried on the trade since the predecessor began to do so (or is treated as having begun to do so).

A *'relevant disposal'* of a trade is:

(*a*)   a transfer of the trade between companies to which *CTA, s 20* applies (see 12.16 (*e*) CORPORATION TAX);

(*b*)   a transfer of the trade from an individual or partnership to a company where at least three-quarters of the company's ordinary share capital is held by the transferor(s) at the date of transfer;

(*c*)   a succession to the trade on the death of the previous owner; or

(*d*)   a transfer of the trade from an individual to his child or to a nephew or niece who has helped full-time in the business for the previous five years.

Where the relevant disposal is within (*a*) or (*b*) above, the trading stock must be transferred at cost or at market value, and the successor must in any case be RI-resident (and if an individual not resident elsewhere) and within the Schedule D, Case I charge in respect of the trade.

[*FA 1984, s 56*].

30.29 UNIVERSITIES

Payments to Irish Universities for purpose of research or teaching industrial relations, marketing or any other subject approved by the Minister for Finance, are allowable. [*FA 1973, s 21*]. Relief is also granted for payments to the National Institute for Higher Education at Dublin or Limerick, the College of Industrial Relations, Ranelagh, Dublin, and certain other colleges established under *Vocational Education Act 1930*. [*FA 1985, s 15*]. See also 30.23 above.

31   Schedule D, Case III—Interest Receivable and Overseas Income

[*Secs 53, 75–77*].

31.1   Tax is charged under Schedule D, Case III on

(*a*)   interest, annuities and other annual payments (but excluding any amounts chargeable under Schedule D, Case V).

(*b*)   discounts.

(*c*)   profits on securities bearing interest payable out of public revenue and not chargeable under Schedule C.

(*d*)   interest paid without deduction of tax on securities issued under authority of Minister for Finance or deemed to be such. [*Secs 53, 466*].

(*e*)   income from foreign securities and not charged under Schedule C.

(*f*)   income from foreign possessions, which include trades wholly carried on and controlled abroad and offices, employments and pensions (*F(MP)A 1968, s 9* exempts certain overseas pensions etc. for past services analogous to RI old age pensions etc.) with benefits in kind taxable to same extent as if arising in RI, see 34.3 SCHEDULE E. [*FA 1976, s 22*].

See 38.120–38.126 TAX CASES for relevant case law.

31.2   **ASSESSMENTS**

All profits assessable under Case III are treated as a single source, except as set out below. Adjustments are not made therefore in respect of each item which is new or ceases, but only when all Case III sources are new, or when they all cease. [*Sec 75; FA 1990, s 17(1)(a)(i)*]. See 38.120 TAX CASES.

Exceptions apply as follows for 1989/90 and earlier years (treated as separate sources):

(i)   income assessable only on remittance (persons domiciled abroad, etc.). [*Secs 75(2)(iii), 76*].

(ii)   untaxed War Loan income of double residents up to 5 April 1976. [*6 Sch Pt III para 5; FA 1977, s 54*].

(iii)   interest which changes from being paid under deduction of tax to being paid gross, and vice versa. [*Sec 75(3)(4) inserted by FA 1974, s 43*].

For 1990/91 and later years, assessment is on actual income arising in the year of assessment. Previously, assessment was on actual income arising in the year preceding the year of assessment, except that

(*a*)   if income first arose **after 6 April** in first year of assessment

1st tax year assessed on 1st year's income, i.e. from date when income first arose to the following 5 April.

2nd tax year assessed on 2nd year's income.

3rd tax year assessed on 2nd year's income with option to taxpayer to substitute 3rd year's income if claimed within 24 months after end of year of assessment.

(*b*)   if income first arose **on 6 April** in first year of assessment

1st tax year assessed on 1st year's income.

2nd tax year assessed on 1st year's income with option to taxpayer to substitute 2nd year's income if claimed within 24 months after end of year of assessment.

3rd tax year assessed on 2nd year's income.

Ceasing to possess source of income. When all sources taxable under Case III cease, or source treated as a separate source ceases, the assessment for the final year is on the actual profits from 6 April to the date of discontinuance. Where the sources ceased before 6 April 1991, the assessment for the penultimate year may be increased (if appropriate) to the tax chargeable on the actual income arising in that year. Death of the taxable person is deemed to be a cesser of income for this purpose, although it is understood that the cessation provisions are, by concession, not applied where a source of income passed on death in its entirety to the surviving spouse. [*Sec 77; FA 1990, s 17*].

Foreign securities and possessions are normally assessable on the full income arising, whether remitted or not. But in the case of persons not domiciled in RI, or RI citizens not ordinarily resident there, the remittance basis still applies to income from such sources (other than sources in Gt. Britain or N. Ireland). Any income arising abroad and not remitted is subject to the same deductions and allowances (including interest relief) as if it had been so received. [*Secs 76, 77, 6 Sch Pt III; FA 1974, ss 44, 45; FA 1977, 2 Sch; FA 1979, ss 9, 10*]. Also, interest on money borrowed to purchase, improve or repair property abroad is deductible from the rents received. [*FA 1974, s 46*]. See 31.4 below for double taxation relief and 27.1 RESIDENTS AND NON-RESIDENTS as regards 1994/95 and subsequent years.

See also 38.164 TAX CASES.

Relief may be given in cases of hardship arising from the assessment of income from an employment exercised wholly outside RI. [*Sec 76(4)*].

See 31.3 below as regards revised definition of 'residence' in relation to individuals working abroad.

Unremittable income. Where a taxpayer satisfies Revenue Commissioners that, owing to legislation or executive action in country of origin, income arising in that country cannot be remitted, tax thereon may be held in abeyance until, in their opinion, that income becomes remittable. Right of appeal to Appeal Commissioners applies to any tax for any year unpaid at date of passing of *FA 1953*. [*Sec 549*].

31.3   DOMICILE AND RESIDENCE

As regards income derived from RI or UK sources the question of domicile or ordinary residence normally makes no difference, but see 29 SCHEDULE C and 19 GOVERNMENT AND OTHER PUBLIC LOANS.

As regards income derived from sources outside those countries (viz., in the Dominions or abroad) the question is of importance.

Persons who are not domiciled in RI, and RI citizens not ordinarily resident there, deriving income from sources outside RI and Great Britain and N. Ireland, are assessable to RI tax on that income on the basis of remittance to the Republic, and not on the whole income arising. But see *FA 1971, s 4* for treating as constructive remittances foreign income set against loans enjoyed in RI.

Working abroad. For 1987/88 to 1993/94 inclusive, when an individual who is domiciled in RI is engaged full-time in a trade or profession carried on wholly outside RI, or in an office or employment the duties of which, apart from incidental RI duties, are performed wholly outside RI, then the retention of a place of abode in RI will be disregarded in determining resident status. [*FA 1987, s 4*].

See also 27 RESIDENTS AND NON-RESIDENTS.

Relief after 10 years residence abroad. Persons who (*a*) are domiciled, resident or ordinarily resident in RI for year of claim and (*b*) were previously resident for an aggregate of 10 years in USA, Canada, Australia, New Zealand, South Africa or any 'British possession' may be given unilateral relief on doubly taxed income arising in that country. [*Sec 365*]. See further 15.14 DOUBLE TAX RELIEF—INCOME AND CAPITAL GAINS.

31.4 DOUBLE TAXATION RELIEF

Income from UK (see also 15.3 et seq. DOUBLE TAX RELIEF—INCOME AND CAPITAL GAINS). While the Convention is in force the Tax Acts are modified by *6 Sch Pt III para 1*.

Tax credit. The income chargeable under Schedule D, Case III on a UK dividend which carries a tax credit under *Convention Art 11(2)(b)* includes the amount of the tax credit. [*FA 1977, s 39(1)*].

32 Schedule D, Case IV—Miscellaneous Income

[*Secs 53, 79*].

32.1 Tax is charged under Schedule D, Case IV in respect of any annual profits or gains not falling under any other case of Schedule D and not charged by virtue of any other Schedule. [*Sec 53*]. Particular items specified as chargeable under Case IV are stated below or under the appropriate headings elsewhere in this book, and can be traced through the index. See 38.127–38.131 TAX CASES for relevant case law.

32.2 **Assessment** is on the profits in the year of assessment or on the average of such period, not being greater than one year, as the inspector directs. [*Sec 79*].

32.3 **Losses** may be set off against Case IV profits of the same year or carried forward indefinitely against subsequent profits assessed under that Case. [*Sec 310*].

32.4 **Illegal and unknown sources of income.** Assessments may be made after 8 June 1983 charging to tax under Schedule D, Case IV as 'miscellaneous income' profits or gains from sources not known to the inspector, or which arose (or may have arisen) wholly or partly from an illegal source or activity. The unknown or illegal nature of the source the subject of such an assessment is to be disregarded in determining liability, and neither that nature nor the general description of the source as 'miscellaneous income' is by itself ground for discharge of the assessment on appeal. [*FA 1983, s 19*]. For the position prior to *FA 1983*, see 38.104–38.106 TAX CASES.

32.5 **OFFSHORE FUNDS** [*FA 1990, ss 62–69, 5, 6 Schs*]

Introduction. After 5 April 1990, 'offshore income gains' arising on disposals of certain interests in 'offshore funds' which are not considered to distribute sufficient income are charged to income tax or corporation tax under Schedule D, Case IV rather than to capital gains tax. Broadly, the capital gains tax regime applies to any part of such a gain accruing before 6 April 1990, but the whole of the gain arising thereafter (without indexation) is taxed as income. Special provisions apply to funds which operate 'equalisation arrangements'.

32.6 **DISPOSALS WITHIN OFFSHORE FUND PROVISIONS**

Disposal of material interests in non-qualifying offshore funds. The offshore fund rules apply to a disposal by any person of an asset if, at the time of the disposal, the asset constitutes either

(*a*) a 'material interest' in an 'offshore fund' (see 32.8 below) which is or has at any 'material time' been a 'non-qualifying offshore fund' (see 32.9 below), or

(*b*) an interest in an RI-resident company or in a unit trust scheme which has RI-resident trustees, provided that at a 'material time' after 31 December 1990 the company or unit trust scheme was a 'non-qualifying offshore fund' and the asset constituted a 'material interest' in that fund (and for this purpose the provisions of *CGTA 1975, 2 Sch 2(2)* equating original shares with a new holding on a reorganisation apply).

[*FA 1990, s 63(1)*].

A '*material time*' is any time on or after 6 April 1990 or, if the asset was acquired after that date, the earliest date on which any 'relevant consideration' was given for the acquisition of the asset. '*Relevant consideration*' is that given by or on behalf of the person making the disposal or a predecessor in title which would be taken into account in determining any gain or loss on disposal under *CGTA 1975*. [*FA 1990, s 63(7)*].

With some modifications, a disposal occurs for offshore fund purposes if there would be a disposal under *CGTA 1975*. Death is an occasion of charge, as the deceased is deemed to have made a disposal at market value, immediately before his death, of any asset which was or had at any time been a 'material interest' in a 'non-qualifying offshore fund'. In addition, *CGTA 1975, 2 Sch 4(1)* will not apply, and there will therefore be a disposal at market value, if an exchange or arrangement is effected under *CGTA 1975, 2 Sch 4, 5* in such a way that securities, etc. in a company, which is or was at a material time a 'non-qualifying offshore fund', are exchanged for assets, etc. which do not constitute interests in such a fund. [*FA 1990, s 63(2)–(6)*].

32.7   **Offshore funds operating equalisation arrangements.** There are specific provisions to enable funds operating 'equalisation arrangements' to satisfy the 'distribution test' (see 32.10 below) which the nature of such funds might otherwise preclude. As a corollary, provision is also made to ensure that the 'accrued income' paid to outgoing investors as part of their capital payments is treated as income for tax purposes when the fund qualifies as a distributor.

For these purposes, an 'offshore fund' operates '*equalisation arrangements*' where the first distribution paid to a person acquiring a 'material interest' by way of 'initial purchase' includes a payment which is a return of capital (debited to the fund's 'equalisation account') determined by reference to the income which had accrued to the fund in the period before that person's acquisition. An acquisition is by way of '*initial purchase*' if it is by way of direct purchase from the fund's managers in their capacity as such or by way of subscription for or allotment of new shares, etc.

'*Accrued income*' *chargeable to income tax—application of offshore fund rules.* A disposal is one to which the offshore fund provisions apply (subject to the exception detailed below) if it is a disposal by any person of a 'material interest' in an 'offshore fund' operating equalisation arrangements where

(*a*)   the disposal proceeds are not a trading receipt, and

(*b*)   the fund is not, and has not at any material time (see 32.6 above) been, a 'non-qualifying offshore fund' (see 32.9 below)

(i.e. the new provisions apply also to distributing funds (see 32.10 below) with equalisation arrangements).

Capital gains tax rules for disposals apply as they do for other offshore fund disposals (see 25.2 above) with some variations. Death is not treated as a disposal in this context. In addition, *CGTA 1975, 2 Sch 2(2)* (reorganisations, etc.) (including that paragraph as applied by *2 Sch 2A* or *4* (exchange of securities) but not by *2 Sch 3* (conversion of securities)) does not apply, and there is a disposal at market value in such circumstances.

Exception. The offshore fund legislation does not apply as indicated above to a disposal where the fund's income for the period preceding the disposal is of such a nature that the part relating to the interest in question is in any event chargeable under SCHEDULE D, CASE III (31) on the person disposing of the interest (or would be so chargeable if residence/domicile/situation of asset requirements were met).

[*FA 1990, ss 63(2)(3), 64*].

32.8   MATERIAL INTERESTS IN OFFSHORE FUNDS

An '*offshore fund*' is:

(*a*)   a company resident outside RI; or

(*b*)   a unit trust scheme which has non-RI resident trustees; or

(*c*)   any other arrangements taking effect under overseas law which create rights in the nature of co-ownership under that law,

in which any person has a 'material interest'. [*FA 1990, s 65(1)*].

A '*material interest*' is one which, when acquired, could reasonably be expected to be realisable (by any means, either in money or in asset form) within seven years, for an amount reasonably approximate to its proportionate share of the market value of the fund's assets. For these purposes, an interest in an offshore fund which at any time is worth substantially more than its proportionate share of the fund's underlying assets is not to be regarded as so realisable. [*FA 1990, s 65(2)–(4)*].

Exceptions. The following are not material interests.

(i)   Interests in respect of loans, etc. made in the ordinary course of banking business.

(ii)   Rights under insurance policies.

(iii)   Shares in a company resident outside RI where:

    (*a*)   the shares are held by a company and the holding is necessary or desirable for the maintenance and development of a trade carried on by the company or by an associated company (within *CTA s 102*); and

    (*b*)   the shares confer at least 10% of the voting rights and, on a winding-up, a right to at least 10% of the assets after discharge of all prior liabilities; and

    (*c*)   the shares are held by not more than ten persons and all confer both voting rights and a right to assets on a winding-up; and

    (*d*)   at the time of acquisition of the shares the company could reasonably expect to realise its interest for market value within seven years only by virtue of an arrangement requiring the company's fellow participators to purchase its shares and/or provisions of either the overseas company's constitution or an agreement between the participators regarding that company's winding-up.

(iv)   Interests in companies resident outside RI at any time when the holder is entitled to have the company wound up and to receive in that event, in the same capacity, more than 50% of the assets after discharging all prior liabilities.

[*FA 1990, s 65(5)–(8)*].

'*Market value*' for the purposes of the offshore funds legislation is determined according to capital gains tax rules with the necessary modification of *CGTA 1975, s 49(5)* (market value in relation to rights in unit trust schemes) where appropriate. [*FA 1990, s 65(9)*].

See also 28.4 RETURNS.

32.9   NON-QUALIFYING OFFSHORE FUNDS

An offshore fund is a '*non-qualifying offshore fund*' except during an 'account period' in respect of which it is certified by the Revenue Commissioners as a distributing fund pursuing a 'full distribution policy' (see 32.10 below). For these purposes, an '*account period*' begins on 6 April 1990 (or, if later, when the fund begins to carry on its activities) and on the ending of an account period without the fund ceasing to carry on its activities, and ends on the fund's accounting date (or on the ending of a period for which it does not make up accounts) or, if earlier, twelve months from the beginning of the period or on the fund's ceasing to carry on its activities. In addition, if the fund is a company resident outside RI, an '*account period*' ends when it ceases to be so, and if the fund is a unit trust scheme with non-RI resident trustees, it ends when those trustees become RI resident. [*FA 1990, s 66(1)(2)(8)–(10)*].

Conditions for certification. Subject to the modification of conditions for certification in certain cases noted below, an offshore fund is not to be certified as a 'distributing fund' for any account period if, at any time in that period:

(*a*)   more than 5% by value of the fund's assets consists of interests in other offshore funds (but see below); or

(*b*)   more than 10% by value of the fund's assets consists of interests in a single company. For this purpose:

    (i)   the value of an interest in a single company is determined as at the most recent occasion (in that or an earlier account period) on which the fund acquired an interest in that company for money or money's worth. However, an occasion is disregarded if it is one on which *CGTA 1975, 2 Sch 2* (equation of original shares and new holding) applied, including that *paragraph* as applied by *paragraphs 3* or *4* of that *Schedule* (reorganisations, conversions of securities, etc.), and on which no consideration was given for the interest other than the interest in the original holding; and

    (ii)   an interest is disregarded, except for determining the total value of the fund's assets, if it consists of a current or deposit account provided in the normal course of its banking business by a company whose business it is to provide such account facilities in any currency for members of the public and bodies corporate; or

(*c*)   the fund's assets include more than 10% of the issued share capital, or any class of it, in any company; or

(*d*)   there is more than one class of material interests (see 32.7 above) in the fund and, were each class and the assets represented by it in a separate offshore fund, each such separate fund would not pursue a 'full distribution policy'. For this purpose, interests held solely by persons involved in the management of the fund's assets are disregarded if they carry no right or expectation to participate in profits and no right to anything other than the return of the price paid on winding-up or redemption.

Where, however, the Revenue Commissioners are satisfied that an apparent failure to comply with any of (*a*)–(*c*) above occurred inadvertently and was remedied without unreasonable delay, that failure may be disregarded.

[*FA 1990, s 66(3)–(7), 5 Sch 14*].

Modifications of conditions for certification. The conditions for certification in (*a*)–(*d*) above are modified in certain cases, as follows.

(A)   *Investments in second tier funds.* If an offshore fund (a 'primary fund') would fail to meet the conditions in (*a*)–(*c*) above because of investments in another offshore fund (referred to below as a 'second tier fund') which could itself be certified as a qualifying distributing fund (without any modification of the conditions in (*a*)–(*c*)), then the primary fund's interests in the second tier fund are left out of account, except for determining the total value of the primary fund's assets, in establishing whether the primary fund is prevented by (*a*)–(*c*) above from being certified as a distributing fund. In addition, where the above applies, if at any time in a primary fund's account period that fund's assets include an interest in another offshore fund or in any company, and the qualifying second tier fund's assets also include an interest in that other fund or company, then the primary fund's interest is aggregated with its proportionate share of the second tier fund's interest in determining whether the primary fund is within the limits in (a)–(c) above. Its share of the second tier fund's interest is the proportion which the average value during its account period of its own holding of interests in the second tier fund bears to the average value during the period of all interests in the second tier fund. [*FA 1990, s 66(3), 5 Sch 6, 7, 9*].

(B) *Investments in trading companies.* Where the assets of an offshore fund include an interest in a company whose business is wholly the carrying on of trade(s), the limit in (*b*) above of 10% of a fund's assets invested in a single company is increased to 20%, and the 10% limit in (*c*) above on the proportion of a class of share in any company is increased to allow holdings of up to 50%. For these purposes companies are excluded if their business consists to any extent of banking or moneylending or of dealing, including dealing by way of futures contracts or traded options, in commodities, currency, securities, debts or other assets of a financial nature. [*FA 1990, s 66(3), 5 Sch 10*].

(C) *Wholly-owned subsidiaries.* Where an offshore fund has a 'wholly-owned subsidiary' company, the receipts, expenditure, assets and liabilities of the fund and the subsidiary are aggregated so that the fund and the subsidiary are treated as one for the purposes of determining whether the fund is within the limits in (a)–(d) above. In the same way, the interest of the fund in the subsidiary, and any distributions or other payments between the fund and the subsidiary, are left out of account. A '*wholly-owned subsidiary*' is one owned either directly and beneficially by the fund, or directly by the trustees of the fund for the benefit of the fund, or, in a case within 32.8(*c*) above, in some other corresponding manner. Where the subsidiary has only one class of issued share capital, ownership of at least 95% of that capital by the offshore fund constitutes the subsidiary a wholly-owned subsidiary for this purpose, and only a corresponding proportion of the subsidiary's receipts, expenditure, assets and liabilities are then aggregated with those of the offshore fund. [*FA 1990, s 66(3), 5 Sch 11*].

(D) *Subsidiary dealing and management companies.* The investment restriction in (*c*) above does not apply to so much of an offshore fund's assets as consists of share capital of a company which is either

  (1) a wholly-owned subsidiary of the fund (as defined in (C) above) whose sole function is dealing in material interests in the offshore fund for management and administrative purposes and which is not entitled to any distribution from the fund, or

  (2) a subsidiary management company of the fund whose sole function is to provide the fund, or other funds with an interest in the company, with advisory services or administrative, management and related property-holding services on arm's length commercial terms. For the purposes of determining whether a company is a subsidiary management company of a fund, that company and any wholly-owned subsidiary companies it may itself have are regarded as a single entity. [*FA 1990, s 66(3), 5 Sch 12*].

(E) *Disregard of certain investments.* Certain holdings which would otherwise fall within the restriction at (*c*) above are not taken into account for the purposes of that restriction. This applies where no more than 5% of the value of the offshore fund's assets consists of such holdings and of interests in other non-qualifying offshore funds. [*FA 1990, s 66(3), 5 Sch 13*].

32.10 THE DISTRIBUTION TEST

An offshore fund pursues a *'full distribution policy'* with respect to an account period if:

(*a*)   a distribution is made for that account period or for some other period falling wholly or partly within that period; and

(*b*)   subject to the modifications specified below, the distribution represents at least 85% of the fund's income and is not less than 85% of its 'Irish equivalent profits' for that period; and

(*c*)   the distribution is made during, or within six months after the end of, the account period; and

(*d*)   the distribution is in a form such that any part of it received in RI by an RI resident which is not part of the profits of a trade, etc. is chargeable under Schedule D, Case III.

These conditions may equally be satisfied by any two or more distributions taken together. [*FA 1990, 5 Sch 1(1)*].

The conditions in (*a*)–(*d*) above are subject to modification in certain cases (see 32.11 below).

A fund is treated as pursuing a full distribution policy for any account period in which there is no income and no 'Irish equivalent profits', but it will not be so treated for any account period for which no accounts are prepared. [*FA 1990, 5 Sch 1(2)(3)*].

'Irish equivalent profits' of an offshore fund are the total profits, excluding chargeable gains, on which, after allowing for any deductions available, corporation tax would be chargeable, assuming that:

(i)   the offshore fund is an RI resident company in the account period in question; and

(ii)   the account period is an accounting period of that company; and

(iii)   any dividends or distributions from RI resident companies are included.

The effect of (i) above is that certain sums received without deduction of or charge to tax on account of the fund's actual resident status are nevertheless brought into account.

The deductions referred to above include a deduction equal to that allowed against a fund's income where legal restrictions prevent distribution (see above), a deduction equal to any foreign capital tax allowed as a deduction in determining the fund's income for the account period in question, and a deduction equal to any income tax paid (by deduction or otherwise) by, and not repaid to, the fund in respect of income of the account period. [*FA 1990, 5 Sch 5*].

Legal restrictions on distributions. Where in an account period an offshore fund is subject to restrictions imposed by the law of any territory on making distributions by reason of an excess of losses over profits as computed according to the law in question, a deduction is allowed from the fund's income of any amount which cannot be distributed but which would otherwise form part of the fund's income for that account period. [*FA 1990, 5 Sch 1(6)*].

Apportionment of income and distributions between account periods. Where a period for which accounts are made up, or for which a distribution is made, covers the whole or part of two or more account periods of the fund, the income or distribution is apportioned on a time basis according to the number of days in each period. A distribution made out of specified income but not for a specified period is attributed to the account period in which the income arose. Where no period or income is specified, a distribution is treated as made for the last account period ending before the distribution. If the distribution made, or treated as made, for an account period exceeds the income of that period, the excess is reallocated to previous periods, to later periods before earlier ones, until exhausted, unless the distribution was apportioned on a time basis as above, in which case the excess is first reapportioned on a just and reasonable basis to the other account period(s). [*FA 1990, 5 Sch 1(4)(5)*].

32.11   MODIFICATIONS OF DISTRIBUTION TEST

The basic rules of the distribution test in 32.10(*a*)–(*d*) above are modified in the following circumstances.

(*a*)   **Funds operating equalisation arrangements.** Where an offshore fund operates such arrangements (see 32.7 above) throughout an account period, an amount equal to any 'accrued income' which is part of the consideration for certain disposals in that period is treated as a distribution for the purposes of the distribution test. This applies to a disposal:

    (i)   which is a disposal of a material interest in the fund either to the fund or to the fund managers in their capacity as such; and

    (ii)   which is one to which the offshore fund rules apply (whether or not by virtue of their application to disposals from distributing funds with equalisation arrangements), or which is one to which the rules would apply if the provisions regarding the non-application of *CGTA 1975, 2 Sch 2(2)* applied generally and not only for the purpose of determining whether a disposal from a distribution fund with equalisation arrangements is brought within the rules (see 32.7 above); and

    (iii)   which is not a disposal within the *exception* referred to at 32.7 above (where the income of the fund is, or would be, chargeable to tax under Schedule D, Case III in any event).

The '*accrued income*' is that part of the consideration which would be credited to the fund's equalisation account if the interest were resold to another person by way of initial purchase (see 32.7 above) on the same day. However, there are provisions to ensure that this accrued income figure is reduced where the interest disposed of was acquired by way of initial purchase (by any person) after the beginning of the account period by reference to which the accrued income is calculated. In addition, where an offshore commodity dealing fund (and see (*c*) below) operates equalisation and there is a disposal within (i)–(iii) above, one-half of the accrued income representing commodity profits is left out of account in determining what part of the disposal consideration represents accrued income.

For the purposes of the distribution test, the distribution which the fund is treated as making on a disposal is treated as being paid to the person disposing of his interest, in the income form required by 32.10(*d*) above, out of the income of the fund for the account period of the disposal. Where a distribution is made to the managers (in their capacity as such) of a fund operating equalisation arrangements, it is disregarded for the purposes of the distribution test except to the extent that it relates to that part of the period for which the distribution is made during which the managers (in that capacity) held that interest. [*FA 1990, 5 Sch 2, 4(4)*].

(*b*)   **Funds with income taxable under Schedule D, Case III.** Where sums forming part of the income of an offshore fund within 32.8(*b*) or (*c*) above are chargeable to tax under Schedule D, Case III on the holders of interests in the funds (or would be so chargeable were the necessary residence, etc. rules met), any such sums which are not actually part of a distribution complying with the part of the distribution test in 32.10(*c*) and (*d*) above are treated as distributions which do so comply made out of the income of which they are part and paid to the holders of the interests in question. [*FA 1990, 5 Sch 3*].

(*c*)   **Funds with commodity dealing income.** Where an offshore fund's income includes 'commodity dealing' profits, one-half of those profits is left out of account in determining the fund's income and Irish equivalent profits for the purposes of the distribution test in 32.10(*b*) above. '*Commodities*' are defined as tangible assets dealt with on a commodity exchange, excluding currency, securities, debts or other financial assets. '*Dealing*' includes dealing by way of futures contracts and traded options. Where the fund's income includes both commodity dealing profits and other income, its expenditure is apportioned on a just and reasonable basis and the non-commodity dealing business is treated as carried on by a separate company when determining what expenditure, if any, is deductible under *CTA s 15* (management expenses) in computing Irish equivalent profits. See also (*a*) above for position where a commodity dealing fund operates equalisation arrangements. [*FA 1990, 5 Sch 4*].

(*d*)   **Wholly-owned commodity dealing subsidiaries.** In a situation within 32.9(C) above, the fund and the subsidiary dealing company are similarly treated as a single entity for the purposes of the distribution test. [*FA 1990, 5 Sch 11*].

(*e*)   **Investments in second tier funds.** In a situation within 32.9(A) above, the Irish equivalent profits of the primary fund for the period are increased by its 'share' of the 'excess income' (if any) of the second tier fund in determining whether not less than 85% of the primary fund's Irish equivalent profits are distributed. The '*excess income*' of the second tier fund is the amount by which its Irish equivalent profits exceed its distributions. There are provisions for apportioning excess income between periods on a time basis when the account periods of the primary and second tier funds do not coincide. The primary fund's '*share*' of the excess income is the proportion which the average value during its account period of its own holding of interests in the second tier fund bears to the average value of all interests in that fund. [*FA 1990, 5 Sch 6, 8, 9*].

32.12   CERTIFICATION PROCEDURE

Fund requesting certification. Application for certification as a distributing fund for an account period must be made within six months of the end of that period (or, if later, by 1 January 1991). The application must be accompanied by a copy of the fund's accounts covering or including the account period for which certification is sought, and the Revenue Commissioners must be furnished with such information as they may reasonably require for that purpose. If they are satisfied that nothing in *FA 1990, s 66(2)(3)* (see 32.9 above) prevents certification, the fund will be certified as a distributing fund for that period. Certification may be withdrawn retrospectively if it subsequently appears to the Revenue Commissioners that the accounts or information supplied do not fully and accurately disclose all the relevant facts and considerations.

An appeal may be made to the Appeal Commissioners against a refusal or withdrawal of certification within 30 days of the date of the relevant notice. The normal income tax appeal provisions apply generally to any such appeal. [*FA 1990, 5 Sch 15,16*].

Investor requesting certification. No appeal may be brought against an assessment (see 32.13 below) on the grounds that a fund should have been certified as a distributing fund in respect of an account period. However, where a fund does not apply for certification, an investor who is assessed to tax for which he would not be liable if the fund were certified may by notice in writing require the Revenue Commissioners to take action with a view to determining whether the fund should be so certified. If more than one such request is received, the Revenue Commissioners are taken to have complied with each if they comply with one.

Broadly, the procedure is as follows.

(i) The Revenue Commissioners invite the fund to apply for certification. The time limit for application (see above) is then extended, if necessary, to 90 days from the date of the Board's invitation.

(ii) If the fund does not then apply for certification, the Revenue Commissioners must determine the question as if such application had been made, having regard to any accounts or information provided by the investor.

(iii) If, after the Revenue Commissioners have determined that the fund should not be certified, other accounts or information are provided which were not previously available, the Revenue Commissioners must reconsider their determination.

(iv) The Revenue Commissioners must notify the investor who requested them to take action of their decision.

(v) The Revenue Commissioners have wide powers enabling them to disclose to interested parties information regarding their, or the Appeal Commissioners', decisions or details of any notice given to a fund regarding a lack of full and accurate disclosure of information (see above).

[*FA 1990, 5 Sch 17–20*].

32.13 CHARGE TO INCOME OR CORPORATION TAX ON OFFSHORE INCOME GAIN

Where a disposal to which the offshore fund rules apply gives rise to an 'offshore income gain' (see 32.14 below), then (subject to below) that gain is treated for all purposes as income assessable under Schedule D, Case IV arising to the investor at the time of the disposal.

The following provisions have effect in relation to income tax or corporation tax on offshore income gains as they have in relation to capital gains tax:

(*a*) *CGTA 1975, s 4* (persons chargeable) except that

(i) in the case of non-residents carrying on a trade in RI through a branch or agency, the requirement that assets be situated in RI does not apply, and

(ii) in the case of individuals resident and ordinarily resident but not domiciled in RI, *section 4(3)(4)* have effect as they do in respect of gains from assets situated outside RI;

(*b*) *CTA s 8(2)(b)* (gains accruing to non-resident companies carrying on a trade in RI through a branch or agency).

Charitable exemption applies similarly to that for capital gains tax (see 9.7(*k*) CAPITAL GAINS TAX).

Where a disposal to which the offshore fund rules apply is one of settled property, any offshore income gain will escape the Schedule D, Case IV charge provided that the general administration of the trust is ordinarily carried on outside RI and a majority of the trustees is not resident or ordinarily resident in RI. [*FA 1990, s 67*].

32.14 COMPUTATION OF OFFSHORE INCOME GAIN

The computation of the gain depends upon whether the disposal is of an interest in a non-qualifying fund or of an interest involving an equalisation element.

Disposals of interests in non-qualifying funds. A '*material disposal*' (i.e. one to which the offshore fund rules apply otherwise than by virtue of the provisions regarding distributing funds operating equalisation arrangements (see 32.7 above and further below)), gives rise to an *'offshore income gain'*, i.e. a gain of an amount equal to the 'unindexed gain' or, if less, the 'post-6 April 1990 gain'.

Subject to the modification to the CGT rules mentioned in 32.6 above and to the exceptions detailed below, the *'unindexed gain'* is the gain calculated under capital gains tax rules without indexation allowance and without regard to any income tax or corporation tax charge arising under the offshore fund rules. The exceptions are as follows.

(*a*)   If the material disposal forms part of a transfer to which *CGTA 1975, 2 Sch 6* (rollover relief on transfer of business to company) applies, the unindexed gain is computed without any deduction falling to be made under that *paragraph* in computing a chargeable gain.

(*b*)   Where the computation of the unindexed gain would otherwise produce a loss, the unindexed gain is treated as nil, so that no loss can arise on a material disposal.

[*FA 1990, 6 Sch 1–3, 5*].

Post-6 April 1990 gains. A person making a material disposal who acquired, or is treated as having acquired, his interest in the offshore fund before 6 April 1990, is treated as having disposed of and immediately reacquired his interest at market value on that date. The offshore income gain from 6 April 1990 to the date of disposal is then calculated in the ordinary way. If the person making the material disposal acquired his interest after 5 April 1990 by way of a deemed no gain/no loss disposal (other than by virtue of the indexation provisions of *CGT(A)A 1978, s 3(3)*), the previous owner's acquisition of the interest is treated as his acquisition of it, and this provision may continue to apply to earlier owners where they in turn acquired the interest after 5 April 1990. [*FA 1990, 6 Sch 4*].

Disposals involving an equalisation element. A disposal to which the offshore fund rules apply by virtue of the provisions relating to distributing funds operating equalisation arrangements (see 32.7 above) (a *'disposal involving an equalisation element'*) gives rise to an offshore income gain of an amount equal, subject to below, to the 'equalisation element' relevant to the asset disposed of. [*FA 1990, 6 Sch 6(1)(3)*].

The *'equalisation element'* is the amount which would be credited to the fund's equalisation account in respect of accrued income if, on the date of the disposal, the asset disposed of were acquired by another person by way of 'initial purchase' (see 32.7 above). However, where the person making the disposal acquired the asset in question after the beginning of the account period by reference to which the accrued income is calculated, or at or before the beginning of that period where that period straddles 6 April 1990, there are provisions to ensure that the equalisation element is reduced to exclude any part which accrued prior to either 6 April 1990 or the investor's period of ownership. Where any of the accrued income represents commodity dealing profits (see 32.11(*c*) above) one-half of that income is left out of account in determining the equalisation element. [*FA 1990, 6 Sch 6(2)(4)–(6)*].

Part I gains. Where the offshore income gain as computed above would exceed the 'Part I gain', the offshore income gain is reduced to the lower figure. If there is no 'Part I gain', there can be no offshore income gain. The *'Part I gain'* is, broadly, the amount which would be the offshore income gain on the disposal if it were a material disposal within the rules in *FA 1990, 6 Sch 1–5* described above, as modified by certain consequential amendments. [*FA 1990, 6 Sch 7, 8*].

32.15 MISCELLANEOUS

Offshore income gains accruing to persons resident or domiciled abroad. There are consequential provisions made in connection with gains accruing to certain non-resident investors in offshore funds, which modify, for the purposes of the offshore funds legislation, provisions relating to

32.15   Schedule D, Case IV—Miscellaneous Income

(*a*)   chargeable gains accruing to certain non-resident companies under *CGTA 1975, s 36* (see 9.17 CAPITAL GAINS TAX),

(*b*)   gains of non-resident settlements under *CGTA 1975, s 37* (see 9.17 CAPITAL GAINS TAX), and

(*c*)   avoidance of tax by the transfer of assets abroad under *FA 1974, ss 57, 58* (see 3.8 ANTI-AVOIDANCE LEGISLATION).

To the extent that an offshore income gain is treated by virtue of (*a*) or (*b*) above as having accrued to any person resident or ordinarily resident in RI, that gain is not deemed to be the income of any individual under *FA 1974, ss 57, 58* or any provision of *Pt XXVIII, Chs I, II* of *ITA 1967* (settlements). [*FA 1990, s 68*].

Deduction of offshore income gain in determining capital gain. There are provisions to prevent a double charge to tax when a disposal gives rise to both an offshore income gain and a chargeable gain for capital gains tax purposes.

Where an offshore income gain arises on a 'material disposal' within 32.14 above, the gain is deducted from the sum which would otherwise constitute the amount or value of the consideration in the calculation of the capital gain arising on the disposal under *CGTA 1975* (the '1975 Act disposal'), although the offshore income gain is not to be taken into account in calculating the fraction under *CGTA 1975, 1 Sch 6* (part disposals).

Where the 1975 Act disposal forms part of a transfer within *CGTA 1975, 2 Sch 6* (rollover relief on transfer of business to company) then, in determining the amount of the deduction from the gain on the old assets, the offshore income gain is deducted from the value of the consideration received in exchange for the business.

Where an exchange of shares or securities constitutes a disposal of an interest in an offshore fund (see 32.6, 32.7 above), the amount of any offshore income gain to which the disposal gives rise is treated as consideration for the new holding.

Where the offshore fund provisions apply to a disposal of an interest in a fund operating equalisation arrangements (see 32.7 above) and the disposal

(*a*)   is not to the fund or to its managers in their capacity as such, and

(*b*)   gives rise to an offshore income gain in accordance with 32.14 above, and

(*c*)   is followed subsequently by a distribution to either the person who made the disposal or to a person connected with him (within *CTA s 157*) and that distribution is referable to the asset disposed of,

then the subsequent distribution (or distributions) is (are) reduced by the amount of the offshore income gain.

[*FA 1990, s 69*].

33   Schedule D, Case V—Property Income

[Secs 80–94; FA 1969, ss 22–29, FA 1975, ss 19–22 and 2 Sch].

33.1   Tax is charged under Schedule D, Case V in respect of rent for any premises in RI and receipts for any easement (not falling under *Sec 93*, see 33.7 below) which are deemed to arise from a single source. The basis of assessment is as for SCHEDULE D, CASE III (31) *[Sec 81; FA 1969, s 22; FA 1990, s 18]*.

See 38.102 TAX CASES regarding rental income falling within Schedule D, Case I.

33.2   **Computation** is on the aggregate of gross rents receivable *less* (i) any rent payable in respect of the premises by the lessor; (ii) any rates borne by him; (iii) interest on borrowed money used to purchase, improve or repair the premises; (iv) the cost to the lessor of goods or services (other than maintenance and repairs) which he is bound by the lease to provide and for which no separate consideration is receivable; and (v) the cost to him of maintenance, repairs, insurance and management (which does not include accountancy fees). *[Sec 81; FA 1969, s 22]*. But (i) or (iii) (the rent payable or interest on borrowed moneys to purchase, improve or repair premises) will not be an allowable deduction to the lessor *for any period prior to the first occupation by a lessee* (as to which see 38.132 TAX CASES). *[FA 1974, s 62]*. See 33.8 below.

Industrial buildings allowances are claimable against income. *[Sec 267; CTA 1 Sch 26]*. See 8.5 CAPITAL ALLOWANCES.

For premises which are 'controlled dwellings' under the *Rent Restrictions Acts 1960 and 1967*, the amount otherwise chargeable (profit rent) is reduced by two-fifths. The aggregate of such reductions to any one taxpayer is not to exceed £200, but the relief given on lettings where the lease was granted for a term not exceeding 50 years at a rent which, after deduction of rates payable by the landlord, does not exceed £52 p.a. is excluded from the calculation for the purposes of the restriction. Special provisions apply where spouses have each let property. *[Sec 82; FA 1969, s 23]*.

33.3   **Farm land.** A deduction may be allowed from the total income of a 'qualifying lessor' of 'farm land'. Where total income includes profits or gains chargeable under Schedule D, Case V, and in computing the amount of those profits or gains a surplus arising from rent from any farm land let under a 'qualifying lease' has been taken into account, a deduction is allowed to the lessor of the lesser of

(*a*)   the 'specified amount' in relation to the surplus, and

(*b*)   the amount of the profits or gains chargeable under Schedule D, Case V.

The deduction is treated as if it were a personal allowance under *Secs 138–143*.

A *qualifying lessor* is an individual aged 55 or more, or permanently incapacitated by reason of physical or mental infirmity from carrying on a trade of farming, who has not, after 30 January 1985, leased the farm land in question (with or without others) from a connected person (within *F(MP)A 1968, s 16*) (with or without others) on other than arm's length terms.

Farm land is land in RI occupied wholly or mainly for husbandry, including a building (other than a dwelling) on the land used for farming that land.

A *qualifying lease* is a lease of farm land in (or evidenced in) writing, for a definite term of five years or more, made on an arm's length basis between qualifying lessor(s) and 'qualifying lessee(s)'.

A *qualifying lessee* is an individual not connected (see above) with the qualifying lessor (or with any of the qualifying lessors), who uses the leased farm land for a trade of farming he carries on solely or in partnership.

The *specified amount* in relation to a surplus is the amount of that surplus (or aggregate amount of such surpluses), limited to

(i)   £2,000 for leasing contracts taken out before 20 January 1987, or after 31 December 1987 and before 30 January 1991,

(ii)   £2,800 for leasing contracts taken out between 20 January 1987 and 31 December 1987,

(iii) £4,000 for leases for a definite term of seven years or more under contracts made after 29 January 1991,

(iv)   £3,000 for leasing contracts taken out after 29 January 1991 not within (iii) above,

subject to an overall limit of £4,000 or £3,000 as appropriate (£2,800 before 30 January 1991).

The specified amount is proportionately reduced when the rent(s) taken into account are less than the rent(s) receivable for a full year.

Where a wife's income is, by election, treated as that of her husband, the deduction under these provisions is determined separately in relation to each spouse's income.

There are provisions for apportionment by the inspector where a qualifying lease relates partly to farm land and partly to any other goods, property or services, so that only the part of the surplus properly attributable to the farm land attracts relief. His decision is subject to review by the Appeal Commissioners or Circuit Court on appeal. The inspector has power to require the lessor to furnish such information as the inspector considers necessary. [*FA 1985, s 10; FA 1987, s 2; FA 1991, s 10*].

33.4   **Residential premises.** In computing rental income, a deduction may be allowed for certain expenditure incurred between 29 January 1981 and 31 March 1987 inclusive or between 27 January 1988 and 31 March 1992 inclusive (the '*qualifying periods*') on the construction of premises for rent. The deduction is allowed for the period in which the premises are first let under a 'qualifying lease'.

The qualifying period is extended to 31 July 1992 where expenditure is incurred on the construction of qualifying premises the foundations of which were completed before 29 January 1992.

To qualify, the premises must consist of a building or part of a building (together with any outhouses, gardens, etc.):

(i)   used solely as a dwelling;

(ii)   of floor area not less than 30 sq. metres or more than 90 sq. metres (75 sq. metres for expenditure incurred before 1 April 1984) in the case of a self-contained flat or maisonette in a building of two or more storeys (but restricted to 75 sq. metres in relation to expenditure before 1 April 1987 unless it contains three or more rooms designed and constructed as, and suitable for use as, bedrooms); or of not less than 35 sq. metres or more than 125 sq. metres in any other case;

(iii) in respect of which, if it is not a new house (within *Housing (Miscellaneous Provisions) Act 1979, s 4*), there is in force a 'certificate of reasonable cost', granted by the Minister of the Environment, in which the construction cost specified is not less than that actually incurred; or, in the case of a new house provided for sale in respect of which a claim was made before 23 May 1984, a 'certificate of reasonable value', as defined in the *Housing (Miscellaneous Provisions) Act 1979, s 18*, in which the amount stated to be the reasonable value of the house is not less than the net price paid for the house;

(iv) first let (without having previously been used) in its entirety under a 'qualifying lease' and continuing to be so let throughout the ten years following the first letting (ignoring reasonable temporary void periods between lettings);

(v) open to inspection by persons authorised in writing by the Minister of the Environment at all reasonable times; and

(vi) complying with such conditions as to construction standards and services as the Minister may lay down under the *Housing (Miscellaneous Provisions) Act 1979, s 4*.

Premises occupied by a person 'connected with' (as defined by *Finance (Miscellaneous Provisions) Act 1968, s 16*) the person claiming the deduction do not qualify unless the terms of the lease are such as might have been expected to result from arm's length negotiations.

A *'qualifying lease'* is one granted in consideration of rent payments falling within Schedule D, Case V, with any premium not exceeding 10% of the 'relevant cost' of the premises. Specifically excluded, however, are leases under the terms of which anyone can at any time directly or indirectly acquire an interest in the premises at less than market value.

'Relevant cost' is the aggregate of expenditure on both land and construction (with any necessary apportionment of expenditure on larger projects, see below).

In relation to expenditure incurred after 31 March 1984 and before 1 April 1987, the deduction allowed in any chargeable period (year of assessment for income tax, accounting period for corporation tax) in respect of qualifying premises is restricted to the amount of rent from those premises. See below as regards the necessary apportionments. Unallowed expenditure is carried forward to the next and subsequent chargeable periods as if incurred in such periods, but subject to the same overall restriction on allowance to gross rent.

The **allowable expenditure** is that incurred in the 'qualifying period' on the construction of the premises, which includes that incurred on the development of the land (including gardens, access, etc.) such as costs of demolition, groundworks, landscaping, walls and mains supplies, and any other buildings for use by the occupants of the premises. Where, however, a premium or like sum is payable directly or indirectly to the lessor or to any person 'connected with' him (as defined by *Finance (Miscellaneous Provisions) Act 1968, s 16*), and all or part of it is not treated as rent under Schedule D, Case V, the allowable expenditure is reduced by the amount of the premium, etc. not treated as rent, or, where any part of the construction cost falls outside the 'qualifying period', to the same proportion of the premium, etc. as the allowable expenditure bears to the whole construction cost. Such a reduction for a period straddling 31 March 1984 is allocated to the part falling on or before and the part falling after that date in proportion to expenditure treated as incurred in each part.

Any question of whether (or how much) expenditure was actually incurred in the 'qualifying period' (or in the part thereof falling after 31 March 1984) on construction work or land development is to be determined by the inspector, subject to review on appeal to the Appeal Commissioners or Circuit Court. Where qualifying premises form part of a building or consist of a building which is part only of a larger development, any necessary apportionment of cost is similarly determined, both for this purpose and in determining 'relevant cost' (see above).

Any allowance given under these provisions is treated as rent received by the person to whom the allowance was given if the **premises cease to qualify**, or if the lessor disposes of his interest, within ten years after the first letting. If the lessor disposes of his interest but the premises continue to qualify, the new owner of the interest is entitled to the same deduction as was granted to the original lessor, but ignoring any reduction in respect of a premium, etc. (see above), and limited to the '*relevant price*' paid by the new owner. This is the same proportion of the total price paid by him as the allowable construction expenditure by the original lessor bore to the 'relevant cost' of the premises, see above. For the purposes of restriction of relief (see above) in respect of expenditure actually incurred on qualifying premises in a period straddling 31 March 1984, but partly on or before and partly after that date, the deduction granted to the new lessor is treated as incurred on or before and after that date in proportion to the actual expenditure incurred in each part.

Where premises on which expenditure was incurred in the 'qualifying period' are sold unused, the buyer (or, if the premises are sold unused more than once, the last such buyer) is treated as having in that period incurred construction expenditure equal to

(i)   if the original expenditure was incurred as a trading expense by a builder, the lesser of the 'relevant price' (see above) paid to the builder and that paid on the last sale unused;

(ii)   in any other case, the lesser of the allowable expenditure actually incurred on construction of the premises and the 'relevant price' on the last sale unused.

Expenditure is apportioned, where necessary, as for the new lessor of qualifying premises in the preceding paragraph.

Expenditure on **conversion** into two or more dwellings of a building, not in use as a dwelling or in use as a single dwelling prior to the conversion, will similarly qualify for relief as if the expenditure had been incurred on the construction of the premises, with necessary modifications to the scheme of relief. Planning permission must have been obtained. The restriction of relief to the amount of the rent arising from the premises in a chargeable period applies to conversion expenditure incurred after 26 January 1988 and before 1 April 1992 as it applies generally to earlier expenditure (but see below as to certain urban renewal reliefs). [*FA 1981, ss 23, 24; FA 1983, ss 29, 30; FA 1984, s 37; FA 1988, s 27; FA 1991, s 56; FA 1992, s 34(a)(ii)*].

For expenditure incurred between 1 April 1985 and 31 March 1987 inclusive or between 27 January 1988 and 31 March 1992 inclusive (and not met directly or indirectly by the State or any statutory body or public or local authority), relief is further extended to:

(*a*)   expenditure on the conversion into a dwelling of a building not previously in use as a dwelling; and

(*b*)   expenditure in the course of a conversion on 'refurbishment' (see 33.5 below), but excluding expenditure attributable to any part of the building which, on completion of the conversion, is not a dwelling (with any necessary apportionment of overall expenditure being made on the basis of floor area), or which otherwise attracts relief under any other provision of the *Tax Acts*.

The extended reliefs applicable to expenditure on urban renewal (see below) apply equally for these purposes. 'Refurbishment' is defined slightly differently in relation to buildings in the Temple Bar Area, to require that the work be in character with the existing building, and for this purpose all conversion work is treated as refurbishment.

[*FA 1985, s 22; FA 1988, s 29; FA 1991, ss 56(2), 58; FA 1992, s 34(c); FA 1993, s 32(c)*].

Urban renewal. The above reliefs are extended in the case of qualifying premises on a site wholly within the Custom House Docks Area (as designated in *FA 1986, 4 Sch Pt II* or by subsequent order) to include expenditure incurred in the period 25 January 1988 to **24 January 1999** inclusive. The reliefs are also extended in the other areas designated by *FA 1986, 4 Sch Pts III–VII* (or by subsequent order under *FA 1987, s 27*) to include expenditure incurred up to 31 July 1994 (and where at least 15% of the total construction expenditure on qualifying premises was certified before 24 February 1994 by the relevant local authority (under the relevant guidelines) to have been incurred before 26 January 1994, further such expenditure incurred between 1 August and 31 December 1994 inclusive is treated as having been incurred in the qualifying period), and in the Temple Bar Area (see *FA 1991, 2 Sch*) to include expenditure on buildings approved by Temple Bar Renewal Ltd incurred up to **5 April 1998**. In relation to expenditure on conversions (within *FA 1981, s 24*, see above), the restriction of allowances to the amount of rent arising from the premises in a chargeable period does not apply to expenditure in any of the above areas after 29 January 1991. For expenditure incurred after 25 January 1994 on the conversion of flats and maisonettes in the Custom House Docks and Temple Bar Areas, the maximum permissible floor area is increased from 90 to 125 square metres, and from 12 April 1995 this applies also to construction expenditure. [*FA 1986, ss 41, 43, 4 Sch; FA 1987, s 27; FA 1991, ss 56, 58; FA 1992, ss 29(a), 34(a)(c); FA 1993, s 32(a); SI 1988 No 314; FA 1994, ss 36, 37(b)(d); FA 1995, ss 32(1)(a), 33, 34(1)(a)(c)(2)*]. See also 33.11 below and 2.22 ALLOWANCES AND RATES, 8.10 CAPITAL ALLOWANCES and 30.22 SCHEDULE D, CASES I AND II.

For 1989/90 only, income tax relief under these provisions in relation to a deficiency in respect of rent is determined without regard to the provisions of *FA 1990, Pt I, Ch II* introducing the current year basis of assessment generally, and as if no surplus arose from premises other than qualifying premises in that year, unless the current year basis in fact applied to the Schedule D, Case V assessment for that year. [*FA 1990, s 20(4)*].

33.5   **Refurbishment of residential premises.** The provisions described at 33.4 above apply *mutatis mutandis* to expenditure incurred between 1 April 1985 and 31 March 1987 inclusive or between 27 January 1988 and 31 March 1992 inclusive on the 'refurbishment' of a building in which, prior to that refurbishment, there are two or more dwellings and which, after refurbishment, contains two or more dwellings. They do not, however, apply to expenditure attributable to any part of the building which, after the refurbishment, is not a dwelling (with any necessary apportionment of overall expenditure being made on the basis of floor area). Relief is given as if the refurbishment expenditure was expenditure on the construction of the building.

'*Refurbishment*' means either or both of

(a)   the carrying out of works of construction, reconstruction, repair or renewal, and

(b)   the provision or improvement of water, sewerage or heating facilities,

provided that the Minister for the Environment grants a certificate of reasonable cost certifying that the work was necessary to ensure the suitability as a dwelling of any house in the building. It is not relevant whether or not the number of dwellings in the building, or the shape or size of any such dwelling, is altered in the course of the refurbishment.

Relief is *not* available unless any required planning permission is obtained, and is also denied where the expenditure is met directly or indirectly by the State or by any statutory board or public or local authority, or is otherwise relieved under any other provision of the *Tax Acts*.

Specific variations to the provisions described at 33.4 above include the following.

(i)   The reference to a premium, etc. in the definition of 'qualifying lease' is to a premium, etc. payable after completion of refurbishment, or payable before completion in connection with the refurbishment. Market value is substituted for 'relevant cost' in the definition.

(ii)   References to the first letting of the premises are to the letting on completion of the refurbishment or, if not then let, to the first subsequent letting.

    (iii)   References to the 'relevant price' are to the net price paid on sale or, if only a proportion of the refurbishment expenditure falls to be treated as having been incurred in the qualifying period, that proportion of the net price paid on sale.

    (iv)   The restriction of relief to the amount of the rent arising from the premises in a chargeable period applies to refurbishment expenditure incurred after 26 January 1988 and before 1 April 1992 as it applies generally to earlier expenditure (but see below as to certain urban renewal reliefs).

The extended urban renewal reliefs detailed at 33.4 above apply equally for these purposes. In the Temple Bar Area, a slightly different definition of 'refurbishment' applies, requiring the work to be in character with the building.

[*FA 1985, s 21; FA 1988, s 28; FA 1991, s 57; FA 1992, s 34(b); FA 1993, s 32(b); FA 1994, s 37(c)(d); FA 1995, s 34(1)(a)(d)*].

33.6   **Premiums etc.** payable under the terms of a lease not exceeding 50 years (including cost of works so required to be borne by the lessee) are treated as additional rent then due equal to the premium reduced by one-fiftieth for each complete year (other than the first) comprised in the lease. Where a premium is payable other than to lessor, the assessment is under Schedule D, Case IV on the recipient. Sums received for waiver, surrender, assignment at undervalue, etc. are included. Sums so taxable on recipient are treated as rent paid by payer. [*Secs 83, 91, 92; FA 1969, s 33*]. For assignments of short leases and sales with terms of reconveyance, see *Secs 84 and 85*.

Where a premium is payable by instalments, the tax chargeable may be paid by agreed instalments over a period not exceeding eight years before the last of the premium instalments is payable if the Revenue Commissioners are satisfied that undue hardship would otherwise be caused. [*Sec 83(6) as amended by FA 1975, s 20(a) and 2 Sch 4–7; CTA 2 Sch 3, 49*].

'Premium' includes any like sum, whether payable to the immediate or a superior lessor or to a person connected with either of them. [*Sec 80; FA 1975, s 19(a)*].

The duration of a lease is determined by provisions under *Sec 80(2) as amended by FA 1975, ss 19, 20(b)(c) and 2 Sch 1–3*, with transitional provisions where reliefs for earlier years are affected.

Provision is made for both lessors and lessees (and any other affected person) to take part in appeal proceedings to determine the taxable amount of any premium. [*FA 1975, s 21 and 2 Sch 1–3; CTA 2 Sch 49*].

For a case involving a sale and lease-back avoidance scheme, see 38.73A TAX CASES.

33.7   **Mining etc. rents.** Rents and payments for easements, where the leased premises or easements are used or employed for mining etc. assessable under Case I (see 30.1 SCHEDULE D, CASES I AND II), are subject to DEDUCTION OF TAX AT SOURCE (13) under *Sec 433 or 434* and are not allowable as deductions from trading profits, and (so far as not otherwise chargeable) are charged with tax under Schedule D, Case IV. The same applies to other annual payments, royalties, tolls etc. in respect of any premises. [*Sec 93; FA 1969, s 29*].

33.8   **Losses and deficiencies.** Rent irrecoverable, or voluntarily forgone by reason of hardship, is a subject of adjustment of the assessment (with further revision if later recovered) [*Sec 90; FA 1969, s 28*]. Profits and losses in a year are aggregated, and net losses on letting may be carried forward against future profits under Case V [*Secs 81(4), 89; FA 1969, s 24; FA 1990, s 18*]. Where rent receivable under a lease does not cover the admissible expenses borne by the lessor, he is neither chargeable under Case V, nor eligible for loss relief under Sec 89. [*Sec 86*]. See also 33.2 above.

33.9 **Non-residents.** Tax under *Sec 434* is deductible at source from rental payments, etc., made (whether in or out of RI) to a non-resident, the latter being entitled to claim repayment of any tax so suffered in excess of his liability as under Case V. [*FA 1969, s 25*].

33.10 **Returns.** For the purposes of obtaining particulars of profits or gains chargeable to tax by virtue of *Secs 80–93* (see 33.1, 33.6, 33.7 above), the inspector may by written notice require lessors, lessees and occupiers of premises to provide specified information in relation to leases and payments thereunder. Managing and collecting agents for premises, and certain public bodies making payments in the nature of, or for the purpose of, rent or rent subsidy in relation to premises, may also be required to deliver details of the premises and the owner(s) thereof, and of the rents and other payments arising, and of other specified particulars (and such returns may be required without notice, see 28.14 RETURNS). [*Sec 94; FA 1992, ss 226, 227(a), 228; FA 1995, s 14*].

33.11 **URBAN RENEWAL—RESIDENTIAL ACCOMMODATION**

Construction expenditure. In computing rental income, a deduction may be claimed for certain construction expenditure attributable to work carried out between 1 August 1994 and 31 July 1997 inclusive (the '*qualifying period*') on 'qualifying premises' for rent. The deduction is allowed for the period in which the premises are first let under a 'qualifying lease'.

'*Qualifying premises*' means a house (which includes any building or part of a building suitable for use as a dwelling, and land or outbuildings appurtenant thereto or usually enjoyed therewith) used solely as a dwelling:

(*a*) the site of which is wholly within an area designated for the purpose by the Minister for Finance, which designation may specify a shorter period within the qualifying period referred to above;

(*b*) of floor area not less than 30 sq. metres or more than 125 sq. metres (90 sq. metres as regards expenditure incurred before 12 April 1995) in the case of a self-contained flat or maisonette in a building of two or more storeys, or of not less than 35 sq. metres or more than 125 sq. metres in any other case;

(*c*) first let (without having previously been used) in its entirety under a 'qualifying lease' and continuing to be so let throughout the ten years following that first letting (ignoring reasonable temporary void periods between lettings);

(*d*) in respect of which, if it is not a new house (within *Housing (Miscellaneous Provisions) Act 1979, s 4*), there is in force a 'certificate of reasonable cost', granted by the Minister for the Environment, in which the construction cost specified is not less than that actually incurred;

(*e*) complying with such conditions as to construction standards and service provision as the Minister may lay down under *Housing (Miscellaneous Provisions) Act 1979*;

(*f*) open to inspection by persons authorised in writing by the Minister at all reasonable times; and

(*g*) which (or the development of which it is part) must comply with guidelines issued by the Minister for the Environment concerning:

    (i) design, construction and refurbishment of the houses;

    (ii) total floor area and dimensions of rooms;

    (iii) provisions of ancillary facilities; and

    (iv) the 'balance' between the houses, the development and the location.

A house occupied by a person connected (within *F(MP)A 1968, s 16*) with the person claiming the deduction is excluded unless the lease is on arm's length terms.

A '*qualifying lease*' of a house is a lease the consideration for the grant of which consists of periodic payments of rent within Schedule D, Case V, with or without the payment of a premium not exceeding 10% of the 'relevant cost' of the house. There is, however, an exclusion for leases under the terms of which anyone can at any time directly or indirectly acquire an interest in the house at less than market value. The '*relevant cost*' of the house is the aggregate of expenditure on the land and construction of the house (with any necessary apportionment of expenditure on whole buildings or on larger developments).

The expenditure for which a deduction is allowable is that incurred on the construction of the house, including expenditure on the development of the land (including gardens, access, etc.), in particular demolition, groundworks, landscaping, walls, mains supplies and outhouses, etc. for use by the occupants of the house. Where, however, a premium or like sum is payable directly or indirectly to the lessor or to any person connected (within *F(MP)A 1968, s 16*) with him, and all or any part of it is not treated as rent under Schedule D, Case V, the expenditure for which a deduction is allowed is reduced by the amount of the premium, etc. not treated as rent or, where any part of the construction cost falls outside the qualifying period, to the same proportion of that amount as the expenditure for which a deduction is allowable bears to the whole construction cost.

Expenditure met directly or indirectly by the State, a statutory board or a public or local authority is excluded.

Where qualifying premises form part of a building or consist of a building which is part of a larger development, any necessary apportionment of cost is made.

If the house ceases to be qualifying premises, or if the lessor disposes of his interest, within ten years after the first letting under a qualifying lease, any deduction under these provisions is treated as rent received by the person to whom the deduction was allowed. If the lessor disposes of his interest but the house continues to be qualifying premises, the new owner of the interest is entitled to the same deduction as was granted to the original lessor, but ignoring any reduction in respect of a premium, etc. (see above), and limited to the '*relevant price*' paid by the new owner, i.e. the same proportion of the total price paid by him as the expenditure for which a deduction was allowable to the original lessor bore to the relevant cost (as above) of the house.

Where a house on which construction expenditure was incurred in the qualifying period is sold unused, the buyer (or, if the premises are sold unused more than once, the last such buyer) is treated as having in that period incurred construction expenditure equal to:

(i)   if the original expenditure was incurred as a trading expense by a builder, the lesser of the relevant price (as above) paid to the builder and that paid on the last sale unused;

(ii)   in any other case, the lesser of the construction expenditure actually incurred on the house and the relevant price (as above) on the last sale unused.

An appeal lies to the Appeal Commissioners on any question arising under these provisions as it would in relation to an assessment to tax.

For capital gains tax purposes, a deduction under these provisions is treated as if it were a capital allowance, and any rent treated as received as above as a balancing charge.

[*FA 1994, ss 38, 39, 43, 47; FA 1995, s 35(1)(a)(b)(h)(2)*].

See 33.4, 33.5 above as regards earlier reliefs, which continue in certain areas.

Conversion expenditure. The provisions described above in relation to construction expenditure apply *mutatis mutandis* to certain 'conversion expenditure' attributable to work carried out between 1 August 1994 and 31 July 1997 inclusive (the '*qualifying period*') on 'qualifying premises' for rent, provided that planning permission has been granted for the conversion under the relevant Acts. The deduction is similarly allowed for the period in which the premises are first let under a 'qualifying lease'.

'*Conversion expenditure*' is expenditure incurred

(*a*)   on the conversion into a house of a building, not previously in use as a dwelling, the site of which is wholly within a designated area, or which fronts onto a designated street, etc. (or part), or

(*b*)   on the conversion into two or more houses of a building, not previously in use as a dwelling or in use as a single dwelling, the site of which is wholly within a designated area, or which fronts onto a designated street,

including expenditure on the carrying out of works of construction, reconstruction, repair or renewal, and on the provision or improvement of water, sewerage or heating facilities, in relation to the building and any outoffice appurtenant thereto or usually enjoyed therewith, but excluding expenditure attributable to any part of the building which (after the conversion) is not a house (any necessary apportionment being on a floor area basis), or otherwise attracting tax relief. Conversion expenditure also includes expenditure on development of the land on which the building is situated (as for construction expenditure, see above).

Designated areas and streets, etc. are those designated for the purpose by the Minister for Finance, which designation may specify a shorter period within the qualifying period referred to above.

'Qualifying premises' and 'qualifying lease' are defined broadly as in relation to construction expenditure, except that premises fronting onto designated streets, etc. are included (see above), the maximum permitted floor area in the case of a self-contained flat or maisonette in a building of two or more storeys is 125 sq. metres (instead of 90), and references to the relevant cost of the house are references to the market value of the house after conversion (apportioned on a floor area basis where necessary).

[*FA 1994, ss 44, 47*].

See below as regards earlier reliefs, which continue in certain areas.

Refurbishment expenditure. The provisions described above in relation to construction expenditure also apply *mutatis mutandis* to certain 'refurbishment expenditure' attributable to work carried out between 1 August 1994 and 31 July 1997 inclusive (the '*qualifying period*') on 'qualifying premises' for rent, provided that any necessary planning permission has been granted for the 'refurbishment' under the relevant Acts. The deduction is similarly allowed for the period in which the premises are first let under a 'qualifying lease'.

'*Refurbishment expenditure*' means expenditure on the 'refurbishment' of a building wholly within a designated area, or fronting on a designated street, etc., in which (both before and after the refurbishment) there are two or more houses, other than expenditure attributable to a part which, on completion of the work, is not a house (any necessary apportionment of general expenditure being on a floor area basis). Expenditure otherwise attracting tax relief is excluded.

Designated areas and streets, etc. are those designated for the purpose by the Minister for Finance, which designation may specify a shorter period within the qualifying period referred to above.

'*Refurbishment*' of a building means either or both of

(*a*)   the carrying out of any works of construction, reconstruction, repair or renewal, and

(*b*)   the provision or improvement of water, sewerage or heating facilities,

certified by the Minister for the Environment, in a certificate of reasonable cost relating to any house contained in the building, as necessary to ensure the suitability as a dwelling of any house in the building, regardless of whether or not the number of houses in the building, or the shape or size of any such house, is altered in the course of the refurbishment.

'Qualifying premises' and 'qualifying lease' are defined broadly as in relation to construction expenditure, except that premises fronting onto designated streets, etc. are included (see above), the maximum permitted floor area in the case of a self-contained flat or maisonette in a building of two or more storeys is 125 sq. metres (instead of 90), and references to the relevant cost of the house are references to the market value of the house after refurbishment (apportioned on a floor area basis where necessary). The ten year period referred to in (*c*) above commences on the completion of the refurbishment if that is earlier than the date of first letting.

[*FA 1994, ss 45, 47*].

Earlier reliefs. See 33.4, 33.5 above as regards construction, conversion and refurbishment expenditure on houses in the Temple Bar or Custom House Docks Areas of Dublin, and as regards earlier reliefs for expenditure in certain other areas. See also 2.22 ALLOWANCES AND RATES, 8.10 CAPITAL ALLOWANCES and 30.22 SCHEDULE D, CASES I AND II.

33.12 QUALIFYING RESORT AREAS—RESIDENTIAL ACCOMMODATION

The provisions described at 33.11 above apply also to construction, conversion and refurbishment expenditure incurred in a '*qualifying period*' **1 July 1995 to 30 June 1998** inclusive on a dwelling the site of which is wholly within a '*qualifying resort area*', i.e. a part of Achill, Arklow, Ballybunion, Bettystown, Bundoran, Clogherhead, Clonakilty, Courtown, Enniscrone, Kilkee, Lahinch, Laytown, Mosney, Salthill, Tramore, Westport or Youghal described in *FA 1995, 3 Sch*, with the difference that the requirement (see 33.11(*g*) above) that for a house to be qualifying premises it must comply with Ministerial guidelines is replaced by a requirement that:

(*a*)   throughout the period of ten years beginning with the first letting under a qualifying lease (or, in the case of refurbishment expenditure, and if later, the date of completion of the refurbishment), the house is used primarily for letting to and occupation by tourists, with or without prior arrangement;

(*b*)   during that period, the house is not let or leased to, or occupied by, any person for more than two consecutive months at any one time or for more than six months in any year; and

(*c*)   a register of lessees of the house is maintained, containing particulars of the name, address and nationality of each lessee during that period, and of the dates of their arrival and departure.

The definition of qualifying lease is correspondingly framed to remove the references to lease premiums (while allowing for single rental payments), and the reduction of the allowable deduction where a premium or like sum is payable is not applicable.

[*FA 1995, ss 46, 50–53*].

See also 8.10A CAPITAL ALLOWANCES, 30.22 SCHEDULE D, CASES I AND II.

34   Schedule E—Emoluments

[*Secs 109–133*].

34.1   Tax is charged under Schedule E on the emoluments of offices and employments including salaries, fees, wages, perquisites, profits, or gains, or the amount of annuity pension or stipend. [*Secs 109, 110*]. Benefits received under an approved permanent health benefit scheme are taxable. [*FA 1979, s 8(4)*].

Pensions to former employees or their dependants are assessable even though voluntary or capable of being discontinued. [*Secs 190, 225*]. Also widows', orphans' and old-age pensions under the *Social Welfare Acts*, but not death grants. [*Sec 224; FA 1971, s 12*].

See 38.133–38.138 TAX CASES for case law regarding scope of Schedule E.

Foreign employments are charged under SCHEDULE D, CASE III (31).

See 27.1 RESIDENTS AND NON-RESIDENTS as regards special relief for 1994/95 onwards for certain income earned outside RI.

34.2   The basis of charge is the actual emoluments of the year under the Pay As You Earn system, except where, for 1986/87 onwards, the inspector notifies the employer that deduction of tax by him is impracticable. Such notice may be cancelled by further notice if changing circumstances so warrant. Emoluments of an office or employment for a year in which the office, etc. is not held are treated as emoluments of the last year in which it was held or, if it has never before been held, of the first year in which it is held. For 1985/86 and earlier years, emoluments were excluded from the PAYE system where Revenue Commissioners notified the employer that deduction of tax by him was impracticable, or that emoluments were included in the Schedule D assessment on the recipient's trade or professional practice, and there was no provision for withdrawal of such notice. See also 38.139 TAX CASES. Before 1990/91, where the income was not within the PAYE system, the basis of assessment is the same as under SCHEDULE D, CASE III (31) but no adjustment is made in the case of a penultimate year. [*Secs 110, 111, 125; FA 1985, s 6; FA 1990, s 19; FA 1991, s 6*].

Unpaid remuneration which has been allowed as a business deduction under Schedule D will be deemed to have been paid as an emolument (on the last day of the period of account in which it accrued or, if that period is longer than twelve months, on each 5 April in the period; or on the date the employment ceased, if earlier) subject to PAYE for which the employer is accountable, *unless* (i) such emoluments are included in the Schedule D assessment on the professional practice etc. of the recipient or (ii) payment is actually made within six months of the date payment is deemed to have been made as above, or, if later, eighteen months from the first day of a period of account which is for longer than one year. [*FA 1976, s 17*].

34.3   **DIRECTORS AND EMPLOYEES**

Directors, and employees receiving £1,500 p.a. or more, are chargeable on all expenses, provision of accommodation, entertainment, services (including domestic), benefits or facilities whatsoever, paid in respect of them by their employer and not refunded, but relief may be claimed under *2 Schedule 3* (see below). Exceptions apply to accommodation, supplies or services provided in employer's premises and used solely in performing duties, costs of meals in canteen in which meals are provided for staff generally, cost of providing death or retirement benefits, cost of acquisition or production of asset remaining property of employer (but assessable benefit arises on use of asset by employee and if asset transferred to him), and provision of certain art objects (see below). [*Secs 116–123, 178*]. Also see these sections and *FA 1973, ss 41–42* for employers to which these provisions are applicable.

Preferential loans. Also treated as an emolument of such a director or employee is the benefit (calculated as below) of certain preferential loans. The loans concerned are those

(i)   made in 1982/83 or later years, directly or indirectly by the employer (or future employer) of the recipient or his spouse, or by any person connected (as defined by *FA 1978, s 8*) with the employer, other than in the normal course of domestic, family or personal relationships, and

(ii) at no interest or at a rate of interest less than the 'specified rate'.

For this purpose, 'loans' include replacement loans, loans taken over from the original lender, and the arranging, guaranteeing or in any way facilitating a loan or the continuation of a loan.

For 1989/90 onwards, a loan is not a preferential loan if the rate of interest is at least that charged on similar arm's length loans made in the course of the employer's trade to non-employees.

The *'specified rate'* for 1995/96 onwards is 7% where the interest is (or would if any were payable be) 'qualifying interest' (see 20.3(*a*) INTEREST PAYABLE) or certain other interest payable to non-residents, 11% in any other case (both rates being subject to variation by regulations by the Minister for Finance), or, if the employer makes fixed term, fixed interest house purchase loans as part of his trade, the rate normally charged by him on such loans at arm's length (other than to employees) at the time the preferential loan was made (if less than 7% or that rate as varied). For 1994/95, the figures were 7.5% and 11.5% respectively, for 1992/93 and 1993/94, they were 11% and 15% respectively, and for 1989/90, 1990/91 and 1991/92, they were 10% and 12% respectively. Previously, the rate was 12% (variable as above) or the lower rate charged on arm's length house purchase loans by the employer (as above).

The sum charged as an emolument of a year of assessment is the difference between the aggregate amount of interest payable in the year (if any) and interest at the specified rate on the outstanding loan(s).

A similar charge arises in any year of assessment in which such a loan, or any interest payable on such a loan, is released or written off, in whole or part. The charge is on the amount so released or written off in the year.

Any amount charged under these provisions in respect of preferential interest rates or the release or writing off of interest is treated as interest paid in the year of assessment of the charge, eligible for relief subject to the usual conditions (see 20.3 INTEREST PAYABLE). It is not treated as emoluments for the purposes of employee allowance (see 2.12 ALLOWANCES AND RATES).

Notification. The employer may be required by the inspector to give details of preferential loans as above.

[*FA 1982, s 8; FA 1989, s 6; FA 1992, s 9; FA 1994, s 9; FA 1995, s 9*].

Cars provided by employer. The 'cash equivalent' of the benefit of a car provided by an employer for use by *any* employee, *less* any amounts which the employee is required to, and does, make good to the employer, is treated as an emolument of his employment for the year of assessment, unless there is no *private use* in the year *and* such use is prohibited. Where the employer is an individual, cars provided in the normal course of his domestic, family or personal relationships are excluded. A car provided for the employee's spouse, children and their spouses, parents, servants, dependants or guests is treated as provided for the employee's use.

Private use is use other than *business use*, meaning travel in the car which the employee is necessarily obliged to do in the performance of the duties of the employment.

The '*cash equivalent*' of the benefit is 30% of the car's original market value (i.e. its price, including VAT and duty, in an open market retail sale immediately before its first registration). It is reduced, where the employer bears no part of the cost in the year of

   (i)   fuel for private use by the employee, by 4.5% of that value, and

   (ii)   insuring the car, by 3% of that value, and

   (iii) repairing and servicing the car, by 3% of that value, and

   (iv)   vehicle excise duty, by 1% of that value.

Where the car is made available to the employee for part only of the year of assessment, the cash equivalent for the year is correspondingly reduced.

The cash equivalent determined as above is further reduced if business mileage in the year exceeds 15,000 miles. The maximum reduction is 95% for 1992/93, 90% for 1993/94, 85% for 1994/95, 80% for 1995/96 and 75% for 1996/97 onwards. The maximum applies where business mileage exceeds 30,000 miles in the year. The reduction where business mileage exceeds 15,000 miles and is less than 30,001 miles is as follows.

Business mileage	Percentage reduction				
	1992/93	1993/94	1994/95	1995/96	1996/97 on
15,001–16,000	2.5%	2.5%	2.5%	2.5%	2.5%
16,001–17,000	5%	5%	5%	5%	5%
17,001–18,000	10%	10%	10%	10%	10%
18,001–19,000	20%	20%	15%	15%	15%
19,001–20,000	30%	30%	25%	25%	20%
20,001–21,000	40%	40%	35%	30%	25%
21,001–22,000	50%	45%	40%	35%	30%
22,001–23,000	60%	55%	50%	45%	35%
23,001–24,000	65%	60%	55%	50%	40%
24,001–25,000	70%	65%	60%	55%	45%
25,001–26,000	75%	70%	65%	60%	50%
26,001–27,000	80%	75%	70%	65%	55%
27,001–28,000	83%	80%	75%	70%	60%
28,001–29,000	86%	82%	78%	72%	65%
29,001–30,000	90%	85%	80%	75%	70%

Before 1992/93, the cash equivalent of the benefit was 20% of the original market value, and the reductions at (i)–(iv) above were 3%, 2%, 2% and 0.5% respectively. Tapering relief began at 10,001 business miles, and rose to 100% at 25,001 business miles.

Car pools. Cars included in a pool for use by employees of one or more employers are treated as not being available for private use. A 'pool' car must be available in the year to, and used by, more than one employee, and not ordinarily used exclusively by one of them; any private use must be incidental; and it must not normally be kept overnight at or near any employee's residence (other than on the employer's premises). Claims to 'pool' treatment may be made by any employee (or by the employer on behalf of all of them), and the inspector's decision is appealable (within two months of its being notified) as though it were an assessment. A decision on appeal applies to all employees concerned, whether or not they took part in the appeal.

Notification. The **employee** must notify particulars of the car, its original market value, and business and private mileages in a year of assessment to the inspector within thirty days of the end of the year, failing which (or if the inspector is not satisfied with the particulars supplied) the figures applicable for the year will be such as are determined by the inspector 'to the best of his judgment'. In the absence of sufficient evidence to the contrary, private mileage of any person's company car(s) will be taken as 5,000 miles. The usual rights of appeal against an assessment based on such figures apply. The **employer** may also be required to give notice of the particulars.

Estimates of liability for a year of assessment may be made before the end of the year by the inspector in the usual way for the purposes of PAYE or Schedule E assessment.

Connected persons. Cars made available, and costs borne, by persons connected with (as defined by *F(MP)A 1968, s 16(3)*) the employer are treated as made available, or borne, by the employer.

[*FA 1982, s 4; FA 1992, s 8*].

Loans of art objects owned by a company to a director or employee are, on a claim by the director etc., exempt from any benefit-in-kind charge or treatment as a distribution (see 12.7 CORPORATION TAX) provided that the object is kept in an approved building or an approved garden (see 22.4 LOSSES) owned or occupied by the director etc.. An '*art object*' is a work of art or scientific collection determined by the Minister for Arts, Culture and the Gaeltacht to be intrinsically of significant national, scientific, historical or aesthetic interest, and determined by the Revenue Commissioners to be an object to which reasonable public access and viewing facilities are afforded (for which see the requirements applied to approved buildings (for determinations after 22 May 1994) under 22.4 LOSSES) at the same dates and times as apply to the building or garden in which the object is kept. A Revenue Commissioners' determination may be revoked for the year of assessment in which such access and viewing facilities cease to be provided and for subsequent years of assessment. There are provisions for inspection of the art object at any reasonable time by certain authorised persons, obstruction of or interference with whom may lead to a fine of up to £500. This exemption applies **for 1994/95** and subsequent years, but may be backdated to years of assessment 1982/83 onwards where the building or garden in which the object was kept was an approved building or garden (see 22.4 LOSSES) and the Revenue Commissioners are satisfied that reasonable public access and viewing facilities were provided in relation to the object.

The capital gains tax exemption of works of art loaned for public display (see 9.7(*u*) CAPITAL GAINS TAX) does not apply to an object which is an 'art object' for these purposes.

[*FA 1994, s 19*].

Expenses. It is understood that various concessions are operated to exempt from tax certain expenses paid or reimbursed by employers, or to allow a deduction from emoluments for expenses incurred by directors or employees. Broadly these fall into the following categories.

(*a*)   Travelling, etc. expenses

   (i)   of a director of two or more companies between the places at which his duties are carried out;

   (ii)   paid to an unremunerated director of a company not managed with a view to dividends;

   (iii)   of a director who holds the position as part of a professional practice, provided that no claim is made to a deduction under Schedule D;

   (iv)   of a wife accompanying a director or employee whose health is so precarious as to prohibit unaccompanied foreign travel;

(v)   during public transport disruption caused by industrial action.

(*b*)   Removal, etc. expenses where an employee has to change residence in order to take up a new employment or to transfer within an employer's organisation.

(*c*)   Provision of home-to-work transport for severely disabled employees.

(*d*)   Certain travelling expenses between RI and overseas for non-domiciled employees of non-resident concerns.

(*e*)   Certain expenses of external training courses.

As regards (*b*) above, the Revenue Commissioners' Statement of Practice SP-IT/1/91 extends the concession to similar payments made to or for an employee taking up employment with a new employer.

Entertainment expenses incurred by an employee on the employer's behalf and reimbursed to the employee are, in practice, not assessed on the employee, but are disallowed to the employer (see 30.10 SCHEDULE D, CASES I AND II).

Returns. Directors and their spouses are generally required to make returns of their income under the self-assessment system. [*FA 1992, s 244*]. See 28.12 RETURNS.

34.4   **SHARE, ETC. OPTIONS** [*FA 1986, s 9*].

For options granted to directors and employees before 6 April 1986, a charge to tax generally arose by reference to the date the option was granted or, if later, the earliest date on which it could be exercised.

Where a person realises a gain by exercising, assigning or releasing (which includes agreeing to a restriction on the right to exercise) a right to acquire shares or any other assets in a company, being a right he obtained after 5 April 1986 as a past, present or prospective director or employee of that or any other company, he is chargeable under Schedule E for the year in which the gain is realised on the difference between

(i)   the market value (as under *CGTA 1975, s 49*) at the time the gain is realised of the shares or other assets (or, in the case of an assignment or release, the consideration received for the assignment or release), and

(ii)   the consideration, if any, (apart from services in the office or employment) which he gave for the grant of the right, plus, in the case of the exercise of a right, the consideration, if any, for acquisition of the shares or other assets.

with just apportionment by the inspector of any entire consideration given, or given in part, for grant of the right.

A person acquires a right as a director or employee for this purpose if it is granted to him, or to another person who assigns it to him, by reason of his office or employment, unless his emoluments are assessable on the remittance basis under *Sec 76(3)* (see 34.2 above and 31.2 SCHEDULE D, CASE III).

If a right can be exercised more than seven years after being obtained, tax liability can arise at the time the right is obtained, as well as on its exercise, etc., and for this purpose the value of the right is to be taken as not less than the market value at the time the right is obtained of the assets over which the right is granted (or exchange assets) less the least possible consideration for which the assets may be acquired. Any tax charged on receipt of the right is then deducted from any tax chargeable on its exercise, etc.. Otherwise, no liability arises under any other provision on receipt of the right where tax may become chargeable under these provisions on its exercise, etc..

There are provisions preventing avoidance by the grant or assignment of the right to a third party, by its assignment, in whole or part, for another right, or by entering into joint arrangements with another person or persons having rights within these provisions.

For capital gains tax purposes, any gain chargeable under these provisions on the exercise of a right is treated as consideration given for the shares or other assets acquired on the exercise.

Any person who, in 1986/87 or a subsequent year, either

(*a*)   grants a right to which these provisions may apply, or

(*b*)   allots any shares or transfers any assets in pursuance of such a right, or

(*c*)   gives consideration for the assignment or release, in whole or part, of such a right, or

(*d*)   receives written notice of the assignment of such a right,

must notify the inspector in writing within 30 days of the end of the year of assessment. There are penalty provisions for failure to comply.

34.5   **RELIEF FOR NEW SHARE SUBSCRIPTION** [*FA 1986, s 12; FA 1993, s 26*].

For 1986/87 onwards, an 'eligible employee' subscribing for 'eligible shares' in a 'qualifying company' is entitled to deduct the amount of his subscription from his total income as if it were a personal allowance, subject to maximum relief of £**3,000** (£750 before 1993/94) in total (i.e. in all years of assessment). Relief is **not** available under these provisions where an entitlement to relief under *FA 1984, s 12* (see 21.2 INVESTMENT IN CORPORATE TRADES AND RESEARCH AND DEVELOPMENT) arises in respect of shares subscribed for after 11 April 1995.

An '*eligible employee*' is a 'full-time director' or 'full-time employee' (as defined in *FA 1978, s 8* (see 20.3(*c*)(ii) INTEREST PAYABLE)) of the 'qualifying company' or, if the 'qualifying company' is a holding company, of a '75% subsidiary' of the 'qualifying company'.

A '*qualifying company*' is a company incorporated and resident in RI, and not resident else-where, which is either a trading company (i.e. its business consists wholly or mainly of carry-ing on trade(s) wholly or mainly in RI) or a holding company (i.e. its business consists wholly or mainly of holding shares or securities of '75% subsidiaries' which are trading companies).

A '*75% subsidiary*' is defined as for membership of a group of companies (see 12.14 CORPO-RATION TAX).

'*Eligible shares*' are fully paid up new shares forming part of the ordinary share capital of the qualifying company, issued after 5 April 1986 to, and acquired by, an eligible employee at not less than market value. They must at no time in the five years following issue carry any preferential rights, present or future, to dividends or assets in a winding up or to redemption, and they must not be subject to any restrictions which do not attach to all shares of the same class. If there is more than one class of ordinary shares in the qualifying company, the majority of issued shares of the same class as the eligible shares must not be eligible shares, and must not be held by persons who acquired them in pursuance of a right or opportunity made available to them as directors or employees of the qualifying company or of any of its 75% subsidiaries.

Withdrawal of relief. Relief is withdrawn if, within five years of acquisition, the shares, or an interest in or right over them, are disposed of, or the eligible employee receives money or money's worth, not constituting taxable income in his hands, in respect of the shares. Only 75% of the relief is withdrawn if the disposal, etc. occurs after the fourth anniversary of the issue. Shares are identified for this purpose in the same way as detailed under 'Disposal of shares' at 21.10 INVESTMENT IN CORPORATE TRADES AND RESEARCH AND DEVELOPMENT.

Where, on a capital reorganisation, a 'new holding' is brought into existence which, for capital gains tax purposes (see 9.15 CAPITAL GAINS TAX), is treated as being the same asset as eligible shares acquired under the current provisions, then it is so treated for the purposes of current provisions. The reorganisation does not give rise to a disposal of the eligible shares to the extent that the consideration consists of the new holding.

For **capital gains tax** purposes, on any disposal of eligible shares, any amount in respect of which relief has been given and not withdrawn under the current provisions is excluded from allowable expenditure in computing the chargeable gain.

Anti-avoidance. There is a general prohibition on relief unless shares are subscribed for and issued for bona fide commercial reasons and not as part of a scheme the main purpose, or one such purpose, of which is the avoidance of tax.

34.6   **APPROVED PROFIT SHARING SCHEMES** [*FA 1982, ss 50–58, 3 Sch; FA 1984, s 31; FA 1986, s 11; FA 1990, s 136; FA 1992, s 17; FA 1995, s 16*].

FA 1982 introduced provisions to allow directors and employees of companies to receive shares in those companies free of income tax under certain conditions.

Provided that the scheme is approved by the Revenue Commissioners, a company will provide funds to RI-resident trustees who will purchase certain defined shares (see below) and appropriate such shares to eligible employees (see below) up to a limit of **£10,000** (*£2,000* for 1992/93 to 1994/95 inclusive, *£5,000* for 1991/92 and earlier years) market value to any one individual in any year of assessment. If the total market value of shares appropriated to an individual in 1991/92 was less than £2,000, the difference is added to the allowance for 1992/93. Shares representing any excess over £2,000 in 1992/93 are treated as having been appropriated on 5 April 1992, and shares issued earlier in 1992/93 are treated as having been so appropriated before shares issued later.

An employee etc. to whom shares are appropriated (a '*participant*') must contract not to assign, charge or dispose of his beneficial interest in the shares within a 'period of retention' (see below); to permit the trustees to retain his shares throughout that period; to pay to the trustees a sum equal to income tax at the standard rate on the 'appropriate percentage' of the 'locked-in value' (see 34.7 below) should he direct them to transfer the shares to him before the '*release date*' (i.e. the fifth (seventh for 1985/86 and earlier years) anniversary of their appropriation to him); and not to direct them to dispose of his shares before the release date other than by sale for the best consideration obtainable. The participant may, however, at any time direct the trustees to accept, in respect of his shares, certain share exchanges or other offers made to all holders of the same class of shares. Where shares appropriated to a participant are replaced by a new holding following a company reconstruction under *CGTA, 2 Sch 2(1)(b)* (other than certain bonus issues following repayment of share capital), the new holding is broadly treated in the same way as the original shares would have been.

Any assignment, etc. of his interest within the 'period of retention' renders the participant ineligible for tax relief (and to a charge to tax as at the time the shares were appropriated to him). Alterations to the scheme must be approved, and approval may be withdrawn if the Revenue Commissioners cease to be satisfied with the conditions. Appeal may be made to the Appeal Commissioners within thirty days of the notification of any decision of the Revenue Commissioners. [*FA 1982, ss 50, 51, 52, 55, 3 Sch; FA 1984, s 31; FA 1986, s 11; FA 1990, s 136; FA 1992, s 17; FA 1995, s 16*].

Period of retention begins on the date the shares are appropriated to the participant and ends two years later or, if earlier, at cessation of employment due to injury, disability, redundancy, death or reaching pensionable age for social security purposes. [*FA 1982, s 52(5)*].

The **shares** must be ordinary shares of

(i)   the company concerned, or

(ii)   a company controlling the company concerned, or

(iii)   a company (or its controlling company) which is a member of a consortium owning the company concerned or a company controlling the company concerned, and which itself owns at least three-twentieths of the ordinary shares of the company so owned,

and they must be either

(*a*)   quoted shares, or

(*b*)   shares in a company not controlled by another company, or

(*c*)   shares in a company controlled by a quoted company (other than a company which is, or would if RI-resident be, a close company).

They must be fully paid up, not redeemable and not subject to any restriction differing from that attaching to other shares of the same class. Where there is more than one class of shares, the majority of the class of shares appropriated under the scheme must be held by persons who are not directors or employees who received special rights of acquisition, or trustees for such persons, or, where the shares are within (*c*) but not within (*a*) above, companies which control the company whose shares are in question or of which that company is an associated company.

Control and associated company are as defined in *CTA s 102*.

[*FA 1982, 3 Sch 5–8, 16, 17*].

Persons eligible for inclusion in the scheme on similar terms must include all full-time employees or directors who are chargeable to tax under Schedule E and who have been employees or directors throughout a qualifying period which may not exceed five years. Also eligible are individuals who were full-time employees or directors in the eighteen months prior to the appropriation of shares to them. A person is not eligible if, in the same year of assessment, shares have been appropriated to him under another approved scheme by the company or group concerned, or if within the previous twelve months he had a material interest (i.e. 15% of the ordinary shares) in such a company, being a company which was a close company, or which would have been close were it RI-resident or were its shares not quoted. [*FA 1982, 3 Sch 2, 9–11*].

Information. The Revenue Commissioners may by notice in writing require any person, within not less than thirty days, to furnish them with such information as they think necessary for the purposes of determining either whether scheme approval should be given or withdrawn, or the liability to tax of a participant. [*FA 1982, s 51(7)*].

34.7   **Charge to tax.** There is no charge to income tax on an eligible employee when the shares are appropriated to him. On disposal before the release date (see 34.6 above) or, if earlier, before the participant's death, tax is chargeable under Schedule E for the year of assessment in which the disposal takes place on the 'appropriate percentage' of the 'locked-in value'. A disposal by the participant of his beneficial interest in the shares (other than on his insolvency or otherwise by operation of law) is deemed to give rise to a disposal of the shares by the trustees for a consideration equal to that obtained by the participant for his interest.

The *appropriate percentage* of the *locked-in value* depends on the date of disposal, as follows.

Disposals after 5 April 1986

before fourth anniversary of appropriation	100%
on or after fourth and before fifth anniversary	75%
on or after fifth anniversary	No charge

If the participant ceases employment with the company because of injury, disability, redundancy or reaching pensionable age for social security purposes before the fifth anniversary, the appropriate percentage is 50%.

Disposals before 6 April 1986

before fourth anniversary of appropriation	100%
on or after fourth and before fifth anniversary	75%
on or after fifth and before sixth anniversary	50%
on or after sixth and before seventh anniversary	25%
on or after seventh anniversary	No charge

If the participant ceases employment with the company because of injury, disability, redundancy or reaching pensionable age for social security purposes before the sixth anniversary, the appropriate percentage is 50%.

Locked-in value of shares is their initial market value when appropriated to the participant (or on any earlier date(s) agreed in writing between the trustees and the Revenue Commissioners) as reduced by any capital receipt charged to income tax under these provisions (see below), or the disposal proceeds if less. Disposal proceeds may be taken as market value of the shares if the disposal is to the participant, or otherwise in a bargain not at arm's length, or is a deemed disposal following the participant's disposal of his beneficial interest (see above). Disposal proceeds are reduced by any payment previously made to the trustees for a rights issue, but payments consisting of proceeds from a disposal of other rights are ignored. Disposals are allocated to appropriations on a 'first in, first out' basis. [*FA 1982, ss 51(4), 52(8), 53; FA 1986, s 11*].

Any **excess or unauthorised shares** (i.e. shares appropriated in excess of the £10,000 (or earlier) limit, or to an ineligible person) are chargeable to tax on the market value at whichever is the earlier of the disposal date, the seventh anniversary of their appropriation, and the participant's death. Any disposal is treated as being of authorised shares in priority to excess or unauthorised shares. [*FA 1982, ss 52(7), 56*].

Capital receipts are charged as if they were consideration for a disposal (see above) for the year in which the trustees or the participant became entitled to them. Excluded, however, are receipts which are (*a*) taxable income in the hands of the recipient, or (*b*) proceeds of disposal of scheme shares, or (*c*) new shares issued in a company reconstruction under *CGTA 1975, 2 Sch 2(1)(b)* (other than certain bonus issues following repayment of share capital), or (*d*) proceeds of rights used to exercise other rights. Capital receipts of £10 or less, and those arising after the death of the participant, are not charged. Where a capital receipt exceeds the locked-in value of the shares to which it is referable immediately before the receipt arose, that value is substituted for the amount of the receipt in determining the charge. [*FA 1982, ss 54, 55(1)(2)*].

If, on the participant's direction, the shares are transferred to him before the fifth anniversary of their appropriation, the **trustees are assessable** to income tax under Schedule D, Case IV on an amount equal to the appropriate percentage (see above) of the locked-in value (see above) at the time of the direction. Credit is given to the participant for the tax so paid. [*FA 1982, s 57*].

Capital gains tax is chargeable on disposal of the shares by the participant, without deduction for any amount determined for purposes of charging income tax under the above provisions. For this purpose, a participant is treated as absolutely entitled to his shares as against the trustees. No capital gains tax is chargeable on the trustees if they appropriate shares to participants within eighteen months of acquisition (shares acquired earlier being taken to be appropriated before shares of the same class acquired later). [*FA 1982, ss 50(3)(a), 51(5)(6)(b)*].

The **company** making payments to the trustee under the scheme **may deduct** them in computing profits (or as management expenses) if (*a*) they are necessary to meet reasonable administration costs of the trustees, or (*b*) they are applied by the trustees in acquiring shares within nine months, or such longer period as the Revenue Commissioners may allow, of the end of the period of account in which the company charges them as an expense. There is an overall limit on the amount deductible of the amount of the trading income (after adjustment for losses, capital allowances, balancing charges and stock relief) or, in the case of an investment company, the income less other management expenses. For accounting periods ending before 6 April 1984, the overall limit was 20% of these amounts. For this purpose, sums are treated as applied by the trustees in the order in which they are received. [*FA 1982, s 58; FA 1984, s 31*]. The amount deductible is also limited to what the Revenue Commissioners consider 'reasonable' in the circumstances. [*FA 1983, s 24*].

Dividends received on shares by the trustees are not liable to the additional rate charge (20%) if the shares are appropriated within eighteen months of acquisition (shares acquired earlier being taken as being appropriated before shares of the same class acquired later). [*FA 1982, s 51(6)(a)*].

34.8   APPROVED SHARE OPTION SCHEMES [*FA 1986, s 10, 2 Sch; FA 1988, s 6; FA 1990, s 137; FA 1992, s 12*].

Where, after 5 April 1986 and **before 29 January 1992**, an individual obtained, as a director or employee of a company, the right to acquire shares in that or any other company, under a scheme approved under *FA 1986, 2 Sch* (see below), and exercises that right in accordance with the scheme provisions at a time when the scheme is so approved:

(*a*)   tax is not chargeable under *FA 1986, s 9* (see 34.4 above) in respect of any gain realised by the exercise;

(*b*)   the market value rules of *CGTA 1975, s 9* (see 9.8 CAPITAL GAINS TAX) do not apply, if they would otherwise do so, in determining the consideration for his acquisition (or for the disposal to him); and

(*c*)   where the shares acquired were in a company which, when the right was obtained, was a 'qualifying company', the 'period of ownership' of the shares for capital gains tax purposes (see 9.3 CAPITAL GAINS TAX) is treated as having commenced on the date the right was acquired.

A company is a '*qualifying company*' at any time when, throughout the preceding twelve months (or, if it commenced trading during that period, throughout the twelve months after it commenced trading) it existed solely for the carrying on of a trade consisting wholly or mainly of the manufacture of goods (including all trades within the manufacturing companies' relief, see 12.17 CORPORATION TAX) or exempt trading operations within the customs-free airport (see 16.2 EXEMPT INCOME AND SPECIAL SAVINGS SCHEMES). For this purpose, the 'wholly or mainly' test is satisfied only if at least 75% of the company's turnover derives from the specified trading activities.

The conditions for approval by the Revenue Commissioners of a share option scheme under *FA 1986, 2 Sch* were as follows.

(i)   The scheme had to provide for directors and employees to obtain rights to acquire shares (see (iii) below).

(ii)   For rights obtained after 5 April 1988, any director or employee of a participating company (see (vi) below) could participate (i.e. obtain and exercise rights under the scheme), although a scheme could permit exercise of rights by persons who had ceased to be directors or employees, and by personal representatives (not more than one year after the death). Before 6 April 1988, only 'full-time directors' (see 20.3(*c*) INTEREST PAYABLE) and 'qualifying employees' could participate.

A '*qualifying employee*' is an employee (not being a director of the company or of any other participating company in a group scheme (see (vi) below)) who is required under the terms of his employment to work for the company for at least 20 hours per week.

A person could not be eligible to participate in the scheme at any time when he had, or at any time in the preceding twelve months had had, a 'material interest' (i.e. 10% of the ordinary shares, with associates) in a close company, or a company which would be a close company if it were RI-resident or if its shares were not quoted (see 12.7 CORPORATION TAX), which was a company whose shares could be obtained under the scheme, or a company controlling that company, or a member of a consortium (as defined) owning such a company.

(iii) The shares over which options are granted had to meet identical conditions to those relating to scheme shares under 34.5 above, except that the restrictions to which shares could not be subject were defined, and excluded any provisions of The Stock Exchange Model Rules set out in the Model Code for Securities Transactions by Directors of Listed Companies (November 1984).

(iv) Rights had to be non-transferable (but see (ii) above as regards personal representatives of deceased participants).

(v) The price to be paid had to be fixed at the time of grant of the right, and had to be not less than the market value of the shares at that time (or at any earlier time if the Revenue Commissioners and the company so agreed). If it subsequently transpired that the price fixed was less than the market value of the shares at that time, the price had to be increased to that market value. The scheme could provide for such variation of the stated price as was necessary to take account of any variation in share capital.

(vi) The scheme could extend to other companies of which the company setting up the scheme had control, and all companies in such a '*group scheme*' were '*participating companies*'.

The Revenue Commissioners would not approve a scheme if it appeared that there were features which were neither essential nor reasonably incidental to the purpose of the scheme. If, after approval, any of the above conditions cease to be satisfied, or any unapproved alteration is made to the scheme, or information required by the Revenue Commissioners (see below) is not provided, approval may be withdrawn. There is a right of appeal to the Appeal Commissioners as if the appeal were against an assessment, and the usual appeal provisions apply. Appeal must be made within 30 days of notification of the decision to withhold or withdraw approval.

The Revenue Commissioners may, by notice in writing, require any person to provide (in not less than 30 days) such information as they consider necessary, and as the person to whom the notice is addressed can reasonably provide, for the performance of their functions under these provisions. The normal penalty provisions apply for failure to comply with such a notice.

These provisions are abolished in respect of any right obtained after 28 January 1992 to acquire shares. [*FA 1992, s 12*].

34.9 EXPENSES

Expenses *wholly, exclusively and necessarily* incurred in performance of duties may be claimed [*2 Sch 3, 4*], including wear and tear (but not initial allowances) of cars, machinery etc. [*Secs 241, 243; CTA 1 Sch 6, 8*]. For many trades, flat rate allowances have been agreed with the trade union concerned, but this does not debar a claim being made instead for the expenses actually incurred. Business entertainment expenditure is not an allowable expense (see also 30.10 SCHEDULE D, CASES I AND II) [*FA 1982, s 20*] but it is understood that, in practice, where entertainment expenses incurred by an employee on the employer's behalf are reimbursed by the employer, the expenses are disallowed to the employer and are not brought into charge on the employee under *Sec 116* (see 34.3 above). See generally 38.143–38.147 TAX CASES for relevant case law. See also 34.3 above as regards concessional relief available in respect of certain expenses incurred by directors and employees.

34.10   PAYE SYSTEM

Under the PAYE system the employer deducts tax on any payment of emoluments in accordance with Regulations designed to equate cumulative allowances and reliefs and to apply them, weekly or monthly, to cumulative gross pay. There are provisions for operation of tax deduction cards, accounting by employer to Revenue, and recovery from him, inspection of wages sheets and other records, penalties, etc. [*Secs 127–128, 131–132; FA 1970, s 5; FA 1972, s 2; FA 1973, s 43; FA 1974, s 72; FA 1976, s 1; FA 1992, ss 233, 234, 238*]. Provisions also apply for charge of interest on deductions from pay not handed over on due dates. [*Sec 129; FA 1973, s 1*]. Also for estimation and recovery of tax, including interest, not paid over or under-remitted and for priority in bankruptcy, liquidation, etc. [*FA 1968, ss 7–11; FA 1975, s 26; FA 1985, s 9; FA 1989, s 10*]. See 25.2 PAYMENT OF TAX as regards collection of certain payments in default, and 25.5 PAYMENT OF TAX as regards waiver of certain interest and penalties.

No formal Schedule E assessments made except where taxpayer (within five years) so requires, or payments in year refer to other years, or liability to tax at the higher rates exists. [*Sec 133*].

See 38.140 TAX CASES regarding allowance in assessment for PAYE deducted.

34.11   RETIREMENT, COMPENSATION ETC.

Payments by the employer for the provision of retirement benefits under schemes etc. are generally assessable under Schedule E unless under

   (i)   a statutory superannuation scheme

   (ii)   certain Government schemes

   (iii) an approved scheme (as defined) [*FA 1972, s 16*].

[*FA 1972, ss 18, 19*].

Similar reliefs apply in relation to schemes under the earlier legislation in *Secs 226–234*. [*Sec 228(2)*].

Payments received on retirement or loss of office are chargeable to tax under Schedule E unless they

   (*a*)   result from the death or disability of, or injury to, the holder of the office or employment, or

   (*b*)   consist of payments for restrictive covenants liable to tax at higher rates (see below), or

   (*c*)   arise from schemes, the premiums for which were chargeable on the holder of the office or employment, or

   (*d*)   are paid under such a scheme as is mentioned under (i)–(iii) above, or

   (*e*)   arise in part from foreign service comprising

(i)   three-quarters of the whole period of service, or

(ii)   (where service exceeds ten years) the last ten years, or

(iii)   (where service exceeds 20 years) half of the period of service including ten of the last 20 years, or

(*f*)   do not exceed the appropriate limit (see below) (with provisions to prevent the splitting of payments to take advantage of this exemption). Only the excess over the exemption limit is chargeable in appropriate cases.

(*d*) above does not apply to certain allowances paid to members of the Oireachtas and certain public servants after (variously) 31 October 1992 and 5 May 1993, and such allowances (other than certain lump sum elements) paid after 31 October 1992 are taxable under PAYE (see 34.10 above).

The *appropriate limit* referred to at (*e*) above is the greater of the 'basic exemption' and the Standard Capital Superannuation Benefit, the latter being calculated by deducting the 'relevant capital sum' from one-fifteenth (one-twentieth as respects payments made before 6 May 1993) of the product of the average annual remuneration of the last three years of service (or the whole period of service if less than three years) and the number of complete years of service. If the claimant has not previously made a claim for exemption or reduction of liability under this provision, and the 'relevant capital sum' received or receivable in respect of the office or employment is less than £4,000, the appropriate limit is increased by the shortfall below £4,000.

The '*basic exemption*' is £6,000 plus, for payments made after 5 May 1993, £500 for each complete year of service.

After 19 April 1990, the '*relevant capital sum*' is the aggregate of all non-chargeable lump sums received and the value of all non-chargeable lump sums receivable (including any which may be received by exercise of an option or right to commute a pension, whether or not such option or right is exercised, unless the option or right has been irrevocably surrendered under scheme rules) under a scheme within (i)–(iii) above. Previously, it was more narrowly defined to exclude the references to commutation rights.

The tax liability on such a payment is computed by treating the payment as additional income of the year of assessment of retirement, etc. An amount calculated by the following formula is substituted, however, where a reduced liability would result.

$$P \times \frac{T}{I}$$

where P is the lump sum payment less the exempt amount
      T is the claimant's total tax liability on income for the previous five years of assessment (before any double tax relief)
      I is the claimant's total taxable income of the previous five years of assessment.

[*Secs 114–115, 3 Sch; FA 1980, s 10, 1 Sch; FA 1990, s 12; FA 1993, ss 7, 8*].

Sums received on reorganisation as compensation for actual or possible reduction of future remuneration, change of duties or place of employment are charged under Schedule E but the income tax thereon is limited to three times the tax on one-third thereof. [*FA 1968, s 3*].

After 23 April 1992, payments etc. received in respect of certain restrictive covenants entered into by a person who holds, has held or is about to hold an office or employment are treated as remuneration from the office or employment (if they would not otherwise be so treated) and subject to PAYE where appropriate. A corresponding deduction may be available to the payer as a trading deduction or as a management expense. [*Sec 525; FA*

1992, s 18]. Previously, such payments, etc. were treated as net receipts after deduction of tax at the standard rate, and the gross amount was assessable to the higher rates. [*Sec 525 as originally enacted; FA 1974, 1 Sch Pt II para I (xii); FA 1976, s 8*].

---

35   Schedule F—Distributions

Cross-references. See also CORPORATION TAX at 12.10 for distribution, at 12.22 for tax credit and at 12.25 for advance corporation tax.

35.1   Schedule F was introduced by the *Corporation Tax Act 1976, s 83* for 1976/77 and subsequent years of assessment. It applies to all dividends and other distributions in the year of assessment made by a company resident in RI, unless specially excluded from income tax. All such distributions are deemed to be income however they fall to be dealt with in the hands of the recipient. No distribution chargeable under Schedule F is chargeable under any other income tax provision.

35.2   **Tax credit.** Any distribution taxable under Schedule F which carries a tax credit is treated as an amount of income equal to the aggregate of the distribution and the tax credit. Tax is then charged on that aggregate and the amount of the credit is set against the individual's total tax liability, and any balance of credit remaining may be reclaimed.

From 6 April 1992, a person who is neither resident nor ordinarily resident is entitled to a tax credit in respect of any distribution received, to be set against the liability to income tax for the year of receipt, and its liability to income tax in respect of the distribution is reduced by the amount by which that liability exceeds the available tax credit. In certain cases of individual non-residents claiming proportionate personal allowances under *Sec 153(2)*, any excess tax credit may be repaid. Previously, no tax credit was available to non-residents (unless provided for in a double taxation agreement or in relation to *Sec 153(2)* claims, see above).

For 1976/77 and 1977/78 and for 1983/84 to 1987/88 inclusive, the credit corresponds to tax at the standard rate of 35% on the distribution (a ratio of 35/65ths). For 1978/79 to 1982/83 inclusive, the credit was equal to tax at a rate of 30% (a ratio of 30/70ths); for 1988/89 it is equal to tax at a rate of 32% (a ratio of 32/68ths); for 1989/90 and 1990/91, it is equal to tax at a rate of 28% (a ratio of 28/72nds); for 1991/92 to 1994/95 inclusive, it is equal to tax at 25% (a ratio of 1/3rd); and for 1995/96 onwards, it is equal to tax at 23% (a ratio of 23/77ths). [*CTA ss 83, 88; FA 1978, s 28; FA 1983, s 28; FA 1988, s 31, 2 Sch; FA 1990, s 36, 1 Sch; FA 1992, s 38; FA 1994, s 27; FA 1995, ss 39, 45*].

36 Settlements

[*Secs 438–448; FA 1971, s 16; FA 1973, s 15; FA 1976, s 13; FA 1979, s 33*].

Cross-reference. See also 7 CAPITAL ACQUISITIONS TAX.

36.1 **Trustees** of settlements are taxed (at the standard rate) in their representative capacities under the Schedule appropriate to the income received. In addition a surcharge of 20% is assessed on income of *accumulation* and *discretionary* trusts unless it is (i) distributed during the year of assessment or within eighteen months thereafter, or (ii) before being distributed, treated as the income of the settlor or any other person, or (iii) income of a charity or of an occupational pension scheme, or (iv) less than the trustees' expenses for the year.

For 1990/91 and subsequent years of assessment, the surcharge is chargeable for the year of assessment in which ends the period of 18 months beginning immediately after the end of the year of assessment in which the income arose. Previously, the liability was that of the year in which the income arose. [*FA 1976, s 13; FA 1990, s 8*].

Beneficiaries receive income from settlements which is treated as net of standard rate of income tax (but any surcharge suffered by the trustee is ignored).

Income deemed to be that of settlor or disponer. In such a case (see below) the income is deemed to be the 'top slice' of the settlor's or disponer's income. The settlor/disponer is entitled to reclaim the amount of tax paid by him from the trustees (and must repay to the trustees any excess tax recouped). [*Secs 441,446*].

36.2 **DISPOSITIONS OF INCOME**

See 38.148–38.153 TAX CASES regarding existence of settlement.

In the following cases, income disposed of (by trust, covenant, agreement or arrangement) is deemed nonetheless to be income of the disponer and of nobody else. [*Secs 438–442*].

(*a*) *Revocable dispositions*, i.e. subject to a power of revocation exercisable, without the consent of anyone except spouse, by the disponer or his spouse so that beneficial enjoyment of the income could revert to him.

(*b*) *Dispositions of income not made for valuable and sufficient consideration*, except where the disposition absolutely divests the disponer of the income-producing capital, and except for the exempt deeds of covenant below.

(*c*) Before 6 April 1995, *dispositions to unmarried minor children*, except where the rules in 36.3 below applied (and which see also for the post-5 April 1995 position).

See also 38.152 TAX CASES.

Deeds of covenant. From **6 April 1996** (or, in certain cases involving hardship, **6 April 1998**), income under such a disposition is *not* deemed to be that of the disponer, who is not taxable thereon, where:

(A) the period for which it is payable can exceed three years and the beneficiary is

    (i) an RI university or college, where the covenant is for the purpose of promoting research, or

    (ii) an RI university, college or school, where the covenant is for the purpose of assisting the teaching of natural sciences, or a fund making grants to such institutions for such purposes, or

    (iii) a human rights body having consultative status with UNO or the Council of Europe; or

(B)   the period for which it is payable can exceed six years and the beneficiary is an individual who is either

(i)   aged 65 years or over, or

(ii)   permanently mentally or physically incapacitated (but see 36.3 below as regards incapacitated persons aged under 18 and unmarried).

Where, however, such a disposition or dispositions (other than within (B)(ii)) is or are made by an individual, the exemption does not apply (and the settlor, if living, is accordingly taxable) to the extent that the income for a year of assessment under such dispositions amounts in aggregate to more than 5% of the settlor's total income for the year (the aggregate payments within the 5% limit being apportioned, where necessary, in proportion to the beneficiaries' entitlements).

For payments made in 1995/96 (or earlier where the disposition was made after 7 February 1995), the above provisions apply except that the exemption under (B) applied to *any* individual beneficiary (although, as under the post-5 April 1996 rules, only dispositions in favour of permanently incapacitated individuals are excluded from the application of the 5% limit). Previously, the 5% limit applied only to dispositions in favour of grandchildren or adult children of the settlor (again excluding those permanently incapacitated) (those in favour of minor or unmarried children of the settlor being caught by *Sec 440*, see 36.3 below).

[*Sec 439; FA 1973, s 15; FA 1979, s 33; FA 1995, s 13*].

Except for (A) above, covenants in favour of charities are *not* relieved of income tax.

36.3   SETTLEMENTS ON CHILDREN, ETC.

Income paid under a settlement to a child, under 18 and unmarried, of the settlor is deemed to be income of the settlor if he is taxable as an RI resident. 'Settlement' is widely defined and includes transfer of a business or admission of child into partnership. Income is deemed to be paid in cases of future or contingent interests or discretionary trusts and where it is not allocated. [*Secs 443, 447, 448; FA 1971, s 16*]. From 6 April 1995 (and in respect of payments before that date under settlements made after 7 February 1995), this is extended to all settlements on persons under 18 and unmarried unless, not being a child of the settlor, such a person is permanently mentally or physically incapacitated. [*FA 1995, s 12(1)(2)*].

Exceptions are

(*a*)   income accumulated under a trust (contained in an 'irrevocable instrument' as defined) of property, and payments out of such property or accumulated income. [*Secs 444, 445; FA 1995, s 12(1)(b)(c)*].

(*b*)   payments before 6 April 1995 not exceeding £60 p.a. to incapacitated children over 16 whose other income does not exceed £40 p.a. [*Sec 443(4); FA 1995, s 12(3)*].

See also 36.2 above.

36.4   FOREIGN TRUSTS

With effect from a day to be appointed for the purpose by the Minister for Finance (related to the enactment of legislation governing the regulation of trustees by the Central Bank of Ireland), income and assets of certain foreign trusts are not regarded as belonging to any person resident or ordinarily resident in RI, so that the income and any gains in relation to the assets are not taxable in RI. The trusts concerned are those in respect of which:

(*a*)   the settlor was not domiciled, resident or ordinarily resident in RI when the trust was created (or on death in the case of a will trust);

(*b*)   none of the beneficiaries is resident, ordinarily resident or domiciled in RI;

(*c*)   none of the trustees (other than certain 'relevant persons', see below) is resident or ordinarily resident in RI; and

(*d*)   all the assets of the trust are situated outside RI (under *CGTA s 48*) and all the income arises from sources outside RI.

As regards (*d*) above, in determining whether all the assets are situated outside RI, an RI bank account held by a trustee who is a 'relevant person' solely for the processing of transactions in relation to assets outside RI is disregarded.

A *'relevant person'* is a person authorised by the Central Bank of Ireland to engage in trust management business, and carrying on such business in RI, who is involved in the management of trusts and who is either:

(i)   a trustee of an authorised unit trust scheme;

(ii)   a trustee of an authorised UCITS;

(iii) in the opinion of the Central Bank of Ireland, a suitable person to be a trustee; or

(iv)   a holder of a licence under *Central Bank Act 1971, s 9* (or exempt from holding such a licence under *SI 1992 No 395, reg 11*).

[*FA 1993, s 49; FA 1994, s 31; FA 1995, s 28*].

37   Social Welfare System

37.1   The RI Social Welfare system is broadly similar to the social security system in the UK. There are four basic kinds of benefit schemes.

(a)   *Social Insurance*, funded in part by contributions from insured persons and their employers and, from 6 April 1988, by self-employed contributors, and providing certain benefits such as unemployment benefit, disability benefit and retirement pension, some subject to contribution conditions. A separate scheme ('wet time' insurance) applies for building labourers who lose working time due to bad weather.

(b)   *Occupational Injuries Benefits*, with no contribution conditions, available to insured persons injured at work.

(c)   *Social Assistance*, distinct from the insurance benefits and paid directly out of State funds on the basis of a means test, providing such benefits as unemployment assistance, allowance for deserted wives and non-contributory old age pension.

(d)   *Miscellaneous benefits*, notably children's allowances but also including free travel for disabled persons, footwear for children and certain supplementary allowances.

Only aspects of the Social Welfare system which affect tax and PAYE deductions are discussed below.

37.2   SOCIAL INSURANCE CONTRIBUTIONS

Compulsory insurance. Almost all kinds of employees over the age of 16 and under 66 must be insured and periodic contributions must therefore be paid in respect of their employment. The main exceptions are persons employed by their spouses or employed under oral contracts at home or on a farm by prescribed relatives. Part of the total contribution is paid by the employee (usually by deduction by the employer under the PAYE system) and the other part by the employer.

Pay-related social insurance ('PRSI') took effect on 6 April 1979 and, for self-employed contributors, on 6 April 1988. From those dates contributions are calculated as a percentage of the contributor's earnings accountable for tax purposes (ignoring, for 1995/96 onwards, the first £50 p.w.), with any amount of earnings over £5,500 for 1979/80, £7,000 for 1980/81, £8,500 for 1981/82, £9,500 for 1982/83, £13,000 for 1983/84 and 1984/85, £13,800 for 1985/86, £14,700 for 1986/87, £15,500 for 1987/88, £16,200 for 1988/89, £16,700 for 1989/90, £17,300 for 1990/91, £18,000 for 1991/92, £19,000 for 1992/93, £20,000 for 1993/94, £20,900 for 1994/95 and **£21,500 for 1995/96** being ignored. For 1995/96, the first £50 p.w. of earnings (£10 p.w. for contributors paying Class B, C and D contributions) are ignored in calculating the PRSI payable. Eleven contribution Classes are laid down, according to the kind of employment, and the percentages for the employer's and employee's contributions are laid down for each class (with variations within each class depending on level of earnings and whether the employee has a medical card or is a woman in receipt of certain benefits).

Self-employed contributions took effect on 6 April 1988. From that date contributions are calculated as a percentage of reckonable emoluments or income as follows.

From **6 April 1988 to 5 April 1989—3%** of reckonable emoluments or income

From **6 April 1989 to 5 April 1990—4%** of reckonable emoluments or income

From **6 April 1990**   **—5%** of reckonable emoluments or income

subject to a minimum of £208 to 1990/91, £234 to 1992/93 and £250 from 1993/94. No contribution is payable where the aggregate of reckonable emoluments and reckonable income before deducting capital allowances or pension scheme contributions is below £2,500.

The annual contribution is £124 where no return is required by the tax authorities. For 1995/96 onwards, the first £10 p.w. is ignored in calculating the contributions payable.

Earnings in excess of £21,500 are ignored, and provisions are laid down regarding persons exempted from making contributions.

[*Social Welfare Act 1988, s 10*].

Voluntary contributions. A person under age 66 who ceases to be employed or self-employed, after at least 156 weeks in insurable employment or insurable self-employment throughout which contributions were paid, may elect to pay voluntary contributions to maintain their insurance record. Before 6 April 1988, this applied to employed persons becoming self-employed. Voluntary contributions are also, from 6 April 1979, a percentage of the contributor's reckonable income, ignoring any excess over a maximum figure as for employee PRSI contributions (above). The percentage payable is 6.6% where contributions previously paid provide insurance for old age contributory pension purposes, otherwise 2.6%. A minimum income, currently £4,750, by reference to which contributions are calculated, is prescribed by the Minister for Social Welfare. Voluntary contributions by a person previously self-employed who ceases self-employment after 6 April 1988 are limited to £208 p.a. to 1990/91, £234 p.a. to 1992/93, £250 p.a. from 1993/94.

Intermittent unemployment insurance contributions payable by building labourers over 16 and their employers under the *Insurance (Intermittent Unemployment) Acts 1942–1978* are paid in a different way, by affixing stamps in a book. Benefits are taxable.

Health contributions under the *Health Contributions Act 1979* are also generally payable, where the person is over the age of 16, of 1.25% of assessable income less superannuation contributions and capital allowances. Before 6 April 1991, there was a contribution limit of £208.75 from 6 April 1990, £200 from 6 April 1989, £193.75 from 6 April 1988 and £187.50 from 6 April 1987 (previously 1% with a maximum of £140 for 1986/87, £130 for 1985/86, £120 for 1984/85, £110 for 1983/84, £95 previously). No contribution is payable where income is less than £9,250 (1994/95 £9,000). There is a deduction for any health contribution paid as part of pay-related social insurance contributions deducted under PAYE.

Youth employment and income levies. See chapter 41.

37.3 SOCIAL INSURANCE BENEFITS

Below is a list of available social insurance benefits (excluding occupational injuries benefit) with notes of whether there are contribution conditions and whether they are taxable.

Benefit	Contributions Conditions	Taxable under PAYE [*Sec 224; FA 1971, s 12*]
Unemployment benefit	Yes	Yes**
Pre-retirement benefit	Yes	No
Disability benefit	Yes	Yes**
Maternity benefit	Yes	No
Pay-related benefit	No	Yes**
(Payable with any of the above and with injury benefit in 37.4 below on claims made before 21 July 1994)		
Invalidity pension	Yes	No*
Contributory survivor's pension	Yes	Yes
Contributory orphan's allowance	Yes	Yes
Deserted wife's benefit	Yes	No*
Deserted wife's allowance	No	No

287

Benefit	Contributions Conditions	Taxable under PAYE [*Sec 224; FA 1971, s 12*]
Retirement pension	Yes	Yes
Contributory old age pension	Yes	Yes
Death grant	Yes	No
Treatment benefits	Yes	No
Intermittent unemployment ('wet time') benefit	No	No

*Taxable under Schedule E, but in practice only taxed where the period of payment is one year or more.

**From 6 April 1994, but from 6 April 1995 exclusive of child dependant allowances and of the first £10 p.w. of unemployment benefit. [*FA 1992, s 15; SI 1994 No 19; FA 1995, s 10(1)*]. However, in relation to unemployment benefit of a person employed in short-time employment (as defined) on 5 April 1994, the start date was deferred until 6 April 1995 or, if earlier, until the end of that period of interruption of employment (within *Social Welfare (Consolidation) Act 1993, s 42*) [*FA 1994, s 10*], and for 1995/96 all unemployment benefit of persons employed in short-time employment is non-taxable. [*FA 1995, s 10(2)*].

37.4 OCCUPATIONAL INJURIES BENEFITS

These benefits are available to insured employees who are injured in the course of their employment or who contract prescribed occupational diseases. There are no contribution conditions.

Benefit	Taxable under PAYE
Injury benefit	Yes
Disablement benefit	No, (but taxable under Schedule E)*
Free medical care	No
Death benefits: widow's pension	No, (but taxable under Schedule E)
dependent widower's pension	No, (but taxable under Schedule E)
orphan's pension	No, (but taxable under Schedule E)
dependent parent's pension	No, (but taxable under Schedule E)
funeral grant	No

*The taxability of disablement benefit is currently the subject of an appeal to the High Court.

37.5 SOCIAL ASSISTANCE BENEFITS

The following means-tested benefits are available for persons who do not meet contribution conditions in 37.3 above: Unemployment assistance; Non-contributory widow's pension; Non-contributory orphan's pension; Social assistance allowances for deserted wives and prisoners' wives; One parent allowance; Non-contributory old age pension; and Blind person's pension.

37.6 OTHER BENEFITS

There are a number of other miscellaneous benefits, most notably children's allowances. These are not taxable.

38   Tax Cases

38.1   This chapter gives brief summaries of reported (and some unreported) Irish tax cases relevant to current legislation. See 1.2 ADMINISTRATION AND GENERAL as regards UK Court decisions. Where comparable current provisions have replaced those at issue in a case, the current statutory reference is quoted.

An alphabetical list of the cases summarised below, under the names of the parties, is appended to the end of this chapter.

ASSESSMENTS AND APPEALS PROCEDURES

38.2   **Discovery.** A company carrying on the business of quarrying and of manufacturing concrete blocks and cement pipes deducted in its accounts the estimated value of the sand and gravel extracted from its own land used in its manufacturing. The deduction was not queried by the revenue authorities until 1966/67 when, on appeal, the Circuit Court Judge held the deduction was not permissible. The company acquiesced in this decision but appealed against additional assessments for 1961/62 to 1965/66, withdrawing the deduction, which the inspector then made. The assessments were upheld, rejecting the contention that there had been no 'discovery'. *W Ltd v Wilson H/C 1974, TL 110.*

38.2A   **Discovery.** In the case, the substantive issue in which is dealt with at 38.73A below, a preliminary point was whether an additional assessment could be raised following a change of view by the inspector, where the original assessment had been the subject of an appeal which had been settled by agreement with the inspector. Held, under *Sec 416(3)(b)* the assessment or amended assessment in these circumstances has 'the same force and effect' as an assessment in respect of which no appeal had been made, and since it was not contested that an unappealed assessment which becomes final and conclusive can be the subject of an additional assessment under *Sec 186(1)*, the position could not be different in this case. *The Hammond Lane Metal Co Ltd v O'Culachain H/C 2 October 1989.*

38.3   **Appeal adjourned for agreement of figures—whether a determination.** A Special Commissioner heard an appeal against an estimated Case I assessment for 1935/36. A relevant point was whether the trade had ceased in that year and he decided that it had, adjourning the appeal for agreement of the figures. New facts came to the knowledge of the inspector and at a subsequent hearing the Commissioner decided he was not satisfied that the trade had ceased in 1935/36. The taxpayer's application for a *certiorari* to quash the second decision was refused. There had been no determination of the appeal. *The State (PJ Whelan) v Smidic H/C 1938, 2 ITC 188; [1938] IR 626.*

38.4   **Res judicata—equitable estoppel.** A company appealed against its excess profits duty assessment for the year to 27 March 1915, objecting to its 'pre-war standard' by reference to which its excess profits liable to the duty were ascertained. After litigation, the appeal was determined by the Court of Appeal. Errors were discovered in the calculation of the standard, and in the assessment for the three years to March 1920 the Revenue used an amended standard. The company appealed, contending that the standard fixed for the year to March 1915 was binding for subsequent periods. Held, the Revenue was free to correct the calculation of the standard. The matter was not *res judicata* nor was the Revenue estopped on grounds of equity. *Bolands Ltd v CIR S/C 1924, 1 ITC 42; 4 ATC 526.*

38.5   **Res judicata—decision purporting to govern subsequent assessments.** The appeal was against an assessment for 1952/53. Included in the assessment was a bad debt recovery in the basis period, to the extent to which, with previous recoveries, it exceeded a doubtful debt allowance made in the 1940/41 assessment. The 1940/41 assessment was determined on appeal by a Circuit Court Judge who said in deciding the matter that any recoveries would not be assessable. In the 1952/53 appeal, the Circuit Court Judge decided he was bound by the decision of his predecessor. His decision was reversed by the H/C, applying *Smidic*, 38.3 above. The jurisdiction of the Circuit Court Judge in the 1940/41 appeal was limited to the determination of the appeal before him. *Bourke v P Lyster & Sons Ltd H/C 1958, 3 ITC 247.*

38.6   **1. Residence. 2. Appeals—evidence of documents.** The taxpayer appealed against assessments under Schedule D, Case III on interest and income from securities and possessions, on the grounds that (i) he was, as regards one year, not resident in RI, having spent a total of twelve months in the Isle of Man, including most of the year in question, and (ii) he had assigned his interest in the securities, etc. to his son by a document executed under seal in the Isle of Man. The document was in the possession of the son in Africa, and the taxpayer had taken no steps to make it available. Held, the taxpayer was resident in RI throughout, and secondary evidence of the terms of any document should not be admitted where the original was in existence. *Hewson v Kealy H/C 1945, 2 ITC 286.*

38.7   **Whether point of law involved.** The Commissioners were upheld in refusing to state a Case, following their confirmation of an estimated assessment, on the ground that no point of law was involved. *R v Special Commissioners (ex parte Stein) S/C 1925, 1 ITC 71.* (*Note*. Later UK cases suggest that, in most such confirmations, it would be a question of law as to whether there was evidence for the decision insofar as it was one of fact.)

38.8   **Whether point of law involved—evidence to be reviewed.** In a capital gains tax case, the only issue for decision by the Circuit Court Judge had been the value of land at 6 April 1974. The appellant contended that no point of law was involved, so that the decision must stand. Held, it was necessary to have regard to the whole of the Case Stated, including the summaries of the evidence of both parties, the findings of the judge as to what evidence he accepted and what he rejected and the expert opinions on values. Unless the conclusions from the primary facts were ones that no reasonable Commissioner or Circuit Judge could draw, the decision could not be set aside. There was evidence here to support the valuation arrived at. *McMahon v Murphy H/C 25 November 1988.*

38.9   **Retirement of Commissioner after Case demanded.** In an appeal, the Stated Case was signed by one of the two Special Commissioners who heard it, the other having since retired. The H/C required the retired Commissioner to sign the Case, before proceeding with the hearing. *O'Dwyer v Irish Exporters and Importers Ltd H/C 1942, 2 ITC 251; 1943 IR 176.* (For another issue in this case, see 38.76 below under Schedule D, Cases I and II—Receipts).

38.10   **Appeal-stated case—'immediate' expression of dissatisfaction.** On an appeal being decided in favour of the Revenue, the appellant company's representative failed verbally to express dissatisfaction with the decision under *Sec 428*. Written dissatisfaction was expressed to the Court on the following morning, with a request that a case be stated for the opinion of the High Court. The request was refused on the grounds that dissatisfaction had not been expressed 'immediately after the determination' of the appeal and that the Court had no discretion in the matter. Held, the requirement for 'immediate' expression of dissatisfaction should not be construed so strictly as to involve its expression at the conclusion of the hearing, and that the requirement was in any event directory and not mandatory. As the Circuit Court's decision had been in accordance with what had been understood to be correct practice, there were no grounds for an order of *mandamus*, but the proper course was for a case to be stated in the normal way. *Multiprint Label Systems Ltd v Neylon H/C 1984, [1984] ILRM 545.*

38.11 **Respondent's notification of Stated Case.** It came to the notice of the Judge that a copy of the Stated Case had not been sent to the respondent until a fortnight after the appellant had transmitted it to the High Court. The Judge, albeit 'with some regret', ordered the case to be struck out of the list, as the requirement of (what is now) *Sec 428(5)* had not been complied with. *A & B v Davis H/C 1946, 2 ITC 350.*

38.11A **Interest on tax paid pending appeal.** Following the decision at 38.109 below, the question arose as to the calculation of interest under *Sec 428(9)* where too much tax has been paid in accordance with a Commissioners' or lower Court decision. It was held that the rate under the *Courts Act* should be applied. *Texaco (Ireland) Ltd v Murphy S/C 15 May 1992.*

38.12 **Application for mandamus.** The taxpayer claimed a repayment of tax under (what is now) *Sec 154*. The Special Commissioners refused the relief, whereupon the taxpayer applied for *mandamus* to them to repay the tax, on the ground that they had misconstrued the law. Held, the Commissioners had been acting in a judicial and not an executive capacity and *mandamus* did not lie to compel them to alter their decision, even if they had misconstrued the law. *R v Special Commissioners (re Spain) H/C 1927, 1 ITC 227; [1934] IR 27.*

38.13 **Application for mandamus.** The company, which was incorporated on 3 August 1983 and manufactured rainwear, applied for a tax clearance certificate which was required in connection with a government contract. The Collector General refused to issue the certificate on the grounds that two of the directors had also been directors of J. Meek & Co (Ireland) Ltd, which had carried on a similar business, employed many of the same staff, and had gone into liquidation in July 1983 owing arrears of £126,414 plus interest in respect of PAYE/PRSI. Melbarien Enterprises Ltd had always discharged its liabilities for PAYE, PRSI and VAT promptly. Held that the Collector General was bound to act judicially and was not entitled to take into account the liabilities of a separate company and the order of *mandamus* should issue to the respondents to consider and deal with the application of the tax clearance certificate according to law. *Melbarien Enterprises Ltd v Revenue Commrs H/C 19 April 1985.*

38.14 **Application for judicial review, certiorari and mandamus.** The taxpayer companies, who were linked, were engaged in the commercial exploitation of a hot car wash system. A complex sequence of transactions involved the payment of substantial advance royalties to Pandion by two other companies, who then granted similar sub-licences to Ospreycare. Ospreycare subcontracted manufacture to OSD Ltd. The taxpayer companies sought what they termed as 'advance rulings' from the Revenue Commissioners, without disclosing the full facts of transactions already entered into. Relief was sought, respectively, under *FA 1973, s 34* for income from a qualifying patent, and under *CTA 1976, s 10* for payments in respect of patents, and letters confirming the availability of relief in given circumstances were received by the representative of the companies from the Revenue Commissioners. Subsequent claims for relief and vacation of an assessment based on the actual transactions were, respectively, partially allowed and denied by the Inspector of Taxes concerned. The Judge observed, *inter alia*, that the Revenue Commissioners were not agents for the Inspector, and that the sequence of transactions did not form a tax avoidance scheme under the principles of the UK case *Furniss v Dawson 1984, 55 TC 324.* The Judge did not allow the claims for *certiorari* and *mandamus* by Ospreycare relating to corporation tax assessments for the calendar year 1984, or a declaration giving that company the benefit of certain 'advance rulings'. A declaration was made, however, relating to a claim by Pandion, resulting in a repayment of tax to that company of £290,824 with interest. *Pandion Haliaetus Ltd, Ospreycare Ltd and Osprey Systems Design Ltd v Revenue Commissioners H/C 21 May 1987.*

38.15   Reopening of settled appeal by Circuit Judge. Some three years after entering in the tax appeal book his decision on an appeal against a partnership assessment, the presiding Circuit Judge re-entered the appeal, heard further submissions by the taxpayers and reduced the assessment. In granting an absolute order of *certiorari* directing the Circuit Judge to quash the later order, the High Court found that the Circuit Judge had no jurisdiction to act as he had done, any claims for hardship following final and conclusive determination of the appeal falling to be dealt with by the Revenue Commissioners. *In re McGahon H/C 1982, 8 February 1982.*

38.16   Legality of proceedings. The Revenue Commissioners had instituted proceedings against two companies for the recovery of customs duties and taxes totalling £1,982,280. It was claimed that the companies carried on business in such a manner as to defraud the Revenue Commissioners and an additional charge relating to the illegal export of large sums of Irish currency had been dropped. In addition to the Plenary Summons in the High Court, assessments were served on the two companies for income tax, corporation tax and VAT totalling £1,926,726 (this excludes customs duties of £55,000), relating to the same matter. Appeals were made and the companies obtained a Conditional Order of Prohibition preventing the Appeal Commissioners hearing the appeals on the grounds that, *inter alia*, the State could not use both the courts and taxing administration to obtain the same amount of tax, which they disputed. The two companies now sought to have the Conditional Order of Prohibition made absolute, but this was refused by the Court. The Judge held that, although the sums claimed may be identical, the two procedures are separate and distinct. By placing the issue before the High Court, the Revenue did not waive their right to have the same issues decided under the tax code. The Appeal Commissioners were not seeking to exercise a judicial power and function, but to determine the tax payable. The application by the two companies therefore failed. *The State (Calcul International Ltd and Solatrex International Ltd) v Appeal Commrs and Revenue Commrs H/C 18 December 1986.*

38.17   Whether estimated assessments and other matters constitutional. The appellant, who was unrepresented, presented a wide-ranging challenge to the constitutionality of several sections of *ITA 1967*. He had not submitted returns or accounts for the four years to 5 April 1985, and estimated assessments were issued, becoming final and conclusive. Subsequently distraint orders were issued for the unpaid taxes under *ITA 1967, s 485(2)*, bringing the total, with costs, to £33,057. The S/C upheld the H/C decision that an incorrect trade description on an assessment and the signature of a subordinate did not make either of the documents invalid, that the authentication of documents and the making of assessments were administrative and not judicial functions and that the taxpayer's constitutional right of access to the courts had not been infringed because he retained the right to apply to the inspector under *ITA 1967, s 416(7)* to re-open the assessments, providing outstanding returns were submitted and tax and interest currently assessed and charged paid. *Deighan v The State (Hearne and others) S/C 1 March 1990.*

38.17A   Interest on overpaid tax. Following the decision at 38.88 below, the taxpayer claimed interest under *FA 1976, s 30* (see 4.5 APPEALS) on the tax overpaid. For certain of the years concerned, the assessments issued and appealed against pursuant to the earlier appeal showed no further tax due (as the full liability had been deducted under PAYE), and for the remainder no assessment had been issued by agreement with the taxpayer's agents pending further progress of the appeal. *FA 1976, s 30* requires interest to be paid only where the tax in question has been charged by assessment. The taxpayer's claim was allowed. In relation to the nil assessments, the tax charged should have been the total specified as being due and payable, and not the net amount unpaid at the date of the assessment. As regards the years for which no assessment was issued, the taxpayer was entitled to rely on the agreement that there was no need for formal assessment and appeals for the years in question. *Mooney v O'Coindealbhain H/C 12 March 1992.*

CAPITAL ACQUISITIONS TAX

38.18   **CATA 1976, 2 Sch 9—whether a business—whether niece worked 'substantially full-time'.** B, a man of advancing years, owned a farm which he let as grazing land under an agreement whereby the landowner was responsible for herding and for the reporting of eventualities. The appellant, his niece, visited the farm every day to herd the cattle and examine the fences, and looked after the management of the farm and buildings. Apart from her household duties, the management of B's lands was her prime concern, and she did work of lasting value for his benefit. Held, relief was due under *CATA 1976, 2 Sch 9*, whereby the rates of tax appropriate to a transaction between parent and child applied to the gift of the farm to the appellant. 'Substantially full-time' could be construed to imply 'continued presence ... on a day-to-day basis whereby ... labour (including expertise) is put at the disposal of the disponer whereby material benefit is conferred, or is attempted to be conferred, on the disponer's business', and the attention given to B's lands was sufficient to indicate that a farming business was being carried on. It was not essential to show that the niece or nephew had taken over the entire running of the business. *A E v Revenue Commrs, Circuit Court (SE Circuit), [1984] ILRM 301.* See 7.4 CAPITAL ACQUISITIONS TAX.

38.19   **See also 38.153 below.**

CAPITAL ALLOWANCES

38.20   **Plant and machinery—poultry house.** The company carried on the business of egg production and incurred expenditure on a deep pit poultry house and equipment. The raised cedarwood poultry house contained tiered stacks of cages, under which ran a deep concrete pit for cleaning purposes. The house was specially designed to provide a controlled environment. The High Court upheld the Circuit Judge's finding that the building was plant within *Sec 241* and *FA 1971, s 26* (see 8.6(*b*) CAPITAL ALLOWANCES) and so attracted 100% wear and tear allowances. *O'Srianain v Lakeview Ltd H/C 1984, TL 125.*

38.21   **Plant and machinery—law books.** A barrister incurred expenditure on certain law books, consisting mainly of a complete set of Irish and English Law Reports. Held, the books must be regarded as plant within *Sec 241* and *FA 1971, s 26* (see 8.6(*b*) CAPITAL ALLOWANCES) and so attracted 100% wear and tear allowances. *Breathnach v McCann H/C 1984, TL 121.*

38.22   **Plant and machinery—suspended ceiling in supermarket.** The company, which carries on business throughout Ireland through supermarkets and stores, had installed a suspended ceiling in the selling area of one of its stores. Other companies within the group had installed similar standard type suspended ceilings. The company contended that the ceiling qualified as plant under *Sec 241* and *FA 1971, s 26* for the purpose of capital allowances. Held, that the suspended ceiling was part of the setting in which the goods were sold and did not constitute plant. *Dunnes Stores (Oakville) Ltd v Cronin H/C 26 April 1988.*

38.22A   **Plant and machinery—filling station canopies.** The taxpayers claimed capital allowances under *Sec 241* as plant on canopies erected over the pump areas of their filling stations. Their claim was allowed by the Circuit Judge, and that decision was affirmed in the High Court. Relying in particular on a *dictum* of Lord Hailsham in the UK case *Cole Bros Ltd v Phillips H/L 1982, 55 TC 188*, the function of the canopies—the provision of an attractive setting for the sale of the taxpayers' products, the advertisement and promotion of those products, the creation of an overall impression of efficiency and financial solidarity in relation to the business of selling petrol, and the attraction of customers to stop and purchase those products—was performed in the actual carrying out of the trade, so that they were part of the means by which the trade was carried on in the appropriately prepared setting. *O'Culachain v McMullan Bros Ltd H/C, [1991] 1 IR 363.*

38.22B Plant and machinery—refurbishment of grandstand. In the case the facts of which are outlined at 38.63A below, it was held, following *McMullan Bros Ltd* (38.22A above), that the grandstand in question was part of the means of attracting people to visit the race-course, and hence part of the means by which the trade was carried on. The net expenditure on items (*a*) and (*e*) therefore constituted expenditure on plant, for which capital allowances were available. The expenditure on the existing and new bar areas (items (*b*) and (*d*)) did not constitute expenditure on plant. *O'Grady v Roscommon Race Committee H/C, 6 November 1992.*

38.23 Plant and machinery—investment allowances. The appellant carried on a trade of plant hire contractor, and incurred expenditure of £100,000 on provision of a crane for use in that trade, the greater part of such use being in 'designated areas' for the purposes of *FA 1971, s 22.* He claimed an investment allowance on the ground that *FA 1971, s 22(1)* required only that the machinery or plant be provided for use in a designated area, without the use of the word 'exclusively'. The inspector contended that as the *subsection* did not use the word 'substantially' either, no allowance was due. In the H/C it was held that the inspector's view was to be preferred, but this decision was overturned by the S/C, where Finlay CJ considered that the statute was ambiguous, and that the clear intention of the legislature was that an allowance should be available in such cases. In the H/C, Murphy J also expressed the view that in any event the use of the words 'provided' in *subsection (1)* and 'provision' in *subsection (2)* made it clear that the expenditure must result in the asset being provided both for trade purposes and for use in a designated area, and that this condition could not be met by a plant hire contractor, as the use in the designated area was provided by the payment of a hire charge by the customer, not by the contractor's expenditure. This ground was not pursued in the S/C. *McNally v O'Maoldhomhniagh S/C 29 June 1990.* See 8.6(*c*) CAPITAL ALLOWANCES.

38.23A Plant and machinery—film production. A company entered into a complex film investment agreement the effect of which was that the £910,000 production cost was met by payment of £217,000 out of the company's own resources and £693,000 out of a loan to the company from RTE, the producers of the film, repayable out of defined profits from distribution. The Circuit Court judge's decision that the company was trading was upheld, but his finding that only the £217,000 attracted capital allowances was overturned. His decision was affected by the benefit of hindsight as to the commercial failure of the film. The £910,000 was paid for the provision of plant and attracted capital allowances in full. *Airspace Investments Ltd v Moore H/C 15 April 1994.*

38.24 Industrial buildings allowance: building within a complex: computer housing. The appellant company had erected a complex of buildings in a number of stages, including factory premises and a separate building housing a computer, showrooms and offices. Held:

    (i)   the building was an 'industrial building' to the extent that it housed the computer, as the computer was principally used for industrial rather than clerical purposes;

    (ii)   in determining whether expenditure on non-qualifying parts was one-tenth or less of the whole (see 8.5 CAPITAL ALLOWANCES), it was expenditure on the whole complex which had to be considered, not just that on the separate building.

O'Conaill v Waterford Glass Ltd H/C 1982, TL 122.

See now *Sec 254(3A)*, inserted by *FA 1990, s 74(c)*.

38.25 Industrial buildings allowance: bonded transit sheds. The company, which engaged in business as shipping agents, stevedores, customs clearance agents etc., stored goods and cargo such as newsprint in bonded transit sheds for short periods. The sheds were used merely as a clearing house for goods unloaded from ships. Industrial buildings allowance under *ITA 1967, s 255* was claimed in respect of a dock undertaking. The Judge held that the company was not carrying on a business as storekeeper or warehouse-man and the transit sheds qualified as industrial buildings and structures in use for the purposes of a dock undertaking within the meaning of *Sec 255(1)(b)*. *Patrick Monahan (Drogheda) Ltd v O'Connell H/C 15 May 1987.*

38.26 Industrial and provident societies—Sec 220(5). In a case turning on the interpretation of *Sec 220(5)* it was held that (i) all capital allowances, not just those under *ITA 1967, Part XVI*, were to be diminished under this provision, and (ii) the words 'capital allowances' were to be construed in accordance with the definition of 'capital allowance' in the interpretation section (*Sec 218*). *Irish Agricultural Wholesale Society Ltd v McDermot H/C 1977, TL 112.*

CAPITAL GAINS TAX

38.26A Abandonment of an option for consideration—whether within CGTA 1975, s 47(3)—application of CGTA 1975, s 8(2)(a). The taxpayer and his wife each granted to the other an option over valuable shares for substantial consideration, a small further amount being payable in each case on exercise. The shares were then sold to a company, subject to those options, for similarly small amounts, whereupon the company offered to pay each spouse a sum slightly more than the payment made on grant of the option for its abandonment. The offers were accepted, and the company subsequently sold on the shares to an industrial and provident society owned by the taxpayer and his wife for full value. A capital gains tax assessment was raised on the basis that a chargeable gain arose in each case on the receipt of the capital sum in return for the abandonment of the option. The taxpayer contended that the transactions fell within *CGTA 1975, s 47(3)*, which provides that the abandonment of an option shall not constitute a disposal. The Revenue Commissioners contended that *section 47(3)* did not apply to the abandonment of an option for consideration, and that if that were not so *CGTA 1975, s 8(2)(a)*, which (subject to the exceptions in the *Act*) deems the obtaining of a capital sum derived from an asset to be a disposal of that asset, applied notwithstanding *section 47(3)*. The Circuit Court Judge found in favour of the taxpayer (reversing the Appeal Commissioners' decision), but in the High Court the taxpayer lost on both counts. On the ordinary meaning of the words, and looking at the substance of the transaction, the 'abandonment' of an option does not include agreeing not to exercise the option in return for payment. On the second point, where *section 47(3)* did apply so that the abandonment was excluded from being a disposal, it did not operate to exempt a capital sum received in respect thereof from the liability clearly arising under *section 8(2)(a)*. *Dilleen v Kearns H/C, 26 November 1993.* See generally 9.6, 9.15 CAPITAL GAINS TAX.

38.27 Compulsory acquisition—adjustment of compensation for capital gains tax liability. An award for compulsory acquisition of land was made with an addendum that an additional award would be made if the compensation was subject to capital gains tax. After the capital gains tax liability had been established, a further award was made by way of special case stated for the opinion of the High Court. Held, the *Acquisition of Land (Assessment of Compensation) Act 1919, s 2* makes no provision for compensation to be adjusted because of claims made subsequent to the initial award. The further award was therefore disallowed. *Re Heron H/C 22 April 1985.*

38.28 Disposals of land, etc.—clearance under CGTA 1975, 4 Sch 11. The company, which was ordinarily resident in Ireland, had applied for *mandamus* following the refusal by the Revenue of a clearance certificate under *CGTA 1975, 4 Sch 11* as introduced by *FA 1982, s 34* (deduction of capital gains tax from proceeds of certain disposals) in relation to a property sale. The case was remitted to the inspector with an order directing him to consider the matter in accordance with the law. The issue of a clearance certificate was mandatory if the conditions laid down in *CGTA 1975, 4 Sch 11(6)* were met, and a wide-ranging investigation into transactions with other companies concerning the property sold was not within the inspector's powers. There was no doubt that, prior to the sale, the company owned the land in question. *Financial Indemnity Co (Ireland) Ltd v O'Ceallaigh H/C 9 November 1983.* (See 9.5 CAPITAL GAINS TAX.)

38.28A **Disposal of land by mortgagee—no clearance certificate—repayment of tax deducted by purchaser.** In a case where the mortgagee was treated under *CGTA 1975, s 8(5)* (see 9.4 CAPITAL GAINS TAX) as having disposed of property as nominee for the mortgagor for the purpose of enforcing its security, and no clearance certificate had been obtained to enable the purchase price to be paid without the 15% deduction under *CGTA 1975, 4 Sch 11(2)* (see 9.5 CAPITAL GAINS TAX), the mortgagee sought repayment by the Revenue Commissioners of the 15% deducted. Held, the 15% deduction had been properly made and paid over to the Revenue Commissioners on account of the mortgagor's liability. The mortgagee's only remedy was to seek reimbursement from the mortgagor. *Bank of Ireland Finance Ltd v Revenue Commissioners H/C 13 October 1989.*

38.29 **Replacement of business assets—'rollover relief'.** The taxpayer and his wife purchased a farm in 1975, and then emigrated to Canada. During their absence the farm was let on conacre, and shortly after return in 1978 it was sold. Another holding of land was then purchased. They had never lived in or worked the original farm. It was claimed that land was deemed to be occupied by the taxpayer and his wife by virtue of *FA 1974, s 17*, and that relief under *CGTA 1975, s 28* in respect of replacement of business assets was due. Held, reversing the decision of the Circuit Court, that the income tax deeming provisions did not apply to *CGTA 1975, s 28*, and that 'rollover relief' applies only to a person carrying on a trade, in this instance the conacre tenant. *O'Coindealbhain v Price H/C 29 January 1988.*

CHARITIES

38.30 **The Pharmaceutical Society of Ireland,** formed by statute to hold examinations for persons desiring to be pharmaceutical chemists and to form a register of them if approved, was held not to be charitable. Its activities of conducting schools and examinations were held to be trading. *Pharmaceutical Society of Ireland v CIR H/C 1937, 2 ITC 157; 17 ATC 587.*

38.31 **Trading by charity.** A hospital established for the relief of the sick poor also admitted paying patients for treatment in an Annexe. The hospital and the Annexe were administered as one undertaking. Held, that the treatment of the private patients was severable from the charitable activities and amounted to carrying on a trade. *Davis v Superioress, Mater Misericordiae Hospital Dublin S/C 1933, 2 ITC 1; [1933] IR 480, 503.*

38.32 **Trading by charity.** The appellant charity was bequeathed an estate including a small retail business, which it carried on, employing for this purpose a disabled man who, if not so employed, would have been a beneficiary of the charity. It claimed exemption under (what is now) *Sec 334* for the profits of the business on the ground that the employee running it should be regarded as a beneficiary of the charity. Held, the employee was not a beneficiary and relief was therefore not due. *Beirne v St Vincent de Paul Society (Wexford Conference) H/C 1932, 1 ITC 413.*

CONSTRUCTION INDUSTRY SUB-CONTRACTORS

38.32A **Haulage contractors.** A firm of sand and gravel merchants entered into arrangements with lorry owners under which the lorry owners purchased materials from a company under the same control and operating from the same premises as the merchants, and undertook to sell the materials to the merchants and to deliver them as directed, receiving only the sale proceeds (which varied according to the distance of travel to delivery) net of the cost of purchase owed to the supplier. It was held that the lorry owners' activities under these arrangements did not constitute 'the haulage for hire of materials', so that *FA 1970, s 17* did not require tax to be deducted from payments to them. *O'Grady v Laragan Quarries Ltd H/C 27 June 1990.* See 13.7 DEDUCTION OF TAX AT SOURCE.

CORPORATION TAX

38.33 **Close company—advertising agency—whether 'service company' within CTA s 162.** The company carried out market research and prepared creative proposals for customers. If these were accepted, the company would then carry out further work, depending on what was required. The High Court upheld the Circuit Judge's finding that the company was not carrying on a profession, nor was it providing professional services. It was thus not liable to surcharge under *CTA s 162* (see 12.7 CORPORATION TAX). *Mac Giolla Mhaith v Brian Cronin & Associates Ltd H/C 1984, TL 124.*

38.34 **Export sales relief—mixed sales—computation of corporation tax relief.** The company's export sales attracting relief under *CTA s 58* amounted to 85.7% of all sales. Losses were surrendered to it which approximately equalled in amount the balance of non-export sales. The question arose as to whether, in determining the proportion of corporation tax liability to be relieved, the proportion of income attributable to export sales should be compared with the overall income net of losses surrendered to the company or before deduction of those losses. Held, as contended by the company, 'total income brought into charge to corporation tax' for this purpose means taxable income, so that the corporation tax liability was relieved in the proportion that income attributable to export sales bore to taxable income for the accounting period net of losses. *Cronin v Youghal Carpets (Yarns) Ltd S/C 1985, TL 129; [1985] ILRM 666.* See 16.4 EXEMPT INCOME AND SPECIAL SAVINGS SCHEMES.

38.35 **Export sales relief—sales into intervention.** The respondent company sold frozen meat to the Minister of Agriculture and Fisheries as agent for the Intervention Agencies of the EC. Product liability was accepted by the company, and the meat was exported under the company's own export licences. Export sales relief under *F(MP)A 1956, s 13(3)* had been granted in the Circuit Court. Held, the fact that the company was not the owner of the meat at the time of export did not prevent its being the 'exporter' within the meaning of *section 13(3)*, so that the relief was due. *Cronin v IMP Midleton Ltd H/C 31 January 1986.* (See now 16.4 EXEMPT INCOME AND SPECIAL SAVINGS SCHEMES as regards the similar successor provisions of *CTA ss 53–68.*)

38.36 **Export sales relief—deposit interest.** The company manufactured ambulances for export, and obtained deposits in respect of items due for delivery several months later. Deposit account interest was earned in respect of these advance payments totalling £8,338 and £12,712 respectively in the calendar years 1978 and 1979. The company claimed export sales relief under *CTA 1976, s 58* on the grounds that the deposit interest formed 'part and parcel' of the sale. Held, reversing the Circuit Court decision, that because it was not income from the sale of goods export sales relief was not due in respect of the deposit interest. *Kerrane v N Hanlon (Ireland) Ltd H/C 6 February 1987.*

38.37 **Export sales relief—deposit interest.** The company moved its residence from RI to Holland in 1975. It continued to carry on a manufacturing business in RI through its Dublin branch, and dividends were paid tax-free (due to export sales relief) into a Swiss bank account. Interest accrued on the account, and some withdrawals were used by the Irish branch. The point at issue was whether the Irish branch was liable to corporation tax on the interest under *CTA 1976, s 8(2)*. Held, that the Dublin branch had no control over the funds in the Swiss bank account, and that the income therefrom was not chargeable to corporation tax. *Murphy v Data Products (Dublin) Ltd H/C 29 January 1988.*

38.37A Franked investment income—date of receipt. An interim dividend payable to the parent company was declared at a Board meeting of the paying company shortly before its year end, and was to be settled through the inter-company account. That account was not written up until some time after the year end. The recipient company wished to claim relief under *CTA s 25* (see 12.13 CORPORATION TAX) for its accounting period coinciding with that of the subsidiary. It was agreed that a dividend may be paid by set-off in an inter-company account, and that an interim dividend is not received until paid. It was held that the dividend was received on the date of the subsidiary company's Board meeting at which it was declared. *Murphy v The Borden Co Ltd H/C December 1991.*

38.37B Group of companies—insolvency—appropriation of tax payments by members to meet other group companies' liabilities. See *Frederick Inns Ltd*, 38.178 below.

38.38 Manufacturing companies relief: 'manufacture'. The appellant company imported green unripened bananas into RI. They were then ripened by subjection to ethylene gas in specially constructed ripening rooms in a process taking from four to twelve days and requiring constant skilled control and testing. It claimed manufacturing companies relief (see 12.17 CORPORATION TAX) on the basis that the ripening process constituted manufacturing within the State within *CTA 1976, s 54*. Held, the relief was due. 'Manufacture' was not defined in the statute and, although it must be construed strictly, it was necessary to look to the scheme and purpose as disclosed by the statute. The relief was manifestly aimed at increasing employment in RI and promoting exports, both achieved by the operation in question. It was then a matter of degree as to whether the process was within the statutory provision. The bananas represented a commercially different product and the process fell within the definition. *Charles McCann Ltd v O'Culachain S/C, [1986] IR 196.* (*Note.* Similar wording applies to the revised manufacturing companies' relief introduced by *FA 1980*, see 12.17 CORPORATION TAX and 38.39 below.)

38.39 Manufacturing companies relief was claimed under *FA 1980, s 41(2)* (see 12.17 CORPORATION TAX) in respect of a company which purchased milk from farmers and resold it after pasteurising and packaging it to make it legally saleable. It was held that the degree of change brought about by the company's activities was sufficient to amount to a manufacturing process, resulting in a commercially different product from the raw milk. Relief was therefore allowed. *Cronin v Strand Dairy Ltd H/C 18 December 1985.*

38.39A The production of J Cloths and nappy liners from bales of fabric was held to be a manufacturing process within *FA 1980, s 42*. The cutting folding and packaging of the material by machine did not bring about any change in the raw material, but the utility, quality and worth of the new product were enhanced by, and could not be dissociated from, the process carried out. See, however, 12.17 CORPORATION TAX as regards the changes introduced by *FA 1990, s 41*. *O'Laochdha v Johnson and Johnson (Ireland) Ltd H/C, 6 November 1991.*

38.39B A company, as part of its trade, 'conditioned' wort purchased from a brewery company. This involves the storing of bottles of wort at a constant temperature of 58 to 60 degrees Fahrenheit for 14 days, during which an irreversible chemical reaction takes place, and is absolutely essential to produce a commercially saleable product. Conditioning was carried out in three insulated and thermostatically controlled conditioning rooms, and was regularly monitored by the brewery company. After such treatment, the bottles are stored for a further 14 days before delivery to retailers. The High Court upheld the Circuit Judge's decision that the conditioning was an integral part of the manufacturing process and not ancillary, and constituted a manufacturing process for the purposes of the relief. *Hussey v M J Gleeson & Co Ltd H/C 2 July 1993.*

38.39C The company carried on the business of producing day old chicks. This involves an elaborate hatching out process of the eggs from the laying hens through a number of stages in 'settler' machines in specially heated and humidified rooms. At 19 days, eggs containing chicks are moved to a hatching room. Finally, the chicks are packed in purpose built containers for despatch in batches of 3,500 females and 450 males for use as breeding stock. The Circuit Court Judge considered himself constrained by the *Charles McCann Ltd* and *Strand Dairy Ltd* decisions (38.38, 38.39 above) to hold that manufacturing relief was due, and his decision was upheld in the High Court. *Kelly v Cobh Straffan IR Ltd H/C 30 June 1993.*

38.39D A company engaged in the import and cultivation of chrysanthemums was held not to qualify for the manufacturing companies relief, overturning the Circuit Court judge's decision. Whilst 'cultivation' and 'manufacture' are not mutually exclusive in the sense that a manufacturing process can be applied to cultivated goods, an alteration in goods achieved by cultivation cannot be said to have been brought about by a manufacturing process. *Brosnan v Leeside Nurseries Ltd H/C 13 May 1994.*

38.39E **Manufacturing companies relief: income from sale of 'goods'.** The advertising revenue of a newspaper publisher was held to be within the relief. It was accepted that newspapers were 'goods' for these purposes, and since the advertising revenue could not arise without the newspaper sales, it arose in respect of those sales. *McGurrin v Champion Publications Ltd H/C 4 February 1993.* See now 12.17(xvii) CORPORATION TAX.

38.40 **Manufacturing companies relief: 'manufactured within the State'.** The company claimed manufacturing relief under *FA 1980, s 41(2)* in connection with the production of advertising materials by means of TV commercials etc. The company carried out the filming, but printing of the film took place in the UK. There was no manufacturing work force or plant in Ireland. Held that the activities of the company were that of a service industry and not a manufacturing company. *O'Culachain v Hunter Advertising Ltd H/C April 1988.*

38.41 **Small companies rate: associated companies.** The limits on profits below which a reduced rate of corporation tax applies under *CTA s 28* are reduced where a company has associated companies within *CTA s 102* (see 12.20 CORPORATION TAX). The appellant company, resident and trading in RI, was under common control with a company resident and trading in Northern Ireland. Held, the scheme of the *Corporation Tax Acts* brings all companies within the charge with an exemption for non-resident companies. The reference to associated companies in *CTA s 28* must therefore be interpreted as including all companies under common control, wherever incorporated. *Bairead v Maxwells of Donegal Ltd H/C 1985, TL 134.*

38.42 **Loss relief—changes of trade and ownership—CTA s 27.** The respondent company had ceased pig slaughtering and the manufacture of meat products, and subsequently acted as a distribution centre for the company which had acquired its share capital. Its intention to recommence the former activities was established. The case concerned claims for the allowance of losses incurred before the change of ownership. Held, confirming the Circuit Court decision, that:

(*a*)   there was no permanent cessation of trade;

(*b*)   there was no major change in the nature or conduct of the trade within the meaning of *CTA s 27(1)(a)*; and

(*c*)   it was not established that the time of the change in ownership of the company was after the scale of the company's activities had become small or negligible and before any considerable revival of the trade, within *CTA s 27(1)(b)*,

so that the company was entitled to the loss reliefs claimed. *Cronin v Lunham Brothers Ltd H/C 1985, [1986] ILRM 415.* (See 12.16 CORPORATION TAX.)

DOUBLE TAXATION

38.42A Government employment. A staff nurse, a national of both RI and the UK, was resident in RI and employed by the Western Health and Social Services Board in Northern Ireland. A claim for relief under *Article 18(2)* of the *Double Taxation Relief (Taxes on Income and Capital Gains) (UK) Order 1976 (SI 1976 No 319)* was refused on the grounds that: (i) the term 'local authority' in that *Article* must be interpreted under UK law, and did not include the Health Board; and (ii) the performance of nursing services for the Health Board were not 'services rendered in discharge of functions of a governmental nature'. *Travers v O'Siochain H/C 24 June 1994.* See 15.7 DOUBLE TAX RELIEF—INCOME AND CAPITAL GAINS.

38.43 Interest paid to non-resident parent company. Under *Article 12* of the Irish/Japanese *Double Taxation Relief Order 1974 (SI 1974 No 259)*, interest paid to a Japanese parent company may be subject to withholding tax not exceeding 10%. *CTA 1976, s 84(2)(d)(iv)*, however, normally requires such interest to be treated as a distribution, not subject to withholding tax. The Revenue contention that the *Order* overrules *section 84* was rejected. The *Order* merely imposes a ceiling of 10% on the tax which may be levied in RI in these circumstances. It does not impose an obligation to levy any such form of taxation. *Murphy v Asahi Synthetic Fibres (Ireland) Ltd S/C 18 December 1986.*

FARM TAX

38.43A De facto repeal of Farm Tax Act 1985—whether enforceable for earlier years. The *Farm Tax Act 1985* was brought into effect on 6 October 1986, but in the 1987 Budget speech, the Minister for Finance stated that it was to be repealed and that tax for 1987 would not be collected. No repealing legislation was, however, introduced. The applicant was assessed to farm tax for 1986, and sought to prohibit the continuance of proceedings for collection of the tax on the ground *inter alia* that, in the circumstances, it would be improper to enforce the *Act*. His application was upheld. The failure to introduce amending provisions meant that the legislation had been interfered with unlawfully, and in that event it ceased to be enforceable not only for the future but for the past also. *Purcell v Attorney-General H/C 14 November 1989.*

LIQUIDATIONS

38.44 Preferential claims in liquidation. The State claimed preferential payment, in respect of a company in the hands of the Receiver, of income tax for one year of assessment (year ended 5 April 1946) and of corporation profits tax for a different year (year ended 31 March 1945). Held that under the terms of the *1908 Companies (Consolidation) Act* the State's rights extended to one year's assessment in respect of each tax assessed separately and distinctly. *Attorney-General v Irish Steel Ltd and Crowley S/C 1948, 2 ITC 402.*

38.45 Tax on deposit interest in voluntary liquidation: whether a charge within Companies Act 1963, s 281. The liquidator sought a determination as to whether corporation tax on deposit interest earned in the course of a voluntary liquidation is a preferential charge within the meaning of *Companies Act 1963, s 281*. The Judge held that the answer to the question was in the affirmative and the decision was affirmed in the Supreme Court. *Re A Noyek & Sons Ltd, Burns v Hearne S/C 25 July 1988.* Note that the liability to pay over corporation tax differs, depending on whether the liquidation is voluntary or compulsory. See also judgments in the cases of *Donnelly 38.47, Hibernian Transport 38.48* and *Wayte (Holdings) 38.49* below.

38.46 Scheme of arrangement with creditors: Revenue priority. The company obtained agreement to a scheme of arrangement at a meeting of all its creditors, at which no distinction was made as to status or quality of the various claims, and at which the Revenue Commissioners were outvoted. Held, the approval of the Revenue Commissioners, as a separate category (having a preferential claim in liquidation in respect of part of their claim), should have been sought at a separate meeting before the scheme was put to the ordinary creditors. *Re Donmac Agricultural Ltd H/C 1981.*

38.47 Expenses of liquidation—whether tax on realisation of assets a 'necessary disbursement'. In a case brought against a liquidator in respect of corporation tax liability on disposal of certain assets, it was held that the tax payable was neither an expense of the realisation nor a 'necessary disbursement' of the liquidation. The liability was therefore governed as to priority in the liquidation by the specific provisions. *Revenue Commrs v Donnelly S/C 24 February 1983.* See now 9.4 CAPITAL GAINS TAX as regards *FA 1983, s 56* provisions. See also 38.48 below.

38.48 Deposit interest in liquidation: liability: whether a 'necessary disbursement': status of Revenue claim. In a case where substantial deposit interest had been earned on money in the hands of the Official Liquidator, it was held that:

(i)   such interest is liable to income tax, corporation profits tax or corporation tax as appropriate;

(ii)   the tax thereon is not a 'necessary disbursement' of the liquidation, following *Revenue Commissioners v Donnelly* (see 38.47 above);

(iii)   the Revenue Commissioners' claim in relation to the tax thereon is not preferential; and

(iv)   the Revenue Commissioners' claim does not rank as an unsecured debt in the winding-up (but see now *FA 1983, s 56*).

In the matter of Hibernian Transport Companies Ltd and Others H/C 1983, [1984] ILRM 583.

38.49 Deposit interest in receivership: liability to tax. A receiver, appointed by a debenture-holder, deposited monies with the Agricultural Credit Corporation in his name as 'receiver' of the company. The Revenue claimed that the receiver was liable to pay corporation tax on the interest earned. The Judge held that *CTA 1976, s 11* does not incorporate the provisions of *ITA 1967, s 105* into the corporation tax code, and that *companies* only, and not their officers, are assessable to corporation tax. *Re Wayte (Holdings) Ltd (In Receivership), Burns v Hearne H/C 9 October 1986.* See also judgments in the cases of *Donnelly* 38.47, *Hibernian Transport* 38.48 and *Noyek* 38.45 above.

38.50 Surcharge on undistributed income of close company. The Revenue sought to impose the 20% surcharge under *CTA 1976, s 101(1)* on a close investment company in liquidation. The company referred to *CTA 1976, s 100(1)* which gives a company a period of 18 months after the end of an accounting period in which to make distributions, and claimed that *CTA 1976, s 84(1)* unfairly penalised a company in liquidation by reducing to 6 months following the penultimate period the time within which a dividend deductible from the amount subject to the surcharge might be paid and reducing to nil the period following the ultimate period within which such a payment could be made. Held that there were no manifestly unfair circumstances in this case, and that the Appeal Commissioner was correct in holding that *Sec 84(1)* did not prevent the application of *Sec 101(1)* in this case. *Rahinstown Estate Company (in Liquidation) v Hughes H/C 15 May 1986.*

38.51 Appropriation of tax payments to earlier years. The Collector General contended that an existing arrangement with the taxpayer entitled him to appropriate payments made for current liabilities against arrears of other group companies. The fact that a new managing director of the company was unaware of the arrangement did not alter the position. The contention of the Collector General was upheld. *Re Metal Products Ltd (In Receivership). Uniacke v The Collector General H/C January 1988.*

MARRIED PERSONS

38.52   **Aggregation of income.** Prior to the amending legislation in *FA 1980*, the plaintiffs sought and obtained a declaration that the provisions of *Secs 192* to *198* inclusive as then enacted (providing for the aggregation of the wife's income with that of her husband for income tax purposes) were repugnant to the Constitution. In a subsidiary judgment, it was held that the provisions in question were void *ab initio*, but that only those taxpayers who had previously challenged through the Courts the constitutionality of the provisions in relation to specific assessments were entitled to seek repayment of tax deducted under such assessments. *Francis and Mary Murphy v Attorney-General S/C 1980, 25 January 1980 and (subsidiary judgment) 25 April 1980.*

38.53   Following the *Murphy* case (38.52 above), *FA 1980, s 21* was enacted (see 23.3 MARRIED PERSONS) to prevent assessments made after 25 June 1980 for 1979/80 or earlier years resulting in a lower liability than would have arisen under the old aggregation rules. In the H/C, this *section* was held to be unconstitutional and invalid, following the *Murphy* decision. *Bernard and Ann Muckley v Attorney-General and Revenue Commrs S/C 12 November 1985.*

RESIDENCE, ORDINARY RESIDENCE AND DOMICILE

(See also *Hewson v Kealy* 38.6 above.)

38.54   **Company registered in Ireland and abroad.** A company registered in both Ireland and the USA merchanted linen goods. Most of its sales were in the USA where its only director resided, but the goods were warehoused in Belfast. The company was held to be resident in Ireland and liable under Case I on the whole of its profits. *Hood (John) & Co Ltd v Magee KB(I) 1918, 7 TC 327.*

38.55   **Jurisdiction of Courts in relation to determination of domicile.** In an income tax case, the High Court reversed a decision by the Special Commissioners that the taxpayer had not given up his domicile of origin. The Supreme Court held that domicile is a question of fact and the Commissioners' decision, if one of fact, could not be reviewed by the Courts. However, in this case the Special Commissioners had approached the question as one of law and had misconstrued the law. The case was remitted to them to determine the question of domicile as one of fact. *Earl of Iveagh v Revenue Commrs S/C 1930, 1 ITC 316; [1930] IR 431.*

38.56   **Domicile and ordinary residence.** The appellant was born in 1870 in Ireland, his father having been born in Italy and having owned residences both in Ireland and in England. The appellant had lived altogether in England up to 1892, when he inherited the English residence and certain entailed property in Ireland. From 1892 to 1922 he resided, whenever not outside the British Isles, at one or other of those properties, neither being regarded as his chief home. His five children were born in Ireland. The property in Ireland was kept permanently ready for his occupation, and from 1922 to the date of the appeal he visited it with his family every year, spending 165 days there in 1923/24, 182 days in 1924/25 and 170 days between 6 April 1925 and 11 December 1925. He also had an interest in an Irish colliery throughout, either as sole proprietor or as director and chief shareholder of the successor owning company. He was admittedly resident in RI for 1923/24, 1924/25 and 1925/26. He claimed that he had elected that his domicile should be in England, and had abandoned his former Irish domicile, although stating that he had not abandoned all intention of returning to his home in RI. In the course of the H/C hearing, it was admitted that he was ordinarily resident in RI, and the Court held that he was also domiciled in RI, having failed to discharge the onus of proof in regard to the claimed domicile change. *Prior-Wandesforde v Revenue Commissioners H/C 1928, 1 ITC 248.*

38.57 **Domicile of choice—acquisition and retention.** The plaintiff's brother, whose domicile at death was in question, had an Irish domicile of origin and was an Irish citizen. He took up residence in France from 1949 until his death in 1984, and on the facts he was held to have acquired a French domicile of choice. Although there was evidence that he had, in 1983, formed an intention to abandon his French domicile, that intention was ineffective in law as he had not in fact changed his residence at the time of his death. He therefore died domiciled in France. *Rowan v Rowan H/C 17 December 1986.*

38.58 **Domicile of choice—acquisition—abandonment.** The taxpayer, of Irish domicile of origin, was born in London and had spent most of his working life in Scotland, with regular annual visits of a month or two to RI. He had inherited the family property in RI, and, on its destruction by fire, had acquired other property in RI. For the last 32 years of his life he lived in RI, with regular visits to Scotland, mainly in connection with his declining business interests. He owned, but not for his own personal use, property in Scotland. In his will he declared that he had acquired and retained a Scottish domicile of choice. Held, the Irish domicile of origin had never been replaced by a domicile of choice. The acquisition of a domicile of choice requires the establishment of an intention to reside in the chosen country for an indefinite time, and the actions of the taxpayer had not shown any such intention, having always indicated that the taxpayer contemplated that he might return to RI. Even if he had acquired a Scottish domicile of choice, there was clear evidence that in the last 32 years of his life he had resolved to make his permanent home in RI, and hence to abandon his domicile of choice. *Revenue Commrs v Shaw and Talbot-Crosbie H/C 1977, [1982] ILRM 433.*

RESIDENTIAL PROPERTY TAX

38.59 **Whether tax unconstitutional.** The appellants in two separate proceedings sought to obtain a declaration that the residential property tax introduced by *FA 1983, ss 95–116* was unconstitutional. The cases referred specifically to the method of determining market value and to the income exemption limit (particularly the aggregation of the income of all persons normally residing in the property), and on the direction of the judge, consideration of the appeals was confined to the facts of each case. Both appeals were dismissed, but with a rider that the decisions need not preclude another appellant bringing a similar case on different facts. *Madigan v Attorney-General; Gallagher v Attorney-General S/C 1984, [1986] ILRM 136.*

SCHEDULE D, CASES I AND II—EXPENDITURE

38.60 **The cost of rebuilding business premises destroyed** in the Irish rebellion of 1916 (less an *ex gratia* Government grant) and of adapting temporary premises, was held to be capital and not an admissible deduction for excess profits duty. *Fitzgerald v CIR S/C 1925, 1 ITC 100; [1926] IR 182, 585.*

38.61 **Improvement of sanitation.** A company carried on business as woollen manufacturers. Following the installation of a new water and sewerage scheme in the locality of its mill, and in compliance with Orders made by the local authority, it replaced the earthen privies at its mill, housed in various sheds detached from the mill building, by water closets in a concrete structure attached to the mill building. Held, reversing the H/C decision, that the expenditure was capital or on improvements, and not allowable. *Vale v Martin Mahony & Bros Ltd S/C 1946, 2 ITC 331; [1947] IR 30, 41.*

38.62 **Replacement of weighbridge building.** For the purposes of its trade as leather manufacturers, a company had a weighbridge in its factory premises, comprising the weighbridge with a ramp in the open next to a small building, separate from the main factory
building, housing the weighbridge machinery and also providing some workshop and storage accommodation. Following severe storm damage, the building was demolished and
replaced by a smaller building, housing only the weighbridge machinery, and no improvement on the old. Held, affirming the Special Commissioners' decision, that the cost of
demolishing and replacing the building was allowable. No new capital was brought into
existence and the replacement was of a small part of the factory premises as a whole which
were the 'entirety'. (A new building was also erected for workshop and storage accommodation, but the cost of this was charged to capital and not claimed as allowable.) *Hodgkins v
Plunder & Pollak (Ireland) Ltd S/C 1955, 3 ITC 135; [1957] IR 58.*

38.63 **Rebuilding of premises.** A company carried on business from a 300-year-old building. It
was in very bad condition and the company was advised that it was not feasible to put it in a
state of good repair. It was therefore demolished except for the rear wall and part of a side
wall and replaced by a modern two storey shop at a total cost of £6,509 of which the archi-
tect allocated £4,919 to 'repairs'. The company claimed to deduct the £4,919. On appeal,
the Circuit Judge allowed £1,276. The H/C disallowed the whole. The expenditure
brought into being new premises and was capital, applying Viscount Cave's test in
Atherton, 10 TC 155, (a UK case). *Curtin v M Ltd H/C 1957, 3 ITC 227; [1960] IR 97.*

38.63A **Refurbishment of grandstand.** The taxpayers promoted and organised horse races at a
racecourse. Extensive works were carried out on the public grandstand. These included:

(*a*)   widening of the steps on the lower terrace (with a consequent 40% increase in the
standing area);

(*b*)   extending the existing bar;

(*c*)   replacing wet and crumbling walls;

(*d*)   construction of a new reserve bar; and

(*e*)   replacement of the existing roof and supports.

It was held that net expenditure on item (*c*) was an allowable repair, but that items (*a*) and
(*e*) constituted renewals and improvements to the grandstand (which was the 'entirety' to
be considered in this case) and were not allowable deductions. Items (*b*) and (*d*) were clearly
capital improvements and not deductible. *O'Grady v Roscommon Race Committee H/C
6 November 1992.* As regards capital allowances for the disallowed expenditure, see 38.22B
above.

38.64 **Quarry—cost of removal of top soil.** A company worked a limestone quarry, using the
limestone mainly to produce limestone flour. To ensure the purity of this product, the top
soil had to be removed before blasting the limestone from the side of the quarry. Held,
reversing the decision of the Special Commissioner, that the cost of removing the top soil
was allowable. It was part of the cost of manufacture of the marketable product. *Milverton
Quarries Ltd v Revenue Commissioners S/C 1959, 3 ITC 279; [1960] IR 224.*

38.65 **Technical information, etc. in return for sum payable in instalments.** In 1958 an
Irish company S Ltd decided to expand its business in plumbers' brassware and for this
purpose agreed to pay W, a leading English firm in the business, 'the capital sum of
£15,000', payable in instalments over some six years, in return for the supply by W for ten
years of technical information and an exclusive licence in Ireland in any patents it held.
Thereafter S's turnover increased substantially and, in the event, it did not call on W for
advice after 1963, although its liabilities under the agreement continued. Its payments

under the agreement were held to be capital and not deductible in computing its profits. *S Ltd v O'Sullivan H/C 1972, TL 108.*

38.66 **Exclusivity payments by petrol company.** The appellant, a petrol company, entered into exclusivity agreements with retailers under which it paid lump sums and, in addition, undertook to reimburse the retailer in respect of sums expended on decoration, re-siting and maintenance of pumps, and other works. The lump sums were calculated by reference to estimated gallonage, although retailers were not aware of this fact. Initially, agreements were for one to three years, but ultimately, they were made for periods of up to ten years or more. The S/C held, by a four-to-one majority, that payments where the agreement was for ten years or less were of a revenue nature and allowable, and, by a three-to-two majority, that there was no ground for according a different treatment to payments where the agreement was for longer than ten years. *Dolan v AB Co Ltd S/C 1968, TL 109.*

38.67 **Expenses of action relating to liability assumed by company on its formation.** With a view to forming a company to take it over, persons contracted with a builder for the construction of a cinema. The cinema was completed and opened for business in November 1947 and a company was registered on 3 January 1948, taking over all the assets and liabilities of the cinema business on the same day. At that time, the balance due to the builder had not been settled. The matter reached the High Court, which awarded the builder £650 with costs, which the company duly paid. The company admitted the £650 to be capital but claimed to deduct its legal expenses of £903 in connection with the court action. The expenses were held to be capital, made in relation to a capital liability and solely referable to the capital structure of the company. *Casey v AB Ltd H/C 1964, TL 104; [1965] IR 668.*

38.68 **Expenses of formation of holding company.** In order to avoid certain consequences of a new system of quotas which might adversely affect the business of three companies in the bacon trade, their shareholders agreed to set up a new holding company, exchanging their shares for shares in the new company. They agreed that the expenses of forming the company should be shared between two of the companies, of which the taxpayer company was one and claimed its share of the expenses as a deduction in computing its profits. Held, the expenses were capital and disallowable. *Per* two of the three judges who heard the case, the expenses were also disallowable as not having been incurred wholly or exclusively for the purposes of the trade; the third expressed no opinion on this. *Kealy v O'Mara (Limerick) Ltd H/C 1942, 2 ITC 265; [1942] IR 616.*

38.69 **Payment to settle action alleging infringement of rights by construction of factory.** A manufacturing company decided to move to another site and to build a new factory there for the purpose. It received all the requisite planning approvals, but while the factory was under construction, tenants of adjacent houses commenced proceedings against it, alleging the factory would infringe their rights to light and air. The company's legal advisers considered the claim unsustainable but advised compromise if possible. In the event the company settled the action, paying the tenants £225 as compensation and £75 for costs, and claimed these amounts as deductions in computing its profits. Its claim was upheld. The expenditure was wholly and exclusively for the purposes of its trade and, applying a *dictum* of Lawrence L J in *Southern v Borax Consolidated Ltd* (a UK case reported at *23 TC 597*), paid to defend its assets and not capital. *Davis v X Ltd S/C 1946, 2 ITC 320.*

38.70 **Settlement of action for nuisance.** A company manufacturing building materials secured the settlement of an action for nuisance and the withdrawal of planning objections by purchasing the complainant's adjacent property, a payment of £8,000, the delivery of building materials to the complainant and payment of costs. The company accepted that the property purchase was capital expenditure, but sought to claim the remaining expenditure as a deduction from profits. The Judge held, noting the different circumstances from *Davis v X Ltd S/C 1946, 2 ITC 320* (see 38.69 above), that the remaining expenditure was capital. *Insulation Products Ltd v Inspector of Taxes Circuit Court (SE Circuit) 1982, [1984] ILRM 610.*

38.71   Costs of promoting private Bills. A gas undertaking was carried on by a committee constituted by a private Act. On modernisation of the works, a number of the employees became redundant and the committee promoted a private Bill (eventually passed) to enable it to pay pensions to its former employees. The Special Commissioners allowed the cost of promoting the Bill and their decision was upheld as one of fact, there not having been a palpable error of law. *McGarry v Limerick Gas Committee H/C 1932, 1 ITC 405; [1932] IR 125.*

38.72   Payments towards statutory sinking fund. Under a private Act of Parliament, a company issued debenture stock to finance its carrying out a Government contract and was required to set aside part of its receipts to establish a sinking fund to repay the debentures. The sums so set aside were held not to be deductible, following *Mersey Docks & Harbour Board v Lucas* (a UK case reported at *2 TC 25*). *City of Dublin Steam Packet Co v O'Brien KB (I) 1912, 6 TC 101.*

38.73   Woodlands—initial planting of new acreage. The taxpayer, who had elected for Schedule D treatment of his woodlands, had cleared 84 acres of waste land preparatory to the planting of young trees, it being accepted that the clearance expenditure was a capital expense. The case concerned whether or not the cost of purchase and planting of the new trees was a revenue expense and it was held to be capital, affirming the High Court decision. *Wilson-Wright v Connolly S/C 20 December 1976.* The judgment distinguished between the cost of the original planting which was regarded as a capital expense and replanting which was regarded as a revenue expense. See now *FA 1979, s 17* (22.2 LOSSES).

38.73A   Lease premium—avoidance scheme. In a relatively straightforward sale and leaseback scheme exploiting the provisions of *Secs 80, 83* and *91*, the inspector's attempt to deny a deduction for the full amount of the premium paid on a lease, where the lessor had validly elected to be taxed on instalments as they arose, was rejected. The legislative provisions were unequivocal and the scheme operated by the company was fully tax effective. *The Hammond Lane Metal Co Ltd v O'Culachain H/C 2 October 1989.* See 33.6 SCHEDULE D, CASE V. For a preliminary issue in this case, see 38.2A above.

SCHEDULE D, CASES I AND II—RECEIPTS

38.74   Compulsory sales of requisitioned goods. The appellant company, being brewers, held large stocks of barley for manufacturing purposes. The barley was not normally sold or traded. Under wartime regulations, the stocks were requisitioned, being thereafter sold as directed to millers at a set price plus commission. The profit on these transactions was assessed as arising from the trade. The Court of Appeal, in a majority decision, held, following the UK case *Glenboig Union Fireclay Co Ltd v CIR H/L 1922, 12 TC 427*, that the receipts were in respect of the taking by compulsion of a capital asset and were not trade profits. *Arthur Guinness, Son and Co Ltd v CIR C/A 1923, 1 ITC 1; [1923] 2 IR 186.*

38.75   Compensation for detention of ships during coal strike. A gas company owned two ships to carry coal to its works. They were compulsorily detained in England during the 1920 coal strike. The company received compensation from the UK Government in 1924. It was treated as a trading receipt in its 1925/26 assessment (based on its 1924 profits) and the assessment was upheld. *Alliance & Dublin Consumers' Gas Co v McWilliams H/C 1927, 1 ITC 199; [1928] IR 1.* (*Note.* The date the compensation should be brought into account was not an issue.)

38.76 **Cancellation of agreement to supply cattle to subsidiary.** In a case in which the facts are special and complex, a decision by the Commissioners that compensation paid by the Minister of Agriculture to a company, on his ceasing to supply cattle to a subsidiary of the company (formed pursuant to an agreement with the Minister), was not a trading receipt, was upheld as one of fact for which there was evidence. *O'Dwyer v Irish Exporters and Importers Ltd H/C 1942, 2 ITC 251; [1943] IR 176.* (For another issue in this case see 38.9 above under Appeals etc.)

38.77 **Merchant bank: sale of investment.** The appellant company, a merchant bank, had a wholly-owned subsidiary investment holding company (TT), which in April 1967 acquired the two issued shares in Hummingbird Ltd, a property investment company, which subsequently made substantial capital profits on certain land investments (see 38.92 below) transferred to it by the appellant company in December 1967. In April 1976, the appellant company, which was experiencing trading difficulties, purchased the two shares in Hummingbird Ltd from TT for £2, and wound up the company, the liquidator paying over £675,000 to the appellant company. Held, reversing the Appeal Commissioners' decision, that the £675,000 was not part of the appellant company's trading profits. All the evidence suggested that the property from which the profits derived was acquired as a long-term investment, and the sale of the Hummingbird Ltd shares to the appellant company by TT could not be regarded as a normal trading transaction. The fact that the realised proceeds were used to defray trading losses was not sufficient to characterise the proceeds as trading profits. *Guinness and Mahon Ltd v Browne H/C 1985, TL 133.*

38.78 **Investment sales by company formed to provide credit for farmers, etc.** A company was established by statute to give credit to persons engaged in agriculture and facilitate borrowing by farmers on the security of their farms. It was accepted as carrying on a banking business for the purposes of *ITA 1918, s 36* (similar to the current *Sec 496*). It was assessed on the footing that its profits less losses on the realisation of its investments were part of its trading profits. In the two relevant years, there were respectively ten and six sales, mostly of Government securities. On appeal, the Commissioners found that the gains or losses were in an operation of business in carrying out a scheme of profit making, and part of the trading receipts. Held, the Commissioners had not misdirected themselves in law and their decision was one of fact for which there was evidence. *Agricultural Credit Corporation Ltd v Vale H/C 1935, 2 ITC 46; [1935] IR 681.*

38.79 **Training grant—whether capital or revenue receipt.** A training grant under *Industrial Development Act 1969, s 39* was held to be taxable as a revenue receipt. The moneys were paid with the object of relieving the company's wage bill, and did not affect the company's capital position. *Jacob International Ltd Inc v O'Cleirigh S/C 1985, TL 128; [1985] ILRM 651.*

38.80 **Ex gratia payment by government on recommendation of 1926 Irish Grants Committee.** In 1926 the UK Government set up an Irish Grants Committee to consider claims from British subjects who had suffered hardship or loss because of their support of the Government before the partition. A taxpayer carrying on business in Ireland claimed an award of £29,469 for losses sustained or profits lost and £11,437 for loss of goodwill. The Government, on the recommendation of the Committee, made an *ex gratia* payment of £14,000 in two instalments in the two years to 31 January 1930. The taxpayer was assessed on the footing that the instalments were trading receipts of the years in which received. Held, the payments were not trading receipts. *Robinson (trading as James Pim & Son) v Dolan H/C 1934, 2 ITC 25; [1935] IR 509.*

38.81 **Recovery under insurance against loss of profits.** A baker's premises were destroyed by fire in May 1942. He was able to continue trading in temporary premises but with reduced turnover and a rise in working costs. He was insured against this for one year, the premiums having been allowed in computing his profits. After negotiation, he received £1,300 in November 1944 under the policy, having incurred professional expenses of £130 in settling his claim. Held, the £1,300 less the £130 was a trading receipt and should be brought into account as at May 1943. *Corr v Larkin H/C 1949, 3 ITC 13; [1949] IR 399.*

38.82   **Gift to professional jockey.** The owner of the winner of the 1921 Irish Derby gave the winning jockey a present of £400. The evidence was that owners sometimes make presents to winning jockeys but this was the only present received by this jockey in the relevant period. Held, confirming the decision of the Commissioners, that the £400 was an assessable receipt of his vocation. *Wing v O'Connell S/C 1926, [1927] IR 84. (Note.* In the report the £400 is sometimes referred to as an 'emolument' or 'remuneration'. Under the law in force at the time, Schedule D, Case II covered employments as well as professions and vocations. The assessment was under Schedule D, Case II and it is thought that the jockey would have been so assessed under present-day legislation).

38.83   **Debt recoveries following death of trader—trade continued by executor.** A trader died and the executor continued to carry on the business on behalf of the residuary legatees. It was held that recoveries by the executor of debts allowed as bad in periods before the death could not be brought into the assessments for periods after the death. *CD v O'Sullivan H/C 1948, 2 ITC 422; [1949] IR 264.* (But see now *FA 1970, s 24.*)

SCHEDULE D, CASES I AND II—TRADE, BUSINESS, ETC.

38.84   **Services supplied without charge—notional receipt.** The appellant company had six subsidiaries and one associated company and operated as a holding company, although it had also been accepted by the Revenue as carrying on a trade of managing and financing the subsidiaries. The appellant company's expenses had previously been charged out to the subsidiaries, but in the two accounting periods in question substantial expenses were incurred and not charged out, thus creating losses. Also in those accounting periods the appellant company received dividends, net of tax credits at 30%, from two of the subsidiaries, and the sum of the dividends received and associated tax credits exceeded the trading loss for each period. The appellant company sought to treat this franked investment income as profits against which its trading losses could be set under *CTA s 25* (see 12.13 CORPORATION TAX). The Appeal Commissioner held that the appellant company's accounts for each period should be adjusted to include notional income in respect of the services provided, and concluded that the appropriate amount to be included was 10% of the income of the paying companies. Held, the decision that a notional amount in respect of services provided should be included in the appellant company's accounts was correct, but there was no evidence to support the basis of computation of the amount made by the Appeal Commissioner. The case was remitted to the Appeal Commissioner to be decided on the basis of its being a bona fide transaction in the ordinary course of business. *Belville Holdings Ltd v Cronin H/C 1985, TL 131.*

38.85   **Meaning of 'trade, business' etc.** The appellant company, which had previously traded by steam vessels out of Dublin, had, by 1920, sold all its boats, but continued to receive a substantial investment income and to make an annual payment of £3,000 under an earlier agreement relating to its previous passenger trade. It appealed against assessments for accounting periods following the sale of its boats, on the ground that it was not carrying on 'any trade or business or any undertaking of a similar character', including the holding of investments', within the charge to Corporation Profits Tax under *FA 1920, s 52(2)(a).* Citing in particular the 'various and elaborate operations ... directed towards the general benefit ... of the company and its shareholders' and the 'repetition of acts' represented by the making of the annual payments, the Court held that the company was carrying on a 'trade or business or undertaking of a similar character'. *City of Dublin Steampacket Co Ltd* *v Revenue Commissioners H/C 1926, 1 ITC 118; [1926] IR 436.* The same conclusion was reached on a later appeal regarding the company's income following its being put into liquidation. *City of Dublin Steampacket Co Ltd (in Liquidation) v Revenue Commissioners H/C 1930, 1 ITC 285; [1930] IR 217.*

38.86 **Meaning of 'trade, business', etc.** The appellant company, founded to make and maintain a railway line, had, under various acts and agreements, passed all the powers and privileges with regard to the line to a working company, and was at the time in question entitled only to a rent of £30,000 p.a. (with an entitlement to profit share which had not in fact been activated). All remaining receipts and expenditure related to investments or to the running of the company itself. A similar contention by the company to that in *City of Dublin Steampacket Co Ltd v Revenue Commissioners* (38.85 above) was again rejected by the Court. *CIR v Dublin and Kingstown Railway Co H/C 1926, 1 ITC 131; [1930] IR 317.*

38.87 **Employment or self-employment—insurance agent.** In a case in which it was held that the defendant was self-employed, the distinction between a contract of service and a contract for services was examined. The test was defined as 'Is the person who has engaged himself to perform these services performing them as a person in business on his own account?'. The nature and degree of control exercised by the employer was only one relevant consideration, others being e.g. whether the person performing the services provides his own equipment, or has his own helpers, what degree of financial risk he takes, what degree of responsibility for investment and management he has, and whether and how far he has an opportunity for profiting from sound management in the performance of his task. *McDermott v Loy H/C 1982, TL 118.*

38.88 **Employment or self-employment—Employment Office manager.** In a case in which the facts were unusual, it was held that the appellant, who was required to provide premises, staff, etc. under a written contract with the Minister for Social Welfare, was engaged under a contract for services and was therefore self-employed. The judgment contains a useful summary of the factors to be considered in distinguishing between a contract for services and one of service, and their application to a written contract. *O'Coindealbhain v Mooney H/C 21 April 1988.* (See also 38.17A above for a case concerning interest on overpaid tax consequent upon this decision.)

38.89 **Employment or self-employment—fishing crew.** The taxpayer was the skipper of a fishing vessel. No contract of service existed for crew members, who were normally re-engaged weekly by custom. Crew members were remunerated by means of a share of the proceeds of sale on an agreed basis, but did not share in losses. The Court had to determine whether an employer-employee relationship existed, and, if so, whether the taxpayer was guilty of failure to submit PAYE and PRSI returns. The Judge held that the skipper and crew members were partners in a joint adventure renewed each Monday morning. *Director of Public Prosecutions v McLoughlin H/C 25 February 1986.* (See also *Minister for Social Welfare v Griffiths H/C 14 February 1992*, where a similar decision was reached in relation to social welfare legislation.)

38.89A **Employment or self-employment—journalists.** In the winding-up of a newspaper company, certain persons who had worked for the newspaper applied to be treated as employees and hence as preferential creditors. All had been dealt with for tax purposes under Schedule D. The liquidator applied to the Court for a ruling as to whether they were employees for this purpose. Held, in the case of a sub-editor working two shifts a week and a regular columnist, that the contracts under which they worked were contracts of service, so that they were entitled to be treated as employees. In the case of another regular contributor, it was held that she was a freelancer who secured commissions in advance, and that she was not employed under a contract of service. *In re Sunday Tribune Ltd (in liquidation) H/C 26 September 1984.*

See also *Louth v Minister for Social Welfare H/C 9 April 1992* as regards deepsea dockers held to be employed under contracts of service. (A social welfare case.)

38.90 **Limited partner—share of losses—avoidance scheme.** The taxpayer was one of seven limited partners in a partnership, five of whom were also directors of the sole general partner, Southern Metropole Hotels Co Ltd ('the company'). Registration of the limited partnership was not in accordance with the *Limited Partnerships Act 1907*, but the finding of fact by the Appeal Commissioners was that the trade was carried on in partnership. Each limited partner contributed £50 as capital in the partnership. The company entered into a five-year agreement with the partnership whereby the company lent money to the partnership, which the partnership used to buy plant and machinery. This was then let to the company at 10% of cost per annum, the partnership being responsible for wear and tear. In the first year the partnership borrowed £30,000, its leasing income was £222 and the amount claimed for wear and tear under *ITA s 241(5)* was £13,000. The taxpayer's claim to relief for his share of the losses (against his personal income), which was allowed by the Appeal Commissioners, was challenged by the Revenue on the grounds that the agreement had no commercial reality and was contrived entirely for its tax advantage. Held, the scheme was not of so extreme a character as to be regarded as having no commercial reality, and it could be regarded as a trading transaction qualifying for the relief sought. *McCarthaigh v Daly H/C 1985, TL 127;* [*1986*] *ILRM 116.* See now 22.5 LOSSES as regards anti-avoidance legislation.

38.91 **Sale of undeveloped land purchased for development—whether within Schedule D, Case I.** A company was set up to purchase, develop and sell land. The owners had previously built houses for sale on land not owned by them. After land had been purchased by the company, the owners had a disagreement and decided not to proceed with development. The land was accordingly sold. Held, upholding an appeal against an assessment under Schedule D, Case I, the transaction was an isolated one by a company which had not commenced any trade and which did not buy the land with the intention of selling it undeveloped. There was no evidence of an adventure in the nature of trade. *Spa Ltd v O'hArgain H/C 1974.*

38.92 **Sale of land during development—whether within Schedule D, Case I.** The appellant company acquired land on which it commenced development with a view to letting. The property was sold during development, and the Revenue assessed the profits under Schedule D, Case I, following *F(MP)A 1968, s 17.* Held, that *F(MP)A 1968, s 17* did not apply, as the entire interest was sold, and that the Appeal Commissioners finding that there was no adventure in the nature of trade should stand. *Mara v Hummingbird Ltd S/C 1977, TL 114.*

38.93 **Farmland rezoned for development—whether sale within Schedule D, Case I.** A land development company acquired farmland unsuitable for development, which it let to a participator until it commenced farming on the land on its own account. A subsequent rezoning rendered the land suitable for development, and the land was transferred to the parent company. Held, there was evidence that the farmland was purchased without any intention to develop the land as building land, but that the company commenced to trade in the land at the time that, following the rezoning, it decided to exploit the land as development land. *O'hArgain v Beechpark Estates Ltd H/C 1979, TL 116.*

38.94 **Purchase and resale of whiskey in bond.** A publican had for many years bought considerable quantities of whiskey in bond from a distillery company. Apart from a small amount used in his public house, he resold it to the distillery after four or five years at varying terms, but generally at cost plus an amount for 'interest'. He was free to sell the whiskey to others but did not do so. On appeal, the Commissioners found that the transactions constituted the carrying on of a business for excess profits duty purposes and their decision was upheld. *Representatives of P J McCall, dec'd. v CIR KB (I) 1923, 1 ITC 31; 4 ATC 522.*

38.95 **Statutory body to operate insurance scheme.** The appellant was a Board set up by statute to carry into effect a scheme for the compulsory insurance of livestock shipped to Britain. The shippers paid levies to the Board to form a Fund out of which were to be met claims under the scheme, the Board's expenses and 'no other moneys'. The Board appealed against Case I assessments on its surpluses. It was conceded for the Board that it was carrying on a trade, but it was contended that its receipts were earmarked to meet its expenses and claims on it, and that the relevant Act did not contemplate that it was a profit-making business. Held, applying, *inter alia, Mersey Docks and Harbour Board v Lucas* (a UK case reported at *1 TC 385*), and dismissing the appeal, that the provision in the Act as to the application of its receipts did not preclude assessment of its surpluses. (Whether there should be any provision for its unexpired risks was not an issue before the court.) *The Exported Live Stock (Insurance) Board v Carroll S/C 1951, 3 ITC 67; [1951] IR 286.*

38.96 **Changes in trade leading to new trade.** A partnership trading as retail fuel merchants acquired interests in coal-bearing land and commenced the production of coal, retaining some of their old customers but thereafter supplying the coal produced mainly to wholesalers and to certain large public concerns. Held that a new trade was set up when coal production commenced. *O'Loan v M J Noone & Co H/C 1948, 2 ITC 430; [1949] IR 171.*

38.97 **Bookmaker—profits from sweepstakes on English races—whether trading receipts.** A bookmaker whose activities included the purchase of Irish Hospitals Sweepstakes tickets relating to races run in both Ireland and England contended that the profits from tickets relating to English races were from private gambling, and not subject to tax, as he did not attend meetings and could not influence the odds. Held, the profits were correctly assessed under Schedule D, Case I. Distinguishing the UK case *Graham v Green K/B 1925, 9 TC 309*, the existence of a bookmaking business was sufficient to require the inclusion of all such profits as trading income. *HH v Forbes S/C 1977, TL 113.*

38.98 **Banking company—Government securities—whether trade under Schedule D, Case I.** The respondent company was a subsidiary of a joint stock bank and engaged in hire-purchase, credit finance and leasing. In order to meet minimum liquidity requirements, Government stocks were purchased and held to maturity, but the company did not otherwise deal in stocks and shares although it had power to do so. The Revenue sought to tax realised gains, treated by the company as exempt capital gains, of £213,375 in 1977 and £922,300 in 1978 as arising from a trade of dealing in securities assessable under Schedule D, Case I. Held, reversing the decisions in the lower courts, that the realised gains were part of the company's trading profits and chargeable to corporation tax. *Browne v Bank of Ireland Finance Ltd S/C 8 February 1991.*

SCHEDULE D, CASES I AND II—MISCELLANEOUS

38.99 **Current cost accounting—whether acceptable for tax purposes.** The High Court upheld the decision of the Appeal Commissioners that accounts for tax purposes are to be prepared on the historical cost accounting convention, and that the current cost accounting convention was not applicable. *Carroll Industries plc and P J Carroll and Co Ltd v O'Culachain H/C 2 December 1988.*

38.100 **Stallion fees.** The appellant company owned a stallion, and mares were brought for service and kept on the farm for about four months, their keep being paid for. Held, that the profits from stallion fees did not accrue from the occupation of farm lands, charged under Schedule B, but from a trade assessable under Schedule D. *Cloghran Stud Farm v Birch S/C 1935, 2 ITC 65; [1936] IR 1.*

38.101 **Land transaction—application of F(MP)A 1968, s 18.** A company in liquidation sold to a director its interest in a lease it had previously acquired from another director at a rent of IR£2,500 without fine or premium. It contended that, under *F(MP)A 1968, s 18*, the profit on disposal of the lease fell to be computed by reference to a deemed acquisition cost based on the capitalised value of the rent. Held, the profit was to be computed on ordinary principles of commercial accounting. *F(MP)A 1968, s 18(2)(b)* did not require a value to be substituted for cost overriding such principles. The assessment must be made on a calculation of the difference between the amount (if any) expended on acquisition of the lease and the amount expended on its disposal, with any appropriate and permissible deductions and additions. *Cronin v Cork and County Property Co Ltd S/C 18 December 1986.*

38.102 A similar decision was reached in another case where a company acquired a lease of land from a fellow subsidiary and the fee simple, with a declaration of merger, from the parent company, and claimed a deduction in its trading accounts based on the market value of the rent reserved in the lease. *O'Connlain v Belvedere Estates Ltd S/C 28 July 1988.*

38.102A Whether rental income falls within Schedule D, Case I. The taxpayer let unfurnished a shop and a number of flats, with no provision of services. She negotiated the lettings and supervised the properties herself. Held, that the letting did not amount to the carrying on of a trade. (The substantive issue was the taxpayer's entitlement to earned income relief.) *Pairceir v E M H/C 1971, TL 107.*

38.103 Grass-cutting rights on military land—whether profits assessable under Schedule D, Case I. A company obtained grass-cutting rights over Government land 'subject to military use of the land'. Assessments for the years 1962/63 to 1969/70 inclusive under Schedule D, Case I on profits from processing the cuttings into grass meal were upheld. The company's contention that the assessments should have been under Schedule B up to 1968/69, and that the profits were exempt for 1969/70 under *FA 1969, s 18*, were rejected on the grounds that the predominant use of the land was military, and that for the purposes of Schedule B and *FA 1969, s 18* there could only be one occupier, here the Government. *O'Conaill v Z Ltd S/C 1976, TL 111; [1982] ILRM 451.*

38.104 Illegal trading. A turf commission agent was assessed on his profits from promoting for charity two large sweepstakes. Under the law then in force, the carrying on of the sweepstakes was a criminal offence, although they were extensively advertised and the State took no steps against them. The S/C reversing the decision of the H/C, held the profits were not assessable. Unless expressly authorised, the Revenue cannot tax profits from activities declared by the State to be unlawful. *Hayes v Duggan S/C 1928, 1 ITC 269; [1929] IR 406, 413.* See now 32.4 SCHEDULE D, CASE IV.

38.105 The appellant's trade consisted of the placing of automatic slot machines in public houses, shops and clubs. In a previous appeal, which had not proceeded to the High Court because of a technicality, the Circuit Judge had determined that the trade was illegal. Held that (i) it was not open to the taxpayer, in support of his appeal, to prove that the trade was illegal, but that (ii) where, as in this case, the Revenue knew the trade was illegal when the assessments were made, the assessments were invalid, following *Hayes v Duggan* (38.104 above). *Collins v Mulvey H/C 1955, 3 ITC 151; [1956] IR 233.* See now 32.4 SCHEDULE D, CASE IV.

38.106 The taxpayers set up an enterprise called Investment International to carry on a chain letter scheme. In the absence of accounts, the inspector raised estimated assessments, against which appeals were made on the grounds that the scheme was illegal. Held, the scheme was illegal and, following *Hayes v Duggan* (38.104 above), the profits could not be assessed. *McMahon v Howard and Patwell H/C 1985.* See now 32.4 SCHEDULE D, CASE IV.

38.107 Tickets issued by shipping company paid for in advance abroad. To facilitate the emigration of Irish citizens to America, a UK shipping company whose activities included carrying on business in Ireland through an Irish branch office, and with agents in America, operated a scheme under which someone in America, e.g. a relative of a would-be emigrant, could purchase a 'Prepaid Certificate' in America which entitled the would-be emigrant to a ticket from the company's Irish agents for the journey to America. If the would-be emigrant did not take up a ticket, the American purchaser of the Certificate was refunded his money, less a cancellation fee. The S/C held that the passenger's ticket was not issued under an Irish contract and hence, applying a *dictum* of Cave L C in *Maclaine v Eccott, 10 TC 481* (a UK case), there was no liability to Irish tax on the profit from the issue of the ticket. *Cunard Steamship Co Ltd v Herlihy S/C 1931, 1 ITC 373; [1931] IR 287, 307.*

38.108 **Trade managed abroad—no control from RI.** The trustees of a will gave an Australian company power of attorney to manage a sheep-farming business in Australia forming part of the estate. Yearly and quarterly accounts were sent to the trustees and the profits regularly remitted to them less a percentage which they directed to be carried to reserve. The trustees and beneficiaries, all of whom resided in Ireland or the UK, did not interfere in any way in the management of the business. The trustees were assessed under Case I on the profits. Held, reversing the decision of the Commissioners, there was no liability under Case I. *Trustees of Ferguson (dec'd) v Donovan S/C 1927, 1 ITC 214; [1929] IR 489.*

38.109 **Scientific research expenditure—exploration.** A claim for relief under *Sec 244* (as expenditure on scientific research) in respect of expenditure on exploring and drilling for oil was allowed. The clear wording of the proviso to *Sec 244(3)* granted allowances for such expenditure, and the further provisions of *Sec 245*, relating to the situation where exploration work proved fruitful, were not relevant. *Texaco Ireland Ltd v Murphy S/C 1991, [1992] ILRM 304.* See 30.23 SCHEDULE D, CASES I AND II. For a subsequent decision relating to interest on tax paid pending appeal, see 38.11A above.

38.110 **Stock relief—payments on account.** A company engaged in the production of prefabricated type houses and buildings normally required a 15% deposit on execution of a contract for supply of a building. The High Court, reversing the Circuit Judge's finding, held that the deposits represented payments on account in respect of trading stock, and hence fell to reduce the amount on which stock relief was available under *FA 1975, s 31* (see 18.8 FARMING). *O'Laoghaire v Avonree Buildings Ltd H/C 1984, TL 119; [1984] ILRM 196.* See also 30.28 SCHEDULE D, CASES I AND II.

38.111 **Stock relief—company with several trades.** A company carried on a number of different activities. If all the activities were taken together, stock relief under *FA 1975, s 31(1)(9)* was not due, but the company claimed the relief for the two individual trades of millers and hardware. The Judge held, reversing the finding of the Circuit Court, that a company may be held to carry on different trades for the purposes of tax, whether or not the different activities were taken on separately, and that it was a question of fact for the Circuit Court Judge to decide whether the company was carrying on a number of separate trades. On the facts, the judge held that two of the activities (milling and the licensed trade) were separate trades and remitted the case to the Appeal Commissioner for a decision on the other activities (including hardware). *Re P McElligott & Sons Ltd H/C 1984, [1985] ILRM 210.*

38.112 **Stock relief—whether company engaged in manufacturing trade.** A company imported components for agricultural machinery, purchased local materials, assembled the machines and then sold them to farmers and agricultural contractors. Approximately 25% of the company's goods were sold direct to farmers, 20% direct to dealers and 55% to farmers with the dealer acting as an intermediary. The company claimed stock relief under *FA 1975, s 31*, either on the basis of carrying on a manufacturing trade, or on the sale of plant and machinery to farmers. In the High Court it was held, confirming the decision of the Circuit Court, that the company's operations were assembly and not manufacture, and that the intervention of an intermediary denied the character of direct sales to farmers for a substantial part of the turnover, but the Supreme Court reversed the decision, finding that the company's operations did amount to manufacture (and accordingly making no finding on the second point). Applying the tests referred to in *McCann Ltd v O'Culachain* (38.38 above), an ordinary adequately informed person would attribute the word 'manufacture' to the process carried on by the company. *Irish Agricultural Machinery Ltd v O'Culachain S/C 1989, [1990] IR 535.*

38.113 Exchange losses. In 1947 an American corporation, with a world-wide trade, commenced trading through an Irish branch. Separate accounts were made up for the branch to 31 December and, immediately after the end of each year, the Irish auditors were told the cost in dollars of goods sent to the branch from America in the year, with their sterling equivalent at the year end rate, and similarly as regards the proportion of the corporation's head office, etc. expenses charged out to the branch. The aggregate amounts so notified for the two years to 31 December 1948 were $24,300 (sterling equivalent £6,075). The $24,300 was not remitted to America. In the branch accounts the £6,075 was charged to profits, allowed as a deduction in arriving at its profits for tax and shown in the Balance Sheet as the balance of a 'Home Office Current Account'. Sterling was devalued on 19 September 1949, and in the 1949 accounts the £6,075 was revalued at the 19 September rate, thus increasing it by £2,603. The company's claim to deduct this £2,603 in computing its 1949 profits was refused. The deductions in the 1947 and 1948 computations concluded the matter. *Revenue Commissioners v L & Co S/C 1956, 3 ITC 205.*

38.114 Statutory reduction of capital in company—whether consequent fall in value of bank's investments allowable. A bank held stocks in a railway; it was common ground that any profit or loss on the realisation of these stocks should be brought into the computation of its profits. The stocks were reduced by the *Irish Railways Act 1933*, holders receiving new stock certificates in place of the old. The bank's claim to deduct the consequent fall in the market value of its investments in the railway company was refused. There had been no realisation or conversion of an investment. *Davis v Hibernian Bank Ltd S/C 1936, 2 ITC 111.*

38.115 Whether unsold investments may be valued as stock-in-trade. The appellant was a company which dealt in stocks and shares, any profits or losses on its sales entering into its trading profits for assessment. It was assessed on the basis that its unsold investments should be brought in at their cost. The company claimed that, as dealt with in its accounts, they should be brought in at cost or market value if lower. The H/C upheld the assessments, applying *Davis v Hibernian Bank Ltd*, see 38.114 above, and finding no precedent, or evidence of usual accountancy practice, to support the company's contention. *A B Ltd v Mac Giolla Riogh H/C 1960, 3 ITC 301.*

38.116 Sale of investments earmarked for reserve fund. Under a private Act of Parliament a gas company was empowered, but not obliged, to set up a dividend equalisation fund. In fact it did so, earmarking investments to form the fund. A deduction for the loss on realising some of the investments was refused as one not connected with, or arising out of, its trade (*Sec 61(e)*); the Act did not impose a duty on the company to create the fund. *Alliance & Dublin Consumers' Gas Co v Davis H/C 1926, 1 ITC 114; [1926] IR 372.*

38.117 Accounts made up for both six and twelve-monthly periods. In an excess corporation profits tax case, a company had, in addition to normal twelve-month accounts, produced six-month accounts at the half and full-year stages. The appeal turned on whether the provisions of *FA 1920, s 54* applied so that, accounts having been produced for periods less than twelve months, it fell to the Revenue Commissioners to determine the accounting periods for taxation purposes. Held that the fact that twelve-month accounts had been made up precluded the operation of the section to impose liability by reference to any shorter or longer period. *Revenue Commissioners v R Hilliard and Sons Ltd S/C 1948, 2 ITC 410.* (*Note.* The provisions of *CTA, s 9* now impose different requirements for the determination of accounting periods.)

38.118 Flour miller and baker—flour milling partly discontinued—whether trade ceased. A company carried on business as flour millers (at two mills) and bread bakers, about half of the flour it milled being used at its bakeries. After making losses, the mills were closed in August 1922, but one was re-opened in April 1923, mainly to supply the bakeries. The Special Commissioners' decision that it had carried on a single trade throughout was upheld as one of fact for which there was evidence. *Bolands Ltd v Davis H/C 1924, 1 ITC 91.*

38.119 'Occupation by a dealer in cattle'—scope of 'cattle'. In a case involving liability under *Sec 78* (now replaced by *FA 1969, s 19*), it was held that the reference in that section to '. . . occupation by a dealer in cattle . . .' referred only to occupation by a dealer in bovine animals, and not by a dealer in sheep or pigs. *De Brun v Kiernan S/C 1981, TL 117;* [*1982*] *ILRM 13.*

SCHEDULE D, CASE III

38.120 Computation of income from different sources treated as one source. The taxpayer had for several years been in receipt of UK interest and dividends, and in the year in question commenced trading in the UK as an insurance underwriter. He was assessed on the preceding year basis in respect of the interest, etc. and on the Schedule D, Case I commencement basis in respect of the underwriting profits, the sum of the amounts so calculated being assessed under Schedule D, Case III. He appealed on the ground that (what is now) *Sec 75* directed that all income under Case III be treated as arising from one source, so that the preceding year basis must be applied to all his income assessable under that Case. Held, upholding the appeal, that the clear direction of (what is now) *Sec 75* took precedence over the provisions of (what is now) *6 Sch Pt III* for an alternative basis of assessment in respect of certain UK possessions. *O'Conaill v R H/C 1955, 3 ITC 167;* [*1956*] *IR 97.*

38.121 Interest received assessable without deduction for interest paid. The appellant County Council was held to be liable under Schedule D, Case III on bank interest received with no allowance for interest paid (in full to the Commissioners of Public Works and others) by various Rural District Councils and Boards of Guardians of Poor Law Unions within the County. *Phillips v Limerick County Council H/C 1925, 1 ITC 96;* [*1925*] *2 IR 139.*

38.122 Bank interest arising during liquidation. Interest credited to a deposit account, into which the liquidator of a company had paid receipts from disposing of the assets, was held to have been properly assessed under Case III. *Irish Provident Assurance Co Ltd (in Liquidation) v Kavanagh S/C 1924, 1 ITC 52;* [*1930*] *IR 231; 4 ATC 115.*

38.123 Voluntary pension from overseas employment. The taxpayer's wife had been managing director of an English family company carrying on business in England. Following her resignation (and eventually becoming resident in RI), the company, under a series of resolutions, made annual payments to her of varying amounts. Held, the payments were correctly assessed as foreign possessions under Schedule D, Case III, since they fell within (what is now) *Sec 225* as voluntary pensions. Certain exceptional payments were excluded. *McHugh v A H/C 1959, 3 ITC 257;* [*1958*] *IR 142.*

38.124 **Foreign pensions.** The taxpayer, resident in RI at the relevant time, was in receipt of a UK National Insurance Retirement Pension in respect of both his own contributions and those of his wife, based partly on voluntary contributions made while resident in RI. He appealed against assessments on the pension payments under Schedule D, Case III, on the ground (inter alia) that there was no related foreign possession as required under that case, since the payments arose from no legal document and were subject to restrictions. Held, the pensions were correctly assessed as arising from foreign possessions. *Forbes v Dundon H/C 1964, 3 ITC 365; [1964] IR 447.*

38.125 **Foreign pension—assignment to company.** On 4 April 1961, C assigned his UK pension to C Ltd, a private company, for £2,805. He did not notify his former employer of the assignment, but continued to receive the pension, handing over the cheques to C Ltd. He claimed that there was a cessation for Schedule D, Case III in 1960/61, so that the assessments for that and the following year should be on the actual rather than the preceding year basis. The Appeal Commissioner took the view that there had been a valid equitable assignment of C's pension to C Ltd on 4 April 1961, and that C's subsequent receipt of the pension had been as trustee for C Ltd. His decision was upheld in the High Court. *Cronin v C H/C 1968, TL 106.*

38.126 **Advance payment of rent—whether a premium.** In an Irish case, the taxpayer company, resident in Ireland, let premises in the UK to a UK company for seven years from 6 April 1950. The rent was expressed to be £625 per annum payable as to £3,000 in advance on signature of the lease and as to the balance by seven annual payments of £196 8s 6d commencing on 5 April 1951. The £3,000 was held to be income arising from overseas possessions for the purposes of Schedule D, Case III, rejecting the contention that it was a premium or fine and capital. *O'Sullivan v P Ltd H/C 1962, 3 ITC 355.*

SCHEDULE D, CASE IV

38.127 **River Conservancy Board surplus.** The receipts of a statutory river conservancy board comprised mainly rates but included also receipts from fishing licences, fines and bank interest. In the relevant years its receipts exceeded its expenses, and it was assessed under Case VI (now Case IV) on the proportion of this surplus which its receipts other than rates bore to its total receipts. Its appeal against the assessments was allowed. It was a rating authority empowered to levy rates to cover its expenditure. If, by faulty estimation, the rates it levied exceeded its expenditure less its 'other receipts', the overall excess was available to reduce future rates and was not liable to income tax. *Moville District of Conservators v Ua Clothasaigh S/C 1949, 3 ITC 1; [1950] IR 301.*

38.128 **Statutory body for registration of veterinary surgeons.** A statutory body whose functions included the maintenance of a register of veterinary surgeons was assessed under Case VI (now Case IV) on the excess of its receipts (registration fees and proceeds of sales of register) over its expenditure. Its appeal against the assessment was allowed. Its activities were not analogous to carrying on a trade and, applying a *dictum* of Lord Dunedin in *Leeming v Jones*, a UK case (reported at *15 TC 333*), its surplus was not income. *The Veterinary Council v Corr H/C 1950, 3 ITC 59; [1953] IR 12.*

38.129 **Statutory body—whether levies received liable to tax.** The Racing Board is a statutory body with two sources of income, the operation of the totalisator (agreed to be within Schedule D, Case I) and a levy on on-course betting (the subject of the appeal). It was held that the levy was not liable to tax. While a public body may be liable to tax on moneys received for services provided for the public, there can be no basis for taxing the receipts from pure taxation as constituting something analogous to a trade. The Board is enabled to raise funds by a levy on bookmakers to whom it supplies no direct service, and to apply the moneys so raised for public purposes. *The Racing Board v O'Culachain H/C 27 April 1988.*

38.130 Ex gratia payment for services. The taxpayer, general manager of Y Ltd, gave advice and assistance to X Ltd (with the permission of Y Ltd). There was no agreement that he would be remunerated for his services. X Ltd was then dissolved by statute and a new company Z Ltd was set up, with the taxpayer as its general manager. Shortly before its dissolution X Ltd made an *ex gratia* payment to the taxpayer which was assessed on him under Case VI (now Case IV). His appeal against the assessment was allowed; the payment to him was a personal testimonial. *McGarry v EF H/C 1953, 3 ITC 103; [1954] IR 64.* (*Note.* An alternative contention for the Revenue that the payment was an emolument of an office or employment held by the taxpayer under X Ltd was not pursued.)

38.131 Fees received after discontinuance. A barrister, who had been assessed on a receipts basis under *FA 1970, s 20*, arranged for fees due prior to his appointment to the bench to be paid to a company in which he had no interest though the entire shareholding was held by his two sons and a son-in-law. Following the decision in *Dolan v K* (see 38.136) the Judge held that the fact that the income was not received directly by the taxpayer did not exempt it from being assessed on him as fees received after discontinuance under *FA 1970, s 20. O'Coindealbhain v Gannon H/C, [1986] IR 154.*

SCHEDULE D, CASE V

38.132 Letting fees and legal expenses were incurred by a company in securing tenants for a building it had constructed and which it intended to let. Held, such fees and expenses were costs of management of the premises constituting an expense of the transactions under which the rents were received. They were thus allowable under *Sec 81(5)(d). Stephen Court Ltd v Browne H/C 1984, T/L 120; [1984] ILRM 231.*

SCHEDULE E AND PAYE—GENERAL

38.133 Voluntary payment on retirement. The president of a college retired after 31 years' service and the governing body granted him, in addition to his maximum pension, etc. entitlements, an additional sum of £1,000 'on account of a great number of services unrewarded, as expressed in a labour of lengthened overtime work during the past seven or more years, and the limited statutory pension to which he is entitled'. The Special Commissioners dismissed an assessment on the £1,000, holding it was a personal gift. Their decision was upheld as one of fact for which there was evidence. *Mulvey v Coffey H/C 1942, 2 ITC 239; [1942] IR 277.*

38.134 Payments under will to manage properties—whether remuneration. Under his father's will, a taxpayer received 10% of certain rents 'so long as (he) continues to manage and look after' the property. He was assessed on the amounts received as remuneration from an employment. Held, the payments were conditional gifts under the will and did not arise from an employment. *O'Reilly v Casey S/C 1942, 2 ITC 220; [1942] IR 378.*

38.135 Children's contributory pension—whether income of widow to whom payable. Under the *Garda Siochana Pensions Order 1981 (SI 1981 No 199)* a children's contributory pension may be payable with the widow's pension (and in certain cases separately therefrom) for the benefit of the children. Held, the children's pension is the beneficial property of the children in respect of whom it is payable, and is thus not assessable as the personal income of the widow to whom it is payable. *O'Coindealbhain v O'Carroll H/C 9 November 1988.*

38.136 Professed nun employed as school teacher. A professed nun employed as a school teacher, but bound by Constitutions of her Order to hand over her earnings to the Order, was held to have been correctly assessed under Schedule E on the earnings. *Dolan v K S/C 1943, 2 ITC 280; [1944] IR 470.*

38.137 Director resident overseas—Schedule E. The appellant, resident abroad throughout the relevant period, was a director of a company incorporated, and carrying on trade, in RI, although managed, controlled and resident in France. None of the duties of his office were carried on in RI. Held, the office was nevertheless 'within RI' and emoluments therefrom thus taxable under the Schedule E provisions. *Tipping v Jeancard H/C 1947, 2 ITC 360; [1948] IR 233.*

38.138 Rent of house occupied by employee paid by employer. A company arranged with the Midleton Urban District Council that the Council would provide houses to be let to the company's employees. An employee of the company occupied one of the houses, the company paying the rent for him. He was required by the terms of his employment to live in Midleton but not in any particular house, whether or not provided by the Council. Schedule E assessments on him, in which the rent paid for him was treated as part of his emoluments, were upheld, applying *Hartland v Diggines*, a UK case (*10 TC 247*). *Connolly v McNamara H/C 1960, 3 ITC 341.*

38.139 Emoluments received after year in which earned. A taxpayer was employed as part-time solicitor by a Harbour Board, his remuneration to be his taxed costs, billed half-yearly. In the event, the employment lasted only from December 1924 to May 1925 and he presented two Bills of Costs in July 1925, covering the whole period of employment and including profit costs of £422 referable to the work done in 1924/25. Held in his appeal against his Schedule E assessment for 1924/25, that the £422 was assessable for that year as the amount earned in that year, rejecting the argument that the assessment could not include an amount not received in that year. *MacKeown v Roe H/C 1927, 1 ITC 206; [1928] IR 195.*

38.140 Remuneration assessed under Schedule E; tax accounted for under PAYE when remuneration paid in subsequent year. A Schedule E assessment for 1962/63 had been made in November 1964 on the taxpayer, a company director, bringing out tax due of £591. The remuneration assessed included a bonus not paid until December 1964, when tax of £646 was accounted for under PAYE. In proceedings taken by the Revenue to recover the tax of £591 with interest, it was held that the assessment had been correctly made. *Bedford v Hannon H/C 1968, TL 105.*

38.141 PAYE—emoluments paid on behalf of employer—liability of payer to account for income tax and PRSI contributions. The defendants, who carried on business in partnership, formed a limited company to provide overseas consultancy services. There was some confusion between the affairs of the two entities, but for the period in question the wages of the limited company's employees were paid by the partnership, on the understanding that the partnership would be reimbursed. The Collector General sought payment from the partnership of income tax (under PAYE) and PRSI contributions in respect of the employees concerned. Judgment was given against the defendants in relation to the income tax (and interest thereon), as the words 'employer' and 'employee' in the relevant regulations (SI 1960/28) were defined as meaning 'any person paying emoluments' and 'any person in receipt of emoluments', so that the partnership, in paying the wages, was obliged to make the appropriate deductions and account for the sums so deducted. As regards the PRSI contributions, there were no such extended definitions in the relevant legislation, so that there was sufficient substance in the defence that the partnership was merely acting as paymaster, and making periodical loans of the amounts paid to persons in reality employed by the limited company, for that part of the claim to be remitted for plenary hearing. *Hearne v J A Kenny & Partners H/C 24 June 1988.*

38.142 **PAYE regulations—defamation—whether procedure unconstitutional.** The Revenue had issued an enforcement notice in respect of unpaid PAYE against the plaintiff, a practising solicitor. He sought a declaration that the operation of *ITA 1967, ss 126, 129, 131 and 485* was unconstitutional and claimed damages on the basis that the enforcement notice had been incorrectly issued, as he had paid the tax concerned. The Judge awarded damages totalling £10,500 for defamation following the publication of the enforcement notice, but held that no issues as to the infringement of constitutional rights arose. *Kennedy v Hearne and others S/C 15 March 1988.*

SCHEDULE E—EXPENDITURE

38.143 **General expenses.** In each of two cases, an engineer claimed a deduction from his emoluments assessable under Schedule E in respect of the cost of

   (i)   subscriptions to professional associations,

   (ii)   renewals of books and journals,

   (iii)   protective clothing,

   (iv)   replacing equipment,

   (v)   entertainment of builders and business callers, and

   (vi)   travelling expenses not reimbursed by the employer,

and in one case

   (vii)   home telephone, and

   (viii)   proportion of maid's wages.

Held, only items (iii) and (iv) were properly allowable, as the remaining items were not 'exclusively' incurred in performance of the duties of the respective offices as required by (what is now) *2 Sch 3. O'Broin v Mac Giolla Meidhre; O'Broin v Pigott H/C 1957, 3 ITC 235; [1957] 159 IR 98.*

38.144 The taxpayer, an officer in the Defence Forces, claimed as a deduction from emoluments taxable under Schedule E

   (i)   room rent in the Officer's Mess,

   (ii)   extra cost of messing,

   (iii)   travelling expenses between home and quarters, and

   (iv)   gratuities to batman.

Held, the gratuities to batman were not wholly, exclusively and necessarily incurred in the performance of his duties, particularly as there was no legal obligation to pay them, and so failed the test under (what is now) *2 Sch 3.* The remaining expenses had already been dismissed on similar grounds by the Circuit Judge. *Kelly v H H/C 1961, 3 ITC 351; [1964] IR 488.*

38.145 **Director's travelling expenses.** A director of five companies incurred travelling expenses in carrying out his duties, the major part of which was reimbursed to him. There was evidence that the balance would have been reimbursed had he so requested. He claimed the balance as a deduction from his emoluments. Held, no allowance was due, as there was no proof that he was obliged to defray the expenses out of his emoluments. *MacDabheid v Carroll H/C 1978, TL 115.*

38.146 **Doctor's travelling expenses.** A doctor employed part-time as a senior house officer in a general hospital claimed a deduction from her emoluments in respect of travelling expenses between her home and the hospital following her being called to the hospital by telephone. She attended the hospital on weekday mornings, but was required always to be available on call when not on duty (or to arrange for a replacement). She could have to give advice and instructions by telephone before returning to the hospital, and considered herself medically responsible for the patient even before her arrival at the hospital. Held, following the UK case of *Pook v Owen, 45 TC 571*, in the very peculiar and exceptional circumstances, the expenses were allowable. As contended for the taxpayer, it was an essential feature of the employment to provide advice over the telephone, and the duties commenced from the time at which she was first contacted by the hospital. *FG v O'Coindealbhain H/C 1985.*

38.147 **Travelling expenses between home and place of employment.** The taxpayer, a schoolteacher, claimed a deduction from his emoluments taxable under Schedule E in respect of the costs of a pony and trap used to convey him between home and school, a distance of some five miles. He claimed that he could not obtain a suitable residence nearer the school, and that his physical condition did not permit him to walk or cycle the journey. Held, the expenditure was neither 'wholly and exclusively' nor 'necessarily' incurred in the performance of his duties, and was thus prohibited as a deduction. *Phillips v Keane H/C 1925, 1 ITC 69; [1925] 2 IR 48.*

SETTLEMENTS

38.148 **Existence of trust: outgoings of residence provided for.** Under the terms of a will, a taxpayer was entitled to the use and occupation of Slane Castle, and to receive a sum not exceeding £3,500 per annum for its maintenance and upkeep other than repairs. Taking one year with another she spent this amount on this maintenance and upkeep. Held, reversing the Special Commissioners' decision, that the £3,500 per annum received by her was impressed in her hands with a trust under which it was to be expended on the property, and was not part of her income for super-tax purposes. *Conyngham (Marchioness) v Revenue Commissioners S/C 1928, 1 ITC 259.*

38.149 **Whether Partnership Deed, etc. a settlement.** On 29 March 1944 a taxpayer carrying on a business as cafe proprietor entered into a Deed of Partnership with three of his sons, hitherto full-time employees in the business, and his mother-in-law, aged 80, who took no part in the business. The Deed gave him extensive powers which conferred upon him a commanding position in the partnership and the conduct of its business. On 3 April 1944 the mother-in-law by Deed irrevocably assigned her interest in the partnership to the taxpayer in trust for his other four children. The partnership assessments for 1944/45 and 1945/46, at the beginning of which all seven children were unmarried minors, were on the footing that the whole of the income was income of the father. On appeal, the Special Commissioner found that the partnership was a *bona fide* commercial transaction; that the two Deeds were separate and not part of a scheme; and that the partnership income should be treated as income of the persons entitled to it under the two Deeds. His decision was upheld by a majority of the S/C, reversing the decision of the H/C. The Revenue relied on *FA 1922, s 20(1)(a)* (similar to *Sec 438*) as regards the income of the children who became partners; and on *FA 1937, s 2* (similar to *Sec 443 et seq.*) as regards the income of all seven. Although the father's dominating position might enable him effectively to terminate the partnership, that would not enable him to obtain the beneficial ownership of income treated as that of the other partners by virtue of *ITA 1918, s 20* (similar to *Sec 26*). The Deed of Partnership in itself was not a settlement and the Commissioner's finding that the two Deeds were not an arrangement was one of fact and conclusive. *O'Dwyer v Cafolla & Co S/C 1948, 2 ITC 374; [1949] IR 210.*

38.150 Whether Deed of Appointment a settlement. The appeal related to income under a settlement appointed, pursuant to a power in the settlement, to a minor unmarried daughter of the settlor, and the issue was whether the Deed of Appointment was a settlement for the purposes of the relevant legislation (similar to *Sec 438 et seq.*). It was held that the appointment was a settlement. *E G v Mac Shamhrain H/C 1957, 3 ITC 217;* [*1958*] *IR 288.*

38.151 Sec 438—settlement income deemed income of settlor. In a case in which the facts are special, it was held (by a majority decision) that income arising in a settlement, which was to be applied to certain charitable and religious purposes for as long as the settlor was a member of a religious Order, was income of the settlor under the predecessor of *Sec 438*. *Hughes v Smyth H/C 1932, 1 ITC 418.*

38.152 Religious order—right to income under deed of covenant. Three members of a religious order entered into a deed of covenant under which they covenanted to pay sums to their Prior for the benefit of each of 17 other members of the order. Individual members of the order subscribed to a vow of poverty and did not hold individual bank accounts, but in this instance the money was held by the Prior as a trustee for each beneficiary, and they could use the covenant income for their own purposes. It was contended that tax deducted from the covenant income should be repaid to the beneficiaries, as *Sec 439(1) (iv)* had been complied with. Held, that the money had been applied for the benefit of the beneficiaries, and the covenants were valid for tax purposes. *Revenue Commrs v HI H/C 1984, TL 126.*

38.153 Capital acquisitions tax—discretionary settlement. A discretionary trust entitled the taxpayer to income from trust property at age 21, and she would become absolutely entitled to the property at age 35. A power of appointment was exercised in her favour before she reached the age of 35. The taxpayer claimed she had a defeasible absolute interest from age 21 (before capital acquisitions tax was imposed) and that no benefit was received by her on appointment (in 1978), so that no CAT liability arose. Held, the interest received at age 21 was a limited interest, and the appointment in 1978 resulted in her receipt of a further interest, bringing a liability to CAT. *Revenue Commrs v Jacob S/C 11 December 1984.* See 7.2, 7.14 CAPITAL ACQUISITIONS TAX.

VALUE-ADDED TAX

38.154 Meaning of 'installation of fixtures'. The appellant, whose trade was the erection of television aerials, sought a determination that his work entailed the 'installation of fixtures' within the meaning of *VATA 1972, s 10(8)* and was, as such, liable to VAT at the then lower rate of 3% (now designated as activities within the *Sixth Schedule*—see 39.9 VALUE-ADDED TAX). Held, having regard to the substantial work involved in securing them to premises and their purpose that television aerials were fixtures. *John Maye v Revenue Commrs H/C 1985,* [*1986*] *ILRM 377.*

38.155 Whether interest payable on VAT refunds. In the first motion the Judge granted judgment in the sum of £15,887.84 with costs in respect of interest on late payments of PAYE and PRSI. As part of their defence the company had cross-claimed for interest on £354,389.30, this sum being late refunds of VAT due to the linked plaintiff company of the second motion. The Judge refused this claim as the two cases involved different companies. There is no provision in *VATA 1972* for payment of interest on refunds due to taxpayers, no matter what the delay is by the Revenue, and the Judge pointed out that under *VATA 1972, s 20(1)* a claim for a refund had to be 'shown to the satisfaction of the Revenue Commissioners' and an enforceable right might not arise until this was done. However, he accepted that there was an arguable case which should be put down for Plenary Hearing.

Hearne v North Kerry Milk Products Ltd. Kerry Cooperative Creameries Ltd v Revenue Commrs H/C 25 June 1985. (*Note.* The Plenary Hearing was not set down by the plaintiffs and the issue remains open. The proceedings in the second motion had the effect of producing a quick refund. In *Navan Carpets v O'Culachain* (see 38.163 below) the Court did use its discretion under *Courts Act 1981, s 22* to award interest on a repayment of corporation tax.)

38.156 **Charge card company—whether exempt supplier.** The appellant company sought judicial review of the Revenue Commissioners' decision that its activities were exempt under Schedule 1 to the *VAT (Exempted Activities) (No 1) Order 1985 (SI 1985 No 430).* It contended that the services it supplied were akin to debt factoring, and that they did not involve the 'reimbursement' of the trader (as specified in the *Order*). It was held, refusing the judicial review sought, that in the context of the three mutually dependent agreements involved in a transaction, the word 'payment' is to be substituted for the word 'reimbursement' in interpreting the *Order. Diners Club Ltd v Revenue Commissioners H/C 24 July 1987.* See 39.6(*c*) VALUE-ADDED TAX.

38.157 **Place of supply of services.** A Dublin firm of solicitors acted for defendants in the Irish courts under instructions from various Lloyd's syndicates whose establishments were in London. VAT was charged on the services on the basis that they were supplied in RI to the defendants for whom they acted, but it was contended for the solicitors that the services were supplied to the Lloyd's syndicates and were thus not chargeable to VAT. Held, the primary commercial transaction was with the Lloyd's syndicates, so that the services were not chargeable to VAT. *Bourke v Bradley H/C 28 July 1988.* See now *FA 1989, s 54* and 39.7 VALUE-ADDED TAX.

MISCELLANEOUS

38.158 **Anti-avoidance—transfer of assets abroad—information powers—FA 1974, s 59(4).** The plaintiffs sought a declaration that, under *FA 1974, s 59(4),* they were excluded from the requirement under that section to provide certain information to the Revenue, on the ground that the transactions concerned were 'ordinary banking transactions carried out in the ordinary course of a banking business'. Two types of transaction were involved: Type A, under which a client would request a personal advance from a Dublin bank on security of a letter of hypothecation of funds on deposit with a sterling area bank; and Type B, under which a client would approach a Dublin bank with a cheque or other negotiable instrument and request that the funds be transferred on deposit with a sterling area bank. He would then separately request a loan on security of a letter of hypothecation over the funds in question. Held that Type A transactions were in the ordinary course of the banking business, and covered by the exclusion, but that Type B transactions were not. *Royal Trust Co (Ireland) Ltd and Whelan v Revenue Commrs H/C 1977,* [*1982*] *ILRM 459.* See 3.8 ANTI-AVOIDANCE LEGISLATION.

38.159 In another case involving *FA 1976, s 59(4),* a notice dated 24 August 1974 was served on the plaintiffs requesting them to furnish within 40 days particulars of transactions entered into by any of their individual clients relating to ten named countries (e.g. Channel Islands, Cayman Islands etc.) over a six-year period. The transactions specified included the formation or acquisition of companies or partnerships, the creation of settlements and the transfer of assets to settlements, and the notice also requested the names of others to whom clients were introduced for the purpose of any of the specified transactions. Held, the notice was not *ultra vires* the *section* on the grounds that it requested information relating to transactions before 6 April 1974, the date of implementation of the charging *section*; neither was it invalid either because it sought information substantially beyond that required for the purposes of the *section* or because of the high cost of compliance. The plaintiffs had not established that the notice was unduly burdensome and oppressive. *Warnock and Others (practising as Stokes Kennedy Crowley and Company) v Revenue Commrs H/C 21 May 1985.* See 3.8 ANTI-AVOIDANCE LEGISLATION.

38.160 Tax avoidance scheme—application of 'Ramsay' principle in Ireland. The appellants entered into a complicated tax avoidance scheme of pre-ordained steps, the purpose of which was to obtain relief for an allowable loss in excess of £1 million under *CGTA 1975, s 35(5)*. No actual loss of this amount was made, although the transactions entered into were real as distinct from sham. The Appeal Commissioners took the view that the doctrine of 'fiscal nullity' developed by the UK cases of *W T Ramsay Ltd v CIR H/L 1981, 54 TC 101* and *Furniss v Dawson H/L 1984, 55 TC 324* applied. Held, that the legislature in Ireland has not enacted a general prohibition of tax avoidance schemes, and it is for the Oireachtas to determine such a prohibition. Accordingly the scheme succeeded. *P, S and J McGrath v McDermott S/C, [1988] IR 258.* See now 3.1 ANTI-AVOIDANCE LEGISLATION.

38.160A Following *McGrath* (38.160 above), a tax avoidance scheme (now closed off by *FA 1989, s 89* (see 3.10 ANTI-AVOIDANCE LEGISLATION)), involving the payment of a capital sum by a subsidiary for an annuity geared to the profits of the parent company granting the annuity, succeeded. The payment for the annuity was allowed as a charge on income, and, following actuarial evidence, the Circuit Court judge held that the greater part of the annuity was a capital receipt. His decision was upheld. *McCabe v South City and County Investment Co Ltd H/C 11 January 1995.*

38.161 Assessability of transactions in basis period for year for which legislation introduced. A builder appealed against his 1935/36 assessment, based on his profits of the year 1934. *FA 1935* imposing income tax for 1935/36, included a provision which, in effect, included in builders' profits fines, etc. received, and the capitalised value of ground rents created, on their disposals of houses built (thus overruling an Irish court decision and bringing Irish law in step with UK law as interpreted in *CIR v John Emery & Sons H/L 1936, 20 TC 213*). The assessment included fines and the value of ground rents relating to houses disposed of in 1934. The assessment was upheld, rejecting the contention for the taxpayer that the legislation did not apply to transactions before 6 April 1935. *Connolly v Birch S/C 1939, 2 ITC 201; [1939] IR 534.*

38.162 Personal representatives—liability in respect of estate income. The respondents claimed that income received by them as executors of an estate was not assessable on them, as the *Succession Act 1965, s 10(3)* indicated that personal representatives were no longer 'receiving or entitled to the income' within *Sec 105*. It was held that that *section* is a re-enactment of *Administration of Estates Act 1959, s 7* and does not alter the legal position that, until administration is completed, the income of an estate is the income of the personal representatives. *Molony v Allied Irish Banks Ltd H/C 26 February 1986.*

38.163 Order of deduction of reliefs. The appellant company was entitled to relief for 1975/76 (i) under *FA 1974, ss 33, 35(5)* in respect of interest £277,661, and (ii) under *ITA 1967, s 307* in respect of trading losses £246,022. The company's only income was a dividend of £500,000 received from a subsidiary under deduction of tax £175,000. Under (i), relief was agreed to be due on £253,978 (i.e. on income £500,000 less trading losses £246,022), giving rise to a repayment of £88,892.30. As regards (ii), it was agreed that £229,552 of the £500,000 dividend was to be left out of account, leaving £270,448. The inspector considered that relief was only available on the residue of £16,470 after deducting the interest charge under (i), whilst the taxpayer considered the full £246,022 could be relieved against the gross income before deduction of the interest charge. Held, income in *Sec 307* means gross income and not income after deduction of charges. An Order was subsequently made for payment of interest on foot of the repayment of tax as found to be due, under *Courts Act 1981, s 22. Navan Carpets Ltd v O'Culachain S/C 16 December 1987.*

38.164 Compulsory sale of dollar balances to State. Under wartime emergency powers, a taxpayer was compelled to sell to the Minister of Finance dollars to her credit in a New York bank representing US income collected on her behalf by the bank. The Minister credited the sterling equivalent to her credit in an Irish bank. It was held that there had been a remittance to Ireland of the US income. *O'Sullivan v O'Connor H/C 1947, 2 ITC 352; 26 ATC 463.*

38.165 Agricultural societies. A committee which managed annual races was held not to be established for the promotion of livestock breeding, and so not an 'agricultural society' exempt from income tax under (what is now) *Sec 348. Trustees of Ward Union Hunt Races v Hughes H/C 1937, 2 ITC 152.*

38.166 Farming—whether large scale piggery qualifies. A partnership carried on a large scale piggery on a nine acre holding of land, of which the sixteen pig houses occupied three acres. Six thousand pigs could be accommodated, and the annual output of twenty-four thousand pigs was sold to a bacon factory of which three of the partners were directors. Apart from sick pigs, all the animals were kept in the pig houses. The partnership claimed to be carrying on farming and so to be within *FA 1969, s 18* and *FA 1974, s 13* (see 18 FARMING). Held, the use of the land for the purposes of rearing and fattening pigs and generally attending to their health and welfare was farming the land. *Knockhall Piggeries and Others v Kerrane H/C, [1985] ILRM 655.*

38.167 Promoting athletic or amateur games or sports—Sec 349 exemption. The appellants, a solicitor and an accountant, formed and funded a club with themselves as trustees '... for the sole purpose of promoting athletic or amateur games or sports ...', and claimed exemption under *Sec 349* for income from the funds provided on the ground that they were a body of persons established for those purposes. The only members other than themselves were four people, being members of their families or employees, and most of the income was donated at the trustees' discretion to financing members' sporting activities. Held, upholding the H/C decision and reversing that of the Appeal Commissioner, that a body of persons for this purpose means an appreciable number of persons, not merely two, united by some common tie, and that the two trustees did not qualify. Their appeal was dismissed. *Revenue Commrs v O'Reilly and McGilligan S/C 1983, [1984] ILRM 406.* See now *FA 1984, s 9* (17.2 EXEMPT ORGANISATIONS).

38.168 The making of investments. A company formed to acquire, *inter alia*, a large family estate in land with a view to its management and development, and a life interest in land in England, was held not to be 'a company whose business consists mainly in the making of investments, and the principal part of whose income is derived therefrom' for management expenses purposes, as required by (what is now) *CTA s 15(6)*. *Howth Estate Co v Davis S/C 1935, 2 ITC 74; [1936] ILTR 79.* This case was followed in another case involving a family estate company, in which part of the estate was sold, the proceeds being invested in Stock Exchange securities. In the relevant year, however, the bulk of the company's income was rental income from the estate, the income for this purpose being the actual rental income rather than the amounts of the Schedule A or B assessments. *Casey v Monteagle Estate Co H/C 1960, 3 ITC 313; [1962] IR 406.*

38.169 Penalties under Sec 500—whether constitutional. Following failure by the plaintiff to deliver returns required by notice under *Sec 172*, the inspector sued the plaintiff claiming a penalty of £500 under *Sec 500* in respect of each of the years in question. The plaintiff claimed that the relevant provisions were unconstitutional, the point at issue being whether the penalties were criminal in character and not civil penalties recoverable as a liquidated sum in the civil courts. The S/C upheld the H/C decision that the requirement to pay a penalty into the Central Fund is not indicative of a criminal offence and is not repugnant to the Constitution. *McLoughlin v Tuite, Revenue Commrs and Attorney-General S/C 13 June 1989.*

38.170 Penalty—criminal or civil proceeding. A prosecution had been taken out against the taxpayer for the recovery of a penalty for failure to make a return under *ITA 1967, s 127.* The Court was asked to decide whether the recovery of the penalty was a criminal or civil proceeding. The Judge held that the recovery of a penalty under *ITA 1967, s 128* is not a criminal proceeding. *Downes v Director of Public Prosecutions H/C 2 February 1987.* See also *McLoughlin v Tuite* at 38.169 above.

38.171 Penalties awarded while assessments open. In a case turning on legislation similar to that now contained in *Sec 500*, a taxpayer failed to make a return. Estimated assessments were made on him against which he appealed, but before the appeals had been determined, penalties were awarded against him for his failure to make his return. The Supreme Court held that the action for penalties should not have been brought before the assessments had become final and it failed accordingly. *A-G for Irish Free State v White S/C 1931, 38 TC 666.*

38.172 Returns—bank accounts—Order sought under FA 1983, s 18. An application, seeking an Order to direct a bank to furnish to the inspector full particulars of all accounts maintained by the taxpayer, was refused. A condition precedent to the granting of such an Order is that the taxpayer has been duly required by an inspector to deliver a statement of the profits or gains arising to him from any trade or profession (i.e. under *Sec 169*) or a return of income (i.e. under *Sec 172*). The inspector's request for accounts under *Sec 174* did not satisfy this condition. *J B O'C v P C D and a bank S/C 24 January 1985.* See 28.1 RETURNS.

38.172A Power under Sec 174(1)(a) to call for documents in support of returns. The taxpayer's accountants refused to produce to the inspector the nominal ledger they had drawn up from the taxpayer's primary records and from discussions with the taxpayer, on the grounds that they were the property of the accountants and subject to professional privilege. Held that the inspector was entitled to demand such evidence in support of the accounts, and that in the circumstances the determination of the taxpayer's profits at the figure stated in the accounts could not stand. *Quigley v Burke H/C, 30 April 1991.*

38.173 Damages—adjustment for tax. A director was awarded damages for breach of contract, including an element for loss of future earnings which exceeded the £3,000 limit of exemption of such payments under *FA 1964, ss 8, 9.* Held, following *BTC v Gourley* (a UK case reported at *[1955] 3 All E R 796*) that the first £3,000 of the award, which was tax-free, should be reduced by an allowance for the tax which would have been payable on it as earnings. *Glover v BLN Ltd H/C 1973, [1973] IR 432.*

38.174 Ex gratia payment—tax exemption limit. The taxpayer was made redundant in May 1981 and received a lump sum *ex gratia* payment, a statutory redundancy payment, and a refund of pension contributions. The matter in dispute was whether the refund of pension contributions net of tax was a 'relevant capital sum' for the purposes of *ITA 1967, 3 Sch 6*, thereby reducing the maximum exemption against the *ex gratia* payment to £6,000. The Appeal Commissioners held that a refund of pension contributions is not a lump sum and that *FA 1972, s 21(4)* totally excludes its treatment as income for any other purposes of the *Income Tax Acts.* The effect of this decision was that the higher exemption limit of £10,000 was due against the *ex gratia* payment. *JK v O'Coindealbhain, Appeal Commissioners June 1986.*

38.175 Interest on debts out of Funds in Court. In a case in which the facts are complex, the substantive decision was that the Courts are not bound to deduct tax under (what are now) *Secs 433* and *434* when paying interest on debts out of Funds in Court, and that the practice of the Courts to provide retrospectively at final allocation for payment of income tax in respect of income accruing to Funds in Court, even though no formal assessment has been made, should not be upset. *Re Colclough dec'd., Colclough and Others v Colclough and Robb S/C 1964, TL 103; [1965] IR 668.* (*Note.* Although subsequent legislation (*FA 1974, ss 31, 50*) limits the application of this decision, it still has relevance to e.g. interest payable to non-residents and to the practice of the Courts generally.)

38.176 Annuity 'free of tax': whether annuitant entitled to retain refund of tax. The annuitant was able to reclaim from the Revenue Commissioners tax paid by trustees in respect of a payment by way of annuity 'free of income tax'. Held, the annuitant was under no liability to account to the trustees for the tax refunded to her. *In re Swan decd., Hibernian Bank Ltd v Munro and Others H/C 1944, [1945] IR 216.*

38.177 Income tax—exemption of earnings under FA 1969, s 2. The appellant, a distinguished journalist, claimed that newspaper articles written by him were original and creative works within the meaning of *FA 1969, s 2*, and therefore exempt from tax. He had previously been granted exemption in respect of earnings from his book 'Death of an Irish Town' (which had first appeared as a series of newspaper articles) and all subsequent newspaper articles until 1974/75. The Judge held, confirming the decision of the Circuit Court, that the newspaper articles concerned did not come within the exemption tests of *FA 1969, s 2. Healy v Inspector of Taxes H/C 12 March 1986.*

38.178 The appellant, a primary school principal and teacher, wrote a series of four original books, intended primarily for the education of children, entitled 'Pathways to History'. He claimed exemption under *FA 1969, s 2*. The Appeal Commissioner reversed the Revenue Commissioners' refusal of exemption, and the High Court upheld that decision. The Appeal Commissioner had heard evidence on which he had come to the decision that, essentially as a matter of fact, the works were 'original' and 'creative' as those words were used in *FA 1969, s 2*, and there was ample justification for that decision. *Revenue Commissioners v O'Loinsigh H/C 21 December 1994.* See 16.19 EXEMPT INCOME AND SPECIAL SAVINGS SCHEMES.

38.179 Appropriation of tax payments between separate companies in a group. In a case in which a number of companies in a group were insolvent, with substantial amounts of tax outstanding, the Revenue Commissioners negotiated with the companies as a group for a payment on account of tax liabilities to be made out of the proceeds of sale of properties by certain members of the group. These payments, when received, were appropriated to meet the tax liabilities of group members in the proportion that each member's liability bore to the total tax liabilities of the group. It was held that any contribution by a company to the payment on account of group tax liabilities which exceeded its own tax liability was *ultra vires,* and that the Revenue Commissioners were obliged to repay to each of the contributing companies the difference between its contribution and its tax liability. *In re Frederick Inns Ltd (in liquidation) and Others S/C 5 November 1993.*

The following is an alphabetical list of all the tax cases summarised above. Each case is listed under the names of both parties except where the CIR or Revenue Commissioners, etc. are a party, when only the taxpayer's name is listed.

39   Value-Added Tax

Headings in this section are:

39.1   Value-Added Tax is charged under the *Value-Added Tax Act 1972 (VATA)* and came into force on 1 November 1972, replacing turnover tax and wholesale tax. This chapter deals with VAT law *from 1 March 1976* onwards, contained in the *VATA* as amended by subsequent *Finance Acts* and the *1978 VAT(A)A* (see below). Further detailed provisions are made in regulations and orders.

The *Value-Added Tax (Amendment) Act 1978 (VAT(A)A)* was passed on 20 December 1978 and took effect on 1 March 1979 by Ministerial order. It implemented the requirements of the *EEC Sixth Directive on VAT (17 May 1977)*.

Administration. VAT is administered by the Revenue Commissioners (VAT), Castle House, South Great George's Street, Dublin 2, and is collected by the Collector-General, Apollo House, Tara Street, Dublin 2, who deals with returns, payment etc.

39.2   SCHEME OF TAX

VAT is a tax borne indirectly by the consumer of goods and services. It taxes the 'value added' at each stage in the chain of transactions leading to the non-trading or exempt consumer. The tax is charged on supplies by taxable persons i.e. traders (and on imports, see 39.19–39.25 below) but they can generally recoup the amount charged in a combination of two ways. As regards *supplies by* a taxable person, he can invoice the buyer of the goods or services (who may in turn be a taxable person) for the amount chargeable on the supply, and must then account to the Revenue Commissioners for this amount. [*VATA s 35(2)*]. As regards supplies *received by* a taxable person for business purposes, he may claim repayment of any 'deductible tax' which he himself has paid over to his supplier under an invoice. The non-trading or exempt consumer cannot reclaim any of the tax and his invoiced VAT payment on the final price funds the entire charge.

VAT is charged on any supply in RI of taxable goods or taxable services by a taxable person in the course of his business. [*VATA s 2*]. *Imported goods* are charged to VAT on their *value* and the tax operates like a customs duty (see 39.19 below). From 1 January 1993, special arrangements apply to imports from EEC Member States (see 39.20 *et seq.* below). *Supplies* of taxable goods and taxable services are charged on the *total consideration* (net of VAT) to which the taxable person making the supply becomes entitled (see 39.10 below).

Cash receipts basis. A taxable person may opt to account for VAT on the basis of cash actually received if most of his business consists of sales to non-registered persons or his turnover is less than £250,000 p.a. (see 39.11 below).

39.3   **RATES** [*VATA ss 11(1), 15(1); FA 1986, s 83; FA 1987, s 40; FA 1988, s 61; FA 1989, s 56; FA 1990, ss 98, 102; FA 1991, s 80; FA 1992, s 173(1)(2); FA 1993, s 87; FA 1995, s 128*].

From 1 March 1986 onwards, the rates are

General	25%	(to 28 February 1990)
	23%	(from 1 March 1990 to 28 February 1991)
	21%	(from 1 March 1991)
Second Schedule	0%	
Third Schedule	10%	(from 1 March 1991)
Sixth Schedule	10%	(to 28 February 1991)
	12.5%	(from 1 March 1991)
Seventh Schedule	16%	(from 1 March 1992* to 28 February 1993)
Eighth Schedule	12.5%	(from 1 July 1995)
Livestock (including, from 1 January 1991, horses), live greyhounds and the hire of horses	2.4%	(to 30 April 1987)
	1.7%	(from 1 May 1987 to 29 February 1988)
	1.4%	(from 1 March 1988 to 28 February 1989)
	2.0%	(from 1 March 1989 to 28 February 1990)
	2.3%	(from 1 March 1990 to 29 February 1992)
	2.7%	(from 1 March 1992 to 28 February 1993)
	2.5%	(from 1 March 1993)
Electricity supply	5%	(from 1 March 1988 to 28 February 1990 (thereafter in Sixth Schedule))

*Strictly, the Seventh Schedule was effective from 28 May 1992, but the goods in the Sixth Schedule transferred to create the Seventh Schedule were charged at the 16% rate in the period from 1 March 1992 to 27 May 1992, so that in effect the Seventh Schedule came into effect on the earlier date.

39.4   **SCHEDULED GOODS AND SERVICES** [*VATA 1–7 Schs; FA 1976, s 60; VAT(A)A ss 25–28; FA 1979, s 49; FA 1982, ss 88, 89; FA 1983, ss 86–88; FA 1984, ss 85, 92–95; FA 1985, ss 49–52; FA 1986, ss 89–91; FA 1987, ss 46, 47; FA 1988, s 63; FA 1989, ss 62, 63; FA 1990, ss 106, 107; FA 1991, ss 86, 87; FA 1992, ss 195–198; FA 1993, ss 95–98; FA 1994, ss 100, 101; FA 1995, ss 140, 141*].

First Schedule (Exempted Activities)—see 39.6 below.

Second Schedule (Zero-rated) includes: children's clothing (not fur skin) and footwear (not for skating or swimming) for average size child aged under eleven and sold on basis of size or age; food and drink for humans (but *excluding* dutiable beverages, manufactured beverages other than tea, coffee, cocoa, etc., ice creams, etc., sweets, biscuits and chocolates, etc., crisps and nuts, etc., and bakery products other than bread, and see also *Sixth Schedule* below); human oral medicines; food and oral medicines for animals other than pets; medical equipment and appliances (other than artificial teeth and, from 1 November 1989, corrective spectacles and contact lenses); electricity (to 29 February 1988, see new *Sixth Schedule*); candles (other than certain ornamental ones); certain fertilisers; food-producing seeds, etc.; goods supplied for transport out of RI or to a taxable person within the customs-free airport, or by one taxable person within the customs-free airport to another in the customs-free airport or in a free port, or by one taxable person in a free port to another, and (from 1 January 1993) certain tax-free supplies to travellers; agency and certain other services connected with the export of goods; supply, hiring or repair, etc. of certain sea-going ships and of international commercial aircraft (and, from 28 May 1992, of equipment incorporated or used in such aircraft and, from 17 June 1993, goods supplied for fuelling or provisioning such ships and aircraft); work on imported goods intended for export; supply of gold to the Central Bank of Ireland; most printed books (including bound volumes of music), booklets and atlases; sanitary towels and tampons; certain services provided by the RNLI or by the Commissioner of Irish Lights. From 1 August 1993, also included are the supply of qualifying goods and services to, or the intra-Community acquisition or importation of qualifying goods by, an authorised person (excluding certain self-supplies, see 39.7 below) within *VATA s 13A* (introduced by *FA 1993, s 90*). This applies to most supplies etc. to or by persons most of whose turnover is dispatched or transported outside RI (and who are duly authorised for this purpose by the Revenue Commissioners). See also 39.21 below as regards zero-rating of certain intra-community transactions.

Third Schedule (10%) is generally abolished after 28 February 1993. It is retained in relation to the following supplies under contracts entered into or arrangements made before 25 February 1993: a domestic dwelling supplied under a contract made with a private individual; and the letting of immovable goods (other than in the course of provision of certain sporting facilities) by a hotel etc. or in holiday accommodation, campsites, etc., and the short-term hire of motor vehicles, at charges fixed at the time of the agreement for the supply. Before 1 March 1993, it included: land and services consisting of the development, maintenance or repair of immovable goods (so long as the value of any *movable* goods supplied therewith does not exceed two-thirds of the total consideration) (excluding routine cleaning and agricultural services); concrete ready to pour and certain concrete blocks; newspapers and periodicals (at least fortnightly) dealing mainly with current affairs; (from 1 July 1991) letting of immovable goods (other than in the course of provision of certain sporting facilities) by a hotel etc. or in holiday accommodation, campsites etc. (previously letting of immovable goods in a hotel trade); (from 1 January 1992) provision of holiday accommodation; tour guide services; short-term hire of passenger vehicles and boats (under 15 tons), or of sports or pleasure craft or caravans, tents etc.

Fourth Schedule (Services taxed where received). Advertising services; services (not connected with land) of consultants, engineers, lawyers, accountants, data-processors, and information-providers; staff recruitment; banking, financial and insurance services; non-competition agreements; transfers and assignments of copyrights, patents, trade marks, etc.; agency services connected with any of the above; and hiring out of movable goods other than means of transport.

Fifth Schedule (Farming, etc.): Part I lists agricultural production activities ('Annex A' activities); Part II lists agricultural services ('Annex B' services).

Sixth Schedule (12.5%) includes: coal, peat and other solid fuels; (from 1 March 1990) electricity supply; gas for heating or lighting (excluding welding, cutting and lighter fuels and motor vehicle gas); most heating oils; agricultural services of field work, reaping, mowing, threshing, baling, harvesting, sowing, planting, disinfecting and ensilage of agricultural products, destruction of weeds and pests, dusting and spraying of crops and land, and lopping and tree felling and similar forestry services, and, after 30 June 1992, of stock minding and rearing and farm relief and advisory services (excluding management and accountancy services); certain goods and services supplied in connection with the repair and maintenance of agricultural machinery; prepared food and drink otherwise within *Second Schedule* (see above) supplied by vending machine or in staff canteens, restaurants, hotels or other catering establishments; ice creams, etc., sweets, biscuits and chocolates, etc., crisps and nuts, etc. and bakery products other than bread (all excluded from *Second Schedule*), and non-alcoholic fruit juices, supplied with meals in staff canteens, etc.; hot take-away food and drink and other food and drink supplied with it (excluding drink otherwise excluded from *Second Schedule*); promotion of and admission to cinema performances; live entertainment supplied in connection with the supply of meals and drink; certain funfairs; waste disposal services; admissions to certain exhibitions of a kind normally held in museums or art galleries (not within 39.6(*t*) below). After 31 December 1991, professional services supplied by veterinary surgeons were added (extended from 1 July 1994 to services of a kind supplied by veterinary surgeons), and after 30 June 1992 the provision of sports facilities other than by non-profit-making organisations (see 39.6(*j*) below). From 1 March 1993, also included are immovable goods (i.e. land); services consisting of the development of and work on immovable goods (including the installation of fixtures), so long as the value of any *movable* goods supplied therewith does not exceed two-thirds of the total consideration, and routine cleaning of immovable goods; newspapers and periodicals (at least fortnightly) dealing mainly with current affairs; letting of immovable goods (other than in the course of provision of certain sporting facilities) by a hotel etc. or in holiday accommodation, campsites, etc.; provision of holiday accommodation; tour guide services; short-term hire of passenger vehicles and boats (under 15 tons) or of sports or pleasure craft or caravans, tents etc.; certain works of art and important literary manuscripts and antique furniture, silver, glass or porcelain; repair and maintenance of most movable goods and alteration of most used movable goods; services (other than *First Schedule* health services) consisting of care of the human body, including health studios etc.; professional services supplied by jockeys; certain supplies of photographic, cinematographic and video software and related services; driving instruction not within 39.6(*d*) below; certain cakes, biscuits etc. not included in *Second Schedule*. From 1 July 1993, the categories of cakes and biscuits included are further extended, and concrete ready to pour and certain concrete blocks added (unless within the auction or margin schemes, see 39.7 below). From 1 July 1995, greyhound food supplied in bulk is added, and works of art, etc. within the auction or margin schemes (see 39.7 below) are excluded (and see *Eighth Schedule* below). From 1 January 1996, certain member-owned and public golf club green fees in excess of £20,000 p.a. are added. Before 1 March 1991, also included were: land and the related services now included in *Third Schedule*; concrete ready to pour; certain concrete blocks; daily newspapers and certain similar newspapers (and, from 1 July 1990, periodicals) published at least fortnightly; letting in the course of a hotel business; short-term hire of boats, caravans, mobile homes, trailer tents, tents and road passenger vehicles; and tour guide services; and, before 29 May 1991, land drainage and reclamation.

Before 1 March 1992, the items subsequently included in *Seventh Schedule* were included in *Sixth Schedule* at the 12.5% rate. They remained in the *Schedule* until 27 May 1992 at a special 16% rate before being transferred to the *Seventh Schedule*.

Seventh Schedule (16%) is abolished after 28 February 1993. Previously it included (from, in effect, 1 March 1992, see footnote to *Sixth Schedule* above): motor vehicle gas; certain works of art and important literary manuscripts; telecommunications services; clothing (not fur skin) and footwear (not for skating or swimming) other than children's clothing and footwear within *Second Schedule*; clothing fabrics etc.; textile handkerchiefs; shoe leather; corrective spectacles and contact lenses; repairs and maintenance of most movable goods and alteration of most second-hand movable goods; work (including routine cleaning) on immovable goods not already included under *Third Schedule* (development etc. services) or *Sixth Schedule* (agricultural services); services (other than *First Schedule* health services) consisting of care of the human body, including health studios etc.; professional services supplied by jockeys; certain supplies of photographic, cinematographic and video software and related services; driving instruction not within 39.6(*d*) below; services of auctioneers, solicitors, estate agents etc. related to the supply of immovable goods for agricultural production activities; and farm accountancy and management services.

Eighth Schedule (12.5%) was introduced with effect from 1 July 1995 in implementation of the margin and auction schemes (see 39.7 below). It applies to a specific list of art, antiques and collectors' items which under certain circumstances are liable to VAT at the Eighth Schedule rate but, when supplied under the margin or auction schemes, are liable at the general rate on the appropriate margin.

39.5   CHARGE ON SUPPLIES WITHIN THE STATE

Up to 31 December 1992, VAT is only chargeable on supplies of goods and services in RI (and on imports of goods into RI). The definitions of the place of supply mean that the following are chargeable to RI VAT.

(*a*)   Supply of goods located in RI at the moment of supply or the transport of which begins in RI (see 39.19 for exports);

(*b*)   Supply of services by a person whose establishment (i.e. fixed place of business) or, if he has no establishment anywhere, whose usual place of residence is in RI;

(*c*)   Supply of RI land and buildings and any associated services supplied by estate agents, architects or on-site supervisors;

(*d*)   Receipt for business purposes of *Fourth Schedule* services (see 39.4 above) (not within (*g*) below) by a person whose establishment (or, if none, usual place of residence) is in RI, unless, broadly, he also has an establishment in another State and the services are most directly for use in that establishment; or by an RI department of State, local authority or statutory body where supply is by person with no establishment in the Community, or with an establishment in another Member State such that VAT is not payable in that State (and see Statement of Practice SP-VAT 1/90, March 1990);

(*e*)   Supply of transport taking place in RI;

(*f*)   Physical performance in RI of: valuation of work on movable goods; artistic, entertainment, sporting or scientific, etc., services; handling etc. of goods for transport;

(*g*)   Services consisting of the hiring out of movable goods by a person established outside the Community where the goods are, or are to be, effectively used in RI;

These rules may be added to by Order.

[*VATA ss 3(6), 5; VAT(A)A s 5; FA 1985, s 42; FA 1986, s 81; FA 1990, s 100; FA 1992, ss 167(c), 169*].

From 1 January 1993, special rules apply in relation to supplies within the EEC. See 39.20 *et seq.* below.

39.6   EXEMPTED ACTIVITIES

No VAT is chargeable in respect of any exempted activity. [*VATA s 6*]. Persons carrying on such an activity are not taxable persons, unless they can and do waive the exemption. The exempt activities are listed in the *First Schedule* of the *VATA* as amended (the list may be added to by Order).

Effect of exemption is that although a person is not liable to account for VAT on his own supplies he suffers VAT, in the same way as a non-trading consumer, on any taxable supplies *received by him* in the course of the activity. He cannot claim any deduction of tax under 39.11 below. *Relief* is available in certain cases by way of repayment of VAT suffered (see 39.18 below).

Waiver of the exemption is available in the case of (*a*)(i) and (*g*) below. It means that a person must account for tax on supplies by him and can claim deduction of tax on supplies received. It also means that the person can pass onto his business customers the right to claim such deduction. Waiver must apply to *all* the person's supplies (i.e. limited waiver is not allowed) and continues in effect until cancellation by the taxpayer. Waiver is claimed by notifying the Collector-General. [*VATA s 7; FA 1991, s 78*].

Exempted activities are:

(*a*)   Professional services, comprising:

(i)   (before 1 January 1992) services supplied in the course of their profession by veterinary surgeons;

(ii)   medical services not within (*a*)(iv) below, except such services supplied in the course of a business of selling goods;

(iii)   professional services of a dental or optical nature, except (before 1 November 1989) such services supplied in the course of a business of selling goods; and

(iv)   from 1 July 1986, dental technician services and dentures, etc..

(*b*)   Insurance services and related agency services.

(*c*)   Financial services, i.e. banking and money lending services, shares and securities dealing, from 20 December 1985 credit and charge card schemes, and from 1 November 1987 underwriting services, credit guarantee, unit trust and, from 1 July 1989, collective investment management, and related agency services (excluding certain share and security management and safekeeping services and, from 1 September 1994, the services of loss adjusters). See also 38.156 TAX CASES.

(*d*)   School and university education, and vocational training provided by recognised establishments and similar bodies, including, from 30 May 1990, heavy goods vehicle driving instruction.

(*e*)   Hospital and medical care provided by a hospital, nursing home, etc..

(*f*)   Catering services for hospital patients and school pupils.

(*g*)   Letting land, but not by an hotel etc., nor machinery, etc. let separately from land, nor provision of parking facilities, nor hire of safes, nor (from 1 July 1992) provision of sports facilities (but see (*j*) below).

(*h*)   Non-profit-making services for the protection or care of children and young persons; supplies given free to members (except for any membership subscription) by non-profit-making bodies of a political, religious, philanthropic etc. nature; supplies closely related to welfare and social security made by non-profit-making bodies.

(*j*)   Sports etc. facilities provided by a non-profit-making body; promotion of and admissions to sporting events (but not promotion of facilities by persons other than non-profit-making organisations, see *Sixth Schedule*). See also Statement of Practice SP-VAT 4/92, July 1992. From 1 January 1996, exemption is withdrawn from member-owned, and State- or local authority-owned, golf clubs to the extent that their non-member green fees exceed £20,000 p.a..

(*k*)   Passenger transport or accommodation, and related agency services.

(*l*)   Supplies of goods used in the course of a business which were charged to VAT on being acquired but without the VAT being deductible (see 39.10 below).

(*m*)   Funeral undertaking.

(*n*)   Broadcasting (excluding advertising).

(*o*)   The acceptance of off-course bets, or on-course bets on horse or greyhound races, and the issue of lottery tickets.

(*p*)   Agency services connected with collection of insurance premiums and, before 1 September 1982, debts and rents.

(*q*)   Blood bank services and similar services relating to human organs and human milk.

(*r*)   Before 1 January 1991, supply of live horses and live greyhounds.

(*s*)   From 1 March 1985, promotion of or admission to most live performances (but not dances or where simultaneous provision of food or drink facilities).

(*t*)   From 30 May 1990, certain services and closely linked goods supplied by recognised cultural bodies.

(*v*)   From 30 May 1990, services supplied by certain independent groups of persons to members.

(*w*)   From 1 January 1992, public postal services.

[*VATA 1 Sch; VAT(A)A s 24; FA 1980, s 82; FA 1982, s 87; FA 1985, s 49; FA 1986, s 89; FA 1987, s 45; FA 1989, s 61; FA 1990, s 106; FA 1991, s 85; FA 1992, s 194; FA 1993, s 94; FA 1994, s 99; FA 1995, s 139*].

The supply of **racehorse training services** is taxable at the *Third Schedule* rate. In general, the Revenue Commissioners are prepared to regard 10% of the gross fees charged as being appropriate to training only, the remaining 90% being for the keep and care of the horses and still considered an agricultural service for which the farmer may or may not elect to register and charge VAT. However, liability arises on the whole of the gross fees where either a taxable activity other than farming or racehorse training is carried on the turnover from which exceeds the exemption limit (see 39.3 above), or a farmer elects to register for VAT (see 39.17 below).

39.7   SUPPLIES OF TAXABLE GOODS AND TAXABLE SERVICES

Taxable goods and taxable services are goods and services the supply of which is not an exempted activity. [*VATA s 1(1); FA 1992, s 165(a)(viii)(ix)*].

Goods means all movable and immovable objects, new or second-hand, but does not include things in action or money. It includes land and buildings (see below). The provision of electricity, gas or any form of power, heat, refrigeration or ventilation is a supply of goods. [*VATA s 1(1); VAT(A)A s 4(c)*].

Supply in relation to goods means transfer of ownership by agreement, handing over goods under a hire-purchase agreement (although hire purchase services are exempt), handing over goods manufactured or derived from other goods of the customer, compulsory acquisition, and certain self-supplies. A self-supply arises where business goods, on the purchase, import etc. of which the person is entitled to a tax deduction, are appropriated to a non-business use or disposed of free of charge. Self-supply also occurs where goods are applied for business purposes in circumstances where a full deduction of input tax is not available. Such self-supplies are deemed to have been made for consideration in the course of the business, except gifts of industrial samples or gifts costing no more than £15 each to the donor. Disposals by e.g. receivers and liquidators of goods forming part of the assets of a taxable person's business (including 'immovable goods'—see below) are deemed to be supplies by the taxable person. Where ownership of goods is transferred as security for a loan or debt or in connection with a transfer of a business, the transfer of goods is outside the charge to VAT. Where agreements amongst a chain of buyers and sellers are fulfilled by delivery by the first seller to the last buyer, the delivery is treated as a simultaneous delivery by each seller. The supply by auction, or through an agent, of livestock (including live horses) or live greyhounds, and the supply by auction of vegetables, fruit, flowers, poultry, eggs or fish are treated as the simultaneous supply to and by the auctioneer or agent. From 1 July 1995, a special auction scheme is introduced. This covers secondhand movable goods apart from the aforementioned. It allows the auctioneer effectively to act as principal and account for VAT on the margin. In addition, *FA 1995* gave statutory effect to the margin scheme which was in practice brought into effect from 1 January 1995, and which works on the same principle, i.e. VAT is accounted for on the dealer's margin. Special rules apply in both cases as to the status of the supplier of the goods, in particular in relation to imported goods. [*VATA ss 3, 10A, 10B; VAT(A)A s 4; FA 1982, s 75; FA 1983, s 78; FA 1990, s 99; FA 1992, s 167; FA 1995, ss 119, 120, 126–128, 141*]. For the special rules applying to the supply of alcohol products from 1 August 1993, see *VATA s 3B*, introduced by *FA 1993, s 84*.

Services are not separately defined but *supply* of services is widely defined as the performance or omission of any act or the tolerance of any situation, other than a supply of goods. Where consideration is received in respect of services without there being any legal entitlement, the services are nonetheless treated as supplied for that consideration. Where the services of a barrister or solicitor are, after 24 May 1989, paid for under a policy of insurance, the services are nonetheless deemed to be supplied to the person indemnified under that policy. See also 38.157 TAX CASES for earlier position. Supply of food for immediate human consumption by vending machine, cafe, restaurant etc. is deemed to be supply of services. [*VATA ss 3(1A), 5; VAT(A)A ss 4, 5; FA 1982, s 76; FA 1989, s 54; FA 1992, s 169; FA 1995, s 123*]. Transfer of goodwill or intangible business assets in connection with transfer of a business is outside the charge to VAT. Special provisions apply to services supplied through an agent. A self-supply of services occurs when a person supplies himself, his family, his staff or his business with services which would be taxable if supplied to anyone else (only self-supplies of catering services are at present taxable). Certain imported services not giving rise to liability in the source country are treated as supplies by the importer, unless the tax would be wholly deductible as input tax. [*FA 1986, s 81*].

See also 39.20 *et seq.* below as regards transactions between EEC Member States.

Land and buildings are termed 'immovable goods'. With certain exceptions, a delivery of immovable goods only occurs where a person disposes of or creates an interest in (*a*) land which has been developed by him or on his behalf, or (*b*) land for which he was entitled to claim deductible tax. 'Development' is defined in *VATA s 1* as amended by *FA 1981, s 43*. No charge arises if the person owned the land on 1 November 1972 and it has not been developed between then and the date of disposal, or where there was no right to claim deductible tax. 'Interest in land' means any estate or interest for a period of at least ten years, but not a mortgage. [*VATA s 4*]. From 7 July 1995, and subject to approval by the Revenue Commissioners, where tax is chargeable in respect of the letting of immovable goods, there is provision for the lessor and lessee jointly to apply for the tax to be payable by the lessee (so that, in normal circumstances, the lessee receives a simultaneous credit for the tax). [*VATA s 4A; FA 1994, s 93; SI 1995 No 184*].

39.8 TAXABLE PERSONS

The following are taxable persons and liable to VAT. A taxable person must, within 30 days of becoming a taxable person, supply particulars to the Revenue Commissioners, who keep a register of taxable persons to each of whom a registration number is issued. [*VATA s 9; VAT(A)A s 7; FA 1992, s 171; SI 1993 No 30*].

(*a*) Any person who otherwise than as an employee of another person engages in the supply in RI of taxable goods or taxable services (subject to the exemptions below).

(*b*) In the particular event only, a person who disposes of an interest in land in connection with the disposal or development of the same land by a taxable person.

(*c*) Any person receiving *Fourth Schedule* services in RI (see 39.5(*d*) above).

(*d*) So far as specified by Order, the State and local authorities.

(*e*) (from 1 January 1993) Any person engaging in intra-community acquisitions of goods (see 39.20 below).

[*VATA ss 4(5), 8; VAT(A)A s 6; FA 1986, s 82; FA 1992, s 170(2); FA 1995, ss 122, 124*].

Similar requirements are imposed, after 31 August 1983, in respect of certain liquidators, receivers, etc. whose disposals are treated as supplies by a taxable person (see 39.7 above). [*FA 1983, s 80*].

Certain interlinked business activities may be treated as carried on by one of the persons carrying on those activities. [*VATA s 8(8); FA 1991, s 79*].

The licensee of **licensed premises on which dances are held** (or the company whose nominee he is) is, after 27 May 1992, deemed to be the promoter of such dances, and to have received the admission money (less tax) and any proceeds in connection with the dances. [*FA 1992, s 170(1)(b)*]. Statement of Practice SP-VAT 6/92, July 1992 states that, where the dances being promoted are for the benefit of non-profit making organisations, no liability will arise on the admission charge.

Exemptions. A person is not a taxable person, and therefore not required to register, unless he elects to be a taxable person, if

(i) after 30 June 1992, a farmer (see 39.17 below) for whose supply of agricultural (other than insemination, stock-minding and stock-rearing) services the total consideration has not exceeded, and is not likely to exceed, £15,000 (£20,000 after 30 June 1994) in any continuous twelve-month period (before 1 July 1992, *any* farmer); or

(ii) the total consideration for his supplies of taxable goods and services has not exceeded, and is unlikely to exceed, a given limit. From 1 July 1994, the limit is £20,000 (previously £15,000, and £12,000 before 1 March 1989) in any continuous twelve-month period; or

(iii) as (ii) above, with higher limit, if 90% of receipts are derived from supplies of taxable goods (excluding goods chargeable at the 21% rate produced wholly or mainly from zero-rated materials). From 1 July 1994, the limit is £40,000 (previously £32,000, and £25,000 before 1 March 1989) in any continuous twelve-month period; or

(iv) he (1) carries on a sea fishing business and his supplies of taxable goods or services consist exclusively of supplies, in the course of the business, of unprocessed fish to taxable persons or non-taxable overseas buyers, or (2) his taxable supplies are as in (1) together with supplies of either or both of machinery, equipment, etc. used in the business, and of other supplies the consideration for which has not exceeded that which would cause the limit under either (ii) or (iii) above to be breached if there were no other supplies. Before 1 July 1994, the requirement was that the consideration for other supplies had not exceeded, and was unlikely to exceed, £15,000 (£12,000 before 1 March 1989) in any continuous twelve-month period.

With effect from 17 June 1993, these exemptions do not apply in relation to services within (*c*) above. Where a person who is a taxable person by virtue of the receipt of such services is a farmer (or would be so but for the provision of racehorse training services, see 39.17(ii)(*b*) below) or fisherman (see (i)–(iv) above), he is (unless he otherwise elects) a taxable person only in respect of the receipt of such services and intra-Community acquisitions of goods (see 39.20 below) and (where relevant) the provision of racehorse training services. See also 39.21 below.

For the purposes of (ii) and (iii) above, the consideration received by certain linked persons must be aggregated in determining whether the relevant limits are exceeded. This applies where a person exercises control (see *VATA, s 8(3B)* inserted by *FA 1984, s 86*) over one or more other persons and supplies of the same type of goods or services are made by any two or more of those persons (whether or not including the person exercising control).

The registration limits above do not apply from 1 January 1993 to foreign traders who are not established in RI and who make taxable supplies in RI. They are obliged to register for VAT irrespective of the level of their RI supplies. [*SI 1992 No 413, reg 7*].

See also 39.6 above and 39.17 below as regards provision of racehorse training services.

[VATA s 8(3); VAT(A)A s 6; FA 1980, s 81; F(No 2)A 1981, s 11; FA 1982, s 77(a); FA 1983, s 79; FA 1984, s 86; FA 1989, s 55; FA 1992, s 170(1)(a), (2)(e); FA 1993, s 85; FA 1994, s 94].

A person who is a taxable person as a result of an election that the above exemption shall not apply may (subject to conditions) apply for the cancellation of the election. Other taxable persons may be treated as not being taxable persons if the Revenue Commissioners are satisfied that they would not be taxable persons unless they elected to be so. *[VATA s 8(5)(6); FA 1992, s 170(2)(f); FA 1993, s 85(e)].*

By concession, landlords who undertake to provide insurance, cleaning, security services, etc., otherwise than by means of their own labour or resources, to VAT registered lessees, may apply to be registered for VAT and, also by concession, transmit the deduction for VAT charged on such goods and services to those lessees. Landlords already registered may similarly apply to avail themselves of this concession.

See also 39.20 *et seq.* below as regards persons engaging in intra-community acquisitions of goods.

39.9 AMOUNT TAXABLE

VAT is charged on the total consideration receivable from the transaction (excluding the amount of VAT itself) except as follows. *Open market price* (exclusive of VAT) applies where all or part of the consideration is not in money and where, for a non-business reason, the consideration is nil or is less than the open market price. A deduction was previously given for the open market price of similar second-hand goods given in exchange or part-exchange, but this provision is deleted with effect from 1 July 1995, and replaced by the margin scheme, see 39.7 above. Special arrangements apply in relation to hire purchase transactions. *Cost of provision* by the relevant person applies to self-supplies of goods or services, and statutory seizure. Goods subject to excise duty (other than certain alcohol products) but supplied before payment of duty to an unregistered person are chargeable on the consideration plus the duty payable had it become due at the time of supply. Regulations deal with valuation of goods supplied in return for trading stamps, coupons etc. and 'simultaneous supplies' to and by auctioneers, agents etc. *[VATA ss 10, 10A, 10B; VAT(A)A s 8; FA 1982, s 78; FA 1992, s 172; FA 1993, s 86; FA 1994, s 95; FA 1995, ss 125–127].* See also Statement of Practice SP-VAT 3/94, July 1995.

Net receipts. From 6 June 1987, when income tax is deducted at source from the consideration receivable in the case of construction industry sub-contractors and certain fees for professional services (see 13.7, 13.9 DEDUCTION OF TAX AT SOURCE), VAT is charged on the *gross* amount before such deduction of tax. *[FA 1987, s 39].*

Livestock (which, from 1 January 1991, includes horses) are charged in full at a substantive rate of **2.5%** from 1 March 1993 (2.7% from 1 March 1992 to 28 February 1993, 2.3% from 1 March 1990 to 29 February 1992, 2.0% from 1 March 1989 to 28 February 1990, 1.4% from 1 March 1988 to 28 February 1989, 1.7% from 1 May 1987 to 28 February 1988, 2.4% from 1 March 1986 to 30 April 1987, 2.2% from 1 March 1985 to 28 February 1986). From 1 January 1991, live greyhounds and the hire of horses are also within these charging provisions. See 39.19 below for imports. *[VATA s 11(1); FA 1985, s 43; FA 1986, s 83; FA 1987, ss 39, 40; FA 1988, s 61; FA 1989, s 56(b); FA 1990, ss 98, 102(c); FA 1992, s 173; FA 1993, s 87(a)].*

Racehorse training services. See 39.6 above, 39.17 below.

Mixed supplies. Detailed rules are laid down for computing and apportioning consideration. *[VATA ss 10(8), 11; VAT(A)A ss 8, 9].*

Fourth Schedule services are taxed on the consideration paid for them by the recipient. *[VATA s 10(5); VAT(A)A s 8].*

39.10 INVOICES AND RECORDS

An invoice must be issued by a taxable person whenever he supplies goods or services to another taxable person (or, from 1 January 1993, he supplies goods to a person other than an individual in another Member State or, from 17 June 1993, he supplies goods under the distance selling arrangements, see 39.24 below) in such circumstances that VAT is chargeable. An invoice must also be issued by a flat-rate farmer who supplies agricultural produce or services (see 39.17 below). The form of invoices, time for issue, etc. are prescribed by regulations. Special rules apply where there is a subsequent increase or deduction in the consideration or where tax is invoiced at a rate higher than should have applied. From 1 November 1992, a taxable person with supplies of taxable goods to other taxable persons in excess of £2,000,000 in the previous twelve months had to issue to taxable persons to whom he made taxable supplies a monthly control statement in prescribed form in respect of all such supplies. See Statement of Practice SP-VAT 7/92, October 1992. From 1 May 1995, there is no longer a requirement to issue monthly control statements. Provision is made for these requirements to be met where electronic data processing systems are employed. See Statement of Practice SP-VAT 9/92, October 1992. [*VATA s 17; VATA(A) s 15; FA 1986, s 86; FA 1990, s 105; FA 1992, s 180; FA 1993, s 91; FA 1995, s 132*]. See also *SIs 1992 Nos 230, 269, 276.*

Every taxable person must keep full records of all transactions affecting his VAT liability. Any non-taxable person who, in the course of business, supplies goods or services must keep all invoices issued to him in respect of goods and services supplied to him for the purposes of his business and, in respect of goods imported by him before 28 May 1992, copies, stamped on behalf of the Revenue Commissioners, of the relevant customs entries. In each case the documents, together with suitable receipts, accounts, books etc., must be kept for six years. [*VATA s 16; FA 1992, s 179*]. Authorised offices of the Revenue Commissioners have powers of entry, search, inspection and removal of records, etc. as respects VAT liability or entitlement to repayment, and may require details of customers and suppliers and of gifts, inducement payments, etc. in connection with supplies to customers. [*VATA s 18; FA 1979, s 48; FA 1982, s 85; FA 1984, s 89; FA 1992, s 181; FA 1995, s 133*].

39.11 CASH RECEIPTS BASIS

Instead of the usual sales (or invoice) basis, a taxable person may, subject to regulations, be authorised to determine the tax due during any taxable period on the basis of cash actually received during the taxable period if either

(i)   90% of the consideration on which he is chargeable to VAT comes from supplies of taxable goods or taxable services to *non-registered persons* (i.e. in most cases, if he is a retailer selling almost entirely direct to the public), or

(ii)   (from 1 July 1994) the total consideration he is entitled to receive from taxable supplies has not exceeded, and is not likely to exceed, £250,000 in any continuous period of twelve months. The Minister for Finance has the right to increase this limit by order.

Before 1 January 1993, the cash receipts basis was available to a person making supplies of taxable services (or services which would be taxable if supplied in the period) without having to meet the 90% requirement.

The Revenue Commissioners have powers to cancel or limit any such authorisation. The cash receipts basis is not in any event available in respect of imported goods (whether from within the EEC or not).

[*VATA s 14; VAT(A)A s 13; FA 1982, s 83; FA 1992, s 177; FA 1994, s 97; SI 1994 No 259; FA 1995, s 131*].

Detailed rules are contained in *SI 1992 No 306* (as amended), with certain transactions deemed to result in cash receipts, etc.. An eligible person wishing to opt for the cash receipts basis can do so either initially on his VAT registration form or by applying to his inspector of taxes.

See also Statements of Practice SP-VAT 2/92, April 1992 and SP-VAT 16/92, October 1992.

Schemes for retailers. A number of schemes are approved by the Revenue Commissioners for the computation of VAT where a retailer sells many kinds of goods chargeable at different rates (see VAT leaflet No 1).

39.12 DEDUCTIBLE TAX

From his liability to VAT for his supplies of goods and services in a taxable period, a taxable person may deduct the total amount of VAT charged to him in that period

(*a*)   on supplies, *for which invoices were issued*, to him by other taxable persons and by flat-rate farmers; and

(*b*)   on goods imported by him (but see 39.20 *et seq.* below as regards imports from EEC countries from 1 January 1993), on *Fourth Schedule* services received by him, on certain self-supplies and on certain business services.

Special arrangements apply in relation to the auction and margin schemes (see 39.7 above).

Where *VATA s 4A* applies in relation to the lessee of immovable goods (see 39.7 above), a deduction is allowed in respect of the tax for which the lessee is liable.

From 1 November 1987, there is an additional requirement that the goods and services are used by the taxable person for the purposes of his taxable supplies or of certain overseas activities. This replaces the prohibition on deduction at (iv) below which applied before that date.

With effect from 17 June 1993, a farmer or fisherman who is a taxable person only in respect of intra-Community acquisitions of goods and certain services received from abroad (and, in certain cases, the provision of racehorse training services) (see 39.8 above, 39.21(*b*) below) is not entitled to such a deduction (except in relation to racehorse training services, where applicable).

Where a taxable person's deductible tax exceeds his VAT liability for his supplies in a taxable period, the excess is refunded to him. This will occur e.g. if his supplies are of zero-rated goods.

From 1 July 1995, a special scheme permits second-hand car dealers to claim a deduction for residual VAT included in the purchase price of dealing stock.

No deduction is allowed on the following supplies received

(i)   non-taxable supplies of food and drink, accommodation, or personal services, to self, agents or employees;

(ii)   entertainment expenses for self, agents or employees;

(iii)   purchase or hiring of motor vehicles (except as trading stock or by driving schools) or purchase of petrol (except as trading stock);

(iv)   (from 23 May 1994) expenditure on provision of food, drink, accommodation or other entertainment services as part of a taxable advertising service;

and before 1 November 1987

(v)   supplies of goods or services which were not used in a business or which were used in an exempted activity (except for certain overseas activities).

From 23 May 1994, (i) above includes expenditure on, or on the fitting out of, a building to provide such accommodation, and (ii) above similarly includes expenditure on, or on the fitting out of, a building or facility to provide such entertainment.

Apportionment of input tax. From 1 November 1987, input tax is apportioned where it relates partly to taxable supplies, and partly to other supplies or activities. The allowable proportion is determined in accordance with regulations. Detailed regulations applicable to second-hand motor vehicles are set out in *SI 1988, No 121*. (This statutory instrument will no longer be applicable when the motor dealer's margin scheme (see above) is fully implemented.)

[*VATA ss 12, 12B; VAT(A)A s 10; FA 1982, s 80; FA 1986, s 84; FA 1987, s 41; FA 1991, s 81; FA 1992, s 174; FA 1993, s 88; FA 1994, s 96; FA 1995, ss 129, 130*].

39.13 RETURNS

Taxable period means a period of two months beginning on the first day of January, March, May, July, September or November. [*VATA s 1(1); FA 1973, s 90*].

VAT becomes 'due' (as distinct from payable) on the issue of the invoice (or expiry of the time for issue of the invoice), or at the time of delivery or rendering, or (in cash trading) on receipt of the cash. The latest time at which the tax can become due is the receipt of the total consideration. For certain intra-community transactions after 1 January 1993, the due date is the 15th day of the month following the transaction, or on earlier issue of an invoice by the supplier. [*VATA s 19(1)(1A)(2); FA 1992, s 182(a)(b)*]. See *SI 1992 No 413, regs 8, 12* as regards foreign currency, and Statement of Practice SP-VAT 15/92, November 1992 on postponed accounting on intra-Community transactions.

A return must normally be furnished to the Collector-General *within nine days after* the tenth day of the month immediately following each taxable period. The return must state the amount of tax which became due in the taxable period and the amount (if any) of deductible tax. The return must be accompanied by a remittance of the balance of the tax payable, net of any advance payment (see below). Special rules apply in relation to certain intra-community transactions involving motor vehicles and other new means of transport and to certain supplies of excisable goods. [*VATA s 19(3)–(5); FA 1973, s 82; VAT(A)A s 16; FA 1992 s 182(c); FA 1993, s 92; SI 1993 No 247*]. Similar provisions apply to liquidators, receivers, etc. whose disposals are treated as supplies by a taxable person (see 39.7 above), and who must issue a statement to the taxable person on making such a return. [*FA 1983, s 84*]. From 24 May 1989, the Collector-General may authorise a taxable person to submit returns for longer periods containing up to six consecutive taxable periods (which may, in certain cases, be aligned with the commercial accounting period), subject to such conditions as he considers proper and, if he so requires, to a payment on account at the normal due dates. Authorisation may be withdrawn in various circumstances, and will be if the taxable person so requests. The preferential status of the Revenue Commissioners in a liquidation or bankruptcy is preserved. [*VATA s 19(3)(aa); FA 1989, s 58; FA 1995, s 134*].

If no return is furnished, the inspector, or other officer authorised by the Commissioners, may estimate the amount payable and serve notice on the taxable person for payment of that amount. A reduced estimate may be substituted where the original estimate was excessive. The inspector may also serve notice for an assessed amount of tax where he has reason to believe that the amount of tax paid by the taxable person was less than his true liability or that he was given a greater refund than was properly due to him, although where an appeal is made against such an assessment, interest under *VATA s 21* (see 39.14 below) may be avoided by the payment with the appeal of at least 80% of the final liability and the payment of the balance within one month of determination of the appeal. The estimate or assessment must be made within ten years. [*VATA ss 22, 23, 30; VAT(A)A s 17; FA 1985, s 47; FA 1992, s 185; FA 1995, s 136*].

Advance payment. On 1 December 1993 and annually thereafter, an advance payment is required of one-twelfth of the total net tax due for the 'relevant period', provided that the total net tax due for that period exceeds £1,000,000 (£300,000) (or such higher amount as the Minister may substitute by Order). The *'relevant period'* is the year ending on 30 June immediately preceding the 1 December in question (or where the person concerned became a taxable person during that year, the part of that year during which he was a taxable person). There are provisions for a late payment surcharge at the rate of 0.25% per day. [*VATA s 19(6); FA 1993, s 92(c); SI 1993 Nos 303, 345; SI 1994 No 342*].

39.14   PAYMENT AND REFUND

The time for payment of the tax 'payable' for a taxable period (i.e. the amount by which the VAT chargeable on his supplies exceeds his deductible tax) is the same as for the return. Liquidators, receivers, etc. making a return (see 39.13 above) may deduct the sums accounted for from proceeds of the related disposals.

Refund of tax will be due if the taxable person's deductible tax exceeds his VAT liability on his supplies. Refund is made after receipt of the return. Refund may, however, be deferred where the business activities of the taxable person are closely interlinked with those of one or more other persons who are in arrears with returns or payments, and security may be required before repayment is made where the Revenue Commissioners consider it necessary. Tax overpaid may be repaid unless the repayment would unjustly enrich the claimant (e.g. if the claimant had charged VAT at too high a rate and those overcharged could not be reimbursed). [*VATA s 20; FA 1986, s 87; FA 1989, s 59; FA 1991, s 83; FA 1992, s 184; FA 1995, s 135*]. A refund may be increased by the amount of any advance payment made in the period (see 39.13 above) or consist of the excess of any advance payment over the net tax due for the period. [*VATA ss 19(3), 20(1); FA 1993, ss 92(a), 93*].

Security. From 28 May 1992, the Revenue Commissioners may serve notice on any taxable person requiring him to give security, as a condition of his supplying taxable goods or services, for the payment of any tax which is or may become due. An appeal may be made against the requirement within 21 days of the date of service of the notice. [*VATA s 23A; FA 1992, s 186*].

Interest at 1.25% per month or part-month is charged on unpaid tax payable by virtue of a return or an estimated liability notice. [*VATA s 21; FA 1978, s 46*].

39.15   APPEALS AND PROCEEDINGS

On application, the Revenue Commissioners may determine (subject to appeal) into which *Schedule*, if any, particular goods fall and whether a particular activity is an exempted activity. [*VATA s 11(1B); FA 1973, s 80(d)*].

Recovery of tax and **appeals** are in general governed by similar provisions as for income tax, see 4 APPEALS and 25.2, 25.3 PAYMENT OF TAX. [*VATA ss 24, 25; FA 1983, s 85; FA 1988, s 73; FA 1991, s 84; FA 1992, s 187; FA 1995, s 137*].

Penalties are laid down for failure to comply with various provisions, for making fraudulent returns, etc. Provision is made for the recovery of such penalties, generally within six years. [*VATA ss 26–31; FA 1973, ss 83, 84; FA 1976, s 57; VAT(A)A ss 18–20; FA 1982, s 86; FA 1984, s 90; FA 1992, s 188–191; FA 1994, s 98*]. See 25.5 PAYMENT OF TAX as regards waiver of certain interest and penalties.

Regulations may be made by the Revenue Commissioners on a large number of matters. [*VATA s 32; FA 1973, s 85; FA 1976, s 58; VAT(A)A s 21; FA 1984, s 91; FA 1985, s 48; FA 1986, s 88; FA 1989, s 60; FA 1992, s 192; FA 1995, s 138*].

39.16 PERSONS RESPONSIBLE

The secretary or any other officer acting as secretary for the time being of a *body of persons* is answerable, in addition to the body itself, for the compliance of the body with VAT law. [*VATA s 33*].

Agents etc. The Revenue Commissioners may serve notice on any person who acts on behalf of a taxable person not established in RI in relation to supplies of goods or services, or allows such supplies by a taxable person to be made on land owned, occupied or controlled by him, deeming him, from the date of service of the notice, to have made such supplies in the course of business. Before 28 May 1992, similar provisions applied to an RI resident agent, manager or factor acting on behalf of a non-resident taxable person. [*VATA s 37; FA 1992, s 193*].

See also 25.2 PAYMENT OF TAX as regards collection of certain payments in default.

39.17 FARMERS AND FISHERMEN

Farmer means a person who engages in at least one 'Annex A activity' in the *Fifth Schedule* and whose sales consist exclusively of either

(*a*)   supplies of agricultural produce (other than live greyhounds) and/or of 'Annex B service', or

(*b*)   supplies as in (*a*) above and of one or more of

   (i)   supplies of machinery, plant or equipment used in farming,

   (ii)   racehorse training services the total consideration for which has not exceeded, and is unlikely to exceed, £20,000 in any continuous period of twelve months (£15,000 before 1 July 1994, £12,000 before 1 March 1989), and

   (iii)   supplies other than those mentioned in (*a*) or in (i) or (ii) above, the total consideration for which has not exceeded that which would cause the limit referred to in either 39.8(ii) or 39.8(iii) above to be breached if there were no other supplies. (Before 1 July 1994, the requirement was that the consideration for other supplies had not exceeded, and was unlikely to exceed, £15,000 (£12,000 before 1 March 1989) in any continuous period of twelve months.)

Where a person would be a farmer under this definition but for exceeding the limit in (*b*)(ii) above, he is a taxable person only in respect of the supply of racehorse training services and, from 17 June 1993, any intra-Community acquisitions of goods and certain services received from abroad. See further 39.6, 39.8 above, 39.21(*b*) below.

[*VATA, s 8(3A)(9); FA 1982, s 77(b)(c); FA 1983, s 79; FA 1989, s 55(b)(c); FA 1990, s 101; FA 1994, s 94(c)(d)*].

See 39.8 above as regards exemption of certain farmers from treatment as taxable persons. A farmer, or a person who would be a farmer but for the provision of racehorse training services (see above), who is not a taxable person (or is only taxable in respect of intra-Community acquisitions of goods and certain overseas services, see above) is a 'flat-rate farmer' and is entitled to levy a flat-rate addition on his supplies (see below). [*VATA s 12A; VAT(A)A s 11; FA 1982, s 81(1)(b); FA 1993, s 89(b)*].

Flat-rate addition on supplies. A flat-rate addition of 2.5% (2.7% from 1 March 1992 to 28 February 1993, 2.3% from 1 March 1990 to 29 February 1992, 2.0% from 1 March 1989 to 28 February 1990, 1.4% from 1 March 1988 to 28 February 1989, 1.7% from 1 May 1987 to 29 February 1988, 2.4% from 1 March 1986 to 30 April 1987) of the agreed consideration is recoverable by the purchaser on supplies by a flat-rate farmer of agricultural produce or services. The person supplied can treat the addition as deductible tax, if an invoice is issued. It is the responsibility of the purchaser to prepare the invoice and to give the farmer a copy; if this is not done the farmer is not obliged to issue the invoice. Special rules apply to a subsequent increase or reduction in the consideration. [*VATA ss 12A, 13(3)(c), 17; VAT(A)A ss 11, 15; FA 1986, s 85; FA 1987, s 42; FA 1988, s 62; FA 1989, s 57; FA 1990, s 103; FA 1992, ss 175, 176(a), 180(c); FA 1993, s 89(a)*]. The flat-rate addition is regarded as compensation for the inability of a flat-rate farmer (being not a taxable person) to deduct VAT suffered on his purchases.

See also Statement of Practice SP–VAT 2/93, July 1993.

Fishermen. Fresh water fishing and fish farming are both 'Annex A activities' so that a person carrying on either of these activities will be a 'farmer' unless his turnover from non-fishing or non-fish-farming activities exceeds the limit referred to in (*b*)(iii) above. If he chooses not to be taxable, such a person will be entitled to the flat-rate addition, like any flat-rate farmer. A *sea fisherman* is not a taxable person (unless he elects) unless his turnover from sales to non-taxable persons (excluding non-taxable overseas buyers) exceeds the limit referred to in 39.8(iv) above. There is no flat-rate addition for sea fishermen. Instead, seafishing vessels exceeding a gross tonnage of 15 tons are *zero-rated*, as are modifications, repairs and maintenance to such vessels, and fishing boats of 15 tons or less (and repairs etc. to them), and fishing nets and other equipment, and marine diesel used in a registered sea-fishing vessel carry a right to *repayment* of VAT suffered (see 39.18 below). [*VATA ss 8(3)(9), 12A, 13; VAT(A)A ss 6, 11, 12; VAT Regulations 1979; F(No 2)A 1981, s 11; FA 1983, s 79; VAT (Refund of Tax) (No 16) Order 1983; FA 1989, s 55(a)(c); FA 1994, s 94(b)(d)*].

See also 39.20 *et seq.* below as regards persons engaging in intra-Community acquisitions of goods.

39.18 RELIEF BY REPAYMENT

VAT borne by a non-taxable person may be repaid in certain cases specified in the *VAT Regulations 1979* and subsequent *Orders*. [*VATA s 13; VAT(A)A s 12; FA 1982, s 82; FA 1985, s 45; FA 1987, s 43; FA 1989, s 92; FA 1992, s 176*]. See also Statement of Practice SP-VAT 2/94, July 1995. The main transactions in which the person supplied (who suffers VAT as part of the consideration paid) will be entitled to repayment by the Revenue Commissioners are

(*a*)   construction etc. of farm buildings, and works of land reclamation or drainage, as regards costs incurred by a flat-rate farmer;

(*b*)   supply, modification, repair or maintenance to a fishing boat not exceeding 15 tons gross tonnage, in circumstances which qualify for State financial assistance, and supply of fishing nets and other equipment and, after 31 April 1983, marine diesel used in a registered sea-fishing vessel;

(*c*)   purchase of radios by an institution for the blind;

(*d*)   purchase of importation, or adaptation, of a car for a disabled driver or passenger;

(*e*)   purchase of a caravan etc. for use as a residence (provided it is rateable);

(*f*)   supply of goods and services within RI for the purposes of his business to a person trading only outside RI (if a non-exempt trade) where the tax would be deductible if the business were carried on in RI (but excluding, from 9 July 1987, means of transport for hire out for use in RI);

(*g*)   medical equipment purchased by a hospital, university, etc., laboratory (repayment of excess over *Third Schedule* rate only).

39.19 IMPORTS AND EXPORTS

From 1 January 1993, the following applies only to transactions with non-EEC countries. See 39.20 *et seq.* below as regards intra-community transactions.

Imported goods are chargeable to VAT at the appropriate rate (see 39.3 above) on their *value* and the tax is administered in the same way as a customs duty. Imports of exempt and zero-rated goods are both exempt. [*VATA ss 11(1), 15; VAT(A)A s 14; FA 1990, s 104; FA 1991, s 82; FA 1992, s 178*].

VAT is collected at the point of importation. [*FA 1982, s 84*]. See also *VAT (Imported Goods) Regulations, 1982* (*SI No 279 of 1982*). The Revenue Commissioners may, under regulations, repay tax chargeable on imports in certain cases (see *VATA s 15(5A) inserted by FA 1992, s 178(c)* and 39.18(*f*) above).

Imports of Fourth Schedule services are chargeable, see 39.5 above. Imports of other services are not chargeable.

Services connected with imports and exports are exempt, see 39.4 above.

Goods exported by the supplier are zero-rated as are goods transported to the Shannon customs-free airport.

Certain **goods and services supplied to exporters** are, from 1 August 1993, zero-rated, see 39.4 above.

39.20   SUPPLIES BETWEEN EEC MEMBER STATES

From 1 January 1993, a new system replaces that previously applicable to imports and exports (see 39.19 above) in the case of 'intra-Community acquisitions of goods' and 'intra-Community transport of goods'. This includes most supplies of goods and certain supplies of transport services, with special arrangements relating to 'new means of transport' and distance selling (including mail order). The existing arrangements continue to apply to imports and exports from and to countries outside the EEC, either directly or through another Member State or States where VAT has not been chargeable, and to supplies of services other than the transport services referred to above.

An '*intra-Community acquisition of goods*' is the acquisition of goods despatched or transferred from one Member State to another as the result of a supply by a person in one Member State to a person in another. Except in the case of 'new means of transport', they must also be supplied by a VAT-registered person (or by a person carrying on an exempted activity) in one Member State to a person in another Member State other than an individual who is not a taxable person. Goods which have been subject to VAT under the margin or auction schemes (see 39.7 above) are excluded. [*VATA s 3A(1)(1A); FA 1992, s 168; FA 1993, s 83; FA 1995, s 121*].

The '*intra-Community transport of goods*' is the transport of goods which actually starts in one Member State and actually ends in another. [*VATA s 5(6)(h); FA 1992, s 169(b)*].

'*New means of transport*' means land vehicles of cylinder capacity exceeding 48cc or power exceeding 7.2kW, sea craft of any type (including hovercraft) exceeding 7.5m in length, and aircraft with a take-off weight exceeding 1,550kg, intended for the transport of persons or goods, supplied either within three months of entering into service (from 1 January 1995, six months in the case of land vehicles) or with usage not exceeding 3,000km (6,000 from 1 January 1995), 100hrs sailing or 40hrs flying time respectively. Sea vessels and aircraft within the *Second Schedule* (see 39.4 above) are excluded. [*VATA s 1; FA 1992, s 165(a)(vi); FA 1994, s 84*].

An outline of the effect of these changes is contained in 39.21 *et seq.* below. These and the very large number of detailed amendments to *VATA 1972* to give effect to the changes are (together with other general provisions) contained in *FA 1992, ss 165–195*. See also *SI 1992 No 413, SI 1993 No 54* and *SI 1994 No 448*.

39.21   Intra-community acquisition of goods (other than new means of transport, see 39.22

below). The liabilities in respect of such transactions depend on the status of supplier and purchaser.

(a) *Purchase by taxable person in one Member State from taxable person in another Member State.* The supply is zero-rated in the Member State of the supplier. The supply is taxable in the Member State of the purchaser at the rate applicable in that State, the tax being payable by the purchaser through the normal VAT return. The tax will normally be simultaneously deductible (subject to the usual rules as to deductibility). [*VATA ss 2(1A), 3A(2), 8(1A)(2B), 10(5A), 19(1A), 2 Sch (i); FA 1992, ss 166, 168, 170, 172(g), 182(a), 195(2)(a)*]. See also Statement of Practice SP-VAT 8/92, October 1992.

(b) *Purchase by person not registered for VAT in one Member State from taxable person in another Member State.* VAT is payable in the Member State of the supplier at the rate applicable there. The transaction is not taxable in the Member State of the purchaser. In the case of RI purchasers:

  (i) persons who make supplies in the course or furtherance of business, but who come within the small turnover exemptions from registration (see 39.8 above) are required to register (and accordingly fall within (a) above) if their intra-Community acquisitions of goods (other than new means of transport and dutiable goods) exceed, or are likely to exceed, £32,000 in any continuous twelve month period;

  (ii) non-taxable entities and exempt businesses are similarly required to register if the £32,000 limit is exceeded (and see Statements of Practice SP-VAT 11/92 and SP-VAT 13/92, October 1992);

  (iii) private individuals are not subject to any limitation, but see 39.24 below as regards direct selling (e.g. by mail order);

  (iv) (from 17 June 1993) farmers and fishermen (see 39.17 above) who would be exempt from registration (see 39.8(i)(iv) above) but for intra-Community acquisitions of goods or the receipt of certain services from abroad (see 39.8(c) above) are, unless they otherwise elect, taxable persons only in respect of such acquisitions and services. Similarly a person who would be a farmer but for the provision of racehorse training services (see 39.17(ii)(b) above) and who is a taxable person by virtue of intra-Community acquisitions of goods or the receipt of certain services from abroad (see 39.8(c)) is, unless he otherwise elects, a taxable person only in respect of racehorse training services and such acquisitions and overseas services.

[*VATA ss 2(1A), 8(1A)(3), 19(1A); FA 1992, ss 166, 170, 182(a); FA 1993, s 85; FA 1994, s 94(a)*].

A purchase from a non-registered person in another Member State is not an intra-Community acquisition of goods and gives rise to no VAT liabilities.

39.22 **New means of transport.** The intra-Community acquisition of new means of transport is, regardless of the status of the purchaser, zero-rated in the Member State of the supplier, and taxable at the applicable rate in the Member State of final delivery. There are special arrangements for payment of the tax by a purchaser who is a private individual (see *SI 1992 No 412*) or a trader not entitled to a deduction for the tax, and for repayment of the tax where the vehicle etc. is subsequently re-exported. [*VATA ss 2(1A), 8(1A)(2B), 13(3A), 19(1A)(4), 2 Sch (i); FA 1992, ss 166, 170, 176(b), 182(a)(c), 195(2)(a); FA 1993, s 92(b); SI 1992 No 413, reg 7; SI 1993 No 248*].

39.23 **Intra-Community transport of goods** (and related ancillary and agency services) supplied to a person registered for VAT are taxable in the Member State which registered that person, who must account for the tax, and who will normally obtain a simultaneous deduction (subject to the usual rules as to deductibility).

Such supplies to a non-registered person are taxable in the Member State in which the transport of the goods actually started (or in the Member State in which the services are physically performed in the case of ancillary and associated agency services).

[*VATA ss 5(3A), 6; FA 1992, s 169*].

See also Statement of Practice SP-VAT 12/92, October 1992 (with Addendum April 1993) regarding transport services.

39.24 **Distance selling** (including mail order), where goods (other than new means of transport, see 39.22 above) are despatched by a supplier in one Member State to a non-registered person in another Member State, gives rise to VAT liability in the Member State of the supplier (see 39.21 above) *unless* the total consideration for such supplies by a supplier to a particular Member State (excluding dutiable goods) exceeds, or is likely to exceed, a certain limit. Where the limit is exceeded, liability arises in the Member State where the goods are delivered, and the supplier is required to make arrangements for registration in that Member State and for accounting for the tax on such supplies.

[*VATA ss 2(1A), 3(6), 8(1A)(2B), 19(1A); FA 1992, ss 166, 167(c), 170, 182(a); SI 1992 No 413, regs 5, 10*].

See also Statement of Practice SP-VAT 14/92, November 1992.

The limit referred to above is required to be set in each Member State at the local equivalent of either 100,000 ecus or 35,000 ecus. The limit in RI is £27,000, that in the UK £70,000. France, Germany, Italy, Luxembourg and the Netherlands have indicated their intention to apply the higher limit, whereas Belgium, Denmark, Portugal, Spain and Greece intend to apply the lower limit.

39.25 **Miscellaneous.** See also:

(a) *VATA ss 3(1)(g), 10(4B), 12(1)(a)(iib) as inserted by FA 1992, ss 167(a)(iii), 172(f), 174(a) and amended by FA 1993, s 82, FA 1994, s 92 and SI 1992 No 413, reg 5* as regards certain transfers between branches of a business operating in different Member States and transfers of 'new means of transport' (see 39.20 above);

(b) *VATA s 3A(4) inserted by FA 1992, s 168* as regards goods supplied to a non-taxable person in RI from outside the EEC but liable to tax on importation into another Member State;

(c) *VATA s 3B inserted by FA 1993, s 84 and SI 1992 No 413, reg 14* as regards supplies of alcohol products from 1 August 1993 (and see Statement of Practice SP–VAT 3/93, July 1993);

(d) *VATA ss 12A(1), 13(3)(c) inserted by FA 1992, ss 175(2), 176(a)* as regards repayment of flat rate addition (see 39.18 above) on intra-Community transactions;

(e) *VATA s 13A inserted by FA 1993, s 90* which, in conjunction with *paragraph (via) of 2 Sch inserted by FA 1993, s 95(b)*, zero-rates certain supplies to, and intra-Community acquisitions and importations by, persons whose output is mainly transported or dispatched from RI (and see Statement of Practice SP-VAT 1/93, January 1993);

(f) *VATA s 19A inserted by FA 1992, s 183* as regards returns of intra-Community supplies;

(g) *SI 1992 No 413, regs 5–7* regarding 'triangulation' (i.e. transactions involving more than two countries).

40 Wealth Tax

40.1 Wealth tax (WT) was introduced by the *Wealth Tax Act 1975 (WTA)* **and suspended, pending abolition, by the Finance Act 1978, s 38**. For details, see 1983/84 or earlier editions of this book.

41 Youth Employment and Income Levies

41.1 YOUTH EMPLOYMENT (EMPLOYMENT AND TRAINING) LEVY

Under the *Youth Employment Agency Act 1981*, a Youth Employment (now Employment and Training) Levy is payable by (or in respect of) any individual over the age of sixteen years, subject to certain exemptions (see below). The levy is charged at the rate of **1%** (subject to variation or suspension by regulation, but not so as to exceed 1%) on all emoluments of the individual and all other income (net of superannuation contributions, etc.), but excluding non-pecuniary emoluments and social welfare payments received, and disregarding the married persons' provisions of *FA 1980* (see 23.1 MARRIED PERSONS). No contribution is payable where income is less than £9,250 (1994/95 £9,000). There are special provisions for determining the income of certain farmers. [*Youth Employment Agency Act 1981, ss 1, 15–19; Youth Employment Levy Regulations, 1982, SI 1982 No 84; Employment and Training Levy (Amendment) Regulations 1988, SI 1988 No 53*].

Exemptions. Emoluments are exempt where the individual to whom they are payable is in receipt of certain widow's, deserted wife's or social assistance benefits or other corresponding payments. Prior to 1994/95, where the individual has full eligibility for services under *Part IV* of the *Health Act 1970* (a 'medical card holder'), liability arises only if the individual is an 'employed contributor' (under the *Social Welfare (Consolidation) Act 1981*) or in certain other employments, and is then imposed on the employer rather than the employee. From 6 April 1994, contributions are not payable by either the employee or the employer in these circumstances.

Liability for payment of the levy in respect of emoluments rests in the first instance on the employer, who (where liability is not finally his—see above) is entitled to make a corresponding deduction from the emoluments. Levy payable in respect of other income is payable in all respects as if it were income tax.

41.2 INCOME LEVY [*FA 1983, s 16; FA 1984, s 10; FA 1985, s 11; FA 1993, s 9*].

For 1993/94 only, an additional levy is imposed on incomes at the rate of 1%. The provisions relating to Youth Employment Levy (now Employment and Training Levy) (see 41.1 above) apply with the necessary modifications to this levy. There is, however, exemption from the income levy where either

(i)   reckonable income consists only of emoluments, and these are payable at a rate not exceeding £173 p.w., or

(ii)   reckonable income does not consist only of emoluments and does not exceed £9,000,

and exemption also applies to medical card holders.

A similar levy applied previously in 1983/84, 1984/85 and 1985/86.

See also 15.3 DOUBLE TAX RELIEF—INCOME AND CAPITAL GAINS.

42   Finance Act 1995—Summary of Provisions

(Enacted 2 June 1995)

TAXATION MATTERS

s 1   **Exemptions from income tax.** The general and age exemption limits are increased for 1995/96. See 2.7, 2.8 ALLOWANCES AND RATES.

s 2   **Rates of income tax.** The standard rate band is increased for 1995/96, the standard and higher rates being unchanged. See 2.3 ALLOWANCES AND RATES.

s 3,   **Personal reliefs** are increased for 1995/96. See 2.9, 2.10, 2.11, 2.16 ALLOWANCES AND
1 Sch   RATES.

s 4   **PRSI allowance** is continued for 1995/96, but reduced to £140. See 2.13 ALLOWANCES AND RATES.

s 5   **Rent allowance** is extended to all tenants in privately rented accommodation from 1995/96, and generally brought onto the current year basis. See 2.23 ALLOWANCES AND RATES.

s 6   **Relief for fees paid to private colleges** is introduced from 1996/97. See 2.26 ALLOWANCES AND RATES.

s 7   **Allowance for service charges** up to £150 for local authority services is given for 1996/97 onwards. See 2.27 ALLOWANCES AND RATES.

s 8   **Tax relief for designated charities.** Donations to certain third world charities will generally be treated as received under deduction of standard rate tax. See 17.5 EXEMPT ORGANISATIONS.

s 9   **Beneficial loans.** The specified interest rates are reduced to 7% (from 7.5%) and 11% (from 11.5%). See 34.3 SCHEDULE E.

s 10   **Social welfare benefits.** Certain short-term benefits are non-taxable from 6 April 1995. See 37.3, 37.4 SOCIAL WELFARE SYSTEM.

s 11   **Savings and investment taxation.** From 6 April 1995, the rate of tax on special savings accounts is increased from 10% to 15%. See 13.8 DEDUCTION OF TAX AT SOURCE, 16.21, 16.23 EXEMPT INCOME AND SPECIAL SAVINGS SCHEMES.

s 12   **Settlements on minors.** Generally from 6 April 1995, income dispositions in favour of minors (other than certain permanently incapacitated persons) are ineffective for tax purposes. See 36.3 SETTLEMENTS.

s 13   **Dispositions for short periods.** The restrictions on the tax effectiveness of such dispositions are broadened. See 36.2 SETTLEMENTS.

s 14   **Information returns** are to be required from certain bodies making rental subsidy payments. See 33.10 SCHEDULE D, CASE V.

s 15   **Error or mistake relief** is extended to Schedule F. See 10.4 CLAIMS.

s 16   **Profit sharing schemes.** The ceiling on annual appropriations is increased from £2,000 to £10,000. See 34.6 SCHEDULE E.

s 17   **Investment in corporate trades.** A number of changes are made to the relief scheme. See 21.2, 21.4, 21.7, 21.8, 21.9, 21.11 INVESTMENT IN CORPORATE TRADES AND RESEARCH AND DEVELOPMENT, 34.5 SCHEDULE E.

s 18   **Sub-contractors in the construction industry.** A number of changes are made to the deduction scheme. See 13.7 DEDUCTION OF TAX AT SOURCE.

s 19   **Short-lived businesses** are to be assessed on the current year basis throughout. See 30.4 SCHEDULE D, CASES I AND II.

s 20   **Relief for expenditure on significant buildings** is extended to certain buildings in use as guest houses. See 22.4 LOSSES.

s 21   **Farming: stock relief** is continued for a further two years, at an increased rate of 100% in the case of certain young trained farmers. See 18.8 FARMING.

s 22   **Compulsory disposals of livestock.** Certain receipts in respect of such disposals may be spread over two years, and additional stock relief granted for replacement expenditure. See 18.4 FARMING.

s 23   **Capital allowances: vehicles.** The £13,000 capital value limit is increased to £14,000. See 8.6(*b*) CAPITAL ALLOWANCES, 30.9 SCHEDULE D, CASES I AND II.

s 24   **Capital allowances: industrial buildings.** Amendment relating to balancing adjustments on cesser of use. See 8.5(*c*) CAPITAL ALLOWANCES.

s 25   **Capital allowances: machinery and plant.** Certain balancing charges in relation to the decommissioning of fishing vessels may be spread over three years. See 8.6(*d*) CAPITAL ALLOWANCES.

s 26   **Capital allowances: unrestricted allowances** are brought to an end by various dates. See 8.5, 8.6 CAPITAL ALLOWANCES.

s 27   **Capital allowances: accelerated allowances** are brought to an end by various dates. See 8.5, 8.6 CAPITAL ALLOWANCES.

s 28   **Foreign trusts.** Certain RI bank accounts are disregarded in considering the requirement for all trust assets to be situated outside RI. See 36.4 SETTLEMENTS.

s 29   **Branch profits.** Certain profits from foreign branches of companies creating employment in RI are exempted from corporation tax. See 12.12 CORPORATION TAX.

s 30   **Late returns.** The tax-based surcharge for late submission of certain returns is graded and capped. See 28.12 RETURNS.

s 31   **Payment of tax.** A fixed date is introduced for payment of the balance of tax for a chargeable period, and an alternative basis of calculation of preliminary tax provided. A loophole concerning preliminary tax of married couples is also closed. See 28.12 RETURNS.

ss 32–35   **Urban renewal reliefs** are extended for two years in certain cases, and a number of changes made to the reliefs, including the introduction of new reliefs in certain 'enterprise areas'. See 2.22 ALLOWANCES AND RATES, 8.10 CAPITAL ALLOWANCES, 30.22 SCHEDULE D, CASES I AND II, 33.4, 33.5 SCHEDULE D, CASE V.

s 36   **Relief for investment in films.** Certain requirements are clarified, and a loophole as to benefits to be received by investors closed. See 12.22 CORPORATION TAX.

s 37   **Non-distributing investment companies** will be able to redeem their own shares without accounting for ACT. See 12.10 CORPORATION TAX.

s 38   **Collective investment undertakings** are extended to include certain investment companies in the International Financial Services Centre or the Shannon Zone whose non-RI resident investors are themselves collective investors. See 12.21 CORPORATION TAX.

s 39   **Distributions to non-residents.** The changes made by *FA 1994, s 27* are backdated two years. See 12.10, 12.18, 12.23 CORPORATION TAX, 35.2 SCHEDULE F.

s 40   **Certain interest** paid to non-ordinarily resident persons by international financial services traders is exempted from income tax. See 16.6(iv) EXEMPT INCOME AND SPECIAL SAVINGS SCHEMES.

s 41   **Offshore funds: material interests** required to be reported by RI residents are extended. See 28.4 RETURNS.

s 42   **Petroleum taxation** changes. See generally 12.19A CORPORATION TAX.

s 43   **Employment grants to certain undertakings** are disregarded for tax purposes. See 16.3 EXEMPT INCOME AND SPECIAL SAVINGS SCHEMES.

s 44   **The Irish Horseracing Authority, Irish Thoroughbred Marketing Ltd and Tote Ireland Ltd** are exempted from corporation and capital gains taxes. See 17.12A EXEMPT ORGANISATIONS.

s 45,   **Tax credits in respect of distributions.** The standard rate is, for 1995/96 onwards,
2 Sch   assumed to be 23%, and other technical amendments are made in relation to distributions. See 12.10, 12.23 CORPORATION TAX, 13.5 DEDUCTION OF TAX AT SOURCE, 35.2 SCHEDULE F.

ss 46–53,   **Reliefs for renewal and improvement of certain resort areas** are introduced
3 Sch   similar to those applicable to urban renewal. See 8.10A CAPITAL ALLOWANCES, 30.22 SCHEDULE D, CASES I AND II, 33.12 SCHEDULE D, CASE V.

s 54,   **Rate of corporation tax** is reduced from 40% to 38% from 1 April 1995. See 12.2,
4 Sch   12.17 CORPORATION TAX.

s 55   **Surcharge on undistributed income of service companies.** The fraction of distributable non-investment or estate income taken into account is reduced from 80% to 50%. See 12.7 CORPORATION TAX.

s 56   **Credit for bank levy.** Technical amendment relating to set-off of levy payments. See 12.21 CORPORATION TAX.

s 57   **National Co-operative Farm Relief Services Ltd.** Certain payments are exempt from corporation tax. See 12.12 CORPORATION TAX.

s 58   **Particulars to be supplied by new companies.** Further information is required from certain Irish-registered non-resident companies. See 12.5 CORPORATION TAX.

s 59   **Research and development expenditure.** Enhanced relief is available in certain cases on incremental expenditure. See 12.9 CORPORATION TAX.

ss 60, 61   **Double taxation relief.** Changes are made in relation to the corporation tax attributable to certain foreign income. See 12.11, 12.17 CORPORATION TAX.

s 62   **Manufacturing companies: double taxation relief.** Certain non-banking financial service traders may set withholding taxes on certain interest against corporation tax on other income. See 12.17 CORPORATION TAX.

s 63   **Manufacturing companies: credit for foreign tax.** A number of technical changes are made to the basis of relief. See 12.17 CORPORATION TAX.

s 64   **Overseas life assurance companies.** Minor clarification regarding investment income. See generally 12.15 CORPORATION TAX.

s 65   **Manufacturing companies: financial services traders** may in certain cases deal in commodities futures and options previously excluded. See 12.17 CORPORATION TAX.

s 66   **Corporation tax returns.** The tax-based penalties for late filing are graded and capped. See 28.12 RETURNS.

s 67   **Gifts to First Step.** Relief is extended to 31 May 1997. See 12.9 CORPORATION TAX.

s 68   **Insurance companies: reinsurance contracts.** Gains or losses on disposals of rights under certain foreign contracts will be charged or allowed. See generally 9.7(*f*) CAPITAL GAINS TAX.

s 69   **Insurance companies: unrealised gains and losses.** Spreading is to be phased in. See generally 12.15 CORPORATION TAX.

s 70   **Capital gains tax: tangible movable property.** The reporting threshold is increased from £5,000 to £15,000. See 9.4 CAPITAL GAINS TAX.

ss 71, 72 **Capital gains tax: retirement relief.** The threshold is increased from £200,000 to £250,000 and a number of other changes made to the relief. See 9.7(*g*) CAPITAL GAINS TAX.

s 73   **Capital gains tax: rollover relief** is made available in respect of certain development land disposals. See 9.16 CAPITAL GAINS TAX.

s 74   **Capital gains tax: reinvestment relief.** The conditions for relief are relaxed. See 9.7(*t*) CAPITAL GAINS TAX.

s 75   **Capital gains tax: reduced rate** is to apply to certain non-qualifying shares acquired in exchange for qualifying shares. See 9.3 CAPITAL GAINS TAX.

s 76   **Capital gains tax: certain disposals to non-residents.** The requirement for the vendor to account for 15% tax where a clearance certificate is not produced is extended. See 9.5 CAPITAL GAINS TAX.

s 118   **Value–added tax: definitions.**

s 119   **Value–added tax: interpretation.** Terms used in the auction and margin schemes (see *sections 126, 127* below) are defined. See 39.7 VALUE-ADDED TAX.

s 120   **Value–added tax: supply.** The related supply of financial services is separated from the supply of the goods. See generally 39.7 VALUE-ADDED TAX.

s 121   **Value–added tax: intra-Community acquisitions of goods** excludes goods subject to the auction or margin schemes (see *sections 126, 127* below) or the special arrangements for second-hand car dealers (see *section 130* below). See generally 39.20 VALUE-ADDED TAX.

s 122   **Value–added tax: immovable goods.** VAT is chargeable on the full value (including the site) in the supply of new houses. See generally 39.8 VALUE-ADDED TAX.

s 123   **Value–added tax.** Amendment in relation to the place of supply of goods or services. See generally 39.7 VALUE-ADDED TAX.

s 124   **Value–added tax: taxable persons.** The definition is amended in relation to the registration of certain golf clubs (see *sections 139, 140* below) and of suppliers of certain commercially competitive sport, health and fitness services. See 39.8 VALUE-ADDED TAX.

s 125   **Value–added tax: amount chargeable.** The trade-in rule is abolished (following the introduction of the margin and auction schemes, see *sections 126, 127* below) and the hire purchase rules revised. See 39.9 VALUE-ADDED TAX.

s 126   **Value–added tax: margin scheme** is introduced. See 39.7, 39.9 VALUE-ADDED TAX.

s 127   **Value–added tax: auction scheme** is introduced. See 39.7, 39.9 VALUE-ADDED TAX.

s 128   **Value–added tax: rate.** A new (*Eighth Schedule*) rate is applied to certain supplies of works of art, etc.. See 39.3, 39.7 VALUE-ADDED TAX.

s 129   **Value-added tax: deductible input tax.** The rules are revised in relation to the margin and auction schemes (see *sections 126, 127* above) and the arrangements for second-hand car dealers (see *section 130* below). See 39.12 VALUE-ADDED TAX.

s 130   **Value-added tax: dealers in second-hand means of transport.** Residual input tax on purchases may be deducted. See 39.12 VALUE-ADDED TAX.

s 131   **Value-added tax: cash basis.** The turnover limit may be increased by order. See 39.11 VALUE-ADDED TAX.

s 132   **Value-added tax: monthly control statements** are no longer required. See 39.10 VALUE-ADDED TAX.

s 133   **Value-added tax: inspection.** Details of gifts, promotional items, etc. may be required. See 39.10 VALUE-ADDED TAX.

s 134   **Value-added tax: annual returns** may be aligned with commercial accounting periods. See 39.13 VALUE-ADDED TAX.

s 135   **Value-added tax: refunds** may be made direct to a nominated account. See generally 39.14 VALUE-ADDED TAX.

s 136   **Value-added tax: estimated assessment** may be reduced. See 39.13 VALUE-ADDED TAX.

s 137   **Value-added tax: appeals.** Procedural changes. See generally 39.15 VALUE-ADDED TAX.

s 138   **Value-added tax: regulation-making powers** are extended. See generally 39.15 VALUE-ADDED TAX.

s 139   **Value-added tax: First Schedule.** Exemption is withdrawn from certain golf club green fees and extended to hire purchase, etc. interest. See 39.6 VALUE-ADDED TAX.

s 140   **Value-added tax: Sixth Schedule** is amended. See 39.4 VALUE-ADDED TAX.

s 141   **Value-added tax: Eighth Schedule** is introduced. See 39.4, 39.7 VALUE-ADDED TAX.

s 151   **Residential property tax: application.** The changes made by *sections 135–138* below apply from 5 April 1995. See 26.3, 26.6, 26.7 RESIDENTIAL PROPERTY TAX.

s 152   **Residential property tax: charge.** A flat rate of 1.5% of net market value is reintroduced. See 26.3 RESIDENTIAL PROPERTY TAX.

s 153   **Residential property tax: market value exemption limit** is reset at £94,000. See 26.7 RESIDENTIAL PROPERTY TAX.

s 154   **Residential property tax: income exemption limit** is reset at £29,500. See 26.8 RESIDENTIAL PROPERTY TAX.

s 155   **Residential property tax: repeal** of *FA 1994, 7 Sch* following *section 135* above. See 26.3 RESIDENTIAL PROPERTY TAX.

s 156   **Capital acquisitions tax: interpretation.**

s 157   **Capital acquisitions tax: minor technical change.**

s 158   **Capital acquisitions tax: agricultural property.** The reliefs are increased. See 7.9 CAPITAL ACQUISITIONS TAX.

s 159   **Capital acquisitions tax: appeals.** Minor procedural change. See 7.12 CAPITAL ACQUISITIONS TAX.

s 160   **Capital acquisitions tax: heritage objects.** Clawback will apply in the case of certain gifts within the six year retention period. See 7.5(*c*)(*d*) CAPITAL ACQUISITIONS TAX.

s 161   **Capital acquisitions tax: business relief** is increased. See 7.9 CAPITAL ACQUISI-TIONS TAX.

s 162   **Capital acquisitions tax: business relief.** Certain agricultural assets used by a farming company may qualify for relief. See 7.9 CAPITAL ACQUISITIONS TAX.

s 163   **Capital acquisitions tax: business relief** clawback is not avoided by certain prior gifts. See 7.9 CAPITAL ACQUISITIONS TAX.

s 164   **Capital acquisitions tax: instalment payment** terms are made more favourable in relation to agricultural and business property. See 7.11 CAPITAL ACQUISITIONS TAX.

s 165   **Capital acquisitions tax: certain inheritances taken by parents** on the death of a child are exempted. See 7.5(*s*) CAPITAL ACQUISITIONS TAX.

s 166   **Capital acquisitions tax: heritage property of companies.** Shares in companies holding such property may be correspondingly exempt. See 7.5(*t*) CAPITAL ACQUISI-TIONS TAX.

ss 167, 168   **Residence: interest payments.** Deposits by non-residents, rather than non-ordinary residents, may be excluded from the deposit interest retention scheme, and the reporting requirements for such payments are correspondingly amended. See 13.8(vi) DEDUCTION OF TAX AT SOURCE, 28.4 RETURNS.

s 169   **Residence: foreign investment income** up to £3,000 p.a. of non-resident but ordinarily resident individuals is exempted from tax. See 27.1 RESIDENTS AND NON-RESIDENTS.

s 170   **Residence: deduction for income earned outside RI.** The first 15 days abroad may now qualify for relief, which is based on total earnings of the year. See 27.1 RESIDENTS AND NON-RESIDENTS.

s 172   **Revenue offences.** Auditors and certain other persons are required to notify certain revenue offences by companies. See 1.11 ADMINISTRATION AND GENERAL.

s 173   **Appeals.** Certain procedural changes are made. See 4.1, 4.2 APPEALS, 16.19 EXEMPT INCOME AND SPECIAL SAVINGS SCHEMES.

s 174   **Liability to tax of holder of fixed charge.** See 25.2 PAYMENT OF TAX.

s 175   **Power to obtain information** is provided in relation to certain payments made by Ministers. See 1.10 ADMINISTRATION AND GENERAL.

s 176   **Relief for donations of heritage items.** Donations to national collections may qualify for non-refundable tax credits. See 25.2 PAYMENT OF TAX.

s 177   **Tax clearance certificates.** The conditions for issue of certificates required in relation to certain public sector contracts are laid down. See 1.12 ADMINISTRATION AND GENERAL.

s 178   **Care and management of taxes and duties.**

s 179   **Short title, construction and commencement.**

OTHER MATTERS

ss 77–117, 5–7 Schs   **Customs and Excise.**

ss 142–150   **Stamp duties.**

s 171   **Capital Services Redemption Account.**

BUSINESS & INFORMATION

43   Table of Statutes

Index

This index is referenced to paragraph numbers. The entries printed in bold capitals are main subject headings in the text. Abbreviations used are:

Index

Cars,
benefit in kind, 34.3
capital allowances, 8.6
running expenses, 30.9
Cash trading, VAT, 39.11
Certificate of registration, 2.23
Certificates of deposit, 3.5
Charges on income, 12.9, 12.19
manufacturing companies, 12.17
Charities,
CAT, 7.5
CGT, 9.7(*k*)(*p*), 9.13(*d*)
DTR, 15.11
exempt, 17.5
retained tax, repayment of, 13.8
third world,
—donations to, 17.5
Child,
allowance, 2.7, 2.8, 2.15, 2.16
definition, 2.16
education (CAT), 7.5(*k*)
gift or inheritance to, 7.4, 7.5, 7.9
maintenance, 7.5(*k*), 23.4
RPT relief for, 26.9
settlement on, 36.2(*c*), 36.3
support (CAT), 7.5(*k*)
Children's allowance, 16.1, 37.6
C.I.E. stock, 19.1
CLAIMS, 10
contingent interest income, 10.2
personal allowances, 2.6 *et seq.*
stock relief, 18.8, 30.28
time limits, 10
Clearance certificate, 1.12, 9.5
Close company,
CT, 12.7
interest payable, 20.1
loans to participators, 12.7
service, 12.7, 38.33
undervalue transfers, 9.15
undistributed income, 12.7
Closing years, 30.5
Coal mines, 24.1
Collective investment undertakings,
7.5(o), 9.14, 12.21
Colleges, 36.2(B)
fees, relief for, 2.26
Commencement of trading, 30.4
Commodities, 9.7(b), 9.12
COMPANIES, 11
ACT, 12.25
assessment, 12.5
capital distributions, 9.6(*d*), 9.15
CAT, 7.15

change of ownership, 12.16, 12.25
chargeable gains, 12.8
close, 12.7
computation of profits, 12.8
control, 12.7
CPT, 12.1
CT, 12
distributions, 12.8, 12.10, 12.13, 12.17
employment, relief for increase in, 12.9
farming, 18.3
foreign branch profits, 12.12
holding company, 12.14
interest payable, 20.1(*a*)
management expenses, 12.9
mining groups, 24.5
mutual business, 12.21
non-resident, distributions of, 12.11
not trading, 12.21
participator, 12.7
partnership, 12.21
payment of IT, 25.1
private, 7.15
purchasing own shares, 12.10
reconstruction, 12.5
relief for increase in employment, 12.9
reorganisation, 9.15
reportable offences, 1.11
research and development, 21
service company, 12.7, 38.33
State-controlled, 12.7
trading company, 12.7, 12.14
—investment in, 21
undistributed income, 12.7
Compensation, 7.5(h), 9.6(c), 9.7(n)
Composers, 16.19
Compulsory acquisition, 9.6, 9.7(s)
Computer repair,
manufacturing companies' relief, 12.17
Computer software,
capital allowances, 8.6
Confidentiality of information, 1.7
Consortium, 12.14
Construction,
companies, 12.17
sub-contractors, 13.7, 38.32A
Continental shelf, 9.2, 9.3, 9.5, 29.1(iv)
Contingent beneficiary, 10.2
Co-operative societies, 12.21
Copyright, returns of, 28.8
Corporate trades, investment in, 21
CORPORATION TAX, 12
accounting periods, 12.3
administration, 12.4
advance, 12.25

Index

Index

Index

Index

Index

Index

Index